THE HISTORY OF TERRORISM

Publié avec le concours du Ministère français chargé de la culture, Centre national du livre. Published with the assistance of the French Ministry of Culture's National Center for the Book.

The publisher gratefully acknowledges the generous contribution to this book provided by the Literature in Translation Endowment Fund of the University of California Press Foundation, which is supported by a major gift from Joan Palevsky.

THE HISTORY OF
TERRORISM
FROM ANTIQUITY TO AL QAEDA

Edited by

Gérard Chaliand and Arnaud Blin

Translated by Edward Schneider,
Kathryn Pulver, and Jesse Browner

UNIVERSITY OF CALIFORNIA PRESS
BERKELEY   LOS ANGELES   LONDON

University of California Press, one of the most distinguished university presses in the United States, enriches
lives around the world by advancing scholarship in the
humanities, social sciences, and natural sciences. Its activities are supported by the UC Press Foundation and
by philanthropic contributions from individuals and institutions. For more information, visit
www.ucpress.edu.

University of California Press
Berkeley and Los Angeles, California

University of California Press, Ltd.
London, England

Library of Congress Cataloging-in-Publication Data

Histoire du terrorisme. English
    The history of terrorism : from antiquity to al Qaeda
/ edited by Gérard Chaliand and Arnaud Blin ; translated by Edward Schneider, Kathryn Pulver, and Jesse
Browner.
        p.   cm.
    Includes bibliographical references and index.
    ISBN-13: 978-0-520-24533-4 (cloth : alk. paper)
    ISBN-13: 978-0-520-24709-3 (pbk. : alk. paper)
    1. Terrorism—History.   I. Chaliand, Gérard,
1934–.   II. Blin, Arnaud.   III. Title.
HV6431.H5713   2007
363.32509—dc22   2006032389

15   14   13   12   11   10   09   08   07
10   9   8   7   6   5   4   3   2   1

Contents

Preface

Throughout history, power has more often than not been wielded through terror—that is, by inciting fear. All despotic societies have been founded on fear, as have so-called totalitarian regimes in the modern era. Submission to the established order and to force has been most of humankind's sole avenue to security and, ultimately, to freedom. Without reaching all the way back to prehistory—itself ruled by terrifying insecurity vis-à-vis nature, wild beasts, and other men—the use of terror to govern began at the very birth of organized society as a means of dissuasion or punishment.

Terrere means "to make tremble" in Latin. The first Mesopotamian empire, that of Sargon of Akkad, was founded on terror. The same was later true of antiquity's first military empire, the Assyrian, whose brutal methods of reprisal were intended to crush the spirit and break the will. Announced with warlike violence, terror remains suspended like a sword in times of peace over the heads of all who dare to rebel. In the despotic societies that make up the major portion of history's fabric, it has served as the tool of enslavement and guarantor of mass obedience. State terror, whether implicit or overt, has haunted the centuries as war's bogeyman, the specter of mass murder. Once unleashed, it can set an example to constrain behavior without the necessity of fighting. The Mongols and Tamerlane used terror in this way to reduce cities without having to resort to siege.

Historians of terrorism may point out that the word "terror" applies to the state terror of the French Revolution, but they often neglect to add that, to varying degrees, the phenomenon was a constant of earlier eras and has also been prevalent ever since. Indeed, terrorism, the principal aim of which is to terrorize, is a historically far broader phenomenon than suggested by the term's current usage, which essentially boils it down to the description or analysis of the illegitimate use of violence in terrorist-type activities.

The fact that the most notorious instances of contemporary terrorism have a religious dimension, notwithstanding their political aims, should serve to remind us that this has also been true historically of most forms of terrorism, such as that of the Jewish Zealots of the first century C.E., for example, or of the Isma'ili sect of Assassins from the eleventh to the thirteenth centuries. Indeed, the religious point of reference was long central to most societies, and this phenomenon has not yet exhausted itself.

Nowadays, terrorism beats out guerrilla warfare as the preferred and practically exclusive weapon of the weak against the strong. Its primary target is the mind. In that sense, terrorism is the most violent form of psychological warfare, and its psychological impact is commonly understood to be far greater than its physical effects. Stooping to often pathetic means, terrorism is a way of creating power in the hope of seizing from below that which the state wields from on high.

Gérard Chaliand and Arnaud Blin

CHAPTER 1

INTRODUCTION

Gérard Chaliand and Arnaud Blin

Of all the passions capable of enslaving man's will,
none is more incompatible with reason and liberty
than religious fanaticism.

Robespierre

It happened in Washington, D.C., at a conference on terrorism—or,
more precisely, counterterrorism—organized by the Pentagon's Defense
Intelligence Agency (DIA). Most of the participants worked for the diverse (and numerous) American intelligence services, which had all, to
varying degrees, become involved in the war on terrorism. After the Cold
War, most of these cloak-and-dagger men had moved into the specialized
and growing field of "new threats"—threats that also include nuclear
proliferation, weapons of mass destruction, and organized crime. This
strange gathering of identically dressed men listened attentively to a series of speakers hold forth on the essence of the counterterrorism struggle. Late in the day, however, as the last speaker was about to take the
floor, a bizarre figure strode up to the podium carrying a briefcase and a
bag. With his long hair and black hat, his thick beard, sunglasses, torn
pants, and leather vest, he stood out like a sore thumb from the intelligence bureaucrats. Suddenly, opening the briefcase and bag with lightning speed, the stranger threw two hand grenades into the crowd and
pointed an M16 rifle into the paralyzed audience.

There was no explosion, and the M16 remained mute. The man
calmly took the microphone and began to address the audience. The lis-

teners, many of them at least, immediately recognized a familiar voice. In fact, it was the director of the DIA, a general who had disguised himself as a "terrorist" to demonstrate the ease with which anyone could gain entry into the building where the colloquium was being held (on the campus of George Washington University, where no security measures had been installed) and wipe out the cream of the American counterterrorist crop. Back in uniform, the general had these prophetic words to say: "One day, terrorists will attack a building like this, in Washington or New York. They will kill hundreds of people and deal us an unprecedented psychological blow. The question is not whether such an attack will occur on American soil, but when and where. It is up to you, gentlemen, to be prepared. The security of our territory is in your hands." The colloquium took place in 1998. Three years later, nineteen determined men killed some three thousand people in the worst terrorist attack in history, striking New York and Washington, D.C. The Pentagon itself, headquarters of the DIA, was hit. In their negligence, the American intelligence services had been unable to prevent the operation.

In hindsight, this scenario seems almost surreal: first, because of the warning issued by the Pentagon intelligence chief and second, because of his staff's inability to follow his advice despite its specificity. There was also a disconnect between the quaint picture of a marginal fanatic—practically the living image of the cartoon anarchist in black cape, bomb in hand—prepared to blow the place to smithereens and the speechifying on the imminence of high-tech terrorism, the notorious "hyper-terrorism" against which all new policies were being drafted.

The terrorist phenomenon is more difficult to conceptualize than it would at first appear to be. The issue tends to be confused by ideological interpretations, along with the temptation, especially on the part of governments, to resort to diabolical imagery whenever the term is trotted out. A good place to start might be by recalling that the point of terror is to terrorize—a role historically assumed by organized force, be it state or army, at least when it comes to despotic regimes. That has always been the case with nondemocratic countries. In other contexts, in times of war, terror may be legitimized, even when deployed against civilians. In the modern era, the bombing of Coventry, Dresden, and Tokyo,[1] and the atom bombs dropped on Hiroshima and Nagasaki, come to mind.

Terror in the name of religion, holy terror, is a recurring historical phenomenon. A well-known example of this were the first-century Jewish Zealots, also known as the *sicarii*. This murderous sect helped to incite an uprising against the Roman occupation that resulted, inter alia, in the destruction of the second temple in 70 C.E. and the Diaspora. The Ismaʿili sect known as the Assassins was an Islamic correlate.[2] For two centuries, between 1090 and 1272, it made the political assassination of Muslim dignitaries by the blade its trademark. No Christian sect ever used terror to such harrowing effect, although we might note the fifteenth-century Taborites of Bohemia, the sixteenth-century Anabaptists, and the active anti-Semitism of the first crusade in 1095, not to mention the excesses of the Inquisition. In any case, messianic movements traffic in and thrive on terror.[3]

Messianism postulates that one day in the not-too-distant future, the world will be completely transformed by an event marking the end of history. In early Christianity, the belief in an imminent end signaling the Second Coming of Christ (Parousia) was common. The idea of an apocalypse is closely linked to various messianic schools of thought, and not exclusively among the revealed religions. The Aztecs believed that four suns (four worlds) had come and gone. They were haunted by the fear that the world would end if the sun failed to receive its due tribute of human blood.

The messianic spirit lived on within Judaism (in the seventeenth-century movement of Sabbatai Zevi, for instance). Immediately following Israel's victory in the Six-Day War, the return to the "promised land" provoked a messianic revival in the form of the creation of Gush Emunim, with its dynamic push to colonize Judea and Samaria (the West Bank). Christian messianism is manifest today among certain fundamentalist Protestant sects with roots in the nineteenth century. Among such sects, the powerful Evangelical movement is especially attuned to Israel's fortunes, since its adherents believe that Israel's ultimate victory is a precondition for the Parousia. Islam has its own movements of this kind, especially with respect to the awaited coming of the Mahdi, its counterpart to the Christian Messiah. Messianism is central to the Twelver Shiism of Iran, with its anticipation of the twelfth imam. Although theirs is a political conflict, the events and antagonisms that fuel the violent clashes between radical Islam and the United States, such as the Israeli-Palestinian conflict, also have a messianic dimension to them. Contrary to a fairly widespread view, they have nothing to do with a "clash of civilizations." Such animosity is equally raw within societies as between them, as evidenced, for instance, by the 1979 attack on the Great Mosque in Mecca by radical, mostly Saudi, Sunnis, or the 1995 assassination of Yitzhak Rabin, deemed by a member of Gush Emunim to be complicit in the abandonment of Judea and Samaria.[4]

Religious terrorism is seen by its practitioners as a transcendental act. Justified by the religious authorities, it gives full sanction to actors who thus become instruments of the divine. The number and identity of the victims is of no importance. There is no judge higher than the cause for which the terrorist has sacrificed himself. The perpetrators of the first, only partially successful attack on the World Trade Center in 1993 had first obtained a fatwa from Sheikh Omar Abdel Rahman, now imprisoned in the United States.

Despite this brief digression into religion, or at least one facet of it, our main focus of study is terrorism, which for many contemporary readers may boil down to Islamic terrorism. Let us recall in this respect that theological and political issues are closely bound up with each other in Islam. This distinctive aspect of Islam can be traced to its early days, when the high chief—to draw on more familiar vocabulary—was both religious and political leader. This ideal was later abandoned. A political apparatus arose, relatively distinct from the religious and legal apparatus, but in Muslim thought that ideal remained a unique structure, Islam, via the Qur'an, embodied in the concept of *din wa dawla* (religion and state). The Christian Church arose in very different circumstances. Even when Christianity became the official religion of empire in the fourth century, the religious and political apparatuses remained separate, although the Church was briefly inclined to impose its rule over temporal leaders in the Middle Ages.

Religious movements have always broken up into sects. Schismatic movements have always claimed to be the true interpreters of the original creed. Nowadays, sectarians affiliated with radical Islam, having flirted with and abandoned guerrilla warfare, are characterized by their use of terrorism colored by religion, interpreted to promote mobilization and involvement to further political ends.

We shall not dwell here on the never-ending parade of despotic regimes that have left their mark on Chinese history, from the foundation of a unified Chinese state in the third century B.C.E. to Mao Zedong; nor on the societies of the ancient Orient and India (except to note the surprising exception in India of Aśoka, a sovereign who sought to rule in accordance with the precepts of Buddhism); nor on the Islamic empires, which, like all governments, preferred injustice to disorder, and the last of which, the Ottoman empire, unscrupulously exploited terror. Nor was the West deficient in that regard until the emergence of embryonic democracies in Switzerland, the Netherlands, England, the United States, and France. Moreover, the first French republic lapsed in the name of virtue into terror, which reached its zenith in 1794 with the Law of 22 Prairial prohibiting witnesses and legal representation for the defense and authorizing the Revolutionary Tribunal to pass death sentences on the basis of conviction alone.

History—or, more precisely, the chronicles of the vanquished whose perspective has colored the historical record—continues to reverberate with the generalized terror incited by the Mongols and their explosive emergence in the thirteenth century, equaled only by Tamerlane and his pyramids of heads after the fall of Baghdad. Our own twentieth century, which produced Nazism and the Stalinist terror, will be remembered as the century of genocides—from those of the Armenians of the Ottoman empire in 1915–16 and in Rwanda in 1994 (committed to general international indifference) to that of the Jews and the Gypsies from 1942 to 1945. It will also be remembered for its massacres of specific social groups, such as the kulaks in Russia, real or suspected counterrevolutionaries, so-called inferior races, and so on.

Legion, too, are the religious sects or other groupings on a holy mission that have wielded terror with abandon. Until their elimination in the nineteenth century, the so-called Thugs terrorized travelers throughout India. Thuggee was a sect of stranglers, membership in which began at an early age, often passing from father to son, but also through the kidnapping of very young children. At the age of ten or eleven, boys were allowed to accompany the killers and watch from a distance, under the guidance of a tutor, to learn the skills of the sect's trade and, above all, how to keep quiet. They actively participated from puberty on.

The sect worshiped Kali, Hindu goddess of death. According to the Thugs, she had created two men from the perspiration of her armpits to help her battle demons; in reward, she had given them permission to kill without remorse, so long as they did not spill blood. Thuggee religious tradition held that, in the beginning, the goddess had removed the corpses by devouring them. One day, however, a novice had turned and seen the goddess at her meal. In punishment, she had thenceforth refused to dispose of the bodies herself. Instead, she ordered the faithful to chop them up and bury them, and then to perform a ceremonial ritual.

Right up to the early nineteenth century, thousands of travelers disappeared every year. When a Thug was taken prisoner, the Mogul authorities had him immured alive or cut off his hands and nose. In 1830, the British set about dismantling the sect, and it ultimately vanished.

Terrorism is above all a *tool* or, if you will, a *technique*. This technique is as old as warfare itself, contrary to the widespread notion that terrorism was the offspring of nineteenth-century nationalist movements. The confusion may be a result of the late appearance of the term in the French Revolution and its Terror.

Like all political phenomena, terrorism is defined by the duality between professed ideas and their implementation. And, like all political phenomena, terrorism exists only in a cultural and historical context. For three decades, the activities of terrorist movements were closely linked to Marxist ideology; Marxist terrorist groups are in the minority today, whereas they predominated in the 1970s and 1980s. The same applies to the entire history of terrorist movements, shaped by the political context in which they are born, live, and die. While terrorism is a phenomenon that is continuously reinventing itself, the lack of continuity between each generation of terrorists often entails a signal break with the past.

These days, the importance of the cultural component is more evident in terrorist movements of religious inspiration than in those of a nationalist or strictly ideological bent. It is the religious movements that are making themselves heard. Hamas and al Qaeda, in particular, combine political or pseudo-political aspirations (the destruction of Israel and/or the United States) with a religious undertone that serves the primary purpose of recruitment and thus finds an echo in the ideology of other movements. It should be noted that the early phase of Palestinian terrorism was essentially political and secular, only drifting into religiosity in the 1980s, following the Iranian revolution.

A terrorist organization is virtually by definition opposed to the state apparatus. The nature of that opposition often defines a movement's character. Where the state apparatus is essentially rational, the terrorist party will tend to appeal strongly to emotion. Where the state machinery operates on the basis of "realist" policies and an understanding of the balance of power, the terrorist movement will imbue its politics with a powerful moral tone (whose code varies depending on the ideology in play) and a weak-versus-strong strategy reliant for the most part on its psychological impact on the adversary. Raymond Aron had a felicitous way of getting to the heart of the matter: "A violent action is deemed terrorist when its psychological effects are disproportionate to its purely physical results."

Today's terrorism is what specialists call group or bottom-up terrorism, but top-down (state) terrorism has been far more prevalent throughout history. It enjoyed its heyday in the twentieth century with the advent of totalitarianism. In terms of victims, top-down terrorism has taken a vastly higher toll than its bottom-up counterpart.

In this study, our focus is on bottom-up terrorism, but not exclusively. As a tool, whether it be top-down or bottom-up, terror espouses the same strategic principle: to bend one's adversary's will while affecting his capacity for resistance. Until very recently, no one spoke of "state terrorism." State terrorism, as it is understood today, applies above all to the support provided by certain governments (Libya or Iran, for instance) to terrorist groups, but it takes many other forms. It is also a tool employed systematically by totalitarian regimes. A state's terrorism is also manifest in the military doctrine of its armed forces. The doctrine of "strategic bombing," for example, developed in the West in the 1930s, was based entirely on the terror incited by the mass bombing of civilian populations to compel governments to surrender. This doctrine resulted in the bombing of Dresden and the atomic destruction of Hiroshima and Nagasaki.

The boundaries between top-down and bottom-up terrorism are often blurred, as exemplified by Lenin before 1917 and after he seized power. We have all seen today's terrorist become tomorrow's head of state, with whom governments will have to deal at the diplomatic level. Menahem Begin exemplifies this typical metamorphosis.

Western tradition considers violence legitimate only when it is practiced by the state. Such a limited definition takes no account of the terror practiced by those who have no other means of redressing a situation they deem to be oppressive. The legitimacy of a terrorist act lies in the objectives of its agents. We need only imagine interviews with terrorists of yore to grasp the idea that "the end justifies the means" is the engine of most terrorist activity. It is the cause embraced by a terrorist movement, rather than its mode of action, that is subject to moral evaluation. In the context of the wars of national liberation of the 1950s and 1960s, terrorist activities are often seen in a positive light because they hastened the liberation of oppressed peoples. Those agents of terrorism—be they in Algeria or Indochina—are heroes. For the most part, they harbor no regrets. It all boils down to idea of a "just war" that legitimates violent action.

In the West and elsewhere, however, there is the tendency to label an action "terrorist" when it is deemed to be illegal. This always dangerous confusion between the moral interpretation of a political act and the act itself clouds our understanding of the terrorist phenomenon. An act is deemed "terrorist" when it smacks of fanaticism or when the aims of its perpetrators seem neither legitimate nor coherent. The observer becomes lost in the labyrinth of terrorist movements, which have varied down the centuries and evolved in distinct historical and cultural contexts. Another confusion arises from the idea that the terrorist act is by definition one aimed at civilians.[5] The civilian population becomes a target of the indirect strategy when its fate as a potential victim can influence the decisions taken by its leaders. The notion that the fate of civilians automatically sways the political leadership represents a contemporary, contingent understanding of politics. It is commonly accepted that the concept of popular sovereignty—exploited, incidentally, to justify state terror—emerged only with the Enlightenment. Somewhat later, political terrorism evolved with the shift in mentality—nineteenth-century Russian populists, for instance, were heavily influenced by the romantic tradition.

If modern terrorism tends in practice mainly to target civilians, the phenomenon derives in fact from the general evolution of political structures and the emergence of the mass media. In the West, political structures have evolved toward democracy since the late eighteenth century. The modern media, a critical component of liberal democracy, emerged in tandem. Now, the political legitimacy of a democracy and its elected representatives lies by definition with its citizens, which is why terrorism is more effective against democratic countries than against dictatorships. This is not, as is widely thought, because dictatorships are more efficient at finding and punishing terrorists—although they do have greater leeway than democracies in doing so—but because the impact of an attack is broader in a free country than in one whose people have no voice in government and the media serve or are controlled by the state. It is therefore not inaccurate to affirm that modern terrorism is in part a consequence of democracy.

That does not mean, however, that the phenomenon of terrorism is necessarily linked to democracy, as the exploitation of terror predates the modern democratic state. And yet—and this is where confusion tends to arise—"predemocratic" terrorism was practiced in other forms, which, at first sight, would seem to be quite distinct from the terrorism we know today.

One of the earliest manifestations of the terrorist technique is what was once called "tyrannicide"—a term long fallen into obsolescence. Traditionally, an attack on a tyrant was carried out in the name of justice. Tyrannicide was the most widespread form of terrorism of the premodern era. The most fearsome organization of that period, acting in the name of ideological purity, was the Assassin sect, active in the thirteenth and fourteenth centuries. It bears some resemblance to certain contemporary terrorist organizations.

No society has a monopoly on terrorism, and over the course of history, terrorist acts have left their mark on any number of geographical and cultural spheres. The Zealots (or *sicarii*) and the Assassins, for instance, were active in the Middle East, which remains a haven for important terrorist organizations to this day. Following World War II, the state of Israel forced its way onto the scene via a strategy that drew on terrorist tactics. The Palestinians draw on terrorism today against Israel. For several centuries, Central Asia and the Middle East were prey to the terror practiced by various nomad armies, including those of Genghis Khan and Tamerlane. Since the nineteenth century, Russia has been the theater of numerous acts of terrorism, including the state terror on which the entire Soviet edifice relied for seven decades. Today, terrorism in Russia is once again "bottom-up." In Europe, the Thirty Years' War (1618–48) demonstrated the readiness with which opposing armies resorted to terror. More recently, Europe has been swept by diverse waves of terrorism: anarchists, Irish terrorism, the activities of ideological groups such as the Red Brigades in Italy and the German Red Army Fraction, and, most recently, the Basque and Corsican movements.

The United States experienced anarchist attacks in the late nineteenth century. Moreover, the assassination of political figures (Lincoln, McKinley) owes something to the tradition of tyrannicide—John Wilkes Booth cried out "Sic semper Tyrannis!" ("Ever thus to tyrants!") as he killed Lincoln—and is deep-rooted in American history. The activities of a semi-clandestine organization like the Ku Klux Klan are also based on terror through the practice of lynching. Organizations of the far right, to a certain degree following in the KKK's footsteps, continue to deploy terrorist tactics (such as the Oklahoma City bombing) but by increasingly sophisticated modern means. Long spared international terrorism on its own soil, the United States was tragically struck on September 11, 2001.

Sub-Saharan Africa, which had long seemed immune, has in recent years fallen victim to the terrorism of regular armies, irregulars, and armed bands. The problem is particularly acute in the Great Lakes region, where the conflict in the Democratic Republic of the Congo has claimed three million victims, mostly civilians. The use of terror in Africa echoes that of the Thirty Years' War. In the context of globalization, Africa has, tangentially, become a terrorist target, as evidenced by the bombings of the U.S. embassies in Tanzania and Kenya. For its part,

Latin America was once the theater of myriad guerrilla conflicts, including in the cities. The guerrillas naturally resorted to terrorist tactics, especially in the kind of guerrilla warfare waged by the Tupamaros in Uruguay.

In Iran, in 1979, radical Islamism burst onto the scene in its Shiite incarnation. That same year, the war in Afghanistan—with the help of the United States, Saudi Arabia, and Pakistan—abetted the rise of radical Sunni Islamism. The movement was swelled by elements from virtually all Muslim countries, other than those of sub-Saharan Africa, and turned against the United States once the USSR had withdrawn from Afghanistan. Its hostility to the United States was manifest in a series of attacks in the mid 1990s. That of September 11, 2001, marked its acme and led to Washington's punitive expedition against the Taliban regime in Afghanistan and the entity known as al Qaeda. The Bush administration accused Iraq of harboring weapons of mass destruction, having links to al Qaeda, and representing a threat to world peace and to U.S. security. Ostensibly part of the global struggle against terrorism, the ensuing war, unilaterally decided on, has been a source of difficulties unforeseen by Washington's hawks.

One cannot condemn terrorism without condemning all violence of every stripe. One must, at the very least, consider why and by whom it is being practiced. Like war, and perhaps even more so, terrorism preys on minds and wills. At first glance, the democracies would seem to be especially vulnerable. And yet, if the challenge is great or even fundamental, people prove themselves surprisingly capable of enduring it and the psychological tensions it begets. Terrorism is justified as a last resort. In the real world, the weak have no other weapon against the strong. Many movements that later became legitimate have used it. As for states, the monopolists of legal violence, they are designed and duty-bound to defend themselves.

Generally speaking, any movement with a certain degree of social substance practices terrorism as a pressure tactic in order to squeeze concessions and a negotiated solution from the state. In the case of militant Islamism, the characteristic that sets it apart from all other movements, past and present, is that it has nothing to negotiate. The truth is that its fight is to the death.

As an international phenomenon, terrorism is more of a galling nuisance than a truly destabilizing force, except for its psychological impact. Terrorism is the price—ultimately, a rather modest one—paid by the West, and especially the United States, for its hegemony. The trick, if one has the political acumen to learn it, is to avoid fueling it while claiming to fight it.

NOTES TO CHAPTER 1

EPIGRAPH: Artarit, *Robespierre*, 71.

  1. The firebombing of Tokyo in March 1945 killed between 80,000 and 100,000 people.

  2. See, e.g., Lewis, *Assassins*.

  3. See, e.g., Cohn, *Pursuit of the Millennium*.

  4. See Sprinzak, *Brother against Brother*, and "Fundamentalism, Terrorism and Democracy."

  5. Carr, *Lessons of Terror*, 66–67, for instance, sees terrorist acts as targeting civilians exclusively, which would exclude the Assassins.

CHAPTER 2

TERRORISM AS A STRATEGY OF INSURGENCY

Ariel Merari

Political terrorism is a mode of warfare. Insurgents' mode of struggle is dictated by circumstances, and whenever possible, they adopt a variety of strategies. Terrorism, which is the easiest form of insurgency, is almost always one of these. This essay examines terrorism's unique characteristics by comparing it with other forms of violent conflict, delineating the main strategic ideas by which terrorists have hoped to realize their objectives, and evaluating their success in doing so and the conditions that affect it.

Before getting to these subjects, however, I need to clarify what I mean by "political terrorism." This term has been used by governments, the media, and even academics to denote phenomena that have very little in common. Thus, for some, terrorism means violent acts of groups against states; for others, a state's oppression of its own citizens; and for still others, warlike acts of states against other states.

A major hindrance in the way of achieving a widely accepted definition of political terrorism is the negative emotional connotation of the term. "Terrorism" has become merely another derogatory word, rather than a descriptor of a specific type of activity. Usually, people use the term as a disapproving label for a whole range of phenomena that they do not like, without bothering to define precisely what constitutes ter-

This article first appeared in slightly different form in *Terrorism and Political Violence* 5, no. 4 (Winter 1993): 213–51, published by Frank Cass, London.

roristic behavior. This essay treats terrorism as a mode of struggle rather than a social or political aberration, approaching the phenomenon technically rather than moralistically.

A WORKING DEFINITION OF TERRORISM

As mentioned above, "terrorism" has different meanings for different people. Terminology is always a matter of agreement for the purpose of common understanding. There is no point in searching for logic-based definitions of terms that belong to the realm of political or social science, especially when the term in question carries a negative emotional connotation. Absent general acceptance of the basic assumptions and semantics necessary for the definition of terrorism, there is no way on earth, for example, for the United States to prove logically that the Libyan-sponsored attacks on the Rome and Vienna airports in 1985 were acts of terrorism. The United States is certainly consistent with its own definition of terrorism, but Colonel Mu'ammar Gadhafi may still maintain that the term "terrorism" should be reserved for acts such as the U.S. punitive raid on Libya in April 1986, and that the Rome and Vienna attacks are more properly described as forms of revolutionary violence, armed struggle, or fighting for freedom.

Achieving a consensus on the meaning of the term "terrorism" is not an important end in itself, except, perhaps, for linguists. Still, for students of political violence, classification of the phenomena that fall under this general category is an essential first step of research. It is necessary to differentiate between various conditions of violence and to distinguish between diverse modes of conflict, whatever we name them, if we want to gain a better understanding of their origins, the factors that affect them, and how to cope with them. The purposes, circumstances, and methods involved in a state's violence against its own citizens are entirely different from those that characterize violence by states against other states or by insurgent groups against governments. The application of the term "terrorism" to all three situations is obfuscating and disrupts both academic research and addressing these problems in political action. As long as the term "terrorism" simply denotes a violent behavior that is deplorable in the eyes of the user of the term, its utility is in propaganda rather than in research.

An interesting approach to the problem of defining terrorism was taken by two Dutch researchers from the University of Leiden, Alex Schmid and Albert Jongman.[1] They collected 109 academic and official definitions of terrorism and analyzed them in search for their main components. They found that the element of violence was included in 83.5 percent of the definitions and political goals in 65 percent, while 51 percent emphasized the element of inflicting fear and terror. Only 21 percent of the definitions mentioned arbitrariness and indiscriminate targeting, and only 17.5 percent included the victimization of civilians, noncombatants, neutrals, or outsiders.[2]

A closer look at the assortment of definitions quoted by Schmid and Jongman shows that official definitions of terrorism are fairly similar. Thus, the U.S. vice president's 1986 task force defined terrorism as "the unlawful use or threat of violence against persons or property to further political or social objectives. It is generally intended to intimidate or coerce a government, individuals or groups to modify their behavior or policies."[3] The definition of the Office for the Protection of the Constitution of the Federal Republic of Germany is: "Terrorism is the enduringly conducted struggle for political goals, which . . . [is] intended to be achieved by means of assaults on the life and property of other persons, especially by means of severe crimes as detailed in art. 129a, sec. 1 of the penal law book (above all: murder, homicide, extortionist kidnapping, arson, setting off a blast by explosives) or by means of other acts of violence, which serve as preparation of such criminal acts."[4] A British legal definition contains the same ingredients in a more succinct form: "For the purposes of the legislation, terrorism is 'the use of violence for political ends, and includes any use of violence for the purpose of putting the public or any section of the public in fear.'"[5] There are three common elements in the definitions quoted above: (1) the use of violence; (2) political objectives; and (3) the intention of sowing fear in a target population.

Compared to official definitions of terrorism, those offered by academics are, unsurprisingly, more diverse, although most of them contain the three cornerstones of government definitions. Before we become overly euphoric about the evolving consensus about terrorism, let us remember that the sample of definitions offered by Schmid and Jongman reflects, by and large, the perceptions and attitudes of Western academics and officials. Syrian, Libyan, and Iranian opinions of what constitutes terrorism are quite different, and so too, most likely, are those of the many other Third World countries. The evolving Western consensus about the essence of terrorism is probably not shared by the majority of people on earth.

Moreover, the three basic commonly agreed-upon characteristics of terrorism delineated above do not suffice to make a useful definition. As working definitions, the official ones quoted above are too broad to be useful. The main problem is that they do not provide the ground to distinguish between terrorism and other forms of violent conflict, such as guerrilla or even conventional war. Clearly, both conventional and guerrilla warfare constitute the use of violence for political ends. Systematic large-scale bombing of civilian populations in modern wars was explicitly intended to spread fear among the targeted populations. For example, a leaflet which was dropped over Japanese cities by American bombers in August 1945 stated:

> These leaflets are being dropped to notify you that your city has been listed for destruction by our powerful air force. The bombing will begin in 72 hours.
> We give the military clique this notification because we know there is nothing they can do to stop our overwhelming power and our iron determination. We want you to see how powerless the military is to protect you.
> Systematic destruction of city after city will continue as long as you blindly follow your military leaders.[6]

The dropping of atomic bombs on Hiroshima and Nagasaki that ended World War II can also be viewed as fitting the definitions of terrorism, albeit on a huge scale. Clearly, these were acts of violence, committed in the service of political ends, with the intent of spreading fear among the entire Japanese population.

The history of guerrilla warfare also offers ample evidence of systematic victimization of civilians in an attempt to control the population. During its struggle for the independence of Algeria, the Front de libération nationale (FLN) murdered about 16,000 Muslim citizens and kidnapped 50,000 others, who have never been seen again; in addition to these, an estimated 12,000 FLN members were killed in internal "purges."[7] A Vietcong directive of 1965 was quite explicit about the types of people who had to be "repressed"—namely, punished or killed: "The targets for repression are counterrevolutionary elements who seek to impede the Revolution and work actively for the enemy and for the destruction of the Revolution." These included, among others, "Elements who actively fight against the Revolution in reactionary parties such as the Vietnamese Nationalist Party (Quoc Dan Dang), Party for a Greater Viet Nam (Dai-Viet), and the Personality and Labor Party (Can-Lao Nhan-Vi), and key reactionaries in organizations and associations founded by the reactionary parties or the U.S. imperialists and the puppet government." Also to be "repressed" were "Reactionary and recalcitrant elements who take advantage of various religions, such as Catholicism, Buddhism, Caodaism and Protestantism, actively to oppose and destroy the

Revolution, and key elements in organizations and associations founded by these persons."[8] A more recent example is the practice of the Peruvian Sendero Luminoso, or Shining Path, organization of killing and maiming villagers for such offenses as voting in national elections.

If the definition of terrorism is equally applicable to nuclear war, conventional war, and guerrilla warfare, the term loses any useful meaning. It simply becomes a synonym for violent intimidation in a political context and is thus reduced to an unflattering term, describing an ugly aspect of violent conflicts of all sizes and shapes, conducted throughout human history by all kinds of regimes. If both the midair bombing of a commercial airliner by a small insurgent group in peacetime and strategic bombing of enemy populations by a superpower in a world war are "terrorism," social scientists, policy makers, and legislators can but sigh. If we wish to use the term "terrorism," in a political science analysis, we ought to limit it to a more specific type of phenomenon, distinguishable from other forms of political violence. Despite the ambiguities and disagreements discussed above, the concept of terrorism in modern usage is most commonly associated with certain kinds of violent actions carried out by individuals and groups rather than by states, and with events that take place in peacetime rather than as part of a conventional war. Although the original usage of the term in a political context referred to state violence and repression (the "Reign of Terror" in the French Revolution),[9] from a practical point of view, the recent definition of the term by the U.S. Department of State is a better anchor. According to this definition, terrorism is premeditated, politically motivated violence perpetrated against noncombatant targets by subnational groups or clandestine state agents, usually intended to influence an audience.[10] Practicality is the only reason why, in the remainder of this essay, the term "terrorism" is used to connote insurgent rather than state violence. In the following sections, I shall identify terrorism more precisely among the other forms of insurgent violence.

THE UNIVERSE OF POLITICAL VIOLENCE

Theoretically, there are an infinite number of ways to classify politically motivated violence. Nevertheless, with the criteria of utility and parsimony in mind, a basic classification that relates to the initiator of the violence and to its target, distinguishing between states and citizens, is presented in Table 1.

Table 1 is a useful way to circumscribe this essay's focus of interest. It

Table 1 A Basic Classification of Political Violence

		Target	
		State	*Citizens*
Initiator	*State*	Full-scale war; belligerent activity in peacetime (e.g., cloak-and-dagger operations and punitive strikes)	Legal and illegal law enforcement oppression
	Citizens	Guerrilla war; insurgent terrorism; coup d'état; Leninist revolution	Vigilante terrorism; ethnic terrorism

encompasses, in a gross manner, all forms of political violence carried out by humans against other humans, while differentiating between their main types. Each one of the four cells includes a distinct category of truculent behavior. These will be described briefly in the following paragraphs.

States against States

Violence initiated by states can be conceptually divided into two main types: (1) state violence directed against other states, and (2) violence that states inflict on their own citizens.

Aggressive actions of states against other states have often taken the form of conventional war: a clash of sizable regular armies. This has, undoubtedly, been the most consequential form of violence in history. Various aspects of conventional wars, such as military strategy and the laws of war, have been studied extensively and have become recognized academic disciplines or subdisciplines. Obviously, states have also used a plethora of lower levels of violence in their contests with other states, such as limited air force strikes, commando raids, or the assassination of enemy agents. Yet, in all cases, these acts can be characterized as organized and planned, and they reflect the capability of a large bureaucracy.

States against Citizens

The use of force by states against their own citizens includes two main subcategories. One is the ordinary, overt legal process by which states enforce their laws. The other is the clandestine use of illegal violence by a government, designed to intimidate and terrorize citizens with the intention of preventing them from opposing the regime. Sometimes illegal state violence is exercised in the context of internal strife in the name of efficiency: cutting corners of due legal processes that hamper the struggle against the insurgents. Examples are abundant. The most extreme instances have involved the enormous totalitarian regimes of Nazi Germany and Stalinist Soviet Union. "Death squads" in several Latin American countries, usually manned by members of the security forces, provide a less efficient, albeit quite repugnant example of a different brand.

Citizens against Citizens

The most mundane form of citizens' violence against other citizens is, of course, common crime. Unlike the types of violence shown in Table 1, common crime is usually motivated by reasons that have nothing to do with political objectives. Much of it is committed for personal economic gain and another significant part is stimulated by personal animosities. Thus, the great mass of citizens' violence against other citizens is unrelated to the subject of this essay, namely, political violence. There are, however, also phenomena of citizens' violence committed for political or social motivations. Some of these are related to racial or ethnic rivalries or strifes; others are associated with right-wing or left-wing social ideologies; and still others have to do with a variety of idiosyncratic issues, such as abortion, environment conservation, or animal rights.

A special case of citizens' violence, vigilantism, merits special mention.[11] Vigilante violence has sometimes been associated with an unauthorized attempt to control crime, but sometimes with violence against ethnic or political minorities.

Citizens against the State

Citizens' violence against states may be organized or spontaneous. Sometimes it is an impulsive expression of discontent, having neither clear political goals nor organized leadership or plan. In its organized form, citizens' violence falls under the category of insurgency, aimed at overthrowing the government. The main forms of insurgency are distinct strategies of uprising that differ from one another in several important characteristics. Before turning to examine them in greater detail, however, it is necessary to cope with the definition of terrorism and to distinguish between this mode of violence and other forms of conflict.

FORMS OF INSURGENT VIOLENCE

Insurgent violence may take various forms. These include revolution, coup d'état, guerrilla war, terrorism, and riots. In recent years the term "intifada" has gained publicity, referring to the Palestinian uprising in the Israeli-administered territories. With the exception of riots, these forms of political violence can be also viewed as strategies of insurgency. Table 2 lists these forms in a framework that distinguishes between them according to several characteristics. The table's purpose is to help in the characterization of terrorism as a mode of struggle, emphasizing the differences between this and other forms of insurgent violence.

Before I turn to focus on the characteristics of terrorism as an insurgent strategy, let me briefly describe the other forms of insurgency, emphasizing their unique attributes.

Coup d'État

A coup d'état is "a sudden, forceful stroke in politics; especially, the sudden, forcible overthrow of a government."[12] It is the seizure of power by an individual or a small group of persons who control important positions in the state's machinery. Edward Luttwak, who wrote a highly informative and amusing book on coup d'état, characterized this strategy as "the infiltration of a small but critical segment of the state apparatus, which is then used to displace the government from its control of the remainder."[13] Usually, but not always, a coup grows from the ranks of the military. In any event, for a successful completion of a coup, the rebels must ensure the cooperation of at least part of the armed forces. The success of a coup depends upon surprise, in order to catch the government off guard. It is, therefore, imperative that preparations for the coup are made in utmost secrecy. Compared to other strategies of insurgency, a coup usually involves little violence, and sometimes it is achieved without bloodshed. A coup is always planned to be swift and is ordinarily a brief episode, regardless of its success, although failed coups have occasionally developed into prolonged civil wars. In sum, a coup d'état can be characterized as a planned insurgency at a high level of the state's ranks, by a few people, involving relatively little violence during a very brief period of time.

Table 2 Comparison of Forms of Insurgency

Form of Insurgency	Insurgency Level	Number Involved	Duration of Struggle	Violence	Threat to Regime	Spontaneity
Coup d'état	High	Few	Short	Varied	Great	No
Leninist Revolution	Low	Many	Short	Great	Great	No?
Guerrilla	Low	Medium	Long	Great	Varied	No
Riot	Low	Medium	Short	Little	Small	Yes
Terrorism	Low	Few	Long	Little	Small	No
Nonviolent Resistance	Low	Many	Long	No	Varied	No

Leninist Revolution

Revolution is usually meant in the sense of a radical social, political, or economic change. Unlike a coup d'état, a revolution is a change of the system rather than a strategy. In some cases the revolutionary change of the system has been achieved with little or no violence (e.g., the transformation of the form of government in Czechoslovakia, East Germany, and Poland in the late 1980s and 1990s, or, using a very different example, the Industrial Revolution of the eighteenth century in England).[14] In other instances, revolutions have involved enormous bloodshed, as in the case of the Chinese Communist Revolution. Some revolutionary changes have involved protracted convulsions, and others were relatively quick. "Revolution is one of the looser words," Crane Brinton's classic treatise on the subject starts out by saying.[15]

In the context of this essay, however, the term "revolution" is used in a much more limited sense, connoting a strategy rather than a social or political outcome. Although revolutions in history have sometimes been spontaneous, unplanned events and have utilized a variety of forms of struggle, since this essay's interest is primarily in the nature and implications of the strategy of insurgency, I shall focus on the Leninist concept of revolution. The Russian Social Democratic Party under Lenin's leadership, and especially its Bolshevik branch, sought to realize the Marxist revolution through a thorough process of clandestine preparations.[16] The period of violence was meant to be brief, but the actual seizure of power was conceived of as a cataclysmic episode that might involve immense violence.[17] Before this final decisive confrontation, however, a long, arduous period of groundwork designed to prepare the revolutionary organization was envisaged. The three most important elements in this preparatory period were recruiting, educating, and organizing the revolutionary cadres. At the opportune moment, the prepared mechanism would be put to action. This moment, according to the Marxist theory, would come when the inherent economic characteristics of the capitalistic regime brought about its collapse.[18] Of course, not all of the activity of the revolutionary party was clandestine. There were front organizations and other tools of propaganda that performed the important task of preparing the hearts and minds of the people. But the most important element of Leninist revolution was the tightly knit clandestine party apparatus. The Leninist model of revolutionary strategy can, therefore, be characterized as an insurgency from below, involving numerous people. The period of preparation is very long, but the direct violent confrontation is expected to be brief.

Guerrilla War

In Spanish, *guerrilla* is a diminutive meaning "small war." This form of warfare is, perhaps, as old as mankind, certainly older than conventional war. Guerrilla war is a diffuse type of war, fought in relatively small formations, against a stronger enemy. In numerous instances guerrilla warfare has merely served as an auxiliary form of fighting, especially behind enemy lines, with the main military effort taking the form of conventional war. In many insurrections, however, guerrilla warfare has been the main form of struggle, at least for a while. As a strategy, guerrilla warfare avoids direct, decisive battles, opting instead for a protracted struggle consisting of many small clashes. In some guerrilla doctrines, final victory is expected to result from wearing out the enemy.[19] Other doctrines, however, insist that guerrilla war is only an interim phase of the struggle, intended to enable the insurgents to build a regular army that will, eventually, win through conventional warfare.[20]

Guerrillas try to compensate for their inferiority in manpower, arms, and equipment by adopting a very flexible style of warfare, based on hit-and-run operations. For this, the guerrillas utilize the terrain to their advantage, blend into the population, or, sometimes, launch their attacks from neighboring countries. The principle is always to prevent the government forces from employing their full might in the contest. Tactically, however, guerrillas conduct warfare in a manner similar to conventional armies. When guerrillas stage an ambush or attack a village, they do it in the same way that a regular infantry unit would.

Riot

Riot is mob violence. Riots are usually unorganized, in the sense that the rioters are neither totally controlled by a leader nor organized in units or some other hierarchical structure.[21] However, riots have sometimes been intentionally incited by organized political activists and at least partly directed. Unlike the other forms of violence discussed in this chapter, riots cannot be characterized as a strategy of insurgency or a form of warfare. Although a major insurrection has sometimes started with riots, such as in the cases of the French Revolution of 1789 and the Russian Revolution of February 1917, the spontaneous street violence was not part of a carefully planned scheme to topple the regime. In contrast to guerrilla and terrorist struggles, riots are brief, unplanned episodes. They may recur over weeks or months, but they nevertheless constitute a spasmodic eruption rather than a planned, organized, protracted campaign.

Nonviolent Resistance

By definition, nonviolent resistance is beyond the scope of an essay on political violence. It encompasses methods such as demonstrations, labor strikes, hunger strikes, boycotting of goods, refusal to pay taxes, and other variations of challenging the authorities without spilling blood. This form of uprising has been included in Table 2 for the purpose of comparison with violent strategies. Moreover, comment on nonviolent resistance seems called for because of the moral and practical importance attached to it as an alternative to violent modes of uprising.[22]

Famous examples of nonviolent struggles that succeeded in inducing a major political change include Gandhi's movement in India, Martin Luther King's civil rights campaign in the United States, and, of course, the 1989 protest movements in eastern Europe. In view of these stunning successes, one wonders why have nonviolent struggles been so rare in history. Some have suggested the reason to be that nonviolent resistance was only discovered in the twentieth century. This is certainly not true. Gene Sharp mentions several cases in history that prove the contrary.[23] A more plausible explanation is that nonviolent resistance is of practical value only when the challenged government refrains from using its power to break the resistance by force. In this sense, the change of political standards after World War II, which has been expressed in a global recognition of the right of self-determination and in a general trend toward further liberalization in democracies, gave nonviolent resistance a better chance than ever before.

Nevertheless, even in the second half of the twentieth century, there was not a single case of a successful nonviolent challenge to a totalitarian regime or external power that was determined to face it by force. This lesson was dearly learned by the Hungarians in 1956, the Czechs in 1968, and the Chinese students in 1989.

At first glance, the success of the nonviolent movements in East Germany, Poland, Czechoslovakia, and Bulgaria in changing the regimes in those countries in 1989 seems to contradict this generalization. It should be remembered, however, that these movements were prompted by the liberalization in the Soviet Union, and they succeeded only because the USSR changed its previous policy of intervention and refused to render the communist regimes of its former satellites even minimal political backing in their effort to retain power. The difference between the successful Czech uprising in 1989 and the failure of 1968, or between the success in East Germany and the failure in China, cannot be attributed to the greater determination or capability of the insurgents in the successful cases, but to a lesser determination on the part of the governments. The Iranian Islamic Revolution of 1979 and the failure of the August 1991 coup in Moscow are other seeming demonstrations of the effectiveness of nonviolent resistance. Yet in these examples too, the success of the unarmed civilians was a result of the rulers' indecisiveness and ineptitude. In all likelihood, greater determination on the part of the shah in Iran or the coup junta in the USSR would have resulted in a bloody crushing of the resistance. In short, nonviolent resistance is a practical mode of strife only when the government allows it to take place. It is absolutely useless against repressive regimes determined to remain in power.

In addition, only rarely has nonviolent resistance existed as the only mode of struggle. Alongside Gandhi's nonviolent struggle against British rule were numerous instances of terrorism and rioting in India.[24] Black dissatisfaction in the United States in the 1960s was not only expressed in peaceful marches and sit-ins but in violent riots as well. A broad uprising is usually expressed in several concurrent forms, and it is hard to evaluate the effects of the various aspects of the comprehensive struggle singly.

TERRORISM

How does terrorism fit into the spectrum of political violence? As suggested above, the customary modern usage of the term refers, at least in the West, to actions such as the bombing in midair of Pan Am Flight 103 in December 1988, the attacks on passengers in the Rome and Vienna airports in December 1985, and the seizure of the Saudi embassy in Khartoum in March 1973. These actions represent a form of political violence different from guerrilla war, conventional war, and riots. Actions of this kind, when they are carried out systematically, constitute a distinct strategy of insurgency. This strategy should have a name, be it "terrorism" or another, and "terrorism" has the advantage of familiarity. In fact, practitioners and advocates of this form of struggle have themselves often used the term to describe their method.[25] Yet the definitions of the term leave several questions to be answered. I shall now examine some of the areas of confusion.

Terrorism and Guerrilla War

The terms "terrorism" and "guerrilla war" are often used interchangeably. Apart from some carelessness in the use of technical terminology by the media, politicians, and even academics, this faulty synonymy reflects confusion concerning the definition of terrorism and, often, a wish to avoid the negative connotation that the term has acquired. "Guerrilla war" does not have defamatory overtones, and its usage therefore seems to many writers to convey objectivity. As Walter Laqueur pointed out, the widespread use of "urban guerrilla warfare" to describe a strategy of terrorism as an extension of or substitute for guerrilla warfare probably contributed to the confusion.[26] As strategies of insurgency, however, terrorism and guerrilla warfare are quite distinct. The most important difference is that unlike terrorism, guerrilla warfare tries to establish physical control of territory. This control is often partial. In some cases, the guerrillas rule the area during the night and government forces have control in the daytime. In others, government forces are able to secure the main routes of transportation but guerrilla territory starts as little as a few hundred yards to the right and left. In many instances, guerrillas have managed to maintain complete control of a sizable portion of land for long periods of time. The need to dominate a territory is a key element in insurgent guerrilla strategy. The territory under the guerrillas' control provides the human reservoir for recruitment, a logistical base and—most important—the ground and infrastructure for establishing a regular army.[27]

Terrorist strategy does not vie for a tangible control of territory.

Notwithstanding the fact that terrorists try to impose their will on the general population and channel its behavior by sowing fear, this influence has no geographical demarcation lines. Terrorism as a strategy does not rely on "liberated zones" as staging areas for consolidating the struggle and carrying it further. As a strategy, terrorism remains in the domain of psychological influence and lacks the material elements of guerrilla warfare.

Other practical differences between the two forms of warfare further accentuate the basic distinction of the two strategies. These differences belong to the tactical domain, but they are actually an extension of the essentially divergent strategic concepts. They relate to unit size, arms, and types of guerrilla and terrorist operations. Guerrillas usually wage war in platoon- or company-sized units but sometimes even in battalions and brigades. There are well-known historical examples in which guerrillas have even used division-sized formations in battle.[28] Terrorists operate in very small units, usually ranging from a lone assassin or a single person who makes and plants an improvised explosive device to a five-member hostage-taking team. The largest teams in terrorist operations have numbered from forty to fifty persons.[29] These, however, have been very rare. Thus, in terms of operational units' size, the upper limits of terrorist units are the lower limits of guerrilla units.

Differences in the weapons used in these two types of warfare are also evident. Whereas guerrillas mostly use ordinary military-type arms, such as rifles, machine guns, mortars, and even artillery, typical terrorist weapons include homemade bombs, car bombs, and sophisticated barometric pressure–operated devices designed to explode on board airliners in midair. These differences in unit size and arms are merely corollaries of the fact noted above, that tactically, guerrilla actions resemble a regular army's mode of operation. Because terrorists, unlike guerrillas, have no territorial base, they must immerse themselves among the general civilian population if they do not wish to become sitting ducks for their hunters. This is why ordinarily terrorists cannot allow themselves to wear uniforms, while guerrillas usually do. In a somewhat simplified comparison, therefore, one may say that whereas guerrilla and conventional war are two modes of warfare that are different in strategy but similar in tactics, terrorism is a unique form of struggle in both strategy and tactics. Table 3 summarizes the differences between terrorism, guerrilla war, and conventional war as modes of violent struggle.

Table 3 Characteristics of Terrorism, Guerrilla War, and Conventional War as Modes of Violent Struggle

	Conventional War	Guerrilla War	Terrorism
Unit size in battle	Large (armies, corps, divisions)	Medium (platoons, companies, battalions)	Small (usually fewer than ten persons)
Weapons	Full range of military hardware (air force, armor, artillery, etc.)	Mostly infantry-type light weapons but sometimes artillery pieces as well	Hand guns, hand grenades, assault rifles, and specialized weapons (e.g., car bombs, remote-control bombs, barometric pressure bombs)
Tactics	Usually joint operations involving several military branches	Commando-type	Specialized: kidnapping, assassinations, car bombing, hijacking, barricade-hostage, etc.
Targets	Mostly military units, industrial and transportation infrastructure	Mostly military, police, and administration staff, as well as political opponents	State symbols, political opponents, and the public at large
Intended impact	Physical destruction	Mainly physical attrition of the enemy	Psychological coercion
Control of territory	Yes	Yes	No
Uniform	Wear uniform	Often wear uniform	Do not wear uniform
Recognition of war zones	War limited to recognized geographical area	War limited to the country in strife	No recognized war zones; operations carried out worldwide
International legality	Yes, if conducted by rules	Yes, if conducted by rules	No
Domestic legality	Yes	No	No

Method and Cause: Terrorists and Freedom Fighters

Terrorist groups normally describe themselves as national liberation movements, or fighters against social, economic, religious, or imperialist oppression, or any combination of these. On the other side of the barricade, in an understandable attempt to degrade terrorism, politicians have presented the terms "terrorists" and "freedom fighters" as contradictory. Thus, then Vice President George H. W. Bush wrote in 1988: "The difference between terrorists and freedom fighters is sometimes clouded. Some would say one man's freedom fighter is another man's terrorist. I reject this notion. The philosophical differences are stark and fundamental." [30]

Without passing judgment on the self-description of any particular group, trying to present the terms "terrorists" and "freedom fighters" as mutually exclusive is in general a logical fallacy. "Terrorism" and "freedom fighting" are terms that describe two different aspects of human behavior. The first characterizes a method of struggle, and the second, a cause. The causes of groups that have adopted terrorism as a mode of struggle are as diverse as the interests and aspirations of mankind. Among the professed causes of terrorist groups are social changes in the spirit of right-wing and left-wing ideologies, aspirations associated with religious beliefs, ethnic grievances, environmental issues, animal rights, and issues such as abortion. Some terrorist groups undoubtedly fight for self-determination or national liberation. On the other hand, not all national liberation movements resort to terrorism to advance their cause. In other words, some insurgent groups are both terrorists and freedom fighters, some are either one or the other, and some are neither.

Terrorism and Morality

The hero of the moralistic approach to terrorism is a Russian named Ivan Kalyayev, who was a member of the "combat organization" of the underground Social Revolutionary Party, which adopted assassinations of government officials as its main strategy in the struggle against the tsarist regime. Kalyayev was chosen by the organization to assassinate Grand Duke Sergei. On February 2, 1905, Kalyayev waited, a bomb under his coat, for the arrival of the Grand Duke. When the latter's carriage approached, however, Kalyayev noticed that the intended victim was accompanied by his wife and two young boys, his nephews, the children of Grand Duke Pavel. In a spur-of-the-moment decision, Kalyayev refrained from throwing the bomb so as not to hurt Sergei's innocent brood. Two days later, Kalyayev completed the mission and was caught and subsequently tried and executed.[31] Kalyayev's insistence on a very strict definition of permitted targets of revolutionary violence gained him the status of a saint in the gospel of moralistic analysts of terrorism and something like a litmus test for a quick identification of right and wrong in revolutionary violence.[32]

The most concentrated treatment of the question of the morality of terrorism is probably that offered by Michael Walzer.[33] His basic position is summarized by the following quotation: "In its modern manifestations, terror is the totalitarian form of war and politics. It shatters the war convention and the political code. It breaks across moral limits beyond which no further limitation seems possible, for within the categories of civilian and citizen, there isn't any smaller group for which immunity might be claimed. . . . Terrorists anyway make no such claim; they kill anybody."[34]

Walzer's morality litmus test is the responsibility of the victims for acts that are the subject of the assailants' grievances. In line with this criterion, he offers what one might call a crude scale of "assassinability": government officials who are part of the presumed oppressive apparatus are "assassinable." A case in point is Kalyayev's victim. People in government service who are not related to the oppressive aspects of the regime (e.g., teachers, medical service personnel, etc.) make up a questionable category. Walzer's somewhat ambiguous verdict is that because "the variety of activities sponsored and paid for by the modern state is extraordinary . . . it seems intemperate and extravagant to make all such activities into occasions for assassination."[35] Private persons are definitely not assassinable, according to Walzer. These cannot spare their lives by changing their behavior. Killing them is, therefore, unequivocally immoral.

Walzer's analysis leaves several principal problems with no satisfactory answer. The most important one has to do with the essence of moral judgment. The fundamental question is whether moral norms in general and war norms in particular are absolute, unchanging over time, and identical in all societies, or a changing reflection of the human condition and therefore varying across societies and perennially modified to fit new situations. Absolute moral norms may presumably stem from one of two sources: a divine edict or a universal psychological trait, common to men and women in all societies in history. In the first case, there is no point in arguing: divine rules are not negotiable, they are a matter of belief. For those who believe in their divine source, they are fixed regulations of human conduct, which do not change over time. Walzer admits that his treatise rests on the Western religious tradition,[36] but it is not clear whether this attribution is a statement of cultural identification or an announcement of personal religious conviction. Cultural norms are certainly a powerful influence on attitudes, opinions, and behavior, and they can be portrayed as the cast in which personal values are molded. But to claim the status of an absolute value of the human race, it is necessary to show that the value under consideration is shared by all cultures. Given the tremendous diversity of cultures, the assertion that a certain value is universal must rest on the assumption that this value stems from a set of attitudes and emotions that prevail in all societies.

With regard to the specific issue under consideration, namely, moral values related to political violence, the universality assumption is untenable. This is proven by the very fact that divergence from the moral code of war presented by Walzer as the absolute dictum is so common. Flagrant breaches of Walzer's rules in modern history cannot be explained merely by the personal craziness or immorality of individuals who happened to head totalitarian regimes that enabled them to act in contradiction to the will of most of their countries' inhabitants. In many cases, violations of morality have been supported by the majority of the population in the nation that committed them. Large-scale departures from the laws of war have been practiced even by democracies, a form of regime where government action is limited by public will. Thus, the massive bombing of the Japanese civilian population, with the intent of damaging its morale, and the total destruction of Hiroshima and Nagasaki by atomic bombs in World War II were undoubtedly supported by most of the American people.

It is obvious that in actual application, the moral code in general, including the rules of war, is a product of people's needs, perceptions, and convenience and is subject to cultural and circumstantial influences. Cultural differences concerning the status of noncombatants have been expressed, for instance, in the utilization of hostages. Whereas most Westerners regarded the usage by Iraq in 1990 of civilian hostages—men, women, and children—as a human shield against the possible bombing of strategic targets as a repugnant, immoral act, for many in the Arab world, this was a legitimate, morally justified tactic. It seems, however, that situational factors have a much greater role than cultural diversity in determining conduct in war. The form of government is, perhaps, the single most important factor. Some of the most severe violations of human rights in modern history have been committed by totalitarian Western regimes. Perceived necessity plays a major role as well. In fact, all states have repeatedly broken the rules of war. In almost all modern wars, civilian populations have been victimized intentionally, and the magnitude of the transgression has been determined by capability and need as much as by moral principles.

Terrorism is not different from other forms of warfare in the targeting of noncombatants. Yet terrorism, more than any other form of warfare, systematically breaches the internationally accepted rules of war. In both guerrilla warfare and conventional war, the laws of engagement are often ignored, but terrorism discards these laws altogether in refusing to distinguish between combatants and noncombatants and, with regard to international terrorism, in rejecting the limitations of war zones as well. Unlike conventional and guerrilla wars, terrorism has no legal standing in international law (from the viewpoint of domestic law, all insurrections are treated as crimes). For this reason, terrorism as a strategy and terrorists as a warring party have no hope of gaining a legal status. Hence, terrorism may be correctly described as an illegal form of warfare, but characterizing it as an immoral one is meaningless. Terrorists wage war by their own standards, not by those of their enemies. Both sides' rules of conduct stem from capabilities and necessities and undergo changes for reasons that are basically pragmatic. Of course, people and states pass moral judgment on wars and on particular acts in war. Their judgment, however, reflects nothing but their own existing cultural norms at best and—too often—a partisan view, influenced by direct interests. Yet morality, although it cannot be coherently treated as an absolute value is, in a given time, society, and context, a psychological and, therefore, a political fact. Publics do pass moral judgments on persons, organizations, and actions. They react based on moral standards, no matter how emotional and irrational these may be. In fact, it is the emotional rather than the logical component that makes morally based attitudes so powerful.

Morality is a code of behavior that prevails in a certain society at a certain time. As such, morality closely corresponds to the existing law, but the latter has the advantages of clarity, precision, and formality. As a reflection of current norms, terrorism is an immoral form of warfare in twentieth-century Western societies. The power of this characterization is weakened, however, by the fact that in virtually all modern wars, moral codes of behavior (and, indeed, the laws of war) have been breached by all parties on a massive scale, at least with regard to the targeting of civilians. In this respect, the difference between terrorism and other forms of warfare is a matter of comprehensiveness. Terrorists usually dismiss the law altogether, without even pretending to abide by it, whereas states pay tribute to law and norms and breach them only under extreme circumstances; but it should be noted that the relativity of morality has been also expressed in the changing rules of combating terrorism. If laws reflect the prevailing moral standards in a given society, one may find interest in the fact that all states, when faced with the threat of insurgency, have enacted special laws or emergency regulations permitting the security forces to act in manners that would normally be considered immoral. Indeed, under such circumstances, states have even tended to sanction security forces' breaching of these laws or, at best, to punish such "excesses" rather leniently.

TERRORISM AS A STRATEGY OF INSURGENCE

In practice, terrorists' operational inventory is rather limited. They place explosive charges in public places, assassinate political opponents, carry out assaults by small arms on the public at large, and take hostages by kidnapping, hijacking, or barricading themselves in buildings. In most cases, their capability is rather slim. Consider, for example, a notorious group such as the German Red Army Fraction (widely known as the Baader-Meinhof gang). At any given period throughout its existence, it had fewer than thirty active members, who were able to assassinate several public officials and businessmen, to kidnap two, and to stage one barricade-hostage incident. How did they expect to achieve their far-reaching political goal of overpowering the German government and instituting a Marxist regime? The same conundrum also applies to much larger organizations, such as the Irish Republican Army (IRA), which according to one British estimate in the 1990s had an estimated active membership of 200–400 men and women and a much broader body of supporters. How could they win the battle against Great Britain? In this section of the essay, I examine the main elements and variations of terrorism as a strategy, trying to explain how terrorists think they may be able to bridge the gap between their meager means and grandiose objectives.

The Psychological Element

Essentially, terrorism is a strategy based on psychological impact. Many authors have noted the importance of the psychological element of terrorism,[37] which is also recognized in official definitions of the term. References to terrorism's intention "to influence an audience," in the U.S. Department of State's definition, or to its purpose of "putting the public or any section of the public in fear," in the British legal definition of 1974, relate to the psychological effects of this mode of warfare.[38]

Actually, all forms of warfare have a significant psychological ingredient, both in trying to damage the enemy's morale by sowing fear in their ranks and in strengthening one's own forces' self-confidence and will to fight. In his famous treatise *Strategy: The Indirect Approach,* Sir Basil Liddell Hart, one of the most eminent theoreticians of strategy of the twentieth century, went as far as to assert that in almost all great battles in history, "the victor had his opponent at a psychological disadvantage before the clash took place."[39] A similar idea was expressed about 2,500 years ago, in a very concise form, by the ancient Chinese strategist Sun Tzu.[40]

Nevertheless, conventional wars are first and foremost massive collisions of material forces, and they are usually won by the physical elimination of the enemy's ability to resist, by destroying its fighting forces, its economic infrastructure, or both. Even if Liddell Hart's contention is correct, the psychological impact of the crucial maneuvers of indirect approach stems from the enemy's belief that resistance is useless for material reasons. Although in many cases, this conclusion is a product of the military leadership's surprise and confusion and does not reflect the true balance of power, it still rests on material assessments, wrong as they may be. Hence, the psychological feat described by Liddell Hart may be characterized as a swift deceptive move, which succeeds in throwing the enemy off balance in a single, surprising jujitsu-type maneuver. The psychological basis of the strategy of terrorism is entirely different in nature. Like guerrilla war, terrorism is a strategy of protracted struggle. Guerrilla warfare, however, notwithstanding its psychological component, is primarily a strategy based on a physical encounter. Although twentieth-century guerrilla theoreticians emphasize the propaganda value of guerrilla operations in spreading the word of the revolution, attracting supporters, and awakening dormant opponents of the regime and providing them with a recipe for resistance, the importance of these psychological elements remains secondary. All insurgent guerrilla doctrines insist that the battleground against government forces is the countryside. The very concept of staging the struggle in rural areas, far from the eyes of the media, weakens the significance of the psychological factor. Indeed, psychological impact is the most essential element in terrorism as a strategy.

The validity of this generalization rests on the basic conditions of the terrorist struggle. Terrorist groups are small. Their membership ranges from a few individuals to several thousands, and the majority number from the tens to a few hundreds. Even the weakest of governments has a fighting force immensely larger than that of the terrorist insurgents. Under such circumstances, the insurgents cannot expect to win the struggle in any physical way. Describing the strategy of terrorism as a form of psychological warfare does not specifically explain how terrorists hope to win by it. Although terrorists have rarely been clear enough as to lay down a complete, coherent strategic plan, it is possible to discern several strategic ideas that terrorists have held as the cardinal practical concept of their struggle. These are described below as distinct notions, although they are not necessarily mutually exclusive, and terrorists have often espoused them concurrently.

Propaganda by Deed

The essentials of the psychological basis of a terrorist struggle have changed little since the nineteenth century, when anarchist writings first formulated the principles of this strategy. The basic idea was phrased as "propaganda by deed."[41] This meant that the terrorist act was the best herald of the need to overthrow the regime and the torch that would light the way to doing it.[42] The revolutionary terrorists hoped that their attacks would thus transform them from a small conspiratorial club into a massive revolutionary movement. In a way, the original concept of propaganda by deed, as explained and practiced by nineteenth-century revolutionaries, was more refined than its modern usage in the post–World War II era. Whereas the earlier practitioners were careful to choose symbolic targets, such as heads of state and infamous oppressive governors and ministers, in order to draw attention to the justification of their cause, the more recent brand has turned to indiscriminate attacks aiming to cause multiple casualties. In doing so, they have exchanged the propaganda value of justification for greater shock value, ensuring massive media coverage. This change seems to reflect the adaptation of the strategy to the age of television. Anyway, this basic concept of the nature of the terrorist struggle does not constitute a complete strategy. Like some other conceptions of terrorism, in the idea of propaganda by deed, terrorism is only meant to be the first stage of the struggle. It is a mechanism of hoisting a flag and recruiting, a prelude that will enable the insurgents to develop other modes of struggle. In itself, it is not expected to bring the government down.

Intimidation

Another salient psychological element in the strategy of terrorism has been, as the term implies, the intention to spread fear in the enemy's ranks. The notion is simple and does not need elaboration. For the regime and its key functionaries, whose very existence is challenged by the insurgents, the struggle is a matter of life or death, and they are generally unlikely to give up because of the terrorists' threat. Nevertheless, terrorists have sometimes succeeded in intimidating select categories of people, such as judges, jurors, or journalists, through a systematic campaign of assassination, maiming, or kidnapping. An extension of this idea of coercive terrorism applies to the general population. Not only government officials and employees are punished by the terrorists, but also all those who cooperate with the authorities and refuse to assist the insurgents. Examples of a large-scale use of this strategy have been the murders of actual or presumed collaborators with the authorities by the Vietminh and the Vietcong in Vietnam, the FLN in Algeria, and the Palestinian "Shock Committees" in the Israeli Occupied Territories. An even more extensive use of this type of intimidation is designed to force the population to take a stand. Actually, it is mostly intended to affect neutrals who, in many cases, constitute the great majority of the public, rather than to intimidate the real opponents. Alistair Horne notes that in the first two and a half years of the FLN's war against the French in Algeria, the FLN murdered at least 6,352 Muslims, as compared with 1,035 Europeans. The killings were often carried out in a particularly gruesome manner in order to maximize the terrorizing effect.[43]

Insurgent organizations have sometimes imposed pointless demands on the population with the sole purpose of exercising and demonstrating their control. In the 1936–39 Arab rebellion in Palestine, the insurgents demanded that the urban Arab population refrain from wearing the tarboosh—the hat popular among townsmen—and wear the kaffiyeh instead. Those who ignored the edict were punished severely.[44] In a similar vein, in 1955, the FLN demanded that the Muslim population in Algeria refrain from smoking. They punished those who broke the ban by cutting their lips with pruning shears.[45] Again, it is hard to find any logic behind this edict, other than the demonstration of power to control the population.

Provocation

An important constituent in terrorist strategy is the idea of provocation. Like the theme of propaganda by deed, this notion is found in the writings of nineteenth-century revolutionaries.[46] However, it is given special prominence in Carlos Marighella's 1969 "Minimanual of the Urban Guerrilla," one of the most influential terrorist handbooks (although the author himself was an unsuccessful terrorist). Marighella wrote that as a result of terrorist attacks,

> The government has no alternative except to intensify repression. The police networks, house searches, arrests of innocent people and of suspects, closing off streets, make life in the city unbearable. The military dictatorship embarks on massive political persecution. Political assassinations and police terror become routine. . . .
> The people refuse to collaborate with the authorities, and the general sentiment is that the government is unjust, incapable of solving problems, and resorts purely and simply to the physical liquidation of its opponents.[47]

The idea is, in general, simple and true, not only in the political environment of a Latin American dictatorship but in many liberal democracies. Terrorist attacks tend to evoke repressive responses by any regime, which necessarily also affect parts of the population that are not associated with the insurgents. These measures, in turn, make the government unpopular, thus increasing public support of the terrorists and their cause. When government counterterrorist actions are not only draconian but ineffective as well, anti-government sentiment is bound to be even more prevalent.

A special version of the provocation doctrine is relevant to a conflict that has an international dimension. When the insurgents represent a radical nationalist faction of a larger political entity, or are supported by a state, they may hope that their acts of terrorism will spark a war between their target country and the state that sponsors them. This was al-Fatah's initial strategy, as Khaled al-Hassan, a leading al-Fatah ideologue, explained:

> The armed struggle technique was ostensibly simple. We called this tactic "actions and reactions," because we intended to carry out actions, the Israelis would react and the Arab states, according to our plan, would support us and wage war on Israel. If the Arab governments would not go to war, the Arab peoples would support us and would force the Arab governments to support us. We wanted to create a climate of fighting spirit in the nation, so that they will arise and fight.[48]

The Strategy of Chaos

Government ineptitude is the basis for another psychological lever in the strategy of some terrorist groups, which attempt to create an atmosphere of chaos so as to demonstrate the government's inability to impose law and order. This "strategy of chaos" or "strategy of tension" is typical of right-wing insurgents.[49] The insurgents hope that the public will, under such circumstances, demand that the "weak" liberal government be replaced by a strong regime. In order to create an atmosphere of disorder and insecurity, the terrorists resort to random bombings of public places. Thus, the Italian neofascist Ordine Nero (Black Order) group placed a bomb on a train on August 5, 1974, arbitrarily killing 12 passengers and wounding 48. Another ultra-right Italian group, the Armed Revolutionary Nuclei, was charged with the bombing of the Bologna railway station in August 1980, which caused the deaths of 84 and the wounding of 200.[50] The same idea presumably motivated German extreme right-wing terrorists, who detonated a bomb in the midst of a joyous crowd celebrating the Oktoberfest beer festival in Munich on September 26, 1980. Thirteen persons were killed and 215 were wounded in the explosion.[51] A similar tactic was employed by a Belgian ultra-rightist terrorist group that, during 1982–85, murdered almost 30 people in random shooting of bystanders during supermarket robberies. There was no apparent reason for the killings other than to create panic in the population.[52] Like the other strategic concepts of terrorism described above, the "strategy of chaos" is not a comprehensive plan for seizing power. It is merely a way to create a public mood that, the insurgents hope, will give them a better chance to continue their struggle in an unspecified way.

The Strategy of Attrition

Some insurgent groups have viewed terrorism as a strategy of protracted struggle, designed to wear out the adversary. In fact, this is the only conception of terrorism that has viewed this mode of struggle as a complete way of achieving victory, rather than as a supplement or prelude to another strategy. The insurgents were fully aware of their inferiority as a fighting force compared to the strength of the government and, unlike in the concepts of struggle delineated above, they did not expect that they would ever be strong enough to defeat the government in a physical confrontation. Nevertheless, they assumed that they had more stamina than the government and that, if they persisted, the government would eventually yield. Because this strategy assumes that the insurgents can prevail by greater perseverance rather than by building a stronger force, it is patently suitable for conflicts where the issue at stake is not of vital importance for the government.

If the government sees the struggle as a matter of life or death, it will not succumb to terrorist harassment, however protracted and unpleasant it may be. Moreover, when a government is fighting for its life or for the existence of the state, it is likely to take off the gloves and employ all means necessary to quell the insurrection, ignoring restraints and controls normally imposed on security forces or instituting emergency laws and regulations that suspend such restraints. In a bare-knuckle showdown, an insurgent group using terrorism as its main strategy has a very slim chance of winning, as long as the security forces are loyal to the regime. If, however, the government's interests in the dispute are a matter of utility rather than the defense of its very existence, its approach to the problem is likely to be one of cost-benefit analysis. The government weighs the political, economic, or strategic losses that it is likely to bear if it yields to the insurgents' demands against the price it is likely to pay if the struggle continues.

This process of cost-benefit analysis is rarely, if ever, a clear-headed, methodical evaluation of the situation and the prospects. Usually, it is a matter of trial and error, marked by fluctuations as a result of political pressures and public disagreements and debates among analysts and decision makers. Nevertheless, what eventually determines the outcome is the relative importance of the struggle for the government and for the insurgents, respectively, and the terrorists' nuisance value and durability.

Expressive Terrorism

So far terrorism has been treated as a strategy, implying an organized plan to achieve a political end, usually to seize power. Nevertheless, in several cases, terrorism has been an emotional response with no clear strategic aim, although the acts of violence have been perpetrated by a group in a tactically organized manner. Admittedly, this assertion takes us into the obscure territory of the rationality of terrorists and terrorism. Retrospectively, judging by its meager success in achieving the declared political goals, terrorism is not an effective strategy, and terrorists may, therefore, be considered in general to be irrational, at least inasmuch as their political behavior is concerned. Nevertheless, in some cases, the terrorist struggle seems hopeless to the extent that its irrationality is particularly striking.

A case in point is Moluccan terrorism in the Netherlands in the 1970s. The Moluccan community in the Netherlands is a remnant of the Dutch colonial era. After the Dutch evacuation of their colonies in Southeast

Asia, a South Moluccan republic was established in 1950 but was soon conquered by Indonesia. About 15,000 South Moluccans, most of them associated with the old Dutch administration, found refuge in the Netherlands. Political and social frustrations bred a terrorist group (the Free South Moluccan Youth Movement) within this small community, which carried out several spectacular terrorist attacks in the Netherlands. The most notorious of these were the concurrent takeover of the Indonesian embassy and a passenger train in 1975 and the concurrent takeover of a school and another train in 1977. In return for the release of their hostages the terrorists demanded that the government of the Netherlands recognize their nonexistent state and release comrades who had been arrested in previous operations.[53]

Armenian terrorism in the 1970s and 1980s is another example. The two main Armenian terrorist groups, the Armenian Secret Army for the Liberation of Armenia (ASALA) and the Justice Commando for the Armenian Genocide (JCAG), carried out numerous terrorist attacks in 1975–85, most of them against Turkish diplomats. The motivation behind these acts was revenge for the massacre of Armenians by the Turks in 1915, in which an estimated 1.5 million Armenians perished. The terrorist groups demanded official Turkish admission of responsibility for the massacre, which the government of Turkey has consistently refused to grant. In addition to this explicitly emotional demand, ASALA also demanded the reinstitution of an independent Armenian state, which would include the old Armenian provinces in Turkey.[54] At present, only about 50,000 Armenians live in Turkey, very few of them in the historic Armenian region. About four-fifths of the Armenians live in the former Soviet Union, most of them in the former Armenian Republic of the USSR.[55] Yet Armenian terrorist activity has been primarily directed against Turkey.

Both Moluccan and Armenian terrorism are manifest examples of expressive terrorism. The dominant motivation of the young men and women who carried out the acts of violence belonged to the emotional realm, rather than to the domain of rational political planning. Terrorism in these instances expressed an emotional state, rather than serving as an instrumental tool in the framework of a strategy of insurgency. Undoubtedly, the emotional element is also part of the driving force behind the activity of other terrorist groups. In most cases, however, the hopelessness of the political case is not as clear as in the Armenian and Moluccan examples, rendering an outside judgment about the weight of the emotional factor impossible.

HOW SUCCESSFUL IS TERRORISM?

The evaluation of terrorism's success as a strategy depends on how success is defined. Most terrorist groups strive to depose the current government and to seize power. By this criterion of success, taking into account only insurgents who have used terrorism as their main strategy, only some anti-colonial groups have fully accomplished what they set out to do. The struggles of EOKA, the Ethniki Organosis Kyprion Agoniston (National Organization of Cypriot Fighters), in Cyprus and the Mau Mau in Kenya against British rule and the FLN in Algeria against the French are well-known examples. The overwhelming majority of the many hundreds of terrorist groups that existed in the second half of the twentieth century failed miserably to attain their declared goals.[56] The fact that terrorist success has been limited to anticolonial struggles is not incidental. The main reason is that it is only in these cases that the issue at stake is far more important for the insurgents than for the government. Where the terrorist organization's struggle is aimed at changing the sociopolitical nature of the regime, such as in the case of right-wing or left-wing insurgents, the incumbent government is fighting for its life and is ready to do whatever it takes to quell the insurgency. For the governments of France, Germany, and Italy, the struggle against Action directe, the Red Army Fraction, and the Red Brigades was an all-or-nothing matter. There was no room for compromise: the terrorists' success would have meant the demise of the government.

The same is also true of most cases of separatist struggle, where the insurgents' aspirations are perceived by the government as threatening the sovereignty and territorial integrity of the state, such as in the Basque separatist struggle in Spain.[57] Differences in the degree of success of separatist terrorists stem primarily from the extent to which secession of the disputed part of the country seems, to most citizens of the state, to be the equivalent of severing one of their own limbs. For France, for instance, leaving the protectorates of Tunisia and Morocco or the colonies of Mali and Madagascar was much less painful than relinquishing its rule of Algeria, which was legally part of France and had more than one million Frenchmen living among its mostly Muslim population; and giving up Brittany or Normandy is unthinkable. In this sense, the success of separatist terrorism in obtaining its goals is a yardstick for the degree to which the disputed territory is truly a separate entity.

It is also true, however, that a nationalist cause is generally much more powerful in motivating people than a social issue, and all else being equal, the intensity of violence stemming from nationalistic sentiments is therefore usually greater than that generated by socioeconomic grievances.

Whereas achievement of the insurgents' goals in full is rare, terrorists have often succeeded in accomplishing partial objectives. Four types of partial terrorist success can be discerned: (1) recruitment of domestic support, which enables the terrorists to move on to a higher level of insurrection; (2) drawing international attention to the terrorists' grievances; (3) acquiring international legitimacy; and (4) gaining partial political concessions from their adversary. These are discussed below.

It has already been mentioned that the most basic notion of terrorism as a strategy is the idea of "propaganda by deed," which views this mode of struggle as a tool for spreading the word of the insurrection, expanding its popular base, and thus serving as a lever for and prelude to a more advanced form of insurrection. For most terrorist groups, even this elementary doctrine has not worked, however. Although their acts of violence gained tremendous publicity, as terrorist attacks always do, they failed to attract public sympathy and support and to generate the broad popular insurrection they had hoped to propel. This was, for example, the case with radical left-wing and right-wing movements in western Europe and in the United States in the 1970s and 1980s.

Nevertheless, there have been cases in which terrorism apparently helped in sparking and arousing a broader movement. One example is the Russian Social Revolutionaries at the beginning of the twentieth century. Although they failed to turn their own clandestine apparatus into a political instrument capable of seizing power, and notwithstanding the fact that the October 1917 Revolution was eventually executed by the broader-based, better-organized Bolsheviks, the terrorist acts of the Social Revolutionaries probably contributed much to keeping the revolutionary torch aflame. Throughout the years that the Social Democrats (the Bolsheviks and the Mensheviks) were building their clandestine infrastructure with no dramatic actions to ignite people's enthusiasm, the Social Revolutionaries, by their assassination of oppressive state ministers and other government functionaries, kept the idea and spirit of struggle alive among potential revolutionaries. Ironically, it seems that Social Revolutionary terrorism, although much criticized and ridiculed by the Social Democrats, enabled the latter to reach 1917 with the capability of seizing power.

The most common outcome of international terrorism is bringing the terrorists' grievances to international consciousness. In itself, this awareness is not enough to effect changes desired by the insurgents and sometimes results in repercussions that are deleterious to the terrorists' cause. Yet, under favorable conditions, it grants the insurgents a ladder by which they can climb further. Among Western publics, the initial reaction to a terrorist campaign is, invariably, one of vehement condemnation. This response, however, is often followed by readiness to examine the terrorists' case more closely, with a tendency to view their grievances favorably. Paradoxically, the public may end up approving of a cause while denouncing the method by which it was brought to its attention.

A benevolent attitude to the terrorists' cause is most likely to occur in publics that suffer from the terrorists' attacks but have nothing to lose from the fulfillment of their demands. In this situation, the initial rage is soon replaced by the wish that the problem would disappear. When a positive political attitude to the terrorists' cause seems to be able to buy peace, governments often adapt their policy so as to gain the terrorists' goodwill. There is an element here of what is known in psychology as "cognitive dissonance," and it is not necessarily conscious. Essentially, it involves finding an acceptable excuse for a course of behavior that may produce conflict because it contradicts some principles or beliefs. It is certainly much more palatable for a government or public to think that, on a closer examination, the terrorists have a point, than to admit caving in to terrorist pressure.

When other pressures and interests are added to the will to end terrorist attacks, such as accommodating influential patrons of the terrorists, the likelihood of adopting a favorable attitude to the terrorist cause is greater. Western responses to international Palestinian terrorism are a salient example of this process. Palestinian terrorist attacks in western Europe began in 1968 and reached a peak in 1973. They were condemned strongly by the European Community. In a few years, however, the Palestine Liberation Organization was allowed to open missions in practically all European countries, and in 1974, about a year after the Arab members of the Organization of Petroleum Exporting Countries (OPEC) proclaimed an oil embargo against nations that supported Israel, with the subsequent increase in oil prices, PLO Chairman Yasser Arafat was invited to address the General Assembly of the United Nations, and the PLO was granted UN observer status.

"An initial problem in assessing the results of terrorism is that it is never the unique causal factor leading to identifiable outcomes," Martha Crenshaw has correctly observed. "The intermingling of social and political effects with other events and trends makes terrorism difficult to isolate."[58] Admittedly, it is impossible to isolate the net effect of terrorism and to assess its relative contribution to the legitimization process of the PLO accurately alongside other factors, such as economic and political pressures by Arab states. There can be little doubt, however, that in the final analysis, terrorism has had a beneficial rather than a deleterious effect on the PLO's legitimacy.

The PLO's case is unique in that other nationalist and separatist insurgent movements have not enjoyed the backing of powerful patrons. The Kurds and the Kashmiris, to name just two examples of separatist movements that have been active in recent decades, have not gained nearly as much international legitimacy and support, although their grievances are arguably as convincing as those of the Palestinians. On the other hand, it is also true that these movements have not resorted to nearly as much international terrorism as the Palestinians (which, in itself, can be explained by the lack of state sponsorship).

Some terrorist groups that have been unable to materialize their political objectives have nevertheless succeeded in driving their adversary to make significant concessions. A typical example is ETA, or Euskadi ta Askatasuna (Basque Homeland and Freedom), whose long violent campaign for secession from Spain has not produced the independence they aspired for but has undoubtedly been a major factor in Spain's decision to grant the Basque provinces extensive autonomy. Another case in point is the IRA's struggle over Ulster. Although no actual steps have been taken yet toward changing the status of Ulster, there has been a growing readiness in Britain to get rid of the Irish problem by any solution that would end the violence. The British-Irish Accord of 1985 guaranteed that Ulster would become part of the Republic of Ireland if its people decided to do so by popular vote. For the time being, Ireland was granted a say in the affairs of Ulster in the framework of an Anglo-Irish conference. Clearly, these changes in Britain's policy were prompted by the IRA's struggle.

THE MIXED FORMS OF UPRISING

Strategies of uprising are usually treated as separate entities or phenomena. In a theoretical analysis, this separation is necessary if we want to understand the essentials of a strategy and its characteristics. The real world, however, is always more complex than academic classifications. In reality, it is sometimes hard to distinguish between terrorism and guerrilla war even with the help of the criteria offered above. By these criteria, the basic strategy used by the IRA, for example, belongs to the category of terrorism: the IRA does not try to seize territory in order to establish "liberated zones," and the tactics used by the organization are mostly well within the typical terrorist brand, namely, assassinations and placing explosive devices in public places. Yet some of this group's operations, such as a mortar attack on a police station and blowing up bridges, have utilized tactics and weapons usually associated with guerrilla warfare. Palestinian groups controlling territory in Lebanon (and in Jordan during 1967–70) outside their main theater of operations are another case in point. Although they used the areas they dominated for the classic guerrilla ends of recruiting, training, and establishing a regular force, their adherents were recruited from the Palestinian diaspora in these countries, rather than from the populace in the Israeli-held territories. Moreover, with some exceptions, they have used terrorist rather than guerrilla tactics. Their operations inside Israel and the Occupied Territories have mostly involved explosive charges placed in supermarkets, residential buildings, bus stations, and so on. Their incursions into Israel have usually been by small teams sent to randomly kill civilians.

Aside from the fact that it is sometimes difficult to make a clear distinction between terrorist and guerrilla tactics, it is even more confusing that in many cases, insurgent groups systematically use a mixture of the two strategies. In Peru, Sendero Luminoso has used a classic guerrilla strategy in the mountainous Ayacucho region, where it has occupied towns, carried out attacks on police stations and military convoys, and established control over large areas. At the same time, however, it has conducted a typical terrorist campaign in the cities, in which it has committed assassinations, bombings, and kidnappings. A similar mix is found in the activities of many other Latin American groups, such as the Colombian Ejército de Liberación Nacional (ELN), M-19, and Fuerzas Armadas Revolucionarias de Colombia (FARC), the Salvadoran Farabundo Martí National Liberation Front, and the Guatemalan Guerrilla Army of the Poor. A dual guerrilla-terrorist strategy has also characterized groups in other parts of the Third World. The Vietminh and, later, the Vietcong insurgencies were instances where regular warfare, guerrilla strategy, and terrorism flourished side by side. Similar examples, albeit on a smaller scale, are abundant in Asia and Africa.

A closer examination reveals that the coexistence of guerrilla and terrorist strategies is not incidental. Apparently, all insurgent organizations that have adopted guerrilla warfare as their main strategy have also used terrorism regularly. Some may claim that resistance movements that have fought against occupying armies are a noticeable exception to this generality. This reservation, however, rests on dubious ground. Fighters against a foreign army in their homeland, such as the French Resistance and the Russian, Yugoslav, and Greek partisans in World War II, only attacked the enemy's military and official apparatus for the simple reason that civilian members of the enemy's nationality were not present on the scene of battle. Failure to target enemy noncombatants was not a matter of choice; it reflected availability. The underground movements did attack civilians of their own nationality—actual and suspected collaborators with the occupiers. In addition, although in some places, such as the Soviet Union and in Yugoslavia, the strategy adopted by the partisans was, by and large, guerrilla warfare, employing large units that operated from liberated or semi-liberated areas, in western European countries, such as France, the strategy of the insurgents can at best be characterized as falling into the gray zone between guerrilla war and terrorism. No territorial control was established by the French underground, and its operations consisted of attacks on individual members of the occupying forces, as well as of blowing up bridges, mining, and similar tactics typical of guerrilla warfare. Presumably, many readers would feel insulted by the classification of the anti-Nazi warriors as terrorists, rather than as guerrillas. For them, I must reiterate that the terms "terrorism" and "guerrilla war" are used here to denote different strategies of warfare, which may be utilized in the service of a variety of just or unjust causes, and that they do not imply any moral judgment whatsoever.

The absence of a genuine anti-Nazi guerrilla campaign in western Europe during World War II draws attention to the fact that there has not been even a single guerrilla organization in western Europe among the many insurgent organizations that have operated in this region since the 1960s. This fact is particularly conspicuous against the backdrop of the abundance of such organizations in Third World countries. How can it be explained? Is it because Western insurgents have decided that they like terrorism better than guerrilla warfare, making it their strategy of choice? The answer is, of course, that in western Europe and North America, they have had no choice. The only short-term rational option has been terrorism. Imagine the IRA in Ulster or the Red Brigades in Italy trying to launch a guerrilla campaign: establishing liberated zones and carrying out company-sized attacks on military installations. Had they tried this strategy, it would, undoubtedly, have been the shortest guerrilla war in history. For the incumbent government forces, elimination of the insurgency would, at most, have been a matter of days.

There are several examples in history that show quite clearly what happens when a group of insurgents aims too high in its choice of strategy. The most dramatic in the second half of the twentieth century is, probably, Ernesto (Che) Guevara's Bolivian venture. Guevara, a leader of the 1956–58 guerrilla campaign in Cuba, drew the wrong lessons from the rather peculiar circumstances that brought about the insurgents' success there. Guevara believed that the Cuban experience could be readily applied in several other Latin American countries that he considered ripe for a revolution. In autumn 1966, he led fifteen men to Bolivia to start a Cuban-style guerrilla campaign. The insurgency, however, never succeeded in taking off. Although the terrain was favorable for guerrilla warfare, Guevara failed to attract popular support. Despite the fact that government forces' efficiency was far below Western standards, their superiority in numbers was enough to encircle and wipe out the insurgency within a year.[59]

Terrorism, on the other hand, however hopeless it may seem to most people as a way of effecting a radical political change, is at least a mode of struggle that is not immediately suicidal, even when the circumstances are not favorable for the insurgents, and it can be sustained for a considerable time. In all likelihood, western European insurgents would have liked to be able to wage a guerrilla war as their major strategy. One might say that all terrorist groups want to be guerrillas when they grow up.[60] They are unable to do so for practical reasons. Guerrilla warfare requires a terrain that favors small bands of insurgents and is disadvantageous for mechanized and airborne government forces. In western Europe, this kind of terrain—thick jungles or extensive, rugged mountains inaccessible to motor transportation—cannot be found. Guerrillas can sometimes compromise and use less than perfect terrain, providing that other conditions are met, in particular inefficient and poorly equipped government forces on the one hand and massive popular support for the insurgents on the other hand. In contemporary Western countries, none of these conditions exists, however, and terrorism is the only strategic option for insurgents who are determined to resort to violence to advance their cause.

It still has to be explained why those who can conduct a guerrilla campaign resort to terrorism at the same time. Again, the answer is to be found in the difference between academic classifications and real life. In a way, the distinction between guerrilla warfare and terrorism is artificial. To be sure, it is a valid differentiation, but only as an external observation. Academics may sit in their armchairs and categorize strategies of insurgency. The point is that the insurgents themselves rarely do so when they come to select their actions. Although rebels have often delineated their strategic concepts, the arguments have almost always been of a practical nature. The key has been what could be realistically done to promote the political cause. That does not include an attempt to fit the actions into a rigid doctrinaire framework. The primary considerations are capability and utility. Because terrorism is the lowest, least demanding form of insurgency, it has always been used simultaneously with other strategies. The relative importance of terrorism in the overall struggle depends on the circumstances, but it is always part of the strife. A case in point is the Palestinian struggle. Abu Iyad, one of the PLO's main leaders, noted in his memoirs:

> I do not confuse revolutionary violence, which is a political act, with terrorism, which is not. I reject the individual act committed outside the context of an organization or strategic vision. I reject the act dictated by subjective motives which claims to take the place of mass struggle. Revolutionary violence, on the other hand, is part of a large, structured movement. It serves as a supplementary force and contributes, during a period of regrouping or defeat, to giving the movement a new impetus. It becomes superfluous when the grassroots movement scores political successes on the local or international scene.[61]

In fact, terrorism has been a perennial part of the Palestinian struggle since the early 1920s. Abu Iyad is referring to the 1971–73 period, when al-Fatah, the PLO's main organization, engaged in an intensive campaign of international terrorism under the guise of the Black September organization. Abu Iyad himself was allegedly one of the principal chieftains of the clandestine apparatus of international terrorism that carried out a series of spectacular terrorist attacks, including the hostage-taking at the Munich Olympic games of 1972. Al-Fatah's decision to launch a spectacular campaign of international terrorism followed the PLO's expulsion from Jordan by King Hussein in September 1970 (an event after which the Black September organization was named). The wave of international terrorism was designed to boost PLO members' morale after the debacle in Jordan, at a time when they lost Jordan as a base for operations.

A similar increase in international Palestinian terrorism took place in the wake of the 1982 war in south Lebanon, in which the PLO lost most of its bases there. Within Israel and the Occupied Territories, however, terrorism has always been considered by the Palestinian insurgents to be an integral part of the struggle. Changes in the number of terrorist attacks have, therefore, reflected capability rather than motivation. The question has never been whether terrorism should continue, but what else could be done. In the course of the seventy years of the Palestinian violent struggle, the insurgents have, at times, been able to wage guerrilla warfare in addition to terrorism, such as in the 1936–39 Arab rebellion, but most of the time, terrorism has been the only mode of violence at their disposal. Riots have occasionally erupted throughout this period and have sometimes developed into large-scale popular uprisings, which have included several forms of political violence concurrently.

The second intifada (literally, shaking) is the most recent of these uprisings, albeit not the most intense one. Like similar phenomena in Algeria, South Africa, Azerbaijan, Soviet Armenia, and in the Jewish struggle for independence in the 1930s and 1940s, the intifada is not a pure form of insurgent violence. It has included violent as well as nonviolent components. The violent elements of the intifada have consisted of riots, petrol bomb and rock throwing at military and civilian vehicles, and ordinary terrorist-type attacks, such as explosive charges and assassinations. The nonviolent elements have included labor and business strikes, road blocks, and an attempted boycott of Israeli goods and government services.[62] One might suppose that embarking on the more effective strategy of mass protest during the intifada would result in reduction in terrorist attacks, which represented a lower-grade, less effective form of struggle. The contrary is true: the frequency of terrorist incidents and the number of casualties have increased considerably.[63] Thus, the intifada has not been a distinct strategy but a mixture of several modes of struggle, including terrorism.

The 1989 bloodless change of regimes in several eastern European countries seems to refute the assertion that terrorism is an omnipresent part of uprisings. By a strict criterion of examination, this reservation is certainly true. It should be remembered, however, that the regimes of the eastern European Soviet satellites drew their strength from an external source—the USSR. Once this hoop was loosened, the barrel fell apart. In other words, the changes in eastern Europe were not a result of a true internal insurgency but of surrender at the top. Had the governments of Czechoslovakia, Bulgaria, and East Germany been more determined to withstand the peaceful uprising, the struggle would have probably been deteriorated into a long campaign, including terrorism as a cardinal mode of insurgency. In fact, this is what happened in several republics of the former Soviet Union.

In sum, the form of insurgency—terrorism, guerrilla warfare, mass protest, or any combination of these—is in reality mainly determined by objective conditions rather than by strategic conceptions of the insurgents. The most important factor is capability. Usually, the insurgents utilize every possible mode of struggle that can advance their cause. Because terrorism is the lowest form of violent struggle, it is always used in insurgencies. Often, because the insurgents are few, the terrain is not favorable for guerrilla warfare, and government forces are efficient, terrorism is the only mode of insurgency available to insurgents. Sometimes, the rebels are able to conduct guerrilla warfare but continue to use terrorism concurrently. The actual form of contest is forged in a continuous process of friction against hard reality, and terrorism is practically always part of it.

NOTES TO CHAPER 2

The work on this essay was supported by a MacArthur Foundation grant to the Center for Criminal Justice at the Harvard Law School. The author is indebted to Professor Philip Heymann and Dr. Daniel McGillis for their invaluable critique, ideas, and advice.

1. Schmid and Jongman, *Political Terrorism* (1983, 1988, 2005).
2. Ibid. (1988), 5–6.
3. Ibid., 33.
4. Ibid., 33–34.
5. Ibid., 34.
6. Daugherty, "Bomb Warnings."
7. Horne, *Savage War of Peace* (1987), 537–38.
8. "Viet Cong Directive on 'Repression,'" 37.
9. For a comprehensive summary of the origin of the term, see Laqueur, *Age of Terrorism*, esp. chap. 1.
10. U.S. Department of State, *Patterns of Global Terrorism: 1988*, v.
11. *Webster's New World Dictionary* (1966) defines "vigilance committee" as "1. a group of persons organized without legal authorization professedly to keep order and punish crime when ordinary law enforcement agencies apparently fail to do so. 2. especially formerly in the South, such a group organized to terrorize and control Negroes and Abolitionists and, during the Civil War, to suppress support of the Union."
12. *Webster's New Twentieth Century Dictionary Unabridged,* 2d ed. (1980).
13. Luttwak, *Coup d'état,* 27.
14. The characterization of some revolutions as nonviolent is controversial: "'nonviolent revolution,' so long as these words retain any precise meaning whatsoever, is a contradiction in terms," Chalmers Johnson maintains, for example. "Nevertheless, it is quite true that many revolutions have been accomplished without any blood flowing in the gutters. What then, sociologically speaking, do we mean by violence? This question is also basic to the analysis of revolution" (Johnson, *Revolutionary Change,* 7).

15. Brinton, *Anatomy of Revolution* (1965), 3.

16. In 1903, the revolutionary Russian Social Democratic Party was split into Bolsheviks and Mensheviks. The division was over the issue of party membership. Whereas Lenin and his supporters envisaged a tight, centrally controlled conspiratorial organization that would include only dedicated activists, the Mensheviks preferred a more general, less demanding and less centralized organization. See, e.g., Deutscher, *Prophet Armed*.

17. In reality, however, the October 1917 revolution was accomplished in a coup-like manner. There were very few casualties in the actual process of seizing power, although the civil war that followed resulted in great bloodshed and destruction.

18. In reality, the dominant factor in the collapse of the tsarist regime in 1917 was the disintegration of the army as a result of a series of defeats in World War 1. See Skocpol, *States and Social Revolutions*.

19. See, e.g., the doctrine of the Popular Front for the Liberation of Palestine (PFLP), in Amos, *Palestinian Resistance,* 192–93.

20. This has been the doctrine advocated by Mao Zedong and his followers. See, e.g., Laqueur, *Guerrilla,* chap. 6.

21. On the basis of empirical findings on riot participation in Newark, New Jersey, Paige, "Political Orientation and Riot Participation," defines riots as "a form of disorganized political protest engaged in by those who have become highly distrustful of existing political institutions" (819).

22. Advocates of nonviolent resistance usually emphasize the moral superiority of this mode of struggle, but in his 1973 book *Politics of Nonviolent Action,* Gene Sharp stresses its practical advantages although his point of departure is that nonviolent resistance is morally preferable.

23. Ibid., 75–90.

24. See Laqueur, *Age of Terrorism,* 21, 44–48.

25. Nineteenth-century revolutionaries have often carried the term "terrorism" with pride. See, e.g., N. Morozov, "The Terrorist Struggle," G. Tarnovski, "Terrorism and Routine," and Johann Most, "Advice for Terrorists," in *Terrorism Reader,* ed. Laqueur and Alexander, 72–84, 100–108. In the second half of the twentieth century, however, most insurgent organizations that adopted terrorism as a strategy shunned the term in favor of a variety of euphemisms. Yet even a modern authority on terrorism doctrine, Carlos Marighella, writes: "Terrorism is an arm the revolutionary can never relinquish" (Marighella, "Minimanual of the Urban Guerrilla," in *Terror and Urban Guerrillas,* ed. Mallin, 103).

26. Laqueur, *Guerrilla,* x, xi.

27. See, e.g., Mao, "Base Areas in the Anti-Japanese Guerrilla War."

28. In the battle of Dien Bien Phu (1954) the Vietminh employed four divisions against a French force of about 15,000 (Dupuy and Dupuy, *Encyclopedia of Military History,* 1296. The battle itself was conducted along the lines of a regular war, although it was waged in the general framework of a guerrilla struggle. See, e.g., Laqueur, *Guerrilla.*

29. The largest terrorist teams have been employed in hostage-taking: thus, e.g., fifty members of the 28th of February Popular League participated in the takeover of the Panamanian Embassy in San Salvador on January 11, 1980, and

forty-one members of the Colombian M-19 group took over the Palace of Justice in Bogota on November 6, 1985 (Mickolus et al., *International Terrorism in the 1980s*, 1: 5–6; 11: 298–300).

30. George H. W. Bush, introduction to U.S. Department of Defense, *Terrorist Group Profiles*, n.p. See also Menachem Begin, "Freedom Fighters and Terrorists," in *International Terrorism: Challenge and Response*, 39–46.

31. Ivianski, *Revolution and Terror*, 274–78 (in Hebrew).

32. Many authors who have addressed the moral issue in terrorism use Kalyayev as an example. A partial list includes Hacker, *Crusaders, Criminals, Crazies*, 294–95; Ivianski, "Moral Issue," in *Morality of Terrorism*, ed. Rapoport and Alexander, 230; Laqueur, *Age of Terrorism*, 83; Walzer, *Just and Unjust Wars*, 198–99; Bell, *Assassin* (1979), 235.

33. Walzer, *Just and Unjust Wars*, 197–206.

34. Ibid., 203

35. Ibid., 202

36. Ibid., xiv.

37. E.g., Crenshaw, "Introduction," in *Terrorism, Legitimacy, and Power*, ed. id., 1; Wilkinson, *Terrorism and the Liberal State* (1977), 110; Wardlaw, *Political Terrorism*, 34–42.

38. U.S. Department of State, *Patterns of Global Terrorism: 1988*; Schmid and Jongman, *Political Terrorism* (1988), 34.

39. Liddell Hart, *Strategy*, 163.

40. Sun Tzu, *Art of War*, chap. 3.

41. Laqueur, *Age of Terrorism*, 48–51; Wardlaw, *Political Terrorism*, 21.

42. See, e.g., Most, "Advice for Terrorists," in *Terrorism Reader*, ed. Laqueur and Alexander, 105–6; Ivianski, *Revolution and Terror*, 106–7 (in Hebrew).

43. See Horne, *Savage War of Peace*.

44. See Arnon-Ohanna and Mi'Bayit, *Internal Struggle*, 282–84 (in Hebrew). The kaffiyeh was the traditional headdress of villagers, and some authors viewed its enforcement on the urban population as a symptom of social rebellion against the bourgeoisie, in addition to the nationalist element that was the main motivation of the rebellion. At that time, the insurgent gangs were mainly composed of villagers. Regardless of the true origin of the insurgents' demand, the kaffiyeh became a symbol of the rebellion, and the insurgents imposed it on the population as a symbol of compliance.

45. See Massu, *Vraie bataille d'Alger*.

46. Laqueur, *Age of Terrorism*, 43, notes, for example, that Armenian revolutionaries of the 1880s and 1890s assumed that their attacks on the Turks would instigate brutal retaliation, which would, in turn, result in radicalization of the Armenian population and possibly also lead to Western countries' intervention.

47. Marighella, "Minimanual of the Urban Guerrilla," in *Terror and Urban Guerrillas*, ed. Mallin, 111.

48. Bechor, *Lexicon of the PLO*, 279 (in Hebrew).

49. See Rentner, "Terrorism in Insurgent Strategies," 51; P. Jenkins, "Strategy of Tension."

50. Janke, *Guerrilla and Terrorist Organisations*, 47–48.

51. The bombing was apparently carried out by members of the neo-Nazi terrorist group Wehrsportgruppe Hoffman (Military Sports Group Hoffman), or the Wehrsportgruppe Schlageter (Military Sports Group Schlageter). See Mickolus et al., *International Terrorism in the 1980s*, 1: 87; Schmid and Jongman, *Political Terrorism* (1988), 558.

52. P. Jenkins, "Strategy of Tension."

53. Schmid and Jongman, *Political Terrorism* (1988), 623. See also Janke, *Guerrilla and Terrorist Organisations*, 57–58; Yaeger, "Menia Muria."

54. Kurz and Merari, *ASALA*. See also Schmid and Jongman, *Political Terrorism* (1988), 673, 675; Janke, *Guerrilla and Terrorist Organisations*, 276.

55. Kurz and Merari, *ASALA*, 14–15.

56. The database at Tel Aviv University's Political Violence Research Unit includes data on more than 800 distinct terrorist groups that operated in the 1980s.

57. For a discussion of the influence of the issue at stake in readiness to yield to terrorism, see Merari and Friedland, "Social Psychological Aspects of Political Terrorism," in *International Conflict and National Public Policy Issues*, ed. Oskamp.

58. Crenshaw, "Introduction," 5.

59. See Kohn, *Dictionary of Wars*, 60.

60. Even Carlos Marighella, the most popular modern advocate of terrorism, viewed terrorism ("urban guerrilla warfare" in his terminology) as a stage necessary to enable the development of rural guerrilla warfare: "it is a technique that aims at the development of urban guerrilla warfare, whose function will be to wear out, demoralize and distract the enemy forces, permitting the emergence and survival of rural guerrilla warfare which is destined to play the decisive role in the revolutionary war" (Marighella, "Minimanual of the Urban Guerrilla," in *Terror and Urban Guerrillas*, ed. Mallin, 83).

61. Abu Iyad, *My Home, My Land*, 98.

62. Merari et al., "Palestinian Intifada."

63. Kurz, "Palestinian Terrorism in 1988."

PART I

THE PREHISTORY OF TERRORISM

CHAPTER 3

ZEALOTS AND ASSASSINS

Gérard Chaliand and Arnaud Blin

THE ZEALOTS

History records one of the first manifestations of organized terrorism in the Middle East in first-century Palestine. The Zealot sect was one of the very first groups to practice systematic terror of which we possess a written account. Our knowledge of Zealots' struggle is based on the reporting of Flavius Josephus in his *Jewish Antiquities,* published in 93–94 C.E., and in his account of the *Jewish War,* a shorter work published between 75 and 79, to the greater glory of Vespasian and Titus, for whom he worked as an advisor on Jewish affairs. Josephus uses the word *sicarii*—a generic Latin term derived from *sicarius,* "dagger-man"—to denote the Zealots.

The immediate cause of the Jewish rebellion against Rome was the census taken by the Roman authorities throughout the empire in the early years of the common era. The Jews resented it and were humiliated by its clear reflection of their submission to a foreign power. The situation turned incendiary in the year 6 B.C.E., some eight years after the death of Herod the Great, an event that marked a decisive turning point in the history of the Jews, who had enjoyed more than a century of relative independence and prosperity since 129 B.C.E. The first rumblings of revolt were heard in 4 B.C.E., but it was in the year 6 that the Zealots launched an organized campaign against the imperial authorities. Under Herod, the Jews had chafed under their circumscribed independence, and they had no intention of passing up the opportunity to win genuine self-determination. Instead, they found themselves forced into a situation that represented the very antithesis of their aspirations. Spontaneous hotbeds of insurrection arose throughout the region. In modern terms, we might say that the Jews were caught up in the anti-colonial dynamic of a war of liberation.

Following the first riots, Varus, the governor of Syria, sent two Roman legions in support of the garrisons beleaguered by the revolt. Varus crushed the rebels and made an example of them by crucifying 2,000 of their number. The idea was to deal a psychological blow strong enough to dissuade the populace from further rebellion. It was the first use of terror in a war that was to last several decades.

According to Josephus, the Zealots were one of the four "philosophical" sects of Judea and the most popular among the younger generation. Their philosophical doctrine was similar to that of the Pharisees, who lived in the strictest observance of the Torah and are accused of dogmatism and hypocrisy in the Gospels. Compared to other Jewish religious movements of the time, the Zealots were reformers; believing that they had to account to God alone, they had an unquenchable thirst for freedom. They were animated by an unswerving faith that was admired both by Josephus, a Pharisee, and by their most violent detractors.

While Josephus commonly refers to the Zealots or *sicarii* as "bandits," his account of their war clearly portrays it as a fundamentally political and religious struggle. All authorities facing a terrorist faction systematically refer to it as a criminal organization. They judge it to be acting beyond the law and to have aims that are intrinsically criminal and immoral. These authorities must seek to brand the terrorists as enemies of society, resolved to destroy it. In Flavius Josephus's telling, the Jewish elite took a dim view of the activities of the Zealots, who threatened their status and their security. On the other hand, the Zealots enjoyed considerable popularity among the lower classes and the young. It would appear that the founders and leaders of the Zealots, of whom very little is known, were educated and therefore probably of prosperous origins. It would also appear that the Zealots sought to recruit their "militants" from the working classes.[1]

The founder of the sect was a certain Judah of Galilee, whose early activities came to naught under Roman repression. After such difficult beginnings, signs of the Zealots resurface in the 60s, although virtually nothing is known about them in the intervening fifty years. One thing is certain: they were able to keep themselves afloat after their initial failure. We also know that Judah's descendants retained the movement's leadership and that they must therefore have had a certain degree of organization. The Zealots had announced their twofold objective right from the start. As a religious organization, they sought, often by force, to impose a degree of rigor in religious practice. For instance, they attacked other Jews whom they felt to be insufficiently scrupulous in their piety. They took up terror as an instrument. As a political organization, they sought to wrest their country's independence from Rome. The party's religious aims were inseparable from its political objectives.

It is here that the idea of purity—religious and political—begins to emerge. This dynamic will be found in almost all such movements. Robespierre, for instance, was animated by the same concept. Moreover, the amalgam of religion and politics is almost systematically present, in one form or another, in the majority of movements resorting to terror. In the nineteenth and twentieth centuries, secular religion, or ideology—Marxism, Trotskyism, Maoism, Fascism, Nazism, and so on—was ubiquitous long before traditional religiosity made its comeback in the late twentieth. In general, exclusively political terrorist organizations are rare in history, as are religious pressure groups with no political ambitions. Maxime Rodinson has elegantly summarized this political-ideological synergy:

> Ideological movements are at the confluence of two series of struggles, conflicts and aspirations. There is, on the one hand, the political dynamic, the eternal struggle for power to be found wherever there are human societies . . . and even in certain types of animal society. On the other hand, we find the no less universal aspiration to be guided in public and private life by a system of standards and rules that spare us the never-ending task of having constantly to construct behavioral models for every occasion, of having continuously to call everything into question. We call such systems ideologies.[2]

This aspiration, individual or collective, together with a burning desire to wield power—or to prevent another from wielding power over oneself, which amounts to the same thing—logically leads to political extremism and its corollary, ideological or religious fanaticism. No less logically, extremism and fanaticism often result in some kind of violence, organized to a lesser or greater degree.

In the case at hand, the Zealots were able to channel the latent violence born of the widespread humiliation felt by the Jewish people. They were able to organize and then direct that violence against the Roman "invader," as well as against those members of the Jewish community whom they considered to be traitors to the national cause. It is in this sense that the Zealots can be thought of as a genuine organization. For, while the party may bear a certain kinship to contemporary millenarian sects, it was distinguished by the political project underlying its activities, which explains the popular support it enjoyed and the resolve demonstrated in adversity by its members.

In a classic pattern that has been reproduced countless times through the ages, from the very start the Zealots had to develop their strategy of operations from a position of weakness. They had two options: either they could organize a guerrilla-style resistance aimed at overcoming the adversary by indirect (military) action, or they could cultivate an indirect strategy aimed at keeping the adversary off balance by waging an essentially psychological campaign.

The documentation shows that the Zealots nevertheless adopted the techniques of terrorism, as evidenced by their designation as *sicarii* by the Roman authorities. In all likelihood, the Zealots waged an armed struggle in the form of guerrilla warfare, including urban fighting, while resorting to a strategy of terror-based psychology. Given that they remained active for decades, it is also likely that their tactics evolved over time and in response to circumstances.

Flavius Josephus has little to say about the Zealots' tactics, preferring to dwell in detail on the organization of the Roman army arrayed against them. And yet, it would appear that their strategy was relatively complex. In the year 66, for instance, the Zealots assassinated a number of political and religious figures. They also attacked buildings used to store archives, including loan documents, with the aim of winning the support of a working class crushed by debt. We know that the *sicarii* used daggers to cut their victims' throats and that they often acted in the midst of a crowd, for instance, in marketplaces. Such operations reveal their desire to foment a sense of vulnerability within the population at large, a classic tactic of terrorists to this day. The *sicarii* could act wherever and whenever they wanted. That was their strength.

The other source of the Zealots' strength was their willingness to confront the enemy at great risk to themselves, thereby winning the support of the populace. On this point, testimony, including that of Josephus, is eloquent. On several occasions, the Roman army captured hundreds of rebels, who were tortured before being put to death in the most painful ways possible. Far from cooling the ardor of the Zealot fighters, such reprisals seem only to have galvanized the men and women in their ranks. After the destruction of the temple in the year 70, a thousand men and women, led by Eleazar Ben Yair, resisted for three years in the fortress of Masada. Encircled by Roman troops, they chose to kill themselves rather than to fall into their enemy's hands.

THE ASSASSINS

The Zealots and the Assassins are the two classic examples of a terrorist organization. There are irrefutable parallels between the two sects, although a lack of information on the former group prevents any kind of rigorous comparative study. While we have few texts on the Zealots, the history of the Assassins is fairly well documented. That history, covering two centuries, unfolded at a particularly splendid moment for Arab-Muslim culture, and one that is therefore abundant in documentation. The history of the Assassins prefigures to a remarkable degree the dynamic of most movements that have resorted to terrorist tactics over the centuries. A thorough analysis of the mechanisms of that fearsome organization is therefore of the essence.

The history of the great monotheistic religions—Judaism, Christianity, and Islam—is inseparable from the idea of struggle. Like any social organization, the religious party is at first a natural rival to political power. The struggle is all the more intense when a religion is universalist in nature, as are Christianity and Islam. The universalist religions, which include Buddhism, naturally cohere as "ideological communities."[3] In other words, they include all those who accept their dogma and exclude all those who do not. Founded on a credo, such communities define and organize every aspect of the society to which their members belong. In their earliest phases, such organizations are mostly interested in religious or philosophical problems. As they grow in number and confidence, however, they extend their influence to other spheres of social organization and ultimately set their sights on definitive social control through political power.

Once a religious party seizes power or grafts itself to political power, we may speak, like Maxime Rodinson, of an

> ideological state, that is, a State that proclaims its adherence and fidelity to the credo, along with its resolve to enforce respect for the rules of common life inferred therefrom. . . . Like many non-ideological states, it seeks to expand where it believes it can, without taking undue risks. In this, however, it seeks not merely to extend the domination of a given group of individuals, let alone an entire nation, but also to extend over the face of the Earth the zone wherein Truth can best exert its beneficial effects.[4]

Among the great monotheistic-universalist religions, Islam has been the most successful at integrating strictly theological issues and political considerations into a common structure. In that sense, it is closest in spirit to the great ideological trends of the nineteenth and twentieth centuries. The priority concerns of Christianity have always been theological, as evidenced by the countless disputes that have punctuated its history. The evident synergy in Islam between religion and politics is the outcome of its historical origins. In the tribal political context of the Arabian peninsula, the first Muslims found it necessary, for reasons of pure survival, to organize themselves into a group similar to the tribal model, an organization in which religious and political power were held in the same hands. It is this primordial model that shaped Islam.

The dichotomy separating Christianity and Islam is fundamental. It allows us to understand how a sect like the Assassins could emerge in the Islamic world, while we find no trace of any such movement in the history of Christianity. The example of Islam, and in particular that of the Assassins, also allows us to grasp the logic of violence in the modern context of the major contemporary universalist ideologies. A fortiori, the history of the Assassins logically encourages us to establish comparisons between it and the terrorist organizations of the modern world, including those that have emerged from and are ideologically modeled by the Islamic world.

In the Christian world, the instance that is clearly closest to the Islamic example is that of the Reformation, in which the boundaries between politics and religions were blurred, as attested by the wars of religion and above all the Thirty Years' War. And yet, even within that specific instance, the boundaries endured, regardless of the many breaches. Ultimately, the history of Europe and Christianity plainly demonstrate the extent to which the two powers, Church and state, are both distinct and compatible. In brief, they are able to coexist.

Within the framework of Islam, on the other hand, no dispute can be said to be merely spiritual or religious. The very raison d'être of a challenging party is defined by its opposition to the reigning power, that is, the power of the state. Its essence is therefore by necessity that of a "political party." The Assassins fall within that rule, in that their organization operated within the logic of political power plays. The fusion, as seen in the Assassins, of religious mission and political ambition leads, as it did with the Zealots, to strategic choices and the use of violence. Taking up the arms of terrorism was a logical choice for the Assassins, as it had been for the *sicarii*. Its effectiveness made it the primary weapon in their strategic arsenal and eventually defined the sect's very essence for posterity. In contrast to the confusion born of the terminology associated with their name, the terrorism practiced by the Assassins was far closer in actual fact to modern terrorism than it was to tyrannicide, a different and distinct branch in the terrorist genealogy. The Assassins employed terror against figures associated with power precisely because they were figureheads and not because they had cause against any particular individual, as in the case of the assassinations of political leaders such as Henri IV, Lincoln, or Kennedy.

The Assassins were rooted in two regions, Iran and Syria. They co-opted the use of terror to psychological ends and targeted, among others, a foreign, Christian power: the Crusaders. The terrorists themselves were animated by an unshakable faith that allowed them to sacrifice themselves willingly in the course of a mission in the certainty that they would ascend directly to paradise. And yet some of these similarities are fortuitous. The fight against the Crusaders, which is strongly emphasized in Western accounts, was in fact a very minor aspect of the Assassins' activities. The history of the sect opens a window onto certain mechanisms underlying all forms of terrorism practiced in the name of ideology. In that sense, this history—or, more precisely, this protohistory—provides a kind of blueprint for terrorism as practiced by ideological groups. In 1789, in France, the phenomenon of ideology would expand into a new dimension that would alter its inner workings without replacing them entirely. That is why the history of the Assassins is still of interest to us today.

THE ORIGINS OF THE SECT

Islam experienced its first crisis of succession upon the death of the Prophet Muhammad in 632. Following the nomination of Abu Bakr as caliph—that is, "successor"—certain Muslims contested the choice, preferring Muhammad's cousin and son-in-law ʿAli. These formed the Shiʿatu ʿAli, the party of ʿAli, which gave rise to the Shiite movement. Named caliph in 656 after the violent death of the third caliph, ʿAli was in turn assassinated in 661. Thanks to the resourceful Muʿawiya—himself targeted by ʿAli's assassins, the Kharijites—the Ummayads assumed power, which they held for over a century by establishing a hereditary system. ʿAli's son Husayn sought to regain it, with the help of the Prophet's daughter Fatima, but the attempt failed. The deaths of Husayn, his family, and his supporters at the hands of the Ummayads—along with a second abortive attempt to seize power in 687—served as the founding myth of the Shiite movement. Gradually, what had initially been a classic struggle for power developed an ideological dimension.

The imam became the emblematic figure of the Shiite movement, mandated to overthrow tyranny and to establish justice. By the end of the seventh century, the Shiites had affirmed their desire to seize power from the caliphate so as to vest it in an imam. More generally, they sought to become masters of the Islamic world and to restore "true" Islam. Thus arose the issue of the imam's legitimacy. He was required to be descended from ʿAli or, better yet, from ʿAli and Fatima, and therefore from the Prophet. The establishment of a link of direct filiation between the Prophet and the imam had a moderating influence on the Shiite movement, which, through the first half of the eighth century, gave rise to myriad offshoot sects, particularly in southern Iraq and along the shores of the Persian Gulf. Taking root in Persia, the movement was very soon and thenceforward permanently subject to an essentially continuous conflict between moderates and extremists. This endemic struggle led to the first great Shiʿa schism. The death of the sixth Imam Jaʾfar in 765 ignited a crisis of legitimacy, pitting his two sons, Ismaʿil and Musa, and their supporters against each other in competition for the succession. The majority party of Musa ultimately developed into so-called Twelver Shiism (after the twelve imams in the line of Musa), which has been recognized as the official religion of Iran since the sixteenth century. The Ismaʿilis, less moderate than the Twelver Shiites, evolved into a secret society based on organization, resolve, discipline, and internal cohesion. The Assassins emerged from within the Ismaʿili movement.

The Ismaʾilis were similar to many anti-establishment groups, religious or not. The sect shared many of the characteristics of European reform movements, such as respect for the Book—in this case, the Qurʿan—and for tradition. Like the Protestants, the Ismaʿilis emphasized the philosophical and moral aspects of community life and looked to the classical learning of the Greeks. But where the Protestants were inspired by the Stoics, the Ismaʿilis borrowed from Neoplatonic philosophy. They harnessed religious and philosophical teaching to a formidable political machine that was both durable and cohesive, capable of sustaining a group in which each individual—mystic and intellectual, malcontent and fanatic—was able to find a place. Religious power, intellectual power, political power—all that was missing was a military branch in order to transform the organization into a genuine political, social, and theocratic entity. That military branch became the purview of the Assassins, whose strategies and tools were adapted to the secretive and minoritarian character of the Ismaʿili sect.

For the first fifty years or so after the founding of the sect, the Ismaʿilis lived in entrenched camps. In the ninth century, the failing power and ossification of the Abassid Caliphate left the door open to other movements, the best organized among which—notably, the two Shiite factions—were able to profit therefrom. The Isma'ilis were fired by the missionary zeal of all universalist movements, establishing themselves in several regions, including southern Iraq, Syria, and Yemen. Their theological and philosophical credentials, having evolved over the course of decades, were highly effective instruments for propaganda and conversion that won over entire populations. Supported by the Fatimid empire of Egypt, the Isma'ilis insinuated themselves throughout the region, including the great centers of learning, such as Cairo. Their influence expanded exponentially. They became an ever more present danger to the power of Baghdad. However, certain external factors ultimately favored the Sunnis, in particular, the arrival of the Turks, who, once converted, became fierce defenders of the Sunni cause. Moreover, the emerging threat from the West compelled the Sunni powers to reorganize and fortify themselves. These elements helped the Sunnis to tilt the balance back in their favor.

Moreover, the successes enjoyed by the Isma'ilis with the support of the Fatimids were also the cause of their retrenchment when the empire crumbled. In the late eleventh century, the crisis led to a rupture within the sect, creating on the one side, the Mustalis, who clung on at the margins of the Islamic world, and on the other, the Nizaris, who, from their base in Persia, came to play a significant role in its heartland. The advance of the Seljuk Turks, which began in 1040 in Iran and continued throughout the eleventh century, and the defeat of Byzantium by Alp Arslan at Manzikert in 1071 drew every malcontent of the regime to the Isma'ilis, including the former elites marginalized by the new power.

Isma'ilism had set down sturdy theological and philosophical roots over the course of the two centuries preceding the crisis. The Isma'ilis universalist approach served their missionary activism. However, in a context wherein, as we have seen, the religious mission cannot be distinguished from political power, the Isma'ilis had yet to establish a political base commensurate with their theocratic aspirations. That would require the emergence of a providential figure to lead the Isma'ili revolution. The Muslim world, it might be said, was in a state of latent crisis that the Isma'ilis were able to exploit to their own advantage.

Like all revolutions, theirs had an inspired manager. Hasan-i Sabbah was the son of a Twelver Shiite of Yemeni origin who had settled in Persia. Hasan was most likely born around the middle of the eleventh century. A chance encounter led him to adopt the Isma'ili faith, and he was sent on mission to Cairo, where he met Nizam al-Mulk, vizier of the Seljuk emperor, and the mathematician and poet Omar Khayyam. Like him, they were Persians, and they became friends. Nizam al-Mulk was the political and bureaucratic architect of the vast empire that, for nearly 1,000 years, determined the governmental organization of the larger part of the Muslim world. Founder of the University of Baghdad, Nizam al-Mulk, together with his descendants, unified the adherents of Sunni Islam. Until the emergence of Western political science, his *Book of Government, or, Rules for Kings* served as the basic handbook for the administrators and political leaders of Iran and the Ottoman and Mogul empires. He devoted a significant portion of the book to the counterinsurrection techniques he would rely on in his fight against the Isma'ilis. Assassinated by the latter in 1092, he became one of the first victims on a long list of ranking dignitaries killed by the Assassins.

In Egypt, Hasan had troubles with the local authorities and was jailed before being deported. He later undertook a lengthy mission that gave him the opportunity for extensive travels, especially in Persia. His journey brought him into contact with all sorts of peoples and numerous communities, some in remote areas. He came to appreciate the diversity of these communities and to discern those areas where his mission was likely to find fertile soil. One region in particular attracted his attention.

The mountainous Daylam region of northern Persia was home to a population of rough, hard, and fiercely independent men who had never been conquered by force. The area, pacified without bloodshed during the Islamic conquest, was an early center of Shiism. It was there that Hasan chose to focus his energies. The people were receptive to the Isma'ili mission and had the further advantage of belonging to a warrior culture. Moreover, the topography of Daylam was ideal for someone looking for a safe haven. Hasan nurtured the hope of one day overturning Seljuk power. To that end, he needed an isolated and naturally protected spot where he could develop his political and military plans.

After several years of prospecting, during which the authorities became increasingly concerned by his activities, Hasan chose the fortress of Alamut in the Elburz mountains, north of modern Tehran and not far from the Caspian Sea. Alamut was built on a rock some 2,000 meters high, overlooking a valley. It was difficult to reach and strategically situated to detect the approach of an enemy from afar. The castle belonged to a local chief, and Hasan had first to prepare its seizure. With the help of local converts who infiltrated the compound, Hasan took the castle in 1090. He made it his headquarters and did not leave until his death in 1125.

THE STRATEGY OF TERROR

From his base in Alamut, Hasan set out to gain control of the entire region. To that end, he sought first to secure the support of its peoples. In this, his strategy was identical to that practiced by the various revolutionary movements of the twentieth century. Such poor, rural populations, under the yoke of petty local lords, were primed to espouse the Isma'ili cause. Missionary activities were top priority, and the propaganda work was intensive. Having won popular support, Hasan would then try to persuade the feudal nobility to hand over control of the neighboring castles and citadels. Where he failed to convince them, he was merciless, deploying every means necessary to take their strongholds, including clandestine subversion and force. In such cases, he used terror to persuade the other nobles to offer no resistance. Hasan gradually gained possession of every strategic position in the region. His military tactics and his politico-strategic acumen grew keener with every victory.

His early successes encouraged him to pursue his activities in farther-flung territories. In 1092, he dispatched a mission to another mountainous region, Quhistan, near the current border between Iran and Afghanistan. There he found fertile ground. The region, which had once been one of the last refuges of Zoroastrianism, was home to a people that jealously guarded its religious and political independence from the central powers and was welcoming to dissident political minorities like the Isma'ilis. At that time, they were proving hostile to Seljuk rule and its vassals. Hasan's man in Quhistan, Husayn Qa'ini, was wildly successful at exploiting this discontent and took control of the region, including its cities. Hasan pursued his conquests in other regions, usually mountainous ones such as Fars and Khuzistan. From such strategic bridgeheads, he sent off armies of missionaries, who slowly but surely infiltrated zones under Seljuk rule. A confrontation between the authorities and Hasan's agents was inevitable. The first such recorded incident took place in the town of Sava.

The Isma'ilis had tried to convert the town's muezzin to their cause. When he refused, they killed him. The vizier, Nizam al-Mulk, responded swiftly. The mission's leader was captured and executed and his corpse dragged through the streets. This clash represented both the first assassination undertaken by the Isma'ilis and the first response by the authorities. It set off an armed conflict between the sultan's forces and the Isma'ilis, with a double offensive against Alamut and Quhistan. At the same time, Hasan was preparing an ambitious action targeting none other than the grand vizier himself, Nizam al-Mulk.

Had Nizam al-Mulk been imagining just such a confrontation when he wrote his *Book of Government* several years earlier, in 1086? The following passage suggests that he had given some thought to the possibility of internal unrest:

> The sovereign has the power to prevent all excesses, all unrest and all sedition. He instills respect in every heart and fear before his majesty, made manifest to all, so that his subjects may enjoy perfect security and wish to see his reign prolonged. But the spirit of revolt may seize his people, and should he scorn sacred law and neglect the duties required by his faith, should he break the divine commandments, God will wish to punish and scourge him as he has deserved. . . . Undoubtedly, the dire consequence of such rebellion will be to bring holy wrath down upon the people and lead God to forsake them. A good prince will die, unsheathed sabers will be raised, and blood will flow. The strongest will act at his own pleasure and those who are devoted to sin will perish in the unrest and bloodshed.

If, as the saying goes, a man forewarned is worth two men, the vizier's strategy of prevention ought to have forearmed him against the murderous attack being planned against him. In his *Book of Government,* Nizam al-Mulk recommends the following precautions:

> Spies should be constantly moving along the roads of the various provinces, disguised as traders, travelers, Sufis, apothecaries, and so on, and prepare detailed reports on what they hear so that nothing may in any way pass unnoticed. If, once such information has been collected, it is determined that something is going to take place, steps must be taken immediately. Governors, feudatories, officials and military leaders are very often prone to opposition and revolt and cherish evil designs against the sovereign. But the spy who has hastened to court will have already informed the prince, who then will leap on his horse, fly to the field, order his troops on the march and, attacking the rebels where he may find them, nip the rebellion in the bud.

The grand vizier would not have undertaken his offensive against Hasan if he had not been informed of his clandestine activities. Even so, Nizam al-Mulk was unable to protect himself adequately from the conspiracy against him. Today, the name of Nizam al-Mulk is inextricably associated with that of the Assassins. His assassination by one of Hasan's agents, a certain Bu Tahir Arrani, on October 16, 1092, during the month of Ramadan, was one of the great terrorist attacks of all time, and its contemporary impact was at least as great as that of the assassination of the Archduke Franz Ferdinand or the attacks of September 11, 2001, in their own eras.

Nizam al-Mulk was a figure of unrivaled repute in the Muslim world of the eleventh century. His place in history had already been ensured by all he had accomplished in his lifetime. In death, he unwittingly opened one of the decisive chapters in the history of terrorism. For a trial run, Hasan could not have hoped for better. Upon learning of the death of his rival, he exclaimed, "The murder of that devil is the beginning of bliss." The incident launched the notoriety of Hasan and his organization, which, through this founding act, gave its name to the violent deed committed against the vizier, which would soon become its trademark: assassination.

As with the attacks of September 11, the government's domestic police and intelligence services were caught napping despite efforts to ensure the effectiveness of its security sector. Nizam al-Mulk's assassin, disguised as a Sufi, had managed with a simple blade to deal a psychological blow of unprecedented impact to an empire ruled by an iron rod. The Seljuk empire in the late eleventh century was a power of the first order. The assassination of the grand vizier was one of the first great terrorist assaults to be identified as such. It came at a propitious moment for Hasan. On the military front, he had successfully repulsed two incursions by the Seljuk army that year.

The most serious of the two attacks, that against Alamut—and thus against Hasan himself—ought from a military standpoint to have gone well for the sultan's forces. Indeed, Hasan found himself boxed into his stronghold with a mere sixty men. As is always the case in situations in which the besieged is the weaker force, the only possible deliverance was to find external reinforcements to come to their assistance. In that regard, Hasan's policies were to yield great dividends. His propaganda over the years had won him the support of the neighboring populations. Seeing their leader in trouble, his missionaries had sprung into action. They cobbled together a small army, which, exploiting the element of surprise, took the besieging army from the rear.

Hasan's rise to power certainly contributed to the crisis of succession that erupted in 1094, during which the Isma'ilis of Persia broke away from their Egyptian tutelage. At the same time, the Seljuk empire was being shaken by a crisis of authority that facilitated Hasan's offensive. He pursued the seizure of castles and secured control of ever more strategic vantage points. The Isma'ili conquest of Shahdiz, near Isfahan, was a terrible military and psychological reversal for the Seljuk authorities. It was around this time that the Isma'ilis began to deploy the tactics of subversion by waging terror campaigns against urban populations. In Isfahan, in the grip of a full-blown political crisis, the Isma'ilis sought to unleash chaos through one such campaign. However, as in other cities, the Isfahan campaign backfired on its organizers, who fell victim to an uprising of the terrorized population.

From the start, the Isma'ilis had a well-defined political project and had developed a strategy commensurate with their ambitions, which sought to deploy a variety of means to choke off the central power. These means included propaganda, the military conquest of strategic positions, and campaigns of terror waged against the public and against political and religious figures. The philosophical-religious platform developed earlier by the Isma'ilis underpinned an ever more sophisticated, multidimensional strategy. Within the Persian branch of the Isma'ilis, the use of terror became an increasingly popular strategic option, first because it meshed well with other, specific characteristics of the sect, such as its penchant for secrecy, and secondly because, during the years of bloodshed, terror—especially that targeting the elite—had proved to be highly successful. Those entrusted with assassinations, the "devotees"—*fidai'in*, or *fedayeen*—formed a sort of elite corps within the sect.

The Persian faction of Isma'ilism, which would soon extend itself beyond Iran, was on its way to becoming the notorious sect known as the Assassins. The term "assassin," which means "murderer" in many languages, is itself derived from the sect's name. The word's etymology is uncertain. It may derive from the word "hashish," meaning herbage, and by extension cannabis. In this interpretation, the Assassins are *hashishiyyin*—hashish-takers—a sense that may have some validity but is not corroborated by any evidence of cannabis use by the Assassins. It may be an expression of contempt and thus not based on any hypothetical cannabis consumption—it was in Syria that the name "Assassin" gained currency to denote a sect whose early members were all foreigners, that is, Persians.

With hindsight, it is obvious that the Isma'ili sect had virtually no chance of driving the Seljuk Turk dynasty from central power. As it happens, it is a characteristic of many terrorist movements to strike at a political entity from a position of extreme weakness that could never allow them to seize power or to eliminate the powers that be. At the very most, such organizations are capable of waging campaigns of harassment, while remaining sufficiently organized to resist the military offensives of the authorities.

From that standpoint, the case of the Assassins is not fundamentally different from that of al Qaeda today. From his sanctuary in the mountains of Afghanistan, Osama bin Laden led a campaign against the West similar to that of Hasan against the Seljuks, with sometimes very similar tactics, including the use of bladed weapons. The propaganda drives and recruitment and training of terrorists in both cases were very much alike, often undertaken among the same social classes and in similar topographies (rural or mountainous regions with populations hardened by warfare). Like Hasan, bin Laden could not hope to topple his adversary—in his case, the West or the United States—with a simple terrorist attack, whatever its nature. Nevertheless, like al Qaeda today, Hasan's organization knew how to exploit the Achilles' heel of the governing (Seljuk) power—unrest linked to succession disputes and power struggles—to weaken his adversary and benefit his own movement. Today, al Qaeda exploits certain weaknesses of the Western democratic system, as well as the mentality of the masses—in particular the desire of Westerners to live in absolute security—to contest religious orthodoxy in the Muslim world in the hope of toppling certain regimes.

The complex interplay between unachievable ideological objectives and realistic goals of lesser ambition determined the Assassins' activities throughout the two centuries of their viability as a sect. Following his victories over the Seljuk besiegers in 1092 and his consolidation of his strategic strongholds in Persia, Hasan decided, with the help of his emissaries, to extend his activities into Syria. Why Syria? After all, the borderlands of Iraq were closer and Egypt was more important. But Hasan and his supporters were thinking strategically. Syria was a mountainous country that had never really established cultural cohesiveness. A variety of Muslim confessions flourished there, including some groups that were close to the Isma'ilis. For their part, the Isma'ilis had managed to gain permanent footholds in certain regions. As in northern Persia, the populations of those regions were receptive to the teachings of Hasan's people. Furthermore, the Syrians were in conflict with the Crusaders from Europe. This European, non-Muslim presence served the Assassins' interests in their propaganda campaigns among the people and, through the accounts brought back by the Crusaders, introduced Europe to the sect and enhanced its notoriety.

Some time around the turn of the twelfth century, the men of Alamut began their work in Syria. The large majority of missionaries were Persian, and thus culturally foreign in an Arabic-speaking world. At first, the missionaries' efforts were far more arduous than they had been in Persia, where success had been quick in coming. In Syria, however, their early campaigns were met with repeated failure. And yet, their strategy was essentially identical to that deployed in Persia. The mission of Hasan's people was to capture strategic points—mountain strongholds, as always—and to launch an opening campaign of terror against the Syrian elites. Their purely missionary work, too, was concurrently most intense.

At first, Isma'ili propaganda had little impact. While targeting foreigners, Turks, and Westerners, it was itself orchestrated by other foreigners and suffered from a serious legitimacy problem. Ultimately, however, the Assassins were able to take advantage of domestic rivalries to win the backing of a number of important political leaders, including among the Turks, who used the sect to eliminate certain challengers. In time, the Assassins incorporated Arab elements. They obtained the support of leaders in Aleppo and Damascus and were thus able to use those two urban bases as headquarters. As always, however, it was in isolated campaigns that they were able to mobilize their troops.

The first assassination perpetrated in Syria took place in 1103, eleven years after that of Nizam al-Mulk. The technique used was the same as that deployed against the grand vizier—the use of bladed weapons had rapidly become an intrinsic part of the ritual. The Assassins found fulfillment in the ultimate sacrifice, since most of them died in the course of committing their crimes. Over the centuries, such volunteers for death would become an integral element of the history of terrorism, as can still be seen today in the status enjoyed in certain quarters by the nineteen dead terrorists of September 11, 2001, or by Palestinian and Tamil suicide bombers.

The Assassins, like the Zealots, killed exclusively with daggers and orchestrated their assassinations in mosques or in markets, where the use of projectile weapons, for instance, might have been easier. For their first assassination in Syria, the Assassins disguised themselves as Sufis and threw themselves, daggers in hand, on the ruler of Homs as he said his prayers. Several murderers died in the attack. As in Persia, the success of the assault led to the perpetration of others.

From the outset, the Assassins enjoyed the significant support of a Seljuk overlord named Ridwan. Thanks to him, they were able to launch an attack against the fortress of Afamiya, a kind of Syrian Alamut that was held by Isma'ilis—of the faction beholden not to Persia but to Egypt—who had seized it ten years earlier, to Ridwan's disadvantage.

Following a daring ruse by which they entered the citadel in disguise, the Assassins seized the place. The success was short-lived, however. Exploiting the crisis, the Crusaders, led by Tancred, prince of Antioch, retook the fortress.

The complexity of the Syrian situation ill served the Assassins' cause. Paralyzed on the military front, they needed a grand gesture to break the deadlock. In 1113, the Seljuk authorities sent an expeditionary force to Syria to lead the response to the Crusaders. The arrival of masses of troops in Syria did not simplify things for the Assassins, who were already unpopular in Aleppo. They decided to eliminate the leader of the expeditionary force, Mawdud. The assassination was successfully undertaken in Damascus, but it did not have the desired effect. Their ally Ridwan was himself killed, and his successor was compelled to disavow the Assassins, whose leaders were rounded up and executed.

Even so, reaping profit from Syrian political rivalries, the Assassins were able to pursue their subversive activities while engaging in the customary political practices of those seeking to overturn the status quo. The time was ripe for alliances of convenience, such as that forged between the Assassins and the Turks. In 1126, they even participated in a joint action against the Crusaders, which ended in failure.

But the Assassins themselves, whose strategy was fundamentally based on exploiting disputes of succession, fell victim to these wars. In 1128 and 1129, for instance, following the death of their Turkish patron in Damascus, they were overwhelmed by popular reprisals led by local militias. Six to ten thousand members of the sect were summarily executed in what constituted one of their greatest reversals. The rulers of Alamut replied by ordering the assassination of the leader of the massacre, but they were nevertheless unable to restore their position in Damascus. Neutralized in Syria, the Assassins turned expediently towards Egypt, where they waged a campaign of terror against the Fatimid caliph, a sworn enemy of the Isma'ilis.

Again, the Assassins launched a series of attacks, of which that against the caliph himself in 1130 was a success. The period that followed is poorly documented, leading us to believe that the Assassins adopted a low profile as they sought to regain a foothold in Syria. This time, they achieved their aim of recovering a number of strongholds previously occupied by the Crusaders.

In the second half of the twelfth century, the Syrian faction of the Assassins finally found its leader of destiny. Rashid al-Din was to the Assassins of Syria what Hasan had been to the Isma'ilis of Persia. A native of Basra, he had spent several years in Alamut before being sent to take charge of the situation in Syria. After a lengthy interlude in which he traveled incognito, Rashid al-Din reached Syria and initiated a vast consolidation of his strategic strongholds. He conquered new territories and undertook great building projects. The length of his rule—thirty years—allowed him to plant deep roots in his work, which eventually proved fruitful. Such was his success that he overshadowed the central power of Alamut, which sought unsuccessfully to have him assassinated.

The political reign of Rashid al-Din coincided with the rise to power of a great leader and uniter of Islam: Saladin. Born in Iraq, the son of a Kurdish father, Saladin had succeeded his uncle as vizier in Egypt. A former theology student, he devoted himself to defending his religion against Christians and heretics alike. Known as the Scourge of the West who crushed Guy de Lusignan and triumphantly entered Jerusalem on October 2, 1187, he was also the toughest adversary the Assassins faced in the twelfth century. In reorganizing his army and navy, Saladin threatened through his drive to unification to eradicate the Assassins. Confronted with the very real danger posed by Saladin's forces, Rashid al-Din decided to resort to the sect's tried and true formula and duly set about orchestrating an assassination.

The first attempt, during Saladin's 1174 siege of Aleppo, was foiled when Rashid's men were recognized. The second took place in 1176, while Saladin was on campaign, but the killers were unable to finish the job. After these two attempts, Saladin became extremely cautious and difficult to approach. He organized a reprisal against the Assassins, but then, for reasons that remain murky, Rashid al-Din and he seem to have concluded some sort of nonaggression pact. Saladin was probably tired of living under a sword of Damocles and perhaps judged that the Assassins did not, on the whole, represent any real threat to his grand design for unification. At the time when this pact was made, he had yet to eradicate the Frankish armies, and the war against the Crusaders was his principal focus. On his side, Rashid al-Din presumably had the intelligence to grasp that Saladin was stronger than he was, and that he had more to gain by making him his "ally" than by treating him as an enemy. Whatever the case, the agreement was sealed, and Saladin no longer had to worry about the Assassins, which did not prevent the latter from prosecuting other assassinations against lesser figures.

In 1192, the Assassins again made themselves heard from. On April 28 of that year, a group of Assassins in Tyre disguised themselves as

Christian monks. In their usual manner, they drew near to their victim and stabbed him in the heart. The marquis de Montferrat, king of Jerusalem, was dead, one of the rare Christian victims of the Assassins. Was the assassination part of the sect's terror campaign? Was it a murder for hire? In their confession, it would seem that the killers swore to having acted on behalf of the king of England. Other sources suggest Saladin as the sponsor. Both theses are credible, since the death of Montferrat benefited Richard the Lionheart and Saladin alike.

The Assassins' behavior was, above all, that of a political organization—unusual, to be sure, yet ready to abandon its principles for alliances of convenience. Following the death of Rashid al-Din, the sect's power was again centralized in Alamut, which regained control of its Syrian cell after three decades of uncontested independence. Concerned that their membership had grown somewhat slipshod, the masters of Alamut instituted a new policy based on reconciliation with the caliphate of Baghdad. This may explain why, in the early thirteenth century, their assaults targeted Western figures rather than Muslims, leading to a trial of strength between Crusaders and Assassins that had to be mediated by the caliph. This struggle pitted the Assassins especially against the Knights Hospitallers and Saint Louis (Louis IX of France), with whom they most likely reached some sort of accord. It was at this time that the Assassins began to seek to profit from their terrorist savoir faire by claiming tribute from Muslims and Crusaders alike, in exchange for which they promised to leave them in peace (although, at one point, they themselves were compelled to pay tribute to the Hospitallers).

Such sidelines are not unusual. A similar situation exists today in Colombia with the Revolutionary Armed Forces of Colombia and the National Liberation Army. Highly ideologized in the 1960s and 1970s, and inspired by Marxist-Leninist national liberation doctrine, these groups gradually evolved into essentially terrorist organizations, using terror—including threats, kidnappings, and murder—to almost exclusively economic ends. Between the two world wars, the Internal Macedonian Revolutionary Organization and the Croatian Ustaše started out with political aims but eventually became semi-criminal organizations. In the case of the Assassins, as in Colombia today, it appears that they succumbed to a certain weariness after decades of fruitless struggle. Since the stated objective of terrorist organizations is to overturn the status quo, failure in that context tends to push such societies into quasi-criminal activities, at least when their leaders decide not to lay down their arms.

DECLINE

Little by little, the Assassins had earned a certain social status, but this political normalization—based on the power they wielded through a strategy of threat, blackmail, persuasion, and dissuasion—would be short-lived. In one single blow, they would be swept from the face of the Earth by a threat greater than any they had encountered in their two centuries of existence: the Mongols.

Under pressure from the Mongols, the Turks—who had also originated in Central Asia—had been driven westwards. Now, the Mongols, unified under Genghis Khan, had caught up with them in Asia Minor and were at the threshold of Europe. In the twelfth century, the Seljuk empire in Iran collapsed, weakened by internal political bickering and the war against the Crusaders. The Khorazmians established their empire there, with its capital in Samarqand, on the ruins of the Seljuk dominion. The men of Alamut briefly enjoyed the benefits of this political upheaval. Between 1210 and 1221, Jalal al-Din Hasan, the new leader of the sect, set a new direction for the movement, whose ideological program had hardened under his father, Muhammad II. Seeking closer adherence to orthodox Islam, he had increased the number of his embassies and had even traveled beyond Alamut. He exchanged terrorism for a classical military strategy aimed at consolidating his holdings. The end of his reign coincided with the arrival of the Mongols.

In 1220, the Mongol army penetrated the empire and took Bukhara, then Samarqand, which resisted a mere ten days, and enslaved all able-bodied men. The Assassins were insignificant by comparison with the Mongols, and were the first to dispatch envoys to the khan seeking a mutual accommodation. Hülegü, Genghis Khan's grandson, definitively subdued Persia and established a Mongol dynasty there in 1256. From the moment he had entered Persia, one of his goals had been to conquer the Isma'ilis and reduce their fortresses. Relations between Mongols and Isma'ilis were punctuated by periods of diplomatic calm interrupted by military confrontation. Head to head with the Mongols, however, the Isma'ilis had few options beyond playing for time. Alamut was invested by the Mongols and its central authority extirpated. Here and there, pockets of resistance persevered for a while—the Isma'ilis were even briefly able to recover Alamut in 1275—but on the whole, the war was lost.

In Syria, too, the Mongol advance wrought turmoil. The country was now under the control of the Mamluks of Egypt, with whom the Assassins had originally been on good terms. Ever since Saladin, the Assassins had sought a rapprochement with the authorities, who had allowed them broader freedom to pursue their missionary work.

The Mamluk Sultan Baybars was the spiritual heir of Saladin. However, he had not only the Crusaders to eradicate, but the Mongol threat to deal with as well. Having sought the assistance of the Assassins to that end, he decided to rid himself of what, to him, was nothing but a gang of heretics and murderers who stood in the way of his ambition to unify the Muslim world under religious orthodoxy. In 1260, while the Assassins were considerably undermined by the eradication of the sect in Persia, Baybars decided to act.

Initially, the sultan exerted economic pressures that the Assassins were compelled to accept, which in itself was evidence of their weakness. Baybars then brought his power to bear on influencing the Assassins' decision-making process. He soon wrested control of the sect, designating a new leader after eliminating his predecessor in 1271. But when discord erupted between him and his appointee, he decided to dismantle the movement. Henceforth, the Assassins ceased to exist. For a short while, Baybars used its members to attack his rivals, such as Prince Edward of England and Philippe de Montfort, or to threaten others, including the count of Tripoli. It was not long, however, before the sect was known only in legend.

The Assassins were not the first secret society to turn to assassination and terror. They were, however, by far the best organized and longest-lived "terrorist" group operating in that context. While they never attained central power, the Assassins nevertheless played a significant role in the geostrategic theater of the Middle East over the course of two centuries, which in itself was quite extraordinary, especially given the political framework in which they operated. Deeply entrenched in regions that were well suited to such movements, the Assassins perfected an effective strategy from a position of weakness. They practiced an indirect strategy based on threat and tactics of persuasion, rather than on classical warfare, and were able to rally the means to make good on their threats. They were virtually unrivalled in the techniques of assassination. This was the comparative advantage that they diligently sought to leverage, exploiting their expertise to win the prestige and reputation essential to political success.

The indirect strategy is a critical element of the strategies that have evolved over the centuries in the Arab world, in contrast to those that have emerged in the West. The indirect strategy, which made a stunning comeback in the twentieth century after the era of revolutionary wars, relies on other than military means in fighting one's enemy. It functions particularly well in a context in which synergy has been achieved between political ends and strategic resources. In the West, where the boundary between the political and the military has a tendency to be impermeable, such an approach was abandoned in favor of a strategy equating political victory with military victory. It is hardly surprising that the indirect strategy should have developed in the context of Arab Muslim culture, in which everything, including religion, has a political dimension.

The Assassins managed to establish a stable centralized regime in Alamut capable of overseeing a complex organization extending across two distinct territories. The system of hereditary succession functioned relatively well, and it was only toward the end, at the moment of final collapse, that dissidents contested the central power. The autonomy enjoyed by the Syrian cell was sufficient to safeguard the authority of the central power in all but a few instances. The religious dimension of the sect, in which its leaders systematically ensured the unfaltering rigor of its members, lent the movement a high degree of legitimacy even as it maintained its extremist nature. And despite everything, this millenarian, marginal, and unorthodox movement was founded on a policy of realism. Its architects were able to exploit the relationships between the complex forces prevailing in that part of the world, and they often got the jump on their adversaries. Far from being the organization of fanatics that they are often imagined to have been, the Assassins were instead able to channel their fanaticism as an instrument for ensuring their own survival. In the end, however, after two hundred years of activity, the sect was never able to threaten Sunni orthodoxy or reach beyond the Persian and Syrian territories it had chosen at the outset of its militant phase. Its political ideal of installing an imam at the head of an Isma'ili Muslim empire acted as a conductor for a militancy that never wavered.

The Assassins' foes, for their part, managed to contain them, but without ever fully eliminating them. The paradigm of the Assassins demonstrates how such an organization, enjoying popular regional support, can take lasting root and integrate itself into the social life of a community. Like any traditional organization, it had its priests, its soldiers, its diplomats, and its teachers. Its meticulous division of labor and the hierarchy of its activities, combined with fanatical zeal stoked by a dynamic theological activism and unflagging loyalty to its leaders, made the sect an actor that, while marginal, always had to be taken into account. The terror that could be inspired by its deadly assaults was virtually unlimited, given that it was capable of attacking anyone at any time. Even in Europe, some heads of state who had been involved in the Crusades feared for their lives within the shelter of their own castles in England and France. There is no evidence to suggest that the Assassins ever attempted such attacks, but it is the irrational fear that terrorists inspire, out of all proportion to their true capacities for harm, that constitutes their strength. The Assassins survived for two centuries thanks to that fear, which they skillfully sustained, and which struck the hearts of the most powerful and best-protected sovereigns of that and perhaps of any era. The aims of twenty-first-century terrorists are not fundamentally different, even if the fear of their threatened attacks is not felt exclusively by the world's powerful. In a democratic context, on the other hand, an attack against civilians can tip an election. Nowadays, while terrorism has yet to enter the age of high technology, our collective subconscious already has us believing that we live in a world of terrorism of mass destruction. One example of this phenomenon is the fact that, since 2001, most of the anti-terrorist measures taken by the American government have been related to weapons of mass destruction, even though terrorists actually rely for the most part on conventional explosive weapons. For years, the experts have been warning against the emergence of cyberterrorism, based on information technologies, whereas to date it has been implicated in one single, victimless incident.[5]

The histories of the Zealots and especially of the Assassins illustrate a fact that is obscured in most analyses of modern terrorism: terrorism is not a recent phenomenon.

While it has evolved and changed form over the centuries, terrorism was not born in the nineteenth century, as terrorism experts would often have us believe.[6] The history of the Assassins is today no more alien to certain contemporary phenomena than the experience of the nihilists and anarchists of nineteenth century. It also undermines another received idea that is currently very widespread, to the effect that the terrorist phenomenon is a direct consequence of the social, economic, and political injustice rife throughout the world, reproducing on a global scale the class struggle of Marxist ideology. After September 11, many voices were raised to accuse the United States, the West, the capitalist system, liberalism, or globalization of having created the conditions for the development of terrorism in disadvantaged countries with no other means of resisting (American, Western, capitalist) imperialism. This analysis is clearly fallacious, and gives rise to another, equally fallacious idea—that the eradication of injustice is the sole possible response to terrorism. The idea that terrorism is a consequence of social and economic injustice is linked to its association with its European roots in the ideological context of modern political doctrines—anarchism, Marxism, nihilism, Fascism—that all challenge the "bourgeois" order embodied today in capitalism and globalization. The terrorist phenomenon cannot be reduced to a modern, subjective interpretation. While every terrorist group is unique in its own way, certain traits seem to be shared by all terrorist organizations, which have more in common than a mere combat technique. We are compelled to recognize that the Zealots and the Assassins had much in common with the terrorists of the twenty-first century.

NOTES TO CHAPTER 3

1. See Brandon, *Jesus and the Zealots,* 56.
2. Maxime Rodinson, preface to Bernard Lewis, *Les assassins: Terrorisme et politique dans l'islam medieval* (Brussels: Éditions Complexe, 1984, 2001), 8.
3. Ibid., 11.
4. Ibid.
5. In Australia in 2000, by altering a software program he had infiltrated, a hacker managed to have waste materials dumped into a river system, killing fish. Although he had himself worked on the installation of the infiltrated program, he had great difficulty in committing this act.
6. Walter Laqueur is the exception in this area. See his *History of Terrorism.*

CHAPTER 4

MANIFESTATIONS OF TERROR
THROUGH THE AGES

Gérard Chaliand and Arnaud Blin

TYRANNICIDE

The assassination of political and religious figures, as we have seen, was the basic tactic of the Assassins as well as of the Zealots. In the nineteenth and twentieth centuries, assassination would again become a weapon in the strategic arsenal of several terrorist organizations. Political assassination is not a monopoly of terrorists, and an organization that commits political assassinations is not necessarily perpetrating a terrorist crime. And yet, from a philosophical perspective, political assassination, within or removed from the terrorist framework, originated in Greek and Roman antiquity with the defense of tyrannicide. Why speak of tyrannicide in the context of terrorism? While it may indeed be difficult to find any sort of link between the philosophy of Aristotle and organizations devoted to sowing terror, such a link does exist, first because political thought in the West and the Arab world has been heavily influenced by their Greek heritage. Furthermore, the direct and indirect influence that the defenders of tyrannicide have wielded over groups engaged in political assassination has been considerable over the centuries. The endorsement of philosophy (or theology) has often been considered a significant source of legitimacy by revolutionaries prepared to seek recourse to violence—and tyrannicide was long considered to be a legitimate means of fighting despotism.

In a nondemocratic context, political assassination represents practically the sole way to challenge political authority. It may be a means either of protest, of destabilizing a political regime, or of eliminating a head of state or political leader, in the hope, perhaps, of an improved replacement. Whatever the case, when a popular uprising is not possible—the norm in most societies—political assassination is the only way left to confront power. The concept of political assassination is associated first and foremost with that of despotism. Most political assassinations are justified by their perpetrators as a blow against despotism. That is true, too, for terrorists, who almost systematically justify their actions as assaults on despotism, whatever form they may take and even when their target is not really a despot at all (the West, the United States, or the Spanish government, for example). The Assassins justified their murders by their declared objective of overturning the despotic rule of the Seljuk Turks. In the final analysis, it hardly matters that most terrorist groups seek to replace one despotic regime with another, since the primary goal is to spark a confrontation.

In truth, anything and anybody can be defined as "despotic." During the war in Iraq in 2003, it was sometimes difficult to discern a difference between a tyrant like Saddam Hussein and the American President George W. Bush in the characterizations of the French media. (Whatever reservations one may have about the latter, he is far from qualified to claim the title of tyrant, if only because he is compelled to face an opposition party in the presidential elections.) In the same vein, the United States is often perceived as a despotic power ready to impose its will on the rest of the world. The terrorists of Corsica justify their activities against the French state in a similar way, describing it as oppressive, when one of its principal failings may be its laxity toward those very terrorists themselves. In the context of such unbridled subjectivity, any action undertaken by a political regime can be justified as a blow against despotism or tyranny.

Among philosophers, the concept of despotism or tyranny is far more precise. For Herodotus, tyranny differs from monarchy in that it lacks the faculties of caution and moderation. For Plato, tyranny is a consequence of the anarchic drift of democratic systems whose laxity compels them to fall back on a tyrant; the latter, as a child of the people, has no qualms about striking out against his own "father." Indeed, according to the philosophers, tyranny is characterized by a dynamic similar to the relationship between a parent and child. Aristotle shares that interpretation, seeing in tyranny a corruption of the political system represented by the monarchy, but one in which the father figure is the monarch or the tyrant rather than the people. This political conception is characterized by a moral interpretation of the system, which may be good or bad. Now, the quest for a just system—and the pursuit of justice is the goal of politics—implies the destruction of an unjust system. In Aristotle's three-part political scenario, which held sway for centuries—monarchy/tyranny, aristocracy/oligarchy, democracy/timocracy—the corrupt version of each system alienates society from justice. It is therefore the duty of citizens to restore the corresponding system by ridding it of all corruption; in plain terms, the physical elimination of the tyrant is in a certain sense a civic duty. This gives rise to an entire mode of political thought approving and even encouraging the practice that came to be called tyrannicide—that is, political parricide.

In Greek culture, the tyrant's assassin is hailed as a hero. Aristotle claims that he who kills the tyrant is a hero because he has eradicated the perpetrator of excess. By contrast, he who kills a thief is no hero because the latter's crimes are motivated solely by his vital needs. From the outset, Aristotle dissociates tyrannicide from simple crime. Such a philosophical distinction has little value in civil law, but it was an important element of ancient political culture and of those cultures arising therefrom in Europe and the Arab world. The Romans, their imaginations fired by the example of Brutus, were fascinated by the concept. Appian, Dio Cassius, and Plutarch draw on his example to justify tyrannicide. Cicero, a contemporary of Brutus, asserted that, while assassination is the most heinous of all crimes, tyrannicide is the most noble of actions, delivering humanity as it does from "the cruelty of a savage beast."

In the twelfth century, John of Salisbury, bishop of Chartres, took up the torch once again, analyzing the phenomenon of tyrannicide in similar terms, while discussing the problem of the legitimacy of the act from the religious perspective. For Salisbury, it is right to eliminate tyrants in order "to free the people at long last so that they may serve God." Even so, the method used must be morally acceptable: "[A]s for the use of poison, although I see it sometimes wrongfully adopted by infidels, I do not read that it is ever permitted by any law."[1]

This justification of tyrannicide, supported by the desire to bring the act into conformity with the law and to associate it with certain moral rules, is akin to the doctrine of the just war, whereby the use of violence is justified in instances that, while very specific, may be open to interpretation. One of the fathers of the doctrine of just war, Saint Thomas Aquinas, addresses the act of tyrannicide in similar terms, that is, as justified exclusively by the requirements of self-defense. In the early fifteenth century, the sixteenth Ecumenical Council of Constance officially proscribed tyrannicide. Nevertheless, Catholic and Protestant philosophers continued to defend the right to kill a tyrant. This was particularly true of the Protestant Philippe de Mornay, known as Duplessis-Mornay (1549–1623), who wrote a *Vindiciae contra Tyrannos* under the pseudonym of Junius Brutus, in which, like Salisbury, he mines the Old Testament for instances of justified tyrannicide. The same year, 1579, saw the publication of another pamphlet on tyrannicide, written by the Scottish humanist George Buchanan. His work elicited outrage and was banned by Parliament. Also in the sixteenth century, the Spanish Jesuit Juan de Mariana, in his *De rege et Regis institutione* (1598), investigates the religious, moral, and political justifications for tyrannicide. Unfortunately, he is sidetracked by such incidental issues as the use of poison (which he condemns)—a problem that may seem of questionable importance to us today, but which was of deep concern to those who wrote on tyrannicide at that time (his text was proscribed by the Sorbonne following the assassination of Henri IV). Mariana's work foreshadowed the political treatises of Hobbes, Locke, and Rousseau on the idea of a social contract by legitimizing tyrannicide on the basis of an analysis of the origin and nature of the state founded on the concept of the "state of nature" that prefigured human society. Half a century later, in 1657, the Englishman Edward Saxby published a pamphlet in Holland entitled *Killing No Murder,* which enjoyed great success, including much later in France during the revolutionary period. Shortly before the revolution of 1789, the Italian Vittorio Alfieri composed a document entitled *Della tirannide,* which would be highly influential in the nineteenth century. According to this Italian writer and poet, only the will of the people or of the majority can keep a tyrant in power or destroy him. Alfieri expanded the notion of tyrannicide to include what he called "moderate tyrannies," which are much more dangerous because less visibly violent, yet capable of annihilating a people little by little by draining it of "a few drops of blood" every day. Alfieri, who was widely read by revolutionary groups, paradoxically heralded the totalitarian systems that some of those revolutionaries would eventually install.

We find in most of these documents on tyrannicide the distant origins of a concept that Jean-Jacques Rousseau would formally situate at the center of political philosophy: the popular will. It is the popular will that motivates men and gives them the right to rise up against a tyrant resolved to destroy his nation. Mariana, while deeply invested in the issue of how to kill a tyrant, endorses not only his assassination (by force of arms), but also civil disobedience where it is justified by reasons other than personal ones and undertaken by the competent entities, and not by individuals or isolated groups. From the sixteenth century on, tyrannicide is no longer, as it was in antiquity, the act of a hero, an individual who sacrifices himself to save the people from despotism. It is up to the people itself, or to one of its representatives, to assume the task. George Buchanan justifies the undertaking by defining it as war against a tyrant who, having broken society's laws, may be considered an enemy of the people and the country and dealt with accordingly. For Saxby, an opponent of Cromwell, the assassination of the tyrant is undertaken in the name of the public honor, security, and well-being. Tyrannicide is a duty an individual or the people takes up on its own behalf, and even on behalf of humanity, with God's blessing. For Saxby, in contrast to Mariana, any method for eliminating a tyrant is acceptable, the ends justifying the means.

Edward Saxby, however, evolved in a radically different political context. His work was published some twelve years after the 1648 signing of the Treaty of Westphalia, which put an end to the Thirty Years' War and launched a new European order. It was a time of political realism—realpolitik, as it would come to be called—and of reasons of state in which moral considerations were no longer of relevance. These radical changes in the European political landscape were accompanied by the emergence of a fundamental principle that would govern international relations until the end of the twentieth century: noninterference in the affairs of other states. This principle stipulates that every state is responsible for its own political management, whatever the nature of its regime, and that its freedom—including that to tyrannize over its own people—is unlimited within that sphere. It was not until the late twentieth century that the principle of noninterference in the domestic affairs of another state was called into question. In practice, the strongest states flout this principle—through colonial and "preventive" wars—to the detriment of weaker, marginal states, but do so in the name of a higher interest: national and international security. Today, the right or duty to interfere is invoked for moral reasons that are practically identical to those found in the philosophical writings justifying tyrannicide. It is worth noting that the Iraq war of 2003, having been initially "sold" by American and British political leaders as a security issue (aimed at destroying Iraq's weapons of mass destruction and stemming the terrorist threat), ultimately hit a sympathetic chord with the public when the propaganda was focused on the elimination of a dictator, which would have been unthinkable a few years earlier. Moreover, the establishment of international criminal courts to try crimes committed in Rwanda and the former Yugoslavia, followed by the creation of the International Criminal Court, has provided international law with a permanent and legitimate mechanism for bringing (deposed) political leaders to justice for crimes committed against their own people—that is, for bringing the law to bear on former tyrants.

Thus, for centuries and until very recently, tyrannicide was a marginal phenomenon defended by a few theologians and philosophers on behalf of a morality that was out of sync with political practice. Nevertheless, that marginalization most probably helped to sell the philosophy to the revolutionary movements that emerged far and wide in the late eighteenth century. Buttressed by Rousseau's theories on the popular will, the doctrine of tyrannicide resurfaced, inspired by the classical and modern texts described earlier and, particularly, by the example of the revolution of 1789, capped by the execution of Louis XVI and Marie-Antoinette. In the nineteenth century, however, tyrannicide became more than a way to get rid of tyrants and restore freedom to the people. The execution of the tyrant was symbolic, because it opened the way to a purification of the political system and the chance for a new beginning, with the goal not only of changing the political regime but also of transforming society. This new interpretation of tyrannicide, though condemned by such moralists as Immanuel Kant, was to mark the entire nineteenth century. The Russian populists were supporters of tyrannicide. For them, the very nature of a despotic regime required the physical elimination of the autocrat as the sole means of changing and regenerating the political system. Lenin was to implement this principle at the end of the 1917 revolution by ordering the extrajudicial execution of the Russian imperial family. For many revolutionary groups and terrorist organizations, tyrannicide is a key element of their philosophy. As we shall see further on, however, tyrannicide also serves as a justification for state terrorism—that is, terror deployed by the state apparatus against the people, which in the modern era emerged from the French Revolution of 1789, whose myth was founded precisely on the assassination of the sovereign.

THE ORIGINS OF STATE TERRORISM:
THE MONGOL CONQUESTS

We shall deal with the French Revolution later on, for it, too, marked a new departure in the realm of terror. But here again, terrorism "from above"—that is, as practiced by the state—does not date from 1789.

Over the course of the centuries preceding the great revolutionary movements of the eighteenth to the twentieth centuries, terror was practiced
above all in times of war, and almost always through recourse to the military apparatus rather than that of the police. The army has always been
a formidable instrument of state terror. In the West, and in sedentary
societies in general, the army has rarely been employed as a terrorist
weapon. The only exception to that rule has been in the particular case
of civil wars, in which the general population becomes an integral component of warfare. In Europe, the horrific Thirty Years' War was probably the only conflict in which terror was used systematically. That war,
however, was in part spawned by the religious conflicts that gripped Europe in the sixteenth and seventeenth centuries, and it always retained
certain features of civil war, while at the same time involving almost
every great European nation of the age, with the exception of England—
then in the throes of its own civil war—and Russia. The case of the
Thirty Years' War is exceptional in modern history and foreshadows
from the seventeenth century the great conflicts of the twentieth. The latter marked the era of total war and were of a kind with the totalitarianism that attended them—that is, with a system fueled by terror.

Before the emergence of modern totalitarian systems, nomad warrior
societies practiced large-scale terrorism with fearsome effectiveness. Of
all such tribes, the Mongols were the best organized, the most terrifying,
and the most destructive. At the height of its power, the Mongol empire
was the largest of all time, encompassing practically the entire Eurasian
continent.

The Mongols under Genghis Khan had at their disposal a military instrument that was superior to every other army of its time. This superiority was a product of their Spartan way of life, their immersion in the
military arts from earliest childhood, their military organization, their
mobility, and their undisputed preeminence in the rigors of discipline.
One further asset available to them was the systematic practice of terror
against peoples. In his *Discourses*, Niccolò Macchiavelli drew a clear distinction between the kind of warfare practiced by sedentary societies and
that practiced by nomad armies:

> [T]here are two different kinds of war. The one springs from the ambition of
> princes or republics that seek to extend their empire; such were the wars of
> Alexander the Great, and those of the Romans, and those which two hostile
> powers carry on against each other. These wars are dangerous, but never go
> so far as to drive all its inhabitants out of a province, because the conqueror
> is satisfied with the submission of the people, and generally leaves them their

dwellings and possessions, and even the enjoyment of their own institutions. The other kind of war is when an entire people, constrained by famine or war, leave their country with their families for the purpose of seeking a new home in a new country, not for the purpose of subjecting it to their dominion as in the first case, but with the intention of taking absolute possession of it themselves and driving out or killing its original inhabitants. This kind of war is most frightful and cruel. . . .

These tribes migrated from their own countries, as we have said above, driven by hunger, or war, or some other scourge, which they had experienced at home and which oblige them to seek new dwelling-places elsewhere. Sometimes they came in overwhelming numbers, making violent irruptions into other countries, killing the inhabitants and taking possession of their goods, establishing new kingdoms and changing the very names of the countries.[2]

By comparison to sedentary society, nomad society is demographically quite feeble. Thus, the superiority of the nomad warrior had nothing to do with numbers. It was through the concentration of forces and the element of surprise that nomads sought to overwhelm their adversaries, as well as through the psychological impact of their attacks on populations ill-prepared for such a scourge. They therefore relied on the terror they inspired in civilian populations and armies to prevent uprisings in their wake. Thus, terror became a basic tool of the nomad strategy of conquest.

For nomads, the core of their strategy was the physical annihilation of the enemy. Military victory was not enough; it had to be put to maximal advantage by eliminating the foe, crushing his will to resist and ensuring his inability to fight another time.

The systematic use of terror was institutionalized by Genghis Khan in parallel with his reorganization of the Mongol armies. But it was refined to an unprecedented degree under Tamerlane, or Timur Lenk (Timur the Lame), who considered himself to be Genghis Khan's spiritual heir. He was indeed a worthy successor to the great Mongol khan, although his conquests proved less enduring. Tamerlane was a Turkic-speaking Muslim immersed in Persian culture who sought to impose Islam while preserving his Mongol heritage and its customary law (the *Yassa*). In military terms, Tamerlane was Genghis's equal, his every operation enjoying success, even though he sometimes met the same adversaries in battle on several occasions.

The key characteristic of his style of warfare was his frequent assaults on great cities, including Damascus, Baghdad, Aleppo, Delhi, and Ankara. His adversaries were far from negligible. His former protégé Toktamysh was a formidable soldier, as was the Ottoman Sultan Bayezid I.

The systematic use of terror against towns was an integral element of Tamerlane's strategic arsenal. When he besieged a city, surrender at the first warning spared its people their lives. Resistance, on the other hand, was brutally punished by the massacre of civilians, often in atrocious circumstances. When the sack of a city was complete, Tamerlane raised pyramids of decapitated heads. In the 1387 taking of Isfahan, a city of about half a million inhabitants, observers estimated the number of dead at 100,000 to 200,000.[3] After the massacre, Tamerlane had some fifty pyramids built, each comprised of thousands of heads. In so doing, Tamerlane hoped to persuade other besieged cities to surrender at first notice. The tactic did not always work, and many towns still refused to capitulate. After the rape of Isfahan, however, Tamerlane moved on to Shiraz, which offered no resistance. By his reckoning, this approach prevented bloodshed, at least among those reasonable enough to lay down their weapons without a fight. The practice of terror remained methodical at all times, and he took pains to spare the elites: theologians, artists, poets, engineers, architects, and so on.

Those who practice large-scale terrorism generally invoke reasons of state and an ethic justified by the ultimate outcome of their actions: peace. But can we compare Harry Truman, who took the decision to use atomic bombs against Japan, with the ferocious Tamerlane? One paradox of terrorism is that that which may look like an abomination to some may be considered as an act of liberation by others. This may be precisely because the use of terror is a political tool rather than an end in itself. Terrorism always seeks a justification, unlike genocide, which is its own objective. The example of Tamerlane is a forceful illustration of how a conqueror may use terror to achieve his aims. The conqueror must not only vanquish armies and shatter his enemy's state apparatus but also subdue populations. Whenever civilians are thrown into the equation, the use of terror is never far behind.

TERROR IN WARFARE: THE THIRTY YEARS' WAR

While the Mongols and Turks implemented a strategy of conquest that included the use of terror, western Europe was largely spared the phenomenon. European warfare in the Middle Ages was a highly ritualized event that, in ideal principle—in truth, not always achieved or respected—operated under a code in which ethics enjoyed pride of place. The grip of the Church, the importance of knightly culture and the continent's cultural homogeneity helped to limit the impact of warfare.

Armies were small and expensive. In times of conflict, civilian populations were hardly spared. First of all, it was their taxes that financed wars; furthermore, it was they who suffered the usual consequences of warfare: famine, pillage, devastation. But in a world in which the life of the common man was worth practically nothing, and in which the population was mostly rural, there was no reason for the military to target civilians. Warfare was therefore a business that principally involved states and their sovereigns, as well as their armies, which were often private entities. Warfare began evolving in the fourteenth century with the renewed importance of the infantry, requiring new sources for recruitment, but it remained a limited affair and in no way comparable with developments in Central Asia and the Middle East.

It took a religious event—the Reformation and Counter-Reformation—to change the strategic order. Civilians soon found themselves at the center of the conflicts raging between Catholics and Protestants. From a strategic perspective, the Reformation added to the art of warfare a moral dimension born of the Protestant ethic and the humanist culture that heavily influenced the Protestant strategists. The Swedish King Gustavus Adolphus, for example, brought an ethical element to the organization of his armies. Nevertheless, the practice of warfare in the first half of the seventeenth century turned out to be particularly cruel.

Wars of religion, civil wars, and wars of "opinion" all have one thing in common: they involve the civilian population. The wars of religion that erupted in Europe in the sixteenth century differed from "chivalric" wars in their violence and most especially in their lack of "discrimination," which made favored targets of noncombatants, in contravention of all precepts of "just war" established by the Church. Wars of religion have two distinguishing features. First, the armies involved are small; secondly, they focus primarily on reducing the towns held by the enemy. Between 1579 and 1585, the governor-general of the Netherlands, Alessandro Farnese, relied on a strategy of "accessories," consisting of a series of assaults on rebel-held cities and the devastation of the countryside to eliminate the provision of supplies.[4] Whether in the Netherlands, France, or England, religious conflicts were primarily limited to low-intensity military operations; armies were expensive, and less costly methods were favored. Thus, efforts focused on populations, with soldiers concentrating on flushing out the enemy in the countryside, burning crops, and killing or stealing livestock. The number of small-scale operations was inversely proportional to the number of pitched battles. Violence was ubiquitous, potentially striking anyone at any time. In such conditions, even the sacrosanct winter truce was not respected. The massacre of civilian populations became a strategic weapon.

In making targets of civilians, wars of religion also incite their participation in the fighting. In the Cévennes, Calvinist insurgents attacked Catholic missionaries. In Bavaria, peasants organized themselves into guerrilla units. More often than not, however, civilians were the victims of massacres. In France, in the decade between 1562 and 1572, dozens of civilian massacres took place. About thirty towns were hit in 1562 alone. In 1572, the year of the St. Bartholomew's Day massacre of August 24, about 10,000 deaths were recorded between August and October.[5] This period was also fruitful in tyrannicides, though neither the massacre of civilians nor the murder of tyrants was part of a larger organized campaign of terror. Many such massacres were committed by civilians against other civilians. They were crimes of passion—the perpetrators were often seen mutilating the corpses of their victims. Moreover, the massacres provoked more massacres. Nonetheless, terror was also an instrument of state, wielded in the good conscience of one who is confident of acting within his rights. As for the tyrannicides, they were not of the terrorist nature of those committed by the Assassins, but sought rather to eliminate a specific head of state for reasons of passion or politics.

In brief, the use of terror in wars of religion is merely a secondary phenomenon within an atmosphere of general violence. At the outset, the Thirty Years' War (1618–1648) was simply one in a series of religious wars and involved only the domestic affairs of the Germanic Holy Roman Empire. But Europe was changing, and such rising powers as France and Sweden sought to awaken the Habsburgs from their dream of imperial hegemony. Ultimately, the clash between the imperial powers and their enemies fused with the civil war engulfing Germany. It was only logical, therefore, that the entire German powder keg should blow. The latent violence of civil warfare found a new source of energy with the massive armies descending from every corner of Europe. These armies were of two distinct types. Private armies of mercenaries—the most formidable of which was that led by Albrecht von Wallenstein, a Czech on the payroll of the imperial party—clashed in the field with modern national armies, the most famous of which was that of Gustavus Adolphus. Two worlds, two eras, two approaches to warfare coexisted in the theater of battle. Unlike the religious wars of the sixteenth century, the Thirty Years' War was played out by enormous armies of a size previously unknown in Europe—an inflation that would be maintained after the war, notably in France under Louis XIV.

As a result of the combination of uninhibited violence and military mass, civilians found themselves in the thick of fighting of which they were the primary victims. The population of Germany, which stood at about twenty million at the outset of the conflict, ultimately shrank by 50 to 60 percent during the three decades of warfare. First, for the most part, civilians were victims of the war's "collateral damage," as it has come to be known—that is, of epidemics, famine, and the consequences of massive population displacements. Second, they were the direct victims of the regular armies or armed groups (consisting of deserters) ravaging the countryside, where anarchy reigned by force of circumstance. Finally, civilians were also the victims of terror campaigns orchestrated by the armies for strategic ends, precisely as Tamerlane's armies had done.

In this area, every army involved shared in the responsibility. After decades of fighting, the generals, weary of campaigning, hoped to hasten the process along by terrorizing the enemy. As always, campaigns were organized as assaults on cities. Many are the examples of such terror campaigns. The best known, and most widely reported in its time, was the sack of Magdeburg on May 20, 1631. The imperial army led by the Bavarian general Tilly had called on the city to surrender. The imperial forces were concerned that the town's resistance might encourage other cities in northern Germany to ally themselves with Sweden. While its citizens sought to play for time, the imperial forces surrounded the city, which, even with Swedish assistance, was not strong enough to resist. Once inside, Tilly's soldiers, urged on by his second-in-command, Pappenheim, massacred the entire population. The consequences of this action were to backfire on its authors. Shocked by a massacre that had thrown all Europe into turmoil, the Protestants, who had been divided up to that moment, drew from it the inner resources to come together and fight the imperial army as a unified force. Tilly's sterling reputation was forever besmirched, and he was never able to undo the damage caused by that decision. By contrast, the rape of Magdeburg gave the Swedes a second wind.

The imperial party was not, however, the only side to resort to such tactics. Grimmelshausen's celebrated novel *Simplicius Simplicissimus,* set during the Thirty Years' War, catalogs all the horrors that the soldiers of both camps were capable of inflicting on the civilian populations. France was no exception. To cite but one example among many, during his campaign through Lorraine, the marquis de Sourdis, on order from Richelieu, stormed the fortified little town of Châtillon-sur-Saône. On June 4,

Sourdis routed the garrison of four hundred Lorraine and Croat soldiers entrusted with the citadel's defense. Once inside, he ordered his soldiers to set an example to terrorize the entire region. His men summarily executed every soldier who had survived the fighting, then set up an ad hoc tribunal before which the locals were summoned, most of them at random. Among the condemned was the 95-year-old provost, Pierre Vernisson. Having hung his victims from the trees of a nearby forest, Sourdis ordered the corpses to be left hanging. This, he believed, would make the shock effect even stronger and spread the news faster and further. For his noteworthy exploit, Sourdis received a letter of congratulations signed by Richelieu.

The atrocities of the Thirty Years' War led to the renowned accords signed in Westphalia in 1648 that ended the fighting. While they were long in coming to signature, the treaties of Münster and Osnabrück gave rise to one the most successful peace accords of all times. Warfare was not stamped out in Europe, but that had not been the intention of the architects of the peace of Westphalia, for whom the resort to arms was an instrument for maintaining the general geopolitical balance. Far from the arrogant idealism that permeated the climate at the end of World War I— the "war to end all wars"—the spirit guiding the diplomats at Westphalia was concentrated above all on what would today be called "human rights." For those diplomats, the violence and terror that had prevailed throughout the conflict were a scourge that absolutely had to be abolished. To that end, they fell back on two basic principles. The principle of balance was based on maintaining the geopolitical status quo by establishing complex but reliable mechanisms to ensure that no state would be capable of dominating all others. The principle of noninterference stipulated that no state could meddle in the domestic affairs of another country. Since every country, in accordance with the 1648 treaty, was bound to respect the principle of "cujus regio, ejus religio" (the religion of the prince is the religion of the people)—which had grown considerably more flexible since the disastrous Peace of Augsburg of 1555—each religion would prosper in all freedom within its designated territory. In contrast to the contemporary interpretation of the principle of noninterference, which views it as running counter to respect for human rights, the seventeenth century view was that the principle represented a great leap forward in that domain. In fact, the Peace of Westphalia put a total end to wars of religion and the campaigns of terror that accompanied them. The resumption of the practice of terror would have to wait until 1789. At that moment, however, terror assumed an altogether different aspect. No longer a minor instrument of the military apparatus, it had become a basic tool of the apparatus of the modern state. Modern terror was born with the French Revolution—and with it the expression "terrorism."

NOTES TO CHAPTER 4

1. John of Salisbury, *Statesman's Book*.
2. Macchiavelli, *The Prince and the Discourses*, 302–4.
3. Roux, *Tamerlan*, 98.
4. See El Kenz and Gantet, *Guerres et paix de religion*, 20.
5. Ibid., 24.

PART II

TERRORISM FROM 1789 TO 1968

CHAPTER 5

THE INVENTION OF MODERN TERROR

Gérard Chaliand and Arnaud Blin

1. The revolutionary is a doomed man. He has no personal interests, no business affairs, no emotions, no attachments, no property and no name. Everything in him is wholly absorbed in the single thought and the single passion for revolution.

2. The revolutionary knows that in the very depths of his being, not only in words but also in deeds, he has severed all the bonds that tie him to the social order and the civilized world with all its laws, moralities and customs and with all its generally accepted conventions. He is their implacable enemy, and if he continues to live among them it is only in order to destroy them more speedily.

Sergei Genadievich Nechayev,
"The Revolutionary Catechism" (1869)

The French Revolution marked a turning point in the history of terrorism. It gave birth to the term "terror"—or what might equally be called "state terrorism"—prefiguring a practice that was to evolve considerably in the twentieth century with the advent of totalitarianism and large-scale violence. The term "terrorism," of course, derives from the experience of the French revolutionary Terror that raged in 1793 and 1794. The Age of Enlightenment had bequeathed humanity the idea of popular sovereignty, and it was in the name of that sovereignty that the Revolution claimed to defend it through the deployment of state terror, in which the ends justified the means, including extreme violence.

Following the Terror, the nineteenth century marked a long hiatus for state terrorism, which did not reemerge in any significant form until 1917. The hiatus instead saw the development of a new kind of political terrorism that has endured to this day. Terrorism directed against the state is not a new phenomenon, as we have seen in the cases of the Zealots and the Assassins. Even so, modern terrorism was different. First of all, it was no longer religious; in the context of terrorism, religion did not reassert itself until the second half of the twentieth century. In fact, nineteenth- and early twentieth-century terrorism essentially had no religious dimension. Second, this new terrorism was often practiced by marginal groups that did not always have clearly defined political objectives, although they were linked to a wide variety of trends—anarchist, nihilist, populist, Marxist, fascist, racist, and so on.

The terrorists of the late nineteenth century were influenced by the romantic tradition, just as Robespierre was an heir of the Enlightenment. This new terrorism developed in a very specific geopolitical and geostrategic context. Above all, the nineteenth century was one of reevaluation, swept by several waves of revolution. It was a violent century, when war became a mass phenomenon, involving not only heads of state and armies, but entire societies. Lastly, technology and industrialization gave unleashed phenomenally destructive forms of violence. The progress achieved in explosives technology during the second half of the nineteenth century gave considerable impetus to terrorist movements, which, by definition, engage in a form of low-cost struggle with the potential to yield a profit that is inversely proportional to the means invested and, often, the risks taken.

On the geopolitical level, the nineteenth century was marked by the gradual collapse of the order based on the Peace of Westphalia and the balance of powers. It was also the era of rising nationalism. Lying at the divide between two declining empires—the Austrian and the Ottoman—the Balkans became an extremely precarious region. Many of the independence movements that arose there in the late 1870s, when the Ottoman empire lost most of its European territory, would persist until the era of decolonization, almost a century later. It was in this political context that the assassination of the Austrian Archduke Franz Ferdinand in 1914 transcended the regional framework, becoming the spark that ignited World War I.

Prior to that, terrorism was manifest in France and southern Europe in the shape of anarchist movements that promoted "propaganda by deed," and in Russia, where anarchists, nihilists, and populists challenged a society in the throes of full-blown crisis. Ultimately, the Bolsheviks came out on top. Lenin used state terrorism to entrench and consolidate his power once the Russian Revolution was under way. His were the first steps toward state terrorism on an unprecedented scale. His successor at the head of the Soviet empire, Joseph Stalin, exploited a terrorist system that was already well ensconced, thanks to a well-oiled political apparatus, and wielded absolute power concentrated in his person. The Soviet model would be emulated throughout the world, in particular in China and, right up to the 1970s, by the Khmer Rouge in Cambodia.

Ireland offered another terrorist model, which was taken up by numerous nationalist movements throughout the world. By confronting British democracy in the midst of World War I, the IRA won independence for the Irish Free State (Éire) in the war's aftermath. The Irish were the first to understand the complex mechanisms defining the disproportion between extremely weak strategic potential and potentially enormous political gain. The IRA and its strategist, Michael Collins, managed to destabilize British rule with very limited means but first-class organization. Their experiment brought hope to myriad independence movements in Europe and beyond.

Between the wars, terrorism was generally associated with independence and far-right terrorist movements, such as Ante Pavelić's Croatian Ustaša organization, which briefly came to power with the support of Hitler's Germany. The European states manipulated various movements in order to weaken their rivals or adversaries. Unlike the period that preceded it, it was a time when international politics were marked by a common will to overturn the system and upset the status quo. Terrorist organizations played an extraordinarily disruptive role in this game, as in the assassination of the Weimar Republic's finance minister, Walter Rathenau.

During World War II, terrorism was more often deployed in a supporting role for certain resistance movements. After the war, various independence movements followed the trail that had been blazed by the Irish a quarter-century earlier. This time, however, the historical context was favorable to organizations calling for independence, since the colonial empires had lost their legitimacy as a result of the war. When driven to fight for independence, liberation movements, whether nationalist or Marxist-Leninist, tend to rely on guerrilla warfare, supplemented by terrorism.

Alongside the official Zionism represented by Haganah, two groups advocating violence—the Irgun and its offshoot the Stern Gang—used terrorism both to compel the British to withdraw and against the Palestinians. Twenty years later, the Palestinians would take up terrorism themselves against the Israeli state in a conflict that had been territorial in nature from the very outset.

In 1947, Great Britain withdrew from India after overseeing the country's partition. It was in India that the "philosophy of the bomb" had been advanced earlier in the century—a terrorist approach combining elements of Indian culture and the Western culture of violence, and in which Indian terrorists were inspired by the Russian experience at the turn of the century.

In the 1950s, in Kenya, the British were confronted by the Mau Mau rebellion, which they succeeded in repressing. Conversely, in Cyprus and in Aden on the Arabian peninsula, the British were unable to overcome terrorist organizations that had learned that the decolonization struggle was to be played out primarily in the theater of politics, and not on the battlefield. France, another colonial power, had a similar experience in Algeria, where the FLN exploited terrorism to impose itself as the bellwether movement of Algerian independence. General de Gaulle was astute enough to see, as his British counterparts had done a few years earlier, that the political battle was doomed from the start in such a context.

The late 1950s and early 1960s saw the transition from wars of national liberation to contemporary terrorism, inspired both by the earlier national struggles and by the Leninist-Marxist ideology espoused by most independence movements. Terrorism as publicity stunt came into its own after 1968, heralding the arrival of a new era in the history of terrorism.

As we have seen, the use of terror to political or military ends was not born with the French Revolution. There were terrorists long before the expression was invented during the Terror of 1793–94. The words "terrorist" and "terrorism," however, soon entered into general usage. The 1798 dictionary of the Académie française defined the phenomenon of terrorism as a "system or regime of terror." The expression had crossed the English Channel even earlier; in 1795, Edmund Burke described the French revolutionaries as "those hell hounds called terrorists." All nineteenth-century terrorist movements originated in the ideas proclaimed in 1789, while the 1917 Russian Revolution launched what was to become the aberrant rise of the modern politics of terror.

Total war, totalitarianism, and terrorism were born at the same time as liberty, human rights, and democracy. It would seem difficult to reconcile these two apparently contradictory extremes. Whereas the 1776 American Revolution strove for freedom and liberal democracy, the

Russian Revolution went in the opposite direction, toward totalitarianism and state terrorism. The French Revolution fell somewhere in between. It both launched the revolution in human rights and invented state terror in the name of virtue, whence its complexity and the difficulty of interpreting its various components.

Generally speaking, the Terror is to be understood as a phase of the French Revolution, rather than as the "form of revolutionary politics" defined by Patrice Gueniffey as "the use of coercion and violence to political ends in a legal vacuum."[1] Interpretation of the Terror has evolved along with historiographic trends and its treatment by various schools of thought, just as Jean Jaurès and Albert Soboul left their mark on the socioeconomic interpretation of the Revolution, or, for instance, as the anthropological roots of violence have been promoted over its purely political nature in recent studies of the Revolution's cultural history. Jean Atarit's recent psychoanalytical biography of the "Incorruptible," *Robespierre ou l'impossible filiation* (2003), constitutes an interesting advance in our understanding of the Terror. Furthermore, analysis of the Terror has often polarized the various interpretations, for instance, pitting the "reactionary" analyses that define it as evidence of revolutionary irrationality against Marxist analyses that see it as a culmination of class warfare, while the liberal trend is to view the Terror as a "deviation."[2]

As with the history of terrorism in general, historians have too often sought to ascribe the revolutionary Terror to the fanaticism of a few individuals. This unfortunately widespread explanation is no more satisfactory for the French Terror than it is for the Assassins or contemporary Islamist terrorists. It tends to minimize terrorist activity as an instance of psychological distraction outside the realm of rational categorization. As Gueniffey puts it: "The Terror was neither a product of ideology nor a reaction to circumstance. It is attributable neither to the rights of man, nor to the plotting of the Coblenz émigrés, nor even to the Jacobin utopia of virtue. It was the product of the revolutionary dynamic, as it would be, perhaps, of all revolutionary dynamics. In that, it arose from the very nature of the Revolution, of all revolution."[3]

Indeed, revolutions as disparate as the Bolshevik Revolution of 1917 and the Iranian revolution of the ayatollahs both produced regimes founded on policies of terror. The Iranian revolution launched a terrorist strategy extending beyond national borders and skillfully blending a revolutionary policy of terror with the practice of religious terrorism that can be traced all the way back to the Assassins.

Historically, the Terror began on September 5, 1793, under the Convention, and ended on July 27, 1794, with the fall of Robespierre on 9 Thermidor—a period of less than a year. However, acts of terror continued after Thermidor, although they were far less extreme than what had gone before.[4] And just as the Terror did not truly end with Thermidor, it cannot really be said to have begun precisely on September 5, 1793, since all the elements for its unleashing were in place prior to that date. It is not easy to trace the precise origins of the Terror. Massacres and calls to political violence had certainly been around since the outset of the Revolution in 1789. But were they genuine acts of terrorism? Therein lies the very crux of the problem of finding a satisfactory definition of terror and terrorist policy. In order to simplify the issue, we shall treat terror here as a political phenomenon. That, in any case, is the perspective of most French dictionary definitions, often on the basis of the historical experience of 1789.

The *Robert* dictionary: "(Since 1789). Collective fear instilled in a populace or group to overcome its resistance; a regime or political process based on that fear or on the use of emergency measures and violence." Hence, the *Robert*'s definition of terrorism: "Governance by terror." The *Larousse* defines terrorism as the "systematic use of violence to political ends."

Specialized dictionaries on politics and strategy tell a similar story. One French dictionary of political thought, which has no entry for "terrorism," offers the following definition of terror: "A period when measures are deployed to terrify and destroy an enemy; more generally, measures to that end as a whole."[5]

The *Dictionnaire de stratégie* also takes the 1789 experience as the starting point for defining the concept of terrorism: " 'Terror' is an emotional state of heightened fear, whereas terrorism is an action. The two concepts overlap, however, inasmuch as, ever since the French Revolution, terror has also been equated with a political regime, a governmental process even, to break resisters through collective dread, while terrorism often goes beyond isolated initiatives to become 'strategy' postulating the systematic use of violence."[6]

One dictionary of strategic thought defines terrorism first and foremost as a political phenomenon: "An action of egregious violence but brief duration, aimed at breaking an adversary's will to fight. . . . A provisional phenomenon of limited physical extent, terrorism is a means to an end."[7] While this is the only definition not linked to 1789, it nonetheless stipulates the limited nature of the terrorist act in terms of means, physical extent, and time.

More precisely, it might be added that, if terrorism is to persist through time, it must necessarily be limited in means and results. Conversely, terrorism of unlimited means generally endures only briefly—either it is defeated or it attains its goals. Even the great Stalinist terror, which lasted far longer than comparable historical instances, rose to a frenzy only for brief periods, such as in 1937. If the use of terror is to be effective, the state must "pace" its terrorist campaigns and play "good cop / bad cop," just as torturers do in a torture session, as Joseph Stalin understood perfectly.

The French Terror served both as the founding act of modern state terror and as the model defining and delineating the strategic use of violence by a state apparatus. "Terror is the order of the day," proclaimed the Convention, which sought to "strike down the enemies of the Revolution with terror." A distinction should be drawn between the collective violence that prevailed at the onset of the Revolution, in particular, and the "strategic" terror that also took hold during the earliest revolutionary uprisings with the creation of the Comité des recherches of the city of Paris by Jacques-Pierre Brissot on October 21, 1789. This committee was charged with uncovering counterrevolutionary conspiracies, but in the process, it invented all sorts of fictitious plots, thus becoming the precursor of the Comité de sûreté générale, created in 1793.[8] The committee relied on denunciations to foil conspiracies. It therefore went to work setting up a functional network of informers and required its members to "gather information, when necessary, concerning denounced persons, interrogate them, and assemble documents and evidence."[9] Members of the committee had access to funds to pay informers in proportion to the importance of the information they provided. In order to preserve itself—its detractors were many—the committee acted the way all institutions of its type act: it imagined and invented conspiracies and enemies of every stripe. Agencies such as the CIA behave no differently in very different contexts, and always invoke the same reason of state, or revolution: "The ends justify the means." Following the creation of this committee and of the National Assembly's own Comité des recherches, the Tribunal révolutionnaire and the Comité de salut public were set up to implement the terror. In 1791, the Legislative Assembly adopted the same approach to target and victimize the émigrés. In the late summer of 1792, a special criminal tribunal was created to expedite mass arrests and the summary execution of prisoners. The terrorist machinery was up and running.

In 1793 and 1794, a further step was taken toward the institutionalization of terror when it was adopted as official revolutionary policy. The policy of terror reached its high point when the government began implementing its strategy of stamping out "enemies of the people"—as witnessed in the Vendée campaign—and of treating counterrevolutionaries as the nationals of a foreign enemy state. In confrontation with an enemy state, the use of force in self-defense can be morally justified. "Terror," says François Furet, "is government by fear, based on Robespierre's theory of government by virtue."[10] The Terror was thus part and parcel of the Revolution: "Launched to exterminate the aristocracy, the Terror had become a tool for crushing villains and fighting crime," Gueniffey observes. "It had become an integral component of the Revolution, inseparable from it, because only terror could ultimately bring about a Republic of citizens. . . . If the Republic of free citizens was not yet possible, it was because men, warped by their history, remained evil; through Terror, the Revolution—history as yet unwritten and brand-new—would make a new kind of man."[11]

The French Terror prefigured a system to be found in all the great revolutions, especially the Bolshevik Revolution: the exploitation of ideological fanaticism, the manipulation of social tensions, and extermination campaigns against rebellious sectors (of the peasantry).[12] Whereas 2,625 people were executed in Paris, and some 16,600 throughout France, these figures account only for the official victims of the "legal" terror; there were at least 20,000 more. Moreover, the Republican *colonnes infernales* ("infernal columns") killed tens of thousands in the Vendée—between 40,000 and 190,000 by some estimates.[13] All in all, the Terror claimed from 200,000 to 300,000 victims, out of a population of 28 million—a modest number in comparison to the terror campaigns of the twentieth century.

State terrorism should not be confused with genocide, notwithstanding that it can occasionally claim a great many victims. Terrorism seeks not to amass victims but to be selective. Genocide aims at wholesale extermination.

Robespierre himself understood that the effectiveness of the Terror depended on its choice of targets rather than on the proliferation of victims. In response to the case presented against the Girondins by the Comité de sûreté générale on October 3, 1793, he said that "the National Convention must not seek great numbers of the guilty; it must strike at the factional leaders. The punishment of their leaders will terrify the traitors and save the fatherland."

The logic of a terrorist campaign is to attack certain areas while sparing others, to single out certain targets while avoiding others, and yet never to offer a "rational" or discernible reason for its choices. The victim of terror never knows why he, rather than another, has been targeted. The French Revolution was no exception to that rule. Terror was implemented in diverse ways. Some, such as the Vendéens, were assailed with full force. Other regions, such as the Languedoc and the Dauphinois, were almost entirely spared the terror. Moreover, it was dispensed in a highly unequal way; some 2,000 Lyonnais lost their heads to the guillotine, while only five inhabitants of Tarbes were executed. Generally speaking, western France, in such cities as Bordeaux and Nantes, was by far the worst hit. And yet Calvados, for instance, saw only thirteen of its own condemned to death.

The disparity demonstrates above all how the Terror involved every stratum of the state apparatus, from the central agencies to local authorities who had a certain leeway in applying directives from on high. Thus, terror is *unfair;* indeed, that is one of its fundamental characteristics, whatever form it may take and in whatever era. The irony of this injustice inherent in state terrorism is that terror has often been used by regimes that advocate equality. The French Terror also illustrates the extent to which a state, even an authoritarian or totalitarian one, fails to exercise complete control over the mechanism of terror. At the various levels of the state hierarchy, decisions taken by those in positions of authority count for just as much as those taken at the very top. This anomaly encourages the abuse of power, especially among mediocrities whose zeal makes up for other deficiencies, and promotes the propagation of terror. In the Soviet Union, that power terrorized even those who were in charge of applying terror.

In the sphere of terrorist organization, France under the Terror was far from having mastered the finesse found later in the twentieth century. As Roger Caillois quite rightly points out: "It is neither courage, nor aggressiveness, nor ferocity that makes war so intense. It is the degree of the state's mechanization, its capacities to control and constrain, the number and rigidity of its structures. Throughout the course of history, state power has usually been strengthened by war. In turn, the growing power of the state has been responsible for the gradual change in the nature of warfare, steadily pushing it toward what began to be known by the early nineteenth century as its absolute manifestation."[14]

The modern practice of terror is inseparable both from totalitarianism and from the emergence of what would eventually come to be known as "total war." Every great revolution that has applied widespread ter-

ror has been simultaneously engaged in warfare and tantalized by the totalitarian temptation, be it in France, the USSR, Nazi Germany, China,
or Iran.

There is an enduring tendency to distinguish between the phenomenon of war and that of terror, as if they were two elements united only
by a coincidence of historic circumstances. And yet war is always at the
heart of terrorist activity undertaken by the revolutionary or totalitarian state. It both serves to legitimize the state's violence against a foreign
enemy power and allows it artfully to substitute the battle against the enemies of the revolution for the battle against the foreigner. Ultimately,
the police replace the army as the apparatus of internal repression and
become the principal vehicle for terror. The transition is barely apparent. The totalitarian state relies on the support of the masses, which it
manipulates with another basic weapon in the totalitarian arsenal:
propaganda.

The French Revolution highlights all these characteristic mechanisms
of the totalitarian state, but it was an incomplete manifestation thereof,
since practically the entire edifice crumbled with the execution of Robespierre. That is why the Terror of 1793–94 can be seen both as a deviation within the Revolution and as the harbinger of the totalitarian phenomenon. "Total terror," writes Hannah Arendt, "is so easily mistaken
for a symptom of tyrannical government because totalitarian government in its initial stages must behave like a tyranny and raze the boundaries of man-made law."[15] But total terror does not stop at dissolving the
fences that protect men from one another and from the state. It is not
there to facilitate the exercise of power by a despot, for whom any space
between men, however limited, represents a space for freedom. The mission of total terror is to create a new humankind by harnessing the will
of the government to accelerate the natural course of history.[16] It imposes
itself forcibly on the natural course of a history that it seeks to shape, and
in that it differs from the terror exercised by an authoritarian state as a
tool of repression to keep itself in power. In the latter instance, it takes
the form of a campaign to eliminate rivals or potential rivals for power.
"Political" assassination and torture are its main tools of repression.
This was the type of campaign waged, for instance, by General Augusto
Pinochet in Chile after the 1973 coup.

What happened in 1793 and 1794 was altogether different. The idea
of regenerating the human being is based on Enlightenment philosophy,
and in particular that of Rousseau. His concept of education, as set out
in *Émile,* establishes the conditions necessary to the creation of a new

being. In the *Contrat social*, he outlines the political conditions for that transformation: "All of us together place our persons and our full strength under the supreme guidance of the general will, and as a body we receive every limb as an indivisible part of the whole." The influence of Rousseau's ideas on the French Revolution is well known, but another current of thought, that of the "philosophy of history," was to give rise to two visions of history, one liberal, the other Hegelian. The latter was to weigh heavily with Marx.

Marx took the philosophy of history to its ultimate conclusion, progressing in phases, through class struggle, to the dictatorship of the proletariat, leading to the withering away of the state. This deterministic view of history was to leave its mark on the nineteenth and twentieth centuries and would be exploited by Marxist-leaning totalitarian regimes to legitimize their actions, including the use of terror. At the very moment when the Terror raged in 1793 and 1794, Condorcet was writing his masterpiece, *Esquisse d'un tableau historique des progress de l'esprit humain* (Sketch of a Historical Picture of the Progress of the Human Mind), directly inspired by Kant's work, as exemplified in the latter's essay "Idea for a Universal History from a Cosmopolitan Point of View."

But the philosophy of history, as espoused by Kant and Condorcet (or by Turgot, who had written his excellent work on universal history in 1751), is based on freedom: through the various stages of its history, mankind eventually achieves its liberty. This liberation was proclaimed by Condorcet, who associated it with humankind's general progress. In Hegel, the progress of history was no longer associated with liberty but was defined by another concept: that of struggle. Marx took up this interpretation in turn and refined it into his well-known concept of class struggle. Liberty, on which the philosophy of history had originally been founded, was abandoned altogether. With this purging, the Marxist philosophy of history was brought into conformity with the Marxist politics espoused by nineteenth- and twentieth-century revolutionaries. Under such conditions, the opportunistic implementation of a policy of terror does not clash, at least provisionally, with the doctrines advocated by those revolutionaries.

Philosophically, liberty was one of the founding principles of the revolution in 1793, as well as of the historical interpretation underlying the activities of the major players, including Robespierre. Paradoxically, however, the prevailing powers needed the Terror, whereas the Revolution could not be accomplished so long as it reigned. Ultimately, the deadlock was broken with the physical elimination of Robespierre, putting an end to the campaign of terror.

Although France seized the opportunity to shut down the campaign of terror orchestrated by the "Incorruptible," its example gives us a sense of how a revolutionary state, once caught up in the logic of violence, ends up with a political system of terror. And yet the Terror was not merely a temporary period of repression designed to keep the Revolution on course.

In 1793, France's military situation was disastrous, both abroad and at home in the Vendée. The political situation was no less precarious, with the parliamentary balance tipping decisively in favor of the radicals. Moreover, the Convention was under considerable pressure from the mob.[17] On September 25, Robespierre summed up the situation for the National Assembly: "Eleven armies to lead, the weight of all Europe to bear, traitors to unmask everywhere, emissaries corrupted by the gold of foreign powers to outmaneuver, disloyal administrators to monitor and prosecute, endless obstacles and hindrances to the wisest measures to be overcome, all the tyrants to fight, all the conspirators to intimidate . . . that is our job."

Let us briefly recap the major events of that year and the next (the calendar change took place in October 1793). January 21, 1793, saw the execution of Louis XVI (Marie-Antoinette was guillotined on October 16). In the first quarter, the Convention declared war on England, Holland, and Spain. The war in the Vendée began on March 11, two days after the creation of the Revolutionary Tribunal, marking the onset of the Terror. The French were defeated at Neerwinden on March 16, and Dumouriez defected on April 1. The Committee of Public Safety was established on April 6. The coup against the Gironde faction took place on May 31, and further demonstrations against the Convention erupted on June 2. It was at this time that the Girondin deputies were expelled from the Convention. The Convention adopted the constitution on June 24. The Committee of Public Safety was renewed on July 10, disenfranchising Danton, and Marat was assassinated three days later. On August 1, the Convention endorsed armed violence to subdue the Vendée. The *levée en masse* (mass levy of troops) was decreed on August 24—a defining moment that would fundamentally change the practice of warfare and revolutionize strategy for the next 150 years. The sansculottes rebelled on September 5, and the Revolutionary Army was established on September 9.

The adoption of the "Law of Suspects" on September 17 launched the second phase of the reign of terror, which included the first defeat of the Vendéen army at Cholet on October 17 and its final destruction on December 23. This period is marked by the trial and execution of the Hébertistes on March 21 and 24, 1794, and of the Dantonists on April 2 and 5.

The third phase of the Terror began on June 10, 1794, with the adoption of the Law of 22 Prairial, and ended with the execution of Robespierre (along with Saint-Just and some twenty other Robespierristes) on July 28.

The Revolution threatened to bring down the venerable balance of power established by the Peace of Westphalia in 1648, and with it all of ancien régime Europe. The stakes were high. The war in the Vendée combined the passions of civil war with the technology of classical warfare. There, too, the stakes were enormous. With the mass levy, the citizenry became the core of the army, marking the emergence of modern nationalism. It gave birth first to the idea of the armed nation, then to that of absolute warfare—with its ideal of maximal violence—and ultimately to that of total warfare, wherein the principal of absolute warfare is implemented on the ground. Things had not yet reached that point in 1793, but the process had been set in motion.

It was in this context of almost total insecurity, and of the climactic struggle for power, that the Revolutionary Tribunal and the Committee of Public Safety were created. Robespierre, whom posterity would come to see as the embodiment of the Terror, was elected to the Committee on July 27. As Jean Artarit notes, "this development, favored by circumstance, was inevitable. He could only have been deeply, unutterably elated by the opportunity to unleash upon the Nation, metaphorically speaking, the gargantuan process of self-purification to which he had always subjected himself. It would be quite inappropriate to pin the onset of the Terror to a specific date. It had long been brewing in many a mind, and not only that of Robespierre."[18]

The September disturbances compelled the Convention to decree the Terror as the "order of the day" on September 5. The Law of Suspects, adopted on September 17, was based on a definition of "suspects" that would allow the elimination of all the regime's opponents. The decree issued on September 20 gave the Revolutionary Tribunal full powers to draw up the list. The terrorist machinery had been set in motion.

On October 10, Saint-Just placed a decree before the Convention creating an emergency regime: "Revolutionary laws cannot be carried out unless the government itself has been constituted on a revolutionary basis." The first article of the decree stated that "the provisional government of France shall remain revolutionary until peace is achieved." The Committee of Public Safety was put in charge of overseeing the entire state apparatus. Bodies such as the Revolutionary Tribunal, which had hitherto acted with restraint—260 accused and 66 condemned to death—were now able to give full vent to their repressive tendencies. The Tribunal was reorganized into four parts. Fouquier-Tinville became the public prosecutor. The Committee of Public Safety and the Committee of General Security drew up the list of jurors for the Convention, which nominated them. The number of prosecutions and condemnations rose dramatically, amounting to 371 indictees and 177 death sentences between October and December. The Girondins were executed on November 1, while the number of arrests orchestrated by the Committee of Public Safety spiraled. Robespierre, succeeding Danton, believed the Terror to be a restraining mechanism to avoid horrendous bloodshed. Restrained or not, justified or not, the practice of Terror gave rise to the politics of terror.

Confronted by the Vendéen counterrevolutionaries, the Convention chose to dedicate all available means to crushing the rebellious region, in accordance with the decree of August 1, 1793, which also sought to depopulate the area by force. The aim of this scorched-earth strategy was to suppress and prevent through terror, in the Vendée and elsewhere, any will to organize armed rebellion against the Revolution. The first decree had no provision, as Barère had sought, "to exterminate that rebellious race," but the implementation of such a strategy on the ground was facilitated and later encouraged by the Committee of Public Safety in October, and again in February 1794, when it supported General Turreau's terrorist strategy of unleashing his "infernal columns" throughout the countryside in a campaign of extermination following the defeat of the Vendéen army.

On September 5, 1793, Robespierre, as president of the Assembly, defended liberty in the name of the people: "The people have raised their arm and justice will fall upon the heads of the traitors and conspirators, and nothing will remain of that impious race. The land of liberty, too long polluted by the presence of these wicked men, must be free of them at last."

But the bloodiest apology for the Terror was that of Saint-Just, who spoke on October 10 on behalf of the Committee of Public Safety:

> We cannot hope to prosper so long as one enemy of freedom remains to draw breath. You must punish not only the traitors, but even those who are indifferent; you must punish whosoever is passive toward the Republic and does

nothing for her. For, now that the French people has manifested its will, all who oppose it are outside its sovereign power; and all who are outside its sovereign power are enemies. . . . Those who will not be governed by justice must be governed by the sword; tyrants must be oppressed.

This statement was not a mere rhetorical exercise. After Saint-Just spoke, the Convention decreed that the government of France must "remain revolutionary until peace is achieved," that the ministers and generals were thenceforth under the supervision of the Committee of Public Safety, and that the Constitution was suspended. The Committee of Public Safety had become de facto the basic instrument of the machine to be replicated later, under the totalitarian regimes, as the "central committees" dear to the hearts of twentieth-century communist regimes, now working on behalf of the "dictatorship of the proletariat."

The terror campaigns orchestrated by totalitarian regimes assign a generous role to political theater, usually in the form of high-profile trials. The Terror of 1793 exemplified this in the trial of Marie-Antoinette. As a woman, a queen, and a foreigner, she embodied every attribute necessary to turn this farce into a spectacular propaganda success for the Terror. Marie-Antoinette was summoned to appear on October 14. Foremost among the trial's "political" charges—in the haste in which the trial was organized, no evidence of treason was found—were those questioning the queen's virtue. Hébert accused her of having had incestuous relations with her son. It is not far wrong to conclude that she was "judged on the basis of the pornographic fantasies of an entire nation."[19]

The Law of 22 Prairial marked the apogee of the Great Terror. On the one hand, it allowed anyone to be accused of being an enemy of the revolution; on the other, it abolished all the legal guarantees that had survived to that point. The revolutionary government that rose from the ruins of the recently disintegrated state was based on centralization and authority more absolute than those of the ancien régime monarchy. The latter had, in fact, become increasingly and broadly liberal in its final years (one of the causes of the Revolution, according to Tocqueville). The creation of the Committee of Public Safety finished off Montesquieu's 1789 triparte separation of the executive, legislative, and judiciary branches. Thenceforth, the committee commanded every power. Unlike the monarchy, it did not even base its claims on divine right. Lord Acton's famous dictum—that power corrupts and absolute power corrupts absolutely—was perfectly suited to the circumstances.

Robespierre embodied this new power. The Assembly had found its master in him and dared not oppose him, even after the elimination of Danton. Having liquidated anyone who might challenge him, Robespierre established his partisans in key posts, putting his brother Augustin in charge of censorship.

The Terror lost its patina of legitimacy once the domestic and foreign situations had been brought under control. The government had in effect achieved its twofold mission and, by the logic of 1793, the Terror had lost its raison d'être. In the meanwhile, it had been transformed from a provisional instrument of the policy of "recovery" into a system of government whose principal function was ultimately to fuel the Terror itself.

Robespierre had come too far to turn back. In June and July 1794, the Terror condemned 1,400 victims to death, some six times more than in the previous months. Did this increase represent a loss of control or deliberate policy? The Law of Prairial was quite clear in its declaration that "the Revolutionary Tribunal is instituted to punish the enemies of the people." As for Robespierre, right up to the very end, his statements demonstrate unequivocally that the Terror was the vehicle for the reign of virtue that he had sought and that was represented by the terrorist oligarchy, with himself wielding absolute power at its helm.

On 8 Thermidor (July 26), Robespierre exalted virtue in an impassioned speech: "There exists a noble ambition to found on Earth the world's first Republic." It was through that virtue that Robespierre intended to cleanse society of the filth that polluted it so as to begin afresh on new foundations. Robespierre had ceased to evolve politically but continued apace morally. The rupture was complete with Machiavelli's amoral universe, where reasons of state had governed political relations under the old regime and in particular since the Peace of Westphalia. The politics of virtue did not stop at the mere physical elimination of the "enemies of the people." It assumed a missionary zeal tasked quite overtly with reforming the human being by purging society of vice. The cult of the Supreme Being established in the spring was the moral legitimization of this vast revolutionary undertaking guided by Providence and sought to ensure its success by sanctioning the Terror that was to see the Revolution through to its conclusion. However, the Terror was embodied by Robespierre; when he fell, the Terror would fall with him (just as it abated in violence, albeit more slowly, with the death of Stalin). And yet, Robespierre was brought down, not by the enemies of the Terror, but by those who shared his approval of it but were directly threatened by his supreme power. To those who may consider the Terror to be an episode, however necessary or unfortunate, closely linked to the specificities of the French Revolution, history is replete with evidence that state terror has direct causal connections to totalitarianism whenever it is coupled with the ideology of radical social and individual transformation. Modern totalitarianism did not invent state terror, but it did vastly strengthen it, just as nuclear technology transformed the nature of strategic bombing. It would take another century for the machinery of totalitarianism to give full expression to its potential in the era of mass movements.

In the meantime, another form of terrorism was to develop over the course of the nineteenth century. Indirectly, it, too, was in part a product of the French Revolution. It was heralded by the emergence of Russian populists influenced by Enlightenment ideas of freedom and social justice, with a strong romantic taint. Contemporary terrorism was born around 1878 in Russia. In its connection with various revolutionary projects, it has been associated with another revolution—the Industrial Revolution. Modern terrorism was to exploit the technical means made available by that revolution and would soon learn what a tremendous target industrial society offered to terrorists. Along with Dostoyevsky's *The Possessed* (one of whose character's is modeled on Nechayev), Joseph Conrad's novel *The Secret Agent* was the first great literary work to tackle terrorism as a central theme, specifically linking the emergence of a society obsessed with scientific progress to that of terrorism aimed at forcibly accelerating human progress.

NOTES TO CHAPTER 5

EPIGRAPH: Sergei Genadievich Nechayev, "The Revolutionary Catechism" (1869), www.postworldindustries.com/library_text/library_praxis/revolutionary_catechism.html (accessed April 13, 2006).

1. Gueniffey, *Politique de la Terreur*, 13.
2. Cf. Furet and Richet, *Révolution française*, 125.
3. Gueniffey, *Politique de la Terreur*, 14.
4. See Baczko, *Comment sortir de la Terreur*.
5. Colas, *Dictionnaire de la pensée politique*, 253.
6. Dabezies, "Terrorism," in *Dictionnaire de stratégie*, ed. Montbrial and Klein, 581–82.
7. Géré, *Dictionnaire de la pensée stratégique*, 269–70.
8. Gueniffey, *Politique de la Terreur*, 91.
9. Ibid., 87.
10. As reflected in Brissot's comment that "he who desires the ends, desires the means" (Brissot, *À Stanislas Clermont*, 12–13). Gueniffey, *Politique de la Terreur*, 89.
11. Gueniffey, *Politique de la Terreur*, 89.
12. Cf. Courtois, "Pourquoi?" in id., et al., *Livre noir du communisme*, 854.
13. The figure cited by Greer in *Incidence of the Terror*.

14. Caillois, *Bellone*, 16.
15. Arendt, *Origins of Totalitarianism* (1979 ed.), 465.
16. Ibid., 466.
17. Guennifey, *Politique de la Terreur*, 241.
18. Artarit, *Robespierre*, 264.
19. Thomas, *Reine scélérate*, 16.

CHAPTER 6

ANARCHIST TERRORISTS OF THE NINETEENTH CENTURY

Olivier Hubac-Occhipinti

Ah, ça ira, ça ira, ça ira,
Tous les bourgeois goût'ront d'la bombe,
Ah, ça ira, ça ira, ça ira,
Tous les bourgeois on les saut'ra . . .
On les saut'ra!

We'll win, we'll win, we'll win,
All the bourgeois'll have a taste of the bomb,
We'll win, we'll win, we'll win,
All the bourgeois'll get blown up . . .
We'll blow them up!

Refrain of the anarchist song "La Ravachole"

The popular imagination has tended to view anarchist terrorism in a positive light. Like their Russian counterparts, libertarian terrorists are perceived as idealistic, romantic rebels. Classic literature provides a partial explanation for the sympathy accorded to the perpetrators of these extremely violent crimes; indeed, certain authors, despite their condemnation of anarchism, nonetheless had a kind of fascination with such acts. Émile Zola, for instance, spoke of the "eternal dark poetry" of anarchists, and the poet Stéphane Mallarmé of dynamite's "decorative explosion." Esthetics alone, however, cannot explain or help us to understand the motives that drove individuals to use bomb attacks as a means of propaganda, thereby giving rise to modern terrorism. Nor is it possible really to understand the major wave of anarchist terrorism that swept through the second half of the nineteenth century without a solid grasp of the underlying doctrines and without placing anarchism in its proper historical context.

THE EMERGENCE OF THE ANARCHIST DOCTRINE

The anarchist doctrine first took shape during the second half of the nineteenth century—a period conducive to the emergence of revolutionary doctrines. At that time, Europe and the United States were experiencing unprecedented technological progress and economic transformation. The discoveries of the first Industrial Revolution were being exploited, and the second Industrial Revolution was getting under way. In the area of metallurgical techniques, the Thomas-Gilchrist process, discovered in 1879, made it possible to produce steel from phosphoric pig iron, opening the way to the exploitation of Lorraine's iron ore deposits, which previously had been unusable. Also key were the development of the steam engine, the hydraulic turbine, and electricity, with the invention of Gramme's dynamo in 1869; of the telephone by Alexander Graham Bell in 1877; and of the internal combustion engine and the automobile. The progress made in these areas also benefited agriculture. The emerging chemical industry provided dyes, fertilizers, pharmaceutical products, and explosives. Nitroglycerine and nitrocellulose, which were invented in the 1860s, made new types of attacks possible.

These new machines and technical processes, along with the development of trade, boosted production to an unprecedented level. As a result, economic life was profoundly transformed. Fifty years of advances in communications and trade—including railroads, automobiles, aviation, and steamships—had made commerce truly global. Indeed, a new economy was being born that heralded modern capitalism. Both prosperity and financial crises characterized this period. The crisis of 1873, touched off by wild speculation, marked the beginning of an almost twenty-year-long period of economic stagnation.

The economic and technological revolution triggered upheavals that profoundly changed the human condition. On the one hand, a drop in the mortality rate resulted in significant population growth—a trend that was not, however, particularly strong in France. On the other hand, during the second half of the nineteenth century, tens of millions of European emigrants headed out—for political, religious, and, above all, economic reasons—to the American West and to Latin America. Many

Spanish, Italian, Belgian, and German emigrants chose France as their destination. Finally, urban populations also grew considerably. Coal mining—coal being essential not only as a source of energy but also as a primary input for the metal industry—required a considerable workforce. Lured by the prospect of a better life, poor farmworkers began to settle in large urban centers. The development of means of communication accelerated the rural exodus, and in sixty years the number of people living in the main urban areas doubled.

All these social transformations helped to lay the groundwork for the formulation of revolutionary doctrines. The emergence of two main classes—the bourgeoisie, or those who did no manual work, and the proletariat, comprising modern industrial workers—led to radical social changes. While the bourgeoisie as a whole benefited from progress, the working class was typified by an industrial proletariat whose condition was miserable and highly precarious. In cities, the social question was becoming a key issue, given that these two worlds knew nothing of each other and lived in different neighborhoods. The first feared social unrest, while the second harbored a deep-seated resentment of the capitalist system.

WHAT IS ANARCHISM?

It is no easy task to define and elucidate the anarchist doctrine. Indeed, as the French anarchist propagandist Sébastien Faure (1858–1942) said, "there can be no libertarian creed or dogma." The fundamental principle of anarchism—the rejection of all forms of authority—also stands in the way of a clearly established definition of the term. We can certainly say, however, that the common denominator among the various movements and individuals claiming to have acted in the name of anarchy is the rejection of the principle of authority in any form—the violent rejection of control over individuals.

The concept of anarchism, in the political sense of the term, was first put forward by Pierre Joseph Proudhon (1809–1865) during the first half of the nineteenth century. At that point, however, it did not yet advocate the destruction of the state—only its reorganization in a manner that would ensure respect for the individual, as well as political and economic free association. Proudhon proposed the concept of "mutualism"—the abolition of the capitalist profit system and the introduction of interest-free credit, so as to enable the people to buy back the means of production and put an end to social injustice. That was the principle underlying the creation of cooperatives and mutual aid societies. Proudhon's doctrine was more reformist than revolutionary. It had considerable influence on the International Workingmen's Association (IWA), or First International, founded in September 1864.[1]

Mikhail Bakunin (1814–1876) advocated the free association of individuals and postulated that true liberty was a sufficient condition for the organization of political, social and economic relations. He was a sharp critic of religion, which he defined as the "enslavement and annihilation and servitude of humanity for the benefit of divinity."[2] Bakunin disagreed strongly with Karl Marx on the question of the nature of the political system that should rise from the ruins of bourgeois states. While Bakunin's goal was the destruction of all state structures and the total rejection of all forms of power, Marx held that dictatorship of the proletariat was a prerequisite for a new society. When Bakunin was expelled from the IWA at its 1872 Hague Congress, that profound divergence of views resulted in a schism within the organization between "authoritarians" and "anti-authoritarians." The split marked the beginning of the autonomy of the Marxist and anarchist doctrines.

The Russian anarchist theorist Pyotr Kropotkin (1842–1921) was the first to champion acts of violence, although starting in 1891 he began to reconsider the effectiveness of terrorist acts. Along with French geographer Elisée Reclus, he founded a newspaper, *Le Révolté,* in which he encouraged preparations for a revolution and stated that it was necessary to "awaken boldness and the spirit of revolt by preaching by example." He believed in "propaganda by deed," a revolutionary tactic described in 1877 as a "powerful means of awakening popular consciousness."[3] At the international level, on July 14, 1881, the IWA's London Congress, which was attended by the various anarchist delegations, announced that "the time has come to . . . act, and to add propaganda by deed and insurrectionary actions to oral and written propaganda, which have proven ineffective." Among its resolutions, the Congress "recommended that organizations and individuals . . . emphasize the importance of the study and application of the [technical and chemical sciences] as a means of defense and attack." All the preconditions for the emergence of a new kind of terrorism were thus in place.

ITALIAN ANARCHISTS: "PROPAGANDA BY DEED"

Italy was a particularly fertile breeding ground for the anarchist doctrine. In 1864, the Italian Federation joined the International Workingmen's

Association, but in August 1872, it broke with its General Council at the Rimini Congress, opposing Bakunin's expulsion from the IWA at the Hague Congress. However, it was at the October 1876 Florence Congress that the Italian Federation definitively distanced itself from the First International by openly speaking out in favor of the collective ownership of the means of production and its products themselves. The anarchists Carlo Cafiero (1846–1892) and Errico Malatesta (1853–1932), the authors of this statement, defended their belief that "insurrectionary deeds" were the "most effective means of propaganda." In 1877, they carried out a practical demonstration in the province of Benevento, although it ended in failure. Armed anarchists occupied the municipal building in the village of Letino "in the name of social revolution," burned all title deeds, and proclaimed the establishment of libertarian communism. However, the arrival of more than 10,000 soldiers put an end to the revolt. This episode gave rise to the practice of "propaganda by deed" favored by anarchist terrorists.

Beginning in the 1880s, the anarchist movement split into two factions: the first was revolutionary and anarchist-communist, while the second was closely related to the form of socialism that prevailed at the time. Despite an attempt by Malatesta and Francesco Merlino (1856–1930), at the January 1891 Capolago Congress, to bring the two factions closer together, the split became definitive in 1892. From this point on, Italian anarchism shifted between those two modes of action in disseminating its doctrine.

On the one hand, acts of violence by individuals, including assassination attempts—an extreme form of "propaganda by deed"—were not particularly successful. The murder of the president of the French Republic, Sadi Carnot, by the Italian anarchist Sante Caserio in June 1894 was an example of a political assassination motivated by revenge.[4] Caserio, who shouted, "Long live the revolution!" and "Long live anarchy!" as he stabbed the president, was above all seeking revenge for the conviction of French terrorist François Ravachol. The following day, Ravachol's wife received a photograph of her husband inscribed "He has been avenged." Other Italian anarchists, following Caserio's example, were active outside of their country. The August 1897 assassination of the president of the Spanish Council of Ministers, Antonio Canovas, by Michele Angiolillo, as well as the murder of Empress Elizabeth of Austria on September 10, 1898, by Luigi Luccheni, were both the work of Italian immigrants who espoused revolutionary anarchist beliefs.[5]

Italian terrorists also set their sights on eliminating their own country's leaders. In Rome, on June 16, 1894, Paolo Lega shot at, but missed, the president of the Italian Council. Three attempts were made on the life of King Umberto I. The first was carried out by Giovanni Passanante, who tried to stab the king, and the second by the anarchist Pietro Acciarito, who did likewise in Rome on April 22, 1897. But it was only three years later that their goal was achieved: on July 29, 1900, at an athletic competition awards ceremony, the anarchist Gaetano Brecci fired three pistol shots at the king, killing him. His goal was to punish the king for having supported and decorated General Bava Beccaris, who had given the order to open fire on a crowd during January 1898 riots over increases in bread prices.

While the murder of a regime's leading dignitary as a means of propaganda was very popular with revolutionaries and anarchists during the second half of the nineteenth century, the king's assassination took place at a time when the anarchist movement was seriously reconsidering recourse to such violent acts of "propaganda by deed." A number of anarchist publications, although they did not condemn Brecci's action, suggested that it might henceforth be preferable to wage the battle in the economic arena. The Italian anarchist movement had previously organized major strikes, and around 1900, distancing itself from this short-lived terrorist period, it opted definitively for the type of revolutionary syndicalism advocated by Georges Sorel.[6] The resurgence of individual assassination attempts as a technique came later, with the advent of fascism.

SPANISH TERRORIST ANARCHISTS:
FROM ARMED REVOLT TO REGICIDE

The anarchist movement was very successful in Spain in the nineteenth century and even into the twentieth. Its most noteworthy characteristic was the use, over a period of several decades, of every possible form of "propaganda by deed."

This particular phenomenon can be explained partly by Spain's industrial and economic backwardness. The country had serious social problems, which affected the vast majority of the population. Agrarian reform had led neither to the creation of large estates nor to the emergence of a land-owning class of small farmers. As a result, agricultural workers—including millions of *braceros*—low-paid day laborers, who were often unemployed—lived in conditions of terrible poverty. In addition, there was little industrialization, and the factories that existed were often foreign-owned. Only the light industry of textile manufacturing in Catalonia had gained prominence, thereby becoming the "national occupation." Spain's economic problems were exacerbated by the existence of regionalist movements that threatened Spanish unity, because the rich provinces did not want to provide financial support to the poorer ones.

Against this difficult backdrop, there were a great many outbursts of violence in Catalonia in the 1830s, although they were not linked to any particular doctrine. In 1835, workers destroyed a number of machines and pieces of equipment. Spain thus already had a long revolutionary tradition when anarchist movements began to emerge.

Whenever the political situation in Spain grew tense, armed uprisings or strikes multiplied throughout the country. That was the case during the first Carlist war (1833–40), in which supporters of María Cristina de Borbón–Dos Sicilias—queen regent on behalf of her daughter, Isabel II— opposed the brother of the late King Fernando VII, Carlos María Isidro de Borbón, known as Don Carlos, who was proclaimed king by his supporters. This period of instability saw the first individual, socially motivated assassination attempt. In addition, throughout the nineteenth century, numerous attacks were carried out against convents, and against monks and nuns themselves, who were accused, rightly or wrongly, of every evil under the sun.

Bakunin's ideas, introduced into Spain by an Italian, Giuseppe Fanelli (1827–1877), were immediately embraced by the Spanish people. The anarchist movement grew very quickly in the 1860s, and, immediately following the IWA's Hague Congress, the Spanish delegation joined the "anti-authoritarian" IWA. Regional branches of the Spanish Anarchist Federation were established throughout the country. One salient characteristic of the anarchist movement of the time was its close ties with laborers and agricultural workers, which enabled it, inter alia, to retain its influence even at the height of periods of suppression.

It was in the poverty-stricken parts of Spain—mainly in Andalusia and in Catalonia—that the anarchists advocated resort to "propaganda by deed." During the period from 1882 to 1886, anarchist groups such as Mano Negra engaged in expropriation and murdered more than twenty leading figures. On January 8, 1892, in response to the motion adopted at the IWA's 1881 London Congress urging resort to illegal action, the town of Jeres in southwestern Spain was stormed by hundreds of agricultural workers.

Although such insurrectionary violence was condemned by the Anarchist Federation right from the start, terrorist acts were to be committed with frequency for more than twenty years. The first attack against the power of the monarchy took place in October 1878, when Juan Oliva Moncasi, a young worker, opened fire on the king's procession. But it was mainly during the reign of Alfonso XIII in his own right, which began in 1902, following a period of regency, that the number of attacks against the king began to increase. In Paris, during an official visit by the king of Spain to France in May 1905, a bomb was hurled at President Émile Loubet and Alfonso XIII, both of whom escaped without a scratch, although a number of other people were injured. The perpetrator, a man named Alejandro Farras, was never caught. A year later, at the king's wedding to Princess Ena of Battenberg in Madrid, an anarchist by the name of Mateo Morral (1880–1906) tossed a bomb, hidden in a bouquet of flowers, from a hotel onto the nuptial carriage. That attack killed fifteen people and injured at least fifty more, but the royal couple escaped unharmed.

It was mainly during the last decade of the nineteenth century that indiscriminate terrorism began to emerge in Spain. On November 7, 1893, to avenge the execution of Paulino Pallas, who had assassinated General Arsenio Martinez Campos that September, the anarchist Santiago Salvador hurled two bombs into the crowd at the Liceu Opera House in Barcelona, killing more than twenty people. In response, the authorities declared a state of siege in the city and arrested anarchists en masse. Despite intense suppression of the movement and the numerous detentions at the Montjuich military fort, another bombing took place during the Corpus Christi religious procession on Cambos Nuevos street in Barcelona, killing more than forty people.

Unlike in other European countries, where the anarchist terrorist trend was fairly limited and short-lived, in Spain, attacks continued into the twentieth century. Individual acts of violence were committed even after a legal pacifist anarcho-syndicalist system was established. Political assassinations in Spain targeted high-level representatives of the political system, identified as such by terrorists. The king, of course, personified the state and the regime. However, the goal was not necessarily to destabilize society, as was often the case with Russian terrorists, who sought to force the state to respond to attacks with suppression so that they could later denounce such police-state measures. The aim in the latter kind of attack was to link it, not only with the individual perpetrator, but also with the doctrine in whose name it had been committed, thus obliging society to acknowledge the intensity of the rage and sentiments of revolt that had motivated it.

The Liceu Opera House attack was unusual in that, for the first time, a crowd of people was targeted directly. Such acts were aimed at terrorizing the whole of a social class that had been identified as inimical to the anarchist cause. The difference between this kind of attack and more commonly used methods was that the goal here was to kill anyone who collaborated with the bosses or the state or even merely worked within the system. From that standpoint, all members of the bourgeoisie were enemies deserving of death, even if they were assigned no particular responsibility.

NORTH AMERICAN ANARCHIST TERRORISTS

The United States was never a particularly conducive environment for the development of the anarchist ideology. In major industrial centers, the rapid expansion of capitalism gave rise to opposition movements within the working class. However, their goal was not to challenge the capitalist system but primarily to limit its negative consequences for the proletariat. There were several reasons for this. For one thing, workers found it difficult to join forces because of the lack of homogeneity within their social class, given that the vast majority of them were recent immigrants. Moreover, many viewed their social situation as temporary and did not feel enslaved by their proletarian status. Against that backdrop, labor organizations such as the short-lived Knights of Labor and the influential American Federation of Labor were relatively successful, but they consistently stayed out of the political arena. Anarchists garnered a certain amount of attention through their publications and the many meetings they held throughout the country. Key figures such as the theoretician Emma Goldman (1869–1940) and the propagandist Benjamin R. Tucker (1854–1939), who had begun in 1876 to translate the works of Proudhon and Bakunin into English, helped to introduce the concept of anarchy to the United States. Johann Most (1846–1906), a former member of the German Reichstag living in exile in the United States who had been influenced by Kropotkin's ideas, became the spokesman for "propaganda by deed" in America. He published, among other works, a small how-to guide for making bombs, although he later shifted from his advocacy of violence toward syndicalism.

Several American anarchists, like European terrorists, resorted to "targeted" assassinations or to armed acts of revenge. However, the notorious events that took place in Chicago in 1886 had more to do with self-defense than terrorist action. The chain of events started with the numerous strikes that were being held in support of the eight-hour work-day, bringing 12,000 factories to a standstill. In Chicago, the movement had intensified, and a workers' meeting had been violently put down by police. At a second mass meeting, held in Haymarket Square on May 4, 1886, police officers charged into the crowd. A bomb was thrown at them, and they responded by opening fire. A dozen people were killed, including seven police officers.[7] In this case, the bomb was thrown in the context of a clash between strikers and police. This had more in common with armed insurrection than with a terrorist attack.

The attempted assassination of Carnegie Steel Company Chairman Henry Clay Frick by the anarchist Alexander Berkman (1870–1936) in 1892 gives a clear sense of the mind-set of American proponents of "propaganda by deed." Their goal was to target a specific person—a symbol of the bourgeoisie and of the suppression of the proletarian movement. In May 1892, workers at the Carnegie Steel Company's Homestead Works were clashing with the company over a new wage schedule, calling for raises because of higher market prices and the company's increased profits. Frick refused to negotiate and suspended all his workers in order to review each job application individually. The mills were closed temporarily, and workers' families were thrown out of company-owned housing. A few days later, Frick's hired guns opened fire on a crowd of workers besieging the mills; many were killed or wounded. Berkman then decided to kill Frick because "he must be made to stand the consequences."[8] The goal of the assassination was to kill someone the anarchists hated deeply and deemed responsible for the tragedy, while sparing innocent victims. Emma Goldman refused to believe that Berkman could have intentionally wounded Frick's secretary in the attack. Unlike certain French anarchist terrorists, they did not extend the concept of the bourgeois enemy to all those who collaborated, directly or indirectly, with the dominant capitalist system.

However, the motivations of American anarchist terrorists were varied. Berkman had hoped that his act would promote the anarchist cause, but his primary objective was to avenge the deaths of the Homestead workers. Leon Czolgosz, who assassinated U.S. President William McKinley in 1901, stated from the electric chair that his goal had been to liberate the American people.[9] In attacking the president, he said, he had been striking out at "an enemy of the good working people." While Berkman had acted out of a desire for revenge, Czolgosz's deed was politically motivated. The tactic of assassinating a state's highest official is reminiscent of the attacks carried out by the Russian Socialist Revolutionaries, whose objective was to destroy the political system and liberate the oppressed masses by targeting the highest level of the regime's political leaders.

The McKinley assassination marked the end of the phenomenon of "propaganda by deed" in the United States. A number of states, and later Congress, enacted key anti-anarchism laws that struck at the very heart of the movement. The principal measures outlawed anarchist activities and prohibited any person hostile to the U.S. government from entering the country.[10] Not only was the movement barely surviving from an intellectual standpoint, but the vast majority of American anarchists condemned the use of violence. Thus it was difficult for Emma Goldman to endorse such acts publicly.

While anarchist doctrines were fairly well received by the working classes in the United States, there were no real instances of anarchist terrorism. The events that took place were more along the lines of armed revolts or political assassinations—even regicide—than terrorism.

FRENCH ANARCHIST TERRORISTS: THE USE OF DYNAMITE

The evolution of the anarchist doctrine in France is inextricably linked to the Paris Commune (March–May 1871). Many of Proudhon's disciples participated in the Commune and never forgave either republicans or royalists for the repression to which they were subjected. Most of them were deported to New Caledonia. As a result, the Commune was ever-present in the minds of French anarchists during the 1880s as a symbol of the sacrifice made by its revolutionary martyrs.

French anarchism was influenced by the ideas of Kropotkin, who had proposed libertarian communism as the ultimate form of anarchism—that is to say, the application of the principle of "to each according to his need." The return of deported Communards in 1880, among them the staunch doctrinaire Louise Michel (1830–1905), breathed new life into the anarchist movement. Amnesty had previously been called for, to no avail, by Victor Hugo and François Raspail in 1876. However, in parallel with the IWA's Chaux-de-Fonds Congress of September 1880, key figures in the French anarchist movement[11] made haste to specify the tactics that were to be used to trigger a social revolution. They advocated "moving out of the sphere of legality in order to act in that of illegality." That was the first endorsement of recourse to the "technical and chemical sciences," which was reiterated and expanded upon at the London Congress on July 14, 1881.

The adoption of the principle of "propaganda by deed" as an exclusive means of action characterized the French movement until the end of the 1880s. Anarchists preferred to organize themselves into groups—units able to communicate freely with other units. They did allow, however, for a considerable degree of individual autonomy. In an atmosphere of general expectation that the great Revolution was close at hand, groups gave themselves bellicose-sounding names that left no doubt as to their intentions of carrying out "direct action." Examples include "Revolver à la main" (gun in hand), of Montceau-les-Mines, and the Paris-based "Panther of Batignolles."

Once the chosen methods had been announced, the French anarchist press fleshed them out by publishing practical guides to bomb-building. Columns began to appear with headlines such as "Anti-bourgeois Products" and "Scientific Studies," supplemented by suggestions that rural areas and the homes of conservative landowners be set on fire. In 1887, a do-it-yourself guide to the use of dynamite, L'Indicateur anarchiste, was published and translated into English, Italian, Spanish, and German. The booklet explained, in simple terms, how to make nitroglycerin and turn it into dynamite. All this information could be had for 10 francs. However, a closer look at the composition of terrorist bombs shows that, despite the widespread availability of information on their fabrication, such techniques were not often used. Of course, handling explosives, not to mention assembling them, is a fairly dangerous undertaking, which requires caution and experience, and nitroglycerin is a particularly unstable substance. It is most unwise to play at being a pyrotechnist. Many of the bombs did not explode when they were supposed to, or blew up without killing anyone. For that reason, terrorists preferred to use other, more straightforward weapons, such as handguns or knives.

Prior to this wave of attacks, France had witnessed a number of popular uprisings, either orchestrated or simply hijacked by anarchists. Yet another manifestation of the principle of "propaganda by deed," they were harbingers of the increasingly violent acts to come. Such occurrences usually began with a strike, accompanied by the threat of potential insurrection or murder. The first such event of significance was a young worker's attempted assassination of an industrialist following the Roanne strike of February 1882. The anarchist press hailed his act as the work of a revolutionary. But, for anarchists, the authentic revolutionary spirit came to be symbolized by the events that took place in Decazeville in 1886. On January 26, an unplanned strike began at the Société nouvelle des houillères et fonderies, in Aveyron. That afternoon, a group of

150 to 200 miners seized the company's administrative buildings. After the assistant director of the company, an engineer named Watrin, refused to accede to the strikers' demands, rioters threw him out of the window.

On another front, during the 1883–87 economic crisis, anarchists urged the unemployed to take the law into their own hands and to help themselves to whatever they needed. On March 9, 1883, on the initiative of the woodworkers' union, jobless people gathered on the esplanade of the Invalides in Paris. After the police dispersed the crowd, a smaller group, led by the anarchist Louise Michel, headed toward Boulevard Saint-Germain, where they looted three bakeries to the cry of "Bread, work, or lead!"

In the summer of 1882, a secret society, the Bande noire, was running rampant in the Montceau-les-Mines area and Creusot. It was a small group—not truly an anarchist one—and its objectives were ill-defined. It desecrated a number of the region's many wayside crosses, and in mid-August attacked houses of worship. The government, fearing the spread of the revolutionary spirit, suppressed the movement. However, in 1884, the Bande noire reemerged and carried out dynamite attacks. At that point it declared itself to be explicitly anarchist and an advocate of "propaganda by deed."

The wave of individual attacks that took place between 1892 and 1894, set in motion by the anarchist Ravachol, was characterized by a large number of spectacular terrorist acts and by the development, by their perpetrators, of a doctrine of direct action. However, recourse to bombings or to political assassinations was nothing new, numerous precedents having been set in the 1880s. Two assassination attempts against eminent personalities—Léon Gambetta in October 1881 and Jules Ferry in January 1884—failed because their would-be perpetrators were unable to get close enough to their intended victims. Novice assassins, even those who claimed to be anarchists, were clearly motivated more by despair than by any particular political belief. The 1884 murder of the mother superior of a Marseille-area convent by the notorious anarchist Louis Chaves, a recently fired gardener, hewed more closely to the concept of "propaganda by deed." In a letter-testament, he called on all anarchists to follow his example, which he deemed the only effective means of disseminating revolutionary ideas.

But it was the 1886 attack against the Paris Stock Exchange that truly foreshadowed the events to come. Its perpetrator, a former notary's clerk named Charles Gallo (1859–1887), had previously been convicted of counterfeiting and later espoused libertarian beliefs. In 1886, he decided to carry out the attack, for which he prepared carefully. Twice he scouted out the area, later borrowing a gun from a friend and obtaining a bottle of vitriol. On March 5, he threw the bottle onto the floor of the Exchange from one of the galleries and fired several shots at employees. No one was killed, which was a great disappointment to Gallo, who said at his trial: "Regrettably, I did not kill anyone." However, he took advantage of the opportunity to expound on his theories on the need to resort to "propaganda by deed." Gallo was sentenced to twenty years in a penal colony, where he soon died.

From 1892 to 1894, the use of dynamite in France reached its apex. Some ten attacks took place, not all of which were successful and which public opinion viewed with varying degrees of approval. In 1893, a bombing in Marseille targeted General Voulgrenant, and in 1894, an explosive device was placed in front of the Printemps department store in Paris. Newspapers put out a new section headlined "Dynamite." Fake bomb threats were not uncommon, as reflected in Michelet's humorous drawings in *L'Illustration*. People lived in a state of abject fear of further attacks.

On March 11, 1892, an explosion shook the house of Judge Benoît, located at 136 Boulevard Saint-Germain. Despite the fact that no one was killed, the attack came to be seen as the first major act of terrorism. Its perpetrator, arrested on March 30, became the symbol of nineteenth-century French anarchist terrorism. François-Claudius Koenigstein (1859–1892), otherwise known as Ravachol, had been a nonpolitical prisoner who had subsequently attempted to justify his actions on the basis of anarchist theories. Indeed, Ravachol had been tried in 1891 for having desecrated the grave of the baroness of Rochetaillé, hoping to find valuable jewelry, and for the June 1891 murder of an elderly recluse, whom he had also robbed. With the police on his trail, he fled to Spain, seeking refuge with another exile, Paul Bernard. It was probably in Barcelona that he learned bomb-making.

In August 1891, he went to Paris under an assumed name and met up with other Paris anarchists. There he met the wife of Henri Louis Descamps, a militant who had been arrested following the May 1 demonstration in Clichy. During that demonstration, the police had tried to seize the anarchists' red flag, and a violent altercation had ensued. Three of the rioters were beaten by the police and, on August 28, 1891, sentenced to long prison terms. Disgusted by the trial's outcome, Ravachol decided to take revenge against Benoît, the presiding judge, and against Public Prosecutor Bulot. He stole some dynamite from a quarry, and, with Judge Benoît in mind as a victim, assembled his first "infernal machine"—also known as an "infernal cauldron,"[12] using a detonator made of fulminate and filled with bullets.

The second bomb was made up of 120 grams of nitroglycerin, along with saltpeter and pulverized coal, in a mixture of nitric and sulfuric acid. It exploded on March 27, 1891, at the home of Public Prosecutor Bulot on the rue de Clichy, wounding five people and causing significant material damage.

While eating dinner at the Véry restaurant, Ravachol gave himself away by talking too freely with a waiter, Jules Lhérot, who turned him in a few days later. He received life in prison for the bombings and was sentenced to death for the murder of the elderly man. He was guillotined on July 11, 1892, at Montbrison, at the age of 33. Some anarchists saw him as a kind of "violent Christ"—the harbinger of a new era.[13]

In keeping with the anarchist tradition, Ravachol was himself avenged a month after his arrest by Théodule Meunier, who blew up the restaurant where Ravachol had been betrayed. Two people, including the owner, were killed in the explosion. At his trial, Meunier was also found guilty in connection with the March 15, 1892, bombing of the Lobau Barracks—infamous as the site of Communard massacres.

Nonetheless, Ravachol's actions were copied, serving as inspiration for the anarchist Léon-Jules Léauthier. On November 13, 1893, armed with a knife, Léauthier went to the Bouillon Duval restaurant determined to kill "the first bourgeois he saw," who turned out to be the Serbian minister Georgevitch.

The spate of attacks had created an atmosphere of widespread insecurity and the sense of a looming threat, and there was thus a strong response to the bombing of the Palais-Bourbon by Auguste Vaillant (1861–1894). Vaillant, long a committed anarchist, had for a time espoused socialist beliefs and later joined the group Les Révoltés. He tried his hand at various professions but never could manage to eke out a decent living. He left for Argentina dreaming of a better life, but returned to Paris three years later, in March 1893. There he married and had a child. But he was unable to support his family—a situation he found unbearable. He considered suicide as a way out of his misery, but, as he said at his trial, he wanted to die a useful death, one that would symbolize "the cry of a whole class that demands its rights and will soon add acts to words." After assembling a bomb in a hotel room on the rue Daguerre, on December 9, 1893, he went to the Chamber of Deputies and hurled it from the gallery into the Chamber itself. The bomb was not very powerful and wounded only one deputy, but his goal had been achieved: from that point on, the government understood that it was being targeted directly by the anarchists.

During his trial in December 1893, Vaillant effectively conveyed the anarchists' hatred of social injustice: "I shall at least have the satisfaction of having wounded the existing society, this cursed society in which one may see a single man spending, uselessly, enough to feed thousands of families; an infamous society that permits a few individuals to monopolize social wealth. . . . Tired of leading this life of suffering and cowardice, I carried this bomb to those who are primarily responsible for social misery."

Two weeks after his execution, which took place on February 5, 1894, the police were notified by mail of the suicide of a man named Rabardy. Two different locations were specified—two hotels, one in the faubourg Saint-Jacques and the other on rue Saint-Martin. But it was a trap; the hotel room doors were hooked up to bombs, set to go off and kill investigating police officers. Both bombings were traced to Amédée Pauwels (1864–1894), a Belgian anarchist who was very active in the Saint-Denis anarchist groups. But he never had the chance to confess; on March 15, 1895, as he was entering the Church of La Madeleine in Paris, a bomb he was carrying exploded, killing him.

But while all the aforementioned terrorists claimed to have acted in the name of anarchism, none of them reflected the massive upheaval caused by terrorism in the late nineteenth century as clearly as Émile Henry.

ÉMILE HENRY: ADVOCATE OF MASS TERRORISM

Although he had been admitted to the Paris École polytechnique, Émile Henry (1872–1894) abandoned his studies, deciding instead to devote himself to anarchist propaganda. At the outset, he opposed the use of dynamite, condemning Ravachol's bombings because they had killed innocent people. "A true anarchist kills his enemy; he does not blow up houses in which there are women, children, workers and servants." But the August 1892 miners' strike in Carmaux was probably the deciding factor in Henry's shift toward the use of terrorism. When the mining company flatly refused to negotiate, he decided that it was his duty to avenge the miners, to prove that "only anarchists were capable of self-sacrifice."

Henry scouted out the area, and, on November 8, 1892, placed a time bomb in the offices of the Carmaux mining company at 11 avenue de l'Opéra in Paris. The bomb was discovered and taken by an officer to the police station located on the rue des Bons-Enfants, where it exploded, killing five people. Although Henry's act, aimed as it was at a capitalist company, can be categorized as "targeted" terrorism, it is clear that had the bomb exploded in the building, it might have wounded or killed passers-by. He had considered that possibility before taking action—unlike Ravachol, who later expressed regret for having killed innocent people. At his trial, Émile Henry said that "the building was inhabited only by the bourgeois; hence there would be no innocent victims. The bourgeoisie as a whole lives by the exploitation of the unfortunate, and the bourgeoisie as a whole should expiate its crimes."

Henry's second attempt was indeed aimed directly at the bourgeoisie as a whole. On February 12, 1894, he bombed the Café Terminus at the Gare Saint-Lazare in Paris, killing one person and injuring more than twenty others, in addition to causing considerable material damage. The bombing was a response to the measures taken by the government against anarchists following the Palais-Bourbon explosion. Henry explained as follows why he had carried out a mass attack: "The bourgeoisie did not distinguish among the anarchists . . . the persecution was a mass one . . . and since you hold a whole party responsible for the actions of a single man, and strike indiscriminately, we, too, strike indiscriminately."

Émile Henry was arrested a few days later and executed on May 21 1894. Public opinion considered his crimes to be those of a madman, and anarchist intellectuals condemned his actions. Maurice Barrès, who witnessed Henry's execution by guillotine, aptly summed up the problem posed by actions of that kind and the means to combat them: "It was a psychological error to execute Émile Henry. You have created for him the destiny to which he aspired. . . . The struggle against ideas should be waged at the psychological level and not through measures that are only secondary [those of the politician and the executioner]."

The end of the era of attacks against individuals was marked by the assassination of Sadi Carnot in June 1894. The anarchist movement was severely suppressed under the so-called *lois scélérates* (iniquitous laws) passed in 1893–94, and in 1894, a number of alleged anarchists were tried on charges of criminal conspiracy, among them key figures in the movement.[14] Most doctrinaire libertarians condemned the major attacks of the era. As the nineteenth century neared its close, the anarchist Émile Pouget (1860–1931) called for an end to "propaganda by deed" and for the use of less violent methods.

Anarchist terrorist acts in the nineteenth century had some very specific characteristics. They were carried out at the individual level and their logistical requirements, in terms of financing and training, were minimal. No networks existed to devise a strategy of terror at the national or international levels, so terrorists acted on the basis of their personal feelings. Suppression of a workers' movement might motivate one, while another might wish to avenge a comrade.

Recourse to "propaganda by deed" began to take on international dimensions. In addition to the numerous bombings in France, Spain, and Italy, the "language of bombs" spread to parts of the world with active anarchist movements, such as Germany, Belgium, and Argentina. The major media, for the first time, devoted extensive coverage to anarchist terrorism. Hence the discrepancy between the number of victims— eleven people were killed in France between 1892 and 1894—and the extent of the resulting publicity.

As the new century dawned, libertarian thinkers as a whole began to reconsider the effectiveness of such acts of violence. In Europe and in the Americas, anarchist rebellion evolved from "propaganda by deed," with a brief foray into the practice of "repossession" by individuals—that is to say, theft using anarchism as a justification—to the definitive adoption of the doctrine of anarcho-syndicalism by the various libertarian federations.

NOTES TO CHAPTER 6

1. During the London World Exhibition of 1862, French and English workers embarked on a dialogue with a view to achieving international solidarity and creating an autonomous organization of the proletariat, leading to the founding of the International Workingmen's Association at a meeting of delegations from various countries on September 28, 1864.

2. See Bakunin, *Oeuvres.*

3. Brousse, "Propagande par le fait."

4. Throughout this article, political assassination should be understood to mean politically motivated murder—not in the legal sense of the term, which, in defining political assassination, does not require such a motive to be present.

5. Canovas was probably murdered out of revenge. He had condemned to death five Spanish anarchists in connection with an attack on June 7, 1896.

6. The French theoretician Georges Sorel (1847–1922) advocated general strikes as a means of action, an example of revolutionary violence.

7. Following the Haymarket events, the police arrested eight notorious anarchists, whose trial was very controversial. Anarchists saw it as the trial of the anarchist movement, and socialists proclaimed a day of commemoration, which was how May 1 came to be International Workers' Day.

8. Goldman, *Living My Life.*

9. President McKinley was assassinated in 1901 at the Buffalo Exposition in New York State, during a speaking tour.

10. The first law targeting anarchists was the New York State Criminal Anarchy Law.

11. A contemporary police report names Kropotkin, Elisée Reclus, and P. Martin de Vienne.

12. The name "infernal cauldron" came about because an ordinary cooking pot was used to make that type of bomb.

13. The May 1894 issue of *Père Peinard*, an anarchist publication written in street slang, ran an illustration depicting him as such.

14. The first *loi scélérate*, enacted on December 11, 1893, targeted the anarchist press. The second, also enacted in 1893, targeted libertarian groups. The third (July 1894) made anarchism a crime.

CHAPTER 7

RUSSIAN TERRORISM, 1878–1908

Yves Ternon

Terrorism was a latecomer to the revolutionary movement in late nineteenth- and early twentieth-century Russia. Its proponents were convinced that it was necessary and included it in an arsenal that ranged from propaganda to armed uprising. Some saw it as a tactic and others as a strategy, but in everyone's view, it was simultaneously ideological, political, and ethical in nature. Its use was rarely the result of one person's decision; it was the outcome of a team effort, which presupposed plotting, decision-making, and lengthy preparation. The man or woman whom a revolutionary group designated to strike was merely the person in the best position to do so. Everyone participating in a terrorist action knew that they were taking a great risk and that death was the most likely outcome. And the tsarist police were formidably effective: attempts failed more often than they succeeded. Ultimately, the desired effect—raising the consciousness of the Russian people—was not achieved. Political killings did not kindle the spark that set Russia ablaze, and they did little to make those in power enact reforms. To the contrary, they led to increasingly harsh reprisals. Yet, at the same time, tsarist rule was shaken by the repeated terrorist strikes; although these were not the direct cause of its sudden collapse in 1917, they were certainly a factor.

We need to be careful in interpreting the history of this period. In seeking to write a linear history of the Russian revolutionary movement and to depict the Bolsheviks as its sole legitimate heirs, Soviet historians distorted the picture by erasing anything that did not reflect doctrine. At the outset, the Social Democratic movement was opposed to terrorism, while its main political adversary, the Socialist Revolutionary Party, often favored its use. In fact, terrorism as a means of struggle was employed at only two points in the Russian revolutionary movement, and then by two groups that were part of the same continuum: Narodnaya Volya (The People's Will) and the Socialist Revolutionary Party, both of which emerged because of the Russian revolutionary movement's split into two factions (the second of which gave rise to the Social Democratic Party). As to those matters of doctrine, the first was that the Socialist Revolutionary Party should be viewed as a party of terrorists. The second was that pre-Social-Democratic opposition to tsarism should be reduced to mere terrorism, although in fact it took many forms. The nihilists; the propagandists who "went to the people"; the earliest Russian anarchists: these were not terrorists. The rioting peasants; the insurgent workers; the rebellious soldiers and sailors: these were not terrorists. Theoreticians of Russian socialism and revolution only rarely advocated terrorism as the best way to topple the tsar—and when, like Mikhail Bakunin, they did, their words were not matched by deeds. And Russian terrorists were atheists: they sacrificed their lives for others, with no expectation of any reward in the next world.

The Russian revolutionary movement was a vast assemblage, where differing theories and ideas led onto diverse paths, which in turn quickly forked, after following sometimes tortuous routes. These paths were lined with groups, associations, and circles whose members easily moved from one organization to another, spurred by their beliefs of the moment. Some of these people kept away from terrorism; others took it up or dropped it, sometimes condemning its use. A terrorist's career could easily end in death, deportation, or exile. Many revolutionaries never participated in an act of terrorism. Vera Zasulich[1]—who initiated the period of Russian terrorism with an act that was spontaneous, not ordered by a group—was a former comrade of Sergei Nechayev's and later became a populist propagandist. After her 1876 attack on Dmitry Trepov, the governor-general of Saint Petersburg, she opposed terrorism from within Cherny Peredel (Black Repartition), a forerunner of the Social Democratic Party, of which she was a founding member. She remained a determined foe of terrorism, later joining the party's Menshevik faction.

In contrast, the career of Sofia Perovskaya provides an example of an evolution toward terrorism. Perovskaya was a young aristocrat who became first a propagandist, then a terrorist; she remained firm in her beliefs until her death on the scaffold for her part in the assassination of Tsar Alexander II in 1881.

Orbiting around the terrorists were spies, provocateurs, and traitors, paid or controlled by the police, and many ideologues—including the nihilists and the early anarchists—who called for the use of terror but did not themselves practice it. The historian of Russian terrorism has a complex world to understand. That complexity reflects the mentality of the protagonists as much as it does the events themselves.

Still, the central theme of Russian terrorism remains the struggle against tsarist despotism; its convictions were the same as those later held by twentieth-century terrorists. In opposition to state terrorism that enjoyed total impunity, they offered true, immanent justice, which they proposed to deploy against those who embodied such terrorism, whom they condemned as the hangmen of the people. Legitimate questions can be raised about their moral right to take such action, but they cannot be condemned as indiscriminate murderers.

This account of Russian terrorism seeks neither to justify these crimes nor to rehabilitate those who committed them. It seeks rather to relate what took place during that period in Russia and to analyze the revolutionary movement in that country—a movement marked by diversity—and the role that terrorism played in it.

THE POPULISTS

With the historiography he ordered up, Stalin broke the continuity of the Russian revolutionary movement. He divided it into "positive" revolutionaries (the precursors of the Social Democratic Party) and "negative" revolutionaries (a catchall that included all terrorists). In the West, on the other hand, some historians aimed at creating a liberal tradition opposed to the populist revolutionary tradition—which was accused of having lost Russia its chance at democracy. Such conflicting views cannot obscure the fact that between 1848 and 1881, Russian socialism was populist in nature, and that this populism rested on the Russian peasantry. The top priority for the various Russian revolutionary groupings was the peasant community: the *obshchina* or *mir*. The peasant commune was the legacy of ancient Slavic structures. There were two sides to it—an ambivalence that no revolutionary movement was ever able to overcome. On the one hand, the *mir* was rooted in serfdom, and this feudal status was imprinted on the peasant mentality. On the other, it was egalitarian and contained the seeds of peasant socialism.

The 1917 Russian Revolution was the logical culmination of a movement whose first public manifestation was the Decembrist uprising of

December 14, 1825, which, in some measure, was an outcome of the Napoleonic wars: young Russian officers in Paris during the allied occupation of 1814 came into contact with the ideas of the French Revolution. One of them, Pavel Ivanovich Pestel, was the first revolutionary to propose a radical change in the tsarist system—on a republican, socialist footing, and founded on solidarity within the peasant commune. Pestel was radical in his choice of means to that end: he was in favor of eliminating the imperial family. When the Decembrist insurrection had failed and he had been sentenced to death, Pestel expressed only one regret: having "wanted to reap before he had sown."

This first blow against despotism roused the Russian intelligentsia. In spite of that, the thirty-year reign of Tsar Nicholas I (1825–55), which followed the Decembrist uprising, was notable for merciless repression. Speech—spoken and written—was scrutinized by the dreaded and formidable political police of the Third Section; ideas of liberty could rarely be expressed except outside the country. Under Nicholas, there was only one political trial, in 1849: that of the Petrashevtsy, whose inspiration was slavophile and Fourierist-utopian. The "sowing" was done by emigrants. The oath taken by Alexander Herzen and Nikolai Ogarev in 1840 to dedicate their lives to the cause of freedom may have been sworn in Moscow's Sparrow Hills, but it would be fulfilled abroad.

Herzen was the founder of Russian populism. He merged the thinking of the Enlightenment with the principles of the Decembrists. He placed before the Russian intelligentsia a question that would remain central to its ponderings: Should the serfs be freed with or without the land? Here he distanced himself from the slavophiles and the French utopians, who represented the two original trends in pre-1848 Russian socialism. Herzen thought that in Russia, through the *obshchina,* it would be possible to develop a specifically Russian brand of socialism and to skip the stage of bourgeois revolution for which the European uprisings of 1848 were to be the preparation. For Herzen, the only solution was freedom together with land: land and freedom. This was the topic that, with Ogarev's help, he would develop in his journal *Kolokol (The Bell),* which from 1857 was printed in London and which was widely distributed in Russia. The Crimean War of 1853–56, in which Russia faced an Anglo-French-Ottoman coalition, ended in a rout for Russia. Reform of society was a matter of urgency: that was the conclusion that the new tsar, Alexander II (his father, Nicholas I, had died in 1855), drew from this defeat. Serfdom was abolished by the Emancipation Edict of February 19, 1861.[2] Peasants could buy the land they worked. Herzen called on the intelligentsia to explain to country people that even if these purchases bankrupted the peasants, the cost would be lower than that of a rebellion. He urged university students to "go to the people" to show them that it was not enough to gain land and freedom: they had to get an education as well. But Herzen had lost contact with reality: in the countryside, the first people who could be roused were those who already knew how to read, and those people were members of sects.

The two approaches—that of the intellectuals and that of the sects—were incompatible. The roots of the Russian peasantry were steeped in the spirit of Old Russia: nationalist, religious, reactionary, xenophobic, anti-Semitic, and barbarous. Because Herzen did not grasp this conflict, his influence declined. He continued to give priority to social reform rather than to the in-depth political reform demanded by the populist movement he had initiated.

It was Nikolai Gavrilovich Chernyshevsky who outlined the action that the populists would take. He was first a contributor to, then the editor of, *Sovremennik (Contemporary),* the old journal founded by Pushkin in 1836; in the 1860s, it was a forum for liberalism. Chernyshevsky summed up his platform in a single question: Could socialism succeed in Russia before the development of capitalism? Put another way, was it possible to avoid destroying the collectivist tradition of the Russian peasant community? He argued that it would be pointless to eliminate the *obshchina* only to rebuild it after the victory of socialism. By 1859, Chernyshevsky knew that this peaceful course would lead nowhere. A "Letter from the Provinces" addressed to Herzen—anonymous, but probably written by Nikolai Dobroliubov—concluded: "You have done everything possible to help bring about a peaceful resolution of the problem. Now change your tone! Let your *Bell* no longer be a call to prayer! Let it be a tocsin! Call on Russia to take up its axes!"[3] A number of small clandestine groups clustered around *Sovremennik* opposed the reformist trend emerging among the nobility. While stating their desire for democracy, these early populists sought to create a strong revolutionary organization, and they advocated the use of violence. Chernyshevsky's novel *Chto Dyelat? (What Is to Be Done?)*—written in 1862 in the Peter and Paul Fortress, where the writer was imprisoned—would become the bible of the young populist intelligentsia. The novel's hero is a determined foe of absolutism and proposes the creation of cooperatives.

Dobroliubov, who died in 1861 at the age of twenty-five, had earlier stated the views set out in Chernyshevsky's prophetic vision. He had stressed the importance of reforming the political mind-set and the need to move from the world of dreams exemplified in Ivan Alexandrovich Goncharov's 1859 novel *Oblomov* to the world of action—as well as the need to think before acting. By effecting a break between generations—between parents and children—Dobroliubov and Chernyshevsky enabled intellectuals to take the path of the people.

The first populist activists came from the universities. In 1853, students numbered no more than three thousand throughout the Russian empire, but the academic world was transformed following the death of Nicholas I. The gates of the universities were opened, and the first women were admitted. Students held meetings and published newspapers. A shared consciousness emerged, and political subjects were discussed. The holding of the first demonstration, in 1861, led to the closing of several universities that were viewed as hotbeds of subversion. These were reopened soon afterward, however, and calm prevailed until 1869. The first Zemlya i Volya (Land and Freedom) organization, founded in late 1861 by a young nobleman, N. A. Serno-Solovyevich, was the first link in the chain of the populist tradition. Its motto echoed the phrase of Ogarev, whose reply to the question "What do the people need?" was "Land and freedom." The Zemlya i Volya manifesto was published in 1862 in *Molodaya Rossiya* (Young Russia). Now Russia was in a revolutionary period. Zemlya i Volya, the first such clandestine organization in Russia since the Decembrists, was a collection of small groups that first emerged in the provinces. Several of these groups moved away from the populist tradition and adopted anarchist or libertarian positions. In March 1863, the association of students from Kazan who were studying in Moscow requested its members to go on a walk to the people. In the course of their pilgrimage, the young people distributed tracts, but they did not establish any contact with the people. Still, the Polish committee to spark a peasant revolt in Russia relied on this group. Its conspirators were denounced to the Third Section and were arrested. The Russian army's crushing of the Polish insurrection dashed the hopes that had been aroused by the 1862 Emancipation Edict. The tsar's desire for change was spent with the administrative reforms (the creation of the *zemstvo*—local assembly—system) and judicial reforms undertaken in 1864, and the authorities were engaged in Russifying the empire.

Nikolai Ishutin's organization, which lasted from 1864 to 1866, was more directly linked with the revolutionary perspective of Chernyshevsky's *What Is to Be Done?* "[Russian] terrorism thrust its roots into this amalgam of revolutionary Machiavellianism and full-blown populism."[4] The Machiavellianism of Ishutin's student followers lay in their view that the revolutionary movement was not mature enough to replace the state, and that only the execution of the autocratic tsar would trigger a social revolution. They formed a secret society known as The Organization. At its center was a cell called Hell, whose purpose was to carry out terrorism against the government and the landowners. The members of Hell were ascetics who broke all ties with the outside world and lived in deep hiding—all the while keeping a watchful eye on the rest of The Organization. The notion of an attack on the tsar was gaining ground. Ishutin's cousin Dmitry Karakozov announced to his friends that he had decided to kill Alexander II. His friends urged him to change his mind, arguing that the people were not ready: the people viewed the tsar as a mythic figure and, following the Emancipation Edict, saw him as their liberator. Karakozov ignored them and on April 4, 1866, he fired on Alexander II as he was stepping into his carriage. His pistol was turned aside by a drunken peasant who was passing by. This was the first attack by a man of the people against the emperor of all the Russias. The reaction, unleashed by the "hangman" of Warsaw, General M. N. Muraviev, was violent: the White Terror tore the still-fragile roots of the revolutionary movement from the soil of the Russian intelligentsia. Thus, from 1855 to 1875, the first twenty years of Alexander II's reign, the revolutionary movement, while rich in ideas, proclamations, and plans, was still trying to find a course and had no success in breaking through to the peasantry. This period saw the growth of nihilism and of the anarchist movement—two distinct trends within populism—as well as the appearance of Nechayev.

NIHILISM AND ANARCHISM

Nihilism is a philosophical and literary movement that was developed in the 1860s through Dimitri Pisarev's journal *Russkoe Slovo (The Russian Word)*. The idea behind it is absolute individualism: "the negation, in the name of individual freedom, of all obligations imposed on the individual by society, the family, and religion."[5] Nihilism assailed all that lacked a basis in pure reason. Turgenev coined the term "nihilist," with polemical intent, in his 1862 novel *Fathers and Sons,* whose hero, Bazarov, condemns prejudice and believes only in reason and science. The populists were neither the siblings nor the offspring of Bazarov—who despised the people. The nihilists believed in nothing; they recognized no authority and rejected all accepted values. The revolutionaries, on the other hand, believed in the people and fought for human rights. Nihilism led to political radicalism; it was among the sources both of Russian anarchism and of the Jacobinism of the populist Pyotr Tkachev.

Like liberalism and socialism, anarchism was a response to centralization imposed by the development of capitalism, but it offered a third way. Its followers called for a revolution that would abolish all authority and create a society based on voluntary cooperation among free individuals. Anarchism was inspired by Bakunin; its doctrine was influenced by Proudhon: suppression of the state, collectivization of the means of production and preservation of individual freedom. Bakunin saw total revolution as a massive uprising—both in the cities and in the countryside—of all the oppressed, who had nothing to lose but their chains. In Russia, anarchism was a product of Nicholas I's despotism, but its antecedents lay in the religious sects. Ideas approaching those of anarchism were also spread by the slavophiles, who were against the bureaucratic state and its centralization, as well as through the socialism of Herzen, who refused to sacrifice individual freedom for the sake of abstract theories. Despite this rich Russian peasant tradition, however, no revolutionary anarchist movement developed in Russia until the twentieth century.[6] It was the "Nechayevism" episode that caused the misunderstanding that led to the association of populism with nihilism and with anarchism.

"Nechayev's importance should be gauged not by his influence—which was brief, sporadic and short-lived—but by his keen and prophetic vision of the revolutionary struggle."[7] Positioned at the confluence of populism, anarchism, and nihilism, Nechayev proclaimed the dictatorship of a small circle of revolutionaries. He was a major figure in the Russian revolution, opening a chapter of action in the revolution and making terrorism a means of taking such action. In an extreme form, the "Revolutionary Catechism" (see chapter 5 epigraph) that Nechayev wrote with Bakunin in 1869 expresses the ideas that were developing in Ishutin's circle. It demands action and ridicules the armchair doctrinaires and products of university corruption who pressed for revolution but were incapable of carrying it out.[8]

It was Nechayev who induced Bakunin to accept terrorism in his *Principles of Revolution* as a way of preparing the ground for revolution. When Nechayev returned to Moscow in 1869, he formed a small group known as The Axe, whose single grand gesture was the murder of one of its own members: a student named Ivanov, who had groundlessly been accused of being an informer. To escape justice in the wake of this crime, Nechayev fled to Europe. He was extradited in 1872 and imprisoned for life but remained in contact with members of the populist revolutionary movement. After Ivanov's murder, Bakunin realized that he had been duped by Nechayev, whom he accused of being a swindler and black-mailer, and whom he viewed as extremely dangerous. And dangerous he was—like Shigalov in Dostoyevsky's *The Possessed* (also translated as *The Devils* and as *Demons*), who could defend any and all methods in the name of unrestricted freedom. Nechayev was not the precursor of the Russian terrorists. His doctrine that everything was permitted gave rise to the totalitarian revolutions of the twentieth century, in which certain individuals would introduce state terrorism and use ideas to justify millions of crimes. For their part, the Russian terrorists killed and then paid for their crimes. Nechayev heralded the dictatorship advocated by Pyotr Tkachev. Tkachev was among the first to make Marx's historical materialism known in Russia and to introduce it into the debate that was under way in populist circles. As a disciple of Chernyshevsky, whom he considered to be the founding father of the Social Revolutionary Party in Russia, he was in contact with members of the groups that were active in Saint Petersburg in the 1860s, including Karakozov and Nechayev. He formed a political view centered on the idea that social revolution would be possible in Russia only if the development of capitalism were halted. By toppling those in power, it would be possible to prevent Russia from following in the footsteps of the Western countries. The revolution would take place in two stages; the first, to be sure, would destroy, but the second would build. Those two stages could be realized only by a homogeneous, disciplined, hierarchical organization acting according to a predetermined plan; only such an organization could carry the people with it. Here, Tkachev's view ran counter to Bakunin's individualism. But the populist movement, haunted by Nechayev's excesses, would no more accept his Jacobinism than Bakunin's anarchism. The populists wanted to "go to the people." And the currents would carry them there.

THE PROPAGANDISTS

When the populist movement, which had been badly damaged by the White Terror, reemerged in the early 1870s, it drew its inspiration from yet another ideologue: Pyotr Lavrov (1823–1900). His *Historical Letters,* written under the pseudonym Mirtov, explained to the students that they must go to the people in the villages; they should mix with them in order to teach them socialism. But they must not forget the working people, because the solidarity of the workers was key. Lavrov too advocated social revolution carried out in stages. The first stage would be to train revolutionary socialist activists among the intelligentsia, who would then go out into the countryside to rally the best forces among the people. He set out this program in his journal *Vperyod* (Forward), whose first issue was published in Zurich in August 1873.

Thus, the Russian revolutionary movement revived in the 1870s. The Paris Commune prompted Russian socialists to leave their studies and discussion groups and travel to the workshops and villages—in other words, to move to action. The populists might have broken with Bakunin and Tkachev, but they were by no means diehard disciples of Lavrov. They were young and impatient, and eager to get to work immediately on behalf of the people. One early group was formed by Mark Natanson in the Saint Petersburg Academy of Medicine and Surgery. When Natanson was arrested in November 1871, his place was taken by the twenty-year-old Nikolai Chaikovsky (1851–1926). The Chaikovtsi, as they were called, had the single goal of propagandizing among the peasants and workers. They were the first to make ethics a priority in revolutionary action: they wanted to live their ideals; they aspired to purity and were ready to make the ultimate sacrifice. Chaikovsky called on them to be "as clean and clear as a mirror."

The Chaikovtsi fanned out in the provinces, as well as in Moscow, Odessa, and Kiev. Thirty-seven provinces were "contaminated" by revolutionary propaganda. The group took final form in 1871 with the arrival of Sofia Perovskaya, who took charge of the bookshop and of propaganda; of Dimitri Klements, who handled book distribution; and of the Kornilov sisters. It was marked by the role that women played. The struggle for women's emancipation had begun in Zurich, where hundreds of student victims of repression had come as refugees—particularly young women, who were barred from Russian universities. To halt this emigration, the Russian government issued a ukase in 1873 that declared any Russian subject who did not immediately leave Zurich an outlaw. The students returned en masse, providing the revolutionary movement with a corps of activists. In the "Mad Summer" of 1874, hundreds, perhaps thousands of young people, alone or in small groups, left the cities and traveled from village to village, especially in the areas where the great uprisings led by Stenka Razin and by Pugachev, in 1670 and 1773 respectively, had begun, moving southward and following the great rivers. They wanted to teach the people, but also to see how they lived and to learn from them; they wanted to learn a trade and ply it in a village. This crusade among the people took place openly; indeed, it could not be clandestine in an environment where no secret could be kept. The government could easily destroy it through mass arrests. In this way, a whole generation of revolutionaries was born.

THE SECOND ZEMLYA I VOLYA

The propagandists' crusade among the peasants was doomed to failure. They hadn't realized that their culture ran counter to that of the countryside, and that the only thing they had in common with its people was their language. Turgenev's 1877 novel *Virgin Soil* explained this to them. Such was the ambiguity of "going to the people." The collectivist and egalitarian nature of the *mir* had misled the populists; they had embellished it with the whole gamut of libertarian virtues. In fact, it had been infiltrated by Old Believer sects; it was a closed world, focused on its faith and its superstitions; and the myth of the tsar as Redeemer was as much alive as it had been in Pugachev's time.

Only once did they attain success: at Chigirin, near Kiev. Three activists had the idea of fabricating a spurious manifesto in the name of the tsar to make the peasants believe that the emperor had granted their demands, and to encourage them to form an organization to struggle against the landowners and seize their property. The "secret legion" they formed won some 2,000 recruits before it was exposed in 1877.

Among the workers, on the other hand, the propaganda sown in the 1860s blossomed in the 1870s. This success was first of all the result of a change caused by the shift from corporatism (a legacy of the peasant *artel*) to a union-based approach; here, the propagandists helped workers to shed their peasant mentality. The first Kiev Workers' Union was broken up, but it was reconstituted in Zurich as the All-Russian Social Revolutionary Organization, whose action was focused on propaganda and agitation among the workers and whose goal was to create a structure that could unite spontaneous movements. Its members were arrested upon their return to Moscow in 1875.

The failure of propaganda among the peasants and the destruction of the workers' organizations made the populists rethink their methodology and become a party operating in strict secrecy. In Saint Petersburg, one early group of surviving Chaikovtsi organized itself around Mark Natanson, who had escaped internal exile, his wife, Olga, and Alexei Oboleshev. Alexandr Mikhailov, who joined them, was of a different generation, one too young to have "gone to the people." To stress their clandestine nature, the conspirators called themselves the Troglodytes. They met with groups based in the provinces, and it became clear to them that a genuine party would have to be formed. The platform of the Social Revolutionary Party, which took the name of the former Zemlya i Volya, was slow to be formulated. The Troglodytes took up the ideas of the Old-Russia movement of the *raskol,* or schism, and once they had come in contact with the sects, they began to weigh the possibilities of agrarian terrorism. They envisioned kindling peasant uprisings. The platform was repeatedly revised before its final version in spring 1878. The party advocated the use of political terror to disrupt the government. The fact is, though, that in the period 1876–78, Zemlya i Volya boasted no more than thirty-five members.

In 1875, they took action to free imprisoned comrades, including the future anarchist Pyotr Kropotkin (1842–1921). And in 1875–77, there were hundreds to be freed. Some of these operations were organized by Sofia Perovskaya. In *Vperyod,* Lavrov published a regular column detailing these escapes. Although the escape operations were a success, demonstrations had to be quickly dropped following the mass arrest of demonstrators on Saint Petersburg's Kazan Square in December 1876. Those demonstrators were tried and sentenced in January 1877. Like those trials, the trial of 193 party members, which ran from October 1877 to January 1878, helped inform the public about the courage and selflessness of these sons and daughters of the Russian people. Although they were held behind closed doors, the trials enhanced the revolutionaries' prestige in Russian society.

At the same time, the government was arranging for the trial of the propagandists. The first, of fifty members of the Moscow Society arrested in 1874, took place in February–March 1877. Unlike previous trials, this one was held in public, which enabled the Russian public to see that these young people were prepared to make sacrifices. "The propagandists wanted nothing for themselves. They personified the purest self-abnegation. . . . If he could not change [society], he should die. And another had already taken his place,"[9] wrote Sergei Mikhailovich Kravchinsky, also known as Stepniak.

The underground Russian press also kept the public informed about the status of detainees in prison and about police violence; the first such print shop was set up in Saint Petersburg by Aron Zundelevich. One prison incident unleashed a protest movement: a Kazan Square demonstrator, Alexei Bogoliubov, had been beaten on the orders of the governor-general of Saint Petersburg, Trepov, because he had not saluted the latter when he visited the prison. The Organization was considering action against Trepov, but, without telling anyone, a young woman, Vera Zasulich, went to the palace, joined a crowd of petitioners and shot and wounded him. She was quickly put on trial in criminal court. The courtroom was crowded with government ministers, generals, and writers, among other spectators. Zasulich's defense attorney, Pyotr Alexandrov, sought to put the government on trial: he denounced Trepov's cruelty and justified his client's action: "Bogoliubov's tormentor required not the moans of physical pain, but those of the outraged human spirit, of trampled human dignity. Sacrilege was committed. The shameful sacrifice was carried out. Solemnly, a Russian martyrdom [of Bogoliubov] by caning was organized."[10] Vera Zasulich was acquitted unanimously. Spectators applauded the verdict. And once freed, the young woman succeeded in evading the police officers who were under orders from the tsar to arrest her as she left the court.

All of Europe, not just Russia, would be shaken by the shot fired from Zasulich's pistol. A "season of attacks" was triggered by her action. "Assassination attempts in Russia were something between partisan war and anarchist action; they were an attempt—at least partially successful—to unleash a political struggle and open the way to revolution; they were a manifestation of "propaganda by deed" rather than through isolated acts of protest. In short, Russian "terrorism" was but one aspect of the formation of a socialist-revolutionary party and of the beginning of a generalized crisis in Russian society."[11]

The winds of terrorism blew from the south: Russian terrorism first took organized form in Ukraine. Kiev saw the establishment of the Social Revolutionary Party's first Executive Committee, created by Valery Ossinsky in February 1878, which took the decision to disrupt the government by striking out at the means of oppression and at traitors. Its manifesto was distributed in a number of Russian cities; below, it bore a seal—an axe, a dagger, and a revolver, interlaced—and above, an inscription: Executive Committee of the Social Revolutionary Party. The committee ordered the execution of Alexei Matveyev, rector of the university, and Baron Hegking, deputy chief of police. In August of the same year, at Saint Petersburg, Stepniak stabbed General Mezentsev, head of the Third Section, while his accomplice Alexandr Barannikov fired on Mezentsev's aide-de-camp; the two fled in a carriage driven by Adrian Mikahilov. The attack took place two days after the execution of the terrorist Kovalsky at Odessa. "A death for a death," wrote Stepniak, who managed to escape in a fast carriage. Stepniak was a former member of the Chaikovtsi; he had sought refuge in Europe, where in 1876 he participated in the uprising in Herzegovina and then in the revolt in province of Benevento in Italy led by the anarchists Carlo Cafiero and Errico Malatesta (see chapter 6). He then returned to Russia and made contact with the Zemlya i Volya party. The government issued a denunciation of this "gang of malicious individuals" and set up a special commission consisting of the minister of justice, the minister of the interior, and the heads of the Third Section and of the police. The ukase of August 8, 1878, authorized the police to arrest whomever they wished.

From the very outset, the Social Revolutionary Party was divided on the question of terrorism. In its clandestine journal, *Zemlya i Volya,* Klements expressed his concern at seeing terrorists force the party's hand, even though they had been characterized as a protection team. But the majority of party activists felt that the government's repression left them only one option: to expand the use of terrorism. The party had moved from conspiracy to revolution, and political killing seemed the only means of self-defense. In early 1879, the southern Executive Committee was disbanded: Ossinsky and his group were arrested and, in May, those who had been found with weapons in their possession were hanged after a brief trial. These arrests did not put an end to the assassination attempts: on February 9, 1879, Grigory Goldenberg killed the governor of Kharkov, Evgeny Kropotkin (cousin of the anarchist prince of the same name); in March, Police Colonel Knoop was killed at Odessa; the spy Reinstein was executed in Moscow; and on March 13 in Saint Petersburg, Leonid Mirsky fired on the new head of the Third Section, General Boris Drenteln, but he missed and fled. The party set up clandestine printing presses and decided to turn to armed robbery to finance its activities; these were the first "expropriations."

Following Mirsky's failed attempt, Alexandr Soloviev decided to assassinate the tsar. He was to act on his own, but he asked for advice from two party leaders, Kviatkovsky and Alexandr Mikhailov, who hesitated before yielding to the young man's resolve. On April 2, 1879, when Alexander II was out for his morning walk, Soloviev fired six revolver shots at the tsar, but missed and was arrested. In prison, he attempted suicide by taking poison; he was quickly treated and lived to be tried. During the trial, he made a lengthy statement in which he outlined his career: "We, the socialist revolutionaries, have declared war on the government," he declared. On May 28, Soloviev was hanged before a large crowd, which included members of the international press. In a brief work published anonymously in Geneva, Pyotr Kropotkin described the day of the execution: "The cities murmured. And out there on the vast plains watered by the sweat of the still-enslaved laborer, in those grim villages where dire poverty stifled all hope, Soloviev's revolver shots became the cause of muffled unrest: the rumbles of insurrection—the precursor of revolution—were already to be heard."[12]

In fact, nothing of the kind occurred; as usual, the government responded to this act of terrorism by instituting a reign of terror. In six regions where the revolutionary movement had burgeoned—Saint Petersburg, Moscow, Kharkov, Kiev, Odessa, and Warsaw—power was put into the hands of military dictators, who carried out summary justice. Death sentences proliferated, especially in Odessa, where Count Eduard Totleben held sway as governor.

After Soloviev's attack, the Zemlya i Volya party debated the appropriateness of terrorism with a greater sense of urgency, and the previously suppressed internal conflict came out into the open. There had to be a meeting of the party's northern and southern groups. Twenty-five revolutionaries, most of them members of the Zemlya i Volya Executive Committee, met at the Lipetsk congress, held in secret from June 15 to 17. Nikolai Morozov justified terrorism; Georgi Plekhanov stated his disapproval; Mikhailov unleashed a violent indictment of the tsar. A new Executive Committee was formed. Then, the party members went to nearby Voronezh, where they met with former populists. The group of nineteen heard Andrei Zhelyabov argue in favor of terror. Zhelyabov set an immediate goal: the overthrow of absolutism through the assassination of the tsar. At that point, Plekhanov left the meeting. The Zemlya i Volya platform was read out and was adopted without amendment. The plan to assassinate the tsar was put to the vote and was adopted by a majority. By August 26, the Executive Committee had sentenced Alexander II to death. But following the Voronezh congress, several party members went back on the concessions they had made to terrorism. Alexandr Popov and Vera Zasulich followed Plekhanov. There was a breakdown, and that was the end of Zemlya i Volya. The party split into two factions: Cherny Peredel (Black Repartition) and Narodnaya Volya (The People's Will). The two groups divided up the party's assets; Cherny Peredel kept the underground printing shop. Cherny Peredel was in the populist tradition; its creed was equal distribution of the land among the serfs—the "blacks." At the same time, it was a bridge between the socialist propaganda of the 1870s and the social democratic movement that Plekhanov would later establish. Plekhanov's position was unambiguous: he believed that the situation was not conducive to insurrection and that neither the revolutionaries nor the people were ready either. That view was shared by Pavel Axelrod and Osip Aptekman: in the event of an uprising, the peasant masses would not support the revolutionary movement. If the revolt were victorious, it would only have replaced one order with another; the revolutionaries would have been working for the bourgeoisie.

NARODNAYA VOLYA

By 1880, terrorists were no longer solitary figures, but rather members of an organization that included them in jointly planned clandestine operations and assigned them specific tasks. A Narodnaya Volya terrorist knew that he or she was destined for death and accepted that fate as part of the price to be paid for the liberation of humankind. Stepniak defined the terrorist—whom he idealized—as "a convinced socialist" whose single goal was "bringing down this terrible despotism and giving his country the status of all civilized peoples: political freedom. Then he could work in perfect safety for his program of redemption."[13] To Narodnaya Volya, the Russian state was a monster that held more than half of the empire's territory as its private property. More than half of the peasants farmed for it. Narodnaya Volya would combat this monster in order to stop its power from being transferred to the bourgeoisie. The struggle had to begin immediately. "Now or never" was the order of the day. The *narodnovoltsy* were convinced that with a blow to the heart—the assassination of the tsar—the people would take control of the state. They remained populists, and they still conceived of the revolution as the conquest of the land by the *obshchina* and of the factories by the workers. They did not realize that the means they had chosen to achieve their goal—terrorism carried out by a handful of clandestine operatives—limited the spread of their ideas among the intelligentsia, and that the people would never understand their actions without this.

During the autumn and winter of 1879–80, Narodnaya Volya focused all its efforts on assassinating Alexander II. It had modified its approach: it abandoned individual revolver or knife attacks and opted instead for dynamite. N. I. Kibalchich devised a bomb that could be thrown at its target. He also suggested tunneling from adjoining buildings under streets that would be traversed by the imperial carriage and filling the tunnels with explosives. The first such tunnel was dug in May 1879, under the Bank of Kherson in Saint Petersburg, in order to finance the operation. In November of that year, the Executive Committee arranged a series of attacks on the rail line to be traveled by the imperial train returning the tsar to Saint Petersburg from his vacation in the Crimea. Three lines were mined. The first attack, planned by Kibalchich, Kviatkovsky, and Vera Figner, was at a grade crossing near Odessa; but the tsar traveled to Odessa by sea and did not use that rail line. The second, by a team led by Zhelyabov, was at Alexandrovsk, near Moscow; but the devices failed to explode. The third, by a nine-member group led by Alexandr Mikhailov and including Sofia Perovskaya, was nearer to Moscow; the second train in the convoy was blown up, but the tsar was traveling in the first. Stepan Khalturin, a carpenter who worked in the Winter Palace, volunteered his services to the Executive Committee, which accepted his offer. On February 5, 1880, he blew up a room in the palace, killing eleven and wounding fifty-six, but the tsar was not there.

The tsar was frightened and could not decide between two responses, one liberal and the other repressive. In the end, he chose both: he disbanded the Third Section and appointed a Supreme Executive Commission chaired by a liberal, M. T. Loris-Melikov. This new "dictator" was in control of the police and the security machinery, but he brought a liberal majority into the commission and sought public support for the reforms he sought to enact. But the Narodnaya Volya Executive Committee did not change its line. Its strength had been sapped with the arrest of many members, but it continued to recruit not only among students but also among workers and the military. Officers and soldiers as well as sailors from the Kronshtadt naval base were prepared to assist the committee; this amounted to a return to the sources of the Decembrist movement. A whole underground world materialized around the terrorists, who lived a totally clandestine life. One essential cog in this clandestine machine was the *ukryvatel*—literally, "concealer"—who could be anything from an aristocrat or bourgeois to a civil servant or police officer. The job of these fellow travelers was to hide things and people. Most building janitors—*dvorniki*—were police informers, but the ones who were working for the revolutionaries were especially effective, because they knew the layout of the city and which houses had multiple exits. The police response was to infiltrate the organization with informers—who were rarely discovered. One of the first, Oklatsky, passed information to the police from 1880 to 1917 and was identified only in 1924.

The Executive Committee remained determined to kill the tsar. It rejected Mlodetsky's suggestion that it select a new target and assassinate Loris-Melikov. Mlodetsky ignored the committee, however, and on February 20, 1881, fired on the "dictator" at point blank range, but missed.

He was tried the following day, sentenced to death, and hanged on February 22, in spite of Loris-Melikov's request that the tsar commute his sentence. In April 1880, Loris-Melikov had submitted an initial report on the situation in Russia to the emperor, in which he proposed steps to improve it. Alexander II accepted that report, as well as the subsequent ones, submitted in August 1880 and January 1881 respectively. On March 1, 1881, two hours before he was killed, the tsar signed the order to convene a special commission mandated to draft a constitution for the Russian empire.

Loris-Melikov may have been readying liberal reforms, but nonetheless he intensified the repression. The conditions in which deportees were held at the Kara penal colony in Siberia grew worse. One after another, Narodnaya Volya activists fell. Alexandr Mikhailov was arrested in November 1880. But preparations for the assassination attempt continued. In August 1880, Konstantin Zhelyabov and Teterka dug a tunnel under the Kamenny bridge in Saint Petersburg. That winter, the *narodnovoltsy* worked out of a cheese dairy they had bought to dig a tunnel under Malaya Sadovaya Street, along which the tsar would travel. Rumors about an attack were spreading; there was talk of it in the press, and the police increased their surveillance. Zhelyabov was arrested on February 27, and on the 28th, those Executive Committee members who had evaded arrest set the following day for the attack that had been under preparation for months. The final plan combined blowing up the Malaya Sadovaya Street tunnel and throwing bombs. At noon on March 1, the emperor was to travel to the riding school via Malaya Sadovaya Street. Bomb throwers would be deployed along the carriage's probable route in case the mine under the street failed. On the advice of his second, morganatic, wife, Princess Ekaterina, Alexander altered his route, however. Sofia Perovskaya, who was running the operation, sent the bomb throwers to the Catherine (now Griboyedov) Canal, where they awaited the emperor's return from the riding school. On the agreed signal, Nikolai Rysakov threw the first bomb. Alexander's convoy came to a halt; the tsar was unharmed. Then, the second bomb thrower, Ignacy Hryniewiecki, stepped forward and exploded his bomb between himself and the emperor; both were mortally wounded.

Most of the plotters were arrested over the next few days, on the basis of denunciations: to save his skin, Rysakov—who had been arrested as a bomb thrower—revealed all the details of the plot, and another "repentant" terrorist, Merkulov, took the police on a tour of Saint Petersburg's streets, pointing out every revolutionary he saw. Zhelyabov admitted having participated in the preparations for the attack and was among those tried in open court. Although defended by the city's finest lawyers, the six accused—Zhelyabov, Perovskaya, Kibalchich, Rysakov, Mikhailov, and Gesya Gelfman—were sentenced to death for regicide. Liberals such as Count Leo Tolstoy and the poet and philosopher Vladimir Soloviev tried to sway the new tsar, Alexander III, and on March 12, the Narodnaya Volya Executive Committee published an open letter written by Lev Tikhomirov and Mikaïl Mikhailovsky in which they called on the tsar to declare a general amnesty and to convene a constituent assembly. Alexander III would not yield, and on April 3, 1881, five of the condemned were hanged in Semyonovsky Square, including Sofia Perovskaya, the first woman to be executed in modern Russia. Only one sentence was commuted: that of Gesya Gelfman, who was eight months pregnant.

Zhelyabov's statement during the trial summarized the history of the Russian revolutionary movement. Dreamers, he said, had become positivists; they had moved from propaganda to action, from words to struggle; the March 1 attack was part of a continuum with the events of 1878, a transitional year, during which the doctrine of a death for a death came to the fore. He concluded: "My goal—the goal of my life—was to work for the common good. I long followed a peaceful path. In keeping with my convictions, I would have abandoned this final form of struggle [terrorism] if there had been the least chance of succeeding through peaceful struggle."[14] For Albert Camus, Zhelyabov was the symbol of the terrorist redeemed: "He who kills is guilty only if he is still willing to live or if, in order to continue to live, he betrays his brethren. Death, on the other hand, voids his guilt and his very crime."[15] Karl Marx did not condemn the attackers; quite the contrary. In a letter of April 11, 1881, he wrote to his daughter Jenny Longuet:

> Have you been following the trial of the people who carried out the attack? They are solidly honest people, striking no melodramatic poses, unassuming, realistic, heroic. Shouting and doing are irreconcilably contradictory. The Petersburg Executive Committee, which has acted so vigorously, is publishing manifestos of refined moderation. . . . They are seeking to explain to Europe that their modus operandi is a specifically Russian and historically inevitable method; there is no more reason to moralize about it than about the [1881] Chios [Greece] earthquake.[16]

THE SOCIALIST REVOLUTIONARIES

The Narodnaya Volya Executive Committee had failed. It had wagered everything on a single act: regicide. But murdering the tsar could not spark an insurrection among the people of Russia, either in the cities or in the countryside. The assassinated tsar's son, Alexander III, succeeded him, in keeping with the imperial system, and immediately responded to the killing by unleashing state terror. This—like Nicholas I's response to the Decembrist uprising of 1825—smashed the revolutionary movement. A thirteen-year reign of terror began with a wave of pogroms: from April 5 to December 25, 1881, the Pale of Settlement, to which Jews had long been restricted by legislation, was scourged. The pogroms were orchestrated by a group of aristocrats: the Holy Brigade (Svyashchennaya Druzhina), a precursor of the extreme-right Union of the Russian People. The Jews were accused of being responsible for the death of the tsar. Choosing a scapegoat let the authorities deflect popular resentment onto the Jews. Initially, Alexander III was surprised by this strife; he attributed it to the revolutionaries. But he later concluded that this popular movement was spontaneous—although the anti-Semitic riots had been carefully planned by the Holy Brigade. Alexander then promulgated emergency laws that made the situation of the Jews even worse. These pogroms triggered massive emigration by Russian Jews, especially to the United States. The main result of the assassination of Alexander II was the resurgence of anti-Semitism in Russia.

The repression instituted during Alexander III's reign contained the revolutionary movement. During the same period, economic development in Russia, which was a result especially of industrialization, contributed to rousing the proletariat. Unions were formed in factories, and the first strikes broke out. A secret society, the Proletarian Party, founded in Poland in 1882, adopted a platform including the use of political terror. But strikes seemed to be more effective than violence; they forced the government to adopt legislation to shorten working hours and to regulate work by women and children. This workers' movement was a prelude to the founding of the Social Democratic Party, planned in 1883 by émigré members of Cherny Peredel. Nor did the countryside remain quiescent: The terrible famine of 1891–92 affected thirty million Russians and took the lives of a hundred thousand. In its wake came a cholera epidemic, which originated in Persia, crossed the Caspian Sea, and followed the course of the Volga River. The famine and the epidemic sparked peasant uprisings, which were mercilessly suppressed. Then the sects were the object of persecution; this brought them closer to the revolutionary movement—something the populists had never been able to achieve.

Alexander III was determined to destroy what was left of his father's liberal reforms. He turned to K. P. Pobiedonostsev, chief procurator of the Synod of the Russian Orthodox Church, and Count Dimitri Tolstoy, former minister of public instruction, to formulate his reactionary policy. Tolstoy's view was that education was the direct cause of the revolutionary movement, and he promulgated laws removing poor children from secondary schools and limiting university autonomy. On May 30, 1882, the empire's staunchest reactionary became its minister of the interior.

FORMATION OF THE SOCIALIST REVOLUTIONARY PARTY

Notwithstanding the violent response of the authorities, terrorism did not cease during Alexander III's reign. To be sure, Narodnaya Volya never recovered from the arrests that had devastated it since 1881: by May of that year, its entire leadership had either been arrested or was outside the country, with the exception of Vera Figner, who assembled the remaining members and moved the organization to Moscow. Despite her efforts, Narodnaya Volya gradually declined, and in 1887, it ceased to exist as a party. A number of small groups came into being during this period. In 1885, in Saint Petersburg, a "terrorist section of Narodnaya Volya" devised a plan to assassinate Alexander III. The conspirators were arrested before they could act. Forty-two were put on trial; fifteen were sentenced to death and five were hanged, including Alexandr Ulyanov, son of a member of the Council of State and elder brother of Vladimir Ulyanov, later to be known as Lenin. In 1888, a group of officers who had been in communication with a Zurich-based terrorist circle made preparations to attack the tsar. A Saint Petersburg student, Sofia Ginsburg, was in charge of liaison. But the plans were uncovered and the so-called militarist circle was broken up.

Loris-Melikov left the Ministry of the Interior in May 1881 and was replaced by Count N. P. Ignatiev, who centralized police and military police activities and set up special units to investigate political crimes in Saint Petersburg, Moscow, and Warsaw. These were known as "protection sections"—*okhrannye otdeleniya*—and it was with the creation of these units in 1881 that the word Okhrana was first used to mean the entire Russian police service under the two last tsars. When Dimitri Tolstoy became minister of the interior in 1882, he relied on the director of the Department of Police Affairs, Vyacheslav Plehve, who in 1884 was promoted to the post of assistant minister of the interior. Plehve retained that post under both Tolstoy and his successor, P. N. Durnovo, who served from 1889 to 1895. The Okhrana was mandated to carry out "political inquiries." Such investigations depended on the existence of undercover collaborators who would inform on the circles they had infiltrated. There were hundreds of them on the monthly payroll. Whenever they made it possible to thwart a plot or uncover a clandestine print shop or bomb factory, they received a special bonus.[17] The Okhrana also instituted a subtler counterterrorism method with the training of agents provocateurs. General A. V. Gerasimov, who led the Saint Petersburg section of the Okhrana from 1905 to 1909, defined "provocateur" in this way: "a provocateur is one who starts by inciting people to commit revolutionary acts and ends by handing them over to the police."[18] Together, revolutionaries and the police were weaving a tightly interlocked net, in which each hoped to ensnare the other. For example, Sergei Zubatov, a former revolutionary recruited by the secret police, became Moscow chief of the Okhrana, and Pyotr Rachkovsky, a former student who had been compromised among the revolutionaries, became Russia's finest police officer and recruited one of the most enigmatic figures in the history of the terrorism, Evgeny Filipovich (Yevno) Azev. This technique—turning revolutionaries—sometimes boomeranged: Lieutenant-Colonel Grigory Sudeikin, the first head of the Saint Petersburg section of the Okhrana, was assassinated on December 16, 1883, thanks to information provided by Sergei Dagaev—whom he himself had recruited. Degaev had been sent to Geneva to make contact with Tikhomirov and lure him back to Russia, but he confessed to his quarry, who suggested that he redeem himself by killing Sudeikin. This he did, managing to escape to the United States, where he became a professor (of mathematics at the University of South Dakota, under the name of Alexander Pell).

Under Alexander III, increasing numbers of people were deported to camps in Siberia, where life was unbearable. In 1889, reprisal for an uprising in Yakutsk took the form of a massacre. In the same year, at the Kara camp, which had been opened in 1875, deportees committed mass suicide following a revolt; the camp was shut down in 1890. Although badly hit by the repression, the surviving populists gradually organized, both in the provinces and in Saint Petersburg. Clandestine printing presses were set up, but these were regularly confiscated. Tracts and manifestos were then published elsewhere, and populist propaganda was spread in factories—in spite of attacks from Social Democrats, who viewed the industrial proletariat as their private preserve. The split of the Russian revolutionary movement that had followed the Voronezh congress was completed abroad, among emigrants. In 1881, Plekhanov founded the first Russian Marxist group, the Emancipation of Labor movement, but it was not until 1892 that the Social Democratic Party

was established. The party glorified the revolutionary role of the proletariat, which it contrasted with the conservative muzhiks (peasants).
Right from the outset, the Social Democrats condemned the activities of
those they pejoratively referred to as populists, while they spoke of themselves as socialists and revolutionaries. They accused these populists of
having tried to grab power in disregard of the will of the people. Former
populists too subjected themselves to self-criticism and questioned the
use of terrorism. In 1888, Lev Tikhomirov published a booklet in which
he explained why he had ceased to be a revolutionary and denounced the
use of terror:

> [T]error has negative effects below, on the revolutionaries themselves and
> everywhere its influence is felt. Terror teaches scorn for society, for the people
> and for the country; it teaches an arbitrariness that is incompatible with any so-
> cial system. From a strictly moral point of view, what power could be worse than
> that of one individual over the life of another? Many people—and by no means
> the worst—refuse to grant that power to society. And so a handful of people seize
> that power. Then what are these murders? They are because a legitimate gov-
> ernment, recognized by the people, refuses to meet the demands of a handful of
> people who are such an insignificant minority that they do not even try to wage
> an open struggle against that government. . . . The terrorist leads a negative life.
> It is the life of a hunted wolf. . . . It might also be recalled that the personalities
> of Zhelyabov, Mikhailov, and Perovskaya were not forged by terrorism and that
> they died too soon to be able to see the influence of the fight that had begun, a
> fight that, to them, was infinitely vaster that it was for their petty heirs.[19]

Following the death of Alexander III and the enthronement of
Nicholas II in 1894, a movement emerged among former populists, initiated by Viktor Chernov, who demanded the right of individual self-
determination and the establishment of a decentralized, self-
administered federal state. In 1895, old revolutionaries returned from
Siberia, their convictions still intact. Young people were stirred by what
they heard from them. From London, Vladimir Burtsev issued an ulti-
matum to the new tsar: the revolutionaries would resort to terror if he
did not agree to the constitution. Between 1895 and 1900, small groups
spawned by Narodnaya Volya took up the catchwords of the populists
and referred to themselves as socialists and revolutionaries. In 1897–99,
seeking to come together as a party, they held conferences at Voronezh,
Poltava, and Kiev. From the very start, there were two facets to this new
party: the goal of its policies was to create a democratic regime; at the
same time, it was building a war machine, which between 1900 and
1908 unleashed a second wave of terrorism. The Socialist Revolutionaries, or SRs, were determined to continue propagandizing among the

workers—whose numbers had grown from 700,000 in 1870 to 2.8 million in 1900—and intellectuals. Here, the SRs ignored the peasantry—contrary to the later claims of Soviet historiographers, who reduced their role to that very sphere. Of all the SR theoreticians, only Chernov saw the peasants as a priority issue; he was convinced that the party needed support from both the city and the countryside. That view was borne out by events: it was the peasants who felt the effects of the industrial crisis that hit Russia in 1900–1903, and there was unrest in the countryside. In 1900, the Agrarian Socialist League was founded in Paris. Renamed the Peasant Union, it was to join with the Socialist Revolutionary Party in 1902. At that point, the question of agrarian terrorism arose, but it was immediately rejected. The Social Democrats and Socialist Revolutionaries disagreed on the question of the workers; the latter did not wish to control the workers' movement any more than they did the peasant movement. They saw the workers' councils—soviets—as the true embodiment of the proletariat and favored the expansion of trade unions. They feared the effects of a centralization of state power. After years of planning, the Socialist Revolutionary Party was finally established in 1900 through a merger of the southern group, which had initiated the revolutionary movement, the northern group, and the émigré circles led by Chernov. This period of consolidation into a single party saw the formation of the terrorist group that would be known as the Socialist Revolutionary Party Combat Organization.

THE ATTACK ON PLEHVE

During 1902 and 1903, the structure of the Socialist Revolutionary Party was put in place. A Central Committee controlled the local committees (which grew in number from ten or so in 1902 to more than thirty-five the following year), defined party activities, and published and distributed propaganda materials. The Central Committee was in control of propaganda and agitation—meetings and demonstrations—among workers, university students, peasants, and the military (officers and enlisted men alike). The populist Yekaterina Breshko-Breshkovskaya, who had returned from Siberia, distributed revolutionary booklets and tracts in country villages.

Student turmoil began in 1899. This was harshly suppressed by the police. On February 14, 1901, a former student named Pyotr Karpovich assassinated Nikolai Bogolepov, minister of public education. When arrested, he declared himself to be a Socialist Revolutionary. Soon after this, Vassili Lagusky, a member of the Samara Committee of Zemstvos, fired through the windows of the apartment of Chief Procurator Pobiedonostsev. Lagusky too stated that he supported the Socialist Revolutionary platform and that he thought it necessary to use terror against key representatives of state power. Those were individual acts, but they had the same effect on the Socialist Revolutionary Party that Vera Zasulich's attack on Trepov had had on the Populist Party. In the autumn of 1901, on the initiative of Grigory Gershuni, the Central Committee decided to set up the Combat Organization, with Mikhail Gotz in charge of liaison between the organization and the committee. The Central Committee issued instructions to the Combat Organization and set its objectives, but the organization retained autonomy in the selection of members and methods. A number of its twelve to fifteen members were recruited by Breshko-Breshkovskaya, who kept their loyalty under scrutiny. The first target the Central Committee named for Combat Organization action was the minister of the interior, D. S. Sipyagin, whom the committee had condemned to death for the responsibility he bore for a 1901 massacre in Saint Petersburg. The sentence was carried out on April 15, 1902, by Stepan Balmashev, the son of a Narodnaya Volya activist. Balmashev infiltrated Saint Petersburg's Mariinsky Palace wearing the uniform of an aide-de-camp and fired on Sipyagin at point-blank range, killing him. Following this murder, the Central Committee fled to Kiev to prepare the next operation: an attack on Prince Obolensky, governor-general of Kharkov. Here, the wish of the terrorists was to avenge the victims of atrocities perpetrated when Obolensky ordered the repression of peasant uprisings. On July 29, 1902, Gershuni's chosen operative, Tomas Kachura, fired his revolver, loaded with bullets that had been poisoned with strychnine, at Obolensky. The first two shots missed, but the third slightly wounded the governor. The Combat Organization struck again on May 6, 1903, in a public garden in Ufa. There, Yegor Dulebov killed the governor, Boris Bogdanovich, who that March had given the order to fire on workers at Zlatoustov. Not long afterward, Gershuni was arrested in Kiev and was condemned to death. The sentence, however, was commuted and he was transferred to the Schlusselburg fortress on a tiny island where the Neva River meets Lake Ladoga, a prison reserved for the most dangerous terrorists. Between 1884 and 1905, sixty-eight individuals were held there; of these, thirteen were shot or hanged, four committed suicide, and fifteen, including Nechayev, died in custody.[20]

Yevno Azev, Gershuni's second in command, succeeded him at the head of the Combat Organization. Two men dominate the history of Russian terrorism: Nechayev and Azev. The former was on the periphery but embodied the extreme option: fanaticism and a total absence of any moral limits in the choice of means. Azev, on the other hand, raised terrorism to strategic status. He was both a police informer and a revolutionary. He played a double game but was not really a double agent. He was recruited in Paris by Pyotr Rachkovsky, head of the foreign section of the Okhrana from 1884 and 1902 and a former member of Svyashchennaya Druzhina, who was instrumental in the creation of the anti-Semitic counterfeit tract *Protocols of the Elders of Zion.* Rachkovsky dispatched Azev to infiltrate the Socialist Revolutionary Party, and Azev became a close associate of Mikhail Gotz, who brought him into the Party's Central Committee, while Gershuni got him involved in the Combat Organization. In July 1902, the new minister of the interior, Vyacheslav Plehve, and the director of the Saint Petersburg police department, Stepan Lopukhin, asked him to gain access to the leadership of the Socialist Revolutionary Party, unaware that he had already done so—and that he had failed to reveal the plans to assassinate Sipyagin and Obolensky, even though he was aware of the preparations. To bolster the Okhrana's trust, Azev provided nuggets of information and turned in a handful of local committee activists. Within the Okhrana, Azev was Rachkovsky's man, and Rachkovsky was in the orbit of Trepov, governor-general of Saint Petersburg. Now, Rachkovsky and Trepov were plotting against Plehve. And the Central Committee had ordered Azev to plan Plehve's assassination. Moreover, the interior minister was responsible for the Kishinev pogrom of April 19 and 20, 1903, and Azev was Jewish (as were some 15 percent of SRs).

The attack on Plehve was painstakingly planned by a small team led by Boris Savinkov using the same approach to preparations as for the assassination of Alexander II. Men disguised as coachmen monitored the minister's movements. It was decided to use bombs, and four bomb throwers were deployed along a route the minister was to take. The explosives were prepared by Aleksei Pokotilov, who was killed by an accidental explosion on March 31. Savinkov wrote in detail about how volatile these devices were:

> Our bombs contained two intersecting tubes with ignition devices and detonators. The former consisted of glass tubes filled with sulfuric acid along with spheres and lead weights. When the device fell, in any position, these weights would break the glass tube. When the sulfuric acid spread, it heated a mix-

ture of potassium chlorate and sugar. This mixture would ignite and would cause first the mercury fulminate, then the dynamite with which the bomb was filled to explode. The danger—unavoidable when the device was being filled—was that the glass tube could easily break when handled.[21]

Azev alerted the police that the Combat Organization was planning an attack on Plehve and simultaneously explained to his men that it was too soon to act. Twice the minister did not take the expected route at the expected time, and surveillance resumed. Savinkov's team was reinforced with four new members: Dora Brilliant, responsible for explosives; Yegor Sazonov, a follower of Narodnaya Volya; Ivan Kalyayev, a childhood friend of Savinkov's; and Yegor Dulebov, Bogdanovich's assassin. Albert Camus devoted much thought to the personalities of these "delicate murderers." Savinkov's memoirs set him to analyzing their characters, and it was among these terrorists that he found the most profound ethical concerns: "These were rigorous people. They came last in the history of the revolt, but they rejected no part of their situation or their tragedy. While they lived in terror, 'while they had faith in it' (Pokotilov), they never stopped being tormented by it. History provides few examples of fanatics who suffered from their scruples even in the midst of the fray."[22]

In his memoirs, Savinkov sought to analyze his comrades' motivations:

> Taciturn, modest, and timid, Dora [Brilliant] lived solely through her faith in terrorist action. She loved the revolution and suffered deeply at its failures; while she understood the need to murder Plehve, at the same time she dreaded this murder. She could not get used to the notion of bloodshed. For her it would have been easier to die than to kill. . . . And she felt it her duty to cross the threshold leading to actual participation in the endeavor. For Dora, as for Kalyayev, terrorist action was beautified, first and foremost, by the sacrifice offered it by the terrorist.[23]
>
> [Yegor Sazonov] was young, healthy and sturdy. He exuded youthful power from his sparkling eyes and from his face with its vivid complexion. He was enthusiastic and warm, and his heart was loving and kind; his joie de vivre made Dora Brilliant's gentle sadness stand out in even greater relief. He believed in victory, and he expected it. For him, terrorist action was, above all else, a personal sacrifice and a heroic act. Yet he went toward this sacrifice, he went toward this heroic act as though he thought nothing of it—just as he thought nothing of Plehve.[24]
>
> [Kalyayev] loved the revolution with the tender, profound love felt for it only by those who have made it an offering of the whole of their lives. But, as a born poet, he loved the arts. When there were no revolutionary meetings, when there was no talk of practical matters, he spoke of literature, and spoke of it at length, with enthusiasm, and with a slight Polish accent.[25]

Azev and Savinkov made careful preparations for the attack on Plehve, first scheduled for July 8, 1904, and then for July 15. Azev deflected the Okhrana's attention by informing it that another attack was being organized and by revealing the plans against Plehve, but without giving any details. On July 15, Azev was in Warsaw, which provided him with an alibi. On that day Plehve was killed by the first bomb thrower, Sazonov, who concealed the six-kilogram, cylindrical device beneath a newspaper. Sazonov threw it at Plehve's carriage; the explosion blew the minister to pieces, and the wounded Sazonov was arrested.

GROWTH OF THE COMBAT ORGANIZATION

After Plehve's death, Azev traveled to Geneva, where he was given a hero's welcome by the eight other members of the Socialist Revolutionary Party Central Committee. He exploited this success by requesting and obtaining total independence for the Combat Organization, whose August 1904 Statute the party endorsed:

> Article 1: The purpose of the Combat Organization is to struggle against autocracy by means of terrorist acts.
> Article 2: The Combat Organization shall enjoy complete independence in technical matters; it shall possess its own separate treasury and shall be linked to the Party through the intermediary of the Central Committee.[26]

Azev was elected director of the Combat Organization and Savinkov vice-director. The "supreme organ"—the Committee of the Organization—comprised Azev, Savinkov, and Maximilian Shveitser. The organization built a laboratory in Paris to manufacture dynamite and to teach prospective terrorists how to assemble explosives. Azev recruited more activists and appointed three teams tasked with carrying out the sentences passed by the Party Central Committee against three governors-general: Shveitser's team was composed of fifteen activists and was to kill Grand Duke Vladimir Alexandrovich, governor-general of Saint Petersburg. Savinkov's five-member team was to kill Grand Duke Sergei Alexandrovich, governor-general of Moscow. And the seven-member third team, led by Mikhail Borishansky, was ordered to assassinate General Kiepels, governor-general of Kiev. The three teams left for Russia in November 1904. Meanwhile, Azev continued to feed his Okhrana handler, Vassili Ratayev, false information and put him on the wrong track.

These preparations were taking place during the Russo-Japanese war and before the events of 1905. Moreover, the strategy followed by the

Okhrana had changed since 1895 under the influence of Zubatov, chief of its Moscow section. Zubatov hoped to drive a wedge between the workers and the revolutionaries by setting up legal trade unions and by goading the revolutionaries to radicalism and terror. Zubatov's career came to an end with the murder of Plehve, but the unions—called "Zubatov societies"—survived him.

This was how the workers' society in control of the January 1905 Saint Petersburg demonstration came to enjoy police protection. The movement was led by an Orthodox priest, Georgi Gapon, and in 1905 had between 6,000 and 8,000 members. On Sunday, January 22, 1905, 8,000 people marched to the Winter Palace to deliver a petition to the tsar. Gapon led the procession, with Pinkhas Rutenberg, a Socialist Revolutionary Party member, at his right hand. Grand Duke Vladimir gave the order to fire on the crowd, and 1,600 people were killed and several thousand wounded. Thrown to the ground by Rutenberg, Gapon was unharmed, and both men fled. The so-called Red Sunday massacre set off the 1905 revolution. Russia's intelligentsia was shocked by this crime and sympathetic to the revolutionaries. The opera star Fyodor Chaliapin sang revolutionary anthems on the stage of the Imperial Theater, and the writer Leonid Andreyev placed his apartment at the disposal of the Central Committee of the Social Democratic Party.

The tsar had to agree to reforms. A decree granting universities their autonomy was issued in 1905; Count Sergei Witte became prime minister; the Russo-Japanese war ended; and the October 17 manifesto gave Russia a legislature, the imperial Duma. But these reforms did not slow the growth of revolutionary parties, in particular, the Social Democratic Party. Throughout the country, local committees of the various parties were formed. For its part, the Socialist Revolutionary Party played only a secondary role in the strike movement that was spreading among workers, students, and sailors.

Despite the political upheaval of 1905, the three Combat Organization teams continued to plan their assigned assassination attempts. Savinkov and his five-member team—Savinkov, Kalyayev, Brilliant, Boris Moyseyenko, and Fedor Kulikovsky—monitored the movements of Grand Duke Sergei. Those carrying out the surveillance, who were disguised as coachmen, noted when the grand duke left and where he went. Dora Brilliant made the bombs. On February 2, Kalyayev withdrew from the action because he had observed that the grand duke had with him his wife and his nephews, the children of Grand Duke Pavel. He explained this to his comrades, and they approved. The Combat Organization had never before raised the issue of innocent victims. As Camus wrote, "At the same time, these doers of deeds, who so completely put their lives at risk, would involve the lives of others only with the greatest fastidiousness of conscience."[27] On February 4, running, Kalyayev threw his bomb straight at Grand Duke Sergei from a distance of four paces; Sergei was killed. Kalyayev was arrested and taken to the Butyrki prison. A few days later he was visited by Sergei's widow, Grand Duchess Elizabeth, who gave him an icon and told him that she would pray for him. The lengthy statement Kalyayev made at his trial, on April 5, 1905, explained the position of revolutionaries who sought vengeance for state terrorism:

> We are separated by mountains of corpses, by hundreds of thousands of broken lives, by an ocean of tears and blood that is flooding the entire country in a torrent of outrage and horror. You have declared war on the people. We have taken up the challenge. . . . You are prepared to say that there are two moralities, one for mere mortals, stating, "Thou shalt not kill; thou shalt not steal," and another, political, morality for the rulers, for whom it permits everything.[28]

Kalyayev was sentenced to death; he was transferred to Schlusselburg and was hanged on May 10.

In March 1905, Max Shveitser, leader of the team intending to kill Grand Duke Vladimir, was killed when a bomb he was making exploded at the Hotel Bristol in Saint Petersburg. On the basis of information provided by a revolutionary named Tatarov, who had been turned by the police, the whole group was arrested. The final group, assigned to assassinate the governor-general of Kiev, decided not to act. During the same year, 1905, independent local Combat Organization groups carried out attacks on police chiefs and commissioners in Odessa, Vyatka, Nizhniy Novgorod, Dvinsk, Vitebsk, Samara, Tbilisi, Lubny, Kreslavl, Rostov-on-Don, Bialystok, Krasnoyarsk, Kishenev, and Gomel. A number of informers were executed, in Baku and in Vilna.[29]

In order to put himself in the clear, Azev betrayed the Bulgarian network to the Okhrana, but he concealed the existence of the organization's Villefranche laboratory, which was subsequently moved to Geneva. The Socialist Revolutionary Party realized that it had been thoroughly infiltrated by the political police. And indeed, by 1904, the police had several hundred agents in the various opposition parties, in particular the Social Democratic and Socialist Revolutionary parties. In 1908, General Gerasimov, who in 1906 had become head of the Saint Petersburg Okhrana, had 120 to 150 agents in place in the Social Democratic, Socialist Revolutionary, and Constitutional Democratic parties, and among the anarchists, in Saint Petersburg alone. Information about Azev even began to circulate, but for his comrades he remained above suspicion.

THE RUSSIAN ANARCHISTS, 1903–1907

A group of anarchists who took the name Borba (Struggle) emerged in Bialystok in the spring of 1903, with around a dozen members, and others then sprang up in Odessa and in Chernigov province.[30] The anarchist movement grew in particular after 1905, in the western provinces, in the shtetls (market towns in the Pale of Jewish Settlement) and, especially, in the south: in Odessa and Ekaterinoslav, then in Ukraine, the Crimea, and the Caucasus. Everywhere the process was the same: disillusioned Socialist Revolutionaries or Social Democrats would form a small anarchist circle. These groups shared the goal of destroying the state and capitalism, but their members did not agree on the means to reach that goal, especially on the role of terror. It is difficult to define this anarchist milieu, but two main groups can be identified: Chernoye Znamya (The Black Flag) and Beznachalie (Absence of Authority).

Chernoye Znamya was by far the Russian Empire's largest terrorist anarchist group. Its members came principally from among young Jews in the Pale of Settlement. In Bialystok, in the summer of 1904, an eighteen-year-old anarchist named Nisan Farber stabbed and seriously wounded Avraam Kogan, owner of a spinning mill, as he walked to synagogue on Yom Kippur. A few days later, Farber threw a homemade bomb in a police station and was himself killed in the explosion. Other attacks took place in factories and in business owners' apartments in Bialystok, Warsaw, and, in particular, in the south, where Chernoye Znamya members founded combat sections, built bombs, attacked factories, and carried out increasing numbers of expropriations and acts of sabotage. One dissident group, the Bezmotivniki (Without Motive) appealed to the masses to rise up and in 1905 set off bombs at the Hotel Bristol in Warsaw and the Café Libman in Odessa.

Beznachalie, which operated in Saint Petersburg, was smaller, but no less fanatical. The majority of its members were students. They referred to themselves as anarcho-communists, because they wanted to set up a federation of communes. Curiously, the group's founder was named Nikolai Romanov, known as Bidbei. In spite of its frenetic calls for mass terrorism, the group in fact concentrated more on propaganda than on terrorist action. Other groups used the cover of anarchism to engage in robbery and looting.

After the 1905 revolution, the police hunted down the anarchists. The punishment was merciless and justice summary. Hundreds of young people—often under twenty years of age—were sentenced to death or were killed by their jailers. A number of them committed suicide or set themselves on fire. The luckiest managed to flee to western Europe or the United States. The two most spectacular trials were the December 1905 proceedings against the Odessa anarchists who had bombed the Café Libman and the November 1906 trial of the Beznachalie group.

Paul Avrich estimates that some 5,000 anarchists were active in Russia in the period 1905–7.[31] The movement engaged in the same debate as other Russian revolutionary movements: whether or not terrorism should be at the center of revolutionary action. After 1907, the terrorist period had ended, and the anarchist movement shifted in the direction of syndicalism: propaganda and organization among the workers. It seemed that the anarchists' dreams would not come true until 1917, when a new storm of anarchism would burst.

THE SOCIALIST REVOLUTIONARY PARTY AFTER 1905

With the October 17 manifesto, the Socialist Revolutionary Party, which had stood in the background during the events of 1905, emerged from concealment. The Central Committee left Geneva and returned to Russia. The terrorism issue was once again being debated. Azev and Savinkov demanded that the Combat Organization continue, but the Central Committee dissolved it and reestablished it in a different form. It also decided to prepare for armed uprising in Saint Petersburg, and it set up a Combat Committee, with Azev and Savinkov at its head. But the planned insurrection failed, and police searches resulted in arrests and in the seizure of weapons and explosives.

In Moscow, on the other hand, the various revolutionary organizations made preparations for a general strike, in which the Socialist Revolutionary Party participated. The Moscow Soviet of Workers' Deputies announced that the general strike would take place on December 6. Barricades were raised, but the army and police had the upper hand and the strike came to an end on December 18. The Semyonovsky guards regiment under General Lev Mien and the Warsaw-based Lodarsky regiment put an end to the uprising and mopped up remaining pockets of resistance in the Presnya quarter. In the provinces, local committees were involved in strikes and uprisings. Despite the Central Committee's decision to abandon terrorism, there were about a dozen attacks on police officers. Having returned to Russia, the Central Committee convened the Socialist Revolutionary Party congress, the first in the party's four years of existence. It was held in Imatra, Finland, from December 29, 1905, to January 4, 1906, and it decided to "bolster centralized political terror" "until de facto freedoms are gained once and for all; only then can the Central Committee suspend terrorist actions."[32] But the party rejected agrarian terrorism, a decision that caused a split with its left wing, which favored such action. Since 1904, the left had believed that terror in rural areas would be the most effective means of struggle. At the party congress, the so-called agrarians demanded the immediate socialization of land and factories. This demand was rejected, and they broke away from the party to form the independent Union of Socialist Revolutionary Maximalists, led by the Saratov-born agronomist Lev Sokolov, known as Medved ("the Bear").

The Socialist Revolutionary Party decided to liquidate Gapon and Tatarov as traitors. Gapon had tried to turn Rutenberg in February 1906, but in doing so, he told him that he was working for the police and that his assignment was to uncover conspiracies against the tsar, Prime Minister Witte, and Interior Minister Durnovo. Gapon suggested to Rutenberg that he meet Rachkovsky, and Rutenberg immediately informed the Central Committee and sought instructions. Azev and Chernov asked him to agree to meet with Gapon and Rachkovsky and to kill them. Rutenberg therefore led Gapon to believe that he was prepared to cooperate with the police. The meeting was delayed several times. Rachkovsky did not appear at the appointed times. Azev was fed up, and Rutenberg decided to act on his own. He rented a villa on the Gulf of Finland and invited Gapon to come there on March 28, 1906. Party workers hiding in the villa then seized Gapon and hanged him. The party did not acknowledge this execution. On April 4, 1906, Tatarov, who had betrayed the Shveitser group, was executed in Warsaw, where he had taken refuge in his parents' home. Savinkov had proposed the killing to the Central Committee, which had agreed to it. Savinkov then put together a five-man team, which included Nazarov, who stabbed Tatarov to death and also wounded his mother.

Azev's men were planning an attack on Durnovo. Those who were watching the minister's house were discovered, and in mid-April 1906, Azev was arrested in Saint Petersburg by police officers who were unaware of his connection to the Okhrana. Since Ratayev's retirement,

Rachkovsky had been Azev's case officer, but he was no longer in contact with him. He told General Gerasimov, the new head of the Saint Petersburg Okhrana, that Azev had long been among his agents, and Gerasimov made a deal with Azev: Azev would inform the secret services about planned attacks; his salary would continue to be paid; and the police would arrest members of his group before the attacks actually took place, which would result in lighter sentences. The agreement was respected: "Over a number of years, Azev proved to be the best of my collaborators," Gerasimov recalled. "With his help, I succeeded to a great extent in paralyzing terrorist activities."[33] Gerasimov was determined to neutralize the Socialist Revolutionary terrorists, employing new methods to that end. In his memoirs, he lambastes his predecessors for their mistakes: "A weapon of such exceptional value and effectiveness as the secret police should be used only with the greatest caution, for it is a double-edged sword that is extremely dangerous for those who employ it without understanding its use."[34]

In February—that is, before he had been reactivated by the Okhrana—Azev had assigned Savinkov to kill Admiral F. I. Dubasov, governor-general of Moscow and the man behind the suppression of the December 1905 general strike. Several times the assassination attempt was postponed because Dubasov failed to take the anticipated route. Each time, the bomb thrower, Boris Voynarovsky, appeared at the expected place with his three-kilogram parcel wrapped in paper; after each failed attempt, the bomb had to be dismantled, which was a risky operation. On April 10, a bomb exploded in the hands of the young terrorist Olga Benevskaya, who was wounded, then arrested. Nonetheless, Azev agreed to the plan for the attack on Dubasov, which took place on April 23. Voynarovsky, who threw the bomb, was killed, as was Count Vladimir Konovnitsov, Dubasov's aide-de-camp, but the governor-general himself was only wounded.

Following the dissolution of the first Duma on July 9, 1906, the Socialist Revolutionary Party—which had been hesitating—once again called for an armed uprising. It pursued its organizational work, fanned out in the provinces, and set up new committees grouped by region; started newspapers and issued proclamations; and infiltrated the armed forces, especially the Baltic fleet. Of all its organizations, the most active was that formed among the sailors of the Volga fleet, which was deployed from Nizhniy Novgorod, about 400 kilometers east of Moscow, to Astrakhan, on the Caspian Sea. The failure of mutinies at naval bases in Sveaborg, Finland, and Kronstadt, on the Gulf of Finland, about twenty kilometers from Saint Petersburg, bolstered the belief among SRs that the time was not yet ripe for such uprisings, and that the party should resume its former tactic, mass terror, both in the capital and in the provinces. On orders from the Central Committee, Azev assigned Savinkov to kill Admiral Yuri Chukin, commander of the Black Sea fleet, who had directed the suppression of the naval uprisings. A team was formed, and surveillance was begun, but the militants themselves were being watched: unbeknownst to Savinkov, the local committee of the Sebastopol Socialist Revolutionary Party was planning another attack, this one on the commandant of the Sebastopol fortress, General Neployev. A bomb was thrown during a military review on May 14, 1906, but it failed to explode. Another took six lives, including that of the terrorist. During the subsequent roundup, Savinkov was arrested, which dealt a harsh blow to the Combat Organization. For that reason, the Central Committee agreed to Lev Silberberg's proposal that Savinkov be sprung from prison. On July 15, under the nose of the other prison guards, a guard set him free. Ten days later, a naval officer, Boris Nikitenko, got him out of the country.

In autumn 1906, at Gerasimov's instigation, Azev proposed the assassination of Prime Minister Count Pyotr Stolypin. In fact, the aim was to destroy the central Combat Organization. The party had realized that it was experiencing extraordinarily "bad luck": not one of its designated targets had been hit, while the local committees, independent of the central organization, remained active and effective. Indeed, during the first eight months of 1906, the local committees had stepped up their attacks on civilian and military officials and on informers, in particular in the northern and Volga regions. These numbered approximately thirty, including Albert Trauberg's August assassination of General Mien, commander of the Semyonovsky regiment. In December 1905, attacks had been planned against three of those responsible for putting down the Tambov peasant riots of November that year: General Vladimir von der Launitz and two of his associates, Bogdanovich and Luzhanovsky. The vice-governor, General Bogdanovich, was killed on December 28 by Karpovich, and in January, a nineteen-year-old Tambov woman, Maria Spiridonova, killed Luzhanovsky, who had commanded the punitive force. Von der Launitz would be killed a year later.

Once more the Central Committee took up the plan to assassinate Durnovo, the previous attempt at Saint Petersburg having failed. Tatyana Leontieva traveled to Interlaken, Switzerland, where the interior minister was vacationing under the alias of Müller. When Gerasimov learned of the plan, he advised Durnovo to leave town, and the young assassin wound up killing a French tourist named Müller, whom she mistook for her target.

On March 7, after they had broken away from the Socialist Revolutionary Party, Sokolov and his maximalist group carried out a so-called expropriation to finance their operations: they robbed the Moscow Mutual Credit Society. On August 12, Prime Minister Stolypin's villa on Aptekarsky Island, Saint Petersburg, was destroyed in a bombing, which claimed thirty-two lives, including those of the three bombers and Stolypin's daughter. The Socialist Revolutionary Party's Central Committee denounced the crime, which ran counter to its ethical principles and its political program. Following Sokolov's arrest on December 1, 1906, and his execution, the Union of Socialist Revolutionary Maximalists was dissolved. Small maximalist groups were formed in Moscow and in the provinces, but by 1907, maximalism was gradually disappearing, although the term was used by the racist theoretician Boris Pavlov, who held lunatic notions about extreme terror and mass extermination. The Okhrana had tried to infiltrate the SR maximalist group, but it was tricked by a man it thought to be its agent: in July 1906, the secret police had recruited Solomon Ryss, a maximalist. He had been arrested in Kiev just as he was attempting to rob a tax collector, and he offered to work for the head of the local Okhrana. But Sokolov had put Ryss in place to pass false information on to the police. An Okhrana agent who had infiltrated Sokolov's circle discovered Ryss's maneuvers and denounced him to his superiors. Ryss was arrested, tried by a military court, and hanged, after having declared his maximalist beliefs during the trial.

Because of the central Combat Organization's failures, the Central Committee removed Azev from his post and set up a new group: the Central Committee Combat Detachment. Silberberg was appointed as its leader; he set up his command post and dynamite laboratories at Imatra, Finland, and put together a new team. He enhanced the methods used to prepare for attacks, gathering intelligence on two fronts: not only on the target's movements but also on his private life. On December 21, 1906, von der Launitz was killed by Kudryavtsev, who then killed himself. Silberberg himself was in charge of three attacks: Albert Trauberg's assassination of the warden of Deryabinsk prison on January 17, 1907; a second failed attempt on the life of Admiral Dubasov; and the assassination of Prosecutor-General Vladimir Pavlov, also by Trauberg. But the police had penetrated Silberberg's team, and Silberberg was arrested on February 9, 1907. Boris Nikitenko, the naval officer who had helped get Savinkov out of Sebastopol after his escape, became the new head of the Combat Detachment, which set about planning attacks on Stolypin, Grand Duke Nikolai, and the tsar. Azev informed the police, and during the night of March 31–April 1, twenty-eight terrorists, including Nikitenko, were arrested.

The second Socialist Revolutionary Party congress was convened in Finland on February 12, 1907. Gershuni, who had escaped from his Siberian prison camp and traveled initially to the United States, was now back in Russia and traveled to Finland to chair the congress. The 115 delegates knew that the upcoming elections to the second Duma would give them thirty to forty seats. Gershuni dominated the debates and made sure that the party agreed to participate in the Duma and condemned "expropriations," even though these were used to finance anarchists, the Bolsheviks, and Polish and Transcaucasian nationalists. Gershuni favored the use of terror, but the party's decision would depend on the position of the government: if it continued its repressive policies—pogroms, abusive prison conditions, arbitrary arrests, the breaking up of demonstrations, and so on—terror would resume. The second Duma rejected the party's proposals, and the SRs duly responded. The second Duma was dissolved on June 3, 1907; a third was elected, still with Socialist Revolutionary participation, and began its work on November 2.

Following the debacle of the main Combat Detachment—left without leadership by the successive arrests of Silberberg and Nikitenko—a "mobile" Combat Detachment was set up under the direct command of the Central Committee. Albert Trauberg, alias "Karl," was appointed to head it. In August 1907, prison wardens were killed in Saint Petersburg and Pskov, and Constantin Maximovsky, the capital's chief prison administrator, was assassinated on October 15. Then the setbacks began. Plans developed by Karl's group were given away, while local groups operating independently of the Central Committee continued to be effective. Indeed, throughout the empire, regional combat groups killed dozens of military officers, informers, and civilian officials—especially prison and prison-camp wardens.[35] Socialist Revolutionary Party terrorism reached its peak in 1907, in spite of the destruction of the central group.

In August 1907, the Central Committee had once again taken refuge in Switzerland; it continued to debate whether or not it was appropriate to employ terror. Azev, still a committee member, not only defended its use, but proposed the use of technological innovations, particularly remote detonations and aerial bombs. Savinkov, who also remained on the committee, favored reorganizing the terrorist division and dividing it into two sections: intelligence and action. The Central Committee rejected these suggestions and decided to set up a new Combat Organization to plan the assassination of Tsar Nicholas II. Azev was named to head the organization and appointed Karpovich as his assistant. At the same time, he continued to pass information to Gerasimov and betrayed Trauberg's detachment. He then came to a new agreement with Gerasimov: the Combat Organization would not carry out any assassination attempts, while the police would not arrest any of the group's members. In that way, the police received regular information about preparations for the attempt on the tsar's life and were able to protect him. But the police were unaware of the agreements between Azev and Gerasimov, and they committed a blunder. Karpovich had escaped from Siberia and was found and arrested by the police. Gerasimov arranged for his escape but wanted this to be done subtly so as not to arouse his suspicion: the police officer who was to transfer Karpovich to another prison had to move him three times before the prisoner seized the opportunity to get away.

The destruction of the terrorist networks continued in 1908. Assassination plans were revealed; caches of weapons and explosives were seized; underground printing presses were destroyed; and regional combat groups saw their entire memberships arrested. Azev, who was partly responsible for this situation, felt himself under threat, and to regain the Central Committee's trust, he made plans for an attempt on the tsar's life. This was to take place in Reval, where a meeting between Nicholas and Edward VII of Great Britain was scheduled for June 9 and 10 (new style). But Azev also warned the Okhrana. Another attempt on the tsar's life failed in September 1908. Sailors on the Scotland-built cruiser *Rurik* informed the Central Committee that the tsar would christen the ship upon its arrival in Russia, and they offered to kill him. Azev accepted their offer and did not reveal it to the police. The only way he could squelch the escalating rumors about his treachery was to let Nicholas II be killed. But, once they were in the imperial presence, the two sailors assigned to carry out the deed did not have the nerve to fire.

Rumors about Azev's betrayals were nothing new. For years the old revolutionary and Central Committee member Vladimir Burtsev had been accusing Azev of being an Okhrana agent, but the other members did not agree. Gershuni, who died in 1908, had always rejected such accusations, and Savinkov accused Burtsev of trying to discredit the party. A commission of inquiry was appointed and cleared Azev, but Burtsev dug in his heels. He was determined to assemble irrefutable proof and met, on a train, with former police director Lopukhin, who told him that Azev had indeed informed the police about Socialist Revolutionary Party activities, but that he had also organized the attacks on Plehve and Grand Duke Sergei, and that he was planning an attempt on the tsar's life. There was a risk that Nicholas II would be killed unless Azev was arrested, and that was why Lopukhin exposed him.

A jury of revolutionaries met in Paris in late October 1908 to put an end to Burtsev's continuous allegations and to establish Azev's innocence. It included both party members and nonmembers, such as Vera Figner, German Lopatin, and Prince Kropotkin. Burtsev's deposition, backed up by documentation, made an impression on the jury. Then Gerasimov learned that Lopukhin was planning to travel to London to meet with three members of the Central Committee: Chernov, Mikhail Argunov, and Boris Savinkov. He advised Azev to talk with Lopukhin, but Lopukhin refused to give in. He went to London and confirmed to the committee members that Azev was an Okhrana informer, and that he had tried to pressure him not to reveal that fact. Azev fled in fear for his life and moved to Berlin under an alias; he died there of nephritis in 1918.

On January 8, 1909, the Central Committee issued a statement naming Azev as an agent provocateur. The revelations caused a sensation in the international press and led to two interpellations from Duma members. The first accused the government of having planned the assassinations of Plehve, Grand Duke Sergei, and General Bogdanovich as acts of provocation in order to justify its repressive policies. The second called on the government to admit that it was aware of illegal activities on the part of some of its agents. Prime Minister Stolypin appeared before the Duma and publicly acknowledged that Azev had collaborated with the Okhrana. The Social Democratic Party exploited this affair to discredit both the government and the terrorists. The Socialist Revolutionary Party, through Chernov, offered another theory: that this was nothing more than an episode in an interministerial battle: at the time, Rachkovsky had been Trepov's man. Savinkov called on the Socialist Revolutionary Party to get beyond Azev's treachery:

> It was not Azev who created the terror; it was not Azev who breathed life into it; and Azev does not possess the power to destroy a temple he did not build. The Azev affair is a harsh blow to the party and to the revolution. But it is a

harsh blow not because it undermines the moral stature of terror—Kalyayev's terror was pure—or because terror is impossible as a form of struggle: Azev will pass; terror will endure. This blow is harsh and terrible for another reason. . . . The Azev affair will unnerve the weak; it could even confuse the strong. We need enormous love to hold our old banner high; we need burning faith. Law without action is death, and victory comes only to those who hold the sword.[36]

And Savinkov called for the policy of terror to continue. But the blow was too severe: the Central Committee resigned and the Combat Organization was disbanded. In March–April 1909, a third party conference made preparations for the formation of a Party Council, which proposed an end to the use of terror, but reversed itself after a speech from Chernov on the technique of "terrorist war":

Our methods of waging terrorist war must rise to contemporary techniques of war. These are not static. . . . I simply affirm that improving the terrorist struggle means, inter alia, carrying out new technical research; to that end, possessing one or more specialized technical groups; and trying to use state-of-the-art science toward the true goals of our struggle. Terror will be terror in the true sense of the word only if it equals the revolutionary application of the highest scientific technology at any given time.[37]

The Party Council elected a new Central Committee, but the party had been weakened. The end of the Azev affair meant the end of terrorism. Between 1910 and 1913, the Socialist Revolutionary Party continued to decline; this was exacerbated by conflicts among individuals and among ideas. A new Combat Organization was set up, headed by Savinkov, who returned to Russia to plan the assassinations of the tsar and of Stolypin. But he gave up the enterprise, and centralized terror was abandoned. The only notable action was the murder of Colonel Boris Karpov, the new head of the Saint Petersburg Okhrana, by the Socialist Revolutionary Ivan Petrov—and it was denounced by the Saint Petersburg Socialist Revolutionary committee. Local committees undertook some actions in the provinces—two prison wardens were killed in 1911—but local organizations were disbanded by the police. The assassination of Stolypin on September 1, 1911, by Dmitri Bogrov was the act of an anarchist who had been an Okhrana collaborator and who was forced to commit this murder in order to clear himself in the eyes of his comrades. During his trial, Bogrov claimed to be a Socialist Revolutionary, but the Central Committee denied all involvement in the attack.

With World War I and the February 1917 revolution, the Socialist Revolutionary Party would rise again. It held the majority in the Soviet of Workers' and Soldiers' Deputies; it dominated the All-Russia Soviet of Peasants' Deputies; it held the Ministry of Agriculture; it was allied with the populists on the right and the Mensheviks on the left: for a while—until October—the party had the illusion of building the self-administering democratic socialism of which it dreamed.

This history of Russian terrorism is far from exhaustive. It is restricted to analyzing two movements that were part of the same continuum. While mentioning anarchist terror, it is silent about the numerous killings carried out by nationalist parties—Polish Socialist Party militants murdered hundreds of people in the first decade of the twentieth century—and by Alexandr Dubrovin's Union of the Russian People, an extreme-right party that planned an attack on Prime Minister Witte, assassinated a number of legislators, and, in 1916, took part in an assassination that held as much symbolism as that of the tsar in 1881: the murder of Grigory Rasputin.

The upheavals that shook Russia under the three last autocratic tsars undermined government authority and prepared the ground for the 1917 Revolution. Terrorism was only one element of the multidimensional violence—which included peasant riots, mutinies, strikes, and armed uprisings—but it was of particular significance. The history of the populists and the SRs has many lessons to teach. It bridges two epochs; and, first and foremost, it is a Russian history. Although, like all revolutionaries, they identified with the French Revolution, the 1848 revolutions, and the Paris Commune, these men and women were Russians. Beneath the muzhik's *shapka* or the student's cap, they were all Russians, body and soul, in appearance and in language, heirs to a long tradition with its roots deep in a vast, cold land. Terrorists and police officers alike were Russians, often from the same social background and intimately linked by crime: one as perpetrator, the other as preventer. The gulf was greater between generations than between classes. The terrorists understood the value of a life; they knew the crime they were committing, and they believed that their own lives were barely enough to atone for it. When the authorities offered them a platform, they spoke, they explained, they offered justifications. They concealed nothing and they denied nothing; loud and clear, they claimed responsibility for their actions. They were murderers motivated by an ideal. They believed themselves entitled to kill because those they executed had themselves killed or ordered others to kill. They were righters of wrongs rather than avengers. They could not tolerate a one-way justice or that agents of the state should enjoy impunity for their actions. They acknowledged that an organization was needed to confront the petrified monster of the government, and that they needed to do as their party said. In that way alone, they heralded the terrorism of the twentieth century, but they were of another time: the nineteenth century. In no way were these men and women the precursors of twentieth-century totalitarianism and its state terrorism. They lived at a particular moment in history and in a particular place: Russia. As Camus wrote, "It was as though the descendants of Nechayev made use of the descendants of Kalyayev and of Proudhon."[38] Yes, the terrorists were murderers, but they had ethical principles: they had crossed a threshold, but they had not torn down their moral barriers. Their choice remained an ethical one.

NOTES TO CHAPTER 7

1. See *Quatre femmes terroristes contre le tsar: Vera Zassoulitch, Olga Loubatovitch, Élisabeth Kovalskaïa, Vera Figner.*

2. Dates in this chapter are those of the Julian calendar, which was behind the Gregorian calendar by twelve days in the nineteenth century and by thirteen days in the twentieth. Dates given in the style of the Gregorian calendar are indicated by the notation "(new style)".

3. Venturi, *Les intellectuels, le peuple et la révolution*, 2: 341.

4. Ibid., 592.

5. Kravchinsky, *Stepniak*, 16.

6. See Avrich, *Russian Anarchists.*

7. Cannac, *Netchaïev*, 169.

8. Venturi, *Les intellectuels, le peuple et la révolution*, 636.

9. Kravchinsky, *Stepniak*, 50–51.

10. Bienstock, *Histoire du movement révolutionnaire en Russie*, 1: 204–5.

11. Venturi, *Les intellectuels, le peuple et la révolution*, 966.

12. Ibid., 1015 n2.

13. Kravchinsky, *Stepniak*, 66.

14. Bienstock, *Histoire du movement révolutionnaire*, 270.

15. Camus, *Homme révolté*, 214.

16. Poliakov, *Causalité diabolique*, 152.

17. Zavarzin, *Souvenirs*, 13–25.

18. Guerchouni, *Dans les cachots de Nicolas II*, 223.

19. Fauré, *Terre, terreur et liberté*, 224–26.

20. Gerasimov, *Tsarisme et terrorisme*, 131–32.

21. Savinkov, *Souvenirs d'un terroriste*, 53.

22. Camus, *Homme révolté*, 208.

23. Savinkov, *Souvenirs*, 57.

24. Ibid., 18.

25. Ibid., 59.

26. Spiridovitch, *Histoire du terrorisme russe*, 187.

27. Camus, *Homme révolté*, 211.
28. Savinkov, *Souvenirs*, 155, 157.
29. Baynac, *Les socialistes-révolutionnaires*, 200.
30. See Avrich, *Russian Anarchists*, 43–84.
31. Ibid.
32. Spiridovitch, *Histoire du terrorisme russe*, 309.
33. Gerasimov, *Tsarisme et terrorisme*, 114.
34. Ibid., 105.
35. See the list in Spiridovitch, *Histoire du terrorisme russe*, 480–83.
36. Ibid., 563.
37. Ibid., pp. 588–89.
38. Camus, *Homme révolté*, 403.

CHAPTER 8

THE "GOLDEN AGE" OF TERRORISM

Gérard Chaliand and Arnaud Blin

The late nineteenth and early twentieth centuries saw the rise of several international terrorist movements. The examples of the Russian populists and of French and Italian anarchists spawned imitators in the Balkans, Armenia, India, and elsewhere.

The decades preceding World War I were a time of profound political and economic changes. It was a time of industrial revolution and the headlong expansion of capitalism. It saw the apogee of some colonial empires (France, England, Russia) and the decline of others (Austria and Turkey). Lenin employed the term "imperialism" to describe the expansionist trend that overshadowed the decay of the great empires, which he saw as the concluding phase of capitalism. The balance of powers underlying the Westphalian order collapsed with the Great War of 1914–18, which also marked the end, or the beginning of the end, of European world hegemony, which was conclusively dead by 1945. It was a system, moreover, that was powerless to quash the embryonic nationalisms that threatened it.

The very gradual emergence of democratic freedoms allowed malcontents to broadcast their demands on a scale that had previously been unthinkable. And yet, the new winds of freedom blew weakly and very unevenly, depending on the country or the government, thus legitimizing such protest movements.

Elsewhere, violence was the instrument of choice for changing the status quo, which, in most instances, was unstable in any case. The rise of nationalism and the emergence of ideologies of the left and right were fertile ground for a new form of violence: terrorism. The expression had been in common usage ever since the French Revolution, but it came to refer to phenomena that had little in common with the state terrorism briefly introduced by that upheaval, and that would enjoy a stunning revival with the October Revolution in Russia. Terrorism at that time was practiced mostly by groups of the extreme left, and mostly in the form of regicide, the modern version of the ancient tyrannicide. Religion was essentially absent from the new terrorist equation. Nationalism was one of its principal driving forces, along with various other ideologies, including anarchism and nihilism. It would take a few more years for Marxism, in various guises, to come to dominate revolutionary ideology. The Russian Revolution would be the vehicle of its success. Yet another revolution—the Iranian—would much later reinject religion into the terrorist framework.

From a theoretical perspective, the German radical Karl Heinzen (1809–1880) was an early apologist of terrorism as a legitimate means of revolutionary struggle. Written at the height of the feverish aftermath of the 1848 revolutions, his essay "Der Mord" ("Murder") expanded considerably on the concept of tyrannicide: "As our enemies have taught us to do, we take it as a founding principle that murder, both individual and mass, remains a necessity and an essential instrument in the making of history."

In assuming the mantle of apostle of violence, Heinzen integrated the philosophy of tyrannicide, the emergence of democratic society, and revolutionary ideology. Like the champions of tyrannicide, Heinzen sought to reconcile the principles of traditional morality (which proscribe murder) with the political expedients justifying revolution. The result was muddled, to say the least, but Heinzen was one of the founding philosophical fathers of modern terrorism, whereby entire populations, and no longer merely the state, are deemed to be legitimate targets. He was also among the first to recognize the fearsome potential of technology in the hands of terrorists, allowing a small group of individuals to wreak great damage in an urban setting. Heinzen himself never put his principles into practice, and terrorist attacks during the first half of the nineteenth century never reached the scale he envisaged. Like many who followed him, Heinzen made the mistake of linking terrorism with mass destruction. Until recently, however, while terrorism has struck at governments through their civilian populations, communities as a whole have generally not been targeted for their own sakes, except by state terrorism.

The terrorist wave of 1870–1914 ended with an assassination of in-calculable consequences. The assassination of Archduke Franz Ferdi-nand of Austria and his wife on June 28, 1914, in Sarajevo triggered one of history's greatest conflicts, which came to be known as the Great War. The assassination was the work not of anarchists, with whom the pub-lic at large automatically associated terrorism—much as it does today with Islamists—but of Serbian nationalist revolutionaries. The era of an-archist terrorism was over; that of the nationalists had only just begun. The assassination did not cause the war but provided the spark that ig-nited it.

THE ASSASSINATION OF THE CENTURY

The most notorious assassination of the twentieth century was organized by the Serbian nationalist Black Hand Society (Crna Ruka). The mili-tants of this secret organization chose to kill Archduke Franz Ferdinand, heir to the Austro-Hungarian throne, because they were worried about possible concessions on his part that would weaken the resolve of the na-tionalist movement in Bosnia. It is, in fact, precisely when states decide to make concessions that hard-core terrorist movements up the radical ante and intensify their violent activities. That dynamic is being played out today by terrorists in Corsica, for whom each concession is inter-preted as a sign of weakness and rewarded with a new series of attacks. The Black Hand was an organization put together from the bottom up by the Serbian secret services. It was highly active in the years before the war, both in Serbia—where it orchestrated dozens of political attacks—and beyond, in the broader Balkan conflict.

In Bosnia, Serbian nationalists fought for Greater Serbian solidarity by organizing the rebellion against the provisional administration es-tablished by Austria. In response to this assault on Austrian authority, Emperor Franz Josef I decided, on October 5, 1908, to annex Bosnia and Herzegovina, taking advantage of the shock caused by the Young Turk uprising, just as the Bulgarians did by proclaiming their inde-pendence that very day. On February 24, 1909, Serbia—which, like Bosnia and Herzegovina, had for centuries been part of the Ottoman empire before it was shorn of most of its European territories in 1878[1]—reacted with violence, backed by Russian support, and threat-ened to annex Bosnia and Herzegovina, Croatia, Dalmatia, and Slove-nia. Aroused by the pan-Slavic ambitions of St. Petersburg, Serbia dreamed of restoring the fourteenth-century Greater Serbia at the expense of Austria-Hungary, which occupied the larger part of the coveted territory. Along the borders, where they could count on support from the minority Serbs, the agents of the Black Hand orchestrated a series of terrorist attacks against Austria from 1910 to 1914, targeting in particular the governor of Bosnia and Croatian prefects. As Dragutin Dimitrijević, leader of the Black Hand, saw it, Serbia was to play the same unifying role in the Balkans as Piedmont had played in the struggle for Italian unity. At the same time, Serbian nationalist feeling was heightened by the conflict that had festered between Serbia and Bulgaria since the regional dismantling of the Ottoman empire. Russia, seeking to salve the humiliation of its 1905 defeat by Japan, had staked a great part of the success of its foreign policy on its Balkan strategy.[2]

Terrorism was the key component of an ambitious strategy involving several actors: a great power, Russia; a state, Serbia; and extraterritorial minorities. The case of Serbia in the years before the disaster of 1914 foreshadows the highly complex conflicts that marked the twentieth century, exploiting the advantages of indirect tactics that included the use of terrorism. Ultimately, the Middle East would replace the Balkans as the world's foremost hotbed of instability. It, too, would rise on the ruins of the Ottoman empire, after its dismemberment by the English and the French. Turkey's interventions in Cyprus, Pakistan's in Kashmir, and, in a different context, the Arab states' involvement in Palestine, would proceed from the same logic.[3] In such situations, terrorism is almost always one of the weapons wielded by the combatants.

The assassination of Franz Ferdinand marked the end of an era particularly rife with terrorist conspiracies, especially against heads of state and monarchs. Despite many failed attempts, such as that on the life of Napoleon III in 1858, terrorists enjoyed considerable success during this period, reminiscent of the tyrannicidal decades of the late sixteenth and early seventeenth centuries. The year 1881 was a kind of inauguration of the era of regicides. Tsar Alexander II of Russia was blown up that year by the People's Will (Narodnaya Volya) organization. (American President James Garfield was shot the same year, but the killing had nothing to do with terrorism.) A series of attacks were undertaken by Italian anarchists in several European countries. Following the fatal stabbing of French President Marie-François-Sadi Carnot by the Italian anarchist Sante Jeronimo Caserio in 1894, Spanish Prime Minister Antonio Cánovas del Castillo was assassinated by yet another Italian in 1897. The next year, anarchist Luigi Lucheni killed Elisabeth (Sisi), empress-consort of Austria and queen-consort of Hungary. Another crowned head, King Umberto I of Italy, was killed by the anarchist Gaetano Bresci in 1900. In the United States, a third president, William McKinley, was assassinated by an anarchist sympathizer, Leon Czolgosz, in 1901. In 1908, King Carlos I of Portugal and his son were murdered by two members of a secret society, whose motives remain unclear. Three years later, Prime Minister Pyotr Stolypin of Russia, having survived several anarchist attempts on his life, was killed by the revolutionary socialist Dmitri Bogrov while attending a performance at the Kiev Opera House.

THE CONTRIBUTION OF TECHNOLOGY

Bomb attacks came to replace the bladed weapons of yore. The technique has remained more or less unchanged since the late nineteenth century. In that sense, terrorism has not kept up with technological innovations in warfare, and, as of the time of writing, nuclear weapons have yet to make an appearance in the theater of terrorism. Chemical weapons, used by both sides in World War I, have been used just once in a nonstate terrorist attack, and on a limited scale, in the Tokyo subway on March 20, 1995. Only the invention of the motorized aircraft early in the century has had any innovating impact on terrorism, although it took until the late 1960s for the airplane to become a terrorist delivery vector.[4] At the same time, terrorists had been considering ways to exploit the new technology since its earliest days. In 1906, the ingenious Russian Yevno Azev had already foreseen the airplane's potential and had even bought one from an anarchist engineer with the idea of using it in a terrorist attack, which he never had the opportunity to undertake.

Terrorism's style is political and psychological. Making an impression on the popular psyche and political regimes is the objective of any terrorist movement. Technology is a secondary factor in attaining those objectives, because its primary resource is human and psychological. On the other hand, explosives technology had progressed sufficiently by the nineteenth century to serve the needs of terrorists. The difficulties inherent in handling nuclear, chemical, radiological, biological, and bacteriological weapons are great enough (for now) to dissuade terrorist groups from trying to use them. Nowadays, given the increasingly sophisticated detection equipment deployed virtually everywhere, and especially in airports, terrorists have only two options: outdo the authorities at the technological level or revert to such simple means that they elude contemporary detection abilities. While counterterrorist authorities are constantly thinking about the next phase in the "arms race," terrorists are trying to figure out how to frustrate their defensive efforts. In the field of prevention, the simpler a weapon, the harder it is to detect.

From the terrorist perspective, the great technological breakthrough was the invention of dynamite. In the second half of the nineteenth century, industrialization required explosives, most particularly in the digging of mines and the laying of railroad track. Engineers and scientists strove to make explosives easier to handle, more effective, and less heavy. In the mid nineteenth century, black powder was the only explosive in use, but it had many drawbacks. Nitroglycerin, first prepared in 1846, was too dangerous to handle to be of use. The Swedish chemist Alfred Nobel began experiments in 1864 that would lead two years later to the invention of dynamite (nitroglycerin with diatomaceous earth as an adsorbent).

Dynamite radically changed terrorist technology and was a major factor in the rise of anarchist and populist movements in France, Russia, and elsewhere, including the United States. Lightweight, safe to handle, easy to use, and reliable, it is well suited to a terrorist-type attack. It makes a lot of noise and can kill a small cluster of people, which is exactly what a terrorist bent on sowing fear is looking to do. Despite all this, it is dangerous to use, and many terrorists blow themselves up during experiments or attacks. In Russia and Ireland, for instance, terrorists set up clandestine chemistry labs to refine their technique and produce explosives better suited to their needs. Nevertheless, while the invention of dynamite may initially have revolutionized terrorist tactics, it was not altogether the panacea it was at first made out to be. Bombs did become far lighter than they had been, but some thirty kilos were still needed to ensure a powerful explosion. When political figures with close protection were attacked, the bomb had to be larger still in order to penetrate a wider perimeter and still reach the target. The proliferation of armed conflicts over the course of the twentieth century not only contributed to advances in this field—notably in the miniaturization of explosive devices—but also broadened access to weaponry of all sorts by private armed groups. The collapse of the Soviet bloc in 1991, setting off a massive sale of weapons and technology overseas, and to terrorists in particular, is the most recent instance of such proliferation.

Explosives technology in the late nineteenth century also had an impact on the doctrines elaborated by the theoreticians of terrorism. Johann Most was born in Germany in 1846 and pursued a lengthy career as a political activist in his native country and in Austria. Forced to flee his homeland when Bismarck came to power, he took refuge in England, where he launched the weekly review *Die Freiheit* ("Freedom"), in which he preached Marxist doctrine. Around 1880, he abandoned Marxism to embrace the anarchism espoused by Bakunin. His change of heart stirred him to defend and encourage acts of terror throughout the world, including in Ireland and Russia. A *Freiheit* editorial on the assassination of Alexander II in 1881 led to his expulsion from Great Britain. In the years to follow, *Die Freiheit* became the beacon of the anarchist movement. In this organ, distributed by the tens of thousands, Most systematically sung the praises of "propaganda by deed." To achieve it, all that was needed was a group of determined actors with access to the technology necessary to wage a campaign of terror.

Under the influence of the social Darwinist ideas current at the time, Most was convinced that natural selection would produce an elite of revolutionaries to lead the masses to revolt. Only one road to achieving this goal was open to that courageous elite: the use of violence. The new technology represented an unhoped-for advance that would allow this small cadre to challenge the entrenched powers.

In one of his most famous pamphlets, "The Science of Revolutionary Warfare," Most praised the bomb:

> Today, the importance of explosives as an instrument for carrying out revolutions oriented to social justice is obvious. Anyone can see that these materials will be the decisive factor in the next period of world history.
> It therefore makes sense for revolutionaries in all countries to acquire explosives and to learn the skills needed to use them in real situations.[5]

Most foresaw the effects propaganda by terrorism would have: "The entire world now knows first-hand that the better aimed the shot or the explosion, and the more perfectly undertaken the attack, the greater the propagandistic impact will be."[6] Moreover, "We have said it a hundred times or more: when modern revolutionaries act, it is not only their actions that matter, but the propagandistic effects they may achieve. Therefore, we advocate not only action for its own sake, but also action as propaganda."[7] Most goes further still, foreseeing the media campaigns that would be part of the terrorist arsenal: "In order to fully achieve the desired success, immediately after an action has been accomplished, and most especially in the town where it has taken place, posters should go up explaining the reasons why the action was undertaken so as to gain the utmost advantage thereby."[8] But it is not certain that Most understood that the very essence of terrorism is to instill an irrational sense of insecurity.

It was in the realm of technology that Johann Most demonstrated how imaginative and far-sighted he could be. He conducted chemical experiments to create booby-trapped letters. Above all, he imagined ways of exploiting the new technologies of flight to terrorist ends. According to Most, the dirigible (a balloon with a steam engine hung beneath it), invented by Henri Giffard in 1852, would allow terrorists to seize the element of surprise by dropping explosives on crowds, armies, or public figures from the air, where they would be untouchable.

ORGANIZATIONAL PROBLEMS

Another constant of the terrorism that evolved over the course of the nineteenth century was the limited character of terrorist organizations, as Most was at frequent pains to point out. They were restricted in terms of human and, above all, financial resources. These modest organizations were compelled to resort to cost-benefit calculations in setting their strategic options. For the most part, these constraints diverted resources away from investments in high technology and into areas where the funds could be put to optimal use: recruitment, training, intelligence, protection, maintaining secrecy. While certain contemporary terrorist organizations, such as al Qaeda, enjoy significant financial support, the terrorist movements of the nineteenth century were poor. Outside support was rare. The gift of a million francs from a wealthy Frenchwoman to her friend the Spanish anarchist Francisco Ferrer was atypical. The Irish Revolutionary Brotherhood was created in 1858 with an American donation of $400. Terrorists were often forced to turn to crime to fund their activities. In the early twentieth century, a group of Indian terrorists tried, and failed, to counterfeit banknotes, before turning to burglary.[9] In France, the gang led by the anarchist Joseph Bonnot specialized in armed robberies before being apprehended by the police in 1912.

It was not until World War I that terrorist organizations began to be funded by governments, a trend that accelerated after World War II in the context of the Cold War and following the oil crisis, with the manna being distributed by the oil-producing Arab countries. The exploitation of terrorist movements for political ends was not a consideration under the balance-of-powers policies that prevailed right up to 1914, the general idea being to preserve stability and the status quo of a system that was essentially homogeneous from a political perspective. The goal of destabilizing one's adversary did not coalesce until the collapse of the Westphalian system and, most especially, the confrontation between the

Soviet bloc and the West. It should be noted, at the same time, that the attacks of September 11, 2001, were undertaken on a modest budget, spent mostly on preparing and training the attackers, rather than on acquiring up-to-date technology.

Thus, terrorists initially worked with few resources and means. Their capacity to do harm was proportional to their ingenuity in devising strategy and their rigor in implementing it on the ground. Generally speaking, the risk of discovery by the authorities was inversely proportional to the size of the organization. Narodnaya Volya, to cite one example, counted as many as five hundred members, which was a significant number at the time.[10] Most terrorist organizations were far smaller, often operating with just a handful of members, and sometimes fewer than ten. The terrorist movements of the 1970s and 1980s, such as Action Direct and the Baader-Meinhof Gang, were not much larger. A movement's growth, especially if it is rapid, increases its risks. In the 1960s, the Tupamaros of Uruguay—who began with barely 50 militants and ended up with 3,500 five years later—were victims of their own success.[11] Among the national liberation movements, the first of which emerged at the turn of the twentieth century, the organization was usually focused on a small central core but enjoyed a very broad base of support, fielding active, semi-active, and dormant agents.

It has been noted that terrorist attacks tend to come in waves. According to Walter Laqueur, these waves correspond to generational shifts of some twenty years.[12] The authorities generally take a few years to adapt their counterterrorism tactics before infiltrating terrorist movements, while the ambitions of those movements are often far greater than their results.

Nationalist and religious movements are far more stubborn. They have a much broader base of support and little trouble with recruitment. Safe havens are critical to a movement's ability to sit out and overcome the inevitable crises. For small, impecunious groups, the search for safe havens can simply be resumed in exile. A movement can more easily elude the authorities of a targeted country from abroad. It was even easier to do so before World War I, when borders were not hard to cross, legal agreements between states in matters such as extradition were few, and communications between police departments were still rudimentary. To this day, the efforts exerted in this domain and the considerable progress achieved in information technologies remain inadequate in the field of interstate cooperation.

A large proportion of terrorist activity is devoted to organizing a movement and ensuring its survival. Only then can attacks be planned and undertaken. Given the many setbacks caused by poor preparation, inaccurate intelligence (from embedded double agents), and shoddy co-ordination (especially in terms of timing), few attacks succeed in reaching their targets. This phenomenon was particularly apparent in the early days of terrorism in the nineteenth century, but it has endured to this day. Terrorists have made and continue to make lots of mistakes.

And yet terrorism has the special ability to perpetuate itself even in the face of repeated failure. Often, such failures may even drive a terrorist movement to pursue its operations to the extent that terrorism eventually becomes an end in itself and ceases to be carried out in the service of a cause. In that sense, "grassroots" terrorism resembles state terrorism.

We tend to think of Russian terrorism and the era of attacks in France and southern Europe as representative of the terrorism that thrived in the period straddling the nineteenth and twentieth centuries. But other terrorist movements existed elsewhere, for instance, in Ireland, whose nationalist movement is still active today. Poland was hit by a wave of terrorism that continued even after World War I. Terrorist attacks in British India foreshadowed the future wars of national liberation by several decades. Before it was dismantled after the war, the Ottoman empire was compelled, in full decline, to confront two terrorist campaigns, waged respectively by Armenians and Macedonians.

IRELAND

For more than a century, violence in Ireland, and later in Northern Ireland, has been an intermittent presence in the headlines. Most people associate one organization—the Irish Republican Army—with that violence. The IRA was born during World War I with the merger of several nationalist groups, including the Irish Republican Brotherhood and the Irish Citizen Army. By the late 1960s, the IRA was involved in a complex struggle with the Protestant community in Northern Ireland, supported by England and enveloped in the mystique of the independence struggle. The British Parliament voted for home rule in May 1914, but the concession of greater autonomy for Ireland was deemed inadequate by the nationalists, who sought an independent state.

The struggle, which ended with the creation of the Irish Free State in 1922,[13] was a blueprint for the various national liberation movements that would rattle the colonial empires a few decades later, after World War II. The orchestration of urban guerrilla warfare on an unprecedented scale would favor the systematic use of terror in Ireland. The United Kingdom, which was not defeated militarily in Ireland, was one of the first countries to experience the effects of a new strategic equation whereby military victory did not amount to political victory. Another great colonial empire, France, would have to undergo a similar experience in Algeria to draw the same conclusion.

The history of the Irish resistance will be forever associated with the Easter Rising of 1916. On that Easter Monday, April 24, the members of several independence movements decided to strike hard at the very heart of Dublin. They were led by the poet Padraig Pearse and the socialist James Connolly, who had returned to Ireland to take up the cause of independence after having emigrated to the United States. The insurgents seized the General Post Office and raised the green, white, and orange flag of the future Irish republic. They entertained the hope that their exploit would spark a general uprising, but the British army brutally suppressed the insurrection. Under a barrage of artillery, British troops—many of whom were Irish—retook the city after bitter fighting that left some 134 crown soldiers and some 60 rebels dead.

In the heat of battle, the insurrectionists had called for negotiations, but the general in charge of putting the rebellion down demanded unconditional surrender. In the aftermath, the British decided to execute the leaders of the rebellion, including Pearse and Connolly, but other leaders, such as de Valera and Michael Collins, avoided the firing squad. The intransigence of the English would ultimately backfire: as clumsy as it had been, the independence movement now had martyrs. It had lost the military battle but was primed to win the political war.

After the bloody events of Easter, the national movement regrouped and drew its lessons from the fiasco. One architect of the armed struggle was Michael Collins, who created a military structure that allowed units to function autonomously and recruited World War I veterans as his staff officers. In response, the English created their own paramilitary counterinsurgency units, the Royal Irish Constabulary Reserve Force, or Black and Tans (so named for the color of their provisional uniforms), and special counterterrorism police auxiliary units. These units had no qualms about meeting violence with violence, even at the risk of alienating the populace. Better armed and equipped than the irregulars, they nevertheless lost the political battle without ever really dominating on the ground.

The war was merciless. Terror was used on both sides. The militants attacked both the loyalists—those faithful to the crown—and the authorities. The police adopted a policy of reprisals aimed at discouraging the rebels from their mission: two freedom fighters killed for every loyalist murdered. In London, Lloyd George and Winston Churchill endorsed this tactic, but the enemy was obstinate. He understood that victory is won in the theater of politics, where public opinion is a key force. Michael Collins never attacked head on, where he knew himself to be irreparably weaker than his foe. He gained the support of a sector of the population—his struggle financed in part by Irish Americans—and through his network of informers won the crucial battle for intelligence, thereby remaining on the offensive.

Just before Easter 1920, the IRA simultaneously attacked more than 300 police stations. A few months later, on November 21, Collins went one better, eliminating fourteen British undercover officers in eight separate locations at the same time. It was a brilliant psychological blow at the enemy's nerve center. The British responded a few days later by opening fire on the crowd at a Gaelic football game, killing fourteen people and wounding dozens.

Michael Collins decided to carry the struggle to England. That same year, on November 28, he sent a commando unit to Liverpool on a sabotage mission. Two Black and Tans were killed. The Liverpool operation was trivial from a military point of view, but it was a political triumph. With it, the IRA not only impacted English public opinion but also made itself heard internationally. The United States, uncontested victor of World War I and now a world power of the first order, stood with the Irish. It was home to millions of Irish, many of them recent immigrants. Supporters of Irish independence, their opinion was politically important in the United States. British Prime Minister Lloyd George was compelled to negotiate, and about a year later the Irish Free State was established. A fratricidal struggle erupted within the independence movement between those, like Collins, who accepted the partition of Ireland, and those, like de Valera, who rejected the accord. Collins had scant time to savor his victory. He fell in an ambush on August 22, 1922.

Several elements had to come together for the independence movement to achieve victory, or at least a semi-victory, since Ulster remained part of the United Kingdom. Who, other than they themselves, would have believed a few years earlier that the Irish independence fighters could win? The nationalist movement was fractured and poorly organized and enjoyed feeble public support. The factors that contributed to success included American support—financial at first, then political; nationalist resolve, which remained firm even in repeated failure; and the strategic genius of leaders like Michael Collins. The context of the war and the weariness of British public opinion did the rest. Throughout the struggle, and especially at the onset, the IRA had stumbled again and again, while the British were brutally efficient. Nonetheless, the latter had made an irreversible miscalculation in forgetting that the conflict had to be played out on the stage of politics. In responding to terror with terror, they fell into the IRA's trap.

The use of terror is not an option for a democratic nation and will lead to defeat, except perhaps in very exceptional cases and in distant theaters overseas (the colonies, for instance). And yet the British had ample experience from their colonies. Captain C. E. Callwell of the British Intelligence Division had theorized in the 1890s about the strategy of undertaking "small wars." The architects of the British counterinsurgency strategy had mostly had to deal with rebellions within the empire, but the context was different when violence erupted on national territory. In the case of Ireland, everything changed when the violence came home to British soil. The situation was similar for the United States after the September 11 attacks: American targets had been hit before, but far from the national territory. (It was no accident that U.S. embassies had been targeted on previous occasions, since they are legally part of national territory.) But when it comes to bona fide homeland territory, the scale of violence is radically different. A simple terrorist attack can have enormous repercussions.

THE BIRTH OF TERRORISM IN INDIA

While the Irish were attacking the British crown, the Indians, too, had begun contemplating the prospect of an India free of the English yoke. There again, Russia's example had transcended borders, and Russian terrorists had even helped Indians to build bombs. The emerging Indian nationalism was a mixture of Western ideology and the native cultural and religious traditions of the subcontinent. For the most part, nationalist leaders were members of the highest caste, the Brahmans (the priestly class). Bal Gangadhar Tilak, a spearhead of Indian nationalism and apostle of terrorist violence in the early twentieth century, preferred a show of force over the strategy of nonviolence rooted in Indian tradition. Here, too, the tradition of tyrannicide had enjoyed a revival. Nationalists in India, like those in Ireland before the Great War, were relatively ineffective. They did manage, however, to assassinate a member of the English government in London in 1909.

Vinayak Savarkar, leader of the Hindu movement Akhil Bharatiya Hindu Mahasabha and its military branch, the Rashtriya Swayamsevak Sangh (RSS), took a sectarian approach to the nationalist struggle, whereby any enemy of the RSS was an enemy of the people. His struggle targeted not only the English but Muslims as well. It was one of Savarkar's disciples who assassinated Gandhi in 1948.

Many members of the terrorist movements fighting for the liberation of India were defectors from Gandhi's movement. Disappointed by its lack of results, they turned to movements that sought to sway Great Britain through violence. Thanks to Gandhi, India enjoyed a well-founded reputation for nonviolence in the West and elsewhere, but the nonviolence associated with India's "peaceable" religions represents only one aspect of a society where violence is rife. In the struggle for Indian independence, these two aspects of Indian society competed against one another. Gandhi was resolutely opposed to recourse to violence, which he repeatedly denounced in public. Conversely, the Hindustan Socialist Republican Association, founded in the late 1920s, was firmly dedicated to violence and inspired by Marxist doctrine. It advocated revolution to abolish capitalism, erase class distinctions and privileges, and institute a dictatorship of the proletariat. In 1930, the movement published and distributed throughout India a manifesto entitled *The Philosophy of the Bomb,* in which it issued a justification of terrorism, without which, the authors believed, revolution was not possible. Terrorism, they wrote, "is a phase, a necessary, an inevitable phase of the revolution. . . . Terrorism instills fear in the hearts of the oppressors, it brings hopes of revenge and redemption to the oppressed masses."[14]

Equal parts revolutionary pamphlet and apologia for terrorism, *The Philosophy of the Bomb* is above all a personal attack on Mahatma Gandhi and his methods, saying: "It is a pity that Gandhi does not and will not understand revolutionary psychology in spite of the life-long experience of public life."[15] The moral basis of *The Philosophy of the Bomb* was yet another reversion to the concept of tyrannicide: "We shall have our revenge—a people's righteous revenge on the tyrant. Let cowards fall back and cringe for compromise and peace. We ask not for mercy and we give no quarter. Ours is a war to the end—to Victory or Death. LONG LIVE REVOLUTION."[16]

Despite such jarring declarations, the terrorist movement in India would be limited in both its impact and its duration. Another manifesto, issued in 1930, called for the orchestration of attacks on Western civil-

ians and certain infrastructures. The terrorists undertook a few assassinations here and there, but on the whole their statements about the class
struggle had little impact on a society still deeply immersed in the caste
system. The British response to these insurrectional movements had been
crowned with success by the mid 1930s. As in Ireland, it was war—this
time, World War II—that triggered the resurgence of terrorism. Here,
too, it eventually led to independence. Gandhi—having long understood
that the violence sparked by terrorist practices would be hard to control
and would ultimately backfire against the Indians, even after independence was achieved—was its most prominent victim.

MACEDONIANS, CROATS, AND ARMENIANS

In the nineteenth century, the Ottoman empire, which had occupied the
Balkans for some four hundred years (Sofia fell in 1385, Kosovo in 1389,
Belgrade in 1520), was under challenge by its Christian subjects in the
region, who sought freedom in the name of nationalism. Greece tore
loose in 1830 with the help of the European powers. Serbia rebelled in
1815 and the Bulgarians in 1878; their brutal suppression justified the
intervention of Russia, champion of the Slavs. The Ottomans withdrew
from a large portion of the Balkans in 1878, but remained fully in control in Albania, Macedonia, and Thrace. A remnant of empire, Macedonia, populated by Orthodox Christians as well as (Albanian) Muslims,
was claimed by Bulgaria, Greece, and Serbia.

Macedonia had received a raw deal in the 1878 Berlin agreements that
stripped the Ottoman empire of most of its European possessions. Well
known as a hornet's nest of multiple ethnicities and religions, it was one
of the most unstable regions in the Balkans.

Macedonia's neighbor Bulgaria, freed from the Turkish yoke in 1878,
offered safe haven to Macedonian independence fighters—many of
whom were Macedonian-born Bulgarians—determined to win for their
country what most of their neighbors had obtained at the Congress of
Berlin. The Macedonians' struggle, drawn out over the course of some
four decades, would eventually become an instrument of Bulgarian foreign policy, demonstrating yet again how frequently terrorist groups
come to be manipulated by states.

The Internal Macedonian Revolutionary Organization (IMRO) was
founded in 1893 at the initiative of Goce Delčev, a schoolteacher. IMRO
was born as a nationalist movement dedicated to achieving independence

for Macedonia. It was initially manned by civilians but later evolved into a standing paramilitary organization under the leadership of Todor Alexandrov.

IMRO's "comitadjis" (that is, its Committee members, a term borrowed from French and the French Revolution) went into action in April 1903, sinking a French ship delivering weapons to the Sublime Porte in Salonika. Bombs were set off in areas frequented by Europeans (casinos, cafes, etc.), but could not, as intended, provoke the powers into intervening. Changing tactics, IMRO attacked a Turkish garrison in Albania in August of that year. The reprisals were fierce, claiming tens of thousands of victims, but the European powers merely called for increased rights for the empire's Christian minorities. IMRO nevertheless pursued its activities, with an emphasis on terrorism, until the Young Turks revolution of 1908, which at the outset was enthusiastically welcomed by the populace, and especially by non-Muslims such as Christians and Jews, with the proclamation of equal rights for all subjects of the empire.

The movement had developed in Salonika, the base for numerous enlightened figures hoping to modernize the empire. Very soon, however, the "Ottomanism" program, based on the equality of all ethnic and/or religious communities, gave way to pan-Turkism. The empire was in acute crisis. In fact, it had been in its death throes since 1878 and had survived only because the powers, and Great Britain in particular, were concerned about how the spoils would be divided, and especially about Russian ambitions in the Dardanelles.

Tensions within the empire were high as the powers put it to the screws, reducing Turkey, at the financial level at least, to the status of a quasi-colony. The Ottoman empire lost Tripolitania (Libya) to Italy in 1911. In 1912, Bulgaria, Greece, and Serbia declared war and essentially drove the Turks from Europe. Constantinople did not fall, in part because of internal rivalries within the Balkan League. Albania became independent but did not recover territories with large Albanian majorities (Kosovo and the western part of what is now the state of Macedonia). Macedonia, which had fought for autonomy, or at least for annexation to Bulgaria, was swallowed up within Yugoslavia. IMRO continued its terrorist activities long after the end of the Great War. The movement hardened, and its struggle against Greece and, above all, Yugoslavia was even more violent than the one it had waged against the Turks.

Still operating from its base in Bulgaria, IMRO's leadership found itself cajoled by the USSR, which had inherited Russia's deep interest in the Balkans. Alexandrov was hostile to a rapprochement with Moscow and was assassinated by a pro-Soviet faction (Italy would later provide the Macedonians with arms and funds). The ensuing fratricidal struggle produced another dominating figure, Ivan Mihailov, who took command of the organization in 1928. Mihailov was a formidable administrator and businessman, but IMRO, whose tentacles were becoming ever more dangerous wherever they penetrated (notably, the Macedonian party in Bulgaria), gradually transformed itself into a mafia-type organization that accepted "contracts." Supported—although at arm's length—by Bulgaria and other interested powers, such as Italy, it was unable to survive when the source of that funding dried up. It was IMRO that would commit the most deadly terrorist attack of the first half of the twentieth century, however: a bombing in the Sveta Nedelia cathedral in Sofia that killed over one hundred people.

In the late 1920s, IMRO began offering training to the Croatian nationalist movement, a fellow enemy of the Yugoslav state that launched a series of attacks, bombing trains and assassinating public figures. Ante Pavelić, a Croatian lawyer in exile who had pleaded the Macedonian cause, joined up with Mihailov to create an independence organization worthy of the name. The Croatian resistance, known as the Ustaše, would make a name for itself in the years ahead; to this very day, it is seen as the embodiment of interbellum terrorism. Having settled in Vienna, Pavelić was ordered by the Austrian authorities to leave the country. He turned to Mussolini's Italy, which offered the Ustaše havens in the Lombard countryside and on the Adriatic coast where they could safely train. Hungary, equally hostile to the Serbs, likewise offered Pavelić its support.

Like IMRO, the Ustaše were committed to attacking civilian targets (unlike the IRA, for instance). Foreshadowing the hijackings of the 1970s and 1980s, they attacked trains, including the prestigious Orient Express, with the aim of bringing their cause to the world's attention. This was one of the first manifestations of the kind of publicity-minded terrorism that came to the fore in the late 1960s. In 1934, the Croatian resistance reached its acme with the assassination of the Serbian King Alexander I of Yugoslavia.

A commando unit of terrorists was sent on a mission to France to coincide with a long-planned visit by the king to Paris. Led by an Ustaša cadre, Eugen Kvaternik, it included a veteran IMRO murderer, "Vlada." The team got off the train in Fontainebleau and went on to Paris by car. There, the little group split in two, with one three-man team, including Kvaternik, heading for Marseille, where the king was to make his first stopover. A first attempt was planned to take place in Marseille; if that failed, a second would be undertaken in Paris.

Once their preparations were complete, Kvaternik left Marseille, while Vlada and Krajli, a trusty Ustaša hired hand, remained behind. The two were armed with handguns and grenades. The attack was to be undertaken at point-blank range during the motorcade procession through the streets of Marseille, a little like the Sarajevo assassination. On October 9, at 4:15 P.M., "Vlada" boldly leaped onto the runningboard of the king's vehicle, a Delage cabriolet, and shot him dead. The assassin took several bullets and a saber to the head, dying later that night. In the confusion, the French foreign minister, Louis Barthou, took a policeman's stray bullet in the shoulder, from which he later died. The other three members of the commando unit who had remained in France were captured and confessed.

The political nature of the crime provoked the intervention of the League of Nations, which in 1937 adopted a resolution that was the first piece of international legislation on terrorism. The Convention on the Prevention and Punishment of Terrorism, signed at Geneva on November 16, 1937, by twenty-five countries (not including Italy and the United States), defined terrorism as "criminal acts directed against a State and intended or calculated to create a state of terror in the minds of particular persons, or a group of persons or the general public." These include "[w]ilful destruction of, or damage to, public property or property devoted to a public purpose belonging to or subject to the authority of another High Contracting Party," and, finally, "[t]he manufacture, obtaining, possession, or supplying of arms, ammunition, explosives or harmful substances with a view to the commission in any country whatsoever of an offence falling within the present article."

Once their culpability had been established, the Ustaše were unable to exploit the assassination, the crowning achievement of their struggle, to further their ends. A paradox of terrorism is that when an attack succeeds too well, the perpetrators are caught up in the ensuing political maelstrom that they had sought to unleash. The September 11 attacks are a further illustration of this: the enormity of the attacks on New York and Washington, D.C., triggered the American response that brought down the Taliban regime in Afghanistan and dealt a very serious blow to al Qaeda. No matter how spectacular a strike may be, there is no guarantee that its results will be those sought by the terrorists. The death of Alexander I did nothing to help Croatia's cause, and September 11 brought down neither the United States nor the moderate Muslim regimes that bin Laden had hoped it would. Terrorists almost always demonstrate a greater aptitude for orchestrating violence than political acumen.

Like al Qaeda today, the Ustaše managed by hook or by crook to keep going. They lost the support they had previously enjoyed from Italy and Hungary. Ante Pavelić and Eugen Kvaternik were arrested by the Italians, who declined, however, to extradite them. The assassination caused a great sensation in Croatia, as well as in the world media.

The Croatians were briefly able to benefit from events that were beyond their control. In 1941, following the German advance into the Balkans in April, the Croatian state declared independence for itself and for Bosnia and Herzegovina. Pavelić took power, with German support, while Josip Broz, known as "Tito," went underground. Croatia's fate was dependent on the outcome of the war, so Pavelić's success was necessarily short-lived; in 1945, the former dictator and Ustaša leader fled to South America, and Tito took control of Yugoslavia.

Among all the independence movements of the first half of the twentieth century, that of the Armenians ended most tragically. Like other anti-Turkish nationalist movements, it took off in the late nineteenth century. Young Armenian students studying in Geneva, Paris, and Saint Petersburg, fired by Enlightenment ideas and socialist ideals, were inspired to fight against despotism upon their return home, some of them by force of arms. Between 1890 and 1908, several thousand Armenian *fedais* led a small-scale armed revolt against the empire. The earliest groups, made up for the most part of young urbanites, were quickly suppressed, but core cells gradually sprang up throughout eastern Anatolia, their aspirations nourished by the example of the Balkan insurrections against the empire. The Bulgarian uprising seemed to provide a particularly useful model. Armenia, however, was at the very center of the empire, unlike the peripheral Balkan states of Europe. The Ottoman empire may well have been "sick," but it remained a military power with a fearsome apparatus of repression.

On August 26, 1896, a commando unit of twenty-six Armenians undertook a terrorist operation intended to snap the European powers to attention. Militants overran the empire's primary financial center, the Ottoman Bank. The raid was strategically successful, in that foreign powers interceded to ensure the unit's escape, and the Turkish government pledged to undertake reforms. That did not, however, prevent the sultan from ordering massacres in Constantinople and numerous towns of Anatolia that claimed between 100,000 and 200,000 victims. The public outcry in Europe and America made the "Armenian question" a key factor in the "Question of the Orient."

The Young Turk rebellion, proclaiming equality among all the peoples of the empire, was warmly welcomed in 1908. The *fedais* laid down their arms, but their euphoria was short-lived. The radical elements in the government forced the moderates into opposition. Pan-Turkism replaced Ottomanism. The empire lost Libya and even loyal Albania. The Balkan wars almost entirely ousted the Turks from the European continent.

The Great Powers may have hoped for reform favorable to the Armenians, but the Great War buried those hopes. Having met with setbacks against the Russians in the Caucasus, the Young Turks decided to resolve the problem of Armenia by eliminating its population. The Armenians were ordered deported and a dedicated entity was mandated to oversee the murder of a nation. Armenian soldiers in the Ottoman army were liquidated in small groups. On April 24, 1915, Armenian political and intellectual leaders were rounded up and killed. Armenians throughout Anatolia were eliminated and half the empire's Armenian population died in the course of the twentieth century's first genocide.

Turkish leaders and the ringleaders of the crime were condemned in absentia by court-martial during the Allied occupation after World War I. Many had fled to Germany, and Berlin refused to extradite them. In response, the Armenian socialist Dashnak Party launched "Operation Nemesis," one of the very rare instances of a terrorist undertaking to avenge the annihilation of a people and to right a wrong. The "special mission" of Nemesis was in a direct line of descent from the tradition of tyrannicide.

The attacks were planned in Boston, Constantinople, and Yerevan, relayed through Geneva and carried out in Berlin, Rome, Tbilisi, and elsewhere. This little-known manhunt was one of the most extraordinary of the century.[17] Its instructions were clear: those responsible, and *only* those responsible, were to be assassinated.

The first attack took place in Berlin on March 15, 1921. Its target was Talaat Pasha, a member of the Young Turk triumvirate with Jemal Pasha and Enver Pasha. It took four months to plan. A 24-year-old who had lost his entire family in the war shot Talaat in the head on Hardenberg Strasse. Brought to trial, the assassin was unanimously acquitted by the jury.

The second assassination took place on December 5, 1921, in Rome. A 22–year-old approached the fiacre of Sayid Halim Pasha, former grand vizier of the Young Turk government, shot him in the head, and vanished from sight. Another flawless attack was carried out in Berlin, despatching Behaeddin Shakir, one of the organizers of the genocide, and Jemal Azmi, "the butcher of Trebizond." Triumvir Jemal Pasha was gunned down in Georgia in front of the Tbilisi headquarters of the secret police. But Operation Nemesis failed to eliminate the former police chief of Constantinople and Dr. Nazim, another chief organizer of the massacres and deportations. The latter was hanged as a conspirator by Mustafa Kemal a few years later. Enver Pasha was killed in Turkestan in 1922, fighting alongside the Basmachi against the Bolsheviks.

TERRORISM OF THE EXTREME RIGHT

Between the two wars, several high-profile assassinations received widespread publicity, including that of Walter Rathenau, the German foreign minister, by the Freikorps in 1922, and that of Italian deputy Giacomo Matteotti by the Fascists in June 1922. The Iron Guard succeeded in killing two prime ministers in Romania, Ion Duca in 1933 and Armand Călinescu in 1939. The extreme right, which enjoyed relatively broad popular support in a number of countries, was particularly partial to targeted assassinations. Its terrorism was aimed above all at eliminating political opponents. Its victims were often members of "outsider" groups, as defined by the extremists. In France, for instance, the extreme right relied far more on the press than on terror, although some tiny, marginal groups, such as Eugène Deloncle's Comité secret d'action révolutionnaire (the "Cagoule"), also carried out killings. (The CSAR murdered two anti-Fascist Italian exiles in 1937, but the *cagoulards* were dispersed soon thereafter.) Unlike the Soviet system, whose basic structure was cemented by institutionalized terror, the Fascist project was driven by violence that was motivated just as much by instinct as it was by reason. The same held true of National Socialism, in which state terror reached its acme.

NOTES TO CHAPTER 8

1. In 1875 and 1876, the populations of Bosnia and Herzegovina and Bulgaria had risen in revolt. William Gladstone, leader of the English Liberal Party, took up the cause of the insurgents, publishing a ringing panegyric entitled *Bulgarian Horrors and the Question of the East*. The 1878 Congress of Berlin stripped the Turkish empire of Serbia, Montenegro, Romania, Bosnia and Herzegovina, Thessaly, Epirus, and Bessarabia. In order to block Russian expansion in the region and to prevent the unification of the southern Slavs, Bosnia and Herzegovina were placed under Austrian trusteeship.

2. Venner, *Histoire du terrorisme*, 37.

3. Ibid., 32.

4. The IRA used a helicopter to drop bombs in 1974.

5. Most, "Science of Revolutionary Warfare," in *Confronting Fear*, ed. Cronin, 17.

6. *Die Freiheit*, September 13, 1884.

7. *Die Freiheit*, July 25, 1885

8. Ibid.

9. Laqueur, *History of Terrorism*, 87.

10. Ibid., 85.

11. Ibid.

12. Ibid., 86.

13. The partisans of Irish independence declared independence on January 21, 1919. After three years of conflict, the treaty conference in London concluded the Anglo-Irish Treaty, dividing Ireland into two entities. The Irish Free State (Éire), with twenty-six counties, became a co-equal dominion of the British Empire; Ulster, with its six counties, remained part of the United Kingdom. On January 8, 1922, the treaty was ratified in Dublin over the objections of President Éamon de Valera.

14. Laqueur, ed., *Terrorism Reader* (1978 ed.), 139.

15. Ibid.

16. Ibid., 140.

17. Derogy, *Opération Némésis*.

CHAPTER 9

LENIN, STALIN, AND STATE TERRORISM

Gérard Chaliand and Arnaud Blin

LENIN AND STRATEGIC TERRORISM

In its various forms, Russian terrorism had helped to weaken the Russian state and set the stage for the 1917 Revolution, whereupon the tactics of terror soon merged with the Soviet state. Lenin installed a system that Stalin would take to extremes.

For the young Lenin, terror was only one of the tools of revolution. Although he rejected its use in 1899, it was only because he believed there to be critical organizational problems at the time. In 1901, he claimed in an article in *Iskra* that he had not rejected the "principle of terror," yet criticized Socialist Revolutionaries (SRs) for their reliance on terrorism without having explored other forms of struggle.

Lenin felt that terrorist tactics were part of a larger political-military strategy and that they should be deployed methodically and cautiously; he believed that the SRs, for whom terrorism had become an end in itself, had failed to grasp this point. For Lenin, terror was not the principal instrument of revolution and should therefore not become a "standard tool" of the armed struggle.

If terrorist tactics were to be effective, Lenin believed, they had to go beyond attacks perpetrated by individuals or small cells. It was popular terror carried out by the masses that would ultimately lead to the overthrow of the monarchy (and capitalism) when the armed forces joined the people. Lenin was firmly opposed to regicidal terrorism, in which he saw no future. At the second congress of the Russian Social Democratic Workers' Party (RSDWP) in 1903, he spoke heatedly against terrorism. It was at this time that the party split into two factions, the Bolsheviks on one side and the Mensheviks one the other.

Because he systematically denounced the terrorism practiced by the SRs, Lenin is sometimes perceived as having been unfavorably disposed toward terrorism. In fact, he had been an apostle of terror ever since his earliest days as a political activist, but from an entirely different angle. While he criticized such "duels" with the tsarist authorities, which led only to popular apathy, with the mass audience awaiting the next "duel," his position remained unchanged right up to the Bolshevik seizure of power in 1917: "Terror, but not yet." The delay only amplified the force with which terror was unleashed once power fell into Lenin's hands. Indeed, it was not an excess of terror that he condemned, but precisely the opposite. Terror, if it was to be applied effectively, had to be mass terror directed against the Revolution's enemies.

As of the third congress of the RSDWP, held in London in the spring of 1905—the 1905 Revolution had taken place in January—Lenin began talking of mass terror, taking his cue from the French Revolution. Lenin believed that, once the revolution began, if any number of Vendée-type mutinies were to be avoided, it would not be enough to execute the tsar. If the revolution were to succeed, "preventive measures" would need to be taken to nip any manifestation of anti-revolutionary resistance in the bud. Terror tactics would be the most efficient means to that end. He felt that Jacobin-style "mass terror" would be needed to crush the Russian monarchy.

It was also in 1905 that Lenin drafted his instructions for the revolutionary takeover. He advocated two essential activities: independent military actions and mob control. He encouraged ongoing terrorist activities but from a strategic perspective, because he continued to denounce terrorist attacks undertaken by lone individuals without connection to the masses: "Disorderly, unorganised and petty terrorist acts may, if carried to extremes, only scatter and squander our forces. That is a fact, which, of course, should not be forgotten. On the other hand, under no circumstances should it be forgotten that a slogan calling for an uprising has already been issued, that the uprising has already begun. To launch attacks under favourable circumstances is not only every revolutionary's right, but his plain duty."[1]

The revolution of 1905 had failed because of lack of will, resolve, and organization, Lenin believed. Revolutionaries had to go further and unleash widespread violence. At that time, however, Lenin was powerless, restricted to composing virulent critiques of the revolutionaries from his distant exiles in Finland and Switzerland. In 1907, he sent the following message to the SRs: "Your terrorism is not the result of your revolutionary conviction. It is your revolutionary conviction that is limited to terrorism."

The following year, he endorsed the assassination of King Carlos of Portugal and his son, but lamented that such attacks were isolated phenomena without specific strategic goals. It always came down to the revolutionaries' lack of strategic perspective, despite their courage. The 1917 Revolution substantiated his warnings: at precisely the right moment, when the situation was sufficiently "ripe," direct action succeeded in tipping the scales.

When war erupted, Lenin distanced himself even further from the other socialist movements, with which he rejected all collaboration. He laid out his position in his classic essay, "Imperialism, the Highest Stage of Capitalism": socialist revolution can be achieved in an economically backward country only when it is led by a vanguard party prepared to go the distance—that is, prepared to resort to extreme violence and undaunted by massive bloodletting. The time was ripe for the dictatorship of the proletariat—that is, de facto, of the vanguard party.

The Bolsheviks, with Lenin at their head, plunged headlong into the vast abyss suddenly opened up by Russia's dramatic collapse. In this political vacuum, the Bolsheviks, with fewer than 25,000 members, were able to seize power because the other revolutionary political parties proved incapable of bringing events under their control following the February revolution.

To a certain extent, the historiography of the October Revolution follows that of the French Revolution of 1789. Russian historians have embraced the "accident" theory ever since the collapse of the Soviet Union in 1991, following decades of Soviet interpretation of that event as the historical culmination of the people's revolution under the guidance of the Bolsheviks.[2] Between both is the "hijacking" theory whereby the revolution launched by the masses was appropriated by a small group that abused its power. We subscribe to Nicolas Werth's analysis, according to which the 1917 Revolution "would appear to be the temporary convergence of two movements: a political power play, the outcome of meticulous insurrectionary planning by a party whose practices, organization, and ideology set it radically apart from all other protagonists of the Revolution; and a vast, multifaceted, and autonomous revolution."[3]

Whatever the case, the tiny Bolshevik Party found itself running an immense country in the grip of a crisis that would lead to civil war and in the middle of the most terrible conflict Europe had ever known. The Bolshevik Party, however, was strong enough to weather the combined impact of all these forces and, through the skill of its leaders, hold on to power.

Lenin was quick to reveal his true character and political convictions. When, on October 26 and November 8, 1917, the Congress of Soviets decided to abolish the death penalty, Lenin declared this "error" to be "unacceptable" and hastened to reinstitute it. Shortly thereafter, a few lines in *Izvestia* unobtrusively announced the establishment of one of the most fearsome instruments of terror ever conceived: "By decree of the Soviet of People's Commissars is created on December 7, 1917, the All-Russian Extraordinary Commission to Combat Counter-Revolution and Sabotage [the Cheka]. Cheka Headquarters at 2 Gorokhovaya Street is open to inquiries every day from noon to 5 P.M."[4]

Thus was created the Soviet secret police, forebear of the KGB, that would send millions of people to the Gulag over the course of thirty-five years. Only a few months later, a new decree announced the establishment of "local chekas to combat sabotage and counterrevolution." Naturally, these chekas were mandated to "prevent counterrevolution, speculation, and abuses of power, including by means of the press. . . . Henceforth, the right to undertake arrests, searches, requisitions, and other aforementioned measures attaches exclusively to those chekas, both in Moscow and in the field."

"Terror" became a term evoked more and more often by political leaders, as seen in the following letter sent by Lenin to Zinoviev when he learned that the workers were threatening a general strike in support of the Bolshevik reaction (including mass arrests in late June 1918) to the assassination of one of their leaders, Volodarsky:

> Only today we have heard at the C.C. that in Petrograd the *workers* wanted to reply to the murder of Volodarsky by mass terror and that you (not you personally, but the Petrograd Central Committee members, or Petrograd Committee members) restrained them.
> I protest most emphatically!
> We are discrediting ourselves: we threaten mass terror, even in resolutions of the Soviet of Deputies, yet when it comes to action we *obstruct* the revolutionary initiative of the masses, a *quite* correct one.
> This is im-poss-ible!

The terrorists will consider us old women. This is wartime above all. We must encourage the energy and mass character of the terror against the counter-revolutionaries, and particularly in Petrograd, the example of which is *decisive*.[5]

The situation in the summer of 1918 was highly precarious. Suddenly, everything seemed to be hanging in the balance for the Bolsheviks. Not only did they control only a very small amount of territory, but they were also fighting on three anti-revolutionary fronts and were compelled to put down 140 uprisings over the course of the summer. The instructions issued to local chekas for dealing with the crisis grew increasingly specific: arrests, hostage-taking among the bourgeoisie, the establishment of concentration camps. Lenin asked for the promulgation of a decree to the effect that "in every grain-producing district, twenty-five designated hostages from among the wealthiest local inhabitants should answer with their lives if the requisition plan is not fulfilled."

Throughout that summer, the Bolshevik Party undertook the systematic destruction of legal protections for the individual. Some members believed that civil war knew no "written laws," which were reserved for "capitalist warfare." Terror, launched long before their power was secure, would allow the Bolsheviks to entrench themselves definitively. The revolutionary logic was the same as that in France in 1793–94. Lenin seized the opportunity offered by two incidents to launch a terror campaign. On August 30, 1918, two unrelated attacks targeted the top Cheka official in Petrograd and Lenin himself.[6] The first was an act of vengeance committed by a young student acting alone. The second, attributed to the young militant anarchist Fanny Kaplan—who was executed without trial immediately thereafter—was perhaps an act of provocation originating with the Cheka. Whatever the case, the Petrograd *Krasnaya Gazeta* set the tone the very next day: "As we recently wrote, we will answer a single death with a million. We have been compelled to action. How many lives of working-class women and children does every bourgeois have on his conscience? There are no innocents. Every drop of Lenin's blood must cost the bourgeoisie and the Whites hundreds of lives."[7] The party leaders sounded the same death knell in a statement signed by Dzerzhinsky: "May the working class use mass terror to crush the hydra of the counterrevolution!"[8] The following day, September 4, *Izvestia* editorialized that "no weakness or hesitation will be tolerated in the implementation of mass terror."[9]

And indeed, what would come to be known as the "Red terror"[10] was embodied in the official decree released on September 5: "It is of the first necessity that security behind the front be maintained through terror. . . . Furthermore, in order to protect the Soviet Republic from its class enemies, the latter must be segregated in concentration camps. All persons involved in White Guard organizations, conspiracies or rebellions must face the firing squad."[11] The decree ended with the following order: "Lastly, the names of all those who have been shot, along with the reasons for their punishment, must be published." In fact, only a small number of those who were executed was officially inventoried. As to the "reasons" for their execution, they must be sought in the arbitrary rationales of institutionalized terror. There are no precise figures for the Red terror, and for good reason. Estimates of the number of its victims between 1917 and 1921 place them anywhere between 500,000 and nearly two million.[12] Clearly, institutional terror had no need to wait for Stalin to make its mark. A comparative study with the tsarist period is even more telling: more death sentences were meted out in the first two months of the Red terror—some 10,000 to 15,000 executions—than throughout the nearly 100 years from 1825 to 1917 (6,321 political executions, of which 1,310 took place in 1906).

From the very onset of the regime of terror in September 1918, we find most of the elements that would characterize the terror practiced not only by Lenin—and later, far more intensively, by Stalin—but also by other political regimes claiming the Marxist-Leninist mantle, including in China under Mao Zedong, Cambodia under Pol Pot, and, more recently, in North Korea. Throughout the twentieth century, state terror directed against the masses claimed far more victims than did terrorism directed against the state, often in the name of those self-same masses. While the toll of those who died in anti-state terror amounts to a few thousand victims, those who fell to state terrorism number in the tens of millions. According to the authors of the *Livre noir du communisme,* state terror in the Soviet Union claimed some twenty million.[13] China can claim some sixty-five million. In a very brief span of time, Nazi Germany far exceeded the ten-million mark.

"What is terror?" asked Isaac Steinberg, who, as people's commissar for justice, was in the vanguard from December 1917 to May 1918. His answer:

Terror is systematic violence from the top down, acted upon or ripe for action. Terror is a legal blueprint for massive intimidation, compulsion and destruction, directed by power. It is the precise, sophisticated and scrupulously weighted inventory of penalties, punishments and threats employed by the government to induce fear, and which it uses and abuses to compel the people to do its will. . . . The "enemy of the revolution" assumes vast proportions when a timorous, mistrustful and isolated minority wields total power. The criterion expands without constraint, gradually embracing the entire country, ultimately applying to all but those who hold the power. The minority that rules by terror always ends up broadening its actions by dint of the principle that there are no rules when it comes to the "enemy of the revolution."[14]

And yet, state terrorism—that is, terrorism wielded by the strong against the weak—and terrorism wielded by the weak against the strong have much in common. A terror campaign seeks to instil a sense of general insecurity by threatening to strike anyone at any time. During the great Stalinist purges, officeholders at the highest level of the terrorist regime were potential victims, and no one but Stalin was safe.

Once certain victims begin to be targeted over others, arbitrariness becomes the hallmark of almost all forms of terrorism, with the exception of tyrannicide. A system of arbitrary hostage-taking was put in place at the very outset of the Red terror. In Novosibirsk, for example, the authorities established a random periodical day of house arrest for the entire population to facilitate roundups. In Moscow, a raid was carried out in a department store.[15] The initial reaction of any victim of Soviet terror was incomprehension: he or she was innocent, and would surely be released once the mistake had been discovered. The same holds true for the victim of al Qaeda; in a terrorist attack in Riyadh on October 9, 2003, one victim interviewed by journalists was baffled by the fact that a bomb had targeted Muslims rather than Westerners, whereas the logical aim of the operation was to destabilize the Saudi government. This is the very essence of terrorism, regardless of its origins; its strength lies in its arbitrary selection of victims. Whether he holds power or is fighting it, the terrorist seeks to broadcast that psychosis. The only difference between them is that anti-state terrorism seeks to destabilize authority, while state terrorism seeks conversely to stabilize it and to destabilize the population at large. A terrorist state has often been established following a struggle in which terrorism played a role, thereby preempting control of that strategic and psychological weapon. The means employed by these two forms of terrorism vary. The terrorist state enjoys every resource of the state apparatus. The "private" terrorist, in contrast, seeks to exploit the weaknesses of the state, or of the society that he is supposed to be representing and protecting. To a certain extent, the terrorist state acts preventively so as to nip in the bud any attempt to contest its power, including by terrorists.

Having come to power, the terrorist state has to eradicate every vestige of the old power, as the Bolsheviks did symbolically by assassinating the tsar and his family. Its second objective must be to eliminate all potential aspirants to power and all its opponents. This was the situation with the French Revolution as early as 1793–94. Lenin drew on the lesson of Robespierre's downfall by mastering the instrument of terrorism and got right down to the work of eliminating his political or ideological adversaries, starting with the anarchists, who were the first to denounce the co-optation of the Revolution and the Bolshevik dictatorship. The anarchists became the earliest victims of the Red terror. The anti-anarchist terror began even before September 1918 and intensified once the state apparatus, the army in particular, was strong enough to promote widespread terror. In April, Trotsky led the first terror campaign against the "anarcho-bandits." After Russia, the persecution of anarchists spread to the Ukraine. The anti-anarchist campaign sought not only to eliminate a political adversary; anarchist thought itself was soon outlawed. The authorities used the repression to crush any will to resist that might be entertained by other groups.

The terror touched even those who were only vaguely associated with the anarchists, such as distant relatives. Logically, the terror targeted all political rivals of the Bolsheviks, starting with the Mensheviks and the SRs, both on the right—their most dangerous rivals—and on the left. The latter quit the government after the signing of the Treaty of Brest-Litovsk in the spring of 1918, while the former were expelled from the All-Russia Central Executive Committee. The leader of the Left Socialist Revolutionary Party, Maria Spiridonova, denounced the terror and was promptly removed by the Bolsheviks in 1919. Sentenced by the Revolutionary Tribunal, she was the first person to be incarcerated in a psychiatric hospital for political reasons (she later escaped and secretly resumed leadership of her party, which by then had been banned). The Mensheviks and Right SRs, occasional allies, were targeted by the Cheka beginning in 1919.

The workers, on whose behalf the Revolution had ostensibly been fought, were not spared. A strike could bring an entire factory under suspicion of treason. Its organizers, naturally, were arrested and put to death, along with some of the workers. In November, the Motovilikha weapons plant was subject to such repression by the local Cheka, urged on by the central authorities. Some 100 strikers were executed.[16] The same scenario unfolded the following spring at the Putilov factory. Elsewhere, numerous strikes were harshly suppressed, such as in Astrakhan and Tula. Anti-worker terror reached its apogee in 1921 during the Kronstadt uprising, where, on Trotsky's orders, the Red Army was sent in to massacre the mutinous sailors of the battleship *Petropavlovsk*.

Rebellious peasants, too, in Tambov and elsewhere, were subject to the same law. Among the units of the Red Army, manned for the most part by soldiers of peasant stock, mutinies erupted and were put down with equal brutality. The suppression of the Cossacks demonstrated that the terror was not limited to social and economic categories, but that it could be aimed at specific groups as well.

It became necessary to identify a legal basis for the internment of prisoners as soon as possible, which was accomplished through the systematic institution of concentration camps. A decree of 1919 distinguished two types of camps: corrective labor camps and bona fide concentration camps; the distinction was entirely theoretical. The concentration-camp universe of the Gulag, with its millions of "zeks," would become one of the foundations of the Soviet regime and the symbol of state terror bequeathed to posterity by the USSR.

Lenin, who had been ailing since March 1923, died on January 24, 1924, and from 1923 to 1927, the country enjoyed a "truce," which lasted until the succession could be secured. Calls went up within the government for the system to be relaxed. In the context of the struggle for succession, however, the political police came to serve Stalin's interests, which lay in eradicating his rivals, Trotsky first among them. Once their power was assured and their rivals done away with, Stalin and his cronies were able to revive the political terror, which had temporarily, and only relatively, eased off. By the late 1920s, the terrorist system was well entrenched in Soviet policy. Stalin made full use of the head start Lenin had given him to push the limits that had been established by his mentor. It took the horrors of Nazi terror to overshadow those of the USSR in the eyes of the world, however briefly. As Hannah Arendt rightly noted, by some ideological sleight-of-hand, the vision of the horrors of the Nazi camps served to mask the realities of the Soviet ones.

STALIN, OR STATE TERROR

In the early 1930s, Stalin experimented with using terror against the peasantry through his infamous "dekulakization" campaign. Forced collectivization unleashed a famine that claimed almost six million victims. The 1930s also witnessed a revival of generalized terror against certain sectors of the populace, in anticipation of the Great Terror of 1936–37. Stalin took the state apparatus established by Lenin—party dictatorship—and transformed it into the instrument of power of just one man. In order to impose this new system—which he believed was the answer to the problem of modernizing and industrializing the country—Stalin drew on his policy's sole means of enforcement: terror. Under Lenin, the apparatus of repression had served the party; under Stalin, it was the party that served the apparatus of repression.[17]

The terror of the 1930s was organized in stages. The purges of 1933 were followed by the respite of 1934. The purges resumed in late 1934 and lasted until late 1935. In early 1936, a brief pause preceded the Great Terror of 1936–38, which peaked in 1937. The Stalinist terror touched the base and the elite alike, assailing peasants and workers, on the one hand, and leading figures of the political and military apparatuses, on the other, along with the entire party membership. Stalin's aim was to create a completely new political machine entirely dedicated to his cause. The old guard had managed to survive right up to 1936, when it was struck down headlong by the Moscow trials.

These impressive trials, at which Stalin's former companions confessed their "crimes" before a tribunal, seized the international public's attention. In fact, they partially eclipsed the widespread campaign of terror being waged throughout the country, striking the peoples of every Soviet province without distinction of class or nationality.

For these people, this meant unremitting dread. Dread of hearing a knock on the door in the middle of the night; dread of disappearing forever. Collectively, the psychological toll was appalling and impossible to quantify. Insecurity, fear, and unpredictability were the order of the day. At work and even at home, suspicion was ubiquitous. The least false step or unguarded word could mean death or the Gulag. No prospect of an end was in sight, nor was faultless behavior any guarantee of safety. In terms of actual victims, the Stalinist terror can boast of having eliminated several million people, although the exact or even approximate figure may never be known.[18] Given the psychological impact on a nation of a terrorist attack that kills a few dozen people, it is not hard to imagine the effects on a country in which everyone knew at least one victim of Stalin's terror: a parent, a relative, a neighbor, or a colleague, if not all of these at the same time.

The system that Stalin set in place was of unparalleled perversity; not only was he the grand architect of the nationwide terror, but it was also to him that the people looked to be protected from that terror, whose mechanisms they only dimly understood. Stalin was seen as the final bulwark against the arbitrary nature of the terror.[19] As with all totalitarian regimes, the perversity also lay in the leaders' resolve to impart a semblance of legality to a system based on the rule of fear, arbitrary power, and illegitimacy.

Of all totalitarian regimes, that of the Soviet Union was, between 1929 and 1953, the most perfect embodiment of state terrorism. No other country had ever been so systematically subjected to terror imposed by the apparatus of a police state. On the other hand, the USSR had many emulators in Europe and Asia that occasionally rivaled it for perversity in the implementation of institutionalized terror. The pinnacle, a combination of Soviet-inspired state terrorism and the Nazi taste for extermination, was reached in Cambodia in the 1970s.

NOTES TO CHAPTER 9

1. Lenin, "Tasks of Revolutionary Army Contingents" (October 1905).

2. See Werth, "État contre son peuple," in Courtois et al., *Livre noir du communisme*, 45–46.

3. Ibid., 46

4. *Izvestiya*, no. 248, December 10, 1917, cited in Baynac, *Les socialistes-révolutionnaires*, 57.

5. Lenin, *Collected Works*, vol. 35, letter 149.

6. See Werth, "État contre son peuple," 85.

7. Quoted in Venner, *Histoire du terrorisme*, 61.

8. *Izvestia*, September 3, 1918, cited in Werth, "État contre son peuple," 86.

9. *Izvestia*, September 4, 1918, cited in ibid.

10. As opposed to the "White terror" carried out at the same time, less systematically but equally brutally, by the monarchist Whites in the civil war.

11. *Izvestia*, September 10, 1918, cited in Baynac, *Les socialistes-révolutionnaires*, 59.

12. Ibid., p. 75.

13. Mostly by execution (by firing squad, hanging, beating, gas, poison, and "accidents"), as well as by hunger and deportation. See Courtois et al., *Livre noir du communisme*, 8.

14. Steinberg, "L'aspect éthique de la revolution," in Baynac, *Les socialistes-révolutionnaires*, 363–64.

15. Baynac, *Les socialistes-révolutionnaires*, 142

16. Werth, "État contre son peuple."

17. See Carrère d'Encausse, *Staline*, 41.

18. For more detailed figures on the Great Terror, available since the opening of the KGB archives, see Werth, "État contre son peuple," 216–36. Also see Conquest, *Great Terror*.

19. Werth, "État contre son peuple," 68–69.

CHAPTER 10

TERRORISM IN TIME OF WAR
From World War II to the
Wars of National Liberation

Gérard Chaliand and Arnaud Blin

World War II marked a strategic break with the past and changed everything, among other things transforming terrorism into an instrument of
resistance. Contemporary terrorism did not hit its stride until the 1960s,
but it was born in World War II and in the wars of national liberation
that followed upon it and continued throughout the 1940s, 1950s, and
1960s (and even beyond in the case of Portugal). Throughout that period, which also marked the apogee of the cold war, terrorism was above
all a terrorism of war, serving, through one technology in particular, a
strategy of attrition.

Whereas World War II represented both the apex and the end of the
era of mass warfare, the ensuing decades saw a great strategic upheaval
with, on the one hand, the evolution of nuclear strategy and, on the
other, the emergence of limited warfare, the latter being in part a consequence of the former. The Cold War, beginning almost immediately after
the end of the world war, made the strategy of total warfare obsolete and
unleashed the strategies of limited and indirect warfare, promoting the
outbreak of all sorts of "low intensity" conflicts. At the same time, the
confrontation between two rival blocs polarized ideological conflicts. In
a classic pattern, the wars of colonial liberation profited from this new
dynamic by generally situating national liberation movements in a
"Marxist-Leninist" context, for reasons that were practical as well as

ideological, since they were thereby guaranteed the support of the Soviet Union or China. Consequently, national liberation movements tended to rely on an indirect strategy based on guerrilla warfare and terrorism. It was on the heels of the anti-colonial experience of those national liberation movements, many of which developed during World War II, that most of the terrorist groups of the 1960s emerged, a few of which endure to this day.

THE TRANSFORMATION OF
THE STRATEGIC LANDSCAPE

From a strategic point of view, the twentieth century was, among other things and above all, a century of psychological warfare, the most violent manifestation of which is terrorism. This was due to several factors. First, total warfare created a new center of gravity: civilian populations. They were the fulcrum of full national mobilization and thus became its target as well. As these populations could be struck at physically and directly in only a limited way, they were bombarded with propaganda and psychological violence.

From that point on, technology was designed to provide, at least in theory, instruments capable of affecting the morale of an entire people.

The brand-new technology of aerial warfare introduced a whole new dimension in that regard. Interbellum theoreticians developed an approach that culminated in the doctrine of strategic bombing—that is, the bombing of civilians intended to evoke such a feeling of terror that they would lose the will to fight and compel their government to give up the war effort. It was on such doctrine that the decision was based to bomb Hiroshima and Nagasaki.

With the invention of nuclear weapons, and of the hydrogen bomb in particular, the psychological dimension of warfare became paramount. In the late 1950s, One of the most high-profile architects of the American nuclear strategy, Albert Wohlstetter, coined the phrase "balance of terror" in a 1958 RAND paper. The balance of terror is based on the principle of mutual deterrence, hinging on the hope that the terror evoked by nuclear weapons will be enough to dissuade one's adversary from using them. The confrontation played itself out through indirect conflicts of varying types, including guerrilla warfare and terrorism. The Korean War, from 1950 to 1953, was the first indirect confrontation between the United States and the Soviet Union. The Cold War soon spread to other theaters, and to the colonies in particular, where the British,

French, Dutch, and Portuguese were compelled to confront liberation movements at the very moment when the colonial powers had lost their aura of invincibility following World War II. Such movements were often underwritten by the USSR and the People's Republic of China. For nationalists, the system of the Marxist-Leninist vanguard proved to be a formidable organizational tool for such conflict. Moreover, some of these movements were initially supported by the United States, as in Vietnam, where it sought to counter Vichy France by supporting Ho Chi Minh, somewhat as it would later do with bin Laden in Afghanistan before the latter, like Ho Chi Minh, turned against his patron.

The great European colonial powers became, for the most part, liberal democracies (with the exception of Portugal). A twofold incongruity had thereby evolved over the decades: on the one hand, those countries were no longer powers of the first order, having been supplanted by the United States and the USSR; on the other, they had adopted values contrary to those embodied by the colonial and imperialist spirit. Their governments, whose natural inclination was to maintain their nations' assets and to safeguard the national territory, for the most part resisted the demands of the independence movements. The British and the Dutch adapted more readily than the French to the new spirit of the times. From 1946 to 1962, France fought two long rearguard conflicts. The senescent dictatorship of Portugal pursued three colonial wars before collapsing in 1974.

It was in that very particular context, and against the background of the Cold War, nuclear weapons, and changing times, that a new kind of warfare arose around colonialism, one in which political victory was no longer linked to military victory, at least when the conflict involved a democratic state. This basic shift was understood better and sooner by the national liberation movements, like that in Vietnam, than by the West in general, which struggled to adapt itself to the swiftly changing strategic landscape. From the moment when political victory came to rely as much, if not above all, on psychological warfare as it did on military supremacy, terrorism became one of the keys to such ascendancy. That was one of the lessons of France's war in Algeria.

Isolated, yet protected by its insularity, England's only hope of weakening Germany, which had essentially subdued the entire continent, lay in strategic bombing and nurturing hotbeds of resistance if it wished ultimately to take the military offensive. "Now set Europe ablaze," Winston Churchill proclaimed in summation of his indirect strategy. In order to do so, Churchill created a specialized entity, the Special Operations Executive, or SOE, which, among other things, lent support to resistance movements, including those in France. And in France as elsewhere, the insurrectional struggle attracted communists, who played a significant role in the French resistance once Hitler had breached the Nazi-Soviet pact.

The first terrorist attack took place in Paris on August 21, 1941, as 5,000 Jewish prisoners were being transferred to the camp that had recently been opened in Drancy. Alfons Moser, a naval cadet chosen at random, was shot down at the Barbès metro station and died with two bullets to the head. The Germans reacted with mass reprisals against the civilian population, including the execution of hostages. The repression was out of all proportion to the attack. In any such strategy, the captive population becomes a pawn. The terrorists were seeking to poison relations between occupier and occupied. The Barbès attack, which claimed a single victim (other attacks on German soldiers took place in the following weeks), while thousands of German combatants were dying anonymously at the front, demonstrates the psychological impact of terrorist violence, even in wartime and even when the killing was at its height. Resistance to Nazi occupation arose in various forms in western Europe, but most especially in Poland, Greece, and, above all, in Yugoslavia and Albania.

ETHICS AND TERRORISM

The casuistry surrounding warfare is almost unanimous in its condemnation of terrorist acts. The Just War doctrine, for instance, permits an act of war only if it is undertaken by a bona fide state. It condemns all actions taken against noncombatants, that is, civilians. Lacking a well-defined ethical context in which to consider terrorism per se, we fall back on a political ethic that judges an act by its consequences. The "terrorists" of the French resistance were heroes because they were fighting the Nazis and because, in any case, their tactics avoided direct action against the civilian population. The stakes were so high that the ends justified the means. Those who planted bombs in the Algerian war did not enjoy such unanimous approval, even though the struggle against "colonial imperialism" was waged with historical justification. The ethics of warfare judges motives and motivations, and not necessarily the acts themselves, which are elements of a broader whole. Generally speaking, terrorism is better tolerated when it is part of a comprehensive strategy that embraces other, more traditional instruments of war.

The war in Algeria, for example, was considered by the French authorities to be not a war at all, but a matter of domestic security, since Algeria was French. The tactics deployed by the "rebels" were described as criminal rather than as acts of war, which, from a legalistic perspective, was not untrue.

In general, the less an act of terrorism resembles an act of war, the more likely it is to be condemned. The term "terrorist" is a qualifier with negative connotations. A terrorist rarely describes himself as such. He sees himself, rather, as a combatant or as a revolutionary, for instance, compelled to resort to terror within the logic of the weak fighting the strong in the service of a cause.

Paradoxically, those who espouse a pure and ruthless realpolitik are often the first to judge an act of terrorism according to moral criteria.

WAR AND ITS AFTERMATH

The Balfour Declaration legitimizing the creation of a "Jewish national homeland" in Palestine was based on an ambiguous set of terms, since, ultimately, such a homeland was supposed not to be established at the expense of the local population. Jabotinsky's analysis of the situation therefore seems in retrospect to have been the most lucid and clearly expressed study of the political reality:

> We cannot offer any adequate compensation to the Palestinian Arabs in return for Palestine. And therefore, there is no likelihood of any voluntary agreement being reached. So that all those who regard such an agreement as a condition sine qua non for Zionism may as well say "non" and withdraw from Zionism.
>
> Zionist colonisation must either stop, or else proceed regardless of the native population. Which means that it can proceed and develop only under the protection of a power that is independent of the native population—behind an iron wall, which the native population cannot breach.
>
> That is our Arab policy; not what we should be, but what it actually is, whether we admit it or not.[1]

Confrontations erupted between the two communities as early as 1920. They resumed in 1929 and more ferociously between 1936 and 1939. Guerrilla and terrorist-type actions were undertaken on both sides. From 1937 on, the Jewish Irgun Zvai Leumi (National Military Organization), created by Jabotinsky, met and responded to Arab violence. On February 27, it struck at several villages and Jerusalem's Arab Quarter simultaneously. That year, Great Britain decided to halt Jewish immigration to Palestine in order to avoid alienating the Arabs. The Jews in Palestine numbered some 450,000 at that time.

When World War II broke out, the Jewish Agency offered to contribute to the war effort by establishing a Jewish Brigade Group under British command. The terrorists being held in British prisons in Palestine were released in exchange for their enrollment in the brigade. Among them was Abraham Stern, who soon broke with the Irgun to create his own group to pursue his fight against the Mandate power. He was killed in 1942, the same month that a ship carrying 800 Jewish refugees was refused entry by several Middle Eastern ports and later sank in the Black Sea. The Stern Gang tried to avenge their deaths by striking at the man it held responsible, British High Commissioner Sir Harold McMichael. The commissioner proved to be too well protected, but the Stern Gang later succeeded in assassinating Secretary of State Lord Moyne in November 1944.

In the meantime, the Irgun had declared a cease-fire with the British occupier for the duration of the war. With Jabotinsky's death in 1940, the Irgun leadership was assumed by Menachem Begin, who arrived in Palestine in 1942. Together with the organization's military commander, David Raziel, he restructured the movement.

Following the publication of the British White Paper of 1939 establishing a Jewish immigration quota, British administrative centers in Haifa and Tel Aviv were attacked, along with various other government buildings. The organization's most spectacular attack was directed against the King David Hotel, headquarters of the British Military Command, on July 22, 1946, killing ninety-one and wounding many more, most of them civilians. One leader of the commando unit was Menachem Begin, later prime minister of Israel from 1977 to 1983, and Nobel Prize laureate, with President Anwar Sadat of Egypt, following the Camp David accords of 1978. Begin wrote in his memoirs:

> The historical and linguistic origins of the political term "terror" prove that it cannot be applied to a revolutionary war of liberation. A revolution may give birth to what we call "terror," as happened in France. Terror may at times be its herald, as happened in Russia. But the revolution itself is not terror, and terror is not the revolution. A revolution, or a revolutionary war, does not aim at instilling fear. Its object is to overthrow a regime and to set up a new regime in its place. In a revolutionary war both sides use force.[2]

The emancipation struggle against British colonization enjoyed the support not only of the Jewish community in the United States but also that of the U.S. Congress. A congressional resolution condemned

"British oppression" and reaffirmed U.S. support for a Jewish state in Palestine. The tension reached its height in 1947 when, in reprisal for the execution of three Irgun terrorists, two British noncommissioned officers were hanged. Pressure rose for immigration to be opened to "displaced" Jews, while an enquiry undertaken by a special UN committee for Palestine led it to call for an end to the British occupation. With the consent of the British, who were eager to disengage, a date was set for the establishment of the state of Israel and the consequent partition of Palestine. The Arab states announced their rejection of partition. The creation of Israel was ratified nonetheless by both the United States and the USSR.

The inevitable war erupted, and, thanks to weaponry provided by, among others, Czechoslovakia, it was won by Israel, which battled its way to a substantial expansion of the territory that had been allotted to it. In September 1948, the Stern Gang, under the command of Yitzhak Shamir, assassinated the UN mediator, Count Bernadotte. The Israeli government disbanded the gang following the assassination. The Irgun launched a terror assault against the village of Deir Yassin to provoke an Arab exodus. As a result, some 700,000 Palestinian Arabs sought refuge in the West Bank and neighboring countries. The United Nations established a specialized agency on their behalf, the UN Relief and Works Agency for Palestine Refugees in the Near East, which has functioned continuously since 1949. A UN resolution demanding Israel's resettlement of the refugees was ignored by the Jewish state. Transjordan annexed the West Bank with the assent of certain Palestinian leaders and proclaimed itself the kingdom of Jordan, with a population two-thirds Palestinian.

Until 1968, movements that relied almost exclusively on terrorist tactics were relatively rare. The Irish of the IRA had practiced terrorism because they had had no other option. Their example inspired Jewish terrorist groups, as well as the Ethniki Organosis Kyprion Agoniston (EOKA) or National Organization of Cypriot Fighters.

It should be stressed that most of the liberation movements born during or immediately after World War II were, first and foremost, guerrilla operations. The countryside was the focus of their activities. Terrorism was generally used in only a marginal way, either as a trigger for taking action or to send the message that the adversary was vulnerable even behind the walls of his fortress. The postwar period proved to be conducive to the success of emancipation struggles. The imperial resolve of the European powers was not as serenely confident as it had once been. Japanese forces had time and again defeated the Americans in the Philippines, the Dutch in Indonesia, the French in Indochina, and the British in Malaysia. And the newly minted United Nations had proclaimed the right of peoples to self-determination. With the retreat of the European colonists—with the exception of Portugal—from their last colonial possessions, the years 1945 to 1965 saw most liberation movements make good on their political aspirations.

There were some failures, of course, generally involving the communist movements. The latter were vigorously resisted—the Huks in the Philippines, the Chinese communists in Malaysia, and the Greek communists were all defeated. Other, poorly organized movements, such as the Mau Mau in Kenya, were suppressed, although Kenya won its independence in 1962.

Nationalist struggles, such as that of the Jews in Palestine, who had relied almost exclusively on terrorism from 1944 to 1947, carried the day, as did EOKA, the movement led by George Grivas in Cyprus.

Grivas, who had distinguished himself in the underground struggle against the Nazis, managed, at the head of just a few hundred men, to force Great Britain to withdraw from the island. Cyprus, which had been occupied by the British crown since 1878, sought annexation by Greece. The Turkish minority, with support from Turkey, opposed the move. After two years of assiduous preparations, Grivas launched his assault on April 1, 1955. Although largely outnumbered by British troops, the handful of Cypriot fighters, organized in small, autonomous cells, was effective in the cities and in the countryside alike. In just a few months, the armed struggle overshadowed years of diplomatic effort. Cyprus became yet another issue for the United Nations.

The Turkish army, concerned about EOKA's progress, landed in the northern part of the island, where the Turkish minority predominated. Clashes took place in 1956 between Greeks and Turks. EOKA failed to secure Greek annexation but contributed to the island's proclamation of independence. Cyprus was de facto divided between Turks in the north and Greeks in the center and the south. The United Nations interposed its Blue Helmets between populations in exodus. A similar situation arose in Aden (Yemen) where, from 1964 to 1967, the National Liberation Front compelled Great Britain to withdraw. It should be noted that the movements whose terrorist activities have been described enjoyed deep-rooted social sanction and resorted to terrorism as a substitute for guerrilla warfare.

The French had their turn in Algeria. During the war there, terrorist-type acts were commonly undertaken in tandem with active guerrilla warfare, especially in regions where the nature of the terrain was conducive to such. The FLN used terrorism to various ends: the eradication of colonial agents, the intimidation of the population to establish control, and the liquidation of rival movements, such as the Algerian nationalists under Messali Hadj. The Battle of Algiers was an especially dramatic episode in the history of terrorism.[3]

The FLN sought to radicalize the situation with "blind" attacks, such as that on the Milk Bar, to send the message that it considered all "pieds-noirs" to be the enemy, and to demoralize the Europeans of Algeria. The FLN offensive began with a series of attacks on September 30, 1956, followed by others throughout the next three months. The army, under General Jacques Massu, was assigned to maintain order. The first half of 1957 saw an escalation of violence and a leap in the number of attacks.[4] The use of torture became systematic, although denied by politicians.

In August 1957, Yacef Saadi, the head of the FLN, was arrested, along with other leaders. Militarily, the Battle of Algiers was won by the French paratroopers, with their formidable weaponry. In the meanwhile, France's parliamentary regime was crumbling, and it collapsed on May 13, 1958. Politically, the FLN won the struggle for international public opinion in 1957 and 1958, and that psychological dimension grew ever more significant with the passage of time.

Under General Charles de Gaulle, the French government sought to end the war and recognize Algerian independence and the FLN. Elements of the army, called the Organisation de l'armée secrète (OAS), fought to keep Algeria French, however, and attempted a putsch against de Gaulle in April 1961, which failed. Among others, the OAS targeted de Gaulle himself, who narrowly escaped one of the several assassination attempts directed against him. The last three months of the war were especially lethal. On March 23, 1962, the OAS tried to gain control of the Bab-el-Oued quarter of Algiers. The French army intervened, and fifteen soldiers were killed. On March 18, the Evian accords were signed, endorsing the principle of Algerian self-determination. But the scorched-earth policy of the OAS hastened the end of French Algeria to the extent that it left the Europeans of that country with no choice but to leave. Terrorism had characterized and exacerbated the conflict, and ultimately, as far as the OAS was concerned, proved to be counterproductive.

The era from the end of World War II to the completion of decolonization was one in which terrorist activity was limited to a specialized, minor branch of the military effort. While certain movements, including those described above, were more or less successful in their exploitation of terrorism, the period was marked rather by limited warfare (the Korean War), anti-colonial guerrilla warfare, and the specter of nuclear war. In studying the strategic "literature" of the time, we find those three areas largely dominating the strategic debate, whereas the subject of terrorism—thought at most to be a subordinate branch of guerrilla and revolutionary warfare—barely arises at all.

But if terrorism has persevered down the ages as one of the constant manifestations of political violence, it is because it has proven its effectiveness as an auxiliary weapon. Whereas terrorism has enjoyed a certain success since the late 1960s, thanks to a particular combination of strategic factors and to the advent of mass media and communications, history tends to demonstrate that, in and of itself, it has rarely proven capable of realizing the political objectives of the groups that resort to it. In that regard, the era of decolonization was egregiously favorable to the national and independence movements that opted, often out of necessity, to use terrorism in conjunction with guerrilla warfare.

It was during this period of vast geostrategic upheaval that the complex relationship developed between democracy and terrorism—a relationship that largely defines the essence of contemporary terrorism today. The terrorism of decolonization owed its success to the moral and political contradictions that evolved between democratic values, characterized by the defense of freedom, and the exigencies of colonialism based on domination. The end of decolonization was the crucible, in a very particular historical content, of the new forms adopted by terrorism since 1968.

NOTES TO CHAPTER 10

1. Jabotinsky, "Zheleznoi stene." Jabotinsky was a founding father of the so-called revisionist Zionist movement of the 1920s. In 1937, he created the Irgun Zvai Leumi (National Military Organization).

2. Begin, *Revolt*, 59–60.

3. Resonantly captured in Gillo Pontecorvo's 1965 film *The Battle of Algiers*.

4. The number of deaths resulting from such attacks rose from 78 to 837 between 1956 and 1957.

PART III

TERRORISM SINCE 1968

CHAPTER 11

FROM 1968 TO RADICAL ISLAM

Gérard Chaliand to Arnaud Blin

For the historian of contemporary terrorism, four years stand out as turning points: 1968, 1979, 1983, and 2001. In 1968, Latin American insurgents launched their so-called urban guerrilla strategy, and Palestinians initiated the tactic of terrorism as publicity stunt, which soon evolved into serious violence. As we have seen, both undertook terrorist-type activities as a substitute for the guerrilla warfare that neither was competent to wage.

Another watershed year was 1979, when the Iranian revolution marked the striking success of radical Shiite Islamism; its influence was both direct, as with Hezbollah in Lebanon, and indirect, facilitating the rise of suicide bombings by the traditional glorification of martyrdom. This tradition also inspired the radical Sunni islamists of Hamas, al Qaeda, and others. The Soviet intervention in Afghanistan in 1979 was seized upon by Washington as the perfect opportunity to inflict upon the USSR the same kind of defeat that the United States had suffered in Vietnam.

The United States, with the financing of Saudi Arabia and the collaboration of Pakistan, which provided logistical support, safe haven, and training centers, gave telling assistance to the Afghan resistance fighters. Radical Islamists from the Middle East and other Muslim regions began to pour in from the very onset of the war to participate in the jihad in any number of ways. Many received their religious and military training on the battlefield. As Sunni-inspired militants, they served the United

States, Saudi Arabia, and Pakistan as a counterweight to the mystique of the Shiite revolution in Iran. Among the diverse movements involved in the Afghan resistance, the United States opted to back the most radical of Islamists, Gulbuddin Hekmatyar, leader of the Hezbi Islami, or Islamic Party.

Less than ten years after moving into Afghanistan, the Soviet forces withdrew, allowing the Afghan mujahideen to boast that they had defeated the Soviet army, a claim that is in serious need of qualification. After Mikhail Gorbachev came to power in 1985, the USSR waged war only half-heartedly in Afghanistan, relying on the services of the Afghan secret police, the KHAD, and playing up tribal rivalries in the best ethnostrategic tradition of nineteenth-century colonialism. The initial Soviet troop deployment of 120,000 men remained the same throughout the war, unlike the Americans in Vietnam, whose deployment eventually rose to 500,000, or the French in Algeria, who sent in twice as many as the Americans.

Furthermore, the USSR never undertook a serious counterinsurgency effort. Anybody could sneak into Afghanistan, yet the Soviet forces killed or captured a mere handful of foreigners in eight years of a war that was assiduously reported on overseas. For the most part, the Soviet troops were content to undertake limited raids to dislodge egregiously active pockets of resistance in the Panjshir Valley, Kandahar province, Paktia, and elsewhere. Moscow's mistake was to wage the war with an army of conscripts—the same mistake made by the Americans in Vietnam. Colonial-type wars should be waged only by professionals, preferably volunteers.

The sober, sturdy, and highly motivated Afghan warriors formed units that were inured to warfare but without discipline or group cohesion and ultimately unsuited to evolving into a homogeneous fighting force. It took them almost three years to capture Kabul following the Soviet withdrawal, despite all the material assistance at their disposal. The discipline and cohesion of the Tajik forces under the command of Ahmed Shah Massoud, drawing on Leninist-Maoist organizational tactics, were an exception.

During these years, the 1983 suicide bombings in Beirut were the single most significant development in international terrorism, especially the two that killed 241 American Marines and 53 French paratroopers.[1] These Hezbollah attacks led to the withdrawal of Western troops and were the most important triumph of international terrorism between 1968 and 2000. Indeed, in this instance, the psychological impact was equaled and perhaps even surpassed by the consequence of the attacks: the enemy's retreat.

The lesson was duly noted. It may well have been a factor in Saddam Hussein's calculations in refusing to back down in the months preceding the first Gulf War between Iraq and the U.S.-led coalition mandated by the United Nations in 1991. At a time when the doctrine of no-casualty warfare was being espoused, could the enemy be sufficiently bloodied to precipitate the collapse of the home front?

In France, the years 1986 and 1995 were marked by two bloody terrorist campaigns, the first waged by Iranians, the second by the Armed Islamic Group. With hindsight, we now see that the third important turning point came between 1991 and 1993, corresponding to changes taking place within Afghanistan at the time. Having been exploited as a tool by the United States to weaken the Soviet Union, radical Islamism, pursuing its own dynamic and its own aims, evolved—in part as a result of the 1991 war against Iraq—into a many-headed, independent political-military movement.

The period saw the launching of jihad under favorable auspices in Algeria, and soon thereafter extended to the wars in Bosnia (1993–95), Chechnya, and Kashmir. The year 1993 also saw the first attack on the World Trade Center, by car bomb, which did not achieve its desired result but announced that the United States was henceforth a target of Islamist fighters. The United States underestimated the importance of the attack in Khobar, Saudi Arabia, in which nineteen American soldiers lost their lives. The following year saw another attack in Saudi Arabia, this time in Dahran, and Osama bin Laden's call on the United States to withdraw from holy Saudi territory. From 1994 to 1996, the Taliban, created and supported by Pakistan with U.S. backing, made themselves masters of Afghanistan. Gradually, the influence of bin Laden and the Egyptians Ahmed al-Zawahiri and Muhammad Atef made itself felt on the Taliban regime. In February 1998, bin Laden declared war on "the crusaders and the Jews." U.S. embassies in East Africa were attacked that year, followed two years later by the bombing of the USS *Cole* in the port of Aden.

The fourth turning point, of course, was the attack of September 11, 2001, marking the final evolutionary stage of classical terrorism. That moment gave rise in turn to the most significant counterterrorism operation ever undertaken: the war to overthrow the terrorist haven of Afghanistan.

Subsequently, the Bush administration, heavily influenced by civilians in the Pentagon, went on the offensive. It felt that the time had come to finish the "unfinished war" in Iraq. The war—one of choice and not of necessity—was launched preemptively to avert the potential threat of terrorism of mass destruction, which remained hypothetical, notwithstanding Great Britain's assertions in support of its great ally.

In practice, and quite predictably, the post-conquest situation in Baghdad has proved more complicated than the initial military operation. But no one could have predicted that the circumstances of what can hardly be called a postwar period would be so negative. A significant share of the responsibility for this lies with the U.S. administration—and most especially with the Pentagon, which is running the occupation. The lack of preparation has been confounding, equaled only by the obsession of the first six months with implementing sweeping policies on the cheap. The restoration of essential infrastructure has been neglected, while looting and crime have been neither prevented nor controlled. The gradual transfer of security responsibilities to the Iraqi police and army was begun very belatedly. The idea of asking Turkey to send troops to Iraq demonstrated a total lack of understanding of historical realities on the part of Pentagon decision makers. The Iraqi Governing Council was not given even a modicum of the power it needed. The public information war was a lost cause from the outset. Six weeks after the taking of Baghdad, the Americans had yet to set up Arab-language radio or television stations.

The rural and urban guerrilla war being waged by the opponents of foreign occupation has claimed untold numbers of victims. Its endurance through 2006 has proven to be a sore trial for the United States. The world's greatest military power appears to be struggling to dominate a so-called low-intensity conflict. The Bush administration will no doubt continue to stress the threat from Syria and increase pressure on Damascus. The provisional verdict is that the counterterrorist campaign carried into Iraq has engendered more terrorism than existed before the war. Conversely, the campaign for the nonproliferation of weapons of mass destruction has been fruitful in the case of Libya.

Meanwhile, the jihads in which some radicals have participated or continue to participate have led to no change in the status quo. Regimes targeted by the radical Islamists remain in power in Egypt, Algeria, and Saudi Arabia. Only time will tell whether Sunni insurgencies in these countries will be able to replay what was accomplished in 1979 in Iran by an organized religious establishment unequaled in the Muslim world outside of Shiism, in a context of eroding state power and the discontent of social strata and classes provisionally united by the force of a charismatic personality. The problem faced by those who seek to bring about regime change through terrorism alone is the same one that was faced by the urban terrorist *focos* of Latin America, namely, the limited capacity of strictly underground groups to establish an organized social base of any significance, a precondition for seizing power.

In what country might a similar revolutionary process evolve, based on an organization enjoying majoritarian support or even spun off from the state apparatus itself? No one can say with any certainty. And yet, in the medium term, Pakistan, which is at the very epicenter of the Islamic terrorist crisis, would seem to be the most at risk. Iraq's place in the battle order will become clear soon enough.

THE MANY FACES OF TERRORISM

The year 1967 was an important one in the Middle East, with its striking demonstration of Israeli military superiority. The Western perception of the 1948–49 war had been that of a young nation heroically defending its right to exist and snatching victory from the combined forces of three Arab states. In 1956, the Israeli army had romped its way to the Suez Canal, but that had been as a member of the Anglo-French coalition. The victory of 1967 had been unqualified, the humiliation of the Arab states complete.

But the Arab defeat opened the door to the rise of al-Fatah, the Palestinian National Liberation Movement, or the PLO, which had up to then only marginal. The PLO, after all, had been founded in 1964 in Egypt under the auspices of President Nasser, who had chosen as its leader a man, Ahmed Shukairy, whose only claim to representativity was his status as a Palestinian figurehead.

After the 1968 debacle and the skirmish that year with the Israeli army at Karameh in Jordan, in which the *fedayeen* distinguished themselves, the Palestinians themselves were promoted to center stage as the redeemers of Arab honor. These events highlighted the fact that, territorially speaking, the Israeli-Arab conflict was essentially an Israeli-Palestinian conflict. They also drove home the fact that, despite the guerrilla war against the Jewish colonizers from 1936 to 1939, Palestinian nationalism had been too weak to resist Transjordan's absorption of the West Bank (which had been part of mandate Palestine) and Egypt's mandate over Gaza.

In one of history's little ironies, the PLO was finally ready by the late

1980s to assume sovereignty over territories that had been under exclusive Arab control from 1949 to 1967. Likewise, in 2002—three decades late—Saudi Arabia offered recognition and peace to Israel in exchange for the territories occupied after the Six-Day War.

The full and comprehensive acceptance by the elite Arab leadership of realities on the ground would seem to have been singularly slow in coming. Its grasp of the military disparities involved was equally tenuous. Thus, in late 1968–early 1969, following the adoption of the Palestinian Charter, the various movements that made up the PLO and its fringes were nourished on delusions.

One of these was the dream of defeating Israel in a guerrilla war modeled on those in Vietnam and Algeria; another was the establishment, via the rejection of alliances with any Israeli faction, of a democratic Palestinian state over all the territory of Palestine, in which the Jews would enjoy only the rights of a religious minority.

This dream represented a regression to the sectarian minority millet system of the Ottoman empire, to the status of *dhimmi* for Jews, to which the creation of a national state had been the explicit response. The Palestinian resistance was flawed in its underestimation of the depth of Israeli nationalism. A Palestinian state was at best conceivable on the West Bank, and perhaps in Transjordan with the overthrow of the Hashemite monarchy. The PLO rejected that strategy and sought instead, with pan-Arab assistance, to undermine Israeli society through guerrilla warfare. Could the Israelis, like the Europeans of Algeria, be forced out of the country? To believe they could was a pipe dream. Indeed, Israeli leaders felt at the time that if the Palestinians wanted their own state, they had only to establish it on the far side of the Jordan River. And among the political elite, there were many who had no intention of restoring the 1967 borders, let alone revisiting the question of East Jerusalem. The impossibility of fostering conditions conducive to guerrilla warfare on the West Bank, coupled with the interception of virtually all commando units crossing the river from Jordan, led the Palestinian organizations to focus on terrorism—just as, in Latin America, the failure of the *focos* had led to urban guerrilla warfare. The impossibility of waging guerrilla warfare caused the Palestinian organizations to fall back on terrorist activities.

In July 1968, by diverting an El Al flight between Athens and Cairo, the Popular Front for the Liberation of Palestine launched what was at the time called "publicity terrorism." The Palestinian cause, born of dispossession, had been emphatically brought to the West's attention.

A TYPOLOGY OF TERRORISM

If we are to have a full understanding of the term "terrorism," which encompasses a significant number of highly varied movements and groups, we need to establish a summary typology. Excluding state terrorism, we need to draw a distinction among terrorist groups based on left- or right-wing political ideology (in that regard, it is useful to recall that terrorism is a tactic and has no inherent political coloration); nationalist movements, either separatist or autonomist; and political-religious sects. In most cases, terrorism represents a political strategy. While warfare is based on physical coercion, terrorism seeks to have a psychological impact. In contrast to guerrilla warfare, terrorism is the negation of combat. It is about attacking an unarmed adversary, not about surprise attacks on elements of a regular army.

Among revolutionary terrorist groups, mainly on the left but also on the right, we find the following organizations or groupings:

- in the United States, the Weathermen and the Symbionese Liberation Army
- in the Federal Republic of Germany, the Rote Armee Fraktion, better known as the Baader-Meinhof Gang, led by Gudrun Ensslin and Horst Mahler in addition to the two principals for whom it was named; along with the tiny, more obscure anarchist group "Movement 2 June" (Bewegung Zwei Juni, or B2J), whose name commemorates the date of the police killing of a student at a demonstration against the shah of Iran's presence in Germany
- in Italy, the Brigate rosse or Red Brigades, and, on the far right, various fascistic organizations
- in Japan, the Japanese Red Army

Among the separatist or autonomist ethnic movements in the West, we may cite:

- in Canada, the Front de liberation du Québec (FLQ), short-lived but noted for its kidnapping and murder of a government minister
- in Ireland, the IRA, the most broadly-based of the movements on this list
- in Spain, the military wing of Euskadi ta Askatasuna (Basque Homeland and Freedom), or ETA

- in France, almost preposterous groups that assert that Corsica is a colony and playact the role of a liberation movement, exploiting the laxity of the French state

Autonomist or separatist movements that resort to terrorism are classified as terrorist movements by the U.S. government, although many are first and foremost guerrilla movements. That is the case in Latin America with two Colombian organizations, the Revolutionary Armed Forces of Colombia and the smaller National Liberation Army, as well as the Shining Path in Peru, or what is left of it since the arrest of its leader Abimael Guzman, known as President Gonzalo.

In the Middle East, such movements include the Democratic Party of Iranian Kurdistan (PDKI), led, until his assassination by the Iranians, by Abdul-Rahman Gassemlou. From 1979 to 1984, when it was compelled to withdraw to Iraq, this group never went in for terrorist-type activity. That is also true, to the best of our knowledge, of the Kurdistan Democratic Party and the Patriotic Union of Kurdistan, the Kurdish movements active in Iraq between 1968 and 1991.

The Kurdistan Workers' Party (PKK), active in Turkey from 1984 to the arrest of its leader Abdullah Öcalan, known as Apo, was above all a guerrilla movement. Over its fifteen years of existence, the movement, operating across a large swath of south-eastern Turkey, compelled Ankara to mobilize up to 150,000 troops to stamp it out. The PKK also put terrorism to effective use in its struggle. The Turkish army, for its part, deployed death squads to eradicate all Kurdish opposition, including nonviolent opposition.

The Palestinians, whatever their political persuasion, have had little alternative to terrorism, being unable to launch a guerrilla war.

The Chechen insurgents are less easy to characterize than others. On the one hand, the movement indisputably harbors nationalists devoted to the idea of independence and fighting in a guerrilla context. On the other hand, Chechnya is a jihad attracting Islamist fighters from a number of countries, the best-known being the Jordanian Shamil Basayev, who tried unsuccessfully to drag Dagestan into the struggle. Moreover, Chechen nationalists or radical Islamists have resorted to terrorism, as illustrated by the 2002 hostage-taking in a Moscow theater.

Beyond a shadow of a doubt, the world's most effective organization when it comes to terror is the Liberation Tigers of Tamil Eelam—the Tamil Tigers. But it is primarily a guerrilla movement and has even been able to mount conventional military operations against the Sri Lankan army.

In Nepal, the Maoist movement is a guerrilla operation, as are the faction fighting for the independence of Aceh in Sumatra, Indonesia, and the weaker movements waging armed struggles on the ground in the Molucca Islands and Papua New Guinea.

In the Philippines, the Moro National Liberation Front, or MLNF, on Mindanao, claiming to represent the Muslim minority of 4 percent within a vast Catholic majority, has been calling for autonomy, or even independence, for decades. Over the years, the movement has received assistance from Libya and other Arab countries. The even more extreme Abu Sayyaf Group split off from the MLNF in 1991.

Since no typology can reflect the full complexity of reality, we must include here the sui generis struggle led, with no hope of success, by the Armenians between 1975 and 1983.

Foremost among the political-religious sects resorting to terrorism are the militant radical Islamists who coalesced in Afghanistan and have participated in various armed struggles, some by no means limited to terrorist activities, in Bosnia, Algeria, Chechnya, Kashmir, and so on. The long list of Islamist organizations includes some with memberships of just a few dozen and others that count thousands of adherents. Such movements have arisen in virtually every Muslim country, with the general exception of sub-Saharan Africa. The Hezbollah movement of Lebanon, deemed a terrorist organization by the United States, is above all a militant political movement. It is not chiefly characterized by acts of terrorism.

Aum Shinrikyo, which gained renown with its 1995 sarin gas attack on the Tokyo subway, killing twelve and injuring thousands to varying degrees, is notable among millenarian sects (but hardly the only one).

Instances of state terrorism that took place during the same period include, in Latin America:

- the death squads in Brazil
- the systematic suppression of Indians in Guatemala
- the depredations of the Argentine military throughout its hold on power
- the early years, in particular, of the Pinochet regime in Chile
- the especially brutal counterterrorism and counterinsurgency operations in Peru under President Fujimori

In Africa:

- the Algerian army and its methods
- the use of terror during the fourteen-year dictatorship of Charles Taylor in Liberia
- the dictatorships of Francisco Macias Nguema in Equatorial Guinea and Idi Amin Dada in Uganda
- the civil war in Sierra Leone
- the terror in Burundi under Tutsi rule
- the genocide in Rwanda and its impact on neighboring Congo

In the Middle East:

- state terror implemented by Turkey in the context of the counterinsurgency, including death squads and the policy of systematic deterritorialization in the Kurdish region
- the massacre of 10,000 Sunnis in Hama by the regime of Hafez al-Assad of Syria in 1982
- the systematic deployment of terror at every level by Saddam Hussein, especially with respect to the Kurds, including Operation Anfal,[2] the use of poison gas against the Kurds in Halabja in 1988, and the 1991 suppressions of the Kurds and Shiites

In Southeast and East Asia:

- genocidal massacres in Cambodia
- terror in China's Cultural Revolution
- and, although occurring before 1968, the 1965 massacre of between 300,000 and 500,000 communists or suspected communists by the Suharto regime in Indonesia

This list is not, of course, exhaustive. Let us keep in mind that, as the political scientist Paul Wilkinson puts it, torture is the "extreme form of individualized terror."[3]

TERRORISM AND GUERRILLA WARFARE

Following the repeated failures of the rural *focos* and the death of Che Guevara in Bolivia in 1967, the Brazilian Marxist Carlos Marighella (1911–1969) tried to develop a new strategy that would ultimately combine urban and rural guerrilla warfare. He only had time to launch the urban operation. According to Marighella, the strategy of urban terrorism is "to turn political crisis into armed crisis by performing violent actions that will force those in power to transform the military situation into a political situation."[4]

Marighella calculated that if he could provoke the authorities into reacting repressively, the state would come to be resented. In practice, the repression served to break up the revolutionary organization without eliciting anything more than passive support from the masses. He had little understanding of the depth of the potential social base for such actions and failed to grasp that there is a big difference between sympathy and organized support. Moreover, Marighella himself saw the contradictions of his own strategy. In his manual, he lists the seven sins of the urban guerrilla:

> The third sin of the urban guerrilla is vanity. The guerrilla who suffers from this sin tries to solve the problems of the revolution by actions in the city, but without bothering about the beginnings and survival of other guerrillas in other areas. Blinded by success, he winds up organizing an action that he considers decisive and that puts into play the entire resources of the organization. Since we cannot afford to break the guerrilla struggle in the cities while rural guerrilla warfare has not yet erupted, we always run the risk of allowing the enemy to attack us with decisive blows.

In fact, Marighella's strategy for urban guerrilla warfare suffers from several inherent weaknesses: the lack of organized popular support, given the underground nature of the movement and its considerable numerical inferiority; and the presumption that the state is weak or has been weakened, which was not the case with the Brazilian state, at that time under dictatorship since 1964. Despite his rejection of the rural *foco* strategy, Marighella's "urban guerrilla warfare" was, in effect, an urban *foco*.[5]

Certainly, terrorist activities had been under way in Latin America in the 1960s, beginning in 1963 in Venezuela, where the minister of justice was shot down by the Movement of the Revolutionary Left (MIR), and in Guatemala. But urban guerrilla warfare per se began in 1968 in Brazil, soon followed by Uruguay and Argentina.

In Brazil, the spread of urban violence was swift, intense, and brief. Marighella, a member of the Communist Party, attended the conference of the Organization of Latin American Solidarity (OLAS) in Havana. Following the death of Che Guevara, he set the priorities that he felt the situation demanded: establish a new revolutionary communist party and set the stage for an armed struggle based on the urban scenario—the Rio de Janeiro–São Paolo–Belo Horizonte triangle—and only later in the countryside, in order to compel the police and the army to disperse their forces.

Action was launched in October 1968 with the assassination of a high-ranking American army officer, followed by a series of holdups to finance the organization and attacks on television facilities to generate publicity. The next year, the U.S. ambassador was kidnapped and fifteen political prisoners were released in exchange for his freedom. Marighella, however, was killed in São Paolo in November 1969. The following year, the West German ambassador was kidnapped and exchanged for forty political detainees. Camara Ferreira, who had succeeded Marighella, was killed in turn in October 1970. From that moment on, the movement disintegrated into chaos without having launched its urban guerrilla warfare.

In Argentina, three movements emerged around 1970: the Ejército Revolucionario del Pueblo, or People's Revolutionary Army (ERP)—an inflated name for a very small group—the Liberation Armed Forces (FAL), and the Movimiento Peronista Montonero, or Montoneros. In May 1970, FAL kidnapped the consul of Paraguay, and then the Montoneros kidnapped the former Argentine president Pedro Aramburu, whom they killed after negotiations failed.

Early the following year, the honorary consul of Great Britain in Rosario was kidnapped by the ERP and later released after free provisions were distributed in the slums. In early 1972, the same movement pulled off a holdup that netted $800,000. Shortly thereafter, the ERP kidnapped the chairman of the Fiat subsidiary in Argentina. The hostage was killed after the breakdown of talks with the government, which refused to accede to the movement's demands. The repression was ratcheted up. Sixteen political prisoners were mown down in the course of a supposed escape. In retaliation, the ERP kidnapped some dozen businessmen, for whom it secured sizable ransoms. The situation was so dire that, in 1973, the Peronist party demanded the return from exile of Juan Perón, the populist leader who had run the country from 1946 to 1955. However, this failed to restore calm.

The kidnapping of the head of the Argentine Esso affiliate earned the ERP a $14-million ransom. The death of Juan Perón precipitated an outbreak of extreme rightist violence, spearheaded by the Argentine Anticommunist Alliance (ARA), seeking to establish a dictatorship. The chaotic situation provoked the army into seizing power in a military

coup in 1976. Terror had switched sides, and endured until the downfall of the military regime in the aftermath of the Falklands/Malvinas defeat of 1982.

The most influential of the Latin American movements claiming to be
urban guerrillas were the Tupamaros of Uruguay, the inspiration for revolutionary cells and movements throughout North America and western
Europe. The Tupamaros rightly understood the capital, Montevideo—
home to roughly half the country's population—to be the strategic center of Uruguay. Cities make aviation and artillery useless, depriving the
enemy of certain advantages. Uruguay's population is more than 80 percent urban and the rural zones, broad plains for the most part, were useful only to divert some of the pressure of the armed forces in the city. For
the Tupamaros, Montevideo, like all large cities, also offered ready-made
targets: embassies, administrative buildings, banks, businessmen, media.

After a preparatory phase, the movement got off to a promising start.
In October 1969, to commemorate the second anniversary of Guevara's
death, they seized a medium-sized municipality, Pando, twenty-five kilometers from Montevideo. The operation put them on the map.

They moved on to kidnappings and other well-organized actions,
never killing gratuitously and offering populist critiques of the country's
governance. In July 1970, they kidnapped Dan Mitrione, an American
expert consultant to the Uruguayan police. The episode dragged out for
ten frenetic days during which the Tupamaros negotiated with the government for the release of six of their own, and pulled off several spectacular holdups. FBI agents arrived to assist the police, and members of
the movement were captured. While the Tupamaros undertook a second
kidnapping, one of their main leaders, Raoul Sendic, was arrested. The
Tupamaros made it clear that the hostages' lives depended on that of
Sendic, and a state of emergency was declared. The body of Dan Mitrione was found the next day. Parliament suspended constitutional liberties for three weeks, but the abductions continued, including that of the
British ambassador, who was released after several months of captivity
in 1971. The following year, 1972, saw eight more kidnappings and the
dramatic flight of several Tupamaro leaders.

The Chamber of Deputies voted to depose the president of the Republic, and the country seemed to be on the verge of civil war. In fact,
the stage was set for a right-wing coup.

The Tupamaros were euphoric over the success of their operations,
which were both dazzling and essentially victimless and earned the sympathy of a broad sector of the populace. It should be stressed, however,

that the Tupamaros were not fighting a nondemocratic government. The escalation of terrorism—aimed, according to the movement, at unmasking the social oppression on which state power was based—led to the rise of the extreme right. As time passed, Tupamaro operations enjoyed diminishing favor among a war-weary population. The movement, relying on an infrastructure of collusive camaraderie, gradually came to see that it was using violence as a substitute for popular support. Once again, the organization's *focista* vocation became apparent at the very moment when it needed organized support rather than sympathy. Like Marighella and his Brazilian followers, the Tupamaros of Uruguay were faced with the dilemma of any small-scale armed organization forced underground: how to build a political infrastructure when all its members were occupied by the military effort. In hindsight, it is obvious that the Tuparmaros had a very tenuous toehold in the working classes, including in recruitment. In 1971 and 1972, their attempts to establish rural bases to ease the stranglehold on them in Montevideo collapsed in failure. Their strategy of inciting the authorities to overreact in order to win the people's support is a dangerous game, in which the state, unless it is very weak, usually has the upper hand.

Like rural guerrilla warfare, the urban variant is first and foremost political, aimed at persuading and organizing the people. It is a task that generally seems to be of secondary importance to small organizations obsessed with secrecy, the imperative of successful operations, and assessing their own impact in the media. The execution of operations and the movement's security are, at best, enough to consume the organization's limited energies and personnel. For the most part, the populace remains a passive audience. Notwithstanding the strenuous effort to remain selective, the use of terrorism ends up becoming counterproductive. Exhaustion and a sense of insecurity overwhelm the initial enthusiasm. With time and the passing of the element of surprise, admiring commentaries on the perfection of an effective operation or on the humbling of the forces of order evolve into a general condemnation of violence, whatever its source.

In late 1972, a well-honed counterterror campaign crushed the Tupamaro movement. And the following year, Uruguay fell into a twelve-year dictatorship. The use of terrorism as a destabilization tactic or as a means of ultimately seizing power tends to lead to a rise in extremism.[6] The Tupamaro strategy of using revolutionary violence against a democratic (though class-based) government in order to invite repression that would open the eyes of the masses to the "true nature" of the regime led to the seizure of power by the army. In Europe, the same aberrant strategy failed to move the masses and led states to expand their arsenals of repressive laws.

The failure inherent in the very founding notion of such groups can promote the emergence of nihilist factions whose stated objective is no longer a degree of popular support and who resort instead to banditry to support their bare-bones apparatus. Movements of the extreme right can also operate within a democratic society, with equally minimal opportunity to affect a country's political stability, except in conditions of deep crisis.

The characteristic that has defined North American revolutionary groups—the Weathermen, the Symbionese Liberation Army, or the more formidable Black Panthers—has been the brevity of their existence. All were speedily—and often brutally—demolished.

EUROPEAN AND MEDITERRANEAN
MOVEMENTS AND GROUPS

Of the five small and larger groups or movements that called themselves revolutionary in the post–1968 era, only two remain the objects of attention: the Italian Red Brigades, whose influence in certain Italian social circles was not insignificant, and the German Red Army Fraction. The tiny German anarchist Movement 2 June, the French Action Directe group—a handful of individuals who lived off robbery—and the Belgian communist cells basically only represented themselves politically.

All of these groups emerged in the aftermath of the crisis of May 1968, whose psychological impact in western Europe was considerable. Until 1975 at least, support for the Third World was vigorous, bolstered by the Maoism of the Cultural Revolution and justified by the war in Vietnam, which strengthened the pervasive atmosphere of anti-imperialism. The armed struggles against Portuguese colonialism and opposition to white racism in South Africa and Rhodesia were mobilizing forces. The Tupamaros' urban guerrilla mythos replaced that of rural guerrilla warfare, and Che Guevara, hero and martyr of the revolution, evolved into an icon.

The struggle of the Palestinians, resisting Israeli occupation after the Six-Day War and aspiring to a state of their own, was yet another fight buoyed by the tides of revolution. The chief offender was Nixon's America. On the domestic front, the campaign on behalf of immigrants and their living conditions overshadowed the elevation of the proletariat.

This was the environment that nurtured European revolutionary groups eager to participate in the international struggle against imperialism and the capitalist, class-based state. It will be recalled that all this took place in the highly favorable economic climate that prevailed prior to October 1973.

Italy was the country by far most affected by terrorist activity between 1969 and 1985. For the extreme left and the extreme right alike, the enemy was the Italian political system dominated by the Christian Democrats, who were disparaged for their corruption and opposition to change. The extreme left also criticized the Italian Communist Party, a significant political force, for compromising with the conservative majority. The extreme right believed that the centrism of the Christian Democrats promoted the rise of the left and extreme left. The decade's toll of terror victims was 428, the highest figure recorded in western Europe, and this does not take into account the daily recurrence of political violence of every stripe, including bank raids, kidnappings, the bombing of administrative facilities, sabotage, and so on.

The self-appointed task of the extreme right was to oppose the rise of the extreme left, which was clearly more in tune with the spirit of the times. This opposition was reflected in actions that claimed numerous victims: Milan, December 1969: sixteen dead; Brescia, May 1974: eight dead; railway attack, August 1974: twelve dead; bombing of the Bologna train station, August 1980: eighty-five dead; attack on the Naples-Milan train, December 1984: sixteen dead. These attacks were undertaken to incite an authoritarian response from a government criticized for its laxity in that regard. As for the extreme left—chiefly, but not exclusively the Red Brigades—it sought, by striking at the multinational corporations and humiliating the Italian state, to awaken a working class that had been diverted from its revolutionary vocation by the Communist Party. In December 1969, it inaugurated its "strategy of tension" with bombings in Rome and Milan; the latter, an attack on a bank, claimed sixteen victims and went unacknowledged by the perpetrators.

In September 1971, the Red Brigades issued their first communiqué, in lockstep with the strategic vision of the Tupamaros: to raise the awareness of the proletariat, of which they saw themselves as the vanguard, through an escalating cycle of violence and repression.

In March 1972, the Brigades kidnapped the head of the Fiat-Siemens company in Milan, followed by an Alfa-Romeo executive in June 1973, the Fiat director of personnel in December of the same year, and a judge in April 1974—the first in a series of kidnappings of magistrates. Earlier, the book publisher Giangiacomo Feltrinelli, who was well known for his political commitment, died accidentally while attempting to sabotage an electricity pylon.

Throughout these years, the Red Brigades had the wind in their sails and were making things rough for the Communist Party. But the repression was beginning to pick up steam; Renato Curcio, a founding father of the Brigades, and another leader were arrested in September 1974. Curcio's wife, Margherita Cagol, herself a leader of the movement, led a jailbreak to free him, to the deep dismay of the authorities. Cagol was killed a few months later during the attempted kidnapping of an industrialist. Renato Curcio was rearrested in January 1976 in Milan, but the movement had enough momentum by then to go on without faltering.

From 1976 to 1978, the Brigades pursued their kidnappings and assassinations with relative impunity: the "execution" of a public prosecutor in Genoa in June 1976; the kidnapping of a manufacturer in the spring of 1977; the assassination of a *La Stampa* editorialist in November 1977. In the meanwhile, the Communist Party was cozying up to power, provoking an acute crisis between those who condemned its dealmaking and those who believed that the state had to be shored up before it collapsed.

It was in this atmosphere that the Red Brigades pulled off the kidnapping of Aldo Moro, prime minister of Italy from 1963 to 1968, and again from 1974 to 1976. On March 16, 1978, Moro went to the National Assembly to vote his confidence in the Christan Democratic government of Giulio Andreotti and thereby endorse its "historic compromise" of bringing the Italian Communist Party into the ruling coalition.

Kidnapped following the murder of his escort, Moro was kept captive for two months, during which he was "tried" and the subject of pleas from the pope and the secretary-general of the United Nations. The Red Brigades dominated the headlines throughout this time, while their founding members were simultaneously on trial in Turin. Between mid-March and late April, they launched attacks in Turin on the former mayor, a Christian Democrat leader, and on prison guards and industrial and political figures, in an atmosphere of growing tension. On May 9, Aldo Moro's body was discovered in the trunk of an abandoned car in Rome.

As dramatic as the Moro affair proved to be, the Brigades' key political objectives were not achieved. The state did not collapse, and the masses were unmoved. Six more assassinations were committed in the course of the same year. At the same time, the organization was being systematically hounded by General Carlo Alberto Dalla Chiesa of the Carabinieri, and being forced to go to ground isolated it from the people, with the exception of the intellectual circle of its sympathizers. In fact, its decline was already well under way, despite the continued trickle of actions between 1979 and 1981. In December 1981, a final dramatic coup was pulled off with the kidnapping of an American general seconded to NATO, J. L. Dozier, who was freed by the Padua police after five weeks of captivity. The movement was gradually falling apart, notwithstanding the few operations it managed to undertake. In 1985, it issued a statement announcing its own disbandment. The police made effective use of the "repentants." The movement's leaders, having acknowledged their "errors" or their "transgressions," received reduced sentences, and in some cases were allowed monitored freedom, as was the case with Renato Curcio, the last of the Brigade members to be released, after seventeen years in jail.

In Germany, on June 2, 1967, the suppression of a demonstration in which a student was killed fixed the resolve of one small group to prepare itself for armed struggle. Andreas Baader and Gudrun Ensslin assumed leadership of the gang but were arrested in the course of an armed attack. However, Ulrike Meinhof, the group's leading light, helped Baader to escape. The anarchist-leaning Movement 2 June was succeeded by default by the internationalist Baader-Meinhof Gang. Contacts were established with Palestinian militants, who, in exchange for logistical support, provided weapons and training.

The Red Army Fraction targeted representatives of the German state, which responded with significant repressive force. Civil servants were questioned for their loyalty and the powers of the police were heavily beefed up. Following a series of attacks, the Red Army Fraction was decapitated. Baader was arrested in May 1971, Ensslin and Meinhof in June. In November 1974, one member died on hunger strike.

In April 1977, a "Meinhof action group" "executed" the public prosecutor of Karlsruhe. The government refused to be blackmailed again, however, and proceeded to try the gang's incarcerated leaders. Shortly thereafter, following five years of legal preparations, members of the Red Army Fraction were given life sentences and transfered to a high-security prison. In May, Ulrike Meinhof "committed suicide" in her cell, according to the government account. In July, the president of the Dresdner Bank was assassinated in retaliation. In early September, the president of the Association of German Industrialists, Hanns Martin Schleyer, a former Nazi, was kidnapped after the murder of his four bodyguards.

Fraction members offered to exchange him for the freedom of their im-prisoned comrades. The police were desperate enough to arrest the ter-rorists' lawyer on suspicion of being an intermediary between the kid-nappers and the movement's incarcerated leaders. In mid-October, in the midst of ongoing negotiations, a Palestinian commando with support from the Red Army Fraction hijacked a Lufthansa flight. The plane landed in Mogadishu, Somalia, where it was stormed by German special forces, aided by British experts.

Five days later, three Fraction leaders, including Andreas Baader and Gudrun Ensslin, where found dead in their cells—suicides, according to the police. Schleyer's body was found the next day in Mulhouse, France. After this episode, the Red Army Fraction—which had contacts with the East German intelligence services—survived a few years longer but never regained the momentum of the preceding decade. The Red Brigades had a greater impact on certain social strata—though not those they had sought to mobilize—than did the Red Army Fraction, but the latter struck more violently at the German state and establishment, which proved themselves singularly resolute, if not downright brutal, in the de-fense of their interests and prerogatives.

In comparison to these two groups, the French Action directe group was feeble indeed. In fact, those who had participated actively in the events of May 1968 and might well have been swept up into the armed conflict—hadn't the Maoists been calling for resistance to the country's occupation by the bourgeoisie?—declined to be so. Action directe had lit-tle social or intellectual substance. Two police officers were assassinated in May 1983, and then two Iranian opponents of Khomeini's in Febru-ary 1984. Chief state engineer René Audran was assassinated in January 1985, and the former Renault CEO Georges Besse in November 1986. The group soon stooped to doing "revolutionary" heists. When its members were eventually rounded up, there were only a handful left.

To the impartial observer, all these highly ideological movements would seem to have sought, at least initially, to launch a process leading to the mobilization of the masses. The strategy of tension, seeking to raise the public consciousness through violence and repression, was at base a *focista* or "spontaneist" concept. Moreover, the class in question clearly had no revolutionary aspirations. It was from this struggle that the support movement for the Third World emerged. Furthermore, the moment circumstances permitted, many of these groups collaborated with outside movements. The movement most open to such cooperation was the Palestinian, be it through the Popular Front for the Liberation of Palestine or al-Fatah. Once civil war erupted in 1975, Lebanon became stateless and remained a convenient sanctuary for unimpeded terrorist training until 1982. Libya, too, occasionally served as a staging point for several European groups. Among anti-imperialist movements of this type, we cannot fail to mention the Japanese Red Army, which, in collaboration with the Palestinians, launched an attack at Tel Aviv's Lod (now Ben Gurion) Airport in 1972, killing twenty-six people, most of them Puerto Rican pilgrims.

On the whole, the balance sheet of political successes was pretty sparse. The law retained the upper hand everywhere, but most especially in Germany, and grew more repressive. All these ideological movements and groups evolved with the spirit of the times in the industrialized countries—anti-imperialism and a radical critique of capitalist society—without showing any real understanding of the scope of the democratic progress that had been made in the West or of the oppressiveness of the bureaucratic dictatorships in so-called revolutionary countries.

It is true that the international arena is more complex than it seems when looked at with a Manichean worldview. Western societies, the United States chief among them, are not only the guarantors of democracy; Washington has also been allied with dictatorships whose sole merit lay in being anti-communist. From the coups in which the CIA participated against Mossadegh in Iran and Arbenz in Guatemala in the early 1950s to U.S. support for the shah of Iran, Marcos in the Philippines, Suharto in Indonesia, and many others, American realpolitik has sheltered behind policy statements far removed from reality. Conversely, the Soviet Union's support for national liberation movements since the Khrushchev era could not conceal the fact that the ruling party suppressed nationalist movements, including those in so-called popular democracies like the republics of the USSR, while enslaving the Russians in exchange for mediocre security, as long as they expressed no opposition to the party line.

Leftist movements had little patience for such complexity. Their choices, in the fashion of the times, were clear-cut and peremptory. Thus, on the basis of positions that were debated only in the context of tactical details, terrorist-type actions were perceived as fully justified by revolutionary necessity.

After the Six-Day War, the Palestinians emerged as an autonomous political force for the first time since the creation of al-Fatah in 1956. The shock of defeat brought leftists and extreme leftists, hitherto preoccupied by pan-Arabist struggles, flocking to their cause. Such was the case with the Popular Front for the Liberation of Palestine led by George Habash, which, on July 22, 1968, splashed the Palestinian cause all over the headlines with its hijacking of an El Al flight.

The Palestine Liberation Organization adopted a charter aimed primarily at creating a democratic Palestinian state and, to that end—in a nutshell—at eliminating the state of Israel and offering the Jews religious minority status. But the imbalance of forces, evident after the crushing defeat of the Six-Day War, put paid to the consideration of any such utopian program. Whatever right they might have had to their own state, the Palestinians had adopted a plan that would find no support in adverse public opinion. Under Arab control ever since the creation of Israel and up until that very moment, the West Bank and Gaza ought to have been the objectives of the Palestinian national movement. Creating a Palestinian state on both banks of the Jordan—the West Bank and Transjordania—would have been a more realistic project than an impossible reconquest.[7]

Given the presence of armed elements in Jordan, was Israel really the primary enemy of the Palestinian national movement, or was it the Hashemite dynasty of Transjordan, which, with the support of leading Palestinians, had annexed the West Bank in 1949, thereby transforming Transjordan into the kingdom of Jordan? The headline-grabbing commando operations, victimless and otherwise, undertaken from the far bank of the Jordan, accounted for the bulk of the activities carried out by various movements. What struck any observer at the time was the extraordinary fragmentation of the resistance. In early 1969, when the charter was published, there were al-Fatah, led by Yasser Arafat, the central figure of the Palestine Liberation Organization (PLO) for decades to come; George Habash's more leftist Popular Front for the Liberation of Palestine (PFLP); the Democratic Front for the Liberation of Palestine (DFLP), a recently created splinter group of the extreme left founded by Nayef Hawatmeh; the pro-Syrian al-Saika; the pro-Iraqi Palestinian Arab Front; and another, pro-Egyptian movement. These groups soon broke up into splinter factions, such as the PFLP-GC—the general command under Ahmed Jibril—and that of Abu Nidal, deployed variously in Iraq, Syria, and Libya.

From the outset, the Arab countries had both supported—either financially, like Saudi Arabia, or logistically—and dissipated a national movement that represented slightly more than three million people at the time. A common policy was rarely formulated, and the strategies put forward were often mutually contradictory.

The Popular Front made the mistake of hijacking several American planes in Zarqa, Jordan, and of negotiating directly with other states in setting conditions for the release of the hostages. The incident, in September 1970, allowed King Hussein, who was fed up with the Palestinians behaving as if they were a state within a state, to crack down on their organizations, most of whose members fled to Lebanon.

In their eviction from Jordan, where two-thirds or more of the population was Palestinian, the Palestinian organizations had lost a valuable base. Except in the eventuality of an Israeli or American intervention, it would not have been impossible in time to overthrow the Hashemite monarchy, with its largely Bedouin foundations.

In 1972, the Palestinians, through al-Fatah, pulled off the most dramatic operation of the century: the hostage-taking of Israeli athletes at the Olympic Games in Munich. Instead of exploiting this high-profile opportunity to offer the Western world a peaceful exegesis of the Palestinian dispossession, the action ended in the deaths of the athletes and members of the commando unit. The kidnappers' demands were nonnegotiable for the Israeli state.

Nonetheless, in 1974, in an atmosphere in which the political struggles of the Third World still elicited sympathetic support, the UN General Assembly recognized the PLO as the "representative of the Palestinian people" and welcomed Yasser Arafat to UN Headquarters in New York with great pomp. A gradual evolution from publicity-seeking terrorism to a terrorism of diplomatic coercion was under way, directed from a distance by Iraq, Syria, and Libya, among others.

So long as its key objective was publicity, Palestinian terrorism was little more than a nuisance. But some states' manipulation of Palestinian groups as elements of their indirect strategy to influence Europe had become alarming. Moreover, over time, western Europe, which had mostly served as the theater—with the democratic intermediary of its media— had become the target.

The 1970s offered political organizations big and small every incentive to resort to terrorism. The impact of a single spectacular action in a European capital far outweighed that of years of guerrilla warfare. Unless American troops became involved, most marginal struggles barely rated a second glance. Every so often an article would recall some "forgotten war." What, in 1972, did anyone know about the most effective fight being waged on the African continent—that of the African Party for the Independence of Guinea and Cape Verde, led by Amilcar Cabral? Ten years later, what did anyone know about the struggle against Khomeini in Iranian Kurdistan, under the command of the most remarkable of Kurdish leaders, A. R. Ghassemlou, who joked at a press conference in Paris in 1982 that he hoped his movement wouldn't be penalized by the media because it refused to resort to terrorism?

In any case, it is futile to condemn the media for favoring sensationalism and dramatics. That's the way things are. If you want to be heard—which does not automatically mean being understood—you have to choose your targets with the headlines in mind.

The case of Armenian terrorism is interesting in this regard, and the actions undertaken by it between 1975 and 1983 led the Rand Corporation to note that, throughout the period, "the breadth of their geographical reach was equaled by no other group." These actions took place in some twenty countries, including the United States, Australia, France, Switzerland, Turkey, Yugoslavia, Bulgaria, and others.

What was happening here?

The concerted liquidation in 1915 and 1916 of the vast majority of the Armenians of Anatolia, carried out through a mass deportation in which most victims were executed en route, barely rates a footnote in Western history textbooks. In 1973, a report submitted to a UN Sub-Commission on the Promotion and Protection of Human Rights noted that these events are generally considered to be the "first genocide of the twentieth century." Turkey's opposition led to the suppression of the paragraph, provoking the considerable indignation of Armenians of the diaspora or persons of Armenian origin, whose memory kept the tragedy alive.

The fact that this terrorism emerged after a half-century of silence (punctuated by various futile Armenian approaches to the League of Nations, and later to the United Nations) is explained by the spirit of the times: decolonization, ethnicity, human rights, the terrorism used by other movements for publicity purposes, and so on. Moreover, it was no coincidence that most of the Armenian activities were based in Lebanon.

Armenian terrorism was directed against representatives of the Turkish state abroad, except in 1983, when a bomb attack at Orly Airport in Paris killed eight.[8] Whatever moral judgment might be brought to bear on these acts, they mostly targeted representatives of a state that has obstinately refused to acknowledge the facts and has even sought to pressure countries that are willing to recognize the Armenian genocide.

The two organizations directing these actions offer fairly accurate illustrations of the scope and limits of contemporary terrorism. The first, the Justice Commandos of the Armenian Genocide (an offshoot of the

Dashnak Social Democrat Party), sought only recognition of the genocide, through dramatic action. Attacks took place even in countries such
as Bulgaria and Yugoslavia, where it was difficult to ascribe them to anti-
Western sentiment.

Genocide is considered subject to no statute of limitations, and to
breach the age-old wall of silence, terrorist violence was required. Publi-
cized by other, perfectly legal means aimed at establishing the facts in the
eyes of public opinion (such as the Permanent Peoples' Tribunal, Paris,
1984), the Armenian genocide was recognized in 1985 by the UN Sub-
Commission on Human Rights, and in 1987 by the Council of Europe.[9]

The policy of the Armenian Secret Army for the Liberation of Armenia (ASALA) was oriented towards the Third World and sought nothing
less than the impossible recovery of territories that had once been Armenian or were of majority Armenian population in 1915.

Without a social base or a realistic strategy—in 1975, and in opposition to Turkey, a member of NATO, could anyone reasonably call for the
return of territory?—the movement inevitably and swiftly drifted into
culpable action. In the late 1980s, certain elements of the movement, including Monte Melkonian, became actively engaged in the struggle for
the self-determination of Nagorno-Karabakh.

Palestinian groups continued their attacks from 1975 to 1982, punctuated by two events: the Lebanese civil war, the outcome of Palestinian
interference in the fragile Lebanese sectarian equation, and the 1982 advance of Israeli troops to the very suburbs of Beirut, leading to the PLO's
eviction from Lebanon. It was during this incursion that, with General
Ariel Sharon's approval, Phalangist militiamen massacred civilians in the
Palestinian camps of Sabra and Shatila.

In the meanwhile, Lebanon had become a revolving door and a sanctuary for any revolutionary group seeking military training, including in
the manufacture of explosives. At one time or another, the Red Brigades,
the Red Army Fraction, ETA, the Provisional IRA, the Turkish Dev-Yol,
ASALA, the Japanese Red Army, and many others had all spent time in
al-Fatah or PFLP camps.

The number of international attacks, limited to a handful before 1968,
rose dramatically in just a few years: 110 in 1970; 157 in 1972; 344 in
1974; 415 in 1976; and 738 in 1978. It should be noted, however, that
there is a considerable disparity between the CIA's tally (the figures provided here) and that of the Rand Corporation. For the decade 1968–77,
the CIA counts 2,698 attacks; Rand, less prone to political skewing, sets
the figure at 1,022, and emphasizes that 729 were casualty-less.

While, from a psychological and publicity perspective, terrorism often dominated the headlines in the 1970s, its results were mixed. The North American and European groups of the far left achieved nothing, and this continued to be the case with those that survived through the mid 1980s. Conversely, such nationalist movements as the IRA and, to a lesser extent, the military wing of ETA endured. Hostilities came to an end in Ulster a few years ago.

The Palestinian national movement, its strategic errors, reversals, and difficulties notwithstanding, enjoys considerable social support and, along with the Irish struggle, has been the most durable political movement of the past thirty-five years. It is worth taking a look at how states, and particularly those of Europe, responded during this early phase of the Palestinian struggle before Islamism rose to prominence.

Actions targeting aviation gave rise to dramatic hijackings. In August 1969, two Palestinians—one of them a woman, Leila Khaled—hijacked a TWA plane in Rome, which they evacuated and blew up in Damascus. In February 1970, the PFLP detonated a bomb on a Swissair plane bound for Israel with 47 people on board. In September 1970, four aircraft were commandeered, one of them an El Al flight. When Leila Khaled was captured, a fifth plane was diverted and its passengers released in exchange for her freedom. Three of the aircraft (Pan Am, TWA, and Swissair) were evacuated and destroyed. In December 1973, again in Rome (clearly a weak link), a commando unit bombed a Pan Am plane, killing 32 people. In 1974, a TWA flight exploded en route between Tel Aviv and New York, with 98 dead.

In response to such tactics, states tightened boarding procedures, making it harder to smuggle weapons on board. In 1976, Israel refused to negotiate with PFLP members who diverted an Air France flight carrying 246 passengers between Israel and Athens. Having disembarked non-Israelis in Libya, the plane landed at Entebbe, Uganda. Israel dispatched a force of paratroopers to rescue the hostages, losing only one commanding officer.

From the Palestinian perspective, the two most spectacular actions were those in Munich in 1972 and in Vienna in 1975, where members of the PFLP and the Red Army Fraction stormed a meeting at OPEC headquarters. The operation made a household name of Carlos the Jackal, who was eventually arrested in the Sudan in 1994.

ORGANIZING THE RESPONSE

No one, on the eve of the Six-Day War, could have predicted the explosive rise of the terrorist phenomenon. More than fifty embassies were taken by assault. In a throwback to the heyday of anarchism, six heads of state or former heads of state—Aldo Moro in 1978, Anwar Sadat in 1981, Indira Gandhi in 1984, Rajiv Gandhi in 1991, Sri Lankan President Ranasinghe Premadasa in 1993, and Yitzhak Rabin in 1995—were assassinated, not to mention the attempted assassination of Pope John Paul II by a Turk in 1982 and the murder of Lord Mountbatten by the IRA in 1979.

Transnational terrorism has claimed at least 15,000 victims since 1968. Terrorism has given states costly security headaches in the protection of political leaders, embassies, public figures, vulnerable public spaces, sensitive infrastructure, airports, and so on.

What could be done to counter terrorism? The fundamental problem was information-gathering, the linchpin of any effective prevention, infiltration, neutralization, manipulation, and elimination. Building a dossier would give insight into a group's social and political connections: its contracts, weapons suppliers, finances, documentation—its overall social network. Information has two very distinct aspects: the basic, indispensable task of gathering it, despite the fact that most of it may be useless; and interpreting it, which is above all a sociological and political art. Interpretation requires an understanding of the adversary, its ideology, organization, methods, and so on. The regularly updated, computerized files kept by the Federal Republic of Germany exemplify the type. In France, the problem has been less one of obtaining information than of sharing it among the various services. Information remains the key bulwark against terrorism, along with the organization necessary to respond adequately to surprise.

Caught short at first, the democratic states began to take the struggle against terrorism more seriously and to engage in tentative cooperation, especially after 1972. Few retaliated, other than Israel, which not only undertook such actions as the Entebbe intervention but also, for instance, sent a commando unit to assassinate three al-Fatah leaders in Beirut in the 1980s. In 1986, in response to a series of attacks manifestly sponsored by Libya, the United States bombed Tripoli, seeking to kill Mu'ammar Gadhafi. The largest counterterrorist action ever undertaken was that led by the United States against Mullah Omar's Afghanistan in the aftermath of September 11, 2001.

Starting in the early 1970s, national legal codes were substantially amended with respect to such matters as police custody, house searches, and so on. In Great Britain, for example, where freedoms had always been jealously defended, the law was adapted to the new realities of terrorism, especially Irish terrorism. The U.K. Prevention of Terrorism (Temporary Provisions) Act of 1976 legalized extended police custody, the invasion and search of homes, the expulsion of suspects, and so forth. Great Britain proscribed the IRA. It become illegal to provide financial support to it, and anyone convicted of having links to the IRA was liable to be expelled from the country. Detention was extended to forty-eight hours, which could be prolonged by five additional days by the home secretary. In airports and ports, the police were empowered to detain suspects for up to seven days and longer with the approval of the home secretary.

In the Federal Republic of Germany, given the grave challenge posed by the Red Army Fraction, the legislation enacted to counter terrorism was the most severe in western Europe. The 1972 *Berufsverbot* (occupational ban) allowed elements deemed undesirable to be barred from civil service employment, including university professors. From 1974 to 1978, the criminal code was amended to give the authorities the greatest possible latitude in combating terrorism. Sections 129 and 129a of the criminal procedures code authorized sentences of up to five years' imprisonment for anyone who joined a terrorist association or directly or indirectly participated in one. Any lawyer suspected of endangering state security could be disbarred by order of the federal court. Under section 48c of the code, the *Kontaktsperregesetz* (contact ban law), all oral or written contact between lawyer and client could be suspended for a renewable 30-day period, if deemed necessary.

The dangers of counterterrorist legislation targeting "suspects" are obvious. In the guise of counterterrorism, any opposition deemed undesirable can be eliminated. The counterweight to such a threat lies in a country's democratic traditions and the independence of its judiciary. Great Britain also created the counterterrorist Special Patrol Groups for rapid intervention when the government sought to retake an objective occupied by a terrorist group. To that end, several European countries established similar units: the Bundesgrenzschutz in Germany, and the Groupe d'intervention de la Gendarmerie nationale in France, which intervened in the 1994 hijacking of a plane by Algerian members of the Armed Islamic Group in Marseille.

Groups have resorted to deadly blackmail tactics to obtain the freedom of their incarcerated comrades. In France, the Organization of the Armed Arab Struggle—a moniker adopted by a splinter group under Carlos and the Lebanese Revolutionary Armed Fractions—attacked the Publicis Saint-Germain drugstore in Paris, killing two people indiscriminately, to obtain the release of a member of the Japanese Red Army from a French prison, following a hostage-taking at the French embassy in The Hague. The prisoner was released.

The same tactic for obtaining the release of terrorists was used in March 1982 with the bombing of a Paris-Toulouse train, killing five. A month later, a car bomb exploded on the rue Marbeuf in Paris on the opening day of a terrorist trial. In that instance, the suspects were found guilty. On December 31, 1983, a bomb in the Marseille train station killed two people, while another on the Marseille-Paris high-speed train killed three. Carlos and the Organization of the Armed Arab Struggle claimed responsibility for these attacks, as well as for one on the French cultural center in Tripoli, Libya, in response to the presence of French troops in Lebanon.

The issue of how to limit media coverage, either through self-censorship or by decree, was a sensitive one. With security concerns greater than most others', Israel alone among the democracies persuaded its media to tone down their reporting of terrorism. But the evolution of cooperation among states, particularly within western Europe, where geographic proximity allowed easy passage from one country to another, was still in its infancy.

Throughout the 1960s, Italy was manifestly irresolute in combating the terrorism of the Red Brigades and even more so that of the far right. This was undoubtedly a reflection of the Italian state's historical development. France had a very different government tradition, and while one organization or another there may have enjoyed the privilege of negotiations or clemency, except in the case of Corsican nationalist groups, this was a matter of a political choice, not of the state's laxity.

A not insignificant number of American diplomats died because the United States government maintained its refusal to negotiate. Negotiation can, however, be a means of imposing one's will on an adversary, although caving in to the demands of a terrorist group is an invitation to further demands.

Negotiating tactics were developed and perfected either to achieve a desired outcome or, more often, to gain time during a hostage-taking situation, such as an embassy siege or a hijacking. The attitude of the French state in the 1960s, for instance, seems to have been dictated less by the demands than by the nature of terrorist groups. Except in rare instances, yielding was not an option. In 1969, the United States agreed to the exchange of fifteen Brazilian political prisoners for the release of its ambassador. Even the Israelis agreed to negotiate on a few occasions.

Generally speaking, however, that is not the objective of negotiations. The state may offer the possibility of either unopposed withdrawal in exchange for hostages or of a political trial, which is the goal of many terrorist groups.

State resolve, media self-censorship, and public awareness need to be harmonized. In October 1977, during the Palestinian hijacking of a Lufthansa flight to Mogadishu, Somalia, the hijackers learned via the media that the captain had passed information to the authorities during routine transmissions. It cost the captain his life.

The sensational spectacle of violence dished up by the media assists terrorism in its psychological warfare. The repeated re-airing of a terrorist spectacle has a contagious effect and encourages imitators. That tendency was perfectly illustrated in France in the summer of 1984, when two young men tried to pass themselves off as members of a political movement to order to extort money from the state. In the United States, in 1971, D. B. Cooper parachuted from a hijacked plane with a ransom of $200,000. That very week, five others, having seen the headlines, tried the same tactic.

Generally speaking, throughout the 1980s, states significantly beefed up their global capacity to respond to terrorism. Ultimately, certain organizations were seriously weakened. In December 1983, German police captured key leaders of the Red Army Fraction. In Italy, the police exploited the testimony of "repentants" to dismantle most of the Red Brigade cells in 1982 and 1983. Their success was far less conclusive with respect to the terrorist networks of the far right, which appear to have enjoyed the sympathies of prominent figures in Italian society and government agencies.[10] Nevertheless, then as now, the terrorist threat was unequal to the task of destabilizing Western societies, whereas the arsenal of suppression continued and continues to grow, especially since September 11, 2001.

Western Europe was long the theater or target of attacks, whereas the United States was always challenged and hit at beyond its own borders. That situation ended in 1993 with the attack on the World Trade Center; in 1995, with the bombing of the federal building in Oklahoma City by an American extremist, Timothy McVeigh; and at the 1996 Atlanta Olympic Games, again by an American. Mention should also be made of the seventeen attacks perpetrated by Ted Kaczynski, the Unabomber. Then came the stunning attack of September 11.

In the United States, the measures that have been taken to reinforce security are felt by certain civil liberties organizations to be unduly restrictive of such freedoms. Islamist prisoners held at Guantánamo Bay have no legal status, for example.

MINORITY AND RELIGIOUS MOVEMENTS

After the Irish Free State came into being after a hard-fought struggle in the early 1920s, Ulster, with its Protestant majority, remained tied to Great Britain.

In 1969, Catholics in Ulster were second-class citizens by virtue both of their economic status and of the way they were perceived by the Protestants, Presbyterian descendants of Scottish migrants brought over by the English in the eighteenth century. Catholics made up 38 percent of the population, but that figure has risen since. Believing that not all the objectives of the emancipation struggle had been achieved, the IRA launched two terrorist campaigns, both fruitless, on the eve of World War II and between 1956 and 1962.

By the late 1960s, however, the Protestant Unionists' rejection of all reform aimed at the Catholic minority had radicalized the latter. The Provisional IRA emerged with the determination to model itself as a national liberation movement on the example of events in the colonized world.

From the outset, the IRA's military struggle was carried out by just a few hundred men. Not only had recruitment always been easy, but the small number of active members allowed selection to be based on the tightest possible secrecy. Despite every effort of the government forces, the IRA was never in danger of being dismantled. The perceived nationalism of its cause carried greater social weight than the ideological struggles of leftist groups.

In its campaign against the Provisional IRA, the British government emphasized the term "terrorism." Prisoners were denied political status. In protest, some dozen detainees went on hunger strike in the Margaret Thatcher years. When the prime minister refused to back down, the strikers went on to their deaths. A significant sector of British society saw this as a moral defeat for the government.

The IRA has two wings. The official IRA is opposed to terrorist-type action and to violence in general, and encourages mass demonstrations. The Provisional IRA broke away in 1969, and violence erupted anew in 1970 when the Provisionals fired into a group of Protestant demonstrators. The organization had to adapt swiftly to fighting a campaign on two fronts against Unionist militias, on the one hand, and the British, on the other. The violence increased in 1971 when the British government imprisoned suspects and militants without trial.

On January 30, 1972—Bloody Sunday—a clash in Londonderry between the British army and the IRA left thirteen protestors dead. The incident led the British government to impose direct rule on Ulster. London became both the referee and the guarantor of safety in a situation in which it was also the repressor, while simultaneously seeking to prevent clashes between Catholics and Unionists from turning tragic. On July 21, 1972—Bloody Friday—the Provisional IRA launched a series of bomb attacks that left nine people dead and hundreds wounded.

The following year, the Provisional IRA carried the fight to English soil. The London stock exchange, department stores, and other targets were attacked. The suppression was stepped up. London offered expanded self-rule to Ulster, a measure of de facto advantage to the Protestant majority. The IRA's response was its 1979 assassination by means of a bomb planted in his boat in Donegal Bay of Lord Mountbatten of Burma, the last viceroy of India and a scion of the royal family, along with several others, including his fourteen-year-old grandson and another young boy. The Unionists, for their part, organized themselves into armed militias (the Ulster Defence Association, the Ulster Volunteer Force, etc.), which undertook punitive forays into Catholic neighborhoods.

Notwithstanding the bitterness of the confrontation, the total number of dead in over thirty years of fighting was just over 3,000. Negotiations were ultimately initiated. The violence faded away, and Sinn Féin, the aboveground political wing of the IRA, benefited. The Unionists considered themselves to be the losers in the struggle, although Ulster's final status has yet to be determined.

ETA was formed in 1959, defining itself as a national liberation movement with revolutionary socialist leanings. In Franco's time—that is, up to 1975—ETA's primary target was the Guardia civil, and its most effective and dramatic act was the assassination by bomb of the regime's second-in-command, Admiral Luis Carrero Blanco, in 1975. ETA did not only pursue but stepped up its activities after the establishment of democracy. The autonomy granted by the Spanish state in 1980 and the election of a Basque assembly were enough to satisfy ETA's politico-military wing, but not so its offshoot military branch, which sought independence for the Basque provinces of Navarra, Vizcaya, Alava, and

Guipúzcoa. ETA's military activities were crimped when Madrid obtained the cooperation of Paris in dismantling the networks of the Basque country. For its part, the Spanish state deployed special clandestine units to eliminate ETA's militants and cadres, until their exposure resulted in scandal.

On several occasions in the late 1990s, popular demonstrations erupted in the Basque country against ETA's ongoing activities. While not disbanding, ETA's military branch has kept a low profile since September 11, 2001. The theater of conflict seems to have drifted into the purely political arena. Self-rule, in the Basque country, as in Catalonia, would seem to encourage broader claims, although the prospect of independence appears to be excluded.

The Corsican independence movements, displaying either an exceptional lack of understanding or bad faith, stress the "colonial" nature of the French state's attitude toward Corsica. The national liberation movement in Corsica is a parody—no one can claim that the majority of Corsicans want independence.[11] That is a primary reason for the movement's failure. Another is the fragmentation of groups and movements and the number of cadres who have abandoned the cause or been eliminated en route. Yet another is its descent into mafia rule. A further flaw may lie in the political and cultural immaturity of a movement that has locked itself into an egregiously narrow worldview.

The French state, in turn, has shown itself to be as pusillanimous as it is inconsistent. Was it justified in its decision to disband the Association for the Rebirth of Corsica and to arrest its leader, Edmond Siméoni, in August 1975? Perhaps not, but the killing of two police officers during a clash incited by that arrest should have been severely punished. Such facts ought not be whitewashed. In Corsica, more than elsewhere—and in any society based on a code of honor and courage—weakness is taken not as a desire for conciliation but as an invitation to push for more. One must be able to clamp down in such circumstances, but to clamp down fairly so as not to give the activists an opportunity to exploit their own suppression.

RELIGIOUS TERROR

As noted in chapter 1, there is nothing new about terrorist activities with a religious underpinning. They are, however, indisputably on the rise, not only in their radical Islamic fundamentalist embodiment, which is addressed separately elsewhere, but also in other religions. Sikhs, for instance, have waged a religious war in the name of a national ideal against the Indian union, seeking to establish their own Khalistan—"land of the pure." The Indian army's closing in 1984 of the Golden Temple in Amritsar, Punjab—a site sacred to the independence-minded Sikhs—unleashed a conflict that left some 20,000 people dead. Prime Minister Indira Gandhi was assassinated by her Sikh bodyguards in 1986. Clashes between ultra-orthodox Muslims and Hindus—incited by the destruction of mosques and plans to build temples on a religious site venerated by Muslims—rose throughout the 1990s.

In 1983, an Israeli *yeshiva* student was murdered by Palestinians. Settlers of the Gush Emunim (Bloc of the Faithful) sect decided to retaliate. Blessed by a rabbi associated with the movement, a commando unit shot up the entrance to a *madrassa,* killing three and wounding thirty. In 1994, Baruch Goldstein—a U.S.-born member of Kach, an ultra-orthodox organization founded by Rabbi Meir Kahane and advocating the expulsion of the Arabs—opened fire on a mosque at prayer during the holy month of Ramadan. Goldstein fired in bursts, killing 29 and wounding 150 before being lynched. In 1995, Yitzhak Rabin's assassin, a member of an ultra-orthodox religious movement, justified his action by invoking Jewish tradition: "When a Jew betrays his people and his country, he must be killed."

In 1995, the Aum Shinrikyo cult, founded in 1987 by Shoko Asahara, self-appointed leader of the "Army of God," launched a sarin gas attack on the Tokyo subway, killing twelve people and injuring hundreds more. The sect, which counted some 10,000 members, with networks in Australia, Sri Lanka, the United States, Russia, and Germany, claimed nothing less than to be setting the stage for the inevitable apocalypse.

The phenomenon of radical militant Islam is not an isolated one, but it is currently the most significant of all political movements claiming divine inspiration. An international avant-garde of radical Islamists coalesced in Afghanistan. With rare exceptions (such as in Algeria in 1991), it has no permanent roots. Its participation in one jihad or another—Bosnia, Chechnya, Kashmir, and so on—on a model similar to that of the international brigades of the Spanish Civil War, has yet to lead to any significant change in its modus operandi. Militant Islamism is handicapped by two factors.

First, without a political wing, it is difficult for any underground organization to provide training for its members. Secondly, the radical Islamic movement, based on the promise of the revival of the *umma* (the community of the faithful), has been stymied by the solidity of local nationalisms that feel that a Tunisian is not an Afghan and a Saudi is not an Egyptian. Coherence has proven less easy to come by on the popular scale than it is among the elites and the dispossessed.

Al Qaeda, or more precisely militant Islamism, has been handicapped by the same contradiction that felled many European groups and movements of the far left: the inability of a self-proclaimed avant-garde to mobilize the masses if they are not organized and supervised.

NOTES TO CHAPTER 11

1. The figure does not include the fifty-seven killed in the attack on the U.S. embassy. The Italian ship *Achille Lauro* was boarded off the coast of Egypt by a Palestinian commando in 1985, and an American passenger was murdered.

2. See Black, *Genocide in Iraq.*

3. Wilkinson, *Political Terrorism.*

4. Marighella, *For the Liberation of Brazil* and "Minimanual of the Urban Guerrilla."

5. The influence on Marighella and the Tupamaros of the Spanish revolutionary Abraham Guillen cannot be overestimated. See Chaliand, ed., *Guerrilla Strategies.*

6. Turkey is a classic example of terrorism's inability to carry weight except through the prospect of unending chaos. The military's rise to power in 1980 and the ensuing law-and-order dictatorship were the inevitable outcome.

7. See Chaliand, *La résistance palestinienne.*

8. Elements of the Armenian Secret Army for the Liberation of Armenia (ASALA) targeted clients of Turkish Airlines and planned attacks on states that had no involvement in the issue. ASALA fragmented and subsequently ceased its activities.

9. Notwithstanding Turkey's wrath, the reality of the Armenian genocide has since been recognized by France, Belgium, Greece, the Russian Federation, Argentina, Switzerland, and the Vatican. In the United States, the protracted battle between the exigencies of Turkish policy and the supporters of recognition is ongoing.

10. The many neofascist groups included the Armed Revolutionary Nuclei, the Black Order, the New Order, the Rose of the Winds, the Avanguardia Nazionale, the National Front, etc.

11. Indeed, 80 percent of Corsicans are held hostage to a muted terror that can spill over into repressive action at any moment.

CHAPTER 12

THE ROOTS OF ISLAMIC RADICALISM

Philippe Migaux

> Islam is ideology and faith, homeland and nationality, creed and state, spirit and action, book and sword.
>
> **Hassan al-Banna, 1934**

> He whose helping hand has allowed us to survive and He who made it possible for us to defeat the Soviet Union can protect us once again and enable us to defeat America, on the same territory and with the same methods; such is the will of Allah. We therefore believe that America's defeat is possible, if Allah wills it, and that it will be easier . . . than the earlier defeat of the Soviet empire.
>
> **Osama bin Laden, 2001**

> O ye who believe! Stand out firmly for Allah, as witnesses to fair dealing, and let not the hatred of others to you make you swerve to wrong and depart from justice. Be just: that is next to piety: and fear Allah. For Allah is well-acquainted with all that ye do.
>
> **The Qur'an, sura 5:8**

The jihad-by-the-sword—or jihadist—movement, which first emerged in the early 1970s, draws its inspiration from an age-old ideology. But it has taken an aberrant form—the end result of a fundamentalist line of thinking based on a mythicized view of original Islam. Indeed, its goal is the manipulation of excluded and marginalized segments of Islamic societies.

Toward the end of the 1970s, a new generation of radical Islamists embraced that ideology to justify the resort to transnational political violence, considered to be the only means of restoring the caliphate—a symbiosis of the political and religious spheres—and of reunifying the *umma* (the Muslim community). Its most radical manifestation is Islamic mujahideen terrorism, which is based on the teachings of the Salafist school. That form of terrorism—of Sunni origin—is today the principal threat to the international community.

I shall touch more briefly on two other forms of contemporary jihadism—the Iranian Hezbollah and Palestinian Hamas movements—because they do not convey the same message of political terror. Each has a political vision that allows for the possibility of negotiations with its opponent at the appropriate time—although Palestinian Islamism has not yet reached that point.

Militant Shiism emerged simultaneously with the establishment of the Islamic Republic of Iran in 1979. The dissemination of its jihadist ideology was related not only to Iran's continuing regional ambitions but also to the mullahs' desire to weaken the position of the Saudis, considered religious rivals. It was reflected in the increasing power, in the early 1980s, of Hezbollah (the Party of God), which considered Lebanon a favorable setting for politically motivated violence. However, the pattern has shifted. Today militant Shiism is primarily an internal movement in Iran, while Lebanon's Hezbollah, which until recently had maintained a significant capacity for terrorist action, has become a local political actor of significance.

Palestinian Islamism, under the ideological leadership of the Grand Mufti of Jerusalem, was in the 1930s the first protagonist in the struggle against Zionism. Although during the postwar period it was marginalized by the Palestine Liberation Organization (PLO) and its dissident groups, as well as by the growing influence of pan-Arabism, the first intifada (1987) gave it a new lease on life, as did the institutionalization of the PLO in the context of the creation of a partially formed Palestinian entity.

Hamas and Islamic Jihad, on the other hand, have remained local movements. Their followers have a different kind of background—Palestinian camps, not Afghan ones—and their goals are different from those of militant Salafists. It is noteworthy, however, that several high-ranking mujahideen officials are of Palestinian origin.

The mujahideen movement is of particular interest given its utopian political beliefs. It is the most marginal and extreme form of contemporary terrorism, because it does not negotiate. In the movement's view, political violence is no longer merely a weapon; it is, ultimately, the only objective, dooming its followers to extinction. The latter are prepared to kill themselves without a moment's hesitation, seeking, through martyrdom, to perpetuate what they likely view as an epic undertaking.

Finally, the ideology underlying the mujahideen movement is often referred to as "jihadist Islamism," which requires definition. As we shall see later, the term "jihad" has a much broader meaning than the interpretations given it, throughout Muslim history, by hard-liners or extremists. The phrase "jihad by the sword" is perhaps a better indication of the simplistic but powerful manner in which radical thinkers have hijacked the Qur'anic allegory of a "paradise under the shadow of swords."

THE JIHADIST MOVEMENT IN THE CONTEXT OF CONTEMPORARY TERRORISM

From 1970 to 1990, it was customary to divide terrorist organizations into three categories: revolutionary, identity-based, and manipulative.

During that period, revolutionary terrorism was mainly the province of far-left European groups such as the Red Brigades or the Red Army Fraction. Cause-based terrorism was particularly influenced, at the international level, by Palestinian organizations, with their secular ideology and Marxist-Leninist leanings. They had succeeded in forging active ties—in the areas of training, logistics, and mission subcontracting—with European revolutionary groups or other cause-based groups such as the Provisional Irish Republican Army (PIRA) and ETA. Finally, manipulative terrorism, or state terrorism—which uses undercover agents, mercenary groups, or other entities under its control—was considered characteristic mainly of the countries of the Middle East or of the Levant such as Iran, Syria, Iraq, and Libya. All of them, in the framework of their regional power strategies, had availed themselves of the services of PLO dissident groups.

Two trends emerged following the collapse of the Soviet bloc: the near-cessation of state terrorism and the end of Palestinian secular terrorism and of European far-left revolutionary terrorism. Islamic terrorism, however, began to pick up steam. Its many new manifestations either filled the vacuums that had been created—for instance, the Palestinian group Hamas took over from the Palestine Liberation Organization, now a state entity—or set out to fight new battles.

Some believe that today's Islamic terrorism is simply a new form of anti-imperialism and that it can be classified as revolutionary terrorism. Others are of the view that it falls into a fourth category—religious terrorism.

It should be emphasized that this essay does not aim to denounce Islam or its religious schools, nor does it claim to be a scholarly treatise on the struggles waged within Muslim or Muslim-influenced societies. Its more modest goal is to serve as a tool—a kind of filter, perhaps—to better understand the contemporary phenomenon of Islam-inspired political violence.

To state that the phenomenon should be viewed as a holy undertaking smacks of propaganda. To insist that it can be explained solely on the basis of specific religious interpretations or selective analyses is to oversimplify the subject; specialists who make such claims can be very far removed from realities on the ground. In the summer of 2002, an in-depth treatise was published by recognized authors which explained that there was no threat of jihadist terrorism in Southeast Asia. Yet on October 12 next, Bali was struck by the Jammah Islamiya in the deadliest attacks since those of September 11. The book—otherwise very good—has since been reissued with a different conclusion.

It is thus important to move beyond a discussion of actual threats and to situate the mujahideen movement in its proper context in the history of political terrorism, so that its true nature can be fully understood and the full extent of the danger it poses accurately assessed.

This text therefore takes a different tack than do those that have been published since the end of 2001, which appear to favor sensationalism over facts. To view the events of September 11 as representing the emergence of a kind of super-terrorism, lumping together a shoddy analysis of events with a discussion of threats verging on apocalyptic fantasy, smacks more of a sales pitch than of a level-headed process of reflection. Gérard Chaliand, in denouncing the "anxiety sellers," points out that, while terrorism certainly kills large numbers of people, it does provide a livelihood for many others—consider the numerous experts offering erudite explanations who have come out of the woodwork in recent times. But the subject of terrorism merits a more restrained approach, if only because of the respect due its victims.

One thing is certain: jihadist terrorism cannot prevail, because, unlike Islamism, it has no genuine political vision and, as a result, does not engage in negotiations. It has a different goal: to push for mass radicalization in the context of a near-Messianic undertaking. In that sense, the jihadists' message is much more revolutionary than religious, and its approach more long-term than is generally recognized.

The extent to which some authors overestimate the importance of the phenomenon is commensurate only with the depth of their silence in the face of its growing strength during the previous decade. The first attack against the World Trade Center was not the one of September 11, 2001, in which hijacked airliners slammed into it; the first attack took place on February 26, 1993, when a car bomb exploded in an underground parking lot beneath the Center.

Those topics have, however, been dealt with very insightfully by a number of serious-minded authors from various fields, all of whom have approached the topic of jihadist terrorism from a comprehensive perspective. They are listed in the bibliography, and the multidisciplinary approach taken here is greatly in their debt.

GUIDE TO TERMINOLOGY

It must be recalled that the term "Islamism" refers not to a theological doctrine but to the political use of Islam. In that sense, Islamism must be distinguished from fundamentalism, which advocates a return to the founding texts of Islam. Islamic fundamentalism becomes Islamism only when its ideology is used to impose a strictly interpreted model of original Islam based on *sharia,* or Islamic law, on society and on the state.

I therefore use the term "political Islamism" to describe the beliefs of those movements that endeavor—by legal means—to use Islam to reform the institutional structure and sociocultural environment of a particular geopolitical grouping. I use the term "radical Islamism" when attempts are made to completely transform such a geopolitical grouping. The term "activist Islamism" (or "militant Islamism") is used when movements resort to violence to achieve their goals. Finally, the phrase "Islamist terrorism" (or "jihadist terrorism") is used to describe a new stage of that third phase, in which Islamist activists use terrorism—indiscriminate or targeted—to impose their views, or in the context of identity politics.

Thus the term "jihadist movement" encompasses previously fragmented Islamist activist groups that had, at an earlier stage, opted for jihad as a means to an end, but that later embraced it as their sole objective. The term "mujahideen movement," which is close enough to it in meaning that it is often used in its stead, places greater emphasis on individual action on the part of its followers, however, in the context of what is to them a holy undertaking.

Finally, I shall avoid engaging in any kind of scholarly dispute; that I leave to the specialists. Inasmuch as I am addressing a readership that is curious about the realities of contemporary terrorism, and that, in general, lacks in-depth knowledge of Islam, I have chosen to limit references to texts to brief but informative quotations, placing them in the appropriate historical context. While it may seem to some that Arabic terms have been translated too simplistically, the goal here is for such terms to be as widely understandable as possible.

THE IDEOLOGICAL ORIGINS OF RADICAL ISLAMISM

It is not possible, in looking at the evolution of Islam, to summarize the history of the Muslim religion in a few pages. I shall attempt simply to show how the circumstances surrounding its creation, its spread and, later, its decline—periods characterized not only by an extraordinary civilizational influence but also by wars and conquests—gave rise to a limited, reductionist view of Islam, which made possible the birth of radical Islamism and of its militant offshoots.

The Birth of Islam and the Prophet's Struggle

Muhammad was born around 570 C.E. Orphaned at the age of 10, he was raised first by his grandfather and then by his uncle in a Bedouin warrior tribe in the territory of what is now Saudi Arabia. At the time, most Arab tribes were polytheistic and had a superstitious respect for genies. Others had long been converted to one of the two major monotheistic religions, Judaism and Christianity.

Mecca was the religious center of that pre-Islamic pagan world, which Muslim authors later denounced as a product of the age of ignorance *(jahiliya)*. Idol worship was commonplace, as evidenced by the presence of a carved Black Stone, said to have fallen from the sky, in the Ka'ba, which at the time was filled with pagan idols.

From 610 on, Muhammad decided to follow the example of Jews and Christians he knew and go into periods of solitary retreat and reflection. Therein he received divine revelations from the Archangel Gabriel, a well-known warrior figure in the Christian imagination. Muhammad thus became the guardian of the new principles of the Law of God, which he conveyed in a language that would later become the standard for classical Arabic. Those teachings formed the moral and political foundation of the new religion, which was viewed as the final form of monotheism. Islam, meaning surrender to God, was for that reason considered to be closely related, but superior to, Judaism and Christianity.

The Muslim calendar began in 622 with the Hegira. The new Prophet and his followers—al-Ansar—were driven out of Mecca by the city's inhabitants, who wanted nothing to do with a new religion. Muhammad took refuge in Yathrib, which became the city of the Prophet (*medinat al-nabi*, or Medina), and began to put in place the normative structures of Islam. Thanks to a remarkable system of alliances, he was able to round up the necessary forces to carry out guerrilla operations. Caravans, so crucial to Mecca's wealth, were repeatedly attacked as they crossed the desert.

In 628/6, after a peaceful march failed to win over the inhabitants of Mecca, he organized an army which, through an all-out strategy of threats and warfare, succeeded in 632/10 in conquering Mecca without bloodshed and in obtaining the surrender of the Arab tribes.

Galvanized by that lightning-fast victory, which they credited to the will of Allah, Arab horsemen, under the banner of the Prophet, managed, in the span of a few dozen years, to conquer a vast empire that would become the cradle of the greatest known civilization to exist from the eighth century to the fourteenth century. It was thanks to those who engaged in combat that the Muslim world was able to produce a new generation of scientists, doctors, artists, and philosophers. Its military power enabled Islam to launch, in the eleventh century, a second process of conversion through active proselytizing on the part of sailors and tradesmen. In the Muslim worldview, the spread of Islam—the superior religion—remained linked to the force of the sword.

Following Muhammad's death, Islam based itself on absolute respect by the *umma*—the community of believers—for the *sunna*—meaning tradition—consisting of two series of sacred texts. The first was the revelation (the Qur'an), whose 114 suras contain all the divine teachings transmitted to Muhammad by the Archangel Gabriel. Caliph 'Uthman compiled the Qur'an around 680/58. The second, the hadith, sayings and acts of the prophet as reported, directly or indirectly, by his first companions, appeared in final form during the ninth century.

That body of theology soon became the subject of interpretations that were declared infallible, which made it possible to create a juridical model based on sharia, or Qur'anic law. Also important were analogical deductions *(qiyas)*, which were used to resolve problems on the basis of similar situations mentioned in the Qur'an or in the hadith. Religious judges—called *mufti* or *ulama*—were authorized to hand down rulings (fatwa) and in so doing to rely on their personal judgment *(rai)*.

The *ulama,* specialists in the area of the Law *(fiqh)*—which in Islam consists basically of reflection on sources and their interpretations—soon evolved into a kind of substitute clergy, although that did not happen in the Sunni tradition. Their work eventually led to the emergence of four distinct schools of thought.

The first of those was the Hanafite School, inspired by Abu Hanifa, who died in 716/150. It tended toward openness and relied primarily on syllogistic reasoning. The Malikite School, inspired by Malik ben Anas, who died in 795/179, focused on the idea of "common utility" and customs. The Shafiite School, inspired by Al Shafi, who died in 820/204, based itself on the consensus of the Muslim community, or *ijma*. Finally, the Hanbali School, inspired by Ahmad Ibn Hanbal, stricter and more puritanical in nature, rejected any innovation that did not accord with what it considered the foundations of Islam.

Islam also defines itself in relation to an entity—the Muslim community—and therefore rejects the concept of state borders in favor of a geopolitical space belonging to God's people. There are five fundamental principles, or pillars, in Islam, which govern believers' lives.

The first pillar is the oneness of God, as proclaimed in the Declaration of Belief *(shahada)*, which states that "there is no God but Allah, and Muhammad is his Prophet" *(la illaha il Allah—Muhammad rasul Allah)*.

The second pillar is *salat*, or prayer, which takes place five times a day, once one has purified oneself and turned to face Mecca. If possible, at noon on Friday—Islam's holy day—group prayer is held in the mosque—literally, the place where one prostrates oneself *(masjid)*. The prayer service is led by the imam—a religious guide—who stands facing the devout, who are lined up shoulder to shoulder.

The third pillar is *zakat*, or alms-giving to the needy. The pursuit of wealth is allowed, since it is believed that man's earthly goods are only on loan from God, to whom everything belongs, and He demands solidarity among believers.

The fourth pillar is *saum*, or fasting, during the month of Ramadan. The fast lasts from sunrise until sunset. Family, social, and charitable gatherings are held at night, when meals are eaten. It is thus a tradition with a real social function.

The fifth and final pillar consists of the *hajj*, or pilgrimage to Mecca. It must be performed at least once in a lifetime, if materially possible. The *hajj* is a major pilgrimage that takes place each year at Mecca between the eighth and thirteenth days of the twelfth month and is thought to cleanse one of sin. A pilgrim thus purified becomes entitled to the honorific "Hajj" or "Hajji" before his or her name. A lesser pilgrimage known as *umra* can be performed privately at any time.

In early times, however, special dispensations were accorded to those who were in a position to spread Islam, such as soldiers, tradesmen, and seamen. The jihadist movement later used such dispensations, in the context of the struggle against infidels, to justify actions traditionally forbidden by the *sunna*.

Finally, Qur'anic prescripts dictate all of the important events in the life of a Muslim: birth; circumcision (between the ages of 3 and 11); marriage, or marriages; family life; death; and inheritance.

The Epic Saga of the Arab Conquests

In the span of under a century, Islamic militants built an empire through war. But was it a war of conquest or a missionary war? In fact, it was both. The spoils of war enabled Muslim fighters to amass the kind of wealth previously unknown to their tribes and at the same time to convert conquered peoples to Islam, according to the will of Allah, which they believed made them invincible.

Those two aspects of the struggle being waged were evident in the very first attacks carried out by Muhammad. In spring 624, the Prophet, accompanied by several hundred horsemen, took on a caravan traveling from Damascus to Mecca. However, 1,000 Kharijite soldiers arrived to defend it. To galvanize his troops, Muhammad told his followers that angels would ensure their victory and promised that those who died in battle would go to paradise. He then claimed one-fifth of the spoils, which was divided into three parts: one for himself, one for his family, and one for poor people and orphans.

Muhammad was more interested in subduing his adversaries than in crushing them. Although in 627 he ordered the massacre of the Jewish tribe of Banu Quraiza for having broken a treaty of alliance, five years later he conquered the city of Mecca with no bloodshed whatsoever. Within less than a year, he had definitively banned polytheism.

Jews and Christians were allowed to continue practicing their customs, but only under certain conditions. They had to pay taxes to their Muslim protectors, they were not allowed to build houses of worship without authorization, and they were forbidden to bear arms or to ride horses or camels. Nor could they proselytize. Muslims themselves were severely punished if they did not abide by all the tenets of their religion.

The Prophet's death in 632/10 stunned not only the Muslim community but especially his closest companions, who were unprepared and had to make a quick succession decision. They decided to choose from among his oldest companions one who they deemed qualified to carry on his work, but stipulated that he could not be from the same tribe. Abu Bakr, Muhammad's father-in-law, was thus chosen to succeed him over other family members, who then initiated a struggle for succession. Abu Bakr eventually won and a few months later became caliph. Like the Prophet, the new caliph had full religious and political powers.

Three of the first four caliphs were assassinated, falling victim to intra-Islamic rivalries. After ʿUmar and ʿUthman, the fourth caliph elected was ʿAli, Muhammad's cousin and son-in-law, who many Muslims had hoped would directly succeed the Prophet. In 656/34, he scored a victory in the "Battle of the Camel" against the followers of Muhammad's widow. But in the wake of that victory, Kharijite fighters asked for an arbitration process. They underscored the legitimacy of their demand by attaching Qur'ans to the end of their spears. Impressed, ʿAli agreed to arbitration. But it was a trick; he was soon ousted and was later assassinated by a Kharijite in 661/39. His son Hussein took over as leaders of his father's followers, who called themselves Shiites—from shiʿa ʿAli (supporters of ʿAli). Hussein was defeated at the battle of Karbala in 680/58 by followers of Muʿawiya, another descendant of the Prophet, who had proclaimed himself caliph in 658/36 in the Holy City of Jerusalem, renamed Al-Quds, or "The Holy One," which had been conquered twenty years earlier.

The victory achieved by Muʿawiya's troops led to the founding of the Umayyad dynasty (651–750), which, after having forcibly restored unity to Islam, chose Damascus as the new capital of the empire. A century later, in 750, the Umayyads were defeated by Abu al-ʿAbbas, a descendant of ʿAbbas, the Prophet's uncle. That same year, in the name of returning to the principles of Islam, he founded a new, stricter dynasty, the ʿAbbasids, and settled in Baghdad.

But internal political divisions soon emerged. Starting in the tenth century, Seljuk Turks, who had only recently converted to Islam, conquered the Caucasus, then Armenia and Asia Minor—today's Turkey. Their Ottoman caliph successors ruled from Bursa, and then from Constantinople, which came to be known as Istanbul.

But the weakening of the ʿAbbasid dynasty signaled the end of the geopolitical unity of Islam. Several caliphates with regionally limited political powers coexisted. Eventually, in 1924, the Turkish strongman

Mustafa Kemal, dubbed Atatürk, stressed the secular, nationalist character of his regime by officially abolishing the caliphate.

The sudden collapse of Islam in the fourteenth century was a direct consequence of the lightning speed at which the Muslim expansion had taken place.

Starting in 632/10, Muslim armies, led first by Abu Bakr and then by ʿUmar, conquered Iran and later the Byzantine Empire, which had been weakened by a lengthy conflict with Persia and by a series of popular revolts. Arab fighters—often welcomed as liberators by the peoples they had come to conquer—managed, in less than seventy years, to carry out a twofold conquest: in northern Arabia, they annexed Palestine, Syria, Persia and Armenia; and, to the west, Egypt, Libya, Tunisia, the Algerian coast, and Morocco.

The conquest of Spain was undertaken in 711/89 with the help of Berber troops newly converted to Islam. However, the momentum of victory slowed to a halt when the advance of the Saracens was halted at Poitiers in 732/110. Spanish Christians then set out on a territorial reconquest, starting from the kingdom of Asturias. Nonetheless, Islam's military power was able to bring about geographical unity by annexing the principal Mediterranean islands. Between 820/198 and 857/235, Cyprus, Crete, Sicily, Sardinia, the Balearic Islands, and Corsica all were conquered.

Around 850/228, the concept of jihad was further fine-tuned. The word is based on the triconsonantal Arabic root *j-h-d,* which means "to make an effort." Two further concepts, different but complementary, emerged: lesser jihad and greater jihad.

Greater jihad refers to the spiritual work that every Muslim must do with respect to oneself—one's own worst enemy—in order to abide by the rules of Islam. It is Muslims' ongoing duty to keep their religious faith alive and to act as true believers.

Lesser jihad refers to the duty of all Muslims to defend, by all means at their disposal—participation in combat, financial assistance, or encouragement—their religion when it is under attack. Successive reinterpretations of the concept of "lesser jihad" led to the emergence of militant Salafism, which evolved in the 1970s into the international jihadist movement.

Historically, the concept of jihad developed in four successive stages.

During the period from 610 to 632/10, with Muhammad proclaiming the teachings of Islam and leading his followers, the Archangel Gabriel's divine revelations began to receive more bellicose interpretations. The stage was set for confrontation when, prior to the Hegira, Muhammad undertook verbally to persuade Jews and Christians to convert to the new religion. While Qur'anic verses of that time were characterized by tolerance—even compassion—they became much more belligerent in tone later when, following Muhammad's departure for Medina, he launched a campaign—often a very bloody one—first against pagans, and then against those Jewish and Christian tribes that refused to submit.

During the military conquest stage, which lasted from 632/10 until the end of the ninth century, the composition of the hadith provided a justification for the spread by means of war of Islam, which, as the last of the revealed religions, has the mission of providing universal guidance.

During the ninth and tenth centuries, with the conquest phase over, the Muslim world sought to achieve an internal political equilibrium, which required stable relations with neighboring countries. Jihad was no longer on the offensive; its purpose was now to strengthen the unity of the Muslim world—hence the trend toward the development of a defensive "lesser jihad," aimed at preventing infidels from undermining Islam's achievements.

Finally, in the eleventh century, with external threats seemingly under control, the Arab-Muslim world, plagued by instability, turned once again to the religion's fundamental tenets. Jihad came to mean defending the *umma* and reflected the believer's internal struggle against his or her weaknesses.

It was at that time that the Muslim world developed the theory of "three abodes." The *umma,* believing Islam to be the true religion, was called on to spread God's word throughout the universe, either through conversion or by force. In that context, any peace treaties signed with infidels had only a veneer of legitimacy and were really only self-serving truces, to be respected or rejected on the basis of their usefulness to the *umma.*

While the goal of the abode of Islam *(dar al-Islam)* was, in the long term, to conquer infidel lands, considered the abode of War *(dar al-Harb),* that undertaking proved so lengthy and difficult that the *ulama* agreed to coexistence with believers of other religions, on the condition that they acknowledge the supremacy of Islam by paying tributes and abiding by a certain number of prohibitions. Thus a third territorial entity emerged—the abode of treaty *(dar al-sulh).*

The Holy War against the Crusaders

The new three-abode political configuration was, of course, not accepted by the West, which for four centuries had been feeling the pressure of Islam. The Spanish Reconquista was slowly beginning—an undertaking that would be complete in 1492, a year marked by the start of the Western expansion toward the New World—and the Muslim threat continued to loom over Christian kingdoms. However, internal conflicts and the division of the Christian Church between Rome and the Byzantine Empire stood in the way of any serious effort at reconquest, especially since Ottoman soldiers already controlled the Balkans.

Nonetheless, requests for help were arriving regularly from Christians under the yoke of Islam. They were prohibited from practicing their religion freely; the tributes they were forced to pay were increasing; and churches were being destroyed. In addition, the enslavement—even extermination—of entire peoples outraged Western Christians.

Al Hakim, an Egyptian caliph of the early eleventh century, violently suppressed those Christians over whom he had authority. His successor, Darazi, razed dozens of churches before demolishing the Byzantine church that had been built over the Holy Sepulcher, where the Al-Quds Mosque was built soon after. Christ's tomb, however, remained a place of worship for Christian pilgrims, who every year traveled to the Holy Land. However, attacks against them were becoming more frequent. In 1067, a caravan of 7,000 German pilgrims was attacked so often that less than a third of their number managed to return to Europe. At the same time, new conquests by the Seljuks in eastern Europe, which resulted in the massacre or enslavement of local Christians, posed a direct threat to the Eastern Orthodox Church.

In 1095, at the request of the patriarch of Byzantium, the Roman Pope Urban II called upon Christians to undertake the reconquest of Christ's tomb. Thus began the First Crusade, led by Peter the Hermit, which ended in bloodshed and defeat. The Second Crusade, led by an alliance of European knights and Byzantine troops, resulted in the capture of Antioch and Jerusalem in 1099. As was the case with Arab conquests, greed and savagery went hand in hand with religious fervor, and a veritable carnage accompanied the liberation of Christ's tomb. Godefroy de Bouillon, the personification of the rules of Christian knighthood, was unable to stop his troops from pillaging Jerusalem and massacring its people—both Muslims and Jews.

The Church reestablished itself in its place of origin, and by the end of the eleventh century had the support of three Christian territories: the kingdom of Jerusalem, the county of Tripoli, and the principality of Antioch. Cyprus was retaken in 1192.

No sooner was the Third Crusade over than the Muslim reconquest began to take shape. The fall of Akko sounded the death knell for the Christian presence in the East. The determination of Muslim warriors combined with western rivalries doomed to failure the six crusades that were to follow. The Middle East became an Islamic land once again, a domination that would not be challenged again until the process of European colonization began, followed by the 1948 war and the creation of the state of Israel.

The battle waged against the Crusaders, seen as a historical parallel with the struggles of the Prophet's first companions, is very much present in the mythology of today's jihadist movement. It was during the Crusades that war became a central theme in Islam.

One concept in particular is that of the Islamic militant, as personified by Saladin (1138–1193), a warlord of Kurdish descent whose skill in combat earned him a military commandership under Egypt's Fatimid caliph, whom he later deposed through trickery. He conquered Syria and reorganized Islam's military forces, taking on the powerful Christian cavalry and pushing it back eastward.

Saladin, a soldier respected even by his opponents for his courage and fairness, elaborated a code of war for the Arab chivalry. In 1192, he and Richard Lionheart signed a peace treaty under which Saladin promised to respect Christian coastal fortified towns and to guarantee the security of pilgrims on their way to Jerusalem. To seal the agreement, which signaled a reconciliation between two of the revealed religions, he married a Christian woman, King Richard's own sister. Thanks to his authority in matters of both war and peace, he was able to reorganize the caliphate, lay down new political and social rules, and build schools and hospitals. His modest tomb in Damascus is still revered today. It lies a few meters from the magnificent Umayyid mosque, built in the eleventh century over the ruins of a Christian church, which still houses the tomb of Saint John the Baptist.

Some consider the Hashishin sect—the Assassins—to be another historical root of jihadist mythology. From the eleventh to the thirteenth century, the sect developed within the Isma'ili community, which practiced a type of Shiism prevalent mainly in Iran and in Syria. It was founded by Hassan-i-Sabbah—also known as "The Old Man of the

Mountain"—in Iran, which was dominated at the time by the Seljuk empire. The Hashishins were no strangers to political violence. Indeed, the sect's followers were fully prepared to accept martyrdom for the sake of their Fatimid faith, a dissident form of the Isma'ili religion.

Following a dynastic conflict among the Fatimids, Hassan-i-Sabbah founded his own religious order in 1086, calling it "the new doctrine" (al-dawa al-jadida) and seizing the castle of Alamut—"the eagle's nest"—in northern Iran. His followers fell into three categories: those who taught (talimmiya), those who were willing to sacrifice their lives (fedayeen), and those who knew of the Mysteries (batiniya). Indeed, Hassan-i-Sabbah, who claimed to be the only one to know of the hidden Truth, denounced all other Muslim emirs as hypocrites and urged that they be either killed or kidnapped and held for ransom. His sect was feared not only because of its military strength, as reflected by its numerous fortified cities, but especially because of its ability to carry out targeted assassinations.

As Farhad Khosrokhavar puts it in Les nouveaux martyrs d'Allah:

> Disciples were willing to die for the cause. They knew that, by killing their victims, they were signing their own death warrant. To kill the enemy designated by the Da'i and then to die oneself—that is a specific kind of martyrdom. What made a strong impression on the Seljuk authorities in Iran and on the Crusaders in Syria was the unfailing devotion of his disciples to Hassan-i-Sabbah—the Da'i, assistant to the Hidden Imam—and later to his successors. Disciples took their own lives. . . . The sect embraced the concept of millenarianism, believing that end times would come through the establishment of a power paving the way for the Resurrection.

According to legend, Hassan-i-Sabbah's followers would generally infiltrate their intended victim's circle several months before the killing and were invariably drugged with hashish—hence the name "assassin" —before striking, which was always with a dagger, never by poison. The Hashishins managed to kill several hundred people—including three caliphs, a vizier, and a Christian king. Saladin himself barely escaped them.

It was the Mongols' brutal conquest that finally sounded the Hashishins' death knell. In 1220, Genghis Khan's grandson Hülegü, who had formed an alliance with the Shiites, captured and condemned to death the last of the great Hashishin leaders, Rukn al-Din. Fearing for his life, Rukn al-Din had earlier proposed an alliance with the Christians, even considering the possibility of conversion.

While it is tempting to liken the Hashishins to contemporary jihadist martyrs, it is important to recall that their view of martyrdom was based on a sectarian form of Islam. Indeed, they hoped, through their sacrifice, to help bring about a better world. Today's world is facing a different problem: Palestinian members of Hamas and Salafist suicide bombers are motivated primarily by the desire to take revenge against an impious world, while hoping that their actions will earn them the joys of paradise. It was only during the twentieth century that, influenced by 'Ali Shari'ati, an Iranian, the concept of the militant martyr became fully developed in the context of radical Islamism.

Ibn Tamiya and the Origins of Salafism

In the ninth century, Ibn Hanbal of Syria had founded a new doctrine, Hanbalism, which, as we saw earlier, developed into one of the four major Sunni schools of jurisprudence. He took a fundamentalist view of the application of the principles of Islam, insisting on strict conformity with the example set by the Salaf, or "ancient ones" of Medina, as the Prophet's first followers were known. Hanbalism later gave rise to Salafism *(salafiya)*.

However, Ibn Hanbal omitted any mention in his writings of the fact that the Medina model of the caliphate was completely idealized, as it did not survive beyond the time of 'Ali, the fourth successor of the Prophet. The omission was not accidental. Ibn Hanbal, as an Ummayad dynasty theologian, sought to erase historical divisions in order to unite the *umma* around the Prophet's message. He was therefore opposed to any new interpretation of the *sunna,* which he considered definitive—unlike other contemporary *ulama,* who allowed personal views to be taken into consideration.

While Ibn Hanbal froze the *sunna* in time in an attempt to unite the community of believers, some of his disciples took a more restrictive approach. One example was Ibn Taimiya of Syria, who was born in 1263 and died in prison in Damascus in 1328. Ibn Taimiya's views were heavily influenced by the fears prevailing at the time. Indeed, the unity of Islam was in jeopardy. The threat posed by the Crusades in the Holy Land was compounded by the invasion of Muslim Mongols, who plundered Baghdad and put an end to the caliphate.

To foster unity, Ibn Taimiya therefore denounced all original forms of Islam as heretical. The adoration of saints, pilgrimages to tombs, and Sufi practices all were viewed as idolatrous. He declared the Mongol people apostate and accused them of distancing themselves, through their impious acts, from the *sunna*.

His political thinking was encapsulated in a short book of 100 or so pages, "Politics in the Name of Divine Law for Establishing Good Order Among the Affairs of the Shepherd and the Flock." The book—excerpts from which are frequently cited and commented on restrictively by jihadist theologians—sets out the sharia-inspired rules governing relations between the prince (that is to say, the highest political authority) and his subjects in a Muslim society. Abdelwahab Meddeb notes that

> the radicalism emanating from such a book totally fulfills the expectations of the fundamentalists . . . the author makes corporal punishment, as set out by the Qur'an, the very criterion of the law. . . .
> . . . [Taimiya] makes jihad, holy war, one of his main themes. He gives it the same importance as prayer and seems to set it above the other four canonical prescriptions . . . to indicate its high status, he associates it with the image that is meant to represent religion: a column with the base representing submission to God, the shaft representing prayer and the capital representing jihad. Thus he makes the fight against the infidel one of the two functions of the prince. . . . At the end of his manifesto, [he] concludes that by putting all the means of the empire (the financial and military capacities) in the service of religion, Islam will complete its religious edifice.[1]

It is noteworthy that Meddeb is the first Muslim author to have dared to openly raise questions about the type of punishment to be inflicted on political leaders who stray from the path ordained by God.

Ibn Taimiya, considered subversive by the authorities and challenged by the *ulama*, was nonetheless, thanks to his simplistic sermons advocating the use of violence, quite successful among the marginalized classes and those lacking an in-depth knowledge of the Muslim religion. It would seem that, six centuries later, the situation has not changed much.

IBN WAHAB AND THE GENESIS OF SAUDI ARABIAN FUNDAMENTALISM

Muhammad ibn Abd al-Wahab, who was born in the Nejd region of central Saudi Arabia, in the Arabian peninsula, carried on Ibn Taimiya's line of thinking in a sectarian direction.

His writings were not particularly innovative. Indeed, his ethnicity was the basis for his self-proclaimed legitimacy as a guide for true believers along the path blazed by the Prophet's earliest followers. His principal work, the *Book of Monotheism,* contained numerous quotations, to show the reader that his beliefs accorded with the Medina tradition. Unlike Ibn Taimiya, who had developed his own personal views after reading the works of Ibn Hanbal, Ibn Wahab espoused a brand of fundamentalism that brought nothing new to the Muslim religion. Expressing a new puritanism, he advocated a return to an Islam "purified of all its dross and restored to its original strictness." Thus any Muslim who failed to abide by the principles of Islam, in its mythicized original form, faced excommunication *(takfir).* Furthermore, all religious innovations were condemned, Sufism in particular.

Why, then, was he so influential? The reason is this: Ibn Wahab forged close ties with the Saud tribe, providing it with a measure of necessary support with respect to its aspirations to dominate Arabia. Under his iron rule, freshly minted Wahabis spread throughout what would become, less than two centuries later, Saudi Arabia. It took the Egyptian Mamluks several years to overcome these new conquerors. Their capital, Darya, located in the middle of the desert, did not fall until 1817.

A period of regroupment followed. In the middle of the nineteenth century, the Sauds launched another, equally unsuccessful expedition. Their third attempt, which began with the capture of Riyadh, wrested from Ottoman troops in 1902, finally succeeded following World War I. In 1932, the Sauds, having garnered the support of the desert tribes, forcibly or through negotiations, put an end to Hashemite claims to the region by founding Saudi Arabia.

Because of the tremendous wealth generated by its oil production, the country—whose only other assets were the first two holy sites of Islam—was able to become the dominant model of Sunni Islam. It was petrodollars that made possible the dissemination of Ibn Wahab's doctrine and positioned Medina University as a rival to Cairo's al-Azhar.

Islamism's Contribution to Arab Anti-Colonialist Thinking and the Evolution of Salafism

Given the colonial conquest of Islamic countries by the European powers, with their monopoly on science and technology, many Muslims began to ask how Islam could best face modern challenges.

A serious process of oral and written reflection was launched by Muslim theologians, who felt that the weakened state of the Muslim community was due to the abandonment of religious practices and to decadent behavior within Islamic societies, in particular among the ruling classes. They believed that salvation could be achieved by following in the footsteps of the Prophet's first companions. The revitalization of the Salafist doctrine thus took place within the framework of the restoration of the caliphate and the elaboration of a new doctrine of social justice.

A number of theoreticians participated in the ensuing broad-based debate on reform *(islah)*, including Ibn Badis of Algeria and Muhammad Iqbal of India, both of whom died in 1940.

The leading figures of that school of thought at the end of the nineteenth century were, without a doubt, Jamal Eddin al-Afghani of Persia (1839–1897) and Muhammad ʿAbduh of Egypt (1849–1905). However, their struggle was an anti-colonialist one. Neither was anti-Western. They rejected its political and religious domination, but not the West itself.

Al-Afghani was certainly no obscure thinker. His beliefs had varied and sometimes paradoxical roots; an example is his improbable initiation into the order of Freemasons. Al-Afghani wished first and foremost to awaken the conscience of his Muslim brothers. He believed that living in the modern world required Muslims to change their system of social organization and, in order to maintain their identity, find their way back to and embrace the fundamental tenets of their religion. He felt that, while Islam was compatible with modernity, it could not accept all of its aspects.

Al-Afghani later became Egypt's legal adviser. His published works were marked by a high degree of tolerance, conveniently overlooked by hard-liners: "My [main goal] was to liberate the process of reflection by breaking the chains imposed by imitation and to present religion as it was understood within the community before disagreements arose, to come back to the original sources of religious knowledge and to weigh them on the human scale that God created so as to avoid any religious excesses or distortions."

The transition was helped along by the final works of Rashid Rida (1865–1935), a Syrian. By advocating Ibn Taimiya's way of thinking, Rida, a disciple of Muhammad ʿAbduh, introduced a certain intransigence into al-Afghani's reformist movement with respect to Islam's compatibility with modern mores.

Although in his youth Rida had strongly opposed Wahabism, which he considered a destructive departure from Islam, toward the end of his life his views changed. Perhaps that turnaround was the result of anger at seeing his homeland fall into the hands of infidels. In any case, Rida, in his desire to unite the *umma* on the basis of simple concepts in order to fight the influence of Christianity, shortly before his death became a eulogist of Wahabism, saying that it was the religious school most faithful to the original principles of the *sunna,* which supported the caliphate as the guarantor of respect for the will of God in human society.

Rida said in *Al Manar* magazine: "We wore out our pens writing that the unhappiness of men cannot be attributed to their religion but to the innovations they have introduced to it and to the fact that the way they are practicing Islam can be compared to wearing a fur coat inside out."

Hassan al-Banna and the Emergence of the Muslim Brotherhood in Colonial Egypt

Hassan al-Banna, an Egyptian teacher born in 1906, learned from his father—a Sufi and a graduate of al-Azhar University—the pan-Islamic principles put forward by Jamal Eddin al-Afghani. As an adolescent, he was inspired by Abdul Aziz Ibn Saud's conquest of the Saudi Arabian throne. He studied in Cairo, where he first came into contact with Salafism, and went on to become a primary schoolteacher in 1927.

In March 1928, he founded the Muslim Brotherhood, a "religious organization dedicated to doing good and stamping out evil." Twenty years later, the movement had nearly 2 million adherents and had spread throughout the Muslim world. Al-Banna, an excellent speaker, knew how to exacerbate his countrymen's resentment of the English presence and in his speeches laid all of the Muslim community's problems at the doorstep of Western domination.

The Brotherhood, organized along the lines of a religious fraternity, required that its members unquestioningly obey the Guide *(murshid).* Advised by a consultative assembly, it quickly became a genuine, structured political movement, proselytizing at the grassroots level. That gave it considerable power, as it controlled a number of social organizations, such as charitable groups, mosques, health centers, and student associations.

The Brotherhood advocated comprehensive social reform aimed at bringing about social justice, not through individual acts of charity but through legal government handouts, thereby ensuring the equitable redistribution of funds. It was opposed to any form of nationalist ideology—considered a Western concept—and called for the revitalization of the *umma.*

Its message to believers was unambiguous, as is clear from this text from the 1930s: "You are neither a charitable organization, nor a political party, nor a local group with limited interests. No, you are a new soul at the very heart of this nation, into which you will breathe new life through the Qur'an. When they ask you what you are offering, tell them that it is Islam . . . that encompasses government and that believes that ensuring freedom is an obligation. If they tell you that you are engaging in politics, you must answer that there is no such distinction in Islam. If [they] oppose us or stand in the way of our message, then we have God's permission to defend ourselves against [their] injustice."

In that context, an armed branch—the "secret organization"—was created within the Brotherhood, whose leadership was entrusted to a close friend of al-Banna's, Salah Ashmawi. Operating under the guise of a Muslim scouting association—so as not to attract the attention of the British authorities—it grew rapidly into a full-fledged armed entity. Its members fought alongside supporters of the Grand Mufti of Jerusalem during the 1936 Palestinian uprising, then alongside Arab forces during the 1948 war.

It was during that conflict that the Muslim Brotherhood acquired combat experience. As a result, the Egyptian authorities, concerned at the Islamic militias' revolutionary capacity, ordered their disarmament. Al-Banna accepted that move, as he did not wish, or perhaps was not yet able, immediately to engage in acts of direct confrontation. To minimize the level of suppression of his movement, he claimed that it was a breakaway group, marginalized by the failure of the anti-Jewish struggle in Palestine, that, against his orders, had engaged in guerrilla warfare against the British forces stationed near the Suez Canal. However, despite such denials, evidence was mounting as to al-Banna's responsibility for political violence against King Farouk's regime.

Was al-Banna, as his followers have since claimed, the religious leader of a legalist Islamist organization whose ideology inspired dissenting activist forces? Or was he rather, as his detractors insist, the determined head of a revolutionary group with armed branches designed to ensure its ultimate victory? The truth no doubt lies somewhere in between. Because of the ambiguous nature of his activities, al-Banna was scapegoated for all of the terrorist acts that were committed around that time. It seems likely, however, that the 1948 murders of an Egyptian judge, two British officers, and the Egyptian prime minister were indeed perpetrated by members of the Muslim Brotherhood.

Al-Banna was assassinated on February 12, 1949, shortly after his organization was dismantled and almost 4,000 of its members arrested. His followers maintained that the Egyptian authorities had plotted to kill him and were responsible for his death.

Haj Amin al-Husseini and the
First Palestinian Jihad in the 1930s

Following the 1916 Sykes-Picot Agreement, which opened the way for the creation of a Jewish homeland and legitimized Zionist ideology, the British authorities maintained close ties with the Hashemite dynasty even as they instituted the Mandate for Palestine. The Palestinian people were greatly displeased, feeling that they had escaped Turkish domination only to come under that of the British. They were all the more convinced of the duplicity of their new protectors given that the fence-sitting British had promised the leadership of the future independent state to both communities.

The resistance was led by Haj Amin al-Husseini, who, in his capacity as Grand Mufti of Jerusalem, was the highest religious authority of the third Holy City of Islam. Indeed, he had ordered the restoration of the al-Aqsa mosque.

In the early 1930s, al-Husseini decided that the time was ripe to try to force new Jewish settlers to return to their former eastern European homelands. His religious militias began a well-organized campaign of guerrilla warfare against the first kibbutzim, which included isolated killings. One of the principal Palestinian militant leaders killed in 1935 was Izz al-Din al-Qassam. Although the revolt was nationalist in character, it should be recalled that the first Palestinian militants had been galvanized into fighting by their imams' calls to jihad. Al-Husseini's sermons made specific reference to Ibn Taimiya and Ibn Wahab, with references thrown in to the fight against the Crusaders.

The frenzied attacks that ensued, which killed around 100 Jewish settlers, forced the latter to leave Hebron in 1936. But the number of settlers in Palestine had tripled since 1920, and they were now a half-million strong. The British army thus had to intervene against the Palestinians in order to avert all-out war. In 1941, al-Husseini—who had decreed, in the name of Islam, that the struggle should continue until the last of the settlers had left—was expelled and sent to Iraq, where he continued with his subversive activities. Toward the end of 1941, British services at the last minute foiled an attempted coup d'état by nationalist officers, which had been masterminded by al-Husseini and the German Abwehr, with which he had been working for years.

After fleeing to Iran, al-Husseini went to Germany, where he became a successful propagandist among Muslims whose territories had been conquered by the Wehrmacht. His sermons, broadcast in Arabic, could not, however, prevent the defeat of the Afrika Korps. Al-Husseini also participated directly in the creation, within the Waffen-SS, of the Hand-schar division, which consisted of about 1200 Muslims.

In the wake of the defeat of 1948, al-Husseini, who had survived the fall of the Third Reich, was unable to create a government in exile in Jordan because of secret agreements between King Abdullah and the new Israeli government.

He was later suspected of having masterminded the murder of the king, who was killed by a Palestinian activist in 1951 in the al-Aqsa mosque in East Jerusalem, which was under Jordanian mandate. Al-Husseini went into exile once again, this time in Lebanon, where he died in 1974. By then Palestinian activists had long been fighting not under the banner of Islam but for a secular ideology inspired by Marxism-Leninism.

Abu l'Ala Maududi and the Rise of Radical Islamism on the Indian Subcontinent

Abu l'Ala Maududi (1906–1980) was a journalist born in British India to a family of Sufis. Politically involved, he saw Islamism as a comprehensive ideology that applied to society and to the individual. He advocated the need for an "Islamic revolution," which he saw as the only way of putting an end to the ignorance *(jahiliya)* that had characterized pre-Islamic societies and was now afflicting modern Muslims.

In 1941, he founded Jamaat-i-Islami (meaning Islamic group), a movement similar to the Muslim Brotherhood, but whose leader was known as the Emir instead of the Guide. It was not particularly socially active, preferring to proselytize at a higher level, actively lobbying and participating in elections. It infiltrated intellectual circles and the administration, garnering strong support among the young Pakistani army, whose nationalist convictions were imbued with religious feeling. He failed, however, in his quest to make Pakistan into an Islamic state.

Maududi believed that politics as a whole were God's domain. On that basis, he denounced all political systems—starting with democracy—as he felt that legitimacy could be conferred only by the divine. "If a man is realistic, he must choose submission to the only authority that has true authority—God," he proclaimed. "Political leaders, rabbis and priests can never exercise any political authority . . . Islam has said that, by dint of constant struggle—if need be by war and bloodshed—all corrupt governments will be swept away. In their place a system of government must be created that is based on the fear of God and that abides by the laws that He has enacted, with all other interests set aside, be they personal, class-related or national."

Maududi thus denied the right to exist to any society that did not conform absolutely to the Islamic model. The overall picture he painted had a definite, and worrisome, totalitarian appearance, the goal being to leave standing only perfect examples of Muslim society. While he did not systematically advocate the use of violence, his disciples had no such scruples. What they gleaned from their leader was a vision of an ideal society, the sole existing example of which was Wahabism. They did not hesitate to advocate the use of violence in building or protecting such societies.

Thus it was a blend of Maududi's theories in Pakistan and Wahabi proselytizing that gave rise to the Pakistani Deobandi madrassas, which promoted the practice of chanting the Qur'an for years on end, and, in the late 1980s, gave rise to the Taliban generation.

The Paradoxical Influence on Sunni Jihadism of the Shiite ʿAli Shariʿati

The major schism within Islam took place, as noted earlier, at the end of the seventh century, following the battle of Karbala. Shiites who were followers of ʿAli and the original caliphate practiced their beliefs in secret, despite suppression by the Umayyids. Political loyalty thus led to religious autonomy, and a specific theology and legal norms emerged. Shiites are still awaiting the return of the twelfth imam, the "Hidden Imam," said to have disappeared in 873 C.E.

One of the principles to which Shiites adhere that distinguishes their beliefs from those of the Sunnis relates to the role of the imam (imamat). Shiites believe that ʿAli was an imam first and a caliph second. That is a fundamental concept, the caliph's role being primarily political and therefore worldly in nature, while the imam's functions are essentially religious.

In the twelfth century, Shiism, with its strong Persian influence—it became the majority religion in Persia, unlike in today's Muslim world, aside from Iraq and Bahrain—was in the midst of a heated theological debate on the concept of interpretation. Traditionalist mullahs believed—as was also the case in certain Sunni schools—that the wisest among them, the future ayatollahs, were authorized to engage in interpretation. The religious supremacy of the latter led to the creation of an autonomous clergy, endowed with considerable financial resources thanks to followers' mandatory donations.

It was not until the middle of the twentieth century that a radical school of thought emerged within Shiism, under the authority of ʿAli Shariʿati (1933–1977), an Iranian layman from a respected religious family. Shariʿati's thinking was influenced by Marxism-Leninism with respect to both social redistribution and the liberation of the masses. Like advocates of the Catholic Church's liberation theology, he tried to adapt Shiite Islam to modern times by incorporating key tenets of anti-imperialist ideology.

While Shariʿati faced strong criticism from the mullahs, he did pique the interest of his country's younger intellectual classes following the ousting of Iran's radical prime minister Muhammad Mossadegh in 1953, which sounded the death knell for Marxist opposition in Iran.

That radical revitalization of Shiism cleared the way for the Ayatollah Ruhollah Khomeini. Though an influential figure within the religious center at Qom, he was certainly no theological innovator. Khomeini imposed the first model of religious theocracy in the contemporary religious world, and, in the early 1970s, he defined the principle of "governance by jurists" (vilayat-i-faqih), which gives religious leaders political power.

Although at the start Khomeini was looked on favorably by that part of the Western press always willing to engage in self-flagellation, by the end of 1979, the regime of mullahs had put in place a veritable dictatorship. It was also manipulating Shiite communities outside the country, exporting the Hezbollah (Party of God) model and, through it, the religious model advocated by the Shariʿati-inspired "Revolution of the Dispossessed."

The increasing number of terrorist acts and political assassinations outside of Iran soon led to increasing media coverage of religious extremists and "Allah's warriors." That period saw the emergence of the concept of a subversive Islamist movement aiming to reclaim Muslim territories and to strike at Western countries, heirs of the Crusaders.

But two decades later, the built-in limitations of that radical Shiite threat have now become clear. Indeed, three elements were at play that were not fully understood at the time.

Iran never had any internationalist aims, only regional ones, although it did made serious attempts at proselytization outside of Lebanon and the Gulf countries, for example, in the Lebanese Shiite communities of sub-Saharan Africa and in the context of the Moroccan diaspora. Iran's primary goals were supremacy over Iraq, whose population was mostly Shiite, and control over Lebanon. Those two factors, along with the Eurodif litigation and the jailing of the Hezbollah hit man Anis Naccache,[2] led to deep hostility towards France up until 1989. In addition, Iran is a Shiite country, and Shiites constitute only 15 percent of the global Muslim population. Finally, Iran is a Persian, not an Arab, homeland.

But Iran's Islamist revolution provoked an intense emotional reaction in Muslim countries as a whole, creating a model of a radical Islamic society that inspired Sunnis. The latter began increasingly to resent their leaders, who were corrupt, blinkered by narrow-minded nationalism, and unable to get the economies of their countries off the ground. To top it all off, they had been humiliated three times running by the Israeli enemy, which had occupied Jerusalem since 1967.

In the end, only the Lebanese-based Hezbollah has endured, thanks to its leader, Sheikh Fadlallah, who transformed it into an autonomous body. The "Party of God" has changed considerably since its founding as a result of Israel's 1982 invasion of southern Lebanon, or "Operation Peace of the Galilee." In the early 1980s, as a nascent underground group, it garnered worldwide fame as a result of its very effective terrorist actions. Now, several decades later, Hezbollah is a full-fledged Lebanese political party, with representatives in the legislature and its own army. Its success in getting the Israelis to leave southern Lebanon was largely due to its capacity to attack Israel's army and people, in particular through the newly developed tactic of suicide bombings.

Suicide bombings, a terrifying new form of martyrdom, owed much to Shari'ati and his views. In Shiite and Sunni traditions, the concept of martyrdom had until then taken second place to that of jihad. Muslims could certainly meet their deaths in fighting the holy war, but suicide —even with the goal of attacking the enemy—remained an unlawful act that barred the doors of Paradise to the faithful.

Shari'ati believed that there were two different kinds of martyrdom.

To illustrate the first, he cited the fate of Hamza, the Prophet's uncle, who died fighting the battle of Uhud, as an example of a Muslim who had lost his life during jihad, thereby participating individually in the victory of the *umma*. Hamza had not wished to die, but to vanquish the enemy, even if he met his death in so doing. In Muslim mythology, Hamza is still known as the "Prince of Martyrs" *(seyyed al-shahida).*

The second kind of martyrdom was that suffered by Imam Hussein, son of 'Ali, who, having lost the battle of Karbala, refused to return home in defeat and went back into battle, knowing he would die. Death sought out thereby became a kind of accomplishment in and of itself. Shari'ati saw such acts as having all the more religious significance because as there is no possibility of victory. "The philosophy of the mujahid—he who carries out jihad—is not the same as that of the martyr," he wrote. "Martyrdom, strictly speaking, is a commandment that comes after jihad, and the martyr takes over when the mujahid has failed."[3]

It was this concept of martyrdom that inspired al Qaeda's strategists. It was cited, even before 9/11, by those who carried out the 1995 suicide attack against the Egyptian embassy in Pakistan.

The Emergence of Broad-based Fundamentalist Movements

Following World War II and the ensuing decolonization-related conflicts, a number of secular nationalist movements emerged in the Muslim world. But they met with near-total failure, which laid the groundwork for mass religious movements characterized by a return to fundamentalism. Following a period of suppression, the growing influence of such movements was encouraged by those in power, who wished to promote pro-Arabization policies, deflect social demands, and weaken Marxist opposition forces.

That was the case in the Maghreb in the 1970s. Algeria's President Houari Boumédienne and Morocco's King Hassan II—both of whom believed they had control over their *ulama*—accepted many Middle Eastern teachers whose membership in local branches of the Muslim Brotherhood made them suspect in the eyes of their own regimes. Those teachers planted the seeds of Muslim fundamentalism, first in schools and then in universities, giving rise to a new generation of intellectuals. It was particularly easy for the latter to take fundamentalist ideologies to heart because, having witnessed the failure of Marxist-Leninist regimes, they aspired to resolve the problems faced by their societies in ways that were more in tune with their sense of cultural identity.

A similar situation prevailed in Pakistan. General Muhammad Zia-ul-Haq's regime, installed in a 1977 coup d'état, sought to consolidate its authority by basing itself on the religious principles set out a few years earlier by Abu l'Ala Maududi and by giving the nationalist question of Kashmir distinct religious undertones. One of the first measures undertaken was to make the banking system responsible for collecting the religious tax called *zakat*. That decision caused a break with the Shiite community, which usually entrusted Muslim alms-giving to the mullahs, or clergy—an institution that does not exist in the Sunni tradition. For several years, militias on both sides fought to the death, with the Deobandi madrassas receiving the larger part of the *zakat*.

A similar phenomenon took place in Indonesia, which did not adhere to sharia, although its more than 245 million people (July 2006 est.) are 88 percent Muslim. In the wake of a 1965 coup d'état, Suharto encouraged the activities of fundamentalist movements in order to counteract potential communist subversion. The resulting militias, which for a time were trained by army special forces, served as breeding grounds for future Islamist guerrilla movements. The movement spread throughout Southeast Asia, with the tacit approval of the United States.

In the early 1960s, the trend had become evident at the global level. It led to the emergence of Muslim fundamentalism, a new and uncontrollable political movement with multiple demands. It was not a homogeneous movement, however. Gilles Kepel views it as a two-pronged alliance, including

> the younger generation in the cities, a class created by the postwar demographic explosion in the Third World and the resultant mass exodus from the countryside. Though poverty-stricken, these young urbanites had access to some literacy and some education. Second, it included the traditional God-fearing bourgeoisie, the descendants of mercantile families from the bazaars and souks who had been thrust aside during the process of decolonization. In addition to the devout middle class, there were also doctors, engineers and businessmen who had gone away to work in the conservative oil-exporting nations and had rapidly become wealthy while being kept outside the traditional circles of political power.[4]

The regimes in power at the time, unable to meet the demands made of them and fully aware of the threat posed by the example of the Islamic Republic of Iran, sought to divide and conquer the Islamist movement by separating it into its various constituent parts. Accordingly, they strengthened their ties to the devout middle classes and to radical theologians—given their close connections to conservative circles—in order more effectively to silence the protests of the marginalized classes, which were prepared to go to any lengths to improve their living conditions. Thus the groundwork was laid for a fundamentalist Islamization—made possible largely by Saudi money—and Muslim countries joined in denouncing Western values, in particular the concept of secular democracy.

Muslim regimes succeeded in averting the looming threat of a new, Iranian-style revolution, but they did so at a price. Conservative Muslim circles, the recipients of their support, had indeed been distanced from the poorest of the poor, but the latter, with no prospects other than ex-

treme poverty and exclusion, became easy prey for manipulation by proponents of the Islamist jihadist movement.

THE EGYPTIAN JIHADIST MOVEMENT
AND THE DEATH OF THE PHARAOH

Sayyid Qutb—Breaking with the Established Order

The political beliefs shared by both al-Banna and Maududi, which did
not posit the need for an armed struggle and allowed for the possibility
of reformist action, were radicalized by a new generation of Egyptian Islamists, spawned in successive waves by the Muslim Brotherhood tradition. Basing themselves on the tenets of radical Islamism, they moved on
to a new phase—activist Islamism.

Sayyid Qutb (1906–1966) was a prominent figure in radical Islamism,
which was rapidly becoming increasingly subversive in nature. He believed that resort to radical violence could be a religious obligation in the
fight against a political leadership that had lost its Muslim roots. Qutb,
like Hassan al-Banna, was a teacher at a time when many in the profes-
sion harbored strong religious sentiments and hatred for the British Protectorate. He soon joined the Muslim Brotherhood, where, under the
tutelage of the Guide, he helped to write a number of books. Early on,
like Maududi, he emphasized the concept of *jahiliya*, refusing to compromise in any way with impious Muslim regimes *(taghout)*. The latter,
deemed illegitimate because of their failure to abide by Islamic law, were
to be declared unbelievers *(takfir)*.

Qutb thus further developed the theory of "challenging and punishing the prince," elaborated by Ibn Taimiya six centuries earlier, adherence to which had evolved into one of the criteria distinguishing political Islamists from radicals. By labeling governing authorities as
unbelievers, Qutb was in effect calling for civil war. From that point on,
jihad was no longer simply an individual obligation to protect the community from infidels—such persons having refused to heed sincere appeals to convert—but also an individual, imperative duty to fight apostate Muslims.

In the wake of al-Banna's assassination, Qutb gave new and revolutionary momentum to the activities of the Muslim Brotherhood. The organization's leaders, who were still working in quasi-secrecy, shared the
nationalist fervor of the Egyptian Free Officers Movement. Indeed, a seg-

ment of the old "secret organization" fought alongside the military officers who carried out the coup d'état that toppled King Farouk and replaced him with General Naguib. The latter, who was not a member of
the movement, was soon ousted by Colonel Gamal Abdel Nasser.

Nasser, no stranger to power struggles, understood the magnitude of
the threat posed by the Muslim Brotherhood, which was fiercely opposed
to the secular nationalism of the new political leadership, and he wasted
no time in putting the Brotherhood under surveillance. The group was
infiltrated and decimated by the subsequent raids carried out by the authorities. Militants were arrested and sentenced, with no real trial, to
lengthy jail terms. Some of them were tortured or summarily executed.

Qutb's work falls into two main categories: his writings from the time
before his imprisonment and what he produced while incarcerated. His
earlier, Marxist-influenced writings focused on social action, in the context of a struggle against a colonizing force and an alliance with the Free
Officers Movement, which at that time had no association with the
reigning elite.

During his imprisonment under Nasser, Qutb produced his most radical work, suffused with a desire for revenge on the regime that was per-
secuting him—views that were in line with the ideas put forward by Ibn
Taimiya and Maududi. He wrote a revolutionary commentary on the
Qur'an stressing that any political system that fails to recognize divine
sovereignty *(akkimiya)* should be categorized as belonging to *jahiliya*, or
the age of ignorance—a blistering condemnation not only of the Western democratic model but also of contemporary Muslim regimes. Accordingly, he said, such governments were usurpers that must be driven
out or eliminated. In his introduction to the *sura* of the Qur'an entitled
"The Spoils" *(al-anfal)*, he noted that "jihad is not a defensive war, as
some Muslims believe; it is an offensive one."

Militant Islam's new strategy was clearly set out in his best-known
work, *Milestones:* "We must wage total revolution against the sovereignty of human beings . . . we must provoke a total revolt throughout
the world and drive out all usurpers . . . that means the destruction of the
kingdom of man so that the kingdom of God can replace it on earth."

In 1964, a general amnesty was proclaimed, but it proved to be the
prelude to yet another purge. Sayyid Qutb, accused of having conspired
against the state, was hanged on August 26, 1966.

The Muslim Brotherhood's new leader, Hassan al-Hudaybi, was
forced, in order to ensure the survival of his organization—seriously
weakened by suppression—officially to distance himself from Qutb, who

had been one of his key thinkers. In the late 1960s, under pressure from the Egyptian authorities, he denounced Qutb's ideas. Al-Azhar University's *ulama* were invited to issue a fatwa declaring Qutb's writings heretical.

But the authorities' blanket condemnation of Qutb was excessive, relegating his extensive body of work to obscurity. The previously unified Muslim Brotherhood branched out into two main offshoots. The first waged its battle for Islam through appeals to conversion, while the other opted for direct involvement in political violence. But the distinction between the two branches was not as clear-cut as some might wish to believe. The underlying theme continued to be conformity with the will of the Prophet, as enunciated before and after the Hegira. Indeed, it was the Egyptian model of the Muslim Brotherhood that gave rise to the two main branches of contemporary Islamic radicalism—the fundamentalist and the jihadist, with solid ties to one another.

However, the greater part of the Muslim Brotherhood sought mainly to restructure the organization and its international branches through religious appeals and nonviolence. Today, the Brotherhood's influence extends not only throughout the Islamic world but also to Muslim communities in infidel countries. But is their message truly one of peace? Despite the reassuring words of the Muslim author Tariq Ramadan— loyal grandson of Hassan al-Banna and a man well acquainted with Western mores—it is undeniable that a call to radicalism is being made to European Muslims seeking a sense of identity. Nor can the sectarian activities of the organization's European structures—headquartered, of course, in London—be overlooked.

The Muslim Brotherhood produced a number of key figures, including ʿAbdallah ʿAzzam, a Palestinian-born Jordanian, who was the first to unite the Salafist mujahedeen army in Pakistan during jihad against the Soviet regime; Egypt's Ayman al-Zawahiri, exiled leader of the Egyptian Islamic Jihad group and al Qaeda's current number two man; and the Saudi-born Omar Bakri, the founder of the immigrants' movement al-Muhajiroun, who became a vocal supporter of international jihad in the British media.

Two Islamic organizations are offshoots of the Muslim Brotherhood: Hamas, whose involvement in jihad against Israel has been well known since the second intifada, and Hizb al-Tahrir (the Islamic Liberation Party), which has a presence today both in northern Europe and in the Muslim countries of Central Asia, where its various branches have served as a recruitment ground for jihadist groups.

In successive waves, a small minority of extremists opted exclusively for political violence. The first generation—of Egyptian origin—called themselves Qutbists, a newly coined term. As Alain Grignard states, "Underground movements that later became political parties or political pressure groups were considered treasonous. Any cooperation with the authorities was denounced, and ultra-extremists broke away to create small groups championing revolutionary purity. Out of a process similar to that of fractional distillation, new terrorist groups were born."

The Emergence of Jihadist Groups

Abd al-Salam Faraj and the "Absent Obligation." Qutb laid the groundwork for an extreme way of thinking: that jihad was a cardinal Islamic obligation, just like the five pillars; that it had to be offensive in nature; and that it applied also to Muslims whose misconduct was tantamount to apostasy, which is punishable by death.

That new interpretation reflected the views of another Egyptian, Abd al-Salam Faraj. His religious background was not sufficient to give him the legitimate spiritual authority to continue with Qutb's work. He was an electrician, and his theological knowledge was limited to that gleaned during his clandestine apprenticeship to radical causes. But it was that very marginal status that was to ensure his success in the jihadist movement.

Faraj came into his own in the context of preparations to take on the Egyptian leadership. President Anwar Sadat, though a former member of the Muslim Brotherhood, had since the 1977 Camp David accords been considered an apostate ruler, and Egyptian radical Islamists had given him the evocative nickname of "Pharaoh." Indeed, Qutb had viewed ancient Egyptian civilization as an example of the despicable state of *jahiliya*.

In his best-known work, "The Absent Obligation," which was clandestinely distributed, Faraj based his arguments on Ibn Taimiya's limited textual interpretation, stating that jihad was, in fact, the sixth pillar of Islam. He thus elevated the duty of armed revolt, offensive in nature, against an infidel political leadership to the level of a standing religious obligation. He thereby outlined the transition from religious dissent in the political sphere to the perpetration of acts of political violence leading to terrorism, at first targeted and then indiscriminate.

Faraj, a man of action rather than words, put his theories into practice by founding the most hard-line jihadist group in Egypt, al-Jihad—

jihad in the specific sense of "holy war." He was executed on April 8, 1982, following the assassination of Anwar Sadat by militant officers belonging to his organization.

But al-Jihad had a number of predecessor underground movements.

Egyptian Groups Move from Violent Protests to Terrorism. In the 1970s, a number of small groups took shape, coalescing around charismatic leaders. Their acts of violence garnered widespread media coverage and piqued the interest of many young Egyptians from the religious middle classes, as well as from socially disadvantaged segments of society. Underemployed students determined to fight corruption among the elites, as well as impoverished farmers forced into rural exodus, joined different groups, depending on their social and geographical origins.

This period saw the emergence of Saleh Sirriya's Organization for Islamic Liberation (al-Harakat al-islamiya lil tahrir), Sheikh Omar Abdel Rahman's Islamic Group (Gama'at al-Islamiya), and Mustafa Shukri's Muslim Society (Jamaat al-Muslimin), which the press soon dubbed "Takfir wal Hijra" (Anathema and Exile), or TWH, the name by which it is generally known—its use being either pejorative or positive, depending on the speaker. Shukri, an agricultural engineer from a modest background in the plains of southern Egypt, took his cue from the attitude of the Prophet at the time of his return to Medina. He believed that people who claimed to be Muslims but failed to devote themselves to waging holy war against apostate rulers were themselves heathens. True believers—still a minority—had no choice but to "anathematize" *(takfir)* those Egyptians who accepted such a *jahiliya* type of existence, and to retreat *(hijra)* in order better to fight them.

The first stages of the war ordered by Shukri were more along the lines of petty crime. Funds were needed to finance the organization, which was composed largely of illiterate Muslims from rural backgrounds. The group therefore engaged in extortion, targeting wealthy farmers and businessmen, and robbed members of the Coptic community—incidents that usually involved some form of violence. All of this, of course, attracted the attention of the Egyptian security services *(mukhabarat)*, which arrested several members of the group. In an attempt to win their freedom, Shukri ordered the kidnapping of key local personalities, including political figures and judges. During the resulting clashes with the police, a hostage was executed, and Shukri was soon identified and arrested. He was condemned to death in 1974.

After Shukri's execution, some of his followers emigrated to Algeria, where the authorities had recently begun an Arabization campaign and were looking for teachers. Influenced by their views, an Algerian movement led by Dr. Ahmed Bouamra adopted the underground name of TWH. A second wave of Shukri followers also went into exile in Pakistan in 1980; they were among the first to join up with those jihadist groups that were fighting the Soviet army in Afghanistan. They originated a form of TWH that, because it was internationalist in character, hewed more closely to the jihadist model; it met with violent opposition from the Salafist movement.

Several dozen Algerians, veterans of the jihad against the Soviet army, returned to Algeria in late 1989, bringing with them their new ideology and giving fresh impetus to the jihadist spirit of Bouamra's Algerian TWH. They were among the first to advocate the use of violence.

Following the imposition of a state of emergency, many of those *takfiris* fled to Europe. There they established a number of networks—part criminal, part jihadist—which were subsequently dismantled by local police forces during the period 1993–2002. Most of their members subscribed to the group's school of thought in order to reap the benefits of *ghanima*—tolerated behavior. Indeed, that obscure dispensation permits the commission, in the name of jihad, of illegal acts—such as theft, trafficking, even murder—against infidels as long as a portion of the spoils is handed over to the cause.

To add to the particularities of the international form of TWH—also known within the Salafist movement as the Muslim Society (Gamaat al-Muslimin)—its last leader, the emir Al Barkaoui, lost no time in proclaiming himself caliph in 1994, before being forced by other, hostile jihadist emirs to flee Pakistan for Europe. He was eventually edged out by Abu Kutada, the ideological leader of the local European jihadist movement, which the last of the TWH's militants drifted into joining.

The Organization for Islamic Liberation involved mainly low-ranking officers whose nationalist ideals had been shattered following the Arab defeat by Israel in 1967. It was decimated in 1974 in the wake of the Heliopolis garrison's aborted mutiny, but its work was carried on, in a sense, by al-Jihad, which had moved quickly to recruit members within specialized military units. The most famous of those recruits is, of course, Lieutenant-Colonel Khaled al-Istambuli, mastermind of Anwar Sadat's assassination during a military parade on October 6, 1981. His brother, Tawfik, later headed out to the Afghano-Pakistani zone, becoming a follower of Ayman al-Zawahiri and then of Osama bin Laden.

The Gama'at al-Islamiya (GI) undoubtedly represents the most fully developed form of Egyptian jihadism and the one that underwent the most extensive transformation. It started out as a student organization, playing a pivotal social role in universities, while proselytizing heavily. Young students, made vulnerable by the isolation that can come with attending university and lured by cheap rent and free transport, soon came to embrace militant Islamism—a symbol of social solidarity. The authorities quietly encouraged their activities so as to counterbalance the influence of the Marxist unions.

In the late 1970s, the movement, led by Omar Abdel Rahman—a graduate of al-Azhar University known as the "blind sheikh"—had evolved into a highly structured organization comprising dozens of autonomous groups. They had considerable material and financial resources at their disposal, including buses, offices, a print shop, and health centers. Sadat was not viewed with hostility at the time, because he had made sure to enlist the support of religious circles, in particular at al-Azhar, so as to foil any attempted plots by Nasser's old guard. During the first part of his term, religion began to intrude into public life: the family code and the status of women were changed to reflect the rules of sharia.

The situation changed drastically when Sadat joined in the peace process with Israel, launched under pressure from the United States. His rule came to mean a corrupt regime; a rapprochement with the West, Israel's great champion; and the excesses of a leadership that left the Muslim people mired in poverty. Thus Sadat became known as "The Pharaoh."

The protests organized by the GI were brutally suppressed. Its property was seized and its offices shut down, depriving students of a number of social benefits and greatly angering them. Many of them, as a result, joined underground offshoots of Gama'at al-Islamiya and went on to wage urban guerrilla warfare against any and all symbols of power. Attacks and assassinations were rife. In the end, the sole result of such a harsh repression was the creation of a fresh crop of martyrs.

Sadat, who had understood the new dimensions of the threat, was more than willing to accept the American suggestion that he support the Afghan jihad, seeing that he might be able to get rid of the most radical of the militants by sending them off to Pakistan. But he was unable to reverse the revolutionary process that had begun in his country, which culminated in his assassination, before the eyes of the international press, during the military commemoration of the first victories of October 1973. His death sentence, which was carried out by al-Jihad members, had been authorized earlier by a GI-issued fatwa, probably written by Omar Abdel Rahman himself.

Indiscriminate Terrorism and the Defeat of Egyptian Jihadism

The death of the Pharaoh was the first great victory achieved by the jihadist movement, whose strategy was now sketched out in blood. For the first time, an apostate leadership had been shaken to its very foundation. Egyptian paratroopers had to intervene, wresting control of the city of Assiout from the jihadists, who had proclaimed it an Islamist city. By the end of 1981, all of the Middle East regimes were under threat, paralyzed by the failure of pan-Arabism and by their inability to create any kind of economic momentum despite the bonanza of their oil wealth.

Syria's Hafez al-Assad had forgotten none of this when, a year later, he ordered his troops to retake, at any cost, the town of Hama, which had fallen to the local Muslim Brotherhood movement. An estimated 8,000 to 20,000 people were killed in the process—a new crop of jihadist martyrs.

The new Egyptian head of state, Hosni Mubarak, saw clearly that suppression—even when carried out with an iron rod—would not suffice. Nonetheless, in 1982, he sent 14,000 soldiers to the shantytown of Imbaba, in Upper Egypt, which had just proclaimed itself an Islamic republic; it took six weeks to retake it. Mubarak followed in his predecessor's footsteps in diverting Islamist demands by directly supporting the Afghan mujahideen.

Most of al-Jihad's leaders were executed and their followers imprisoned. Most of the latter, once freed, chose to return to Pakistan. That was the case of Ayman al-Zawahiri, a surgeon, and Muhammad Atef, a police officer, who went on to become the leaders in exile of a militant organization whose jihadist activities were focused more on other countries than on their own. Many of the militants who remained in—or returned to—Egypt were arrested in August 1993, just before a planned bomb attack against the minister of defense. However, it was probably al-Jihad members—veterans of the war in Afghanistan—who carried out the first major suicide bombing, using two vehicles, against the Egyptian Embassy in Islamabad on February 3, 1995. Al-Jihad was also responsible for the attempt on Mubarak's life during an official visit to Addis Ababa on February 19, 1995.

Strangely enough, the GI was not as affected, probably because of the organization's size. Omar Abdel Rahman himself, following a lengthy trial, was found not guilty of issuing the fatwa calling for Sadat's assassination. He went into exile in Saudi Arabia and later in Pakistan, and finally, in 1990, requested political asylum in the United States. Until his arrest three years later, he continued from there to guide the decisions of Egyptian leaders in the context of the armed struggle.

Despite the purges carried out within the ranks of the army, soldiers remained who were open to jihadist ideas. Egyptian military officers forged ties in Pakistan not only with the Afghan mujahideen but also with the Arab volunteers who were being trained to fight the Soviet army. It was a long time before the regime could regain trust in its security apparatus, and it thought twice about positioning it in areas where there was support for the GI. The Islamists took advantage of that state of affairs to strengthen their bases and move ahead with the recruiting process, while at the same time forming profitable relationships with their counterparts in neighboring countries such as Libya, Somalia, Yemen, and Saudi Arabia.

The first GI targets were local ones. The groups attacked and robbed infidels—that is to say, Copts—and struck at symbols of power, in particular local authorities, so as to ensure security in Islamist-held areas. In the early 1990s, the Cairo cemetery, in which hundreds of thousands of marginalized Egyptians were living, served also as a GI rear base, which the police dared not enter.

In the early part of the decade, however, the Egyptian security services gradually retook the ground they had lost. The *ulama,* aware of the danger posed by the radicals, lent their support to the ruling authorities, taking a stance against the insidious but very real call that was being made to submit to the rules of Islam. Now the roles were reversed. Successive neutralization campaigns, coupled with the absence of any real external support, drastically undermined the strength of GI militant cells. By 1996, the movement no longer had a strategy, and its seven jailed leaders finally agreed to negotiate a truce. Sheikh Abdel Rahman himself, from his American prison cell, called for an end to the fighting.

For that reason, the last remaining active GI cells, in a senseless, last-ditch effort to bring the government to its knees, began to target tourist areas, so vital to the Egyptian economy. In September 1997, a group of mujahideen carried out a grenade attack against a busload of tourists, killing nine German citizens. That November, a hail of bullets felled fifty-eight Western nationals, the majority of them Swiss tourists, at Luxor; survivors were stabbed to death.

The operation was masterminded by an Afghan veteran, Mehat Abdel Rahman, and probably directed, from Afghanistan, by Rifai Taha, head of the group's external branch. But the Egyptian jihadists, whose actions had doomed hundreds of thousands of Egyptians to many long months of unemployment, had played their last cards. Since then, the Islamist movement has not claimed responsibility for a single local attack.

However, in the 1980s the fight being waged by Egyptian militants—precursors of the mujahideen movement—had acquired a new dimension through its support for external jihads. Forced to take refuge in Afghanistan in the mid 1990s, its militants openly joined forces with al Qaeda, for which it had always been a mainstay.

THE AFGHAN NETWORK:
ARAB MUJAHIDEEN JOIN THE ANTI-SOVIET JIHAD

On December 24, 1979, Russian special forces seized Kabul airport, clearing the way for the Red Army to conquer Afghanistan. Setting aside tribal rivalries, the Afghan resistance organized itself, and the international Muslim community mobilized in support of the mujahideen, who soon were receiving assistance from the United States, logistical support from Pakistan, and financial contributions from Saudi Arabia.

Divergent interests were at stake in the context of that indirect strategy. The United States, taking a containment approach, wanted to halt any progress by the two leaders of the anti-imperialist front, the Communist Soviet Union and Shiite Iran—a brand-new enemy since the fall of the shah and the hostage crisis at the American embassy in Tehran. Saudi Arabia—traumatized by a 1979 incident that took place at Mecca during Ramadan, in which young Sunni protesters took a number of hostages and 1,500 people died—decided to take charge of the Sunni radical movement in order to control its young fundamentalist members and prevent them from being manipulated by pro-Iranian Hezbollah. It was supported in this by the wealthy Gulf petromonarchies, intent on increasing their prestige among the Muslim community. Finally, Pakistan—whose traditional adversary to the east, India, was a Soviet ally—wished to maintain a buffer zone in Afghanistan, on its western border.

Arab volunteers arrived in Pakistan, some by very circuitous routes, to join up with the Afghan mujahideen. Often they were receiving assistance from their own governments, which were more than pleased to see the last of potentially dangerous active political opponents. It is likely that, during the 1980s, more than 20,000 Muslims from the Middle East and the Maghreb were involved in jihad. Most of them were recruited by transnational Islamic networks, headed up by radical *ulama* with ties to the World Islamic League and to Wahabi foundations, who secured the necessary fatwas to ensure support for the anti-Soviet jihad from recognized theologians.

The largest battalions came from the Middle East. Their numbers likely included approximately 6,000 Saudis, 4,000 Egyptians, and 1,000 Yemenis, as well as several hundred Syrians and the same number of Jordanians of Palestinian origin. A smaller number came from the Maghreb— maybe 2,000 Algerians and a few hundred Tunisians, Moroccans and Libyans. Some hailed from farther afield, including a few Westerners and a handful of Indonesians, Malaysians, Filipinos, and Sudanese.

The Founding of Maktab al-Khidmat

Considerable and predictable funding was required to accommodate and organize all of the volunteers and provide them with combat training. The necessary resources were provided by the Saudi authorities or by wealthy private donors. A number of Wahabi nongovernmental organizations—restructured or created for that very purpose—were used to collect such funds anonymously. Furthermore, the hundreds of millions of dollars that were circulating discreetly in circles populated by arms dealers and traffickers—an ideal situation for embezzlement to take place—had to be managed by men who could be trusted.

The task was entrusted to a Jordanian of Palestinian origin, ʿAbdallah ʿAzzam (1941–1979). ʿAzzam, who had fought in the 1967 war, had broken with the PLO on the grounds that it had sacrificed the struggle against Israel in giving priority to acts of subversion against the Hashemite royal family, aimed at gaining gain control over Jordan. Following 1970's Black September, he obtained his doctorate from al-Azhar and taught the Qurʾan at Jeddah's Islamic University. He thus became the educational authority within the World Islamic League, maintaining close ties with the leaders of the Red Crescent. ʿAzzam, a pivotal figure in the context of militant and religious Islam, in 1984 created a new organization in Peshawar to which, given the clandestine nature of its activities, he gave a fairly neutral name, Maktab al-Khidmat ul-Mujahideen ul-Arab (MUKUB), or "Bureau of Services for Arab Mujahideen." Most of its leaders were from the Middle East, aside from a small number of Algerians. Two of ʿAzzam's appointees were Abu Tamin and Abu Sayyaf.

To officially assist ʿAzzam—and, in all likelihood, to monitor his activities—Prince Turki al-Faisal, head of the Saudi intelligence services, chose the son of a wealthy entrepreneur with close ties to the royal family, Osama bin Laden. Bin Laden, who had been active in the family business, was a deeply religious man who had recently finished his training as an engineer. He had also studied not only under ʿAzzam but also under Muhammad Qutb, the Egyptian ideologue's younger brother.

Soon MUKUB had at its disposal a veritable propaganda machine whose most visible activity was the regular publication of the Arab-language magazine *Al-Jihad,* which served as a platform for ʿAzzam. In a document entitled "Join the Caravan," he stated that mujahideen combat in Afghanistan was an individual obligation for all Muslims, who were duty-bound, if they could not actually participate, to provide financial support for it. He stated that when "the enemy has penetrated into Islamic territory, jihad becomes an individual requirement. . . . No parental permission is necessary. . . . Giving money does not exempt anyone from physical jihad, no matter how great the sum. . . . Jihad is a lifelong obligation."

He obtained religious backing from eight high-ranking *ulama,* including Sheikh Bin Baz, who would become Grand Mufti of Saudi Arabia, and Dr. Saleh Abu Ismail, a member of Egypt's Majlis al-Shura. He regularly welcomed to Peshawar charismatic leaders of the jihadist movement, such as Egypt's Omar Abdel Rahman.

This period marked the emergence in ʿAzzam's writings of the concept of a standing international jihad army: "That obligation will not end with victory in Afghanistan, and jihad will remain an individual obligation until we have reconquered all Muslim lands and reinstalled Islam: we still have ahead of us Palestine, Bukhara, Lebanon, Chad, Eritrea, Somalia, the Philippines, Burma, Yemen, Tashkent, and Andalusia."

It is noteworthy that, in speaking of future jihads, ʿAzzam gave priority to the Palestinian struggle. Indeed, the first intifada of 1987 marked the resurgence of Islamic fervor in the context of the anti-Zionist effort.

An Army of Arab Volunteers

At the same time, a comprehensive training program for militants was being set up. Requirements were minimal: some physical and weapons training, and the occasional shooting off of the odd round. Weapons and matériel were mainly reserved for the numerous Afghan militants, who knew the terrain well. To occupy the volunteers' time, religious education classes were held in hastily assembled structures, most of which were set up within the refugee camps in the area around Peshawar, which housed 2 million Afghans. The students were pleased to acquire some basic knowledge of the Qur'an, and it was an easy task for instructors to move on to more radical dogma, teaching them, in a rudimentary but inspiring manner, the views of the theologians of jihad.

However, a few volunteers actually participated in operations on Afghan soil. Early on, they served as reinforcements for specific units, because the Afghan mujahideen—few of whom were open to Wahabism—distrusted these impassioned, jihad-invoking foreigners. The Afghan resistance movement, based in Peshawar, encompassed seven main parties, of which four were openly Islamist. But the volunteers were for the most part accepted by the Pashtun groups Hizb-i-Islami-i-Afghani (HIA), meaning Afghan Islamic Party, headed by Gulbuddin Hekmatyar, and al-Ittihad (Islamic Unity), founded by Dr. Rasul Sayyaf. A small number of them were integrated into the Jammaat-i-Islami-i-Afghani (JIA)—the Afghan Islamic Society—headed up by Professor Muhammad Rabbani, whose military adjunct was a Tajik, Commander Massoud.

Those men, who were viewed either as specially qualified or simply as the most highly motivated—would see action. They included Arab fighters who successfully halted a Soviet offensive in the Paktar region in February 1987. Although the following month, they failed in their attempt to seize Jellalabad, their pugnacity earned them the respect and longstanding loyalty of the Afghan mujahideen. Their names soon became famous in radical Muslim circles throughout the world. Among them were Osama bin Laden; Egypt's Muhammad Atef and Ayman al-Zawahiri; Saudi Arabia's Ibn Khattab; Jordan's Muhammad al-Maqdisi; and the Philippines' Abu Sayyaf. Ten years later, all of them would receive extensive international press coverage.

The rest were assigned to tasks that were not so directly war-related but equally necessary, such as handing out food supplies to refugees, caring for the wounded, and transporting weapons and matériel to the Afghan border.

Far from home and living in difficult material conditions, in an atmosphere of semi-secrecy, they were all participating in a thrilling adventure. They were building up faith in a crude, radical form of Islam, establishing a network of relationships, and acquiring the aura of combatants. Isolation and shared solidarity with other believers from different cultures and with different experiences accomplished the rest. They felt that they were sloughing off their nationalities and forming a new community of holy warriors, like the Prophet's companions. No longer were they Saudis, Egyptians, or Algerians; they were Salafist mujahideen, in the vanguard of the warriors of Islam. At the same time, they came into contact with a shady underworld, populated by dealers of all sorts, passionate theologians, and secret service agents, notably those of Pakistan's Inter-Services Intelligence, which had close ties to the Deobandi madrassas.

Founding myths also emerged that blended fact and fiction. Some famous ones tell of the invincibility of certain mujahideen, who, although riddled with bullets, continued to advance against the enemy, or who could disappear at will. Others speak of the power of God, through which fighters were able to stop tanks by throwing sand at them—sand that instantly changed into fireballs. All these stories met with great success when, years later, the Arab mujahideen, having returned to their communities, recounted them to naïve and fascinated audiences. The storytellers, however, intoxicated by their experiences, truly believed that they had brought the Russians to their knees—forgetting the important material assistance provided by the West.

The End of the Afghan Jihad

Following Soviet withdrawal, and under pressure from the American intelligence services, who knew that their efforts in Afghanistan had forged a double-edged sword, the Pakistanis made an attempt to exert greater control over the Arab mujahideen, who had, at war's end, been abandoned by their former friends. American and Saudi support had melted away. Their fate was of little interest to their Afghan brothers, who were busy looting their country, reaping the benefits of the opium trade, and engaging in inter-clan clashes with an eye to conquering Kabul. The Arab volunteers had no choice but to consider three alternatives.

The first group decided to return to their respective homelands, where they mostly served as radical spearheads for local Islamist movements, creating underground cells with the goal of preparing for jihad against their governments, which they deemed infidel and corrupt. The second preferred to leave for those lands that people of their ethnic origin had traditionally favored—Europe in particular. Some of them found the prestige accorded them by dint of their reputation as mujahideen instrumental in converting to Salafism a second generation of marginalized youths in search of an identity. The third category opted to continue on with international jihad by lending fresh logistical or operational support to mujahideen fighters at the camps located near the Afghan-Pakistan border. The list grew rapidly: Algeria, Bosnia, Kashmir, Chechnya . . .

However, during that period the Arab volunteers' leaders were secretly making plans for the future of their international jihad army.

Certain writers claim that jihadist leaders stood united under 'Azzam until the end, agreeing to the long-term pursuit of his plan to support oppressed Muslims in order to recreate the ancestral *umma*, from Andalusia to the Philippines. They say that al Qaeda was formed to replace MUKUB, which had become obsolete in the context of the fresh struggles that lay ahead.

Others, such as Rohan Gunaratna, believe that it was the debate over the new jihadist plan that led to a parting of the ways between 'Azzam—who was fully aware of the strategic danger involved in terrorist activities—and Osama bin Laden, who had been convinced by the Egyptian al-Jihad, with whom he had forged very close ties, of the need to start out by fighting apostate regimes.

There really is no definitive answer to that question. On November 24, 1989, 'Abdallah 'Azzam died, along with his two sons, in a car bombing in Peshawar. Some saw it as the work of bin Laden, who was known for being duplicitous and who might have wished to rid himself of a troublesome leader overwhelmed by the magnitude of the stakes now involved in jihad. Others believed that the responsibility lay with the Arab intelligence services, which were determined to eliminate the leader of an army of international terrorists before he could bring his fight to their doorstep. In any case, 'Abdallah 'Azzam became the symbol of the mujahideen movement—an exemplary Muslim killed while carrying out the jihad that he had helped to make a reality. He certainly took many secrets with him to the "Paradise in the shadow of swords."

But beyond the creation of this mythology, the future was looking grim for the mujahideen movement. Its members had dispersed, and the former combatants, although relieved that combat had ended, had, however, to face the harsh reality of returning to civilian life and receding into anonymity.

Osama bin Laden, 'Azzam's official heir, returned to Saudi Arabia with a plan that could not yet be carried out, given the realities of the time. Even the most highly motivated Salafist mujahideen had no choice but to go back to their old national projects. It took bin Laden only seven years to rebuild the Afghan network, this time with new opponents in mind.

In the meantime, it was Algerian Islamists, despite the fact that they had represented a minority in the Afghan conflict, who, beginning in 1989, gave additional impetus to the dynamic of jihad. That new struggle led to all-out civil war and to unspeakable horrors.

THE ALGERIAN JIHAD AND
ITS CONSEQUENCES FOR EUROPE

The Islamic Salvation Front

April 1989 witnessed the legalization in Algeria of the Islamic Salvation Front (al-Jabhat al-Islamiya al-Inqadh) (FIS), an Islamist party of recent vintage. Founded in 1987 by Abassi Madani and Ali Belhaj, the FIS was financed primarily by Saudi Arabia. Aiming beyond the Muslim Brotherhood's goal of external influence, it wanted to reproduce, within a Sunni regime, an Iran-style Islamic revolution. It kept up appearances through its apparent respect for democratic principles and participation in the electoral process, but its leaders were organizing intensive proselytization campaigns aimed at winning over a people traumatized by the rule of the corrupt National Liberation Front (FLN), which had been in power for twenty-seven years, and by the socioeconomic repercussions of the 1985 oil crisis.

Two schools of thought coexisted within this new Islamist organization. The Algerianists wanted to confine their struggle to Algerian territory, while the more internationalist Salafists believed that a Muslim victory in Algeria would represent only the first stage of the process, and that it was necessary to collaborate with external representatives of the *umma*. That key distinction was to be ever-present in the ongoing power struggle within the Algerian jihad movement. In addition, a jihadist subgroup emerged within the FIS that included extremists of both persuasions. Its members met regularly in a mosque in the Belcourt area of Algiers, which they renamed "Kabul."

The Algerianist radical contingent was made up of former members of the Armed Islamic Group (al-Harakat al-Islamiya al-Musalaha), the first Algerian militant Islamist organization, founded in 1984 by a former mujahid who had fought in the war of independence, Muhammad Bouhali. Along with a few others, Bouhali carried out targeted attacks against governmental structures to protest the corrupt, apostate regime of the National Liberation Front. He also attempted to manipulate public opinion by claiming to redistribute wealth to the poor, thereby acquiring, in the span of a few months, the reputation of a Muslim Robin Hood. Betrayed by one of his followers, Bouhali was killed in 1987 by security forces. Most of his accomplices had been arrested and imprisoned two years earlier, including a young imam with very strong anti-French views, Ali Belhaj, the son of a partisan killed during the Algerian war. He, too, was freed during the amnesty that was granted in 1988.

The Salafist doctrine had its adherents in veterans of the Afghan war, recently returned to the country, whose dream it was to spearhead, through armed violence, an Algerian Islamist revolution. Some of them even espoused the concept of *takfir*.

That conspiratorial relationship among dissident minorities of varying backgrounds and religious beliefs gave rise to a number of underground organizations, which had been preparing for jihad even before the suspension of the January 1992 electoral process. They included a small group of extremely determined Salafists, founded in West Algiers in mid 1992 by a charismatic figure of the Afghan jihad, Abdelhaq Layada, also known as Abu Adlan, and a neighborhood strongman, Muhammad Allal, also known as Moh Leveilley. This new entity, impatient but highly organized, consisted mainly of Afghanistan veterans; so-called *hittistes*—an Algerian term for the unemployed; and petty criminals. It would later give rise to the Armed Islamic Group (al-Jamaa al-Islamiya al-Musalaha), known by its French acronym, GIA. Some believe that it led the July 1991 attack against the Guemmar military post, in which, working in tandem with some of the post's staff, a group of Islamists got away with arms, ammunition, and explosives. The Islamic Salvation Front had already denounced this as the work of a branch of Algerian military intelligence.

The National Liberation Front was taken by surprise by the Islamic Front's victory in the March 1991 municipal elections, in which the Muslim party won a majority in 55 percent of the city councils, including that of Algiers. The newly elected party wasted no time in taking some disturbing measures: requiring women to veil themselves; closing cafes, considered dens of iniquity; and using municipal resources for the benefit of Islamist organizations. The Algerian authorities decided to put the brakes on the FIS when, emboldened by its recent victory, it organized increasing numbers of street demonstrations. The subsequent suppression measures, which were quite brutal, led to the deaths of dozens of people and included the detention of Abassi and Belhaj on June 30,

1991. At the last minute, the Algerianists scored a victory at the August 1991 Batna conference, also known as the "loyalty conference," and held steady throughout the electoral process. During the first round of legislative elections, at the end of December 1991, the FIS received 43 percent of the vote and was positioned to be the next governing party. The authorities, fearing an Iranian-style takeover, responded immediately. Algerian generals resigned in early January 1992, and President Chadli Bendjedid cancelled the elections and imposed a state of emergency.

In April, the FIS was officially dissolved, and several thousand of its members were jailed or placed under administrative detention in camps located in the southern part of the country (In M'guel, In Salah, Bordj Omer Driss, El Homr, Ouargla, and Tsabit). That led many militants, now at a loss and concerned that they, too, might meet the same fate, to go underground. Some stayed in Algeria and joined the first armed groups to be constituted. Others went to Europe, where they would later play key roles in the context of support networks.

Armed Movements

Starting in mid 1992, militant groups began to form, without any overall coordination. Some of them, such as Said Mekhloufi's Movement for an Islamic State (Harakat al-Daula al-Islamiya), were based in rural areas, engaging in sporadic acts of guerrilla warfare as small units. Others, such as the Islamic Front for Armed Jihad (al-Jabha al-Islamiya lil Jihad al-Musalah) (FIDA), an Algerianist group, carried out localized acts of terror, both targeted and indiscriminate, aimed at government figures, in particular police officers and gendarmes, whose weapons they would steal. The situation was complicated and confusing, given that, in all likelihood, the Islamist cause served as a cover for many crimes and acts of manipulation.

The GIA made its official appearance in 1993. Its hallmark—identical to that of Gulbuddin Hekmatyar's HIA (Hizb-i-Islami-i-Afghani)—was clear evidence of the Afghan roots of the Algerian militant organization. From the very start, the GIA, which had understood full well that a militant group's influence is commensurate with the media coverage it receives, picked easy targets—journalists, intellectuals, unveiled women— that were sure to get the attention of the public. But soon, under the direction of its new emir, the Afghanistan veteran Cherif Gusmi, aka Abu Abdallah Ahmed, the group decided to take its fight to the international level, in keeping with Salafist ideology.

France was the first country to be targeted. In the early stages—during which the Thévenots, a married couple, were kidnapped in September 1993—the GIA ordered all foreign nationals to leave Algerian territory or face execution. The first two victims were French: two land surveyors killed at Sidi Bel-Abbes on October 18, 1993. Their deaths were followed by those of another 200 people—60 of them French nationals.

On December 24, 1994, the GIA for the first time struck outside of the country. It hijacked a Paris-bound Air France Airbus, which was eventually diverted to Marseille's Marignane airport. The perpetrators' inability to carry out their plan—only four Islamists participated in the operation instead of ten, as originally planned—made it that much easier for the French National Gendarmes Intervention Group (GIGN) to overpower them. It is likely, given their attempt to return to Parisian airspace, that they had planned ultimately to crash the plane into the capital. No explosives were found on board after all the hostages—aside, of course, from the three who were killed at the Algiers airport—were freed.

It is noteworthy, however, that no suicide attack was ever committed by the Algerian Islamic movement in Algeria or elsewhere, either before or after the hijacking. In that particular case, the terrorists' outrageous demands, their likely plan to crash the plane into Paris, and their decision to fight to the death were probably the result of the operation's having gone awry. Likewise, in the case of the January 30, 1995, attack against the Algerian headquarters of the General Office of National Security (DGSN), which killed at least 150 people, the driver's death was unanticipated.

Why did the GIA target France directly? There are three possible reasons.

France, because of its colonial legacy, was a traditional scapegoat within Algerian society, which often pointed to the so-called "Party of France" (Hizb Francia) as the cause of all its problems. Algeria's primary economic partner and the holder of a third of its external debt, France was considered by the Islamist movement as a political and therefore military ally of the Algerian government.

The French intelligence services had since 1993 noted that the jihadists threatening French citizens in Algeria had logistical intermediaries in France that funded their assistance through criminal activities, including the procurement of forged documents, counterfeiting, extortion, and theft. As a consequence, October 1993 witnessed the beginning of a process of neutralization of the relevant support structures. The GIA decided to take revenge.

However, the primary reason is this. France was home to approximately 3 million people with direct ties to Algeria: 800,000 legal residents, approximately 100,000 illegal residents, and 2 million French citizens of Algerian origin, who, as a rule, held dual nationality. In that respect, France represented a kind of sounding board for Algerian Islamism, which found accomplices there—whether on a voluntary or forced basis.

The series of attacks that took place from July 25 to October 14, 1995, was preceded by the July 11 assassination in Paris of Imam Abdelbaki Sahrawi. Sahrawi, a founding member of the FIS, was opposed to the GIA's actions and, during his Friday sermons at Paris's Myrha Street mosque, had been denouncing its clandestine operations.

May 1994: Algerian Jihadism Unifies around the GIA

The GIA's media strategy, whose effectiveness had become clear in the context of its external activities, paid off. In May 1994, through a communiqué of unity, it managed to amalgamate all of the Algerian fighting movements. The only group to remain independent was the Islamic Salvation Army (AIS), considered the armed branch of the former FIS, which restricted itself to guerrilla warfare against the security forces.

Under the leadership of Cherif Gusmi, and, following his death in October 1994, that of Jamel Zituni, the GIA established itself in nine regions of Algeria, patterned on the layout of military bases. The organization, which comprised more than 20,000 experienced fighters grouped into autonomous units, at that point revamped its strategy. It stopped its attacks against the security forces and began a campaign of terror against the civilian population, using tactics such as fake roadblocks and car bomb attacks in urban areas. The GIA hoped thereby to force the Algerian people to collaborate with it.

The GIA's External Networks

The GIA now had the support of all of the Algerian underground's assistance networks. Most of them, headquartered in Europe, were composed primarily of youths of North African origin. The GIA also had the backing, in the Afghan-Pakistan area, of Algerians with ties to mujahideen groups.

The GIA's principal rear base was, without a doubt, the capital of Great Britain, which Islamists themselves referred to as "Londonistan." Indeed, the United Kingdom had become the preferred safe haven for many Islamist militants who were wanted in their own countries for terrorist activities. Many were Afghanistan veterans.

Imam Mahmoud Omar Othman, aka Abu Qutada, a Jordanian of Palestinian origin, who headed up first the Finsbury Park Pakistani mosque, then the one on Baker Street, coordinated propaganda activities and financial assistance. Indeed, *al-Ansar* (the Prophet's followers) magazine, a bimonthly Salafist jihad publication, soon began to focus on supporting the GIA. Abu Qutada was assisted by two other Afghanistan veterans, a Spaniard of Syrian origin named Nasser Mustafa Setmarian, aka Abu Mussab, and a Briton of Egyptian origin, Mustafa Kamel, aka Abu Hamza.

In that context, most of the Salafist militants who had fled to Europe—mostly North Africans and Egyptians, and some Turks—served as mercenaries for the Algerian organization, which had become even more famous than Egypt's al-Jihad. However, notwithstanding repeated accusations by Algerian authorities, it cannot be seriously accused of having perpetrated the spectacular 1992 assassination of President Muhammad Boudiaf by a bodyguard.

That transnational evolution and the link with the Afghan network became very clear when the so-called Marrakesh network was dismantled in both France and Algeria. On August 30, 1994, two Spanish tourists were killed during an armed robbery at the Atlas Hotel in Marrakesh. An investigation revealed that four groups, composed mainly of Frenchmen of Moroccan extraction—some of whom had trained in camps in the Afghan-Pakistan zone—were planning acts of armed violence in Morocco so as to trigger a holy war. They were led by two Moroccans, Abdelilah Zyad and Muhammad Zinedine, both former members of the militant Moroccan Islamic Youth Movement (MJIM) and Afghanistan veterans, who had decided to engage in independent jihad. With a network of accomplices in Morocco at their disposal, they had been able to obtain weapons from Europe through channels established by a former Algerian smuggler, Jamel Lounici, the primary supplier of weapons to the Algerian underground. Subsequent investigations made clear the magnitude of the North African support networks that existed on French territory.

Jamel Lounici's network, which specialized in the trafficking of arms and in forged documents, had very close ties with the logistical support group headed by Muhammad Chalabi, an Algerian. That network was dismantled in the Paris region on November 8, 1994. On July 16 of the previous year, six Tunisian Islamists with links to the Tunisian Islamic Front (FIT) had been captured at the Perpignan train station and found to be in possession of weapons that were probably destined for Algeria, by way of Morocco.

In 1995, the French authorities began an investigation into rings that were recruiting French Islamists and sending them to jihadist training camps in Pakistan and in Afghanistan. Cooperation with the police also made it possible to locate in Europe other networks that supported the Algerian underground.

On March 1, the Belgian federal police broke up the Brussels network run by Ahmed Zaoui and Jamel Belghomri, which specialized in propaganda and arms trafficking. It came to light that the network—composed mostly of Algerian Islamists with ties to the GIA—was to have served as a support base for a planned series of attacks against France.

On June 13, the leaders of Milan's Islamic Cultural Institute (ICI) were brought in for questioning. Most of them were Egyptian political refugees, GI militants in exile. The ICI was a focal point for European Salafist networks and played a key role in providing assistance to Bosnian mujahideen. Its former director, Anwar Chaabane, had headed the brigade of Arab volunteers in Zenica, composed of several hundred fighters of mainly North African origin. Chaabane, who was killed in early 1995 in a clash with Croatian forces, had been replaced by an Algerian veteran of the Afghan war, Lahcene Mokhtari, aka Abu el Maali. In September, Jamel Lounici's group was broken up in Milan, Naples, and Rome.

Finally, on June 20, the French police dismantled three more networks, with European ramifications, that supported the Algerian underground.

GIA Attacks in France in Summer 1995

In July 1995, the GIA launched a series of operations on French territory. On July 11, Imam Abdelbaki Sahrawi was assassinated at the Myrha Street mosque, located in Paris's eighteenth arrondissement. Following an explosion at the Saint-Michel regional train network (RER) station on July 25, a string of eleven other attacks were committed in the Paris and Lyon regions, which left 13 people dead and 180 wounded. After the identification and killing of one of its leaders, Khaled Khelkhal, a French citizen, the group was finally dismantled on November 1, just as it was about to carry out a car bombing of the Wazennes market, in the city of Lille.

The network was composed of three groups—located in Paris, Lyon, and Lille—and their members were young, second-generation North Africans of Algerian descent. Their leaders were two GIA emirs, both Afghanistan veterans, Boualem Ben Said and Ait Ali Belkacem, who had come from Algeria on the orders of Jamel Zituni.

The network's financial coordinator, Rachid Randa, was arrested on November 4 in London. An Algerian political refugee, he was a regular contributor to *al-Ansar* magazine and a European GIA leader. But 'Ali Touchent, aka Tarek, managed to escape. A former member of the Zaoui network, he had since 1993 recruited most of its members, who were used in the early stages to provide logistical support to the Algerian underground. Touchent was killed in late 1997 by the security services in Algiers, where he had rejoined FIDA, his original group.

Another, more autonomous jihadist group was also neutralized as it was preparing to launch an attack against a refinery in the Lyon region. Headquartered near Chasse-sur-Rhône, it was headed up by David Vallat and Joseph Jaime, a Frenchman of Spanish descent.

The GIA's Trail of Blood

In late 1995, the GIA's national emir, Jamel Zituni, aka Abu Abderrahman Amin, was at the height of his powers. The Algerian people, living in terror, believed that he would topple the government, whose security forces seemed on the point of being overwhelmed. The GIA had shown that it could strike in the land of infidels—home of the Crusaders—and has thus garnered the support of a new generation of sympathizers in Europe.

Externally, he had the backing of the internationalist jihad movement, as evidenced by the support provided by Abu Qutada and two militant Salafist organizations, Egypt's al-Jihad and the Libyan Islamic Fighting Group (GICL). The latter had made a name for itself in early 1995 by claiming responsibility, in a communiqué issued by its leader, Abu Abdallah Sadek, for an attempt against the Libyan dictator Mu'ammar Gadhafi, which supposedly wounded him.

Intoxicated with his newfound power, Zituni decided that he had to have absolute authority over his organization—an agglomeration of armed groups with varying ideologies. He began a series of violent purges aimed at weeding out potential rivals. Zituni, a Salafist who never left Algeria, was the GIA's first national emir not to have participated in the anti-Soviet jihad. He therefore started by eliminating those emirs who were veterans of the Afghanistan war, whose charismatic image he saw as a threat. Next in line were Algerianist leaders who might use their status as former imams to their advantage. He later tried to blame the Algerian security services, before admitting to what he had done and attempting to justify his actions by inventing an Algerianist plot against him. Finally, in March 1996, he claimed responsibility for the kidnapping of seven French monks from the Cistercian Monastery of Our Lady of Atlas at Tibhirine, south of Algiers. The monks were beheaded several weeks later.

Algerian Jihad in Algeria

In early July 1996, Zituni was killed by Algerianist Islamists belonging to the Islamic League for Preaching and Jihad (Al-Ittihad Al-Islam lil Daawa wal Jihad) (LIPJ), led by Ali Benhajar, the first GIA subgroup to break away. Zituni was succeeded by Antar Zuabri, aka Abu Talha, who inherited an organization weakened by dissidence. To maintain its strategic credibility, he launched a campaign of psychological terror against the civilian population. The massacres began in isolated villages. Ultimately, Zuabri was killed by security forces in November 2002. Today his partner, Abu Anta, has no more than 100 followers, whose actions can be characterized as near-psychopathic.

Algerianist groups were among the first dissident GIA entities engaged in independent jihad. They included Ali Benhajar's Islamic League for Preaching and Jihad; Mustafa Kertali's Islamic Movement for Preaching and Jihad (Al-Harakat Al-Islamiya li Daawa wal Jihad) (MIPJ); the Afghanistan veteran Abu Jamil's Faithful to the Oath (al-Baqoun ala'l Ahd) (FS); and Abu Fida's Islamic Front for Armed Jihad.

Later, other Salafist groups broke away, claiming that they were waging the GIA's true fight: in the west, mainly the al-Hawal, meaning "terror," group; and, in the east, a group led by Hassan Hattab, former emir of the second region of the GIA (Greater Kabylia). Soon they all were embroiled in a fratricidal struggle against their former GIA comrades, who now considered them to be apostates.

The European Jihadist
Movement Seeks a New Cause

On June 22, 1996, Abu Qutada, despite having been the unidentified author of the odious fatwa issued a year earlier legalizing the murder of women and children, stated, in an editorial that appeared in *al-Ansar*, along with Abu Musab Al Syri, that he had broken away from the GIA. The Egyptian al-Jihad and the GICL also ended the alliance by publishing a communiqué in the same issue of *al-Ansar*.

From that point on, Algerian jihad sympathizers in Europe began to distrust the GIA, suspecting that either its leaders were psychopaths who believed in a deviant form of Islam or that it was being manipulated by the Algerian secret services.

At that point, Imam Abu Hamza Al Masri—the only person left at *al-Ansar* after the month of June—also broke with the GIA, in October. He founded a new organization called "Supporters of Sharia," whose membership consisted mainly of Islamists of Pakistani or Bengali origin. The organization had an eponymous web site—one of the earliest instances of the use of a means of propaganda that would later be widely employed by the mujahideen movement.

After several months of uncertainty, the Taliban's victory signaled to the hard-liners—mainly Afghanistan veterans supporting the Bosnian cause—the restoration of Islamic law to Afghanistan. Contact was quickly reinstituted with the Afghan network, and recruitment activities resumed, with a view to channeling more volunteers toward camps in the Afghan-Pakistan zone. As Osama bin Laden's associates gradually began to assume control of these groups, a new Islamist International began to emerge, which had training camps in Afghanistan and stressed mutual assistance among the various militant jihadist groups.

At the same time, two pivotal events took place in France that made clear the shifting nature of the threat. Indeed, the attention devoted to the GIA, although fully justified, had prevented the danger posed by marginal elements from other jihadist movements—those consisting of Bosnia and Afghanistan veterans—from being fully understood.

On March 5, 1996, the Roubaix ring was broken up. The ring, composed of Salafist militants who were veterans of the Bosnian jihad, had been headed by two French converts, Christophe Caze and Lionel Dumont, with close ties with Abu Hamza in Great Britain and with Abu el Maali in Bosnia. They had recently carried out a series of particularly violent armed robberies in the Lille region, and had also attempted a car bombing in Lille on March 4, two days prior to the G-7 summit. The subsequent investigation enabled authorities to dismantle a mujahideen support network run from Canada by Fateh Kamel of Algeria that had ties to Europe, Bosnia, and the Afghan-Pakistan zone.

On December 3, 1996, the Port-Royal RER train station in Paris was bombed, killing four people, including a Canadian tourist and two Moroccan students. The sequence of events seemed clear to the media: the GIA had just sent a letter containing vague threats to the president of the French Republic, and a hasty claim of responsibility on the part of the Algerian organization had been made from a phone booth in the Paris suburbs. However, it soon became clear that the GIA had not, in fact, been involved in preparations for the bombing. On the contrary, given the imminence of the Marrakesh network's trial, set to begin on December 12, and the operational similarities with the bombing of July 25, 1995, it was concluded that the bombing had been committed by lone individuals based in Europe with links to the mujahideen movement.

Clearly, the threat, which theretofore had been strictly of Algerian origin, had become multifaceted. Jihad sympathizers in Europe were on the lookout for fresh causes, as the Bosnian jihad had been over since the Dayton accords of December 1995. The gradual reopening of mujahideen training camps, which the Taliban allowed, triggered a wave of enthusiasm, giving rise to a second generation of Arab volunteers in Afghanistan who would slowly become incorporated into al Qaeda's sphere of influence (see following chapter).

In Europe, however, a small number of former GIA sympathizers, loyal to the Algerian jihad, were still on the lookout for a group embodying the common ideal of May 1994. They soon chose the GIA's second region, led by Hassan Hattab, who wanted to maintain a sense of continuity with Cherif Gusmi's GIA.

To that end, Hattab, in an 20-page interview in the Salafist publication *al-Jamaa*—meaning "the group"—presented a number of justifications for the strategic validity of attacks on France. However, the principal objective of those belligerent statements was to cast his net wide with respect to former GIA supporters. Hattab, aware of his organization's weakness, took care to avoid any fresh adventurism in Europe so as to ensure the survival of his few logistical networks, including Adel Mechat's group in Germany and Omar Saiki's in France, which were engaged primarily in fund-raising and in distributing propaganda related to the GIA's second region. However, they were both dismantled during

European police operations prior to the soccer World Cup in May 1998. The following October, Hattab, wishing to distance himself from the GIA in order to garner fresh support globally, changed his organization's name to the Salafist Group for Call and Combat (GSPC).

The Algerianist Movement
Gives Up the Jihadist Dream

But the Algiers riots had perhaps made the Algerian generals aware of the fact that most FIS sympathizers were not dyed-in-the-wool Islamists but simply citizens wishing for a change in their system of governance. As was happening under other Arab regimes at the time, the FLN elite had taken the dream of independence and used it for its own benefit. The promises made by Houari Boumédienne and his successors had not led to any redistribution of oil wealth but only to unemployment, housing shortages, and a quest for ethnic or linguistic identity. French Algerians' impossible dream of returning to a homeland known to them only through the stories told to them by their parents is often evoked. The fact that many Algerians, despite having been brought up in an atmosphere that glorified independence fighters, long for a French visa, is less often mentioned.

The Islamist crisis in Algeria was above all a social crisis. The Algerian authorities could not resolve it, because doing so would have meant overhauling the entire system, resulting in the loss of certain privileges. Consequently, the only course of action was to divide the emerging popular opposition movement, which was unified around Islamic issues.

Since the suspension of the electoral process, the Algerian authorities had made a consistent effort to divide the Islamist movement—a strategy that explained the doublespeak used by a government lacking any real political or economic vision. Up until the late 1990s, the Algerian gendarmerie, which the people generally loathed, stayed in their barracks, while the GIA openly strutted about in villages throughout the country. Ultimately, the country's security apparatus—a source of both pride and terror for the Algerian people—revealed itself to be totally obsolete. It should not be forgotten, however, that several thousand of its members died in the fight against terrorism.

Large-scale massacres were the work of fanatical GIA elements, not of the Algerian army. The latter's failure to intervene to protect the population was due not to its desire to manipulate the jihadists but to its inability, given the complexity of its structure, to take action without great risk. The mujahideen responsible for the wholesale massacres that took place during 1997 and 1998 acted at night, on familiar terrain. They had accomplices serving as guides, and they booby-trapped all approach roads so as to prevent any kind of quick reaction. There is no doubt that interventions by helicopter-borne troops could have saved some villages, but either the few available helicopters were otherwise occupied or flight authorizations were received too late as a result of Algeria's overly centralized military structure. Partisanship continued to characterize the European debate over who was killing whom.

However, the security apparatus's lack of reactivity to Islamist atrocities cannot fully be explained—even taking account of the physical obstacles posed by the Algerian terrain—by a lack of inclination to defend citizens hostile to it. From the mid 1990s on, supporters of law and order created reasonably effective self-defense structures—the Patriotic Militias and Legitimate Defense Groups. However, populations with ties to GIA-dissident Islamist movements had no protection. Their distrust of authority made them reject any kind of control. Deprived of any kind of protection from the security forces, they became easy targets for the GIA, which was determined to take revenge on dissidents by murdering their relatives.

In 1997, Islamic Salvation Army militants—ill-equipped, worn out by five years of guerrilla warfare and appalled by a jihad gone astray—were spending more time fighting the GIA than fighting the government. Any hope for a fresh legalization of the former FIS was extinguished. Through the intermediary of the Executive Committee of the Islamic Safety Front outside Algeria (IEFE) in Germany, led by Rabah Kebir, which was playing the improbable role of a government in exile, the AIS agreed to negotiate in order to protect its fighters' families. A truce was signed in October, quietly supported by all of the militant Algerianist groups. In the final stage of the process, a civil concord policy—the Algerian version of the "peace of the brave"—was adopted, as proposed in 1999 by President Abdelaziz Buteflika. Few Salafist militants accepted it, but it opened the way for the Algerianist movement's reintegration into Algerian society.

The Algerian authorities had been correct on one point. The FIS had from the start created an improbable alliance between the traditional middle classes with Algerianist leanings, mostly tradesmen and teachers, and the marginalized classes—who were, to a large extent, the product of rural exodus—whose utopian demands made them a natural fit with militant Salafists. The latter had no real common social vision, other than the fantasy of an Islamist Algerian republic. It had taken eight years of civil war to get back to the starting point. The Algerian population, which had lost 150,000 people for no good reason, was left numb and drained.

Residual Terrorism

Successive Algerian governments for years used the expression "residual terrorism," until it became meaningless. Terrorist groups, generally composed of fewer than 1,500 militants, persisted in their struggle, and that state of affairs was used to misrepresent the realities of contemporary Algeria. Militant Islamist elements, however, bore no responsibility for the Kabylian revolt or for the level of dissatisfaction among students.

The situation is changing, however, because the September 11 attacks gave the Algerian anti-terrorist struggle fresh legitimacy, removing any suspicion of its being used as a pretext to reject any democratic reform.

Terrorism has been banished from Algerian towns. The organizations that carried out several bombings in early 2001 in Algiers, using home-made explosive devices, were quickly neutralized, because they had no support structures. The number of victims of terrorism dropped twenty-fold in five years—clear evidence of the level of security now prevailing in the countryside.

The few dozen GIA members left no longer pose any real security threat. They live holed up in their last remaining safe havens in the hills of Medea, near Algiers.

West Algerian underground movements made an attempt to continue jihad independently, refusing Hassan Hattab's proposed alliances. Today, most of them have mutated into criminal gangs, with isolated hamlets the only realistic targets for the operations they need to survive. Only one of these groups, the Jamaa al-Houmat al-Daawa al-Salafiya (Group of Protectors of Salafist Preaching), which still has some support in Europe, retains any operational capacity.

In early 2004, the only substantive operation left was the GSPC, which had finally taken control of all of the militant groups of eastern and southern Algeria. Since 1999, Greater Kabylia—Hattab's traditional stronghold—had been the headquarters of the second region; Lesser Kabylia that of the fourth region; and the Aurès mountains that of the fifth. In late 1999, Hattab persuaded the former sub-Saharan (ninth region) GIA emir, Mokhtar Belmokhtar, to join forces with him. Belmokhtar, who had fought in Afghanistan in the late 1980s, had, after

breaking with Zituni, turned to smuggling weapons and cigarettes between Algeria and the Sahel. His appointment as head of a revitalized
ninth region provided the GSPC with a new route for the movement of
weapons and individuals.

This enabled Hassan Hattab, who was keenly aware of his isolation
in Algerian territory, to try to renew his ties with the mujahideen movement. It should be recalled that relations between the latter and the Algerian jihad had been broken off in 1996 because of the GIA's extremism. Contacts were finally reinstituted in late 2000, thanks to former
GIA sympathizers in Europe who had rejoined the Afghanistan-based
Salafist movement before giving favorable reconsideration to the GSPC's
Algerian model.

In fact, the GSPC was more compliant with mujahideen standards
than the GIA. Hattab had consistently advocated a Salafist form of
Islam, while steering clear of the sorts of bloodthirsty attacks perpetrated
by the GIA. His motto, "no truce, no reconciliation with the apostates"
was respected. His troops focused on guerrilla attacks—sometimes spectacular in their execution—against the Algerian army and militias, although a number of civilians suspected of being informers were also executed. But they did not kidnap women to be sex slaves—a practice
termed "temporary marriage" by a GIA theologian, who had twisted the
meaning of an old Shiite custom that allowed travelers to satisfy their
sexual needs outside of marriage—nor did they massacre people or carry
out indiscriminate attacks.

In the end, attempts to interact did not allow for any real reintegration of the GSPC into the mujahideen movement. Distance was a factor,
compounded by the realities of the time, the events of September 11, and
the destruction of the Afghan base. The combination of all of those factors doomed to failure the plan to loosen the stranglehold of the Algerian armed forces.

The GSPC has since suffered a number of severe blows. Belmokhtar's
group—which masterminded an aborted plan to attack the Paris-Dakar-
Cairo rally during its Nigerian stage in January 2001—is much weaker.
The surviving members, including their leader, have taken refuge in the
no-man's-land of the Sahel, composed of eastern Mauritania, northern
Mali, and northern Niger.

Some thirty tourists were kidnapped in a surprise attack in that area
in 2003. It seems that the operation was planned by the fifth-region
leader himself, a man by the name of Abderrahman, who was clearly
itching to replace Hattab as head of the GSPC. His partial success did

not, in the end, change anything. Indeed, Hassan Hattab was killed in early October during an operation carried out by the Algerian armed forces in Kabylia.

NOTES TO CHAPTER 12

1. Meddeb, *Malady of Islam,* 45, 48.
2. On Eurodif, see http://en.wikipedia.org/wiki/Eurodif; on Anis Naccache, see www.humanite.presse.fr/journal/1990–07–28/1990–07–28–800889 (both accessed April 11, 2006).
3. ʿAli Shariʿati, *Shahadat va pas az shahadat* (Tehran: Sazman-i intisharat-i Husayniyah-i irshad, 1350/1972).
4. Kepel, *Jihad: The Trail of Political Islam,* 6.

CHAPTER 13

AL QAEDA

Philippe Migaux

AL QAEDA'S STRATEGY
OF UNIFICATION (1989–2001)

Any number of theories have been advanced as to the origins of the name "al Qaeda" (the base), from a reference to a computer file revealing the identities of Arab veterans of the Afghanistan conflict (the database), to Osama bin Laden's alleged high-tech headquarters, deep in the mountains of Afghanistan (the secret base), drawings of which—impressive though entirely fictitious—were produced by the American media when U.S. operations began in October 2001.

The name al Qaeda, which instantly became the focus of media attention following the August 1998 U.S. embassy bombings, had long had mythical status. Osama bin Laden himself had contributed to the mystery surrounding the name by never uttering it prior to the events of September 11. The group's leaders, in their internal communications, usually referred to it as "the society," an intentionally neutral appellation.

In fact, it was ʿAbdallah ʿAzzam who had named the organization. In 1988, at the first signs of a Soviet withdrawal from Afghanistan, ʿAzzam decided that he would not disband the army of Arab volunteers he had created four years earlier but would use it to undertake a much vaster mission—the reconquest of the Muslim world.

To that end, he needed a standing vanguard of fighters to serve as leaders of the *umma*. He coined the term *al-qaeda al-sulbah* (the solid base) for this, which was also the headline of an editorial he wrote in issue number 41 of *al-Jihad,* published in April 1988. The article stated: "Every principle needs a vanguard to carry it forward that is willing, while integrating into society, to undertake difficult tasks and make tremendous sacrifices. No ideology, celestial or earthly, can do without such a vanguard, which gives its all to ensure victory. It is the standard-bearer on an endless and difficult path until it reaches its destination, as it is the will of God that it do so. It is *al-qaeda al-sulbah* that constitutes this vanguard for the hoped-for society."

A few lines down, ʿAzzam set out eight moral guidelines governing the behavior of the devout, iron-willed members of such a "solid base":

One must unhesitatingly face the hardest challenges and the worst difficulties.

Leaders must endure, along with their men, the blood and sweat of grueling marches.

The vanguard must abstain from base, worldly pleasures, and its distinguishing characteristic must be abstinence and frugality.

The vanguard must translate into reality the great dream of victory.

Will and determination are necessary for the march ahead, however long it may be.

Three things are essential to this march: meditation, patience, and prayer.

Two rules must be followed: loyalty and devotion.

All anti-Islamic plots that are being hatched throughout the world must be foiled.

ʿAzzam's violent death in Peshawar in 1989 deprived the mujahideen movement of a recognized, victorious leader who had conceptualized his ideology and formed a militant group. His murderers were never identified. Many theories have been floated in that respect—from his killing being the work of Arab intelligence services, for reasons of state, to an internal settling of scores within the mujahideen movement. But the salient point here is that, by killing ʿAzzam, his murderers brought Osama bin Laden into the picture. Bin Laden would give an impetus of a different sort to al Qaeda and a new direction to the jihadist strategy.

Rohan Gunaratna believes that the car bomb that killed ʿAzzam—a highly professional job using a remote-controlled explosive device—was the work of Egypt's al-Jihad group, under the guidance of its new mentor, bin Laden. Indeed, in the wake of the Afghan jihad, bin Laden, eclipsed by ʿAzzam, had been unable to impose his views. Al-Jihad apparently managed to persuade him to concentrate on the struggle against corrupt Muslim rulers instead of on the reconquest of former Islamic territory. That was a key shift, because al Qaeda, in the context of its new strategy of taking the fight onto national territory, adopted the terrorist techniques used by the Egyptians. ʿAzzam, who had been deeply involved with the Palestinian resistance and who had in 1970 strongly criticized the PLO for having abandoned the struggle against the Zionist occupier in favor of efforts to subvert Jordan's Hashemite government, could not allow his organization to experience another Black September.

America Becomes the New Enemy

Saddened by the death of his spiritual father—or, perhaps, secretly pleased at the disappearance of his rival, bin Laden returned to Saudi Arabia, where he was welcomed with the honors due a hero of Islam. He received considerable media coverage—heralding the era, to come a few years later, when every bazaar in Asia and the Middle East would hawk T-shirts and posters picturing him as an Arab horseman in a plain white robe, armed with an AK-74 or a saber of Islam.

By 1990, ʿAzzam's Maktab al-Khidmat (MUKUB) organization appeared to be no more than an empty shell. Its former Saudi and American backers had stopped funding its activities after the USSR pulled its army out of Afghanistan. Apparently bin Laden, during its last months, had, with ʿAzzam's approval, discreetly transferred considerable sums of money in order to ensure al Qaeda's future financial autonomy. Certain Middle Eastern bankers were involved who, because of their business ties to bin Laden, subsequently became the target of American financial investigations following the events of August 1998.

However, Maktab al-Khidmat continued to operate under the radar for a few years in the context of two autonomous groups.

The first, which was still using the Peshawar infrastructure and offices, was led by Sheikh Muhammad Yussef ʿAbbas, aka Abu Qassim, and by Egypt's Ayman al-Zawahiri. Its focus was on providing logistical support to mujahideen groups on the Afghan-Pakistani border, whose objective, in keeping with ʿAzzam's wishes, was to provide support for new jihads throughout the world. It was also involved in a number of humanitarian activities, funded mainly by Saudi Arabia. The money was channeled through World Islamic Relief Fund and the Mufawaq Foundation, future fronts for al Qaeda activities. The group's four main offices were located, respectively, in Afghanistan, Pakistan, Saudi Arabia and Iran, the latter headed by close associates of Gulbuddin Hekmatyar, who in 1999 was bin Laden's principal Afghan supporter.

The second group, better known as the "House of Martyrs" *(Beit al-Shuhada),* was based in Islamabad. It continued to publish *al-Jihad* magazine, albeit on a less regular basis, and was headed by two Jordanians of Palestinian origin, Mahmoud Said Salah ʿAzzam, aka Abu Adil—ʿAbdallah ʿAzzam's nephew—and Abu Aris, a Jordanian Palestinian who had been ʿAzzam's assistant. Both of them had conflicted relationships with bin Laden. Another of their associates was Boujemah Bunnua, aka Abdallah, ʿAzzam's son-in-law. The group was dismantled in 1995 by the Pakistani authorities, which suspected it of having helped Ramzi Yussef flee the United States for Pakistan and of having provided assistance to the perpetrators of the Egyptian embassy bombing. As a result, it relocated to Afghanistan, and publication of *al-Jihad* ceased. Bunnua moved to Great Britain in 1995, after having spent many months in Bosnia, in close contact with the Revival Society of Islamic Heritage (RSIH), a Kuwaiti Wahabi nongovernmental organization, publisher of *al-Forqan,* which was very popular among fundamentalist militants.

Bin Laden kept in contact with Maktab al-Khidmat's remaining members, who provided operational continuity during al Qaeda's formation. He also attempted, by various means, to stay in touch with the most highly motivated members of the former army of Arab volunteers. But after his years in Afghanistan, he had difficulty readjusting to life in his country, where, as he saw it, corruption and hypocrisy were rife. His status opened the way for him to forge useful relationships in religious circles, in Medina in particular, which were very critical of the Saudi royal family. Early on, bin Laden had had very close ties to the royal palace—where his father, Muhammad bin Laden of Yemen, had been an honored guest—but he had quickly distanced himself from it. Close friends and relatives began to give him discreet warnings.

Then, in 1991, Kuwait was invaded by the Iraqi army. The Saudi regime, which had no real army, was immediately under threat. Osama bin Laden's conviction that he had defeated the Red Army in Afghanistan led him to propose to the Saudi authorities that the Arab mujahideen help them take on the Iraqi armored divisions.

Bin Laden was opposed to the presence of Christian troops on Saudi soil because two of Islam's three holiest sites—Mecca and Medina—are located there. (The third, Jerusalem, has been occupied by Israel since

1967.) More than a half-million international coalition soldiers, mainly Americans, were now stationed in Saudi territory. Bin Laden viewed this development as an unbearable humiliation for all Muslims—the land of the Prophet defiled by infidels. To him, the American presence represented a twofold act of aggression: the occupation of Saudi Arabia by infidel soldiers was also evidence of America's desire to plunder the country's wealth under the pretext of protecting it. The United States, having thus humiliated all Muslims, became their principal enemy, inasmuch as it was deemed responsible for the Saudi authorities' corruption and apostasy.

Exile in Sudan and the Creation of the "Solid Base"

Bin Laden—like the Prophet when he left for Medina—chose exile, seeking refuge in Khartoum, in Sudan. He was welcomed there by Hassan al-Turabi, whom he had met in Pakistan. Al-Turabi, the new government's éminence grise, was the secretary-general of the Popular Arab Islamic Conference (CPAI), which, while officially backing Islamist political movements, also clandestinely supported militant Islamist organizations. In the early 1990s, Sudan was a hotbed of activism on the border of an unstable Arab world and an Africa gangrenous with corruption, economic instability, and ethnic conflicts.

Bin Laden had at his disposal in Sudan a large fortune and support of various kinds. He undertook the construction of modern roads and housing, and, in exchange, the state turned a blind eye to his clandestine activities, enabling him, at long last, to establish a "solid base" for the mujahideen. He also kept in close contact with neighboring militant Islamist organizations in the Horn of Africa, in particular the Somali Islamic Unity group, as well as the Aden-Abyan Islamic Army in Yemen.

But such semi-clandestine activities were a source of concern for the Gulf monarchies, especially Saudi Arabia, which were rapidly becoming aware of the threat posed to their internal equilibrium by a jihadist army ready to take on corrupt Muslim regimes. Furthermore, the new Sudanese base was located on the threshold of the Middle East and its oil-fields.

The dissemination of al Qaeda's ideology among radicalized segments of the population of the Middle East had become a tangible threat, especially since bin Laden's denunciation of the infidel occupation and of apostate governments had the more or less tacit approval of certain religious circles. Radical theologians and wealthy Saudi businessmen—

supported, in 1994, by bin Laden—helped to fuel the growth of a political movement of opposition to the royal family—the Advice and Reform Committee. After local committee officials were jailed by the Saudis, the decision was made to set up shop in London. The violence-filled speeches made there, relayed to Saudi Arabia via the sermons preached in mosques, helped to promote the rise of an informal but determined protest movement against the regime.

The Saudi regime—indubitably a religious and political model for the Muslim world but undermined by corruption and by its alliance with the United States, now faced a direct threat on its own territory. In addition, given the worsening state of health of King Fahd, who delegated only limited authority to the forceful Prince Abdallah, succession quarrels were rife.

Bin Laden, whose Saudi funds had been frozen and Saudi citizenship revoked in February 1994, made it known, through the few Saudi intermediaries with whom he was still in discreet contact, that no compromise was possible as to the American presence. The result was a complete break with the authorities of the Middle East, which began to pressure Sudan in an attempt to isolate it.

Bin Laden stated in later interviews that al Qaeda's continued presence in Sudan—several thousand mujahideen were there at the time—was in particular jeopardy, because two attempts had been made on his life, masterminded, he believed, by the Saudi intelligence services. From then on, he used the principle of legitimate self-defense to justify his struggle. In an August 1996 fatwa, he said:

> the people of Islam had suffered from aggression, iniquity and injustice imposed on them by the Zionist-Crusaders alliance and their collaborators; to the extent that the Muslims' blood became the cheapest and their wealth as loot in the hands of the enemies. Their blood was spilled in Palestine and Iraq. The horrifying pictures of the massacre of Qana, in Lebanon are still fresh in our memory. Massacres in Tajakestan, Burma, Cashmere, Assam, Philippine, Fatani, Ogadin, Somalia, Erithria, Chechnia and in Bosnia-Herzegovina took place, massacres that send shivers in the body and shake the conscience. All of this and the world watched and heard, and not only didn't respond to these atrocities, but also with a clear conspiracy between the USA and its allies and under the cover of the iniquitous United Nations, the dispossessed people were even prevented from obtaining arms to defend themselves.[1]

Such narrow escapes made bin Laden increasingly cautious and secretive. Before September 11, he had never once claimed responsibility for any of the attacks he called for periodically. He officially rejoiced at each attack but systematically denied any involvement. That was viewed by certain writers as a typical manifestation of Shiite dissimulation, probably inspired—as was the concept of martyrdom later on—by the writings of Iran's Shari'ati.

The "Solid Base" and Its Pivotal Role in Afghanistan

When the Venezuelan terrorist Ilich Ramirez Sanchez, aka Carlos the Jackal—a convert to Islam who had been living in peaceful retirement in Khartoum—was turned over to the French authorities in 1994, bin Laden became convinced that he was no longer safe in Sudan. A quick overview of the global situation led to the conclusion that Afghanistan, despite its clan rivalries, was the last remaining safe haven for Salafist militants, inasmuch as they still had bases in Pakistan, both in urban areas—in Karachi and Peshawar in particular—and in refugee camps, especially Jalozai, near the Afghan border. Furthermore, Salafist militants were for the most part viewed favorably by the Taliban, which was moving ahead with its territorial conquest.

In an interview with an American reporter, Osama bin Laden spoke of the serenity he found in the mountains of Afghanistan, which reminded him of the deserts of his childhood. Moreover, the area's rugged terrain, harsh climate, and vast expanses, as well as the Pashtun code of honor, served as the best assurance of his safety.

The situation in Afghanistan had changed since bin Laden's departure seven years earlier. The tribal factions fighting for control of the country, in the process plundering it and brutalizing the people, had since 1994 been brought to heel by the Taliban (students of religion) movement. The sons of Afghan refugees, Taliban members were educated in Deobandi madrassas. Indeed, the Pakistani intelligence services, with the tacit approval of the Saudi and U.S. authorities, had promoted the creation of a new Muslim army charged with restoring internal security in Afghanistan, as had happened ten years earlier with Arab volunteers.

Arriving in Kabul in May 1996, bin Laden was welcomed by Gulbuddin Hekmatyar, who had taken charge of some of MUKUB's activities following the 1989 assassination of its founder, 'Abdallah 'Azzam. Hekmatyar, the principal spokesman for the Arab fighters, who had just reached an agreement with his long-standing enemy, Commander Massoud, was preparing to assume the post of prime minister. On August 26, bin Laden issued his first fatwa from Afghanistan—a final warning to the American forces to leave Saudi Arabia.

The second Taliban offensive resulted in the fall of Kabul on September 27. Hekmatyar and his followers fled to Iran. Bin Laden consolidated his ties with the Taliban and suggested a rapprochement with Shiite Iran in the struggle against their common enemy: American imperialism.

The Taliban—whose new leader, Mullah Omar, was a veteran of the war against the Soviet army—now controlled 80 percent of the country and had the people's confidence. Indeed, Afghans hoped that the application of sharia law would put a stop to the robberies and acts of brutality committed against them. But the Taliban lacked funds and technical and administrative know-how, and that was exactly what Osama bin Laden—himself a veteran with great personal charisma and a mujahideen leader with established religious credentials—had to offer.

In early 1997, the Taliban authorized the reopening of training camps for Arab volunteers. Their management was entrusted to bin Laden's close associates—mainly Saudis and Yemenis—whose following now included the majority of Egyptian militants, under the leadership of Ayman al-Zawahiri. A wave of new volunteers had also arrived that, in between military training in the camps and religion classes in the madrassas, participated directly in the combat against the Northern Alliance forces.

A delicate network of alliances, based on honorary positions, marriage ties, administrative functions, financial support, and involvement in trafficking—was gradually being woven between the Taliban and bin Laden's movement. Bin Laden was a member of the Taliban's council of elders, and Mullah Omar was accorded an honorary position in al Qaeda's Majlis al-Shura.

Jihad against the United States

In early 1998, al Qaeda's internal structure was modified in order better to implement the plan of attack against the United States, whose troops were still present on Saudi territory. That simplified structure was subsequently used as a model by most jihadist movements.

Bin Laden was officially appointed al Qaeda's emir, or commander, by the Majlis al-Shura, consisting of its most experienced members. All of them were close friends of bin Laden's, who wanted to ensure a balance, under his authority, among the various belief systems and nationalities represented therein. The most important members were three Egyptians, Muhammad Atef, Ayman Al-Zawahiri, and Abdel Rahman Rajab.

Several committees, each headed by an emir, reported to the Majlis al-

Shura on their respective areas of specialization: training and operations, financing, theological issues, communications, propaganda, and so on.

In February 1998, bin Laden issued a second fatwa, calling on all Muslims to "kill Americans, military and civilian, and plunder their money," which led to the creation of the World Islamic Front against Jews and Crusaders (FIMLJC). Various extremist movements joined forces with it, including al-Jihad and the Egyptian GI, the Followers of the Prophet Movement (Harakat al-Ansar)—which had until then focused on jihad in Kashmir—and the Bangladeshi Jihad Movement (Harakat al-Jihad). At the time, al Qaeda claim responsibility for any of the numerous attacks that had been committed against U.S. interests since 1993, but they bore the imprint of its Egyptian, Saudi, Somali, and even Pakistani accomplices.

On January 25, 1993, Mir Aimal Kansi, a Pakistani, killed two CIA employees and injured three other people in front of the CIA's Langley, Virginia, headquarters. He was not captured until 1997, in Pakistan. On February 26, 1993, a car bomb filled with cyanide exploded in a parking lot underneath the World Trade Center in New York. However, faulty calculations led to the toxic material's combustion in the heat of the explosion instead of its diffusing as planned. In June 1994, eight Islamists were arrested in the United States. Five of them were Sudanese citizens who had been plotting to attack United Nations and FBI headquarters and to blow up a number of tunnels.

The involvement in the subnetworks spawned by the Afghan network of Islamists as varied as Sheikh Omar Abdel Rahman and Ramzi Yussef, a Pakistani raised in Kuwait, is evidence of the fact that such networks were composed of individuals of many nationalities who shared a common resolve to strike at the very heart of enemy structures. It was learned, following Ramzi Yussef's arrest in Manila in 1995, that he had been planning two assassinations—those of Pope John Paul II and of President Clinton—and that he was putting the final touches on a terrorist plot of vast proportions: the destruction of twelve international civil transport aircraft. In a practice run on December 24, 1994, Yussef bombed a Philippine Airlines aircraft en route to Tokyo from Manila, killing a Japanese national.

American interests were also being targeted outside the country. In Mogadishu, Somalia, eighteen members of the American Special Forces were killed in October 1993, during an attempt by to capture aides of the Somali warlord Muhammad Farrah Aidid. Aidid's forces were being trained at the time by members of the Somali organization Islamic Unity (al-Ittihad al-Islamiya), which was reputed to have received regular visits from Egypt's Muhammad Atef. The United States later charged Osama bin Laden with involvement in the attack on American troops.

In Kuwait, on April 15, 1993, seventeen Islamist militants were arrested for planning an attack against former President George Bush during his visit.

In Pakistan, two American diplomats driving through Islamabad were killed on March 8, 1995. As noted earlier, on November 19, a car bomb exploded at the Egyptian embassy in the Pakistani capital. Three Egyptian groups claimed responsibility—al-Jihad, the GI, and an unknown entity, the International Justice Group, which sent a fax demanding the release of Omar Abdel Rahman, as well as that of Sheikh Talaat Fouad Kassem, who had been arrested in Croatia in 1995 and extradited to Egypt.

In Saudi Arabia, a car bomb killed seven American soldiers in front of the National Guard building in Riyadh on November 13, 1995. The Islamic Movement for Change claimed responsibility. Local intelligence services arrested four Saudi citizens—Afghanistan veterans—and summarily executed them. On June 25, 1996, American armed forces stationed at Khobar, near Dahran, lost nineteen soldiers to a suicide truck bombing. Subsequent investigations by the Saudis into possible Shiite involvement came to a dead end. During an interview with CNN on May 13, 1997, bin Laden stated calmly: "I have the greatest respect for those who committed that act. It is a great honor that I cannot claim for myself."

That same level of brutality was characteristic of the Egyptian branch of the FIMLJC, al Qaeda's new front, which carried out several simultaneous attacks against American embassies.

On June 28, 1998, Albanian authorities extradited to Egypt several al-Jihad militants and their leader, Afghanistan veteran Sayd Salama, who had been planning an attack against the U.S. embassy in Tirana. His capture led to the Egyptian government's well-publicized "Albanian network" trial, which sounded the death knell for al-Jihad in Egypt. But on August 7, Ayman al-Zawahiri indicated in a communiqué that he had "received the Americans' message and that he would respond in the only language they understood: violence." On August 8, two suicide bombings tore through the American embassies in Nairobi, Kenya, and Dar es Salaam, Tanzania, killing 224 people, including seven Americans. An unknown organization, the Islamic Army for the Liberation of the Holy Places (AILLS), claimed responsibility.

In fact, the attacks had been masterminded primarily by Egyptians, with the assistance of Sudanese, Yemeni, Somali, and Comorian accomplices. A small group of Libyans, with ties to the GICL and headed by Abu Anes, had planned the operation. Their network had accomplices in Europe—in Italy and Great Britain in particular. In that connection, at the request of the United States, Khaled Al Fawaz—head of the Committee for Advice and Reform and an old friend of bin Laden's—was arrested in London.

In 1999, al Qaeda was busy preparing, from Afghanistan, several major attacks against the United States and its allies. French interests had also been scouted out, particularly military installations in Senegal and Djibouti. However, all those operations—carried out by outside groups with ties to the mujahideen movement—ended in failure.

On August 12, German police intercepted a shipment of detonators coming from Bosnia and arrested a Saudi named Salim, believed to control al Qaeda's European financial networks.

In Jordan, on December 3, an organization of Afghanistan veterans, known as Muhammad's Army (Saif Muhammad) was broken up. The group, led by a Jordanian imam of Palestinian origin, Muhammad al-Maqdisi, had been planning attacks against Israeli and American interests in Amman. It had close ties with Abu Qutada in London and with the Afghan-Pakistani movement, especially Zein al Abideen Abu Zubeida, well known for his role in recruiting and training volunteer mujahideen. Another of the group's leaders, Khalil al-Deek, was arrested in Pakistan and extradited to Jordan.

On December 14, Algerian-born Ahmed Ressam was captured at a border crossing between the United States and Canada. He was transporting 60 kilos of homemade explosives and makeshift detonators, to be used in an attack against the Los Angeles airport.

Concurrently, international efforts were under way to counter the activities of support structures located in areas previously considered safe. Western countries such as Canada and Australia, and even Islamist states such as Malaysia and Pakistan, finally began to grasp the extent of the Salafist threat. In Pakistan, security checks—carried out despite internal reluctance—forced the mujahideen to relocate their bases, which had been in Peshawar for twenty years, to other Pakistani cities, Karachi in particular, and even to Afghanistan.

A new route, via Iran, was mapped out for volunteers headed for Afghanistan, who now had to go by way of Tehran, Qom, and Meshat, then cross the Afghan border on their way to Mazar-i-Sharif and Kabul.

North African networks—which had been marginalized by al Qaeda's subgroups, consisting mainly of Middle Easterners (Saudis, Yemenis, and Egyptians)—took on fresh importance. They were the only ones able to carry out operations in Europe, as Middle Easterners found it more difficult to undertake clandestine activities there.

Al Qaeda's Strategy to Attack the United States

In late 2000, a series of meetings were held among al Qaeda's leaders and a number of highly placed mujahideen at which they decided to take action against their common adversaries. Each would be free to set goals and choose the means to achieve them, and each could count on support from the others. The mujahideen movement was thus joining forces with bin Laden.

But that did not result in the creation of an organization with a pyramid hierarchy. Bin Laden made no attempt to openly impose his authority but established himself as a presence to be reckoned with in Afghanistan. His experience and personal charisma, his ties with radical Saudi *ulama,* his wealth—all earned him respect. A prudent strategist, he refused to support massacres, and he never claimed responsibility for any attacks. He seemed more of a messenger than a guide.

Indeed, bin Laden showed no evidence of personal ambition. Backed by al Qaeda's Majlis al-Shura and its experienced mujahideen, he called for jihad, which they viewed as the only means of restoring the caliphate and reuniting the Muslim community so as to make it a single political and religious entity.

The communications strategy he developed would make him world-famous, enabling him to disseminate information through the American media and securing the loyalty of a number of Muslim journalists. While his strategy focused mainly on the Arabian peninsula, through threats against Americans, his message was a purely Salafist one calling for support for all oppressed Muslims, including Asian and Chechen Islamists and the Palestinian people.

Bin Laden's closest aides were in charge of training camps. Recruitment was more effective that way, and volunteers were placed individually—usually in groups of thirty or so—in progressive stages, starting with basic military training and moving on to more specialized lessons about various poisons, electronic devices for use in bombs, and other techniques.

In between training stages, mujahideen were either placed in accommodations known as "reception houses" *(beit),* usually with individuals of the same ethnicity, or they would go for religious instruction. Volunteers for suicide attacks were generally recruited in the early stages of military training, during rousing propaganda meetings run by the movement's leaders. Others were chosen for specific projects because of their particular operational profile—nationality, technical skills, or local connections. The final stages of training lasted for nearly a year. Those who went through it became very effective fighters, and a new caste of sorts was formed, most of whose members had seen combat alongside Taliban fighters against the Northern Alliance.

Training structures were reorganized and further compartmentalized, becoming increasingly professional with the arrival of a new generation of war-savvy instructors, most of them Yemenis under the age of thirty. All participants were given new, several-thousand-page instruction manuals—available at the outset on diskette and later on CD-ROM—titled *Encyclopedia of Jihad,* in which translated passages from Western military instruction guides alternated with detailed chapters penned by experienced mujahideen. By early 2000, the *Encyclopedia of Jihad* was available on various Internet sites set up worldwide through a complex relay system by mujahideen computer experts.

Once trained, some of the volunteers settled in the area, either sending for their families or marrying Afghan women, and helped to train new arrivals. Others went back to countries where jihad was under way, or they participated in operational missions. Most of them, however, returned to their respective homelands, forming sleeper cells and providing logistical support while awaiting orders to make preparations for, or to participate in, attacks.

That was the scenario in Europe, where restructured mujahideen networks concentrated on four principal missions.

First, recruiting efforts—which had resumed in 1997—were intensified, aimed at signing up volunteers for military training camps, located mainly in Afghanistan but also in the Philippines and in Yemen. Their second goal was to purchase specific items—including computers, communication materials, medicines, and certain kinds of clothing—for militant groups in jihad countries, particularly in Chechnya. Thirdly, they had to somehow secure the considerable financial resources required. That was accomplished through resort to organized crime—trafficking in forged documents, counterfeiting, credit-card fraud, and the drug trade—as well as burglary and armed robbery. Their fourth mission was to provide logistical support to mujahideen operatives in transit through Europe.

Starting in 2000, Europe, too, became the target of operations.

In earlier years, as we have seen, marginalized militants who in the past had been close to the mujahideen movement had independently planned and carried out attacks against France. They believed that, as they were working for the cause of jihad, they were free to act in the absence of specific instructions. New fatwas were therefore no longer necessary. It is likely that their previous involvement in GIA-linked groups led them to target France, given its long-standing status as the principal external enemy of true Muslims.

On December 3, 1996, a bomb exploded at the Paris RER train station Port-Royal. Given its timing—the Marrakesh network trial was due to begin on December 12—and its operational similarities with the July 25, 1995, attack, it was concluded that the perpetrators were lone individuals based in Europe with close ties to the mujahideen movement.

The situation became clearer when, on March 5, the Brussels authorities broke up the group led by Farid Melouk—a French veteran of the war in Afghanistan—and Muhammad Chaouki Badache, an Algerian also known as Abu Qassim, who had been an MUKUB leader in Peshawar from 1992 to 1995. The group, which had been planning an attack in France during the soccer World Cup, was also involved in the trafficking of forged documents, which it needed in order to send its volunteers—who were mostly Moroccans—to the Afghan camps.

The mujahideen movement's involvement in attacks against Europe became evident on December 24, 2000, when German police arrested four Algerians, Afghanistan veterans all, in Frankfurt. They had in their possession weapons and an explosive device of the kind Afghan camps trained volunteers to build. A videocassette was also found showing locations around and in the city of Strasbourg—clear evidence that the group was planning an attack, probably on French soil, before January 1, 2001.

The subsequent investigation, during which the contacts made by the Frankfurt group during the preceding three months were tracked down, made it possible to identify a significant percentage of European mujahideen networks. European police proceeded to dismantle them—little knowing that al Qaeda was gearing up for the most ambitious terrorist operation ever committed on American territory.

In Great Britain, on February 28, Abu Doha, an Algerian, was arrested for having provided logistical assistance in the Ressam case. The

Italian subgroup of the Tunisian Fighting Group (Jamaa al-Muqatila al-Tunsia) (GCT), led by Afghanistan and Bosnia veteran Sami Ben Khemais Essid, was dismantled on April 4 in Milan. Evidence was unearthed of the pivotal role played within the GCT in Belgium by the group led by Taarek Maaroufi of Algeria, two of whose close associates were responsible for the assassination of Commander Massoud on September 9, 2001. The two had been recommended as journalists, slated to cover the Northern Alliance, by the Islamic Observation Center, a London Islamist propaganda group headed by Yussef al Fikri, an Egyptian, who had been sentenced in absentia in his homeland ten years earlier for his participation in GI activities. In Germany, where Islamist militants had been keeping a low profile, major judicial operations were launched, followed a few months later by investigations into the assistance provided by the Hamburg group to Muhammad Atta's group of pilots. In July, the arrest in Dubai of a French-Algerian, Jamel Beghal, tipped off the authorities to a suicide bombing being planned in Afghanistan by Zein al Abideen Abu Zubeida, whose target was probably the American embassy in Paris.

All of those undertakings were part and parcel of the broad-based plan devised by the mujahideen emirs during meetings with bin Laden and his associates. But the emirs were in the dark as to al Qaeda's overarching goal: to attack America on its own territory and to humiliate it in a twofold, symbolic manner, striking at targets representative of its power and using its own equipment against it.

The plan, which was elaborated under conditions of absolute secrecy over a period of more than a year, had been fine-tuned by bin Laden himself. He had entrusted the various stages of the operation's implementation to specific cells in Asia, Europe, and North America, chosen for their effectiveness and discretion.

A CHANGED STRATEGY SINCE SEPTEMBER 2001

On September 11, 2001, at 8:45 A.M., American Airlines flight 11, en route from Boston to Los Angeles, crashed into the north tower of New York's World Trade Center. At 9:05 A.M., United Airlines flight 175, whose itinerary was identical, flew into the south tower of the Trade Center. At 9:39 A.M., Los Angeles–bound American Airlines flight 77 out of Washington crashed into the Pentagon. At 10 A.M., United Airlines flight 93, on a Newark–San Francisco route, plummeted to the ground in Somerset County, Pennsylvania. Its target—the White House—would have been hit as well had it not been for a passenger revolt, and perhaps the flight's pursuit by U.S. fighter aircraft.

Nearly 3,000 people were killed—Americans as well as nationals of seventy-nine other countries. Material damage was in the neighborhood of $7 billion.

Investigations revealed a highly organized network. Each plane had been hijacked by a group of at least four terrorists, most of whom had previously taken reconnaissance flights together. At least six of the nineteen perpetrators had gone to flight school in the United States; several had visited the country in 2000; and all of them had arrived in, or returned to, the United States between April and August 2001.

A letter written in Arabic, found in a suitcase that did not make it onto American Airlines flight 11, gives some insight into the kamikaze pilots' state of mind. A mixture of Qur'anic verses and operational instructions, penned by the group's leader, Muhammad Atta, an Egyptian with a Saudi passport, the letter is a striking illustration of the effectiveness and determination of the operation's perpetrators:

> The tasks to be undertaken individually and by the group, in veneration of the Prophet, have but one objective . . . the end is near and paradise is close at hand. . . . You must pray to God as soon as you enter the plane, because all those who pray to God are victorious. You are doing this for God. As the all-powerful Prophet said, an action undertaken in the name of God is better than anything on earth and better than the earth itself. . . . As soon as you are on board and seated, you will remember what we told you earlier, and your thoughts will turn to God. . . . The hour has come for you to know God. . . . When you act, strike hard, as a hero would, for God does not love those who do not complete their missions. . . . The night before . . . recall that you must forget [your past] and obey . . . because you will be in a very serious situation and the only course of action will be to follow orders to the letter. . . . Tell yourself that you must do this. Check all of your items—your bags, your clothes, knives, your will, your IDs, your passport, all your papers. Inspect your weapon, because you will need it.

The extent of the destruction wrought by the four attacks against the United States on September 11, 2001, was testimony of al Qaeda's strategic skill. In the deadliest terrorist attack in history, it had scored a direct hit against highly symbolic targets.

The operation's extraordinary success was due primarily to three factors: the perpetrators' desire for martyrdom; the compartmentalized nature of the various teams involved in its preparation and implementation; and the use of aircraft as weapons of mass destruction.

Al Qaeda's wiles proved a match for America's technological capacity; the planes it hijacked became mujahideen-controlled missiles. Thus the balance of power between Islam and the realm of the infidels was restored, with al Qaeda spreading terror in the United States just as the latter had done in the Muslim world. The four airborne missiles that struck America in September 2001 were payback for the cruise missiles and Tomahawks that rained down on Afghanistan and Sudan in September 1998.

The events of September 11 were deeply symbolic. The World Trade Center was chosen for a number of reasons: the desire to strike at an icon of American arrogance and economic power, to signal the start of a global war targeting all enemy interests, and to establish continuity with the first mujahideen attack against American territory eight years earlier.

While al Qaeda had focused mainly on its plan to attack the United States using airliners, it also masterminded a number of secondary, less elaborate operations. Compared with the operational profiles of the nineteen kamikaze pilots involved in the September 11 attacks—all of whom were Middle Eastern—those of Jamel Beghal of France and Richard Calvin Reid of Great Britain seem fairly lackluster. The pilots were chosen on the basis of their intelligence and competence, while the latter were selected simply because they possessed European passports and could therefore move around without attracting undue attention.

Reid and Beghal, however, were just continuing the pilots' work. The goal of post-September-11 plots was to ensure that the shock wave of terror continued to resonate. However, what many commentators failed to understand at the time was that al Qaeda lacked the capacity to carry out other, similar attacks. In fact, bin Laden admitted, in a videotape aired in October 2002, that he had anticipated the destruction of only a portion of the towers—the floors above the planes' point of impact. Crafty as ever, he attributed the towers' collapse to divine intervention.

September 11 was thus not the harbinger of an era of super-terrorism, in which ever more terrifying attacks would follow one after the other. It did, however, manage to persuade the non-Muslim community that it would henceforth live in a world haunted by the specter of further attacks. Bin Laden—a top-notch strategist in the area of psychological warfare—unable to carry out a frontal attack against the United States, chose instead to undermine it in the long term by focusing on its rear.

At the same time, the events of September 11 made clear that the strategy elaborated by al Qaeda in the 1990s had reached a breaking point. By unveiling itself in the videotape mentioned earlier—something it had never before done—al Qaeda positioned itself as a determined enemy of the international community as a whole. Did bin Laden, convinced that divine assistance had enabled him to defeat the Soviet army, truly believe that he could do the same with respect to all infidel armies? No doubt many al Qaeda emirs—whose unshakable convictions had been forged in the isolation of the mountains of Afghanistan—believed that to be true. But bin Laden was craftier and more perceptive. He was fully prepared to be identified, hunted down, and eventually eliminated—thereby imposing on himself and on his organization the martyr's fate of the kamikaze pilots—because he believed that such a sacrifice would trigger a new stage of mass jihad.

Al Qaeda's Strategy at the Dawn of the Third Millennium

The Failure to Follow Up. The mujahideen movement's strategy of using jihad networks resulted in a fourfold failure. After twenty years of struggle, no Salafist state had yet been created. The jihad movement had not taken root, either in Algeria or in Bosnia, Chechnya, Kosovo or Uzbekistan. Islamist states, which had been early sympathizers with the cause—in particular Sudan, Pakistan, and Saudi Arabia—had eventually caved in under pressure from America and set limits on the support they provided the movement.

The Taliban regime, which was becoming increasingly isolated within the international community, was unable to extend its authority to the whole of the territory of Afghanistan. Thus the assassination of Commander Massoud represented a kind of rent paid to the Afghan regime by the mujahideen.

The vast majority of armed undertakings failed because mujahideen groups, still split by rivalries, used different strategies: attacks in Algeria, guerrilla warfare amounting to little more than banditry in the Philippines, urban combat by Chechen Islamists in Grozny, suicide attacks in the Horn of Africa, logistical assistance to sleeper cells in Western countries—all based on different philosophies and agendas. The links among al Qaeda's numerous mujahideen satellite groups were based on individual ties and not determined by any kind of pyramid structure.

Operational groups were aware of increasing surveillance by international security services, while financial networks had been under scrutiny since the 1998 attacks against American embassies in Africa.

In that connection, it is noteworthy that almost all local groups were financially self-sufficient, more as a result of criminal activity than of funds raised by sympathizers. Operations were financed, and a portion of the funds were sent directly to the mujahideen movement. Indeed, bin Laden, who had invested considerable sums in his Sudan and Afghanistan projects, was no longer the "terrorist billionaire" who had held such fascination for the Western media.

Jihad Takes on a New Dimension. Despite his previous efforts to safeguard al Qaeda, bin Laden, by striking at the American superpower and claiming responsibility, had put the group's very survival on the line.

His plan was reminiscent of the terrorist doctrines of nineteenth-century Russian revolutionary socialists: an armed group carries out attacks in a stable country; the resulting suppression affects the population; and the people, led by the armed group, revolt.

Action, suppression, revolution; the pattern is identical. The armed group is al Qaeda; the authorities—corrupt though they may be—are those of the Muslim countries; and the people are the Muslim community.

But did the plan to globalize the jihad movement by involving Muslim peoples have any chance of succeeding? Previous versions of it had failed. Western response continued to be measured, and Muslim states saw that they could potentially become the principal victims of Sunni Islamist radicalism. Al Qaeda sustained heavy losses, but Muslims did not rise up, despite the fact that some saw the war in Iraq and support for Israel in the Palestinian conflict as parallel forms of state terrorism and that bin Laden remained a source of fascination for them.

The Transition to Global Warfare. Many authors believe that the Bali attacks marked the beginning of a global terrorist war triggered by al Qaeda's strike against Western economic interests. But al-Jihad and the GI had since the 1980s been targeting tourist sites in a bid to weaken the Egyptian government. Furthermore, the first jihadist attack against the United States involved a World Trade Center tower—not just the embodiment of U.S. power but also an economic symbol.

In the wake of September 11, Ayman al-Zawahiri set three goals for future operations: to inflict maximum casualties, that being the only language understood by the enemy; to concentrate on martyrdom operations as the most successful way of causing damage to the opponent and the least costly to the mujahideen in terms of casualties; and to choose targets, as well as the type of weapons used, with a view to wreaking maximum destruction on enemy structures and thus making clear the true dimensions of the struggle.

Aside from the World Trade Center and Bali attacks, jihadist operations have always aimed more at terrorizing the masses than at massacring them. This is no doubt due more to an insufficiency of funds than to any lack of will to engage in combat. Indeed, bin Laden stated in several interviews that the jihadist movement should have at its disposal the very same weapons of mass destruction as its American opponent.

The vast majority of the attacks that have taken place since September 11 have been of a more conventional nature, due to the need for operational secrecy and the unsophisticated tools available to jihadists. However, upon closer examination, it becomes clear that they have taken place in a strategically consistent manner.

Al Qaeda's goal is to spread terror using limited means. Its targets are chosen to give it the advantage of surprise over its opponent. Indeed, the West, whose wealth has grown excessive, has many weak points. The mujahideen, who cannot possibly succeed in a direct attack against enemy interests, must aim for the spectacular in order to lower their opponents' morale and galvanize their own followers. Al Qaeda and its accomplices are, above all, engaging in psychological warfare.

In that context, while it is true that the mujahideen movement has not fulfilled the predictions made by doomsayers over the past two years, it is inarguable that it has shown a formidable power of imagination. It appears to have a better grasp of the infidel world than the latter could possibly suspect. In the future, its capacity to surprise will serve as a better indicator of its state of health than will the extent of the destruction it inflicts.

This new form of warfare required, first of all, the adoption of a new communications policy, probably elaborated under the guidance of Suleiman Abu Gayth, a Kuwaiti national and a Bosnia and Chechnya combat veteran who had been appointed al Qaeda spokesman in August 2001. Given the West's interception capacities, al Qaeda was forced to revert to more basic means of communication. The use of satellite phones and email—even in coded form—was curtailed as much as possible, and other slower but safer methods were used, such as human couriers.

Likewise, the mujahideen, in order to keep their positions secret, had to stop using a very effective tool: their many and ever-changing web sites. They took on the Western media machine by co-opting its methods and using the Arabic media, starting with the Al-Jazeera television channel. The Western media monitored the channel, watching for news flashes and retransmitting, in real time, every minor Islamist threat. As a result, such threats took on disproportionate importance in the eyes of the public. That strategy was not a new one: for years Egyptian—and later Algerian—militant groups had transmitted their communiqués to London-based Arabic-language newspapers such as *Al-Watan al-Arabi*.

Video and audiotapes, transmitted clandestinely, thus spread al Qaeda's message throughout the world. Such messages supposedly always originated from the group's leaders but could not always be accurately dated. Threats against countries such as Great Britain, France, Italy, Canada, Germany, and Australia, and periodic claims of responsibility, were all the more forceful in their impact given that al Qaeda took care never to boast. Its goal in terrifying the infidel world with threats made in the name of Islam was to force the Muslim world into a clash of civilizations.

The Mujahideen Movement Repositions Itself
(September 2001–October 2002)

Al Qaeda's forces in Afghanistan appeared to crumble rapidly during military operations. Underequipped, poorly trained, grouped mainly by ethnicity, mujahideen units did not have at their disposal the modern infrastructure described by the Western media. Most of them did not keep their promise to die as martyrs. Many died during the bombings or were killed in Afghan score-settling, and several hundred ended up in the American camp at Guantánamo Bay in Cuba, but most of them managed to disappear.

It was believed at the time that the movement's traditional fallback structures had been neutralized. Most of the countries that had welcomed it had, like Pakistan, done a sudden political about-face and either joined the international alliance or agreed to "clean up" their territory. Yemeni special forces launched major military operations to defeat the Aden-Abyan Islamic Army. The GNT and Somali clan leaders, under the watchful eye of neighboring Ethiopia and of the United States, announced that they had control over Al-Ittihad al-Islamiya. The Bosnian authorities arrested dozens of mujahideen and stripped hundreds of others of their Bosnian citizenship.

The seizure of bank accounts and the reaction of the financial world had thrown into disarray the movement's usual system of transferring funds, and, furthermore, the international community, under the auspices of the United Nations, was in the process of elaborating new international legislation to combat terrorism.

The only thing we can be sure of is that the movement, having lost its Afghan network, has been dispersed and no longer has a coherent geopolitical structure capable of providing training and safe haven. For the time being, anyway, no state appears to have the capacity to provide to the mujahideen movement with the kinds of facilities that had been available to it in Afghanistan. Furthermore, the effective action of the anti-terrorist coalition led by the United States, whose president was overly quick to use the expression "crusade of good against evil"—a disastrous choice—has been strengthened by regional agreements.

Unfortunately, it has become clear that the mujahideen movement is still alive and well. Most of its leaders survived the aerial and ground campaigns on Afghan soil, and ways of smuggling them out to other, more secure areas had long been planned. Indeed, al Qaeda had very close ties with Pakistan's seven tribal zones, which, lacking confidence in their own security forces, were all the more resistant to control by the Pakistani authorities.

In the space of a year, the movement quietly repositioned itself geographically. Its key leaders fled to Pakistan and Iran, where long-standing and influential networks existed. Its operational chiefs and their lieutenants regrouped along a second axis, formed by the geographical crescent spanning Georgia, Turkey, Syria, the Gulf states, Malaysia, and Indonesia. Mujahideen sleeper cells took a third tack, remaining in Europe and Asia as well as in the United States.

During that time, the movement continued its fight in traditional jihad regions—in Algeria, Chechnya, and Kashmir and in the context of Asian guerrilla warfare—but al Qaeda carried out relatively few attacks. As usual, none really succeeded, killing fewer than 200 people in total. But most of the attacks perpetrated by the movement had links to Pakistan: either they were committed there or preparations had been made in that country. All of those undertakings had similar characteristics: determined individuals employed the usual methods against media-ready targets, through the now-standard suicide attack.

In Pakistan, several particularly violent attacks—using automatic weapons and grenades—struck Christian communities. But the ones of greatest magnitude occurred in Karachi, a city of 16 million people, where al Qaeda networks had been in operation for twenty years. In January 2002, the American journalist Daniel Pearl was kidnapped and beheaded. On May 11, the bombing of the Sheraton Hotel killed fourteen passers-by, including eleven French naval experts. On June 14, a car bomb was set off in front of the U.S. consulate, killing thirty or so Pakistani civilians. In all of those cases, investigated inconclusively by Pakistani authorities, involvement by al Qaeda operatives was suspected.

Other operations were planned in Pakistan, probably by Khaled Sheikh Muhammad himself, believed to have masterminded the September 11 attacks. He was arrested in 2002, shortly after the capture of other key figures, including Zein al-Abideen Abu Zubeida, of Jordan, and Ramzi bin Al Shib of Yemen.

On December 22, 2001, Richard Calvin Reid of Great Britain, the "shoe bomber"—pentrite was found in his footwear—failed in his attempt to blow up a Miami-bound American Airlines plane out of Paris. Reid had received assistance from Pakistani networks that until that point had devoted their efforts to supporting jihad in Kashmir.

On April 11, 2002, on the island of Jerba, Nizar Nouar of Tunisia carried out a suicide mission against the oldest synagogue in Africa, killing nineteen people. The Islamic Army for the Liberation of the Holy Places (AILLS) claimed responsibility, as it had when the U.S. embassies in Nairobi and Dar es Salaam were bombed in August 1988.

On June 23, 2002, Moroccan authorities arrested three Saudi nationals who were planning suicide attacks by boat against American and British warships off of Gibraltar.

Al Qaeda Franchises Its Activities after 2002

The Maghreb. The problems created by militant Islamism in Morocco have been discussed at length in the previous chapter. It should simply be added that, while the security situation did subsequently improve—although the country remained deeply traumatized—the Casablanca bombings of June 9, 2003, took Morocco completely by surprise, making it all too clear that the threat was capable of taking new forms.

A phenomenon had emerged whose danger had not yet been understood: the radicalization of isolated Islamists, lured, at the local level, by jihadist speeches relayed by representatives of the mujahideen movement, and reeled in by sleeper cells composed of Afghanistan veterans.

The Middle East. Following the events of September 11, the peoples of the Middle East did not give in to the temptation to radicalize, and, in late 2002, the situation seemed to be under control, despite continuing evidence of the existence of underground groups. In 2003, as hopes for a settlement of the Palestinian question faded once again, two pivotal events occurred that led to further destabilization.

The first, of course, was the war in Iraq, strongly condemned by the Islamic world. Poor handling of the situation in the postwar period, marked by Shiite radicalization and a surge in the number of attacks—some of which looked to have been committed by mujahideen who had infiltrated the area—created a new regional hotbed of tension.

The second was the serious crisis affecting the Saudi regime, increasingly challenged by its constituents and viewed with suspicion by its Western allies. The authorities, after denying for years that local groups with ties to al Qaeda were present on its territory—several attacks against British nationals having been classified by police as "score-settling between alcohol smugglers"—and after having been implicated directly in the U.S. Congress's report on the events of September 11, finally responded by arresting radical *ulama* and Islamist militants. But they did not move fast enough: on June 4 and November 9, 2003, major suicide attacks were carried out in Riyadh, killing forty-two and thirty-eight people, respectively, including Western civilians.

Also important is the still-latent threat posed by local Islamist movements to stable regimes. That is the case of Jordan and Syria, two countries weakened by a recent power succession.

The West. In Europe, the participation on a massive scale of British troops in Afghanistan made Great Britain al Qaeda's European enemy No. 1, ahead of France, which, for historical reasons, remained the primary target of North African mujahideen. Al Qaeda's leadership, aware of the fact that the British authorities were taking a sterner stance toward the activities of small Islamist groups in England, had actually considered a strike against the British Parliament. The plan had been to hijack a plane from a British airport and crash it into the building. That operation, which was to have been carried out by Pakistani Islamists simultaneously with the World Trade Center attacks, was eventually cancelled.

In any case, the decision to act against England, guilty of having opposed the mujahideen presence in "Londonistan," was announced on November 12, 2001, in a message said to be from bin Laden. The movement's hostility increased further in the face of British involvement in the second Gulf War. However, in early 2003, the threat to England had become more concrete, as evidenced by a series of failed armed operations ranging from small-scale biological attacks using ricin to a plan to launch a homemade missile at a plane at Heathrow Airport.

Thus al Qaeda, unable to strike at Great Britain on its own territory, chose to attack that country's interests in Turkey. On November 19, two car bombs destroyed the British consulate and a British bank in Istanbul, killing nineteen people. It was the second real show of force by the mujahideen movement in Turkey and testimony to al Qaeda's resolve. It also made clear the movement's inability to carry out direct attacks in Europe. Its decision to shift the struggle to a neighboring country that had served as one of its rear bases meant the sacrifice of logistical networks that had been operating for years with relative impunity. The move also confirmed the fact that the jihadist threat against Europe was aimed primarily at its external interests, specifically at expatriates and tourists.

That was the case of France, which, although it had been able, following December 3, 1996, to thwart all jihadist plots on its soil, was struck on several occasions beyond its borders. The death toll included two residents and a tourist at Jerba on April 11, 2001; a sailor off Yemen on October 6, 2002; four tourists in Bali on October 12 next; eleven technical experts in Karachi on May 5, 2002; and three expatriates in Casablanca on June 9, 2003. Aside from the Karachi attack, in which French naval-engineering personnel appeared to have been chosen because their level of security was inadequate, the other French victims had not been selected specifically because of their nationality but were simply random targets.

Another new development was jihadist groups' choice of Western targets on the basis of regional criteria. Jamaa Islamiya preferred to strike at Australians, killing 132 in the Bali attacks. The group even recruited Australian converts in al Qaeda camps so as to set up local operational networks. That plan had been in place in Europe since the 1990s, with the ongoing recruitment of young, second-generation North Africans in Afghan camps. The trend became evident in December 2001 in the United States, with the capture, in the mountains of Afghanistan, of John Walker Lindh, a convert to Islam. Lindh has since been sentenced to twenty years in prison for treason.

On the American continent, an investigation revealed that the nineteen pilots had acted virtually alone. Since then, other mujahideen cells in the United States have been dismantled—groups in Detroit and Chicago, not to mention the case of José Padilla—but they were rather small and did not appear to have made the transition to an operational phase. Lacking the advantage of surprise, al Qaeda once again proved unable to strike.

In fact, the only attack against the United States was committed by a troubled American adolescent a few days after September 11. During a flying lesson, he crashed his plane into a building in Atlanta, following an incoherent radio transmission proclaiming his support for Osama bin Laden.

Central Asia. In the early 1990s, the Muslim republics of the Caucasus that came into existence following the Soviet Union's breakup witnessed the emergence of radical Islamist groups. Paradoxically, some of their commanders had fought against the mujahideen while serving in the Soviet army in Afghanistan. In 1994, al Qaeda set up a support structure in Baku, Georgia, for Azerbaijani Muslims fighting Armenian troops for control of Nagorno-Karabakh. Several hundred Arab veterans of the anti-Soviet jihad had fought there as a unit until the 1994 peace accords.

In 1991, a former Soviet air force general, Dzhokhar Dudayev, who had been elected president of the Republic of Chechnya on October 29, issued a decree of Chechen independence. Dudayev, backed by the Islamic Liberation Party (Hizb ut-Tahrir)—a Chechen faction of the Muslim Brotherhood—had chosen as military commander Shamil Basayev, an Afghanistan veteran who had been close to bin Laden.

The first Chechen war began in 1994. In early 1995, several hundred mujahideen, including veterans of the Azerbaijani and Bosnian conflicts, were fighting alongside Chechen irregulars against the Russians. Their commander, Ibn Khattab, a Saudi national, and bin Laden had fought side by side during a 1987 battle known as the Lion's Den. Khattab soon became Basayev's operations chief. In June 1995, Basayev, at the head of a Chechen commando unit, carried out a spectacular raid in Russia that led to the Budyonnovsk hostage incident. On August 31, 1996, the Khasaviurt Agreement put an end to the hostilities. Ibn Khattab, who wanted to continue the jihad in the Caucasus, supported Islamist guerrilla warfare in Inguchia and north of Ossetia. Many local volunteers set off to be trained in Afghanistan's new camps.

Basayev and Ibn Khattab, unable to score any decisive victories in neighboring countries, attempted an incursion into Dagestan on August 7, 1999. During the period from 4 to 16 September, 300 Russian civilians were killed in five apartment building bombings, committed, successively, in Boinarsk, Moscow, and Volgodansk. No one claimed responsibility for the attacks, which Moscow authorities said were committed by "Chechen bandits." A month later, direct intervention by the Russian army marked the start of the second Chechen war.

The civilian population, a large percentage of which had fled to Georgia, was particularly affected by the brutality of the conflict; indeed, atrocities were committed by both sides. As had been the case in

Afghanistan, the Muslim world backed the Chechens, specifically through Islamic nongovernmental organizations. Some of them—such as the International Islamic Relief Organization (IIRO)—were used by al Qaeda to channel assistance to Ibn Khattab's troops. Thus the Chechen jihad followed on from the Afghan jihad.

That is why Ibn Khattab, in a September 1999 statement titled "Europe: We Are Still at the Beginning of Jihad in This Region," said,

> The West, and the rest of the world, are accusing Osama bin Laden of being the primary sponsor and organizer of what they call "international terrorism." But as far as we are concerned, he is our brother in Islam. He is someone with knowledge and a mujahid fighting with his wealth and his self for the sake of Allah. . . . What the Americans are saying is not true. However, it is an obligation for all Muslims to help each other in order to promote the religion of Islam. . . . He fought for many years against the Communists and is now engaged in a war against American imperialism.

During this period, several dozen Arab mujahideen arrived in Georgia under the pretext of providing humanitarian assistance to Chechen refugees, settling in the midst of the Pankisi Valley camps. The valley had been chosen by the Georgian authorities as a holding center for Chechen refugees, because the local people—the Kists—were themselves descendants of Chechen migrants who had arrived there in the nineteenth century.

While the presence of mujahideen groups facilitated jihad in Chechnya by providing external logistic support, direct assistance by Arab volunteers to Chechen guerrillas remained limited. The local climate was not to their liking. They did not look Chechen or speak the language, so, unlike local mujahideen, it was hard for them to blend in with the locals. On the other hand, they played a pivotal role in carrying out criminal activities, in particular kidnappings of foreigners, a number of whom were supposedly held in the Pankisi Valley.

In Chechnya itself, the Islamists' religious leader, Sheikh Amar, worked to organize external assistance. As the local head of a Wahabi NGO that had been very active in Bosnia—the al-Haramein Foundation—he had the support of Middle Eastern theologians. The funds received were used to develop propaganda tools that included publications and a web site—"The Voice of the Caucasus"—which advocated the creation of an Islamic emirate in the northern part of the region.

But despite financial assistance from the Gulf, in the end suppression got the best of the Chechen Islamists. Their communications systems were scrambled by the Russian forces, which also relied heavily on bombings and searches, with the help of Chechen loyalists. Basayev had to have a foot amputated in January 2000, and Ibn Khattab died a few months later, probably poisoned.

On October 23, 2002, Chechen Islamists led by Musar Barayev with explosives strapped to their bodies—including widows and sisters of "martyrs"—took 800 people hostage in a Moscow theater, demanding the withdrawal of Russian troops. The Russian special forces intervened, using a sedative gas. Forty-one guerrillas were killed along with more than a hundred hostages.

Georgia, under pressure from the United States, cordoned off the Pankisi Valley—the Chechen mujahideen's last supply base. It is believed that the area also served as a safe haven for the 700 *boiviki* (fighters) led by Commander Ruslan Gelayev, who had in late 2001 failed in his attempt to trigger Islamist warfare in Abkhazia. The network led by Abu Musab al-Zarqawi—a Jordanian of Palestinian origin—also had a presence there. Al-Zarqawi had set up a number of structures to train combat volunteers to fight against the Russian forces. Several members of his group who specialized in explosives and chemicals, unable to get into Chechnya, decided to return to France and to Great Britain to wage jihad there.

The failures of those two European groups sounded the death knell for the Chechen network. Some of the other organizations in al-Zarqawi's network—which was located in Iranian Kurdistan, along with the Ansar al-Islam (Followers of Islam) mujahideen group—had been dismantled when the American bombings started, in February 2003. It is likely, however, that some of the survivors are actively participating in suicide missions against American troops in Iraq—missions that are operationally very similar to those carried out by the mujahideen movement.

Tensions remained high, however, in the Muslim republics of the Caucasus, where many Afghanistan veterans were believed to have found refuge, despite the preventive operations carried out by security forces against local jihadist groups. The security situation in Central Asia remained, in the medium term, closely linked to the development of jihadism in South Asia.

South Asia. Insecurity continued to prevail in the Afghan-Pakistani zone. Indeed, the considerable dollar sums provided following the lightning-quick American victory did not make the Taliban any more open to democratic values. While military operations in Afghanistan were carried out effectively, reconstruction was done on the cheap.

Aghanistan's President Hamid Karzai, who narrowly escaped death in assassination attempts in 2002 and 2004, is arguably in control only of Kabul, and that only because of the presence of the International Security Assistance Force (ISAF) and of NGO activities. Almost everything needs to be rebuilt—the administration, the tax system, the educational system, public services, and transportation.

The Taliban's weakness was overestimated because of their sudden disappearance. But they had simply hidden their weapons and become Pashtuns once again. Have they lost sight of the ideology that kept them in power before the Americans' arrival? It is more likely that they are just waiting for them to leave.

In the meantime, they are keeping busy, for instance by participating in the various kinds of trafficking that are once again endemic throughout the country—especially opium trafficking. The 2002 opium harvest was estimated at 4,100 tons—a record for Afghanistan, only ten months after poppy cultivation had restarted.

Kabul is not yet safe from attacks. Isolated yet significant acts of violence have made it clear that the Taliban and the "Arab Afghans" have not vanished entirely and still want to participate in jihad. The impenetrability of the tribal zone—where traditional Pashtun ties of solidarity have held fast against all foreigners—and the question of Kashmir remain unresolved issues in the crisis affecting the Indian subcontinent, where Afghanistan remains the weakest and most unstable link.

That regional crisis, which had prevailed since the violent partition of British India in 1947, fueled the process of radical Islamization—with a primarily Deobandi influence—in Pakistan. The tensions that exist today in that country are but a new form of the "Great Game" that has long been played in the region by local factions and foreign forces.

Before September 11, Pakistani militant groups had been engaged in two types of jihad, in the conflict in Kashmir and in sectarian fighting against the Shiites. Ties were forged with al Qaeda so as to facilitate the training of their followers. But Pervez Musharraf's outlawing of those organizations in August 2001—a courageous act—led to the formation of underground groups devoted primarily to a third type of jihad—one dedicated to providing support for the mujahideen movement.

It is no accident that, as we saw earlier, all of the attacks committed between September 11, 2001, and October 6, 2002, either occurred or were planned in Pakistan, nor that key arrests among al Qaeda's operational chiefs were subsequently made there. Musharraf, weakened by the conflict with India—which was quick to denounce the Pakistani origin of the attacks committed in New Delhi and in Mumbai—then witnessed the emergence of a legal Islamist opposition movement. Nor could he be certain that his security forces would be loyal, and, in fact, he narrowly escaped several attempts on his life. This was a considerable burden to bear for the ruler of a country in a deep economic crisis, forced by international realities to drastically switch alliances.

Sub-Saharan Africa. Often overlooked is the fact that a third of sub-Saharan Africa's 700 million inhabitants are Muslims. The jihadist influence became evident most rapidly in the Horn of Africa due to the assistance provided in the early 1990s by Hassan al Turabi to ten or so radical groups in Eritrea, Uganda, and Somalia.

In February 1988, Abul Bara Salman, deputy commander of the Eritrean Islamic Jihad Movement (Jamaat al-Jihad Eritrea) stated that "the Islamist strategy in the Horn of Africa is based on several factors: jihad and preaching; educating Muslims about Christian plots . . . the resolve of Arab countries in the face of the Jewish threat; the efforts made in the context of jihad in Palestine."

The most powerful militant group in the region was probably still Al-Ittihad al-Islamiya, which had provided considerable support in connection with the August 7, 1998, U.S. embassy bombings. It is likely that the group is the author of a communiqué issued on August 19, 1988—supposedly on behalf of the apocryphal Islamic Army for the Liberation of the People of Kenya—claiming responsibility for the Dar es Salaam bombing, specifying that "the fight against the United States and its allies, the Jewish people of Israel, is a fight to the death. Before the Nairobi attack, we warned Muslims to avoid any location where there were Americans. . . . We are waging jihad everywhere and at all times." The Somali group was also involved in the two-pronged Mombasa attack of November 28, 2002.

In the late 1990s, threats had emerged in South Africa in connection with the radicalization of an Islamist group known as People Against Gangsterism and Drugs (PAGAD). However, PAGAD is believed to have been neutralized following the bombing of the Planet Hollywood restaurant in Cape Town in 1998.

The situation had become more worrisome in Nigeria since the twelve northern provinces, with a mostly Muslim population, voted for the application of sharia despite opposition from the federal government. Several thousand Christians were killed during the rioting as the international community looked on with indifference. Two Salafist centers—in Kano and Katsina—were located in that area. They both played an active part in arms trafficking in the sub-Saharan region, in support of Algerian militant groups. Nigerian Islamists had close ties—based on the call to jihad as well as on smuggling activities—with a number of groups that were flourishing in the Chad-to-Mauritania geographic crescent. It is worth noting that the Algerian GSPC carried out two operations in that region and that the aborted January 2001 attack against the Paris-Dakar-Cairo rally, as well as the March 2003 hostage incident involving thirty or so European tourists, also took place there.

Southeast Asia. The first signs of al Qaeda's presence in Southeast Asia appeared in 1995, following the arrest of Ramzi Yussef in Manila. At that time, Muhammad Jamal Khalifa, a Saudi national, had set up a financial holding company for al Qaeda in the Philippines, so as to finance the activities of local Islamist groups and forge ties with the mujahideen movement. But Khalifa was not just an average Saudi businessman; he was a veteran of the anti-Soviet jihad and Osama bin Laden's brother-in-law.

In the 1990s, Southeast Asia was a convenient rear base for al Qaeda, which operated from its Afghan fortress. It was a safe area where new volunteers could be recruited, funds raised, fatwas obtained, and forged documents as well as technology procured. The presence in the area of many tourists—particularly Middle Easterners—as well as ineffective security systems, undermined by corruption and excessive bureaucracy, made it an ideal place for a brief, or longer, stay, because they could go about their business unnoticed.

For al Qaeda, Southeast Asia was also a fallback zone. As early as 1997, the organization knew that its strategy of secretiveness—to threaten, strike, and praise but claim no responsibility—was not viable in the long term, and it planned to withdraw to Southeast Asia when the Taliban regime fell. In order to do so, alliances were required, and Asian mujahideen trained in Afghan camps heading back to their respective homelands were given messages for the leaders of their local groups, some of whom were veterans of the anti-Soviet jihad. Camps specializing in explosives training were needed, so al Qaeda sent instructors with particular skills in the area of the building and use of homemade bombs.

As routes to Afghanistan, Pakistan, and Iran were under close surveillance, some of the new recruits were sent for training to Moro Islamic Liberation Front (MILF) camps in the Philippines. One of those recruits, a Frenchman by the name of Claude Sheikh Boulanouar, was arrested in December 1999 at Manila airport as he tried to board a plane with a detonator fuse hidden in his backpack. The first attack in the Philippines by mujahideen was committed in 1997 on the island of Mindanao by two Arab mujahideen sent by al Qaeda to serve as MILF instructors.

Militant Islamism in Southeast Asia has its roots in a clandestine Muslim organization—the Darul Islam (Islamic Unity)—that emerged in Indonesia following World War II. Its primary goal was to secure independence from its colonizers, but it also aimed to create a republic founded on Islam—present in the region since the fourteenth century—that would encompass the Muslim peoples of the region: Indonesia, Malaysia, southern Thailand (the Pattani region), and the southern Philippines (the Mindanao archipelago). Such a state was to be ruled by sharia law and would unite the local *umma* (community of believers), but Darul Islam did not at the time aim to conquer non-Muslims.

Two of its leaders, Indonesians by the name of Abdallah Sungkar and Abu Bakar Bashir—both wanted in their homeland for subversive activities—took refuge in Malaysia in 1985. There they founded an Islamist movement similar to Wahabism, which advocated jihad and evolved into Darul Islam. Their goal to was to agglomerate the various local conflicts pitting Muslims against Christians or the central authorities

In the mid 1990s, several dozen of their followers—mostly Indonesians and Malaysians—headed to the Afghan-Pakistani zone to train in militant Islamism. They managed, if not to actually surpass their instructors, to persuade them to give their stamp of approval to a new dynamic similar to that of the Afghanistan-based mujahideen network, whose ideological bases were located, once again, in Pakistan and in Saudi Arabia.

When he returned to Indonesia in 1999, Abu Bakar Bashir became the undisputed leader of the new Jamaa Islamiya (JI) (Islamic Group), a clandestine transregional organization whose goal was to impose Darul Islam through jihad. At the same time, he founded, quite openly, the Indonesian Mujahideen Movement (MMI), an organization of fundamentalist activists that served as an inspiration for the activities of religious militias and as a JI recruiting ground.

Bashir, though a declared Salafist and despite his incendiary sermons preaching jihad and his sympathy for bin Laden, was more of an ideologue than a fighter. For that reason, he charged his follower of fifteen years, Riduan Isamuddin, aka Hambali—a member of the JI's Majlis al-Shura—with the task of building up the military branch of the organization.

The branch quickly zeroed in on three *mantiqis* (zones of action). The first included Singapore, Malaysia, and southern Thailand—an area of wealth sure to benefit a future Islamic state. The JI had been founded there, and the armed branch's secret headquarters were there as well. The second zone, given the long-standing presence of MILF structures, was used for training. The third, Indonesia, was to be the battleground.

Indonesia, however, was not prepared to act alone. Muslim guerrillas were focusing primarily on local conflicts—in Aceh, Molucca, and Celebes. Hambali, during several clandestine meetings held in Indonesia and Thailand, endeavored to standardize combat practices at the transregional level. Filipino militants affiliated with the MILF or with Abu Sayyaf; Malaysians belonging to the Kampulan Mujahidin Malaysia (KMM) (Malaysian Mujahideen Movement); Indonesian guerrillas from Celebes, Molucca, and Java; Burmese members of the Rohingya Front; and ethnic Pattani Thai nationals participated in the creation of a coordinating body, the Rabitatul Mujahidin (Mujahideen League), along with, in all likelihood, representatives of the Afghan-Pakistani movement.

The first attacks planned in Indonesia (against priests and president-to-be Suhartoputri) came to naught. Amrozi, an Indonesian national who would later be involved in planning the three-pronged attack in Bali, was one of the protagonists. Malaysian mujahideen members of the KMM then launched a series of holdups and attacks against military posts to procure the necessary funds and explosives for future attacks. They also assassinated a state assemblyman, Joe Fernandez, deemed too close to Christian circles.

The jihad waged by the JI thus began in Indonesia. On December 24, 2000, approximately sixty bombs exploded in Christian churches throughout Java, killing forty civilians, including priests. On August 16, 2001, a car bomb went off in Jakarta, wounding the Philippine ambassador and killing four of his aides. No one claimed responsibility for either attack, in a strategic move reminiscent of al Qaeda's modus operandi.

However, the Asian mujahideen movement was not as experienced as al Qaeda. In late 2000, the capture in Malaysia of Abu Jibril, an Indonesian who was one of JI's leaders, led to the identification of Hambali, who was running *mantiqi* 1 directly from Kuala Lumpur. He fled to Pakistan in January 2001, where he was given new instructions, presumably by Khalid Sheikh Muhammad.

Hambali had been the mastermind of the Bali attacks. Indeed, Bali was a perfect "soft target," because the island, with its mainly Hindu population, was a popular tourist destination for Westerners and for many nationals of Australia—Indonesian fundamentalists' bête noire since Timor-Leste's independence.

The three-pronged attack was a complete operational success. Although only a third of the 1,100 kilograms of homemade explosives contained in the car bomb detonated in front of the Sari Club, everything within a 100-meter radius was destroyed. The first bomb had gone off a few minutes earlier in Paddy's Bar, 300 meters away, and people had gathered in the area where the second explosion was to take place. The final death toll was 202, including 88 Australians. The third attack, which caused only material damage near the U.S. consulate, presumably was the operation's anti-American facet.

Evidence soon surfaced of a double suicide bombing and of cell-phone detonation—a technique taught in the camps of Afghanistan—that pointed to a local group with ties to al Qaeda.

It took a few weeks to break up the network, and in the process the JI's regional dimensions became apparent. There could be no doubt that for al Qaeda Southeast Asia had become a key strategic zone. The possibility of getting some of Asia's 300 million Muslims to engage in armed protests was especially appealing to the organization since throughout the areas where jihad had traditionally been waged operational cells were being dismantled and high-level chiefs arrested.

In hindsight, the Jakarta attack of August 5, 2003, was a failure. The suicide bomber was unable to get past security checkpoints and blew himself up too far away from the Marriott Hotel to do any damage. Of the twelve people killed, ten were Indonesian Muslims, which deprived the bomber of the status of *shahid* (martyr).

However, the regional organization for the first time claimed responsibility—a striking similarity with al Qaeda's strategy in the wake of September 11. The goal was probably to ensure a harsh sentence for Abu Bakar Bashir, set to go on trial August 10 for his role in the Indonesian bombings of 2000, which would anger Asian fundamentalists. But the Indonesian justice system responded in a measured and pragmatic way. The aging ideologue was sentenced only to four years in prison for his intellectual responsibility for JI's strategy of violence. For followers of the mujahideen movement, the warning was clear; the Indonesian people as a whole rejected the violence advocated by the organization and its official entities.

On August 11, President Bush's announcement that Hambali had been arrested in Thailand was a major setback for the jihadist strategy in Southeast Asia. His capture was the result of a series of operations that took down a logistical group in Cambodia, al-Qur'an (the Holy Book), and an operational group in Thailand, the Jamaa Salafiya (Salafist Group), which had been planning local attacks against five embassies and three tourist sites.

In early September 2003, the organization's treasurer, Tawfik Rafke, was arrested. As a result, authorities were able to foil another plot and to identify a number of the group's members on the run from Indonesia.

However, in Southeast Asia the threat remains very real, with Indonesia and the Philippines as the weak link security-wise. Thailand, formerly a safe haven for clandestine groups, has taken decisive steps in the anti-terrorist struggle, given that its drawing power as a tourist attraction makes it a potential future target. Malaysia and Singapore, well protected within their borders, are concerned about threats to their external interests. Ultimately, Cambodia and Burma, and even Vietnam and Laos, all of which feature important sites which Westerners visit—look to be the new safe havens for jihadists on the run.

NOTE TO CHAPTER 13

1. See www.pbs.org/newshour/terrorism/international/fatwa_1996.html (accessed April 12, 2006).

CHAPTER 14

THE FUTURE OF
THE ISLAMIST MOVEMENT

Philippe Migaux

THE GROWING POWER OF LOCAL
AND INDEPENDENT JIHADIST GROUPS

Military operations in Afghanistan resulted in significant advances in the fight against Islamist terrorism, making it clear that the international community would not tolerate the existence of a jihadist-controlled gray zone. Under Taliban rule, that country—the only territorial expression of the mujahideen vision—served a threefold function for the movement: as training base, headquarters, and safe haven, just as the Lebanese network did for international revolutionary terrorism in the 1980s.

Only Taliban-ruled Afghanistan could have produced such a large contingent of trained Salafist militants. But they are dwindling in number and will in time disappear if they are not replaced by succeeding generations stamped out of the same mold. While their sacrifices did win the movement some new adherents, since 2001 the latter can no longer hope to equal the degree of cohesion or operational stature of senior members.

The five Casablanca bombings of June 2003 showed that local commanders with qualifications limited to a criminal past and a vague knowledge of the Qur'an were perfectly capable—without attracting undue attention from security forces—of recruiting young radicals, training them, and persuading them to carry out suicide attacks. Martyrdom, as the end of a life devoid of hope, was considered a passport to paradise.

In a 1999 propaganda text titled *Reasons for Jihad,* al Qaeda set out eight key reasons for recruiting new volunteers: "The will to end domination by infidels, the need for new mujahideen, fear of the flames of Hell, the desire to do one's duty by responding to God's call, the example of the Prophet's companions, the desire to provide a solid foundation for Islam, protection of the oppressed, and the quest for martyrdom."

Other factors can influence the decision to make that ultimate commitment. Ego is a key issue, because, in a community context, it is possible, through martyrdom, for an outcast to burnish his image or to fashion an entirely new one. Nor is the promise of seventy-two virgins likely to be overlooked in societies where sexual frustration is the norm from childhood on. Other powerful psychological motivators include a thirst for revenge and the desire to provide one's relatives with material or moral recognition by the community.

In point of fact, the Palestinian movement Hamas has for years methodically capitalized on those factors in its long-term approach to selecting and recruiting martyrs. Israel's strategy of selectively eliminating key members of the Palestinian terrorist organization has not succeeded in stemming the flow of volunteers. Indeed, Sheikh Ahmed Yassin had to intervene personally to make conditions for recruitment more stringent—inter alia, limiting women's access to the group.

But can this self-perpetuating model, fueled by a desire for revenge and tied into the historical suffering of the Palestinian people, be shifted over the long term to other Muslim communities? The answer is, probably not, given that Hamas's structures are the only ones truly able to train and supervise recruits—the result of a successful propaganda campaign aimed at a vulnerable population sympathetic to its cause. Martyrs from poor Sunni suburbs certainly provide no example to follow, nor do they end up contributing to their relatives' emotional or material well-being.

Would-be martyrs, in order to act, require only limited training, but constant supervision is required—with brainwashing generally involved. Such behavior is, in a way, the ultimate form of sectarian conditioning. However, if it is to perpetuate its experience, a sect must live on. Surviving members of local Islamist cells—commanders, recruiters, and instructors—are often neutralized in subsequent suppression campaigns. But while the model of suicide-mission volunteers appears to be viable only in the medium term, it remains particularly dangerous in the short term.

NRBC THREATS

The ongoing threat of major terrorist attacks involving nuclear, radio-logical, biological, and chemical (NRBC) weapons has to date been only minimally realized. No plan of that sort has yet succeeded, although it is possible that a few years hence, scientific, technical, and communications advances might enable underground groups to use such techniques.

The basic problem with NRBC terrorism is that of its methods of de-livery. In what form should the toxin be used—liquid, gas, or powder? How should it be transported and diffused? While the mujahideen movement has without a doubt been able to glean a rudimentary level of scientific knowledge from textbooks and from the Internet, it appears that its chemical specialists do not pose any significant threat. Their ex-periments to date have been more along the lines of sinister do-it-yourself projects.

Nothing much needs to be said about a nuclear threat; it is very un-likely that the mujahideen movement will acquire any fissile material. With respect to radiological materials, the case of José Padilla—a former petty criminal of Puerto Rican origin—comes to mind. Al Qaeda had in-structed him to build a "dirty bomb" (a conventional explosive filled with radioactive particles). When Padilla was arrested upon returning to the United States, it was found that he had no real knowledge of the subject.

Various mujahideen leaders carried out research projects in Af-ghanistan on the use of biological weapons, notably Abu Musab al-Zarqawi, a Jordanian and a former commander of the Herat camp, and Egypt's Abu Khabbab, who had run the Derunta training camp and whose tapes of animal experiments were found by U.S. special forces. Members of the Chechen network did have an operational project in the works in the United Kingdom involving the use of ricin (a poison derived from castor beans), which they had managed to produce, but they were arrested in January 2003. Their stock of ricin was never found, but the makeshift nature of the laboratory indicated that only minimal amounts of it had been produced. There is no antidote to the poison, which kills through suffocation. The group's plan had been to coat doorknobs with ricin to contaminate the skin, but specialists have opined that no fatali-ties would have resulted.

A more serious incident occurred involving chemical weapons. The French subgroup of the "Chechnya network," which was dismantled in December 2002 near Paris, had a more elaborate plan, whose targets were probably Russian interests in France. The group had everything it needed to build a sophisticated explosive device filled with cyanide, which an explosion would then diffuse—assuming that the chemical was not destroyed in the explosion, as had happened in the first attack on the World Trade Center, in 1993. While it is possible that the powder could have been inhaled by the explosion's survivors or by emergency-response teams, it is difficult to ascertain whether its effects would have been deadly in a well-ventilated area. It is undeniable, however, that broadcasting images of infected people coughing in the midst of the rubble would have had a powerful effect on public opinion.

The NRBC threat is primarily a psychological one. As most people do not generally know much about the topic, the result is a vague, irrational feeling of terror. That is why the media pounced on the issue—often, it must be noted, quite irresponsibly—immediately following September 11. Far from serving any educational purpose, they managed only to terrify people needlessly, especially since the main threat at the time—envelopes were being sent within the United States containing powdered anthrax—was, in the end, never linked to the mujahideen movement. The Western media did, however, succeed in giving the movement's most extreme elements some excellent food for thought.

These two examples testify to the difficulties involved in a terrorist group's carrying out a chemical operation. Of the eleven people killed by sarin gas during the 1995 attack in the Tokyo subway, several were members of the Aum sect that carried out the attack. Paradoxically, the only recent example of a chemical attack by a terrorist group is the Moscow theater incident, in which the hundred or so hostages taken were gassed by authorities indiscriminately along with the Chechen terrorists.

Let us use common sense here. While an NRBC attack would certainly qualify as one of the spectacular acts of terrorism advocated by al-Zarqawi, the execution of such an attack is fraught with difficulties related to the use of the substances involved. Makeshift explosive devices are much easier to assemble and to use. Following September 11, American intelligence services feared that nuclear plants would be struck. However, the successful operations carried out by the movement since that date, far from targeting secure sites, have focused on more ordinary places—public or living spaces that are relatively easy to access.

MARITIME TERRORISM

Prior to the twenty-first century, maritime terrorism was infrequent. Its principal manifestation was the September 1984 hijacking of the *Achille*

Lauro by Palestinians belonging to Fatah's Force 17. Their modus operandi (the terrorists blended in with other tourists on the cruise liner, Jewish and Israeli passengers were targeted, demands were made for negotiations with the Israeli authorities, media coverage was sought) made it clear that this sudden innovation was but the transposition into a maritime environment of the more common practice of aircraft hijacking, which had brought Palestinian militants to the attention of international public opinion. The incident's unsuccessful outcome—an elderly, disabled American Jew was murdered, and the perpetrators were captured by American forces, although they were subsequently quietly freed by the Italian authorities—dissuaded terrorists from resorting to such complicated methods.

Also, in 1988, the Abu Nidal group claimed responsibility for the bombing of a Greek day-excursion ship—the *City of Poros*—that killed nine passengers.

Like piracy, maritime terrorism requires specific skills. It is especially important that the perpetrators be trained seamen able to carry out basic operations such as boarding, taking over, and even sailing a ship. However, terrorist groups active during the period 1970 to 1990 had all-landsman memberships.

The threat took on a new dimension with the emergence of the Liberation Tigers of Tamil Eelam (LTTE), who carried out a brilliantly planned operation on October 23, 2000. Four armored rebel boats packed with explosives managed to enter the Trincomalee naval facility at night, destroying one Sri Lankan ship and damaging another. Twenty-four people were killed in the attack, including the operatives. During that same period, the Palestinian Hamas, aiming to enhance its operational credibility, carried out a similar operation, whose outcome was less successful. On November 7, a boat piloted by a suicide bomber exploded prematurely off the coast of Israel before reaching its target.

In February, the Moro Islamic Liberation Front, which few suspected at the time of having ties to al Qaeda, carried out a bomb attack against the vessel *Our Lady Mediatrix* off the coast of the Philippines, killing forty crew members and putting it out of commission.

None of those events received much press at the time, as terrorism had not yet mutated into a global phenomenon. Furthermore, international attention had been focused on the suicide bombing in October 2000 of the USS *Cole* in the port of Aden. But the consequences of the attack— seventeen dead, forty wounded, and the ship disabled—had attracted more attention than the innovative character of the operation. The bombers were members of the Islamic Army of Aden-Abyan, a Yemeni mujahideen group with close ties to al Qaeda.

Acts of maritime terrorism are fully in line with the concept of global war envisaged in *Knights under the Prophet's Banner*. The idea is that surprise attacks against ships or ports have major psychological and economic repercussions. As ports are key links in the global economy, a strike against the maritime sector would trigger a chain reaction in many industrial and service sectors.

A jihadist training manual, the *Mujahidin ki lalkaar* (War Cry of the Holy Warriors), devotes a chapter to attacks by boat: "A warship can be immobilized if 1.2 kilograms of explosives are attached to the driveshaft; an additional 1.3 kilograms will destroy the engine . . . 4 kilograms near the bottom of the hull will sink it."

The bombing of the USS *Cole* was not the group's first such attempt. In May 1998, following a three-day visit by an American ship, the USS *Mount Vernon,* to the port of Aden, the Islamic Army of Aden-Abyan began to hatch a plan. Their first attempt, on January 3, 2000, failed, as the would-be suicide craft, overloaded with explosives, sank in a few minutes.

Following October 12, other attacks were planned but failed for reasons ranging from bad luck and poor preparation on the part of the mujahideen to the effective action by security forces.

In Asia, the KMM—closely linked to Jamaa Islamiya (JI), whose members included veterans of the Afghanistan war—had since 2000 been mulling an assault against an American vessel during its stopover in a Malaysian port. The JI's Singapore cell had since that same date been planning successive operations against U.S. navy and naval facilities in Singapore.

In June 2002, Moroccan intelligence services arrested three Saudi nationals who had been planning suicide attacks, using small explosive-laden crafts, against American or British warships off Gibraltar.

On October 6, 2002, the Islamic Army of Aden-Abyan launched a small explosive-packed boat in an attack against the *Limbourg,* a French oil tanker. The operation was badly planned: only one sailor was killed; the ship did not sink; and two successive claims of responsibility were made, followed by the admission that the suicide bombers had missed their principal target, an American warship moored nearby. It is worth noting, however, the disproprortionate reaction to the operation, which triggered a panic in the stock market and deep concern within oil circles.

For all these reasons, the threat of maritime terrorism by al Qaeda should be taken very seriously, as the organization has loyal allies with well-established seamanship skills in Southeast Asia and in the Gulf of Aden—both major piracy zones. It is worth recalling here the broad media coverage received by the June 2000 Jolo hostage incident, which thrust the Abu Sayyaf jihadist group into prominence.

On September 11, 2001, airliners were turned into air-to-ground missiles with the capacity for mass destruction. It follows that particular care must be taken to protect ships, which terrorists could also use to achieve their goals. Furthermore, the short-term damage caused to the target itself (a ship or a port) could be compounded in the long term by destructive consequences for the environment.

Today the danger that small craft can pose is better understood. Able to travel close to the water's surface, they can duck under surface radar. In choppy seas, they cannot be seen at a distance. And, finally, they can move around easily and dodge fire from a vessel's weapons. In recent years, attacks by the LTTE have shown that, given the speeds that can be reached by small boats and how hard they are to spot, such vessels, when packed with explosives and piloted by trained crews, can become suicide torpedoes that are almost impossible to stop.

There is another danger associated with high-tonnage ships. Because of their size and weight, they can be difficult to stop, even if vital parts are hit by precision strikes. Turning and stopping are maneuvers that take several nautical miles to complete.

A hijacked ship's cargo, crew, or passengers can also represent substantive negotiating capital. The latter can also be used as an effective human shield and as a decoy if a ship is seized as the prelude to a suicide operation. Indeed, it is not so easy to intercept or sink a vessel heading full steam toward a port if hostages can be seen on deck.

THE QUEST FOR AN ALLIANCE WITH PALESTINIAN ISLAMISM

The hatred that Palestinian and Israeli extremists have for one another is fueled in many ways by the recollection of the sacrifices made by their ancestors. Palestinian Islamists, influenced by the Shiite Hezbollah, remember the death of Hussein in 669/47 during the battle of Karbala. Surrounded and outnumbered, he refused to surrender and was decapitated along with seventy-two relatives and companions. Zionists, for their part, have for centuries kept alive the memory of what happened at Masada—a fortified city where the last of the Zealots and their families, under siege by a Roman legion, chose to commit suicide rather than surrender.

The Islamic Resistance Movement (Harakat al-Muqawama al-Islamiya)—its Arabic acronym, Hamas, means "courage"—is an off-shoot of the Palestinian branch of the Muslim Brotherhood, which in the mid 1980s controlled the university and most of the mosques in Gaza through its social programs.

Hamas was founded by Sheikh Ahmed Yassin during the first intifada. Yassin stressed, in his sermons, that "when all doors close, God's doors open." The Israeli authorities turned a blind eye to the group's growing power, as they hoped to weaken the PLO and the militant structures of Force 17—Fatah's armed branch—and of the Popular Front for the Liberation of Palestine, which, despite the elimination of Abu Jihad, remained operational.

Its denunciation of corrupt PLO authorities, the social assistance provided by religious organizations and its fervent religious message soon made Hamas the major political force in Gaza. During the intifada, with stone-throwers dying in increasing numbers, Palestinian nationalism and radical Islamism came together. In 1990, with the stated goal of "launching the attack, working toward the destruction of the state of Israel, competing with the PLO on its own territory, and working towards the victory of Islam," Hamas formed a military branch named after one of the first Palestinian Islamist martyrs, Izz al-Din al-Qassim, who had been killed in 1935 while fighting Jewish settlers.

One of the tasks of Hamas's military branch was to hunt down Israeli spies. Sheikh Yassin was sentenced to life in prison for having ordered the execution of four Palestinians suspected of being informers. However, in 1997, as a consequence of a failed Mossad operation—the attempted assassination of a Hamas leader in Jordan—Israel was forced to free Yassin. One of his first acts was to call for Islamic resistance in Palestine, declaring: "The only solution to the question of Palestine is jihad,"

The campaign of suicide bombings began even before the second intifada of June 2000. Its slogan was: "Israel's planes can bomb us, but we will strike Israel even harder with our human bombs." Israeli soldiers patrolling Gaza began seeing a new graffito on the walls: "Occupation kills." From the very beginning of the second intifada, Hamas developed a new strategy of alliance with the other Islamist group involved in the Palestinian struggle, Islamic Jihad. That smaller organization, with support in Syria and Iran, adopted a strategy of terror similar to that used by Hezbollah. Some of its recruits were Israeli Arabs, and it engaged in simultaneous suicide attacks.

However, up until September 11, Palestinian jihad had been waged independently of the mujahideen movement. As it recruited locally and trained militants and suicide bombers at a fast pace, there was no need for the Afghan camps, and the children of the intifada were not at the time overly concerned with jihad in Afghanistan. In June 2000, Israeli security services arrested two Palestinians, veterans of the Afghanistan war, whom they suspected of planning a suicide attack for Hamas. One of them, Hindawi, was the son of the chief of the Palestinian police in Hebron. He had been recruited in Lebanon in 1998 by mujahideen from a local group called Osbat al-Ansar (The League of Partisans) and had gone for training a few months later to Afghanistan's Khalden camp.

The news of the attacks against the United States gave rise to great jubilation in the Palestinian territories, prompting President Arafat—in full view of the international media—to rush to donate blood to help American victims. Indeed, a strike against Israel's ally could not but give joy to Palestinian extremists. Al Qaeda has since consistently reaffirmed its support for the anti-Zionist movement in order to find fresh recruits among those sympathetic to the Palestinian cause.

Al Qaeda's claim of responsibility for the Jerba attack, which targeted a synagogue rather than an infidel government, was evidence that the organization had made an informed decision to diversify its targets. Let us recall that Richard Calvin Reid, the "shoe bomber," who on December 22, 2001, attempted to blow up an airliner traveling from Paris to Miami, had the previous summer been sent to Israel and Egypt to scout out locations for later attacks. In that context, it seems clear that the mujahideen movement had, as early as 2002, set itself the new objective of exploiting among Muslim peoples the anti-American sentiment stemming from the threat of war against Iraq and support for the policies of Israel's Likud.

In Mombasa, Kenya, on November 28, a suicide car bomb ripped through a hotel where Israeli tourists were staying. Fifteen people were killed, including the three bombers and three Israelis. At around the same time, two missiles narrowly missed an El Al aircraft that had just taken off from the local airport. Responsibility for the attack was claimed by an unknown group, the Army of Palestine, but this was presumably the first time that al Qaeda had openly targeted Israelis. The two Russian-made surface-to-air missiles came from the same batch used in May 2002 in a failed attempt to down an American warplane in Saudi Arabia—an attack already attributed to al Qaeda.

The four Casablanca bombings that took place on June 9, 2004, were aimed at the Sephardic community, with the goal of putting an end to its long-standing coexistence with the Moroccan population. The same motive was behind the November 15 attacks in Istanbul against two synagogues, for which al Qaeda and a small local Islamist group, the Great Eastern Islamic Raiders' Front, immediately claimed responsibility.

It is worth noting that, in March 2003, two young British citizens of Pakistani origin went to Israel to carry out a suicide attack against a Tel Aviv snack-bar, for which Hamas immediately claimed responsibility. Two years earlier, the two martyrs would probably have passed through Afghan camps and joined the jihad movement in Kashmir. It was obvious that new ties had been forged between supporters of the mujahideen movement and supporters of the Palestinian intifada, on the basis of their instinctive sense of belonging to the same militant *umma*. Hamas has always focused on attacking Israel, and its support cells, which exist worldwide—including in the United States—had theretofore limited themselves to propaganda and fund-raising activities. But, clearly, one of them had begun to branch out into recruitment.

THE THREAT OF AN ALLIANCE WITH SHIITE RADICALISM

It should not be overlooked that in the early 1980s, France—at the time regarded as the "Little Satan"—was the preferred target of jihadist Shiism. Since the start of civil war in Lebanon, France, based on its historical ties with that country, had sought to position itself as a protagonist to be reckoned with. Its diplomatic activities were buttressed by the presence of a French detachment, under the aegis of the United Nations, in the southern part of the territory. The arrival of Syrian forces—under the guise of the Arab Dissuasion Force—was of concern to France, which feared that annexation, pure and simple, was the goal of Hafez al-Assad's regime, which wanted to extend its reign to all of the territory formerly under the French Protectorate. It was in that problematic context that the French ambassador to Lebanon was assassinated on September 4, 1981.

However, some were of the opinion even then that the assassination could not have been carried out without, at the minimum, the tacit approval of the Iranian intelligence services, which had recently reached an agreement with their Syrian counterparts. The Amal militia was a tool of the Syrian authorities, and the Iranians were training Hezbollah fighters on the Bekaa plain.

Iran was looking to become an influential player in war-ravaged Lebanon. Indeed, the disproportionate press coverage accorded the kidnapping of a dean of the American University of Beirut led Hezbollah to make greater use of that particular brand of terrorism. Acting under assumed names such as Islamic Jihad and the Revolutionary Justice Organization, Lebanese jihadists, over a six-year period, kidnapped, or arranged for the kidnapping of, a number of Western nationals, including three French citizens. One of them, a sociologist by the name of Michel Seurat, died in captivity.

In parallel with that publicity-seeking form of terrorism—requiring only limited resources but resulting in the kind of media coverage that thrilled Shiite refugees from west Beirut's working-class districts—Hezbollah moved forward with a more offensive strategy. Following the Sabra and Shatila massacres, which were committed by Lebanese Phalangists, four Western powers sent troops to restore peace in Beirut. Shiite militants now had Western military forces, as well as Israeli soldiers, in their sights. On October 23, 1983, at dawn, two explosions shook Beirut. Fifty-eight French paratroopers and 241 U.S. Marines were killed, and the Americans left soon after. The West had lost face.

Two years later, Iranian services took the fight onto French soil. Between December 1, 1985 (the Galeries Lafayette department store), and September 17, 1986 (the Tati department store on the rue de Rennes), the Committee of Solidarity with Arab and Middle East Political Prisoners (CSPPA) carried out fifteen bombings, killing thirteen people. The French segment of the network—consisting of a handful of North Africans led by a Tunisian convert, Fouad Ali Saleh—was neutralized on March 21, 1987.

During his exile in the Sudan, Osama bin Laden—setting aside age-old enmities toward the Shiites in order to fight the common enemy of Muslims—allegedly forged close ties with the Lebanese Hezbollah and, following the failed attack against the World Trade Center, sent al Qaeda instructors to a Lebanese Hezbollah camp to study bombing techniques.

According to statements made by ʿAli Muhammad, an Egyptian member of al Qaeda who was tried in New York in 2000, bin Laden met several times with the supposed mastermind of the two Beirut attacks of October 23, 1983, Imad Mughniyah. Mughniyah, a Palestinian and former Fatah leader, was now in charge of Hezbollah's operations, under the direct authority of Sheikh Fadlallah. Al Qaeda supposedly got the idea of suicide truck bombings from him.

Al Qaeda's good relations with influential members of the Iranian jihadist movement—made easier by Hassan al-Turabi's intermediary services—had to be kept under wraps. Bin Laden had not thought twice about going directly to the Taliban council of elders to ask for an end to the fratricidal attacks against Afghan Shiites. In late 1999, he had major construction work done on the Afghan-Iranian border, further endearing himself to the extremist-dominated Iranian regime.

It is for that reason that some high-placed al Qaeda members were able to take refuge in Iran during the most intensive phases of American operations in Afghanistan. Bin Laden could also rely on his old comrade-in-arms, Gulbuddin Hekmatyar, who had been living in Iran since fleeing Kabul. While the Iranian authorities have consistently denied having any ties to bin Laden, it is clear that influential members of radical circles, setting aside their schismatic disputes, provided—for reasons ranging from ecumenical solidarity and hatred of the Western enemy to sheer venality—discreet but very real assistance to al Qaeda in its repositioning.

The media reported mass arrests of mujahideen militants in Iran by the Iranian security services, which were concerned about the possibility of American retaliation. On June 30, 2003, it was announced that key operatives had been captured in Iran, including Ayman al-Zawahiri; Abu Ali Gaith, a Saudi and the organization's spokesman; and Saad, Osama bin Laden's eldest son. Iran denied everything.

In that context, the tragic turn that the situation has taken in postwar Iraq is even more alarming. The American authorities—having dodged responsibility for the massacres committed against the Shiite community towards the end of the first Gulf War—were not in 2003 expecting hostility on its part, nor had they anticipated its capacity to restructure itself so quickly around fundamentalist clergy. In the end, misleading claims of collusion between al Qaeda and the Iraqi authorities, cleverly woven in with the supposed threat of Iraqi weapons of mass destruction, backfired on those who made them. In February 2003, bin Laden appealed for support for Iraqi Muslims.

It appears that his message has been received loud and clear. Since the fighting ended, a large number of mujahideen have apparently joined up with surviving members of al-Ansar al-Islam. Many observers believe that the high-profile suicide attacks committed against Western interests, such as the destruction of the UN headquarters in Baghdad in August

2003 and the bombing of Italian police headquarters on November 7, were the work of the mujahideen movement. Such observers believe also that there is a strong possibility that an alliance might be forged with Shiite radicals aiming to create an Islamic republic of Iraq.

CONCLUSION

The mujahideen movement continues to pose a serious short-term threat. Its leaders have survived, and its sleeper cells, composed of effective and determined veterans of the Afghanistan war, are scattered throughout the world. Most of the armed operations perpetrated since September 11 have followed the usual pattern, targeting, by various methods, sites that are relatively easy to scout out. However, the attacks committed since 2003 have clearly shown the capacity of jihadist networks to strike at any time at al Qaeda's behest—whether in coordination with it or following its example—at carefully chosen targets in the enemy's strategic centers, in an ongoing endeavor to develop new operational methods.

The backdrop to this growing threat is favorable to al Qaeda: a political solution to the Israeli-Palestinian conflict is still lacking; American forces are bogged down in Afghanistan and in Iraq; and terror alerts are frequent occurrences in Western countries. For the mujahideen movement, all of this spells success. By depicting—albeit prematurely—the American fight against terrorism as a failure, the mujahideen hope to find new supporters within anti-imperialist movements or among champions of the Palestinian cause.

Given the dissolution of the Afghan network and the fact that its structures are scattered far and wide; the difficulties involved in keeping communications secure; and the large-scale international investigations under way, it is possible that the mujahideen movement might disintegrate in the medium term. By committing the September 11, 2001, attacks, it definitively broke with the international community. But the threat posed by jihadist Islam must be viewed from a long-term perspective. Al Qaeda's long-standing hope is to see a mass radical Islamist movement, supported by armed groups, succeed the radical Islamism of the mujahideen.

Let us recall here that, while Islam is an integral component of the contemporary world, radical Islamism is one of the principal current manifestations of the eternal revolt of the excluded—both the marginalized and those who are outcasts by choice—against the well-off. In that sense, militant Salafists are truly the heirs of the anti-imperialist struggle.

The threat looms largest over Islam: the majority of Muslims wish only to practice a "religion of tolerance." The struggle against the mujahideen movement will succeed only if there is close and respectful cooperation by governments with Islamic countries. It is important, in that context, to stop lumping jihadist groups in with moderate Islamic parties.

While we must accept political Islamism, radical Islamism must be defeated. There is no place for naïve optimism in the new world order. The principles that guide the Muslim *umma* must gradually be integrated into the international legal system, which must be characterized by respect for human rights and pluralist democracy. While dialogue is necessary with political Islam, whose influence is important in certain parts of the world, there can be no negotiating with activist Islamism. It is a matter of common sense and of legitimate self-defense. Islamic terrorism must be fought with the full panoply of resources available to a state based on the rule of law. The best way to overcome terrorism is to confront it. The next step is to prevent it from recurring. Thus Islamic peoples must be ensured a future that is free from poverty, illiteracy, and corruption—always fertile breeding grounds for terrorist groups.

CHAPTER 15

SUICIDE OPERATIONS:
BETWEEN WAR AND TERRORISM

François Géré

Homicidal self-sacrifice is when human beings intentionally kill themselves in the process of killing other human beings. It occurs in two contexts: in declared, open war in which regular combatants target other soldiers—their uniformed enemies—and equipment and installations bearing flags, insignia, or other identifying markings; and in undeclared conflicts, which can also be civil, ethnic, or religious in nature. Suicide attackers are indistinguishable from the rest of the populace and are capable of indiscriminately striking military targets or civilian populations and sites.

With that simple distinction, we can differentiate between wartime suicide operations, such as the Japanese kamikaze attacks of World War II, and terrorist suicide operations, such as those carried out on behalf of al Qaeda and certain Palestinian Islamist organizations.

There are overlaps, of course, and, as we shall see, ambiguities remain. But these criteria provide an effective way of drawing distinctions that can be useful for formulating, preparing and implementing strategies to block and defeat the use of homicidal self-sacrifice as a weapon.

WHAT ARE SUICIDE VOLUNTEERS?

The Incidence of Suicide Operations

On the cusp of the new millennium, suicide attacks stamped a new, grimly stunning mark on world conflicts. That is why so many references were made to the apocalypse. The collapse of New York's twin towers was an effective metaphor that etched our collective memory. But it took neither 9/11 nor indeed the final decades of the twentieth century in Palestine for suicide attacks to become a strategic weapon in our planet's wars.

It is true that in a very short period following the summer of 2000, the phenomenon saw unprecedented acceleration: Israel, Palestine, and a detour to Manhattan and Washington; then Russia, Chechnya, Iraq, Saudi Arabia, and Pakistan, where 2003 ended with the foiling of two suicide attacks against the head of state, General Pervez Musharraf. The infection spread through the world along a line of crises stretching from Bosnia to Kashmir, with tangents into the Persian Gulf and the Red Sea. Of course, these did not all involve the same people or the same goals, but the procedure was identical: human beings transforming themselves into weapons in order to kill other human beings.

Suicide attacks are a transhistorical, transnational, and transcultural phenomenon, spanning time and place. This is a constant phenomenon, though not a regular one: it appears in one place, then disappears; then it reemerges somewhere else and for other reasons. These attacks are inherently spectacular, and this is greatly magnified in the media. They are often presented as terrorism, although some consider them to be a weapon of war. Once again, it is important to agree on the terms under dispute.

Definitions

It is no accident that we have a meager ability to describe this phenomenon. It is beyond the ordinary imagination; language fails us. We generally use the word "kamikaze," since it describes the one spectacularly famous class of suicide operations. The 9/11 attacks bolstered that association because they used airplanes as delivery vehicles. The Japanese government was quick to protest—in vain—the use of a metaphor that raised the issue of the difference between war and terrorism. But the analogy arose more from a void in our thinking than from any real analysis. In the same way, we randomly see expressions such as "suicide bombing," *bombes humaines, Lebenbombe,* and "suicide terrorism."

Raphael Israeli, a knowledgeable specialist on terrorism, recently coined the term "Islamikaze." He justifies the coinage in this way: "Islamic suicide attackers are not suicides . . . they are similar to kamikaze pilots in their motivation, organization, and ideology and in the way they perform their task." It is true that this form of suicide is altruistic and is carried out in the service of a cause viewed as infinitely more important than an individual human life. But the comparison ends there: when they struck American warships, the Japanese pilots were waging war. They were engaging in a warrior's self-sacrifice in the tradition of seppuku—which in turn is rooted in a soldierly code of honor whose purpose is to prevent the enemy from enjoying the glory of victory.

I have decided to use the term "suicide volunteers" for these practitioners of self-sacrifice/homicide. That is because of a historical reference that rounds out the philosophical approach.

I refer here to the Indochina war of 1946–54, when French soldiers used the term *volontaires de la mort* to describe individuals who caused deaths by pedaling their rickshaws in front of a police station or into an outdoor café, or especially to describe columns of attackers who broke through barbed wire and burst into fortified positions to hurl their mines.

In the philosophy of action, will is defined as the tension of the mind toward the attainment of a goal. A volunteer (the word comes from the Latin *voluntas* = "will") is someone who, having understood and internalized the value of that goal, chooses the path of action. Leaving contemplation behind, the volunteer embarks on an effort to change a situation.

The notion of suicide-homicide perfectly describes the nature of the act: to kill oneself while bringing death to adversaries, with a view to causing a favorable change in the relationship among material and moral forces within a conflict.

THE EVOLUTION OF THIS "WEAPONS SYSTEM"

While self-sacrifice/homicide has been pervasive both in time and in space, there have been periods, sometimes lengthy ones, during which it has lain dormant. There are also geographical seas of tranquility that have not experienced it. There is little doubt that there have been distinct stages in the development of this form of strategic action. The first coincided with the introduction of modern chemical explosives, principally dynamite and its derivatives, which, because of the size of the devices, could be secretly carried by human beings. Did such explosives change attitudes? Absolutely not: rather, they made killing oneself a certainty.

Previously, one had to consign oneself to the enemy's fury. Explosives solved a technical problem: before, one might be wounded, tortured, manipulated, exchanged, or turned. One thus never knew whether life would go on, with its unpredictable interlacing of the contradictory plans of multiple protagonists. By eliminating the element of chance, voluntary death put an end to such uncertainty.

By inventing dynamite, Alfred Nobel breathed new life into the weapon of suicide, which had become obsolete and, in general, was rarely used owing to its merely adequate effectiveness. With weapons such as knives and swords, there was no need to kill oneself. Without a doubt, explosives changed the technological and tactical situation. Moreover, looking further into the future, it is important to ask whether other technological advances in arms might not ultimately make a human being an infinitely more deadly weapon. This raises the issue of the relationship between suicide attackers and the weapons of mass destruction that could well become a twenty-first-century nightmare.

The second period relates to the Islamic world's return to the ideology of sacrifice. Here, the point of departure might be seen as Iranian Shiism: revolutionary, impassioned, and expansive—not to say expansionist.

The infection led to powerful metastases in an Islamic world that was no longer limited to its Middle Eastern, Arab-Persian core. Islam is a cultural force that is expanding in what has come to be called the Third World. It is spreading, and it is articulating its positions. Above all, it has access to a powerful force for influence: charitable support. At the heart of this structure, which is neither aggressive nor peaceable, ideologies of conquest use violence as one element of a strategy of conquest and seizure of power. For how long? No one can say. Nearly a generation has gone by, and a second generation of rebels has arisen, convinced of the legitimate value of self-sacrifice/homicide. Betting on its rapid self-extinction could be as dangerous as it is premature.

FROM SPONTANEOUS SELF-SACRIFICE TO ORGANIZED STRATEGY

The Tradition of Antiquity

This tradition is based on the existence of slavery, a structure that defined the thinking with respect to conflict. The prisoner became a "thing," stripped of humanity.

In his celebrated *Address to the German Nation* of 1807, Johann Gottlieb Fichte spoke of Germanic forebears who preferred freedom in death to a life of subjugation. That is the dichotomy of antiquity: freedom or death. The framework was honor in battle and the rejection of a life in slavery. The Jews were to add a new, religious dimension linked to monotheism.

There is no doubt that the Jewish Zealots were terrorists imbued with the spirit of resistance mixed with hatred for the Roman occupiers and a yearning for revolutionary social transformation that was, if we may venture an anachronism in terms of Jewish society, "messianic." When in the Nazareth marketplace a zealot flashed his *sica* and slit the throat of a Roman—or of a Jew who had compromised with the occupying authority—he rarely took flight. He remained to bear witness to his act. Remaining stone-still on the murder scene amounted to an abandonment of life. We find this attitude throughout the history of suicide volunteers; it marked the actions of the twelfth-century Assassins.

Who were those unfortunate rebels at Masada? Those who took their own lives in the vanquished fortress killed no one else. They did not even attempt a final sortie that would have led to slaughter at the enemy's hands. Therein lies the profound and tragic strangeness of their act. It was their will to undertake—by their own hand, with certainty and with no element of chance—the liberating task of death, beginning with the weak, women, children, and the aged. Not a single Roman perished in the collective suicide at Masada. Yes, that suicide was altruistic in nature, but it served no strategic purpose.

The real homicidal suicide in the Jewish tradition is Samson. Reduced to slavery, that negation of humanity, he enters into a contract with God, saying, "give me strength only this once, O God, and let me at one stroke be avenged on the Philistines" (Judges 16:28). By agreeing to the bargain, God legitimizes Samson's suicide. That is the essence of the sacrifice: an exchange, reciprocal giving guaranteed by belief in a God who one ensures is on one's side. In God we trust.

Samson's sacrifice and the self-destruction at Masada have become rallying symbols of the State of Israel's will to survive—which is contrasted with the will to die, though both share a single purpose: affirmation of one's own existence while calling into question those others who question it. Or at least, that is the belief held by each side. They are cautionary hints at a hidden object: the nuclear weapon. Without having ever admitted to possessing such weapons, the Hebrew state has adopted a stance known as "deliberate ambiguity." There is no reason to possess nuclear weapons, but if they proved to be essential, they would be there, like Samson, to exterminate the enemy and save the Jewish people—with Masada as the metaphor—from final destruction. These, to be sure, are short circuits in an anachronized history and are dangerous metaphors. Perhaps we can detect there the magical dimension of the ritual of sacrifice and of *devotio*. Anachronism would appear to have its virtues, enabling us to take account of individuals and organizations whose perception of time may respond to representations that are original and deviant, and hence not consistent with dominant Western linearity.

Infectious Devotion

Of all ancient civilizations, it was certainly Rome that attached the highest value to suicide. Far from being denounced, it was viewed as a liberation, a sign of the affirmation of individual freedom in the face of death, whether imposed by one's prince or by one's other master, time.

In combat, it was represented through the ritual of *devotio*. Livy writes that the battle that took place in 295 B.C.E. between the Romans and the Samnite–Senonian-Gaul coalition was going badly. The Roman left wing was overwhelmed, and the roar of the Gauls' chariots was spreading panic among the Roman cavalry. The horses failed their riders; a rout was under way; a massacre was near. Then, Publius Decius

> commanded Marcus Livius, a pontiff, whom, at his coming out to the field, he had charged not to stir from him, to dictate the form of words in which he was to devote himself, and the legions of the enemy, for the army of the Roman people, the Quirites. He was accordingly devoted with the same imprecations, and in the same habit, in which his father, Publius Decius, had ordered himself to be devoted at the Veseris in the Latin war. When, immediately after the solemn imprecation, he added, that "he drove before him dismay and flight, slaughter and blood, and the wrath of the gods celestial and infernal, that, with the contagious influence of the furies, the ministers of death, he would infect the standards, the weapons, and the armor of the enemy, and that the same spot should be that of his perdition, and that of the Gauls and Samnites."[1]

This was a magical-strategic act aimed at reversing the course of the battle.

Devotio may be seen as a magic rite—and black magic without a doubt, because it is accompanied by the casting of spells. There are two stages in this ritual. First, the sacrificer utters an invocation to bring forth the infernal powers. In exchange for his life, he compels them to be a present and potential force. He thus transforms himself into a "weapon of mass destruction": an evil object infected (Livy uses the word *infectio*) with destructive power that he will hurl at the enemy. He turns himself into an "infernal machine" that will contaminate the enemy. As Livy notes, "Thenceforward the battle seemed to be fought with a degree of force scarcely human. . . . The Gauls, and especially the multitude which encircled the consul's body, as if deprived of reason, cast their javelins at random without execution, some became so stupid as not to think of either fighting or flying."[2] This was petrifaction. We shall often encounter this strange psychological phenomenon, which manifests itself in a kind of freezing of physical powers.

The ritual of *devotio* was a form of necromancy by which, as Jean Bayet explains, "a general, in order to save his army by substituting himself for it, dedicates himself to the infernal gods and seeks death among the enemy, who are, so to speak, forced to carry out the sacrifice-substitution and who are at the same time contaminated by cursed contact with it."[3]

The Middle Ages and the Renaissance

The growth of "heretical" sects was fostered by the weakness of state power, the comparative decadence of the way power was handed down and the spiritual strength of Christianity.

It is useful to recall that, when viewed against the numerous sects within Islam, Christian sects more than held their own. In the Middle Ages and the early Renaissance, such sects proliferated in a climate of death, predictions of the end of the world, scorn for worldly things: a climate favorable to suicide.

The members of the medieval Islamic sect of the Assassins, discussed in chapter 3, can be viewed as suicidal only to the extent that they did not try to flee once they had carried out their act. Yet in both a positive and a negative sense, some of their characteristics are of interest if we are fully to understand the death volunteer: first, their complete obedience to their leader; secondly, the high quality of their strategic thinking in terms of selecting their targets; thirdly, the care with which their actions were planned. The fourth relates to an early example of psychological warfare against the Assassins: their reputation as users of hashish, which was intended to present them as irresponsible and, ultimately, powerless dreamers. Thus, these addled spirits would do their deed in an irresponsible state of altered consciousness.

Obviously, not all sects are of a suicidal bent. Only a few consider killing themselves or—like Aum Shinrikyo—taking action to kill their enemies. Yet some view the time of the second coming of Christ—the Parousia—in an eschatological context, which results in a very special relationship to voluntary death. Suicide volunteers per se do not exactly constitute a sect but are rather a deliberately isolated group that is out of the mainstream and that tends to form an elite because of its highly unusual relationship with death.

In the end, at the intersection among these groups we find closely related contexts and similar behaviors and practices that, because they run through history, suggest timelessness. They view as alien, or reject, notions of history and indeed of progress. Such notions are seen as outmoded because of a shift of the territory of the here and now to the Beyond. This fusion of human time and divine timelessness is illustrated by the Cathars, who in the twelfth century sought a new conception of the world and of times defined by the Apocalypse.

We find this recurring in most sects and sectarian organizations. It is seen among the Anabaptists of early-sixteenth-century Münster, who actually inverted time and the order of their day. As "ana-baptists" (literally, "rebaptizers") they returned to the source—the creation myth—to remake humanity, with the fierce complementary goal of the immediate institution of the new kingdom of God. They changed all the rules; they rediscovered primitive rites in a sort of archaizing frenzy. Problems, rivalries, and disputes arose, and the solution was quickly found: massacre or mass suicide. Why? Because they needed to have done with the present and the future—not in order to go backward but in order to bring about the pure origin, timelessness, and eternity. The Anabaptists burned, ravaged, massacred, and committed suicide in order to abolish the whole of history.

A short circuit in time: what does Salafism aim for if not a return to the mythic origin of the pure prophetic word? That is the tradition within which Bin Laden and his cohort seek, through the restoration of the caliphate, to return history to the temporal zero point of absolute origin: the word of the Prophet. This also requires, they would say, a strategy involving the seizure of worldly power, even though such power is held to be materially trivial and has meaning only in relation to the ultimate spiritual goal. Hence the logical dead end of such undertakings, which once they are effective are unable to free themselves from the tyranny of the here and now.

There is a powerful relationship between sectarian ideologies and suicide. Sectarianism is rarely the same as suicide/homicide: either one kills others to save oneself in order to lead the new post-revolutionary, post-chaos times, or one embraces the Apocalypse thorough communal suicide.

That said, knowing the ways in which a sect is established and functions is helpful for a better understanding of the nature and the dynamics of genuine suicide volunteers: their training, their relationship to their leaders, and their connection with their times and their cause. A sect is a miniature world—introverted, paranoid, and potentially suicidal. Russian nihilism was a culmination of this fatal mechanism.

In 1850, it was as though Russian society had been invaded by a contagion, to which Turgenev's 1862 novel *Fathers and Sons* bears early witness. This context gave rise to such warped personalities as Nikolai Ishutin, Dimitri Karakozov, and the better-known Sergei Nechayev, whose "Revolutionary Catechism" (see chapters 5 and 7 above) proclaimed: "The revolutionary is a doomed man. He has no personal interests, no business affairs, no emotions, no attachments, no property and no name. Everything in him is wholly absorbed in . . . the single passion for revolution." In search of "the surest and quickest way of destroying the whole filthy [existing] order," Nechayev's revolutionary studies "mechanics, physics, chemistry, and perhaps medicine. But all day and all night he studies the vital science of human beings, their characteristics and circumstances."[4]

What was Nechayev calling for here? He wanted a physical weapon backed up by the weapon of psychological warfare. His wish would later be granted by the political commissar responsible for training the Vietnamese suicide volunteers.

Ultimately, the most important question raised by nihilism is a moral one; the indiscriminate character of its violence, which is based on a self-proclaimed notion of collective responsibility—of a group, an ethnicity, a social class, and so forth. This was a notion that constantly preoccupied those who advocated propaganda through deeds, as exemplified in France by someone like Émile Henry, who struck indiscriminately (see chapter 6 above).

Nihilists liked to think of their movement as icily realistic and purely Machiavellian. In that sense they were the true forebears of the Leninists, who in the name of the tide of history denounced the moralism of the Socialist Revolutionaries—before liquidating them.

Nihilism is founded on a great ambiguity that barely conceals an opportunistic Phariseeism: "Forward, you, the others!" The militant must give his life massacring the class enemy, while the leader remains safe. Ishutin, founder of the group known as Hell, set the following rules of action for militants: "Lots will be drawn to determine the member who will carry out the action . . . as soon as the attack has been carried out, the author must poison himself."[5]

Does one throw the bomb or is one blown up with it?

There are two reasons to blow oneself up with the bomb: to make sure of the target, and also to ensure that only the target is harmed and that innocent bystanders do not die as well. Such suicide is akin to a duel in which the assailant alone sets the rules and prohibitions that will ensure both operational effectiveness and morality. The self-sacrifice remains pure. The cause wavers in the face of the target: in the absence of a deity, not everything is permissible, as it is in the name of God, and individuals thus bear responsibility vis-à-vis their fellow humans.

Another reason for self-sacrifice is to inflict the greatest possible damage on the enemy. That was the aim, for example, of the young women of the Jewish Zionist socialist youth movement during the Warsaw ghetto uprising in the spring of 1943, who approached Germans—officers if possible—and then detonated grenades when they got close enough. They did not toss their grenades from a distance, as a normal soldier would; they deliberately destroyed themselves along with their enemies. Surprise, proximity, and precision were required: the Nazis understood and learned to fire first from a safe distance, including on women.[6]

Is There an Asian Tradition of Suicide Volunteers?

We now move forward in time toward the earliest explanations of the use of suicide volunteers as a weapon. The conflict must be an intense one, and the group that feels under threat must possess cultural resources that include an understanding and an enduring tradition of self-sacrifice. Without that, even in the face of military superiority and great danger, no one would think of employing such a strategy. On the eve of World War II, its systematic use came about with the early stages of the Sino-Japanese conflict, then with the confrontation with the United States, and finally with the communist war of national liberation against the French in Indochina.

Kamikaze: The Dark Blaze of Glory. We vacillate between utter incomprehension of this tradition—which has been lumped together with that of hara-kiri—and pity for the unfortunate men who sacrificed themselves for a cause that had been lost by hideous militarists in an attempted last stand against defeat.

The very roots of Japanese society are immersed in the sacrificial tradition of the warrior. By a natural tendency of strategic thinking, organized suicide arose as an effective response to the barrage of U.S. military superiority. When it feels imperiled, a society responds in ways defined by its identity and, thus, by its traditions. That was the view of Admiral Onishi, who for months had been advocating the tactic of aerial suicide attacks; when the opportunity arose, he took the initiative on October 19, 1944, three days before the battle of Leyte Gulf, in the Philippines, in which four Japanese aircraft carriers were sunk, stripped Japan of its aero-naval power. The way had been cleared for the enemy to move inexorably toward Japan. The notion of suicide became an obsession. By July 1944, the island of Saipan provided a tragic echo of Masada with the suicide of hundreds of Japanese settlers. To escape the "barbarians," officers disemboweled themselves, and women and children hurled themselves into the sea from the rocky cliffs. The Navy Air Force was then authorized to establish a Special Body Crash Attack Unit (Taiatari Tokubetsu Kogekitai, abbreviated to Tokkotai).

We should consider the importance of these techniques, which were undoubtedly the most important ever used within the framework of self-sacrifice/homicide; nothing comparable in terms of scope, diversity or technical sophistication had ever been ventured. That alone makes the Japanese undertaking unique in the context of a large-scale conflict.

The Oka are less well known, but they provide an example of how radical military action in this area could be. The expression Jinrai oka Butai—Cherry Blossom of the Thunder Gods—refers to type-11 naval suicide attack bombs. These glider-type craft were designed to be released by a bomber; they carried more than a ton of extremely powerful trinitroanisol explosive and were propelled toward the target by three solid fuel rockets at a speed of 570 miles (more than 900 kilometers) per hour.

In January 1945, the Special Unit had 160 volunteer pilots, along with a reserve to replenish the personnel. There were far more volunteers than could be accommodated with available aircraft. Once they had been developed and tested, during the fall of 1944, first-generation devices were placed aboard the world's largest aircraft carrier, the *Shinano*. But three weeks later, in November, four torpedoes launched by an American submarine sent the *Shinano* to the bottom with its cargo of fifty Oka. Only on March 21, 1945, did the first combat trials take place. These were a total failure, not because the system malfunctioned but because the fifteen Mitsubishi G4M2e ("Betty") bombers were shot down by American fighter planes before getting close enough to their target: around twelve and a half miles (twenty kilometers). The glider-bombs themselves could have outrun the U.S. Navy Hellcats, but the Bettys were too heavy and, at speeds of around 200 miles (320 kilometers) per hour, too slow. From the moment their approach was detected, they were easy targets.

1950: The Vietminh. Although there are no official statistics in this regard, the special suicide units set up by the Vietnamese People's Army were numerically speaking the largest such force. The Vietminh's assault tactic was based on the classic dense column, with several hundred men two or three rows abreast. This means that the attack will be concentrated on a point in the opposing defenses that is relatively narrow, no more than perhaps 65 feet (20 meters). By means of furious digging, these units would get to within a few dozen meters of the enemy positions. They still had to break through a defensive perimeter bristling with barbed wire and strewn with mines. The purpose of artillery preparation was to destroy this network of passive defenses, but the remaining large fragments were still capable of slowing the progress of the column under enemy fire. It was therefore necessary to succeed in clearing the width of the corridor in order to deliver the human power of the infantry. That was the mission of the suicide volunteers; to carry it out, they possessed a tried and true tool that had been tested over the course of many years: the Bangalore torpedo.

This device had been well known to sappers since World War I. It consists of a series of connected steel tubes that soldiers can thrust into the enemy defenses while remaining under cover. A rocket is then inserted into the tube and ignited; it explodes in the midst of the barbed wire and chevaux-de-frise protecting the enemy fortifications. The Vietminh did not have access to the same materials, but they adapted the principle by placing explosive charges at the end of very long bamboo poles. These would be carried as far as necessary by men who exposed themselves to defensive fire as they breached the perimeter, within which, as a rule, mines had been laid. Moreover, when the charge was detonated, the man carrying it could be struck by shrapnel thrown off by the explosion within a radius greater than the length of the bamboo pole. Death was a certainty; it was indeed the bearer of the weapon who had to detonate it. All of this meets the definition of voluntary death in the service of a cause. It is true that the soldier did not directly kill his enemy; he contributed to his annihilation by laying the groundwork for his comrades, who would immediately follow. In cases like this, it is hard to draw fine distinctions about intent.

These suicide units appear to have been large; a conservative estimate would be twenty thousand men. It would have been important to be able to replace their members, given how many died in attacks. But the Democratic Republic of Vietnam (DRV) has never provided statistics. Nor do we know the casualty rates during such assaults.

To what extent was this tactic the result of real weakness in the face of French military might? At Dien Bien Phu, Vietminh General Vo Nguyen Giap held superiority on the ground. So, did he need to use suicide units to attack French fortifications when patient and continuous shelling by his heavy artillery would have ultimately smashed the French defenses? He did not. They went to their death because that had become the accepted combat tactic. Suicide volunteers were no longer the exception; in this battle they were a weapon, like any artillery shell. One subsequent focus of the cult of the hero in that politically centered society would be to affirm that each suicide volunteer played a valuable role.

Today: The Shiite Trend

Why should we view 1980 as the advent and epiphany of self-sacrifice/homicide? There is no question but that the return of militant, impassioned, revolutionary Shiism to the Middle East restored to selfless sacrifice and martyrdom a momentum they had not enjoyed for a long time.

Iran. Where does "today" begin? It begins in 1979, when the followers of Shiism reintroduced the dimension of sacrifice.

In Iran's use of suicide volunteers, we can draw a distinction between mass martyrdom and individual martyrdom: groups of "mass" suicide volunteers were used for large-scale military operations in vast theaters, in pursuit of a military strategy, while lone volunteers were employed in isolated operations in Lebanon and Palestine in the prosecution of a conflict that, although different in form, was no less radical.

Suicide volunteers produce an effect that relates to the size and strategic value of their theaters of operations. The larger the theater, the more dilute the impact of their action. Palestinian suicide volunteers have benefited from the small size of the area and the attendant psychological effects of concentration and reverberation.

To fend off Iraq and launch enormous counteroffensives, the Iranian regime—having hastened to destroy the country's real military competence—improvised. This led to the creation of the *bassidje,* or "organized volunteers." These were youths about fifteen years of age. In theory, they could not join the army, which had a minimum enlistment age of eighteen and which was a serious, quite well organized body that was little inclined to be affected by the revolutionary spirit. And for their part, families tried to oppose the enrolment of their children. Albeit with some difficulty, Ayatollah Ruhollah Khomeini removed this legal obstacle, however, once again proving (if proof were needed) the resourcefulness of theological argument.

It was confirmed yet again that the psychological manipulation of adolescents is an indispensable tool. It places the masses in the service of the revolution—whatever sort of revolution it may be. Young people are quick to rebel; also, they can be held in reserve to respond to situations of extreme military peril: their dynamism, enthusiasm, passion, and libido can all be placed at the disposal of the cause. But one must also know how to monitor, organize, and lead them, which is no less important.

Against this backdrop, Khomeini sought deliberately to sow and disseminate a culture of martyrdom throughout Iranian society. "Martyrs are the symbol of Iran's strength," immense propaganda billboards erected along the broad boulevards of Iranian cities proclaimed. And the mullahs' homilies promised the most splendid of rewards in the hereafter. Previously, such themes had never been the subject of systematic preaching. Religion, which here could provide a ready-made corpus, was strategically oriented to meet newly decreed political needs. The recently installed religious leadership adapted religion to the circumstances with genuinely revolutionary and patriotic opportunism. At the time, many theologians disapproved of these interpretations, but they did not have an opportunity to oppose them—except in exile and at danger to themselves.

Given the lack of a military need, one might wonder whether the development of suicide volunteers as a weapon could have been an instrument of control for the leader and the governmental system he ran. Did Khomeini have any military need for the *bassidje*? The same question was posed in relation to the Vietminh in 1954, and the answer remains the same.

Lebanon. The Israeli army's 1982 invasion of Lebanon, in what it called "Operation Peace of the Galilee," succeeded in throwing people into the arms of radical Shiite factions, because it appeared to confirm the main themes of the propaganda spread by those groups. Spiritually weakened and traumatized by the invasion, the population was fertile ground for Islamism and a ready source of suicide volunteers.

This still embryonic organization gained by the "invasion" of Lebanon by the multinational interposition force comprising American,

French, and Italian troops, which deployed to Beirut in late September 1982 but was forced to withdraw following the suicide attacks that occurred in 1983. Two suicide attacks killed some 300 American and French soldiers.

This was an initial victory; it was essentially political in nature, but gradually took on a military dimension, because Hezbollah used it to gain a permanent base in southern Lebanon and a complete infrastructure—whose military level, however, remained modest. It possessed staging posts throughout the country. In spite of the support it received from Iran, Hezbollah was tolerated by Syria because it maintained a second front against Israel, leaving Damascus to focus its attention on the Golan area. Moreover, its ties to Tehran, then in the midst of war, heightened the isolation of Iraq, whose aggressiveness was a constant source of concern for Syrian President Hafez al-Assad.

With those assets, Hezbollah was able to arrange for education and training and the various kinds of ceremonies that enshrined suicide volunteers as an elite weapon.

Hezbollah's radio and television stations enabled it to function as a state within a state; its media strategy helped publicize the glory of its martyrs throughout the Middle East. Yet its military capabilities remained those of a guerrilla force lacking heavy military resources, which was not in fact such a bad thing: in that way it was able to frustrate Israeli army action. It was in this context that Hezbollah gained its second victory.

The Israeli army suffered its greatest losses in a war of attrition in southern Lebanon, in which, by using the weapon of suicide volunteers, Hezbollah took full advantage of the strategic asymmetry. From a moral standpoint, the Israeli troops were in a weak position. On one side, every effort was made to protect the Jewish soldier—a precious resource—on the other, human beings were being sent to their death by the dozen and were seemingly content with that fate. Israeli soldiers were poorly prepared psychologically; they still had a superiority complex vis-à-vis the mediocre Arab fighters, and they did not understand the way this confrontation worked. They were losing their bearings even though nothing had shaken their military superiority.

The July 2000 withdrawal of Israeli forces from Lebanon under those circumstances was seen as a military, political, and symbolic windfall for the suicide weapon, reinforcing the initial effect of the American withdrawal in 1983. Hamas and other Palestinian movements pondered this lesson.

The Palestinians. While they garner most of the attention, Palestinian attacks are described more than they are explained. But why was this method chosen, and why did it become a major tool beginning with the second intifada in 2000?

Starting in 1967, an ideological movement had been forming: the celebration of the Palestinian nationalist fighter, the *fedayeen.* After Black September in 1970, when King Hussein of Jordan crushed a Palestinian attempt to overthrow him, secular Palestinian movements, some of which were Marxist-Leninist in orientation, were radicalized. Special units were created which made death a reference point and a symbol. The point was not to commit suicide, but to demonstrate through action a level of determination that rose to total disregard for one's own life— which, obviously, one was prepared to sacrifice.

Thus, the basis was present. But later, this would become a deliberate strategy, when religious movements such as Hamas revived the notion of martyrdom. This ideological transformation would actually take something less than twenty years: a single generation in countries with high birthrates, countries where people began combat very young, rather like going to school. The shift was built on a twofold awareness of failure: the struggle waged in the name of nationalism and social revolution had not achieved the promised success; and the balance of military power remained consistently unfavorable. The pursuit of parity led to disaster. The extreme military asymmetry required exceptional forms of struggle. Paradoxically, the establishment of an autonomous Palestinian Authority possessing lightly armed police forces only strengthened Palestinians' sense of inferiority.

Thus, turning to the use of suicide volunteers as a weapon was more a strategic than a tactical choice for the Palestinians. It appears that it was not ideologues who initiated strategic consideration of the usefulness of "martyrdom" operations, but warriors such as Yahya Ayyash of Hamas and Fathi Shiqaqi of Islamic Jihad. Their arguments were based on operational effectiveness: the precision, cost-effectiveness, destructive capacity, and psychological impact of really successful attacks.

Between April 1994 and July 1997, suicide attacks by Hamas and Jihad took more than 150 Israeli lives. Between April 1994 and April 2002, 96 suicide volunteers caused 334 deaths and 2,700 injuries among Israeli civilians and soldiers; 53 of these were attributable to Hamas and 28 to Islamic Jihad. What was new was the emergence of an al-Fatah group known as the al-Aqsa Martyrs Brigade, whose name alludes to Ariel Sharon's provocative visit to the al-Aqsa mosque/Temple Mount complex in Jerusalem, one of Islam's most important sites, on September 28, 2000, shortly before the Israeli election. It showed that al-Fatah, a secular organization, felt obliged not to ignore the religious dimension and to compete with Hamas on its own turf. The context of radicalized confrontation, with the Palestinians standing alone in the face of the power of the Israeli army, made al-Fatah reconsider how valuable the suicide-volunteer weapon could be to its operational and political-psychological plans.

This assessment of the strategic situation can be ascribed to one of the key leaders of the Palestinian Authority's law and order organization: Marwan Barghouti, who was arrested in April 2002 by the Israelis. Starting in 1998, he had set up small paramilitary groups known as the Tanzim. The October–November 2000 test of strength was a military disaster for the Palestinians, who accounted for 250 of the 280 recorded victims. It had become clear that conventional asymmetrical confrontation would lead to intolerably disproportionate losses. There was no compensating for the asymmetry in terms of equipment, with its impact on numbers of losses.

So what strategy should take its place, and what weapons should be employed? The answer carried special weight because the Israeli army's complete withdrawal from southern Lebanon was perceived—more erroneously than correctly—as a Hezbollah victory and as proof of the success of its combat techniques, notably suicide attacks.

There is no doubt that the use of suicide attacks proved positive in terms of cost-effectiveness. The intensification of operations in the course of 2002 caused the Israeli government to toughen its response by combining a strategy of the carefully targeted killing of leaders with massive, indiscriminate responses, including against houses in Palestinian areas. It is practically impossible to determine the exact reasons for the lull in 2003. In part, it related to exhaustion on the part of the Palestinians, who had been hard hit, as well as to internal debate over the validity of the overall strategy. But also connected was the episode of Mahmoud Abbas's appointment as prime minister. The attempt to substitute a prime minister for the authority of Chairman Arafat gave rise to a period of dormancy, which appeared to correspond to a cease-fire that enabled the Palestinians to put their operations back together and the Israelis to pursue their separatist strategy and their "decapitation" of Palestinian networks.

Sri Lanka: The Black Tigers. Suicide volunteers have been employed in the ongoing conflict in Sri Lanka between the Sinhalese majority (around

74 percent of the island's population) and Tamil separatists, which began in 1975. The conflict is confined within the region, but it has been very deadly and in that regard extremely intense.

The Liberation Tigers of Tamil Eelam (LTTE), or Tamil Tigers, claim to have some 15,000 fighters at their disposal, including 2,000 to 3,000 women. The Sri Lankan army consists of about 20,000 troops, including a Special Task Force entirely made up of British mercenaries. There is also a 3,000-strong navy.

The Tamil minority can rely on support from southern India (the state of Tamil Nadu), from which they are separated only by a 25-mile (40-kilometer) strait. In keeping with classic strategic tradition, Tamil Nadu serves as a rear base. In their training camps around Madras, the guerrillas attain a high level of proficiency. Also in this movement's favor is the fact that it can draw on assistance from a diaspora in Asia (including in Malaysia and Thailand), Australia, and a few European countries, in particular the United Kingdom.

The Tigers' success is founded on the existence of an effective organization encompassing the entire Tamil population, including a diaspora that is very active worldwide. The supreme leader of the LTTE is Velupillai Prabhakaran; in order to hold onto the Tamil people and to impose his dictatorial sway, he has made use of all the tools of power employed by effective tyrants everywhere.

He ensures that his forces are of high quality, and he provides them with high-level technical resources that contrast with those of Sri Lanka's unsophisticated regular forces. The preparation of minefields and artillery firing zones is precisely calculated by means of global positioning systems, with a view to drawing enemy forces into the most lethal areas.

Confrontations in Sri Lanka are of extreme ferocity. Tamils have often been burned alive by their adversaries. This radicalism suggests a loathing of the enemy verging on a desire for extermination.

The importance attached to fire also has cultural roots; it is the preferred instrument of destruction. Nor can it be overemphasized that killing too is a cultural act: some kill with fire, some with knives used for sheep or pigs. Hatred is not as inventive as we sometimes think. In the study of intercommunal antagonism, this aspect is obscured. Sexuality too plays a key role, both in the determination to humiliate the enemy and in the wish for vengeance. Rape is one part of the trauma and phobic torment that motivate young Tamil women to join the Tigers, or even the Black Tigers, the LTTE's elite suicide squads.

Prabhakaran has developed a holistic strategy that combines guerrilla fighting, terrorism, and the use of suicide volunteers. Here, his originality lies in the use of two resources: women and suicide swimmer-fighters, both male and female.

The first relates to the wish to systematically destabilize the Sinhalese state and its civilian and military governing structure. The suicide volunteers strike at the head, in the tradition of classic violent political struggle. Suicide is used with a view to precision targeting; it is the opposite of indiscriminate.

The employment of swimmers reflects interest in a military strategy that will prevent the guerrilla force from being cut off from its rear base in continental India. The strait separating northern Sri Lanka from Tamil Nadu is extremely narrow: a couple of dozen miles (three dozen kilometers). The Sri Lankan navy could cut lines of communication by interdicting all crossings. The mission of the suicide swimmers is to neutralize this by attacking Sri Lankan ships. This method recalls Japanese experiments with human torpedoes—which in turn were inspired by Italy's disastrous attempts to use pocket submarines in 1941–43. But this technique has been effective for the Tamils. The key is high-quality intelligence. The Tamil command knows the movements of enemy units and can launch suicide operations at the right time and in the right place. Use of suicide volunteers is part of an asymmetric strategy: the Tamils do not possess the vessels that would enable them to confront the Sri Lankan navy, however limited it might be. The targeted nature of the attacks and the situation itself are very similar to those of Japan during World War II. Yet the capabilities of the two sides are not so far out of balance, and developments in the strategic situation would seem—from the strictly operational standpoint—to justify the targeted use of such suicide operations.

The "Septembrists" of 9/11 and the al Qaeda System. Given the complexity of this subject, one should refrain from making any firm judgments and should set out the facts with the possible caution. Even genuine knowledge is subject to political handling that, at best, aims at gaining the greatest possible advantage from any information one may have. The invasion of Iraq by the United States and its allies showed this all too clearly.

The men of 9/11 came out of a long tradition of political and ideological turbulence in the Arab world going back to the founding of the Muslim Brotherhood by Hasan al-Banna in 1928 and of Jamaat-i-Islami in 1941 by Abu l'Ala Maududi.

This tradition came of age with the assassination of Egypt's President Anwar al-Sadat on April 8, 1982, but it had already given rise to a phenomenon that was more original because it was stripped of a territorial aspect: the movement of volunteer Islamist fighters to the battleground of Soviet-occupied Afghanistan.

Up to that point, suicide had not been an issue. To be sure, the spirit of self-sacrifice was glorified, and thinking had become bleak: Sadat's executioners belonged to the group known as Takfir wal-Hijra—Anathema and Exile: constant themes of Osama bin Laden's discourse. The "deterritorialization" of fighters and their leaders—which Westerners take as the internationalization of terrorist networks—has been presented as linked to the Hegira, the prophet Muhammad's departure from Mecca, which marks the beginning of his wandering and the start of the Muslim calendar.

Suicide operations played hardly any part in the Afghanistan war. There are many examples of mujahideen sacrificing their lives, but there has been no evidence of the conception, planning, and systematic carrying out of such actions. That absence is interesting, given that Shiite groups linked to Iran were already present on the ground and that the Sunni would readily adopt this technique a few years later. There is an obvious explanation: the balance of forces, although asymmetrical in favor of the Soviet army, did not seem so unfavorable as to require action of this kind. The terrain was favorable; the population had largely been won over, at least in terms of its hostility to the occupier; money was generously provided by the Americans; and arms were flowing in via Pakistan. Victory and the final collapse of the Soviet Union changed the entire political and strategic picture.

The Afghan territorial and popular base became less necessary, in spite of fairly positive relations with the Taliban. But whether or not they were Islamists, the "Arab legionnaires" constituted a foreign body within Afghanistan's tribal system. There is no doubt that the Kabul regime permitted the presence of al Qaeda training camps, but it was wary of any excessive military power that could have threatened its tenuous predominance. The fact remains, however, that these camps made it possible to train versatile fighters capable of waging a regional war against the Northern Alliance led by Ahmed Shah Masoud and Abdul Rashid Dostum, and indeed of carrying out faraway terrorist actions that could involve suicide.

The group trained by Osama bin Laden and Ayman al-Zawahiri embodied the leadership's complexity and perplexity during those years, which were pivotal with respect to the orientation of the fighting Islamist movement. Two elements, of two different heritages, clearly emerged: the Saudis and Yemenis on the one hand, and the Egyptians on the other. The leadership hesitated about where to deploy them. Bin Laden was drawn by Sudan, where Hassan al-Turabi was trying to set up a theocratic state based on sharia; that experiment came to an abrupt end. Perhaps Afghanistan would be needed as a base from which to seek a presence in former Soviet Central Asia. Ultimately, did the very essence of the movement not lie in its global struggle against the occupiers of Islamic lands: the Jews and the Americans?

Furthermore, direct confrontation with U.S. military power had given rise to a justified sense of weakness for which the spectacular effect of suicide operations could be only partial compensation. What was lacking in terms of actual strength needed to be offset by the suggestive power of self-sacrifice/homicide.

The highly meticulous planning of the 9/11 attacks would conform to this surprising application of asymmetric strategy.

Yet how much of a surprise was it? There was no lack of precedents and signals. Indeed, the first World Trade Center bombing, in 1993, suggested that there was an intention to bring the conflict to the heart of the United States, a state viewed as responsible for aggression against Islam. Had the blind sheikh Omar Abdel Rahman inspired a new radical form of jihad? But the planning of that attack did not suggest suicide, and police investigators have not really looked in that direction.

Yet warning lights continued to flash.

An aerial suicide operation was the plan when in December 1994 the Algerian Groupe islamique armé (Armed Islamic Group), or GIA, hijacked an Air France Airbus on the Paris-Algiers route. When it landed at Marseille, the plane was stormed by the a French gendarmerie special unit. The plot had involved destroying the plane and its 280 passengers over Paris in order to create a spectacular effect of terror and apocalypse. In March 1995, a GIA group known as the Phalange des signataires par le sang (Phalange of the Signers in Blood) killed 45 people in a suicide attack using a car filled with explosives against the El-Biar police station in Algiers. But here again, the context was circumscribed.

There were also a number of suicide operations attributable to Islamists from the Arabian peninsula targeting U.S. bases or forces. First came the June 1996 attack on the U.S. Air Force base at Khobar Towers, near Dahran, Saudi Arabia. Attacks against the U.S. embassies at Dar es Salaam, Tanzania, and Nairobi, Kenya, followed in 1998; these used car bombs parked near the targeted buildings, not steered into the targets by human drivers. The result carnage was horrendous from the attackers' point of view: the victims were passers-by.

The American destroyer the USS *Cole* was attacked in the port of Sanaa, Yemen, in October 2000, this time by a suicide boat. The attack appears to have been planned by Tawfiq bin Attash. Similar actions occurred after 9/11. The French oil tanker *Limbourg* was struck by a boat in September 2002. The November 2002 attack against a Mombassa, Kenya, hotel popular with Israeli tourists was carried out using a vehicle that appears to have been occupied by three attackers; on this, doubts persist, for there are limits to redundancy.

This catalogue of incidents suggests that suicide attacks are not inevitably an indispensable tool. They do not result from any religious imperative favoring suicide, but rather from operational opportunism or from the availability of suicide attackers. No one claimed responsibility for these attacks, or only in a very vague way. We must look behind this anonymity to find the personalities of those involved: What are they thinking? What do they want?

Muhammad Atta, who led the 9/11 operation, was not a direct product of the madrassas: Qur'anic schools for teenage boys at loose ends. The spiritual spark that ignited this involvement was lit in the world of fairly advanced university studies on American and European campuses. How were these men chosen, and in preference to which other people who could have served the purpose? For how long had they been under preparation for martyrdom?

At the same time, another factor—family relationships—plays a key role in motivation and recruitment. The March 2003 arrest of the chief planner of 9/11, Khalid Sheikh Muhammad, enabled us to form a clearer picture of the men of September. Thirty-eight years of age in 2003, he was born in Pakistan and emigrated to Kuwait when young. He studied engineering in North Carolina but quit to join Islamist fighters in Afghanistan in 1985. He seems to be the uncle of Ramzi Yousef, one of those at the origin of the 1993 World Trade Center attack, who has been in prison since 1995.

This man had a comparatively high level of education, especially in technology; he had been a longtime visitor to the United States and was familiar with air transport. Does this explain the choice of airplanes for the 9/11 attacks?

The delivery vehicle (airplanes) and the technique of the attacks (crashing into the target) offer seeming similarities between the "Septembrists" and kamikazes. But all similarities and comparisons stop there. The Japanese pilot considered himself to be striking the enemy in an act of war in which civilians were entirely uninvolved, while for the "Septembrists" inspiration came from elsewhere.

To be sure, suicide attackers of Saudi and Egyptian affiliation had made use of all means, including cars and boats. The idea of an airplane attack had been spreading, at least after 1995, when Bosnian Islamists conceived Project Bojinka, which included the simultaneous hijacking of seventeen civilian aircraft to be crashed into major population centers.

Chechnya and Iraq. The taking of Grozny by Russian forces in 2000, which marked the official end of the second Chechen war, clearly did not put a stop to the activities of pro-independence Islamists. Still, the blow was harsh enough that the warlords had to turn to more targeted guerrilla operations and opt for suicide operations both within Chechnya and in the very heart of Russia itself. The October 2002 hostage-taking in a Moscow theater was but the prelude to a series of suicide actions, generally carried out by women, throughout 2003; these claimed more than two hundred lives. Media exposure was limited. At this point it is difficult to evaluate the effectiveness of the strategy. But the phenomenon itself has interesting characteristics. First of all, it confirms the existence of a Chechen Islamist terrorist ring capable of turning to such actions. The fact that in 2003 one branch was neutralized in the Paris region as it was planning attacks on Russian interests in France indicates that suicide operations can affect any European state and that no one can feel himself to be in a safe haven. Russian President Putin's firmness in October 2002 was nothing to emulate: 120 Russian citizens died because of the Russian special forces' use of a highly concentrated, exceedingly toxic chemical. This firm stand, for which so high a price was paid, had no deterrent effect. Against such an implacable foe, it was clear that hostage-taking would be ineffective and that it would be better to try to sow terror in and around Moscow by seeking to cause as many deaths as possible, and by doing so indiscriminately. Apart from an approach favoring mutual massacre, it is hard to see what form a political solution could take.

The most striking trend of 2003 was the emergence of suicide and other terrorist attacks in Iraq and in Saudi Arabia. Anti-American operations in Iraq display great diversity in both their origin and their methods. There may be reason to think that Arab Islamist volunteers had been present in Iraq even before the U.S. attack began. It is also possible that the porosity of the borders—the result of the disappearance of Iraqi regular forces—allowed infiltration by Islamist fighters capable of carrying out suicide attacks. This would mean a preexisting clandestine infrastructure providing logistical support for these attacks, which cannot occur without such support. Although human resources are plentiful and although explosives are a widespread commodity throughout the country, a minimum of supervision and preparation is required to plan targeted attacks intended to politically isolate and demoralize the invader.

The same reasoning applies to Saudi Arabia, which had been spared until 2002. That country is probably one of the main strategic objectives of the al Qaeda system's strategists. Although ties with the United States remain stronger and more solid than has been somewhat rashly suggested, relations were damaged by 9/11. For its part, the Saudi monarchy can no longer continue the double game it has played for a generation: support for Salafism in the Islamic world, on the one hand, and its special alliance with the United States, on the other. A crisis in the regime is under way, and it gives full meaning to the attacks of 2003. From the strategic standpoint, Riyadh has truly become a hard target. Given the arrival and popularity of violent Islamism, suicide volunteers may well find Saudi Arabia to be both the site and the perfect target of their future sacrifices.

IDEOLOGY AND STRATEGY

While self-sacrifice does not pervade all human societies, it undoubtedly forms part of military tradition. "The supreme sacrifice" is an expression that remains in the vocabulary of traditional warfare. Soldiers kill themselves to save their comrades. They volunteer for delaying actions from which they know they have practically no chance of returning. They refuse to surrender. From Leonidas at the battle of Thermopylae in 480 B.C.E. to the wars of the twentieth century, the record of such altruistic self-sacrifice is long and its tradition powerful.

The philosophy of the suicide volunteer goes beyond the self-sacrifice of the soldier because it is based on a paradox: on the one hand, such actions are altruistic self-sacrifice; on the other, they require total negation of the human being—both oneself and the other. Such all-encompassing nihilism is the result of twofold reification. Suicide volunteers agree to transform themselves into weapons—explosive objects endowed with intelligence. This choice is the first step into the domain of death. They have renounced their lives and are now part of the arsenal available for future operations to be conceived and planned by their leaders. The second form of reification is that of the human target. The adversary is treated as a thing, a pest, sexless, ageless, and faceless: the nonself, the enemy. Underlying the quality of indiscrimination is this absolute indifference, which often lends a chilling calm to the discourse of suicide volunteers.

Are these explanations not the same as those that cause a group to turn to ordinary terrorism? They undoubtedly are. But what is the additional factor? It is the lethal exchange of "my life for their lives."

We have no intention here of dealing with higher causes and supreme goals. They are no different for war than for terrorism. To sum them up in one perfectly apt word, these goals are the cause. This bears different names and takes different forms depending on the time, the place, the conflict and the individual. It goes by the name of homeland, emperor, revolution, Allah, and so on. In the case of self-sacrifice/homicide, the important thing is to know why—and, more precisely, in exchange for what—human beings agree to give their lives in order to destroy the lives of other human beings. What drives them to this deadly volunteerism?

Superficial explanations for this phenomenon abound. They are made on the basis of a total lack of understanding, on clumsy indignation, or—in particular—on a deliberate intention to discredit the suicide attacker. The targets of aggression respond to this denial of their humanity—everyone's humanity—by denying (even sometimes with a touch of pity) the rationality of their aggressors. They are lunatics, dope addicts, poor souls addled by the brainwashing of the real criminals: their leaders, who exploit them with the prospect of concrete rewards in a hereafter filled with delights that are beyond reach in their world, the world below—far below.

Finally, there is the compassionate version: despair born of the poverty, frustration, and physical abuse inflicted by the enemy. Psychiatrists speak of the trauma young children experience when they witness violence carried out by the "enemy" against their parents or elder siblings.

The demands of any serious operation preclude suicide volunteers being under the influence of any substance that could isolate them from the very things that make them valuable: situational awareness and the ability to adapt. Stimulants can make it possible to overcome physical resistance, but that is where drug use stops.

There is no question that suicide volunteers are motivated by an extraordinary internalization of the cause and that they hate the enemy with a hatred so intense that it ceases to be personal. Together, these two factors yield the reification that opens the way to indiscriminate targeting. Training by the leader maintains and bolsters motivation, which is somewhat further developed by the effects of group dynamics. Without a doubt, once they are trained, suicide volunteers give an impression of psychological strangeness, including to friends and family. They are what might be called initiates, and it is as though they exist in another dimension. But that is only the result of their voluntary decision to become weapons. We must go further back to find the underlying motivation.

Unlike ordinary suicides, whose act is purely self-centered, suicide volunteers are not in despair; quite the contrary. They are tragic "players" impelled by the conviction that their death-dealing sacrifice will yield an improved situation for the cause and for the communities to which they belong. The motive force behind the phenomenon of suicide volunteers thus lies at a crossroads between individual psychology and collective strategy. It is in fact the inverse of despair: the expectation of gain.

But what are these gains? Let us be clear: they are certainly not material benefits in the afterlife, in the form of feasting and lewd delights that break all earthly taboos. Can anyone seriously believe that Islamists are offering a grotesque mirror-image of sharia as a reward? While a literature describing the delights of paradise certainly exists, it must not be taken literally.

The Social Psychology of the Leaders and Their Troops

There are two kinds of leaders: inspirers and instructors. The first remain at a distance and are surrounded by an aura of tragic reverence. They both incarnate and express the cause. The second are the trainers who are near at hand: those who train the corps of suicide volunteers. They form a constantly renewed chain ensuring that the suicide volunteers are prepared. The Vietminh had political instructors modeled on Bolshevik political commissars. In parallel, there were also trainers specializing in this specific kind of operation.

The leaders rarely come from among the poor. To the contrary, they generally belong to the privileged minority within Third World developing societies, going two or three generations back. They are intelligent and very well educated; some are professionals such as doctors and teachers, while others are from the priestly class. With the passage of time, their status as "professional revolutionaries" expunges their original affiliations, without completely eliminating them. Sayyid Qutb, who was among the main inspirations for bin Laden and al-Zawahiri, exemplifies the intellectual frustration with the West that gives rise to an aggressive sense of the fundamental incompatibility between the two cultures, an incompatibility based on fear of a loss of identity. Could it be that the anti-colonial hostility experienced by Great Britain and France between 1920 and 1960 has been replaced by anti-American hostility, in a transfer of negation to the dominant power? Indeed, many violent Islamists have lived in the United States.

The social origins of those who carry out the attacks vary widely. When recourse to suicide attacks becomes more of a mass phenomenon (as, for example, in Iran and Vietnam), these social origins and educational levels grow more modest. The Tamils, the Palestinians, and the 9/11 "Septembrists" have drawn on all social classes. There is a high percentage of students who, far from being poorly educated products of Qur'anic schools, possess real university, scientific, or technological learning. Many have traveled and are familiar with the Western world. Obviously, the overall level of their societies influences who is recruited: the poverty of Chechen society means that fighters—and especially suicide volunteers—will be unsophisticated.

In recent developments we see diversity in all spheres. The presence of women—normal among the LTTE's Black Tigers—is becoming more widespread in Palestine and in Chechnya. Islamist groups are by no means averse to recruiting women. Even nowadays women arouse somewhat less suspicion, and they are as highly motivated as men.

Of fundamental importance are the ties between the leaders and those who carry out the attacks. To combat these attacks effectively, those ties must be broken. Those who seek to counter suicide attacks must get to the heart of this relationship and understand what it is made of. We must not shy away from even the most complex psychological interpretations in seeking all the hidden impulses.

Those leaders who call for self-sacrifice/homicide stand out from the rest of the large cohort of political leaders whose organizations employ terrorism. Once it was Admiral Onishi; today it is Velupillai Prabhakaran of the Tamil Tigers and Sheikh Hasan Nasrallah of Hezbollah who are the focus of cults of personality that are acknowledged to varying degrees.

Oath-taking plays an important role. It means that a decisive choice has been made. The transformation from human being into weapon is consecrated through this promise to one's leader and through commitment of a kind that is well known to students of the psychology of voluntary submission.[7]

The leader is a terrifying archetypal father-figure, who produces an effect of counterterror, and is also the guarantor of what the community gives in return: he ensures the development of a cult of heroes and martyrs. He is the celebrant of its rituals and organizer of the funerary structure of memory, preserved in order to replenish the stock of future suicide volunteers. Schools become the vehicle for education that encourages emulation of the exemplary martyr. Special cemeteries honor suicide volunteers. In this way, the community lives alongside its ever-present dead in a sort of adapted grief that has become bearable. Children are proud of their fathers, their elder brothers—even perhaps their sisters. A culture of which Western societies have become ignorant has been put in place. Instruction combines psychological and moral preparation with operational training.

Training: Learning from Example

In groups such as the Vietminh, the Black Tigers, Hamas, and al-Aqsa Martyrs Brigade, recruits always undergo a period of reclusion of varying length, for training (whether by an imam or a political commissar) and for creating the group dynamic that is indispensable for melting individual willingness in the crucible of the collective will. Such retreats promote the urge to emulate by which each individual is possessed, in the name of the cause; this inspires intragroup rivalry: to kill the most enemies, to destroy the most valuable target, and so on. Fanatical enthusiasm makes it possible to forget death and to enter another psychic dimension beyond that of life in the biological sense. Thus, an impatience to take action—viewed as fulfillment—comes about.

As in any military training, the goal here is to gain mastery over the body and to control the mind. Indeed, to succeed in a suicide operation it is critical to overcome obstacles of two kinds, both of which are part of what make a person human: one's body, and one's awareness of one's fellow human being and sense of membership in the community of the human race.

The first issue is the body's natural reactions. Even the most hardened and most motivated troops, those in whom the code of honor is most deeply ingrained, will not indefinitely resist prolonged, intensive bombardment. This is a simple question of the body's resiliency—quite apart from the effects of the imagination. Fear is also—and above all—a form of physiological protest.

It is here that a very mild stimulant drug can be useful. It calms the body, which threatens at the last moment to rebel and refuse to obey the will. It should go without saying that suicide operations require complete clarity of mind. The very reason for choosing to use suicide volunteers is the flexibility of adaptive intelligence and situational awareness that make it possible to see an action through—or if necessary to modify the original plan or even to abort the operation and try again another time.

It is also necessary to consider the possibility of flashes of morality and spasms of humanity. Killing someone is not easy in the absence of personal enmity or proximity hatred. An unknown, anonymous human being calls too-familiar images to mind: images of oneself to start with. This is where ultimate ideological training comes into play, with its purpose of reifying the enemy and obliterating all sense of human community.

Planning

In well-structured organizations that possess comparatively sheltered "liberated" territories—that is, rear bases—training is carried out at a slow pace, and putting together a carefully planned operation takes time. As with any serious military operation, it is preceded by intelligence gathering; defining the mission; and planning for the action—target reconnaissance and, sometimes, rehearsal.

If the target is of high quality in terms of the strategic objective, there may be several months of preparation. Examples are attacking a ship in the Tamil Nadu strait, and attacking the twin towers and the Pentagon.

The Palestinians have extemporized in the urgent context of direct, nearly daily, confrontation with the Israeli army. Although since 1996 Hamas has taken the time to plan its actions in a strategic context viewed from a political perspective, it has also had to make tactical responses of a military nature. Islamic Jihad and the al-Aqsa Martyrs Brigade have had to take the same approach. There has been a shift in the initiative's central issue.

Logistics

The scale of logistic needs varies with the context. Overall, they remain simple—except in the case of Japan during World War II, where the level of sophistication was commensurate with the Japanese war effort, which remained considerable even in its decline. In most cases, we can speak of a lack of sophistication. All that is needed are easily made or easily acquired explosives to be attached to a belt, and sometimes vehicles. That is the yardstick by which the strategic worth of suicide volunteers can be measured.

THE OVERALL STRATEGY:
ASYMMETRY AND COST-EFFECTIVENESS

Why is self-sacrifice/homicide used? What does it offer that could not be gained from the skillful use of an ordinary weapon? There are many answers and these must be considered on several levels.

On the strategic level, it at least partially redresses imbalances in capacities.

On the logistical level, it is a useful, effective, inexpensive, easily renewable weapon.

And on the tactical level, it is effective because it relies on human intelligence.

It is the weapon of the weakest, of those who moreover perceive an aggression that could result in a very serious defeat endangering the human, territorial, and spiritual community to which they belong. The suicide volunteer is the response of last resort in a strategic situation marked by fundamental asymmetry between the adversaries. This response can compensate for military inferiority: "If we had possessed conventional weapons with which to fight the Israeli invader, martyrdom would have been an illegitimate means. It was necessity that permitted recourse to martyrdom operations," said Hezbollah spokesman Sheikh Malek Wehbe in 1999. Islamist religious leaders are perfectly clear on this point: their action is seen in the context of a different set of values that gives rise to different strategies. When its mullahs and ayatollahs affirm that the present world order is unacceptable, Shiism is returning to its tradition. "We do not fight by the rules of the present world," added another Hezbollah official, Mustafa Shamran. "We reject those rules."

The second advantage of using suicide volunteers as a weapon is generally good cost-effectiveness, which is factored in when determining the value of any weapons system. And that is indeed what we are talking about here: selection, training, equipment, operations, and results vis-à-vis the target. The value of suicide volunteers can be assessed in terms of strategic objectives. Quickly—a little too quickly—a spectacular result can be observed.

We must draw a distinction between strategic effectiveness—attainment of the wartime objective—and operational effectiveness: the success rate of a given mission or a series of missions in terms of gains and losses. It is still necessary to define the mission clearly, by selecting the right targets. Clearly, strategic effectiveness is a function of operational success, but only in part. All the other components of the use of the weapon and all the events that have an impact on the conflict are also factors in the equation; the adversary's evolving reactions and responses are another.

For example, it is possible to measure the operational effectiveness of the kamikazes. Nearly 7,000 pilots were trained and, according to the historian Ikuhito Hata, 3,400 died. In the battle of Okinawa alone, 1,035 were used. Between October 25, 1944 (the battle of Leyte Gulf), and January 11, 1945 (Okinawa), 300 U.S. ships were struck and 34 were sunk. The target was hit in less than one in eight attempts. At Leyte, Japan expended 424 planes and 500 men to neutralize 18 ships, including three small aircraft carriers; this was a very poor result compared with German submarine campaigns in the battle of the Atlantic.

Following the battle of the Philippines, Admirals Chester Nimitz and William Halsey acknowledged that one in four kamikazes had hit his target, but noted that only one in thirty-three had succeeded in sinking a ship. It has been confirmed that 26.8 percent hit a ship and that 2.9 percent succeeded in sinking one. After this, operational effectiveness steadily deteriorated.

The Iran-Iraq war of 1980–88 claimed some 800,000 lives. The toll in Algeria's civil war, which began in 1992 and has by no means come to an end, has far exceeded 100,000. Compared with such slaughter, the number of deaths attributable to suicide operations seems trivial. The kamikazes were a tiny fraction of Japan's war dead: 3,500 compared with the 70,000 to 80,000 killed at Hiroshima in August 1945 and the 80,000 to 100,000 who died in the March 1945 firebombing of Tokyo. Compared with thousands of American lives lost on June 6, 1944, on Omaha Beach, the toll of a kamikaze attack amounted to hardly more than a regrettable incident.

When we look at losses among suicide volunteers per se, the picture varies. The Vietnamese, the Japanese, and the Iranian *bassidje* fielded the largest suicide contingents precisely because they were deployed in the context of a large-scale conventional war. The number of Palestinian suicide volunteers remains modest by comparison. Until a sharp increase in 2002, it stood at some 250, about the same as the number of Black Tigers. The meaning of these figures depends on how they are spread out over time. The Tamils' use of suicide volunteers has been spread out over more than ten years, while the more recent Palestinian practice saw a spectacular intensification starting in the summer of 2001.

Palestinian suicide volunteer operations have achieved very good results in terms of operational effectiveness.

Between 1987 and 1993, the ratio of Palestinian to Israeli losses was 6.7 to 1 (1,162 compared with 174). In the first months of the second intifada, the ratio declined, to 5.3 to 1. And starting in the spring of 2001, systematic use of suicide volunteers transformed the situation, with the ratio declining to 1.7 to 1, then to 1.5 to 1 by the end of the summer.

COMPARATIVE EFFECTIVENESS

Japanese suicide volunteers: Several thousand men and airplanes; explosives still readily available; fuel. Effectiveness too limited in strategic terms.

Vietnamese suicide volunteers: Several tens of thousands of men; small quantities of explosives; easily manufactured; good quality; good strategic and tactical results.

Iranian suicide volunteers: Tens of thousands of young volunteers; no specific weaponry; effective if we discount the human cost.

Tamil suicide volunteers: A few hundred; well prepared; high-quality matériel; very effective.

Lebanese Shiite suicide volunteers (Hezbollah): A few hundred; good planning; simple logistics; rudimentary weaponry; very effective.

Palestinian suicide volunteers: A few hundred, growing rapidly; rudimentary methods deployed locally; results uncertain.

"Septembrist" suicide volunteers from the al Qaeda system: Several thousand; rudimentary methods; good logistics; uneven effectiveness; one spectacular, exceptionally massive strike can in no way predict the final result.

Chechen suicide volunteers: A few hundred; large potential human resources; rudimentary means; final results very uncertain.

Costs vary with the situation. A Japanese kamikaze was very costly in terms of fuel, military pilot training, high-quality delivery vehicle, and explosive charge. A Vietminh, Iranian, Tamil Tiger, or Palestinian suicide volunteer costs nothing compared with a World War II Japanese pilot.

The cost ratio is based on the deployment of a human weapon compared with the target. Nowadays, in addition to the military impact, there is also a psychological—and hence highly political—dimension, which the Japanese never really achieved.

What are the advantages compared with a car bomb? They include suddenness, surprise, precision, and the capacity to penetrate the target. When guided by a human being, a device can explode not merely in front of or alongside a target, but actually within it. Then there is the psychological factor of martyrdom-in-action extolled by supporters, while the adversary is left to absorb the emotional shock of this demonstration of absolute determination.

At this point, there is no answer to the question, even for the intelligence and other bodies responsible for understanding the phenomenon in order to better calibrate the means of protection and response.

Depending on the locale and the target, different levels of thinking and different skills may be appropriate.

The Bali discotheque (attacked by a car bomb in 2002) constituted a limited objective; the attackers did what they could, where they were. The wish to harm—which is, to be sure, common and intense—depends on capacity for action and on the intelligence with which such action is devised. Clearly, in al Qaeda, which is an international system, not all leaders are equally brilliant or networks equally effective. There are many shortcomings. Outside observers are insufficiently aware of these vulnerabilities, and they underestimate them; they attach greater importance to spectacular shows of force. But it would be too much to conclude from this that there is a trend toward a weakened al Qaeda.

Westerners observe only their own reactions. They disregard the negative feelings of local populations who are not eager to pay the price exacted by the car bombs that massacre passers-by while sparing embassy buildings. Can anyone believe that the families of the Nairobi and Dar es Salaam victims in the summer of 1998 blithely forgave the authors of those appalling attacks?

Yet the intelligence and similar services draw a distinction.

It could well be that planning is not always so meticulous and that choices are sometimes the result of an opportunity that presents itself. Attackers may strike a target simply because they have information about it.

Once the weapon is available, the planning of a suicide operation is based also on any intelligence that is to hand and that presents a sudden opportunity. There are two categories of action: those based on lengthy planning, against fixed, very high value targets; and far less sophisticated actions based on a set of circumstances, against targets of opportunity. Suicide volunteers are more useful for the former, but if there is a breeding ground of such volunteers for simpler operations, why not use them?

PUTTING AN END TO IT?

Opposing suicidal terrorism means first and foremost—and as a matter of urgency—diminishing its operational effectiveness. Then, in the long term, it means eliminating its ideological legitimacy. We must focus on the concept of the target, both in its material and, above all, in its moral sense, and must work to develop several modes of action to physically protect and to counterattack. Protection will make suicide operations increasingly difficult to carry out and decreasingly worthwhile. Counterattacking means destroying bases and infrastructure. It can mean the "decapitation" of leaders and instructors. Reprisals against populations and property have the effect of somewhat further tightening the bond between leaders and the people they depend on.

It is also important to seek deterrence at an earlier stage. To the extent that suicide volunteers are motivated by the expectation of gain, everything possible should be done to ensure that, following their action, the situation appears unchanged or worse than before. It is important ultimately to make them think that they have more to lose than to gain and that their goals cannot be reached in this way.

It is striking to observe that any ideological system, if circumstances seem to require it, can come up with arguments to legitimize any action whatsoever on the pretext of the end justifying the means. It is thus possible to discredit a position in ideological terms by delegitimizing it. This would include criticizing the methods vis-à-vis the cause. Clearly, this endeavor can be pursued only from within, by raising doubts about the legitimacy of suicide operations. It means quashing any shred of respect for "martyrs" who kill indiscriminately.

The long-term approach is not an economic one; it is political and ideological. The struggle involves values, in particular that of life in a modern society. The decision to volunteer for death is no excuse for trivializing one's relationship with life. The thoughtlessness and rejection that characterize Western societies at odds with the sacred and the symbolic give rise to a basic vulnerability that can never be addressed by the technology of security.

In order to repel suicide volunteers, we must listen to their message and understand the challenge they pose. They claim that their death outweighs our lives and that human self-sacrifice is a higher thing than a human being. To be unable to continue to respond in this arena would be a defeat with unpredictable—but certainly very serious—consequences.

The suicide weapon—the ultimate stage of terrorism—is very much on the rise today, and it will not disappear any time soon. And strategies for countering suicide attacks are still under development.

NOTES TO CHAPTER 15

1. Livy, *The History of Rome,* 10.28–29, trans. D. Spillan and Cyrus Edmonds, Project Gutenberg eBook (http://www.gutenberg.org/dirs/1/0/9/0/10907/10907-8.txt).

2. Ibid., chap. 29.

3. Bayet, *Histoire de la religion romaine,* 134.

4. Sergei Genadievich Nechayev, "The Revolutionary Catechism" (1869), www.postworldindustries.com/library_text/library_praxis/revolutionary_cate chism.html (accessed April 13, 2006).

5. Venturi, *Populismo russo,* 336–37.

6. See Moczarski, *Conversations with an Executioner.*

7. The ultimate embodiment of the psychology of submission and commitment, albeit in degraded form, is nothing other than advertising. This aspect of manipulation is analyzed at length in Géré, *Guerre psychologique.*

CHAPTER 16

THE UNITED STATES
CONFRONTING TERRORISM

Arnaud Blin

Why a special chapter about the United States? After all, countries such as the United Kingdom and France have been confronting terrorism far longer than the United States, and the threat has been far more constant. Yet since September 11, 2001, America has been the epicenter of international counterterrorism. And in a more general sense the world, like it or not, is now defined in terms of the United States. As Pierre Hassner has written, "While things were once defined in terms of the USSR, China and socialism, it is indeed in relation to the United States, to capitalism and to modernization and globalization—of which it appears to be both the incarnation and the beneficiary—that positions are now taken."[1] As the sole superpower—or, if you prefer, "hyperpower"—the United States has traded the Cold War soldier's uniform it had found it hard to shed after 1991 for the garb of a crusader, the scourge of terrorism (anti-Western terrorism). America is never as highly motivated as when it commits itself to the quasi-divine mission of combating the "forces of evil." After standing against the forces of communism, it is now tenaciously standing against the forces of terrorism. How is it responding, why, and with a view to what? Those are the questions I shall try to answer.

First, however, let us briefly review the history of the United States and terrorism. Contrary to the conventional wisdom widely accepted during the 1980s and 1990s—and even now after the 9/11 attacks—the United States was not completely spared the phenomenon of terrorism in the course of its history, although it may be said that until now terrorism never had a significant impact on the country's political and social life.

THE EARLIEST CONFRONTATIONS

Like the members of so many national liberation movements, Americans had to take up arms to free themselves from the colonial yoke. But it was an act not of terrorism but of provocation—the Boston Tea Party of 1773, when three British ships were stripped of their cargoes of tea, which was then tossed into the harbor—that launched the hostilities against Britain. It had the same impact as a deadly attack would have had, but in the eyes of history, America never engaged in terrorism. Nor did its founding fathers. During an exchange at the United Nations General Assembly on November 13, 1974, Yasser Arafat compared his actions with those of the American revolutionaries. Outraged by such a comparison, the U.S. representative responded on November 21: "There were no victims, on either side [in the Revolutionary War], of a deliberate policy of terror. Those who molded our nation and fought for our freedom never succumbed to the easy excuse that the end justifies the means."[2] The Bostonians' action was spontaneous and was enough to trigger the War of Independence. But who can say with certainty that in different circumstances, the founding fathers would never have turned to the weapon of terrorism?

In any event, it did not take long after the War of Independence for the United States to be faced with a problem not unrelated to the phenomenon of terrorism. Historians are not in the habit of referring to the activities of the Barbary pirates in the Mediterranean as terrorism. Strictly speaking, the pirates' objective was economic more than political. The Barbary ships, in the service of dictatorial strongmen, had the job of holding to ransom foreign vessels plying the Mediterranean. The techniques were those of terror: the pirates perpetrated massacres and took the passengers of some ships hostage so that others would submit and pay tribute in order to travel in peace. This practice had the backing of states and grew to the point at which it nearly amounted to policy, with direct contacts between the states taking the hostages and those being held to ransom. This was not exactly terrorism, but the technique was not dissimilar to that employed by present-day terrorists, especially when their acts are state-sponsored. Coincidentally, the technique was practiced by Tripoli then, as it would be two centuries later under Mu'ammar Gadhafi. As the nineteenth century began, the young United

States had already been the victim of hundreds of attacks against its merchant ships, and it decided to respond, in what would be its first large-scale foreign intervention. It was at this time that Washington assembled a naval force and that the United States, spurred by Thomas Jefferson, committed all available means to ridding itself of this scourge. After several unsuccessful attempts, the U.S. Navy helped free the Mediterranean of a peril that had tormented mariners for centuries.

What is interesting here is not so much to compare the Barbary pirates' practices with those of contemporary terrorists as to analyze the U.S. reaction at the time. It is worth noting too that this had been a little-known episode of American history but was the subject of renewed interest in the United States after the 2001 invasion of Afghanistan, which followed the 9/11 attacks. At the time of its Mediterranean intervention, the United States was an insignificant nation absent from a geopolitical chessboard dominated by Europe: it is no coincidence that during the same period Napoleon Bonaparte sold off territory amounting to one-third of the present lower forty-eight American states to help finance his European campaigns. For its part, the American government decided to fully commit itself to a costly military campaign, whereas the Europeans had preferred to negotiate with the Barbary dictators, incident by incident. But Jefferson had already understood what his successors would take more than a century to grasp: that America's interests were not confined to its national territory. Such intervention off the American continent was highly unusual. Only in the early twentieth century, under William McKinley and Theodore Roosevelt, would the United States again engage beyond its sphere of influence in the Americas—and only in the twenty-first would Washington opt to attack terrorism with massive military force and with assurance of its technological superiority. But for the first time, or nearly, the United States had been struck on its own territory, which until then had been considered inviolable.

Although America did not truly become aware of the terrorist threat until after the events of 2001, it had repeatedly faced terrorism on its own territory. In the late nineteenth century, the United States had gone through its own anarchist "era of attacks," although this was by no means as eventful as what Europe experienced during the same period. The wave of terrorism had resulted from the concurrence of several elements. First of all, the influx of European immigrants brought Old World ideas to the New World. Secondly, industrialization gave rise to a trade union movement that sometimes took a violent political approach. Finally, in this society fascinated by technology, some viewed a new invention, dynamite, as a means to further the demands of society's outcasts; some even went so far as to affirm that dynamite was an instrument of democracy that would set everyone on an equal footing. A further factor was the Civil War, whose long-term impact on American society is difficult to gauge. This war, the first of the industrial age, was marked by savagery unknown since the Thirty Years' War, notably in the devastating campaign conducted by the North's General William Tecumseh Sherman with the objective of destroying the enemy's will to resist. That campaign left its mark, foreshadowing twentieth-century psychological warfare and the increasingly extreme violence of war. Following the war, in the southern states, organizations such as the Ku Klux Klan conducted small-scale local terror campaigns whose violence reflected disappointment at having lost the war. Klan members, operating outside the law and garbed in sheets and hoods, targeted minority communities: blacks, obviously, but also Catholics. During the same period, the practice of "tyrannicide" gained a degree of success with the assassination of several presidents, including Abraham Lincoln, who was killed immediately after the war. But these assassins were not motivated by specific political objectives or by any intention to spark a campaign of terrorism. The phenomenon of "tyrannicide" has been a constant in the history of the United States; the most recent instance was the unsuccessful attempt to assassinate Ronald Reagan in 1981 (however, the would-be assassin, John Hinckley, was not acting out of political motives but in an absurd attempt to impress the actress Jodie Foster). Of all the successful and unsuccessful attacks on American presidents, only one was orchestrated by an organized group: the 1950 attack against Harry Truman carried out by Puerto Rican extremists. Then there is the Kennedy case, but, failing proof to the contrary, the Dallas killing was committed by one man acting alone—and in any event, it was not plotted by a terrorist group.

In the 1980s and 1990s, the United States faced two sources of terrorism: domestic, from extreme right-wing movements; and external, from Islamist terrorists. Before that period, it had experienced two comparatively serious episodes of terrorism. The first occurred between the 1870s and 1890s in the working-class environments of major East Coast and Middle Western cities and against the backdrop of anarchist activism imported from Europe. The second wave followed at the turn of the twentieth century and continued until around 1920. Its theater was the American West and, again, it was the work of individuals belonging to trade union movements and often, again, with anarchist affiliations. Because of the threat it posed, the anarchist movement was suppressed by the American authorities, who forbade membership in such movements. The 1927 execution of the Italian immigrants Nicola Sacco and Bartolomeo Vanzetti shocked international public opinion. The two anarchists, who in 1921 had been sentenced to death for murder in connection with an armed attack—with no tangible proof of their guilt having been established—were sacrificed by the American authorities as symbols of the kind of anarchist terrorism—the "red terror"—that it was their intention to eradicate once and for all. Indeed, American anarchism was now a thing of the past, but America would soon have other far tougher adversaries to contend with.

The first wave of terror took place within the strict logic of the class struggle, with the workers' unions on one side and the bosses on the other. During this period, unfettered capitalism emerged in strength, and friction between exploiter and exploited was at its height. It was also a time of urbanization and the emergence of great metropolitan centers such as Chicago, New York, and Philadelphia. In a word, it was a revolution. Like all revolutions, this one spawned its share of confrontation and violence, including massive strikes and bloody riots. That was the context for the creation, in Philadelphia, of the Molly Maguires, a secret organization of Irish miners. They were active during the ten years following the Civil War, from 1865 to 1875, and waged a campaign of terror using a variety of means, including arson and murder, targeting the employers; this claimed a number of victims, including members of the police. The establishment reacted forcefully; after painstaking police work, the movement's leaders were captured and convicted. The Molly Maguires quickly disappeared, but they inspired other groups and movements on both sides of the Atlantic. Bakunin himself planned to come to America in 1874 to observe the situation at firsthand, but for health reasons was unable to do so. Johann Most immigrated to the United States in 1882 and, through his periodical *Die Freiheit,* established himself as the spokesman for anarchist activism. The energetic Most built a small core group of active, determined supporters. Along with two of them, Albert Parsons and August Spies, he created the "Black International," known officially as the International Working People's Association, in Pittsburgh in 1883; its headquarters were established in Chicago. The chaotic economy of the time helped ensure it a measure of success, with its leaders organizing a large number of meetings throughout the country. American anarchists were in the headlines, most of the time reviled for their "anti-American activities"—a recurrent notion in U.S. history, including during the McCarthy era.

The 1886 Haymarket Square episode in Chicago is an enduring symbol of the anarchist terror of that time. In early May, during a workers' strike, a policeman fired on the crowd, killing one person and wounding several others. An outraged August Spies put pen to paper and published an incendiary editorial in the anarchist paper *The Alarm,* whose title was a call to rebellion: "Revenge! Workingmen, to Arms!" A rally was planned for May 4 near Haymarket Square; some three thousand people attended. Forewarned, the police were there in force, with nearly two hundred men. A bomb was thrown at the police, who responded by firing on the crowd, in turn provoking the demonstrators. At least a dozen people died, including seven policemen. The incident, news of which was spread through the great press outlets that were then emerging, shocked the nation. The authorities opted to react forcibly, arresting ten or so leaders, including Spies and Parsons, both of whom were sentenced to death; they were executed on November 11, 1887. Johann Most, who had not been on the scene, was not apprehended, but his time had passed: a new generation of anarchist activists had arisen, led by two Russian émigrés, Emma Goldman and Alexander Berkman.

The Haymarket Square incident had not eased tensions between workers and employers. In the steelmaking capital Pittsburgh—where one of the era's great captains of industry, Andrew Carnegie, had made his vast fortune—about ten people were killed during a confrontation between striking workers and the forces of order (Pinkerton operatives, in this case, not regular police) on July 6, 1892, at the steelworks at Homestead. Following this incident, the state of Pennsylvania restored order and broke the strike by sending 8,000 militiamen to the scene. A furious Alexander Berkman resolved to take action. On July 23, he entered the office of the highly influential Henry Clay Frick—Carnegie's right hand and an important art collector—who had organized the suppression of the strike. Berkman fired several pistol shots at point-blank range. Miraculously, Frick survived the attack with no lasting effects. Berkman (whose action was condemned by Most) was sentenced to twenty-two years in prison, but was released in 1906 following a media campaign on his behalf.

Five years before this, on September 6, 1901, U.S. President William McKinley has been shot by an assassin; he died on September 14. The attacker was Leon Czolgosz, an admirer of Emma Goldman and Johann Most. An 1894 law banned foreign anarchists from emigrating to the United States, but could do nothing to prevent Americans from being sympathetic to anarchist thinking. Although of Polish origin, Czolgosz had been born in Detroit, Michigan, and he belonged to no movement.

Although consistent with a terrorist approach, Czolgosz's attack remained an isolated act for which he alone was responsible, having formed the idea following the assassination of Italy's King Umberto I in 1900. Nonetheless, it had important repercussions for American—and even international—politics: McKinley's vice-president, Theodore Roosevelt, replaced him in the White House and took the country in a whole new direction, intended to enable it to play a leading role on the international political stage. Since Jefferson's time, America had evolved considerably, but apart from the rest of the world. Now it had a president who matched its power. The era of isolation was over, and so was that of anarchist workers' rebellion—or nearly. In the great cities of the American East, the violent anarchism of the followers of Bakunin was giving way to a peaceful form of anarchism.

Now it was on the West Coast that labor unions would turn to terrorist methods. The impact of revolutionary thought imported from Europe was not as great in the West as in the East, because new immigrants had not yet made their way across the country. Yet anarchist thought was not unknown, and a number of unionists declared themselves to be anarchists. Although these terrorist movements did not have a very well developed political organization, the individuals who chose the path of action enjoyed some striking media success. In 1905, the Western Federation of Miners unionist Harry Orchard, born Albert Horsley, was arrested for the murder of Frank Steunenberg, a former governor of Idaho. Upon his arrest, and without supporting evidence, he accused union leaders of involvement, including the treasurer, William "Big Bill" Haywood, an anarchist sympathizer who would end his days in the Soviet Union. In 1910, another attack that attracted heavy press coverage took some twenty lives in Los Angeles: a bomb exploded in the offices of the *Los Angeles Times,* whose editor was openly hostile to trade unions. Those responsible for the bombing included two brothers, John and James McNamara, the first of whom was treasurer of the Bridge and Structural Iron Workers Union. In 1916, another major California city, San Francisco, was the site of a bombing that took ten lives. Another unionist, Thomas Mooney, was accused of the attack, along with his disciple Warren Billings, who had previously been jailed for dynamite possession. This episode is not without parallels to the events that, decades later, would take place in Oklahoma City.

In 1920, this time in New York, an explosion at the J. P. Morgan Bank claimed thirty-four victims; its authors were never identified. This finally sparked a robust reaction from the U.S. government, which arrested thousands of activists. Those it deemed most dangerous, it speedily deported to the Soviet Union. They included Emma Goldman and Alexander Berkman—who wasted no time in leaving that country, where the liquidation of anarchists was in full spate. Once again the U.S. government had acted briskly, not hesitating to show disdain for the very human rights that President Wilson had so recently been championing. In 2001 the authorities would do likewise when they set up the internment camp at Guantánamo Bay in Cuba.

THE NEW LEFT

After this "red scare," terror attacks were far less common in America; only a few isolated acts took place. The country and its leaders were now preoccupied with the Depression, then with World War II and the Cold War. The times of unrest that had punctuated American history were forgotten. It was not until the 1960s that terrorism would reappear in the United States, aside from the Capitol attack in Washington, D.C., by Puerto Rican extremists in 1954, when five representatives were wounded, one seriously. This time, the terrorist violence came from extremist movements spawned by the New Left. Ideologically speaking, the majority of these movements claimed to follow Marxist thought, whether Leninist, Trotskyite, or Maoist. This political trend would be influenced by three events: the civil rights struggle, which President Lyndon Johnson had made one of his priorities; the Vietnam War, which was the object of increasingly powerful opposition; and the wars of national liberation, which inspired a number of groups, including the Black Panthers. This was a period of increasing openness: political (with John F. Kennedy), social (with the sexual revolution), and cultural (with the emergence of the "counterculture"). As ever, California was in the vanguard of America's cultural evolution. The campuses of the major universities—starting with the University of California at Berkeley—were fertile ground for New Left political activism, and it was in California that many small groups were formed and operated. These included the Symbionese Liberation Army (SLA), which, although it had only a dozen or so members, carried out a number of deadly attacks. The SLA achieved the most prominent media coup of the time when it kidnapped Patricia Hearst, the heiress of press magnate Randolph Hearst, who went over to the side of her abductors. There was also Students for a Democratic Society (SDS), of which a small core group operated in secret, and the Weathermen, who were responsible for many bombings. The latter group was much talked about as the 1960s gave way to the 1970s, but it had little real impact on American politics, although its prime objective was to blow up society and bring about a revolution.

The 1960s would see the abscess of racial problems in the United States burst with the civil rights movement of which the Reverend Martin Luther King Jr., assassinated in 1968, was the standard-bearer. It was only logical that radical movements should emerge from this struggle; these included the Black Panther movement, which was created in 1966. The Black Panthers saw the battle waged by American blacks as an anti-colonial war of liberation in the context of the class struggle. At first, the Panthers did not necessarily tread the path of terrorism, but over time, the movement became increasingly radical, just as its weaknesses became more apparent. Before it had a chance to have any real effect on events, the organization collapsed under the twofold weight of its own shortcomings and the tough action the American authorities took against it. Ultimately, nothing much was left behind by these movements, which very quickly faded away. Yet again, the limitations of radical left-wing ideology had become evident in a society where, for various reasons, it had never been widespread. And yet again, the American government, by sparing no means, had succeeded in crushing the revolt. There was no doubt that, under Richard Nixon (elected to the White House in 1968 and again in 1972)—a president brought up on the struggle against communism—America would not let itself be undermined by a handful of no-account movements.

From that point, terror in the United States would be carried out by isolated individuals for a variety of reasons, often personal in nature, and most of the time using explosives. The best known of them, Theodore Kaczynski, long known as the Unabomber, gained notoriety through the letter bombs he sent to random victims over a period of nearly two decades. Having killed seventeen people, he was finally turned in by his brother in 1997. On the model of groups of the 1960s and 1970s, this former Berkeley assistant professor withdrew to a cabin in the woods; he gave in to the desire to see his lengthy neo-Luddite "manifesto" in print, and that was his downfall: it was published in major newspapers, and Kaczynski's brother recognized the author, whose motivations had probably been as much personal as ideological.[3]

THE NEW TERRORISTS

The transition from the period of the sexual revolution and the counterculture to that of the money-mad 1980s reflected a 180-degree turn in

American terrorist activity. Now, the weapon of terrorism was wielded by movements of the far right. This new form of terrorism culminated in the April 19, 1995, bombing of the Alfred P. Murrah Federal Building in Oklahoma City. With its 168 victims, this was by far the deadliest terrorist attack in American history until September 11, 2001.

The new American terrorists, who continue to be active, are of varied origins. On the one hand, they include fringe elements opposed to all forms of government power and falling within the libertarian tradition, but in a radical, violent, and grotesquely exaggerated form. These individuals and small groups are often also linked to anti-government private militias and organizations whose purpose is to defend the "right to bear arms." The very powerful National Rifle Association constantly declares, loud and clear, that this is a constitutional right—without mentioning the context in which this right was included in the Constitution. While lacking real ideological ties, adherents are often drawn to the racist theories enunciated by groups ranging from neo-Nazis to the Ku Klux Klan, which in turn includes a myriad of rival clans.

Then there are the terrorist movements of the extreme right. These are closely allied with the Christian right, which so fervently supported George W. Bush in the 2000 election. The Christian far right has a long history behind it, and over the past two centuries it has fueled quite a number of hate groups, starting with the Know-Nothings, who were already active before the Civil War in their battle against (generally Irish) Catholics and who arose several decades before their counterparts of the Ku Klux Klan. These anti-immigrant nativists were the forerunners of today's survivalists, whose most radical elements have retreated to the vast states of the northwest such as Idaho and Montana, fleeing everything they detest, such as cities, blacks, Asians, Jews, immigrants, and Catholics. The Christian extreme right has always drawn its ideology from certain specific biblical passages and especially from prophetic texts, which they use, for instance, to justify their virulently anti-Semitic positions.

The new fundamentalist terrorists, unlike the fringe elements, focus on a specific cause: their condemnation of abortion. The January 22, 1973, Supreme Court decision in *Roe v. Wade* to permit first-trimester abortion was the starting point for a major protest movement, which in its most radical form was akin to terrorism. In general, the fringe elements are of rural working-class background, while the anti-abortionists belong to the educated middle classes. Both groups used terrorism in the 1980s and 1990s, achieving some media success. During the first two decades of their terrorist activities, anti-abortion groups set nearly one hundred arson fires, detonated around forty bombs, attacked about a hundred people (mainly the medical personnel of clinics performing abortions and their patients) and killed seven. Fringe groups were far less active, but the Oklahoma City bombing had more of an effect on the American public than any other before 2001. The trial of the main perpetrator—Timothy McVeigh, a decorated veteran of the U.S. Army, who was sentenced to death in 1997 and was executed on June 11, 2001— was the subject of vast media coverage.

CONFRONTING INTERNATIONAL TERRORISM

For the Americans, the 1980s began with the Iran hostage-taking on November 4, 1979, which made it possible for Ronald Reagan to enter the White House, and ended with the collapse of European communism, of which event Reagan declared himself the great architect. In between, the Soviet intervention in Afghanistan gave Washington the chance to take revenge for its failure in Vietnam by supporting Afghan resistance movements. This is when a tree took root: the tree that would soon bear the poisoned fruit of terrorism. And those who were behind that terrorism were determined to make America tremble. Among the pawns Washington used to harass the Soviet Union was one Osama bin Laden. The confrontation with the USSR was at its height, and the politicians were thinking about today and perhaps about tomorrow—but almost never about the day after.

The Reagan years were a time of optimism. They followed the stagnation of the 1970s, which had been marked by the domestic crisis of Watergate and by a succession of humiliations including Vietnam and Iran. America wanted to turn the page. It had elected a man who incarnated the can-do optimism of the republic's early years. At the time, few observers took the terrorist threat seriously: it was something of concern to Old Europe but, in their view, the United States had always been protected by its insularity, at least as far as international and transnational terrorism went. And why would that change? In any event, it was more useful to concentrate, first and foremost, on serious matters such as victory over the Soviet Union. Reagan's people were seasoned veterans of the Cold War, and they thought—and acted—in terms of bipolar confrontation. Some of them would reappear surrounding George W. Bush, this time waging a different war: the war against terrorism.

Early warning signs of a terrorist threat from abroad began to be noted. George Shultz, Reagan's second secretary of state, was among the first American leaders to understand that a grave threat was forming on the horizon and that it would be preferable to eliminate it while there was still time. But hardly anyone listened to this visionary. As ever, it was novelists who looked into the future; they were already envisioning various catastrophic scenarios involving terrorists and weapons of mass destruction, as in the 1991 novel *The Sum of All Fears,* by the best-selling author Tom Clancy, who specialized in military subjects. The issue was then picked up by the research institutes, which took this kind of terrorism very seriously. In the 1990s, public counterterrorism funding was largely devoted to projects studying mass-destruction terrorism, at the expense of fieldwork aimed against "conventional" terrorism. Indeed, this was one reason for the intelligence services' inability to predict the events of 9/11. But the Reagan administration—as well as that of the second President Bush—held the conviction (or the fantasy) that America had reached the political, economic, and technological level at which it could acquire an unbreachable shield. Plans for a nuclear shield were drawn up under Reagan and were updated under George W. Bush. From its inception, U.S. anti-terrorism strategy counted on America's unquestioned superiority in the area of military technology. This model was the successor to the venerable policy of containment of the communist bloc, which had been Washington doctrine from the onset of the Cold War. And it gave rise to the strategy of "preemptive war" that Washington unveiled in the wake of the 2001 attacks, although it had been in development since the fall of the Soviet Union in 1991; this strategy provided the framework for the "war on terrorism" declared by the Bush administration.

In 2001, one had the impression that Washington had suddenly realized the full extent of the terrorist threat. Yet there had been many warning signs over the previous two decades. During the 1980s, a number of major attacks had struck America, some at close range and some further off. Among these were the bombing of a Marine barracks in Beirut (1983), the hijacking of TWA flight 847 (1985), the hijacking of the cruise ship the *Achille Lauro* (1985), the airport massacres at Rome and Vienna (on the same day in 1985), and the bombing of a West Berlin discotheque frequented by GIs (1986). Elsewhere, more than a hundred other terrorist attacks affected American citizens.[4] It was in Beirut on October 23, 1983, that the United States paid the highest price—241 deaths—just a few months after a suicide truck bomb had exploded in front of the U.S. embassy, claiming sixty-three lives, including those of seventeen Americans. Attacks on U.S. embassies would increase in number over the years; they were a way for terrorists to attack the United States without having to enter its territory. That was why—in spite of the increasing number of attacks on Americans and American interests abroad—Americans were barely affected psychologically until September 11, 2001: their territory seemed to be inviolable.

But Washington's leaders could not forever stand idly by in the face of such provocations. In part, 1980s terrorism involved states that sponsored terrorist groups. This was a godsend for Washington, which, owing to America's strategic culture, was far more comfortable facing up to states than fighting irregulars or, worse, nebulous elements. Moreover, the Vietnam syndrome was still very much in effect at that time. Therefore, if the problem were linked to a country, a solution seemed reachable. Reagan—the great communicator—had a perfect understanding of this equation. On July 8, 1985, he named five countries as members of a "confederation of terrorist states": Iran, North Korea, Cuba, Nicaragua, and Libya. Later, there would be talk of a rather longer list of "rogue states," then fifteen years later, under George W. Bush, of an "axis of evil" comprising North Korea, Iran, and Iraq. At that time, in the mid 1980s, the Libyan dictator Mu'ammar Gadhafi was in the Americans' sights, as Saddam Hussein (then "allied" with the United States in the context of its anti-Iran policy) would be later.

Another constant of American policy is the desire to identify an adversary and demonize it. Dealing with that adversary thus becomes a biblically inspired struggle pitting the forces of good against the forces of evil. The adversary might be Hitler, Stalin, the Soviet Politburo, or communism. The forces of the World War II Axis combined with those embodied by the Cold War evil empire (to use Reagan's expression) gave way to George W. Bush's famous "axis of evil." At a certain point, Gadhafi cut a very pallid figure as the embodiment of evil, but the media undertook to demonize this monster as Washington waited impatiently for an opportunity to respond to terrorism by mounting an attack against the Libyan leader. On April 5, 1986, a bomb went off in the La Belle discotheque in Berlin, wounding two hundred and killing two (an American soldier and a Turk). Once the link between the Berlin attack and Tripoli had been established, Washington planned an offensive against the Libyan dictator.

On April 14 (the night of the fifteenth in Libya), with the support of the United Kingdom, and without that of France,[5] Washington launched F-111 bombers from British bases with a list of targets including Gadhafi's headquarters. Two hours after the attack, President Reagan appeared on American television and said, "We believe that this preemptive action against his terrorist installations will not only diminish Colonel Qadhafi's capacity to export terror, it will provide him with incentives and reasons to alter his criminal behavior."[6] The operation was a success on many levels. First and foremost, it was an enormous media coup, with all the television networks rebroadcasting the bombing ad nauseam, using raw footage taken from the bombers themselves. The attack helped cool Gadhafi's ardor; subsequently, he was far more subdued. Finally, the greatest victory linked to this attack was the Washington government's demonstration to its European allies that it could take action on its own, even in their sphere. In retrospect we can see that the modest 1986 attack had already set the parameters of the American anti-terror strategy that those surrounding President George W. Bush—who included a large number of former Reagan associates—put in place following September 11, 2001. Among those parameters were the idea of linking a terrorist act to a state, such as the Taliban regime or Saddam Hussein; the idea that massive military response is a way to solve the problem of terrorism; the concept of preemptive war; and the American determination to act alone if necessary.

Despite the success of the attack against Gadhafi, it is difficult to assert that it had a meaningful impact on the global struggle against transnational terrorism, which expanded in the course of the 1990s. Two events would contribute to the surge in transnational terrorism: the collapse of the Soviet Union in 1991, which put an end to the Cold War; and the birth of a major center of terrorism based in Afghanistan, supported in particular by the supposed Saudi billionaire Osama bin Laden. But terrorism would not develop in the direction predicted by American experts (whose ranks suddenly swelled at the turn of the 1990s), the great majority of whom focused on the connection between terrorism and high technology, now far more easily accessible through weapons and technology transfers from the former Soviet republics, starting with Russia.

In the United States, the 1990s were years of renewal under Bill Clinton. Elected in 1992, the young Arkansas Democrat embodied a resurgence of the Kennedy myth. John F. Kennedy had marked the rejuvenation of American society by turning the page on the rigidity of the 1950s. Bill Clinton turned another page: the page of the Cold War, whose final lines had been written by George H. W. Bush. America was ready to move on. The once-weakened economy regained its strength after having derailed the reelection campaign of President Bush, even though he was basking in the glow of his Gulf War victory against Saddam Hussein. Then, in the early 1990s, there was relatively little talk of terrorism. Obviously, the angst-mongers continued to wave their arms, warning about the virtual threat of terrorists using weapons of mass destruction and about cyberterrorism. But they never succeeded in convincing the public or the political leadership. The enemy seemed to be elsewhere: for instance, in a China that was in the midst of an economic upsurge. In any event, Clinton had a different perspective on international relations; he gave economic relations priority over political relations. This was a policy of expanding the American model of democracy and opening international markets. International and transnational terrorism was at most a nuisance, like organized crime or the drugs trade, of which Colombian narcoterrorism—the financing of Colombian guerrilla movements through cocaine production—was the most violent form.

Yet international terrorism would creep onto American territory with the first attack on the World Trade Center, on February 26, 1993. This half-failed bombing of one of the twin towers killed five people and wounded hundreds. The authorities arrested a suspect: Sheikh Omar Abdel Rahman, who had worked with the U.S. clandestine services during the Afghan war. Yet once initial emotions had subsided, Americans' reaction was not as strong as one might have imagined given that this was a first in U.S. history. Curiously, the 1995 sarin gas attack in the Yokohama subway would have a greater impact than the New York bombing. The Yokohama incident, which led to no further attacks, triggered a major reaction among American anti-terrorist officials, who justifiably saw it as the start of a new era in the history of terrorism.

Still, attention needed to turn to the Islamists, and especially to Osama bin Laden. Bin Laden began to attract attention in 1996, when he issued a fatwa against the United States, in which he called on his "Muslim brothers" to kill American citizens: "The decision to kill Americans and their allies—civilian and military—is an individual duty for every Muslim who can do so in any country where it is possible." A truck bomb targeting a U.S. military base at Dhahran in Saudi Arabia that year killed nineteen Americans and wounded several hundred, and Washington pointed to bin Laden as being responsible. In 1998, bin Laden issued another fatwa, against "Jews and Crusaders," and on August 7 that year two car-bomb attacks on the U.S. embassies in Kenya and Tanzania claimed 224 lives, including those of twelve Americans. This time, Washington opted to respond with air strikes against targets in the Sudan and in Afghanistan. The operation became a fiasco from the time when it became apparent that the intelligence services had mistaken the nature of the targeted sites. In any event, the air attacks would do nothing to solve the problem of the terrorist threat.

Washington had responded using its high-tech resources to resolve a problem that called, first and foremost, for human resources on the ground. The U.S. intelligence services—neither very effective nor much heeded since the end of the Cold War, in the wake of an unfortunate series of scandals—showed their limits in the war against terror, especially on the international level. Two years later, on October 12, 2000, the bin Laden network struck again when a small boat filled with explosives was launched against the USS *Cole,* an American destroyer anchored at the Yemeni port of Aden, killing seventeen American sailors. And bin Laden's men had already begun planning their attacks against New York and Washington.

SEPTEMBER 11 AND THE U.S. RESPONSE

Let us briefly recap the events of September 11, 2001. Four U.S. airliners were seized by nineteen hijackers belonging to the bin Laden network. Two planes crashed into the twin towers of New York's World Trade Center and a third struck the headquarters of the Department of Defense, the Pentagon. A fourth aircraft, which might have been headed for the White House or the Capitol, crashed in Pennsylvania. In all, three thousand people died in these attacks, the vast majority of them in the collapse of the New York skyscrapers, whose metal structure melted in the fires caused by the explosion of the two airliners: long-range aircraft had been chosen because of the large quantity of fuel they would be carrying. The 9/11 attacks were the biggest achievement yet by a terrorist group: in media terms (the attacks were broadcast live around the world); symbolically (the attacks struck at the core of America's financial center and military establishment); and statistically, with the large number of victims (the term "megaterrorism" was used). There is no doubt that, psychologically, America and much of the rest of the world, especially in the West, were in a state of shock.

Islamic terrorists had succeeded, through a spectacular act of force, in throwing the West off balance: the West, which they viewed as morally corrupted by its materialism. The Islamist strategy encompassed other elements: it stood against Israel, for example, as well as against the regimes of most Muslim countries. In theory at any rate, this strategy formed a coherent whole. The al Qaeda worldview may have seemed grotesquely distorted, but terrorist movements need powerful ideas and are always subjective when analyzing the state of the world and its future. Westerners too bore a share of responsibility for formulating theories—some more convincing than others, but always provocative—about the decline of the West. Looking at Paul Kennedy's and Emmanuel Todd's ideas about the decline of the United States and at the theories of Samuel Huntington on the "clash of civilizations" and of Robert Kagan on the weakness of Europe, it was easy for the general public to find reasons for concern about the future of Western civilization.[7]

On 9/11, America was caught off guard. But in spite of the state of collective shock, Washington immediately put together a list of strategic options for a response. From immediately after the attacks, an offensive against Iraq figured among these, even though nothing suggested that that country was involved in this act of terrorism. The moderate line of Secretary of State Colin Powell ultimately prevailed, and the White House planned a large-scale operation against Afghanistan, where the Taliban regime was sheltering the al Qaeda network and its training camps. This first reaction, however, reflected a particular climate and in the end those advocating an offensive against Saddam Hussein succeeded in imposing their views and finally got their Iraq war.

Having squeaked into the presidency in a questionable election, George W. Bush had the reputation of a lightweight when he entered the Oval Office in January 2001. He compensated for his lack of experience by surrounding himself with a strong team of veterans driven by powerful convictions and impatient to make up for what they thought of as the time lost by Bill Clinton, who had not exploited the superiority of the United States following the collapse of the Soviet Union. The vast majority of the team members (apart from Colin Powell and National Security Adviser Condoleezza Rice) were right-wing activists, who would become known as the hawks; they wanted at any cost to get the country on track—or get it back on track—by exploiting its superiority and power. From the moment they took office, the hawks openly or not so openly declared some of their objectives: to increase the defense budget to enable the military to carry out the hoped-for technological revolution; to create an anti-nuclear defense system as quickly as possible; to reconceive America's global strategy on a new footing; to tackle the problem of the proliferation of weapons of mass destruction; and to put an end to Saddam Hussein after the "incomplete" Gulf War, in which Bush senior had opted to withdraw his troops before bringing down the Baathist regime.

Most of these objectives would demand a major effort of political persuasion, particularly in Congress, which held the keys to the public treasury. Indeed, the game was by no means won. President Bush's initial steps were hesitant. But overnight, the situation completely changed. George W. Bush now had a unique chance to put his stamp on American policy, and his team had the wit and the presence of mind to seize the opportunity at a time of the highest tension. It is not surprising that some observers saw orchestrated manipulation in the 9/11 attacks: politically, they were a godsend with significant repercussions. In any event, although the White House had nothing to do with the attacks, it did an excellent job of profiting from their consequences.

Now, America had a strategy: the "war on terror." This had the advantage of being comprehensible, free of all moral ambiguity, and consonant both with American political culture (the notion of mission) and with the instincts of George W. Bush, a man who, like Reagan, operated mainly on the basis of conviction and instinct.[8] On September 20, Bush made a speech in which he set this war in a Manichean framework that was in complete harmony with American political culture and in which he indicated Washington's hegemonic ambitions: "Every nation, in every region, now has a decision to make. Either you are with us, or you are with the terrorists. From this day forward, any nation that continues to harbor or support terrorism will be regarded by the United States as a hostile regime."[9] Above all, the war on terrorism would enable the administration's extremist wing—starting with the Pentagon's chiefs, Donald Rumsfeld and Paul Wolfowitz—to claim victory in their battle with the moderate line represented by Colin Powell. For his part, Powell favored a policy of international cooperation giving primacy to diplomacy, somewhat along the lines of the pragmatic policy once followed by Henry Kissinger. Paradoxically, Powell's initial victory with the decision to pursue the Afghanistan campaign would now be turned against him.

Contrary to all expectations, the punitive war against the Taliban regime was an unquestionable success for the American military. While many had predicted another Vietnam or a remake of the Soviet disaster of the 1980s, the U.S. armed forces—thanks to its air power and special forces, and assisted on the ground by troops opposed to the Taliban regime—in a matter of weeks did away with one of the most reactionary regimes on the planet. Although it was not eliminated, the al Qaeda organization experienced a serious reversal, and its chief disappeared. This success galvanized the hawks, who saw in the military triumph (postwar reconstruction was rather less conclusive) a springboard for implementing the strategic vision they wanted to impose on the White House, the country, and the world.

Indeed, after 9/11, funding for defense and counterterrorism, including domestic security, was considerably augmented. The White House began a reorganization to centralize counterterrorism; this resulted, among other things, in the creation of the Department of Homeland Security. Above all, the hawks obtained the resources they desired, benefiting from unwavering public support and not being hampered by their political opposition, which remained silent. The only area of doubt lay in the bitter internal battle against the moderates within the government. Colin Powell was increasingly isolated, and he finally lost the day when a number of allies, starting with France, undercut him during diplomatic exchanges related to the decision to invade Iraq.

Through the sleight of hand that politicians are so good at, the White House had managed to convince the public that overthrowing the Iraqi regime was an indispensable part of the war on terrorism. Following American tradition, Washington's intention was to use military force to solve the problem. But this time, unlike in the Gadhafi episode, the case had yet to be made. Nevertheless, just as Washington's strategic vision had linked the problem of terrorism to that of the proliferation of weapons of mass destruction, it succeeded in selling the idea that Iraq's clandestine production of such weapons—forbidden under UN Security Council resolution 687 (1991), adopted after the Gulf War—was the equivalent of terrorist activity. It remained to be proven that following 1991, Saddam Hussein had actually sought to develop such weapons in defiance of the UN ban. Although nothing was proven, the Iraqi dictator's general stance could have given the impression that he had indeed sought to develop arms of this kind. The report issued by the UN experts was ambiguous enough to be subject to a variety of interpretations, and Washington asserted that the evidence justified suspecting the Iraqi president of illegal activities. This was enough to unleash an operation that some had been awaiting for a decade.

In reality, the twofold threat of terrorism and weapons of mass destruction was nothing more than a pretext to get rid of an enemy who had long been in the Americans' sights—particularly those of Republicans close to the Bush family. The strategic head of the Bush administration's neoconservative camp, Paul Wolfowitz, number-two at the Pentagon, had put forward the idea of regime change in Iraq as early as 1992. Here, Wolfowitz was taking up an old Reaganite concept—preemptive action—and making it a key tenet of his new strategy. The age of deterrence was giving way to the age of preemption. Now, the theoretical concept of preemptive or preventive war became intertwined in practice with the war on terrorism that had begun following 9/11. But this vision went far beyond preemptive war: it was a way to establish American supremacy and to transform the United States into an uncontested hegemonic power for decades to come.

To that end, Wolfowitz proposed intervening in the Middle East and promoting in the region a democratic zone of peace and free trade favorable to the United States. This proposal was a blend of realism and idealism, in the purest American tradition; the underlying principle was that once democracy was established in Iraq, it would inexorably spread and ultimately transform the region. This scenario had many advantages. Saddam Hussein's was an unpopular and weakened regime and would be unable to resist a U.S. military offensive. The long-term exploitation of Iraqi oil fields would ensure greater independence from Saudi Arabia, whose reliability as an ally had been faulted after 9/11. It also would ultimately have a positive impact on the Israeli-Palestinian conflict. Finally, such a solution appeared to provide a way of combating both Islamist terrorism and the threat posed by weapons of mass destruction.

We all know what followed. In the spring of 2003, coalition forces—essentially American and British—speedily dealt with the Saddam Hussein regime, which offered hardly any resistance. As for the overthrown dictator, American soldiers arrested him a few months later. No weapons of mass destruction were found, and a way around the question of the intervention's legitimacy was found in a moral justification: the ouster of a dictator and the establishment of a democratic regime—principles that had barely been mentioned when the decision to act was being taken. Nevertheless, the Bush administration continued to interpret the war in Iraq—and to sell it to the public—as one of the pillars of the war against terrorism. Once the war had been more or less declared to be over—"Major combat operations in Iraq have ended"[10]—Washington encountered far more problems in achieving the second element of its strategy: winning the peace in Iraq and setting up a democratic government to which it could hand over power. Time will tell the extent to which the intervention in Iraq furthered the war against terrorism.

Having earlier severely minimized the terrorist threat, the United States completely changed its position after 2001 and made terrorism the foundation of its strategic vision for the twenty-first century. Domestically, numerous security measures were put in place, including very strict controls at airports and in public buildings. Border controls were tightened, especially with regard to the granting of visas. Immigrants viewed as suspect were detained. Organizationally, the administration sought to centralize the counterterrorist command and control system while simultaneously trying to reshape the vast intelligence community, which was being sapped by infighting. The federal and state governments also granted their respective departments of justice additional resources to take action in this area.

It is hard to gauge the degree to which all these measures helped curb the terrorist threat. They certainly made everyday life for Americans and visitors a little less simple and threatened to undermine civil liberties and human rights. Here, many questions were raised by the decision to intern prisoners suspected of terrorist activities at the naval base in Guantánamo Bay, Cuba: some 660 individuals from 42 countries, mainly veterans of al Qaeda camps who had been captured during the Afghan war. But the creation of this "extra-legal" zone was not the only gray area. The Patriot Act, adopted in the wake of 9/11, enabled the government to acquire personal information on individuals not proven to be engaged in terrorist activities, with all the abuses that this involves.[11]

Abroad, the war on terrorism gave the American government an opportunity to go off in new directions, but using old reference points. The strategy of preemption requires that the new enemy, as in the days of communism, be a centralized entity with more or less well defined objectives, preferably a state or group of states. This requirement poses two problems. First, the terrorist threat clearly cannot be linked solely to the actions of a state. Secondly, the blacklist of states accused of terrorism was not exactly compiled using objective criteria. On the one hand, there is Iraq, whose support for al Qaeda was not at all evident; on the other, we find Pakistan and Saudi Arabia, whose ambiguous policies do not prevent them from remaining America's allies. Therein lies the paradox of a policy whose declared objectives are out of sync with its true objectives. In spite of everything, we are dealing with a democracy, subject to public opinion and, above all, to elections. But the hegemonic ambitions of the neoconservatives are in fundamental opposition to the philosophical, but eminently practical, view of the democratic values the United States claims to promote. Raymond Aron had already observed this in the context of the conflict with the Soviet Union.[12] But in the "war against terrorism," this paradox is even more striking, since ultimately the threat posed by transnational and international terrorism cannot be compared to the threat represented by the Soviet Union. Here, we recall the words of Franklin Delano Roosevelt: "the only thing we have to fear is fear itself." Among the fundamental freedoms that Roosevelt sought to defend was "freedom from fear." It appears that the defense of this freedom in the name of the war against terrorism has given the American government a free hand to fish in troubled waters, both on U.S. territory and abroad. Yet another American historical figure, Benjamin Franklin, once cautioned: "Those who would give up essential Liberty, to purchase a little temporary Safety, deserve neither Liberty nor Safety."

NOTES TO CHAPTER 16

1. Hassner, *Terreur et l'empire,* 149.

2. Official Records of the UN General Assembly, 29th sess., plenary meetings, vol. 2, 2294th meeting, para. 59. See also Parry, *Terrorism: From Robespierre to Arafat.*

3. Like the English Luddites of the nineteenth century, Kaczynski viewed technology as the source of all ills.

4. Wills, *First War on Terrorism,* 7–10, records 126 attacks between 1981 and 1989.

5. When approached by the U.S. government through General Vernon Walters, President François Mitterrand considered that the attack would not be decisive enough to deter Gadhafi from continuing his gadfly policies. Jacques Chirac, then prime minister, was also against any French participation in the operation. On all the negotiations that took place between the United States and Europe, see ibid., 187–212.

6. Text at www.reagan.utexas.edu/archives/speeches/1986/41486g.htm (accessed April 15, 2006). See also Wills, *First War on Terrorism,* 211.

7. See Kennedy, *Rise and Fall of the Great Powers;* Todd, *After the Empire;* Kagan, *Of Paradise and Power.* Kennedy starts with a historical analysis of the decline of the great powers, while Todd offers a historical forecast on the basis of economic and demographic data. Huntington's relatively complex thesis, based on a political assessment of the current situation, has often been reduced by his numerous critics to the first part of the title of his 1996 book *The Clash of Civilizations and the Remaking of World Order.* The most concise thesis is that of Kagan, whose ideological options are clear from his analysis.

8. See Hassner, *Terreur et l'empire,* 194–95.

9. Text at www.whitehouse.gov/news/releases/2001/09/20010920-8.html (accessed April 15, 2006).

10. Text at www.whitehouse.gov/news/releases/2003/05/20030501-15.html (accessed April 15, 2006).

11. See Harold Hongju Koh, "Rights to Remember," *Economist,* November 1, 2003, 24–26.

12. Aron, *République impériale.* See also Hassner, *Terreur et l'empire,* 160–61.

CHAPTER 17

TERRORISM IN SOUTHEAST
ASIA—THREAT AND RESPONSE

Rohan Gunaratna

Al Qaeda is the most hunted terrorist group in history. To grow, adapt, and survive, it has evolved through three distinct phases.

Al Qaeda was originally created by ʿAbdallah ʿAzzam and his protégé Osama bin Laden to sustain the momentum of the anti-Soviet multinational Afghan mujahideen campaign. Since its creation on September 10, 1988, in Peshawar, it has sought to position itself as the "pioneering vanguard" of the jihad groups worldwide.

Then, with the formation of the World Islamic Front for Jihad against the Jews and the Crusaders in February 1998, al Qaeda morphed from a group into a network. By providing training, finance, weapons, and ideology to disparate jihad groups in Afghanistan, it earned the respect of like-minded groups.

Finally, inspired and instigated by its attack on several of America's most iconic landmarks on 9/11, some thirty to forty jihad groups began to emulate al Qaeda's vision and mission of a global jihad as well as its technologies and tactics. Al Qaeda's ideology and operational methodology has been adopted by a number of jihad groups in the global South, including by groups in Southeast Asia.

THE NEW ENVIRONMENT

Since 9/11, especially after the U.S.-led coalition's intervention in Afghanistan in October 2001 and the invasion of Iraq in March 2003, the security environment in Southeast Asia has changed dramatically. To fight back, a weakened al Qaeda has relied on regional and local Islamist groups worldwide including its Southeast Asian counterparts. For instance, since 9/11, Indonesia's Jemmah Islamiyah (JI) group has attacked and plans to attack predominantly targets of the West and its allies and friends. Although JI was specifically established to create an Islamic caliphate in Southeast Asia, it poses a much greater threat to Western targets there.

In February 1998, to consolidate its training and financial assistance to Islamist groups worldwide, al Qaeda created the World Islamic Front for Jihad against the Jews and the Crusaders. The Asian, Middle Eastern, African, and Caucasian Groups within al Qaeda's ideological orbit of global jihad that received support now emulate al Qaeda. They conduct coordinated simultaneous mass fatality bombings including suicide attacks, the hallmark of al Qaeda operations. The coordinated simultaneous bombing of bars frequented by tourists and the U.S. consulate in Denpasar, Bali, in October 2002 remains the world's worst terrorist attack since 9/11. Furthermore, the bombing of Superferry 14 in Manila remains the world's worst maritime terrorist attack. Inasmuch as the intentions and capabilities of Southeast Asian groups to target regional governments and Western interests have not diminished, the region is likely to witness more attacks in the immediate future.

THE CONTEXT

The disruption of al Qaeda–JI plans to bomb American, British, Australian, and Israeli diplomatic targets in Singapore in December 2001 led Southeast Asian governments to uncover the links between al Qaeda and JI. Until the Bali bombings in October 2002, the government of Indonesia, and until the disruption of JI plans to bomb American, British, Australian, Israeli, and Singaporean diplomatic targets in June 2003, the government of Thailand publicly denied the existence of the JI terrorist network on their soil. To meet the current and emerging threat, Southeast Asian governments—with U.S., Australian, European, and Japanese inputs—are slowly but steadily strengthening their intelligence and strike capabilities. As there is lack of trust within ASEAN countries, cooperation is bilateral, or at best, trilateral. Elements of cooperation and coordination include harmonizing legislation, rendition, common databases, exchange of personnel, sharing of experience, transfer of expertise, joint training, and combined operations.

In Southeast Asia, the Islamist threat has moved beyond al Qaeda. Although terrorism is not new to the region, both its scale and nature has changed since 9/11. Since its foundation in March 1988, al Qaeda has imparted ideological, financial, training, and operational support to Moro Islamic Liberation Front (MILF) and Abu Sayyaf Group (ASG) in the Philippines; Lashkar Jundullah in Indonesia; Kumpulan Mujahidin Malaysia (KMM); Jemmah Salafiyah (JS) in Thailand; the Arakan Rohingya Nationalist Organization (ARNO) and Rohingya Solidarity Organization (RSO) in Myanmar and Bangladesh; and JI, a regional group, with a presence in Australia. An al Qaeda dispersed from its Afghanistan-Pakistan core is increasingly relying on these Southeast Asian groups for sanctuary, support, and strike operations.

Al Qaeda ideologically penetrated and made regional and local groups fighting territorial struggles believe in its vision and mission of a universal jihad. They have adopted al Qaeda ideology and tactics. For instance, the Singaporean chief of JI, Ma Salam-at Kastari, was planning to hijack and crash an Aeroflot aircraft from Bangkok, Thailand, onto the Changi International Airport, Singapore. According to Kastari, the choice of a Russian aircraft was to teach Moscow a lesson for what it was doing to the Muslim brothers in Chechnya. Similarly, the attacks on Bali and the Jakarta Marriott Hotel were mass fatality/casualty operations, and one of the Bali bombers and the Marriott bomber were suicide terrorists. The tactic of suicide and inflicting mass death and injury—hitherto alien to Southeast Asian groups—is clearly an al Qaeda concept. Al Qaeda's most enduring impact on Southeast Asian groups has been to instill into them a sense of duty to fight not only nearby enemies but also the distant enemy—the United States of America.

BACKGROUND

Immediately before the withdrawal of Soviet forces from Afghanistan in February 1989, al Qaeda's role changed. In addition to inheriting the anti-Soviet Afghan training and operational infrastructure, al Qaeda benefited from the worldwide network created by its predecessor Maktab-il-Khadimat (MAK: Afghan Service Bureau), with thirty offices overseas. As the international community neglected Afghanistan, the country that won the war against communism, and Pakistan, a frontline state in the fight against communism, both Afghanistan and Pakistan became the international center for ideological and physical war training of Islamist guerrilla and terrorist groups. By the early 1990s, Afghanistan had replaced the Syrian-controlled Bekka Valley in Lebanon as the principal center of international terrorism. As the West looked the other way, Afghanistan evolved into a terrorist Disneyland. Several Islamist groups, principally al Qaeda and al Qaeda together with the Islamic Movement of the Taliban, the ruling party of the Islamic Emirate of Afghanistan, trained 70,000–130,000 mujahideen until the intervention of the U.S.-led coalition in October 2001.

Al Qaeda provided trained recruits and funds to local Islamist groups fighting in conflict zones where Muslims were suffering, including in Tajikistan, Kashmir, Bosnia, Chechnya, Dagestan, Mindanao, and Xingjiang. As the bulk of the Arab mujahideen, including their leader, bin Laden, were unwelcome in their home countries, they remained in Afghanistan and Pakistan. Especially after the first World Trade Center attack in February 1993, when the United States demanded that Pakistan either get rid of the mujahideen or be declared a terrorist state, most of the Arab mujahideen in Pakistan moved to Sudan, where al Qaeda established its new headquarters in December 1991. American and British pressure on Sudan forced al Qaeda to relocate to Afghanistan in May 1996, where Western intelligence agencies failed to monitor it. After having established new and consolidated old relationships with Balkan, Caucasian, Middle Eastern, and East African groups when in Sudan, al Qaeda was able to develop closer and deeper ties with Asian groups after its relocation to Afghanistan. As an organization with a global membership, al Qaeda had diverse capabilities as well as access to unprecedented resources, and it armed, trained, financed, and indoctrinated three dozen Islamist groups from Asia, Africa, the Middle East, and the Caucasus. In addition to its training camps in Afghanistan, al Qaeda dispatched its trainers to establish or serve in the training camps of other groups in Asia, Africa, the Middle East, and the Caucasus.

Beginning in 1988, and persistently since 1994, al Qaeda has penetrated Southeast Asia. In 1988, Osama bin Laden's brother-in-law Muhammad Jamal Khalifa established the Manila branch of the International Islamic Relief Organization, a respectable Saudi charity, to provide assistance to Islamist groups in the region. In 1994, Khalid Sheikh Muhammad—the mastermind of 9/11—and the February 1993 World Trade Center bomber Ramzi Ahmed Yousef traveled to Southeast Asia with the intention of destroying twelve U.S. airliners over the Pacific. Meanwhile, at the MILF's main base, Camp Abu Bakar in the Philippines, a Kuwaiti calling himself 'Umar al-Faruk established "Camp Vietnam" to train Southeast Asian groups in guerrilla warfare and terrorism. The aim was to build a core of fighters to alleviate the suffering of Muslims at the hands of the oppressive and repressive regimes and rulers supported by the United States.

Three generations of distinct but interlocking mujahideen feature in conflicts today. The experience in Afghanistan was pivotal. A few hundred Southeast Asians that fought in the anti-Soviet multinational Afghan jihad (December 1979–February 1989) joined several Islamist groups, including the core of JI. Throughout the 1990s, al Qaeda and Taliban training camps in Afghanistan trained Muslim youth to fight in the Philippines (Mindanao), Indonesia (Maluku and Poso), Myanmar, China (Xingjiang), Kashmir, Bosnia, Kosovo, Chechnya, Dagestan, Nagorno-Karabakh, Algeria, Egypt, Jordan, Yemen, and other regional conflicts. The smaller and mobile camps in regional conflict zones of Asia, Africa, Latin America, and the Caucasus, compensating partially for the loss of Afghanistan, are likely to produce the third generation of mujahideen. Islamist camps active in Southeast Asia since 9/11 have included the Hodeibia, Palestine, and Vietnam camps on Mindanao in the Philippines; the Poso camp on Sulawesi and Balikpapan in Kalimantan (the Indonesian part of the island of Borneo) in Indonesia; and the Rohingya camps on the Myanmar-Bangladesh border. Ideological training occurs in Islamic schools (madrassas), and military training takes place in makeshift camps, which are difficult to detect from the air.

Although al Qaeda has gravely suffered from both the loss of its operational leaders and destruction of its traditional bases in Afghanistan, its intention to attack the United States and its allies and friends is undiminished. With the difficulty of striking targets in North America, Europe, Australia, and New Zealand, al Qaeda and its associate groups are aggressively scouting for targets in lawless zones of Asia, Africa, and the Middle East. When al Qaeda–JI leaders deemed that U.S. and Israeli targets in Manila were not suitable, they shifted the targets to Singapore. When the Singapore operation was disrupted, they shifted the targets to Taiwan, Seoul, Cambodia, and Bangkok. Al Qaeda–JI operatives search out new targets like sharks moving rapidly in search of prey. Inasmuch as many Southeast Asian countries suffer from porous borders, availability of firearms and explosives, lack of law and order, complacency, and corruption, the region remains conducive for the operation of local, regional, and extraregional Islamist groups.

THE EMERGING THREAT

Al Qaeda's traditional roles have changed. Traditionally, al Qaeda members were better motivated—willing to kill and die for the cause—and better trained—capable of hitting strategic, high-profile, and symbolic targets. As such, al Qaeda conducted a fewer attacks but they were all high impact. By its actions, al Qaeda aimed to inspire, instigate, and influence the regional groups and the wider Muslim community to wage war against the United States and its allies and friends. By co-opting leaders, al Qaeda influenced regional groups by arming, training, and financing them to strike at tactical targets. With al Qaeda weakened, its leadership is urging its regional associates to hit both strategic and tactical targets.

After al Qaeda struck America's iconic targets, Islamist groups throughout Southeast Asia perceive it as their pioneering vanguard. As the acknowledged "spearhead of Islam," al Qaeda provides both ideological and strategic direction. Its overarching ideology of a universal jihad facilitates the organization to co-opt regional and local leaders and their respective groups. The al Qaeda umbrella organization, the World Islamic Front for Jihad against the Jews and the Crusaders, attempted to unite its Middle Eastern, African, Caucasian, and Asian groups and give them a common agenda. Similarly, al Qaeda's regional umbrella, the Rabitat-ul-Mujahidin (Legion of the Fighters of God), created by the JI leader Riduan Isamuddin, aka Hambali, in 1999, attempted to unite its Southeast Asian groups. Some groups such as the Free Aceh Movement (both MP-GAM and MB-GAM), in Indonesia resisted attempts by Hambali to absorb the ethnonationalist Muslim group. Driven by the ideals of Muslim brotherhood, MILF, a group that inherited the 500-year Moro struggle for independence from the Christian-dominated Philippines, continued to provide critical assistance to al Qaeda and to Southeast Asian Islamist groups. Despite an active U.S. presence aimed at combating the Abu Sayyaf Group, the MILF works clandestinely with al Qaeda, JI, the ASG, and the Rajah Solaiman Revolutionary Movement (RSRM). Since the detection of JI in Singapore, JI trainers and combat tacticians have persistently worked with Southeast Asian groups to attack Western and domestic targets in the Philippines. In June 2003, the Philippine authorities disrupted multiple attacks in Manila by arresting the MILF Special Operations Group leader Muklis Yunos and his Egyptian counterpart, who were planning to attack the presidential palace, using an oil tanker truck filled with ammonium nitrate mixed with sawdust and gasoline; the U.S. embassy; a U.S. ship in Manila Bay with an explosives-laden speedboat; the Pandacan Oil Depot with a rocket-propelled grenade triggered by mobile phone; Manila International Airport with an explosives-laden vehicle; and a major commercial shipping line plying Philippine waters by remote detonation of a car bomb in a ship's hold. The co-option and integration of al Qaeda and JI elements into the MILF infrastructure has complicated peace talks between the MILF and the government of the Philippines.

Spearheaded by JI, ASG, RSRM, and MILF formed Jayash al Madhi in November 14, 2004. At the meeting of the *majlis shura* (consultative council) in Datu Piang, Mindanao, the leaders of these groups agreed to eliminate their differences and work together. Among the leaders present were Dul Matin, the senior JI leader in the Philippines; Umar Patek, a JI member involved in the Bali attack; and Gaddhafi Janjalani, the ASG leader. Janjalani, involved in criminality, has been reborn as an Islamist. At the meeting, it was decided that they would have a common doctrine and conduct joint training and operations. They all escaped the Philippine government bombing of the meeting venue. A key outcome of the Datu Piang meeting was the Valentine's Day bombing in 2005 where JI-trained RSRM and ASG members in MILF territory attacked three targets in Manila. Although another operation to simultaneously attack targets in Jakarta, Manila, and Mindanao was disrupted in April and May 2005, they are likely to succeed eventually.

IDEOLOGICAL INDOCTRINATION

The ideology of global jihad advocated by al Qaeda has now penetrated Southeast Asian groups. To compensate for its depleted operational capability, al Qaeda has invested extensively in sustained propaganda since 9/11 to inspire and instigate other Islamic movements, as well as the wider Muslim community, to join in the fight against the United States and its allies and its friends. Al Qaeda sent an unequivocal message to the domestic Islamist groups that they must attack not only domestic but foreign targets. In response, JI attacked on Bali in October 2002, the Jakarta Marriott Hotel in August 2003, the Australian embassy in September 2004, and again on Bali in October 2005. JI used the classic al Qaeda modus operandi of suicide bombing, and in many cases, the attacks were coordinated and simultaneous.

Al Qaeda's new role includes advancing its traditional mission by both military and nonmilitary means using the mass media, especially the new communication technologies. The surge of regular pronouncements by Osama bin Laden and Ayman al-Zawahiri communicated by audio, video and print media since the intervention of the U.S.-led coalition in Afghanistan in October 2001 have resonated in the Muslim world especially since the U.S. intervention in Iraq in April 2003. Al Qaeda believes that it can only sustain the fight against the United States and its allies and friends by building a large, committed support base throughout the Muslim world, including diaspora and migrant communities. By continuing to politicize and radicalize Muslims by the dissemination of propaganda, al Qaeda intends to increase the pool of recruits and support, critical for the continuity of jihad programs by multiple groups.

Al Qaeda invested in propaganda before 9/11, but to a lesser degree. In the decade preceding 9/11, al Qaeda's primary mission was to train as many Muslims as possible and to provide specialist assistance to Islamist groups worldwide. Virulent pre-9/11 propaganda was primarily the responsibility of a number of Islamist parties and groups based in Europe and North America. With a number of these parties and groups coming under close scrutiny from Western governments, al Qaeda and its associated parties and groups have taken over the role of information dissemination. In comparison to the pre-9/11 propaganda dominated by other groups, the al Qaeda brand of propaganda is extremely violent, directly calling Muslims to kill. Successfuly instilling its ideology into JI and several other smaller groups has been al Qaeda's greatest success in Southeast Asia.

CRAFTING A RESPONSE

Most Southeast Asian governments are weak and either corrupt or incompetent. Supporting strong leaders with political will and political capital to bring about change; appointing and promoting leaders to the security sector based on merit, ability, and performance; and building partnerships with Western governments is the gravest need of the hour. There is no magic bullet to end terrorism in Southeast Asia. Eventually, counterterrorist measures will have an impact on terrorist groups and their support bases. Although policies and measures will be formulated to fight the Islamist brand of terrorism, it will reduce the threat posed by both Islamist and non-Islamist groups. Legislative and practical measures will also have an impact on ideological (left- and right-wing groups) and ethnonationalist (separatist, irredentist, and autonomy-seeking) groups, eroding their operational and support capabilities. Some groups, such as the MILF, will agree to talks to escape the global counterterrorism measures. As a result, the post-9/11 environment will force several terrorist groups to consider retaining their strike capabilities but consider the political option seriously, at least tactically. The threat of Islamist terrorism and extremism will persist, but it will decrease substantially in the coming years.

Whereas terrorists in the 1970s and 1980s killed in tens, terrorists in the 1990s killed in hundreds. Today, the terrorists want to kill in thousands. Because of the increased lethality of the contemporary wave of terrorism, a government cannot wait until a terrorist attack occurs to act. Counterterrorism must be largely preventive. But the traditional law enforcement mind-set is to wait for an incident to occur in order to begin an investigation. Without preliminary evidence, the criminal justice system will not permit wire-tapping, surveillance, arrests, raids, and searches of premises. Even today, law enforcement systems are designed to act efficiently after the event—to investigate, collect evidence, arrest, charge, and prosecute. Unless there is a lead, the average police officer will not expend time, energy, and resources. A sea change in law enforcement culture is essential to combat terrorism. Instead of building cases by gathering evidence to prosecute, law enforcement authorities must invest their assets in collecting intelligence to detect and disrupt terrorist attacks. This involves effective use of confidential informants, undercover officers, and other covert assets, a mind- and a resource-intensive process.

Winning hearts and minds is key. To prevent terrorists from influencing the public, governments must co-opt ethnic and religious leaders from communities affected by terrorism. Inasmuch as it is communities that eventually defeat terrorism, governments must ensure that Muslims are not demonized. Since no terrorist group can sustain itself without public support, it is critical to win over public support. Like a company, a terrorist group needs to grow in order to survive, and recruitment and flow of support—intelligence, funds, weapons, sanctuary—remain key. To disrupt the public appeal of terrorist groups, it is essential to legally criminalize and then target the terrorist support networks. In Indonesia, JI is still a legal group. These networks disseminate virulent propaganda with the intention of indoctrinating supporters and potential supporters that join terrorist groups. Comprehensive legislation targeting terrorist propaganda, including through the World Wide Web, and fund-raising by extremist groups, should be criminalized. Likewise, religious leaders who spread hatred in schools and elsewhere must be prosecuted.

Developing a zero-tolerance policy toward terrorism in Southeast Asia is essential. International measures must be developed to prevent terrorists from seeking sanctuary or support. When JI was targeted in Singapore and Malaysia in December 2001, the group moved to Thailand and to Indonesia. Terrorists are like sharks—they rapidly move in search of new opportunities. Since postmodern terrorists are highly mobile, fighting postmodern terrorism will involve the universal adoption of measures and countermeasures. As a balloon bulges out in one place when depressed in another place, terrorists will move to another hospitable or less hostile theater. To be effective, counterterrorist action should be coordinated. In the fight against terrorism, to prevent escaping terrorists from relocating their support and operational infrastructures when attacked, the development of governmental measures and countermeasures will have to be coordinated. History has shown that those governments that do not develop zero-tolerance policies against terrorism will eventually suffer. Bali is a classic example. The international community should develop a zero-tolerance terrorism code, and those who defy the code should be punished.

An international fund against terrorism should be developed to assist poor countries or countries that lack the capacity to cope with terrorism. It requires substantial resources and expertise to sustain a counterterrorism campaign. Most terrorist-affected countries in the developing world lack both the trained manpower and the resources to fight a protracted campaign against terrorism. Rich and poor governments must develop a shared response in the fight against terrorism. Over 90 percent of terrorist groups are born in the developing world, but they have established state-of-the-art terrorist support networks in the developed world. Until 9/11, the West tolerated the presence of these networks because they did not pose a direct and an immediate threat to the host countries. Whenever governments in the global South requested the extradition of known terrorists from the West, the host governments spoke of the incompatibility of the criminal justice and prisons systems or of human rights violations by the requesting government. Until 9/11, terrorists raised significant funds in North America, western Europe, Australia, and New Zealand that supported multiple terrorist operations in the global South. Even today, a number of Islamist and non-Islamist groups generate significant support from their diaspora and migrant communities, as well as from charities, companies, and other front, cover, and sympathetic organizations. With persistent calls from al Qaeda leadership that it is the duty of every Muslim to wage jihad, the terrorist support networks in the West are mutating into terrorist operational networks. Furthermore, with increased Western assistance to governments in the South, the terrorist threat to Western governments and societies will increase. Al Qaeda's first wave of attacks were in Middle Eastern and Asian countries, and it was the failure of those governments to degrade and destroy the groups that led to a spillover of the threat to the West. A shared response, where the West works with the rest of the world, will reduce the threat at a global level. Western assistance to Southeast Asia to fight terrorism at home will eventually reduce the threat to the West.

The post-9/11 environment is steadily creating a norm and an ethic that the use of terrorism as a tool will criminalize the political struggles of groups that practice political violence. Increasingly, terrorism as a tool will appeal less to most groups, especially if governmental, nongovernmental, and intergovernmental organizations create institutions to address the grievances and aspirations of marginalized communities. The threat of terrorism will remain, but it will decrease substantially in the coming years with the opening up of new avenues for the latter to vent their anger and frustrations.

Although military response is paramount to reduce the immediate threat, especially if the threat is high, governments need to be aware of its limitations. To end terrorism, it is essential to address the root causes and enact prophylactic measures. A multipronged and a multidimensional response is essential to dissuade serving terrorists and prevent the production of new terrorists. Ideological response, where Muslim clerics condemn the preachers of hatred, is lacking in many countries.

It is critical to extend cooperation from the security and intelligence domain to law enforcement and judicial cooperation. Furthermore, governments must graduate from cooperation to coordination and collaboration where joint and combined action is taken to erode terrorist capabilities. For instance, terrorism will persist in the south of Thailand as long as Bangkok does not work collaboratively with Malaysia.

As terrorists increasingly operate transnationally, future counterterrorism initiatives will depend on building common databases, exchange of personnel, joint training, combined operations, sharing of experience, and transfer of expertise.

SOUTHEAST ASIAN PECULIARITIES

In comparison with other regions, the security threat confronting Southeast Asia is different both in nature and scale. Having lived under the shadow of large Buddhist, Christian, and Hindu populations, the vast majority of the South Asian Muslims are tolerant and moderate. A minority of Southeast Asian Muslims politicized and radicalized by extraregional influences, notably ideology and financing, from the Middle East is willing to use political violence, even terrorism, to create Islamic states. Today, the region hosts a few hundred Islamist and Muslim political parties and guerrilla and terrorist groups campaigning for the enforcement of Islamic law. Although these organizations represent a minuscule segment of the Muslim population, power-hungry political leaders in religious garb have successfully (mis)used religion to mobilize significant support to achieve their political aims. As Southeast Asia hosts one of the largest Muslim populations, many Muslims see themselves as duty-bound to assist fellow Muslims in conflict zones such as Mindanao, Afghanistan, Kashmir, Chechnya, and now Iraq.

Governmental, nongovernmental, and international response must be at three levels—global, regional, and domestic. As the Islamist groups depend on one another for support, a concerted and a coordinated approach is essential. Al Qaeda is the unifier, the coordinator, and the guide, and targeting it is therefore paramount. Although al Qaeda's capability has suffered, its intention to attack has not diminished. Although militarily weak, al Qaeda is ideologically resilient. Despite severe damage to the organization at multiple levels, al Qaeda is still playing a significant role in setting the agenda. As the waves of attacks in October 2002 (against the French oil tanker *Limbourg*, U.S. personnel in Kuwait, and Bali nightclubs) and May 2003 (in Riyadh, two in Chechnya, twenty-one on gas stations in Karachi, and in Casablanca) demonstrated, al Qaeda still retains the ability to coordinate and provide strategic and tactical direction to groups in Asia, the Middle East, the Caucasus, and the Horn of Africa. From Pakistan, Hamza al Rabiyya, the successor to Khalid Sheikh Muhammad, continues to communicate with groups in Southeast Asia, and funds continue to flow to Asian terrorist groups from Saudi Arabia.

Today, the global nature of the threat has changed, and Southeast Asia is no exception.

Since 9/11, rather than being a single entity, al Qaeda has been a conglomerate of organizations. Al Qaeda proper—estimated at 4,000 members in October 2001—has been replaced by al Qaeda plus two dozen associated groups armed, trained, and financed by al Qaeda. With al Qaeda having suffered significantly in its operational capability, it is trying to compensate for its losses by getting groups and members it trained in Afghanistan and elsewhere to join the fight. Al Qaeda's greatest success has been to provide ideological direction despite being aggressively hunted worldwide. Despite the targeting of JI, the group has relocated to Mindanao and continues to operate its training and base camps. In March 2005, twenty JI members graduated, demonstrating the continuing threat. Today, the threat is more diverse, dispersed, and diffused. To counter the post-9/11 threat, a global response is required.

THE FUTURE

The post-9/11 security environment in Southeast Asia presents new challenges and opportunities. With enhanced security in the West and protecting Western targets in the global South, Asia and the Middle East will face the brunt of terrorist attacks. Southeast Asian governments are burdened with the task of preventing attacks on both domestic and Western targets on their soil. For supporting the West in the fight against terrorism, Asian and Middle Eastern countries will earn the wrath of domestic and foreign Islamist groups. Nonetheless, governments in the South have no option but to cooperate with the resource-rich and the technologically advanced West to fight terrorist groups. Until governments worldwide, including in Southeast Asia, develop a common strategy and cooperative structures to fight terrorism at the domestic, regional, and global levels, it will remain a significant threat. The burden of response must be shared by nongovernmental organizations. To overcome the dual loyalties of some Muslim governments in the region and to reach out to Muslims subjected to anti-Western propaganda, public diplomacy, hitherto neglected by the West, is paramount.

As the situation is fluid and dynamic, there is no standard textbook for fighting al Qaeda and its associated groups in Southeast Asia. The current threat can be reduced by maximizing successes and minimizing policy and operational failures. Since the destruction of al Qaeda's camps in Afghanistan and worldwide arrests of its members, Southeast Asian groups have established their own training camps in the region to provide training in suicide operations, assassinations, bombing of aircraft and ships, and so on. As Western intelligence agencies assist Southeast Asian governments to interdict and target Southeast Asian groups, these groups are transforming their operational and support networks, including their modus operandi. In addition to relying on Gulf charities, they also rely on local businesses and individual donors, and with the interception of satellite and mobile phone communications, they are using encrypted email and human couriers, and even shifting from hard to soft targets. Flexibility and agility are thus key for frontline law enforcement and intelligence services engaged in fighting terrorism. The terrorist group must become the mentor of government operational agencies.

CONCLUSION

More than five years after 9/11, the terrorist threat stems from the global jihad movement. Since the U.S.-led coalition's intervention in Afghanistan, the threat has moved beyond al Qaeda, which has lost its preeminent status as the pioneering vanguard of the Islamic movements operationally but not ideologically. It lacks the organizational structure and the resources to mount global operations but is able and willing to inspire, instigate, and coordinate operations by other groups. As al Qaeda diminishes in size and strength, it is increasingly trying to rebuild and regain its influence by relying on its associate groups in Asia, the Middle East, Africa, and the Caucasus to conduct operations. Unless and until the pressure on al Qaeda diminishes, the group intends to survive by working together with its regional associates. The international, regional, and domestic responses to the associate groups will determine whether the remaining al Qaeda will survive or perish.

The nature of the threat is changing rapidly to adapt to security measures and countermeasures. In keeping with its mandate, before 9/11, al Qaeda focused only on conducting spectacular attacks. Although al Qaeda and its associate groups are unable to mount coordinated multiple suicide attacks of the scale of 9/11 inside the United States, they are still capable of mounting medium and small attacks of the scale of Bali, Riyadh, and Casablanca in America. There are three reasons why al Qaeda has failed to conduct another 9/11 attack inside the United States. First, increased human vigilance; second, unprecedented international and domestic law enforcement, security, and intelligence cooperation; third, al Qaeda is being hunted, denying the group time, space, and resources to plan, prepare, and mount dramatic, spectacular attacks. As long as Western governments can place relevant threat information in the public domain to keep the public alert, and can sustain sharing of information with Middle Eastern, Asian, and other governments; and as long as the U.S.-led global coalition against terrorism can remain active, terrorist groups and their support bases will weaken.

To reduce the threat in Southeast Asia, partially compounded by external developments, it is essential to target both indigenous and foreign groups active there. Severing the al Qaeda operational and ideological link is paramount. Despite unprecedented security measures and counter measures since 9/11, al Qaeda remains a formidable threat to the security of the region. Since 9/11, over 100 attacks worldwide by al Qaeda and its associated groups, including a dozen attacks in the region have been aborted or disrupted. Bali, Casablanca, Djerba, Chechnya, Mindanao, and Karachi bombings have demonstrated that the threat has moved beyond al Qaeda. Its regional offspring, such as the Southeast Asian groups, are as lethal as their parent. They have learned and will increasingly use al Qaeda tactics as such hijacking and crashing aircraft, contact poisons, anti-aircraft weapons, and a range of other techniques to inflict mass fatalities. As the East Africa bombings in August 1998, the attack on the USS *Cole* in October 2000, and 9/11 demonstrated, martyrdom operations—or suicide terrorism—will be their most effective tool.

Al Qaeda is the most hunted terrorist group in history. Despite the arrest of Al Qaeda members and associate members in 102 countries, including in Southeast Asia, the response has been inadequate to operationally shut down the group or the network. Despite the relentless hunt, the violent Islamic movements have been able to replenish its wastage in rank and file and continue the fight. The robust Islamist milieu is facilitating the continuation of the fight. Although al Qaeda had existed since 1988, the fight against al Qaeda began in earnest only after 9/11. Al Qaeda is an agile organization, capable of learning, and the fight against its brand of terrorism will be long and hard. Inasmuch as terrorist groups enjoy an average life span of 13.5 years, it is essential to build counterterrorist structures and train personnel to meet both the current and the long-range threat. Al Qaeda is an organization of organizations with a global reach and therefore no one country can fight and destroy it. Furthermore, al Qaeda threatens military, diplomatic, and civilian targets; uses conventional and unconventional weapons; and is capable of operating in the air, on land, and at sea. Therefore, a wide range of security countermeasures are necessary to protect both civilian and infrastructure targets from attack. Al Qaeda ideology appeals to a cross section of society—the group recruits from among both the rich and the poor, the educated and the less educated. As such, governments need to enlist the support of educational and religious institutions and of community and other influential leaders to build a norm and an ethic against the use, misuse, and abuse of religion for political purposes. As the scale of the threat is high, governments have no option but to work with a range of public- and private-sector partners in the fight against terrorism. To counter the threat posed by the global jihad movement, a multipronged, multidimensional, multiagency, and multinational effort is paramount.

Bibliography

Abu Iyad, with Eric Rouleau. *My Home, My Land: A Narrative of the Palestinian Struggle*. Translated by Linda Butler Koseoglu. New York: Times Books, 1978.

Adams, James. *The Financing of Terror*. New York: Simon & Schuster, 1986.

Alexander, Yonah, and Richard Latter, eds. *Terrorism and the Media: Dilemmas for Government, Journalists and the Public*. Washington, D.C.: Brassey's, 1990.

Amos, John W. *Palestinian Resistance: Organization of a Nationalist Movement*. New York: Pergamon Press, 1980.

Arendt, Hannah. *The Origins of Totalitarianism*. 1951. New ed. San Diego: Harcourt Brace, 1979.

Arnon-Ohanna, Youval, and Kherev Mi'Bayit. *The Internal Struggle within the Palestinian Movement, 1929–1939*. Tel Aviv: Yariv-Hadar, 1981. In Hebrew.

Aron, Raymond. *République impériale: Les États-Unis dans le monde, 1945–1972*. Paris: Calman-Lévy, 1973.

Artarit, Jean. *Robespierre ou l'impossible filiation*. Paris: La Table Ronde, 2003.

Aust, Stefan. *The Baader-Meinhof Group: The Inside Story of a Phenomenon*. Translated by Anthea Bell. London: Bodley Head, 1987.

Avrich, Paul. *The Russian Anarchists*. Princeton, N.J.: Princeton University Press, 1967.

Ayanian, Mark Armen, and John Z. Ayanian. "Armenian Political Violence on American Network News: An Analysis of Content." *Armenian Review* 40, no. 1–157 (spring 1987).

Baczko, Bronislaw. *Comment sortir de la Terreur: Thermidor et la Révolution*. Paris: Gallimard, 1989.

Bakunin, Mikhail Aleksandrovich. *Oeuvres*. Edited by James Guillaume and Max Nettlau. 6 vols. Paris: P.-V. Stock, 1895–1913.

Barkun, Michael. "Millenarian Aspects of 'White Supremacist' Movements." *Terrorism and Political Violence* 1, no. 4 (October 1989).

———. "Millenarian Groups and Law Enforcement Agencies: The Lessons of Waco." *Terrorism and Political Violence* 6, no. 1 (Spring 1994).

———, ed. *Millennialism and Violence*. London: Frank Cass, 1996.

Bauer, Yehuda. *From Diplomacy to Resistance: A History of Jewish Palestine, 1939–1945*. New York: Atheneum, 1973.

Bayet, Jean. *Histoire de la religion romaine*. Paris: Payot, 1969.

Baynac, Jacques. *Les socialistes-révolutionnaires*. Paris: Robert Laffont, 1979.

Beaumarchais Center for International Research. *Puissances et influences: Annuaire géopolitique et géostratégique, 2000–2001*. Edited by Arnaud Blin, Gérard Chaliand, and François Géré. Paris: Mille et une nuits, 2000.

Bechor, Guy. *Lexicon of the PLO*. Tel Aviv: Ministry of Defense Publishing House, 1991. In Hebrew.

Beckman, Robert L. "Rapporteur's Summary." In *Nuclear Terrorism: Defining the Threat,* ed. Paul Leventhal and Yonah Alexander. Washington, D.C.: Pergamon-Brassey's, 1986.

Begin, Menahem. *The Revolt: Story of the Irgun*. Jerusalem: Steimatzky, 1977. Los Angeles: Nash, 1977.

Bell, J. Bowyer. *Assassin: Theory and Practice of Political Violence*. 1979. New ed. New Brunswick, N.J.: Transaction Publishers, 2005.

———. *The Secret Army: The IRA, 1916–1979*. Cambridge, Mass.: MIT Press, 1979.

———. *A Time of Terror: How Democratic Societies Respond to Revolutionary Violence*. New York: Basic Books, 1978.

Bienstock, J. W. *Histoire du mouvement révolutionnaire en Russie*. Vol. 1: *(1790–1894)*. Paris: Payot, 1920.

Binder, Patrice, and Olivier Lepick. *Les armes biologiques*. Paris: Presses universitaires de France, 2001.

Bishop, Patrick, and Eamonn Mallie. *The Provisional IRA*. London: Heinemann, 1987.

Black, George. *Genocide in Iraq: The Anfal Campaign against the Kurds*. New York: Human Rights Watch, 1993. www.hrw.org/reports/1993/iraqanfal/ (accessed April 9, 2006).

Brandon, S. G. F. *Jesus and the Zealots: A Study of the Political Factor in Primitive Christianity*. Manchester: Manchester University Press, 1967.

Brinton, Crane. *The Anatomy of Revolution*. 1938. Rev. ed. New York: Vintage Books, 1965.

Brissot, Jacques-Pierre. *À Stanislas Clermont, sur la diatribe de ce dernier contre les comités de recherches, et sur son apologie de Mme Jumilhac, et des illumines*. Paris: Buisson, 1790.

Brousse, Paul. "La propagande par le fait." *Bulletin de la Fédération jurassienne,* August 5, 1877.

Burgat, François. *L'islamisme au Maghreb*. Paris: Payot, 1995.

———. *L'islamisme en face*. Paris: La Découverte, 1985.

Caillois, Roger. *Bellone ou la pente de la guerre*. Brussels: Renaissance du livre, 1963.

Callwell, C. E. *Small Wars: Their Principles and Practice.* 1896. Rev. ed. London: HMSO, 1899.

Camus, Albert. *L'homme révolté.* Paris: Gallimard, 1951.

Cannac, René. *Aux sources de la Révolution russe: Netchaiev, du nihilisme au terrorisme.* Paris: Payot, 1961.

Carr, Caleb, *The Lessons of Terror: A History of Warfare against Civilians.* New York: Random House, 2003.

———. "Terrorism as Warfare: The Lessons of Military History." *World Policy Journal* 13, no. 4 (Winter 1996–97).

Carré, Olivier, and Gérard Michaux. *Les Frères musulmans.* Paris: Gallimard, 1983.

Carré, Olivier, and Paul Dumont, eds. *Radicalismes islamiques.* 2 vols. Paris: L'Harmattan, 1985–86.

Carrère d'Encausse, Hélène. *Staline: L'ordre par la terreur.* Paris: Flammarion, 1979.

Chaliand, Gérard. *Anthologie mondiale de la stratégie: Des origines au nucléaire.* Paris: R. Laffont, 1990.

———. *L'atlas du nouvel ordre mondial.* Paris: Laffont, 2003.

———. *The Palestinian Resistance.* Translated by Michael Perl. Harmondsworth, Eng.: Penguin Books, 1972.

———. *La résistance palestinienne.* Paris: Seuil, 1970.

———. *Terrorismes et Guérillas.* Paris: Flammarion, 1984.

———, ed. *Guerrilla Strategies: An Historical Anthology from the Long March to Afghanistan.* Berkeley: University of California Press, 1982. Originally published as *Stratégies de la guérilla: Guerres révolutionnaires et contre-insurrections, anthologie historique de la Longue marche à nos jours* (Paris: Mazarine, 1979).

———, ed. *Stratégies du terrorisme.* Paris: Desclée de Brouwer, 1999.

Chaliand, Gérard, Alain Grignard, and Olivier Hubac-Occhipinti. *L'arme du terrorisme.* Paris: L. Audibert, 2002.

Chaliand, Gérard, and Arnaud Blin. *America is back: Les nouveaux césars du Pentagone.* Paris: Bayard, 2003.

———. *Dictionnaire de stratégie militaire: Des origines à nos jours.* Paris: Perrin, 1998.

Chalk, Peter. *West European Terrorism and Counter-Terrorism: The Evolving Dynamic.* London: Macmillan, 1996.

Clutterbuck, Richard. *Living with Terrorism.* London: Faber & Faber, 1975.

———. *Terrorism and Guerrilla Warfare: Forecasts and Remedies.* London: Routledge, 1990.

———. *Terrorism in an Unstable World.* London: Routledge, 1994.

Cohn, Norman, *The Pursuit of the Millennium: Revolutionary Millenarians and Mystical Anarchists of the Middle Ages.* New York: Oxford University Press, 1990.

Colas, Dominique. *Dictionnaire de la pensée politique: Auteurs, oeuvres, notions.* Paris: Larousse-Bordas, 1997.

Conquest, Robert. *The Great Terror: Stalin's Purge of the Thirties.* New York: Macmillan, 1968. Reprint. Harmondsworth, Eng.: Penguin Books, 1971.

Corbett, Robert. *Guerrilla Warfare from 1939 to the Present Day*. London: Orbis, 1986.

Corsun, Andrew. "Armenian Terrorism: A Profile." *Department of State Bulletin* 82 (August 1982): 31–35.

Courtois, Stéphane. "Pourquoi?" In id., Nicolas Werth et al., *Le livre noir du communisme: Crimes, terreur, repression*. Paris: Robert Laffont, 1998.

Crenshaw, Martha. "Introduction: Reflections on the Effects of Terrorism." In *Terrorism, Legitimacy, and Power: The Consequences of Political Violence*, ed. id. Middletown, Conn.: Wesleyan University Press, 1983.

——— [Martha Crenshaw Hutchinson]. *Revolutionary Terrorism: The FLN in Algeria, 1954–1962*. Stanford, Calif.: Hoover Institution Press, 1978.

———. *Terrorism and International Cooperation*. Occasional Paper Series no. 11. New York: Institute for East-West Security Studies, 1989.

———, ed. *Terrorism in Context*. University Park: Pennsylvania State University Press, 1995.

Dabezies, Pierre. "Terrorism." In *Dictionnaire de stratégie*, ed. Thierry de Montbrial and Jean Klein, 581–82. Paris: Presses universitaires de France, 2000.

Daguzan, Jean-François, Gérard Chaliand, and Raphäel Prenat. *Le terrorisme non conventionnel*. Paris: FED-CREST, 1999.

Daugherty, William E. "Bomb Warnings to Friendly and Enemy Civilian Targets." In id. and Morris Janowitz, *A Psychological Warfare Casebook*, 359–62. Baltimore: Johns Hopkins University Press, 1958.

Davis, Uri, Andrew Mack, and Nira Yuval-Davis, eds. *Israel and the Palestinians*. London: Ithaca Press, 1975.

Derogy, Jacques. *Opération Némésis*. Paris: Fayard, 1986.

Deutscher, Isaac. *The Prophet Armed: Trotsky, 1879–1921*. London: Oxford University Press, 1954.

Dobson, Christopher, and Ronald Payne. *The Carlos Complex: A Study in Terror*. London: Coronet / Hodder & Stoughton, 1978.

Downes-LeGuin, Theodore, and Bruce Hoffman. *The Impact of Terrorism on Public Opinion, 1988 to 1989*. Document no. MR-225-FF/RC. Santa Monica, Calif.: RAND Corporation, 1993.

Drake, Richard. *The Aldo Moro Murder Case*. Cambridge, Mass.: Harvard University Press, 1995.

Dupuy, R. Ernest, and Trevor N. Dupuy. *The Encyclopedia of Military History from 3500 B.C. to the Present*. 2d rev. ed. New York: Harper & Row, 1986.

Ehrenfeld, Rachel. *Narco-terrorism*. New York: Basic Books, 1990.

El Kenz, David, and Claire Gantet, *Guerres et paix de religion en Europe aux 16e–17e siècles*. Paris: Armand Colin, 2003.

Étienne, Bruno. *L'islamisme radical*. Paris: Hachette, 1987.

Fadl Allah, Ayatollah Muhammed Hussein. "Islam and Violence in Political Reality." *Middle East Insight* 4, nos. 4–5 (1986).

Fauré, Christine. *Terre, terreur et liberté*. Paris: Maspero, 1979.

Fetscher, Iring, and Günter Rohrmoser. *Ideologien and Strategien*. Vol. 1 of *Analysen zum Terrorismus*. Bonn: Westdeutscher Verlag, 1981.

Foley, Charles, ed. *The Memoirs of General Grivas*. London: Longmans, 1964.

Foley, Charles, and W. I. Scobie. *The Struggle for Cyprus*. Stanford, Calif.: Hoover Institution Press, 1975.

Furet, François, and Denis Richet, *La Révolution française*. Paris: Fayard, 1973.

Gerasimov, Aleksandr. *Tsarisme et terrorisme: Souvenirs*. Translated by Thérèse Monceaux. Paris: Plon, 1934.

Géré, François. *Dictionnaire de la pensée stratégique*. Paris: Larousse-Bordas/HER, 2000.

———. *La guerre psychologique*. Paris: Economica, 1997.

———. *Les volontaires de la mort: L'arme du suicide*. Paris: Bayard, 2003.

Goldman, Emma. *Living My Life*. New York: Knopf, 1932.

Greer, Donald. *The Incidence of the Terror during the French Revolution: A Statistical Interpretation*. Cambridge, Mass.: Harvard University Press, 1935.

Grivas, General George. *Guerrilla Warfare and EOKA's Struggle: A Politico-Military Study*. Translated by A. A. Pallis. London: Longmans, 1964.

Gueniffey, Patrice. *La politique de la Terreur: Essai sur la violence révolutionnaire, 1789–1794*. Paris: Fayard, 2000.

Guerchouni, Grigori. *Dans les cachots de Nicolas II*. Paris: Dujarric, 1909.

Guillén, Abraham. *Philosophy of the Urban Guerrilla: The Revolutionary Writings of Abraham Guillén*. Translated and edited by Donald C. Hodges. New York: William Morrow, 1973.

Gunaratna, Rohan. *Inside Al Qaeda: Global Network of Terror*. New York: Columbia University Press, 2002.

———. *War and Peace in Sri Lanka, with a Post-Accord Report from Jaffna*. Colombo: Institute of Fundamental Studies, 1987.

Hacker, Frederick J. *Crusaders, Criminals, Crazies: Terror and Terrorism in Our Time*. New York: Norton, 1976.

Halliday, Fred. *Islam and the Myth of Confrontation: Religion and Politics in the Middle East*. London: I. B. Tauris, 1996.

Hassner, Pierre. *La terreur et l'empire*. La violence et la paix, 2. Paris: Seuil, 2003.

Heinzen, Karl. "Der Mord." *Die Evolution*, February–March 1849.

Heisbourg, François, and the Fondation pour la recherche stratégique (FRS). *L'hyperterrorisme: La nouvelle guerre*. Paris: Odile Jacob, 2001.

Heller, Joseph. *The Stern Gang: Ideology, Politics and Terror, 1940–1949*. London: Frank Cass, 1995.

Hoffman, Bruce. *Inside Terrorism*. New York: Columbia University Press, 1998,

———. "Low-intensity Conflict: Terrorism and Guerrilla Warfare in the Coming Decades." In *Terrorism: Roots, Impact, Responses*, ed. Lawrence Howard. New York: Praeger, 1992.

Horne, Alistair. *A Savage War of Peace: Algeria, 1954–1962*. London: Macmillan, 1977. Reprint. New York: Penguin Books, 1987.

Huntington, Samuel P. *The Clash of Civilizations and the Remaking of World Order*. New York: Simon & Schuster, 1996.

International Terrorism: Challenge and Response. Proceedings of the Jerusalem Conference on International Terrorism, July 2–5, 1979. Edited by Benjamin Netanyahu. Jerusalem: Jonathan Institute; New Brunswick, N.J.: Transaction Books, 1981.

Ivianski, Ze'ev. "The Moral Issue: Some Aspects of Individual Terror." In *The Morality of Terrorism*, ed. David C. Rapoport and Yonah Alexander. New York: Pergamon Press, 1982.

———. *Revolution and Terror*. Tel Aviv: Yair Publications, 1989. In Hebrew.

———. "Source of Inspiration for Revolutionary Terrorism: The Bakunin-Nechayev Alliance." *Conflict Quarterly* 8, no. 3 (Summer 1988).

Jaber, Hala. *Hezbollah: Born with a Vengeance*. New York: Columbia University Press, 1997.

Jabotinsky, Vladimir. "O zheleznoi stene" (The Iron Wall). *Rassvyet*, November 4, 1923. In Russian.

Jamieson, Alison. *The Heart Attacked: Terrorism and Conflict in the Italian State*. London: Marion Boyars, 1989.

Janke, Peter, with Richard Sim. *Guerrilla and Terrorist Organisations: A World Directory and Bibliography*. New York: Macmillan, 1983.

Jenkins, Brian Michael. "International Terrorism: A New Mode of Conflict." In *International Terrorism and World Security*, ed. David Carlton and Carlo Schaerf. New York: Wiley, 1975.

———. *International Terrorism: The Other World War*. Document no. R-3302AF. Santa Monica, Calif.: RAND Corporation, 1985.

Jenkins, P. "Strategy of Tension: The Belgian Terrorist Crisis, 1982–1986." *Terrorism* 13, nos. 4–5 (1990): 299–309.

John of Salisbury, bishop of Chartres. *The Statesman's Book of John of Salisbury*. Englewood Cliffs, N.J.: Prentice-Hall, 1963.

Johnson, Chalmers. *Revolutionary Change*. 1966. 2d ed. Stanford, Calif.: Stanford University Press, 1982.

Joll, James. *The Anarchists*. Boston: Little, Brown, 1964.

Kagan, Robert. *Of Paradise and Power: America and Europe in the New World Order*. New York: Knopf, 2004.

Kahane, Rabbi Meir. *They Must Go*. New York: Grosset & Dunlap, 1981.

Kaplan, David E., and Andrew Marshall. *The Cult at the End of the World: The Incredible Story of Aum*. London: Hutchinson, 1996.

Kellen, Konrad. *On Terrorists and Terrorism*. Document no. N-1942-RC. Santa Monica, Calif.: RAND Corporation, 1982.

Kennedy, Paul. *The Rise and Fall of the Great Powers: Economic Change and Military Conflict from 1500 to 2000*. New York: Knopf, 1989.

Kepel, Gilles. *Le prophète et le Pharaon: Aux sources des mouvements islamistes*. Paris: Seuil, 1993.

———. *Jihad: Expansion et déclin de l'islamisme*. Paris: Gallimard, 2003.

———. *Jihad: The Trail of Political Islam*. Translated by Anthony F. Roberts. Cambridge, Mass.: Harvard University Press, 2002.

Khosrokhavar, Farhad. *Les nouveaux martyrs d'Allah*. Paris: Flammarion, 2002. Translated by David Macey as *Suicide Bombers: Allah's New Martyrs* (London: Pluto Press, 2005).

Kitson, Frank. *Low-intensity Operations: Subversion, Insurgency, Peacekeeping*. London: Faber, 1971.

Kohn, George C. *Dictionary of Wars*. Garden City, N.Y.: Anchor Books, 1987.

Kravchinsky, Sergei Mikhailovich [pseud. Stepniak]. *Stepniak: La Russie souterraine*. Translated by Hugues Le Roux. Paris: Jules Lévy, 1885.

Kuper, Leo. *Genocide: Its Political Use in the Twentieth Century*. New Haven, Conn.: Yale University Press, 1981.

Kurz, Anat. "Palestinian Terrorism in 1988." In *The Middle East Military Balance, 1988–1989*, ed. Shlomo Gazit, 84–97. Boulder, Colo.: Westview Press, 1989.

Kurz, Anat, and Ariel Merari. *ASALA: Irrational Terror or Political Tool*. Boulder, Colo.: Westview Press, 1985.

Lakos, Amos. *International Terrorism: A Bibliography*. Boulder, Colo.: Westview Press, 1986.

Laqueur, Walter. *The Age of Terrorism*. Boston: Little, Brown, 1987.

———. *Guerrilla: A Historical and Critical Study*. Boston: Little, Brown, 1976.

———. *A History of Terrorism*. 1977. New Brunswick, N.J.: Transaction, 2001.

———. *Terrorism*. London: Weidenfeld & Nicolson, 1977.

———, ed. *The Terrorism Reader: A Historical Anthology*. New York: New American Library, 1978.

Laqueur, Walter, and Yonah Alexander, eds. *The Terrorism Reader: A Historical Anthology*. Rev. ed. New York: NAL Penguin, 1987.

Lenin, V. I. "Tasks of Revolutionary Army Contingents" (October 1905). In id., *Collected Works*, 9: 420–24. Moscow: Progress Publishers, 1972.

Lewis, Bernard. *The Assassins: A Radical Sect in Islam*. New York: Basic Books, 1968.

Liddell Hart, B. H. *Strategy: The Indirect Approach*. London: Faber, 1954.

Luttwak, Edward. *Coup d'état: A Practical Handbook*. 1968. Cambridge, Mass.: Harvard University Press, 1979.

Macchiavelli, Niccolò. *The Prince and the Discourses*. New York: Modern Library, 1950.

Mao Zedong. "Base Areas in the Anti-Japanese Guerrilla War." In *Guerrilla Warfare and Marxism*, ed. W. J. Pomeroy, 183–93. New York: International Publishers, 1968.

Maududi, Abu l'Ala. *Jihad in Islam*. Lahore: Islamic Publications, 1976. Address delivered on Iqbal Day, April 13, 1939, at the Town Hall, Lahore.

Marighella, Carlos. *For the Liberation of Brazil*. Translated by John Butt and Rosemary Sheed. Harmondsworth, Eng.: Penguin Books, 1971.

———. "Minimanual of the Urban Guerrilla." In *Terror and Urban Guerrillas: A Study of Tactics and Documents*, ed. Jay Mallin, 67–115. Coral Gables, Fla.: University of Miami Press, 1971

Marret, Jean-Luc. *Les techniques du terrorisme: Méthodes et pratiques du métier terroriste*. Paris: Presses universitaires de France, 1997.

Massu, Jacques. *La vraie bataille d'Alger*. Paris: Plon, 1971.

Meddeb, Abdelwahab. *The Malady of Islam*. Translated by Pierre Joris and Ann Reid. New York: Basic Books, 2003.

Merari, A., and N. Friedland. "Social Psychological Aspects of Political Terrorism." In *International Conflict and National Public Policy Issues*, ed. Stuart

Oskamp. *Applied Social Psychology Annual 6*. Beverly Hills, Calif.: Sage, 1985.

Merari, A., T. Prat, and D. Tal, "The Palestinian Intifada: An Analysis of a Popular Uprising after Seven Months." *Terrorism and Political Violence* 112 (1989): 177–201.

Mickolus, Edward F. *Transnational Terrorism: A Chronology of Events, 1968–1979*. Westport, Conn.: Greenwood Press, 1980.

Mickolus, Edward F., Todd Sandler, and Jean M. Murdock. *International Terrorism in the 1980s: A Chronology of Events*. Ames: Iowa State University Press, 1989.

Moczarski, Kazimierz. *Conversations with an Executioner*. Edited by Mariana Fitzpatrick. Englewood Cliffs, N.J.: Prentice-Hall, 1981. Translation of *Rozmowy z katem*. Based on conversations with SS General Jürgen Stroop.

Moss, Robert. *Urban Guerrillas: The New Face of Political Violence*. London: International Institute for Strategic Studies, 1971.

Most, Johann. "The Science of Revolutionary Warfare: Handbook of Instruction Regarding the Use and Manufacture of Nitroglycerin, Dynamite, Gun-Cotton, Fulminating Mercury, Bombs, Arson, Poisons, etc." In *Confronting Fear: A History of Terrorism*, ed. Isaac Cronin. New York: Thunder's Mouth Press, 2002.

Netanyahu, Benjamin, ed. *Terrorism: How The West Can Win*. New York: Avon, 1986.

Nizam al-Mulk. *The Book of Government, or, Rules for Kings: The Siyar al-Muluk, or, Siyasat-nama of Nizam al-Mulk*. 1086 C.E. Translated by Hubert Darke. 1968. 3d ed., Richmond, Surrey: Curzon Press, 2002.

O'Neill, Bard E. *Insurgency and Terrorism: Inside Modern Revolutionary Warfare*. Washington, D.C.: Brassey's, 1990.

Paige, J. M. "Political Orientation and Riot Participation." *American Sociological Review* 36 (1971): 810–20.

Parry, Albert. *Terrorism: From Robespierre to Arafat*. New York: Vanguard, 1976.

Peci, Patrizio. *Io, l'infame*. Milan: Mondadori, 1983.

Poliakov, Léon. *La causalité diabolique: Du joug mongol à la victoire de Lénine*. Paris: Calmann-Lévy, 1985.

Quatre femmes terroristes contre le tsar: Vera Zassoulitch, Olga Loubatovitch, Élisabeth Kovalskaïa, Vera Figner. Texts translated by Hélène Châtelain. Edited by Christine Fauré. Paris: F. Maspero, 1978.

Ramadan, Tariq. *Western Muslims and the Future of Islam*. New York: Oxford University Press, 2004.

Ranstorp, Magnus. *Hizb'allah in Lebanon: The Politics of the Western Hostage Crisis*. London: Macmillan, 1997.

Rapoport, David C. "Fear and Trembling: Terrorism in Three Religious Traditions." *American Political Science Review* 78, no. 3 (September 1984).

———, ed. *Inside Terrorist Organizations*. New York: Columbia University Press, 1988.

Rashid, Ahmed. *Jihad: The Rise of Militant Islam in Central Asia*. New Haven, Conn.: Yale University Press, 2002.

———. *Taliban: Islam, Oil and the New Great Game in Central Asia*. London: Tauris, 2002.

———. *Taliban: Militant Islam, Oil and Fundamentalism in Central Asia*. New Haven, Conn.: Yale University Press, 2001.

Raufer, Xavier, and Alain Bauer. *La guerre ne fait que commencer: Réseaux, financements, armements, attentats . . . les scénarios de demain*. Paris: Jean-Claude Lattès, 2002.

Rentner, K. S. "Terrorism in Insurgent Strategies." *Military Intelligence*, January–March 1985.

Rodinson, Maxime. Preface to Bernard Lewis, *Les assassins: Terrorisme et politique dans l'islam medieval*. Brussels: Éditions Complexe, 1984, 2001.

Roux, Jean-Paul. *Tamerlan*. Paris: Fayard, 1991.

Roy, Olivier. *L'échec de l'islam politique*. Paris: Seuil, 1992.

———. *Généalogie de l'islamisme*. Paris: Hachette/Pluriel, 2002.

———. *Les illusions du 11 Septembre: Le débat stratégique face au terrorisme*. Paris: Seuil, 2002.

———. *L'islam mondialisé*. Paris: Seuil, 2002.

Savinkov, Boris. *Souvenirs d'un terroriste*. Paris: Payot, 1931.

Schmid, Alex P., and Albert J. Jongman. *Political Terrorism: A New Guide to Actors, Authors, Concepts, Data Bases, Theories, and Literature*. Amsterdam: North-Holland Publishing Company, 1983, 1988. Rev. ed. New Brunswick, N.J.: Transaction Publishers, 2005.

Sharp, Gene. *The Politics of Nonviolent Action*. Boston: Porter Sargent, 1973.

Skocpol, Theda. *States and Social Revolutions*. Cambridge: Cambridge University Press, 1979.

Sommier, Isabelle. *Le terrorisme*. Paris: Flammarion, 2000.

Spiridovitch, Alexandre. *Histoire du terrorisme russe (1885–1917)*. Paris: Payot, 1930.

Sprinzak, Ehud. *The Ascendance of Israel's Radical Right*. New York: Oxford University Press, 1991.

———. *Brother against Brother: Violence and Extremism in Israeli Politics from Altalena to the Rabin Assassination*. New York: Free Press, 1999.

———. "Fundamentalism, Terrorism, and Democracy. The Case of the Gush Emunim Underground." Woodrow Wilson Center Occasional Paper no. 4. Washington, D.C.: Smithsonian Institution, 1986. *Journal of Strategic Studies*, May 1987.

Steinberg, Isaac Z. "L'aspect éthique de la revolution." In Jacques Baynac, *Les socialistes-révolutionnaires*, 363–64. Paris: Robert Laffont, 1979.

Stern, Jessica. *The Ultimate Terrorists*. Cambridge, Mass.: Harvard University Press, 1999.

Sun Tzu. *The Art of War*. New York: Delta, 1988.

Taheri, Amir. *Holy Terror, The Inside Story of Islamic Terrorism*. London: Sphere, 1987.

Talbott, John. *The War without a Name: France in Algeria, 1954–1962*. London: Faber, 1980.

Taylor, Peter. *Provos: The IRA and Sinn Fein*. London: Bloomsbury, 1997.

Thomas, Chantal. *La reine scélérate: Marie-Antoinette dans les pamphlets.* Paris: Seuil, 1989.

Todd, Emmanuel. *After the Empire: The Breakdown of the American Order.* New York: Columbia University Press, 2004.

Tucker, Jonathan B. "Bioterrorism: Threats and Responses." In *Biological Weapons: Limiting the Threat,* ed. Joshua Lederberg. BCSIA Studies in International Security. Cambridge, Mass.: MIT Press, 1999.

Tu peux tuer cet homme: Scènes de la vie révolutionnaire russe. Texts edited by Lucien Feuillade and Nicolas Lazarévitch. Paris: Gallimard, 1950.

United States Department of Defense. *Terrorist Group Profiles.* Washington, D.C.: G.P.O., 1988.

United States Department of State. *Patterns of Global Terrorism: 1988.* Publication 9705. Washington, D.C.: Office of the Secretary of State, Ambassador at Large for Counterterrorism, March 1989.

Venner, Dominique. *Histoire du terrorisme.* Paris: Pygmalion / Gérard Watelet, 2002.

Venturi, Franco. *Il populismo russo.* 2 vols. Turin: J. Einaudi, 1952.

———. *Les intellectuels, le peuple et la révolution: Histoire du populisme russe au XIXe siècle.* Paris: Gallimard, 1972.

"A Viet Cong Directive on 'Repression.'" In *Terror and Urban Guerrillas: A Study of Tactics and Documents,* ed. Jay Mallin, 31–43. Coral Gables, Fla.: University of Miami Press, 1971.

Walzer, Michael. *Just and Unjust Wars: A Moral Argument with Historical Illustrations.* New York: Basic Books, 1977. 2d ed. 1992.

Wardlaw, Grant. *Political Terrorism: Theory, Tactics, and Counter-Measures.* Cambridge: Cambridge University Press, 1989.

Werth, Nicolas. "Un état contre son peuple: Violences, repressions, terreurs en Union soviétique." In Stéphane Courtois, Nicolas Werth, et al., *Le livre noir du communisme: Crimes, terreur, repression.* Paris: Laffont, 1998.

Wieviorka, Michel. *Sociétés et terrorisme.* Paris: Fayard, 1988.

Wilkinson, Paul. *Political Terrorism.* New York: Macmillan, 1974.

———. *Terrorism and the Liberal State.* 1977. London: Palgrave Macmillan, 1994.

———. *Terrorism versus Democracy: The Liberal State Response.* London: Frank Cass, 2000.

Wilkinson, Paul, and Brian M. Jenkins, eds. *Aviation Terrorism and Security.* London: Frank Cass, 1999.

Wills, David C. *The First War on Terrorism: Counter-Terrorism Policy during the Reagan Administration.* Lanham, Md.: Rowman & Littlefield, 2003.

Wohlstetter, Albert. "The Delicate Balance of Terror." RAND P-1472. 1958. www.rand.org/publications/classics/wohlstetter/P1472/P1472.html (accessed April 15, 2006). *Foreign Affairs,* 1959.

Yaeger, C. H. "Menia Muria: The South Moluccans Fight in Holland." *Terrorism* 13, no. 3 (1990): 215–26.

Zavarzin, Pavel Pavlovich. *Souvenirs d'un chef de l'Okhrana, 1900–1917.* Translated by J. Jeanson. Paris: Payot, 1930.

Contributors

Arnaud Blin is a Senior Fellow at the French Institute for Strategic Analysis in Paris. He is the author of several books on terrorism, including *Le terrorisme* (Cavalier Bleu, 2005) and *La terror démasquée* (Cavalier Bleu, 2006).

Gérard Chaliand specializes in contemporary global political and strategic problems, in particular, guerrilla movements and terrorism. He has been a visiting professor at Harvard and at the University of California in Los Angeles and Berkeley and has taught at the École nationale d'administration (ENA) and the Collège interarmées de défense. Most important, he has visited conflict zones in Asia, Africa, and Latin America. Books he has written include the *Anthologie mondiale de la stratégie* (Paris: R. Laffont, 1990); *Stratégies de la guérilla* (Paris: Mazarine, 1979), published in translation as *Guerrilla Strategies: An Historical Anthology from the Long March to Afghanistan* (Berkeley: University of California Press, 1982); *L'arme du terrorisme*, written with Alain Grignard and Olivier Hubac-Occhipinti (Paris: L. Audibert, 2002); and *L'atlas du nouvel ordre mondial* (Paris: Laffont, 2003).

François Géré is director of the French Institute for Strategic Analysis in Paris and gives seminars at the Sorbonne. His publications include *Pourquoi les guerres? Un siècle de géopolitique* (Paris: Larousse, 2003); *Les volontaires de la mort: L'arme du suicide* (Paris: Bayard, 2003); and *Pourquoi le terrorisme?* (Larousse, 2006).

Rohan Gunaratna is the director of the Terrorism Research Institute for Defence and Strategic Studies in Singapore. He is the author of *Inside Al Qaeda: Global Network of Terror* (New York: Columbia University Press, 2002).

Olivier Hubac-Occhipinti specializes in conflict and in piracy. He collaborated with Gérard Chaliand and Olivier Hubac-Occhipinti on *L'arme du terrorisme*

(Paris: L. Audibert, 2002) and on the Beaumarchais Center for International Research's *Puissances et influences* (Paris: Mille et une nuits, 2000). He is the author of *Irak, une guerre mondiale* (La Martinière, 2006).

Ariel Merari is a visiting professor of political science at Harvard University and director of the Political Violence Research Unit at Tel Aviv University. He is the co-author, with Shlomi Elad, of *The International Dimension of Palestinian Terrorism* (Boulder, Colo.: Westview Press, 1986).

Philippe Migaux is the author of *Sécurité intérieure et menaces extérieures* (Paris: Centre d'analyse sur la sécurité européenne, 1993). He teaches at the Collège interarmées de défense.

Yves Ternon has published many books, including *Empire Ottoman: Le déclin, la chute, l'effacement* (Paris: Félin, 2002, 2005): *Du négationnisme: Mémoire et tabou* (Paris: Desclée de Brouwer, 1999); *L'état criminel: Les génocides au XXe siècle* (Paris: Seuil, 1995); and *Makhno: La révolte anarchiste, 1917–1921* (Brussels: Complexe, 1981).

Index

Text: 10/13 Sabon
Display: Franklin Gothic
Indexer: Barbara Roos
Compositor: Binghamton Valley Composition, LLC

CPSIA information can be obtained
at www.ICGtesting.com
Printed in the USA
LVOW12s1808100118
562548LV00004B/629/P